A·N·N·U·A·L E·D·I·T·I

P9-CKT-043

American History, Volume II

Eighteenth Edition

Reconstruction Through the Present

EDITOR

Robert James Maddox (Emeritus)

Pennsylvania State University
University Park

Robert James Maddox, distinguished historian and professor emeritus of American history at Pennsylvania State University, received a B.S. from Fairleigh Dickinson University in 1957, an M.S. from the University of Wisconsin in 1958, and a Ph.D. from Rutgers in 1964. He has written, reviewed, and lectured extensively, and is widely respected for his interpretations of presidential character and policy.

McGraw-Hill/Dushkin

2460 Kerper Blvd., Dubuque, IA 52001

Visit us on the Internet
http://www.dushkin.com

Credits

1. **Reconstruction and the Gilded Age**
   Unit photo—Courtesy of National Archives.
2. **The Emergence of Modern America**
   Unit photo—Courtesy of National Archives.
3. **From Progressivism to the 1920s**
   Unit photo—Courtesy of the Library of Congress.
4. **From the Great Depression to World War II**
   Unit photo—Courtesy of the Library of Congress.
5. **From the Cold War to 2004**
   Unit photo—The White House.
6. **New Directions for American History**
   Unit photo—© Getty Images/PhotoLink

Copyright

Cataloging in Publication Data
Main entry under title: Annual Editions: American History Vol. Two: Reconstruction Through the Present. 18/E.
1. United States—History—Periodicals.   2. United States—Historiography—Periodicals.   3. United States—Civilization—Periodicals. I.   1. Maddox, Robert James, comp. II   Title: American History, Vol. Two: Reconstruction Through the Present.
ISBN 0–07–296881-8   973'.05   74-187540   ISSN 0733–3560

© 2005 by McGraw-Hill/Dushkin, Dubuque, IA 52001, A Division of The McGraw-Hill Companies.

Copyright law prohibits the reproduction, storage, or transmission in any form by any means of any portion of this publication without the express written permission of McGraw-Hill/Dushkin, and of the copyright holder (if different) of the part of the publication to be reproduced. The Guidelines for Classroom Copying endorsed by Congress explicitly state that unauthorized copying may not be used to create, to replace, or to substitute for anthologies, compilations, or collective works.

Annual Editions® is a Registered Trademark of McGraw-Hill/Dushkin, A Division of The McGraw-Hill Companies.

Eighteenth Edition

Cover image © 2005 PhotoDisc, Inc.

Printed in the United States of America   1234567890QPDQPD987654   Printed on Recycled Paper

Editors/Advisory Board

Members of the Advisory Board are instrumental in the final selection of articles for each edition of ANNUAL EDITIONS. Their review of articles for content, level, currentness, and appropriateness provides critical direction to the editor and staff. We think that you will find their careful consideration well reflected in this volume.

EDITOR

Robert James Maddox
Pennsylvania State University-University Park

ADVISORY BOARD

Neal A. Brooks
Community College of Baltimore County, Essex

Jeff Davis
Bloomsburg University of Pennsylvania

Celia Hall-Thur
Wenatchee Valley College

Melvin G. Holli
University of Illinois

Harry Russell Huebel
Texas A & M University

Wilma King
University of Missouri - Columbia

Carl E. Kramer
Indiana University - Southeast

Larry Madaras
Howard Community College

Ronald McCoy
Emporia State University

Robert C. Pierce
Foothill College

John Snetsinger
California Polytechnic University

James R. Sweeney
Old Dominion University

Irvin D. S. Winsboro
Florida Gulf Coast University

Staff

EDITORIAL STAFF

Larry Loeppke, Managing Editor
Susan Brusch, Senior Developmental Editor
Jay Oberbroeckling, Developmental Editor
Lenny J. Behnke, Permissions Coordinator
Lori Church, Permissions Coordinator
Shirley Lanners, Permissions Coordinator
Bonnie Coakley, Editorial Assistant

TECHNOLOGY STAFF

Craig Purcell, eContent Coordinator

PRODUCTION STAFF

Beth Kundert, Production Manager
Trish Mish, Production Assistant
Kari Voss, Lead Typesetter
Jean Smith, Typesetter
Karen Spring, Typesetter
Sandy Wille, Typesetter
Tara McDermott, Designer

To the Reader

In publishing ANNUAL EDITIONS we recognize the enormous role played by the magazines, newspapers, and journals of the public press in providing current, first-rate educational information in a broad spectrum of interest areas. Many of these articles are appropriate for students, researchers, and professionals seeking accurate, current material to help bridge the gap between principles and theories and the real world. These articles, however, become more useful for study when those of lasting value are carefully collected, organized, indexed, and reproduced in a low-cost format, which provides easy and permanent access when the material is needed. That is the role played by ANNUAL EDITIONS.

Some scholars have used the phrase "the velocity of history." By this they mean the rate of societal and technological change over the course of years. A person, who was born in 1700, if he or she lived to be 100, would have found the world in 1800 perfectly familiar. The United States remained primarily a rural, agricultural nation. People traveled mostly by foot or wagon, they read at night by candle or lantern, and they might never have ventured more than a few miles from where they were raised. A person born in 1900, on the other hand, would have found the world of 2000 virtually unrecognizable. Automobiles, trains, and airplanes enable people to routinely travel to places they would only have dreamed about earlier. Massive population shifts, from farms and small towns to cities and suburbs, and from one section of the nation to another, have radically altered the face of the nation. At home, people can listen to the radio, watch television, or explore new worlds of information via their computers. Diseases that once were almost certainly fatal or at least debilitating have now been virtually eliminated, resulting in life expectancies undreamed of in the past.

With all of these "improvements," one would be hard put to argue that people in modern society are happier or more content than they were in the past. Extreme poverty is still with us in a land of untold wealth. Television and motion pictures, furthermore, encourage frustration by allowing even the poorest souls a glimpse of those with lifestyles that only the wealthiest few would have enjoyed a century earlier. Other issues we face today also have echoes in the past: race relations, gender roles, domestic terrorism, and environmental problems, to name just a few. Some people fear that we are destroying the very planet on which we live. And at least one new epidemic—AIDs—has become a scourge just as smallpox once was. Studying history will provide no "answers" to our modern troubles, but perhaps can provide some helpful guidelines.

Someone once said that historians wrote about "chaps," meaning white males who enjoyed positions of power or influence. Older history books tended to concentrate on presidents, titans of industry or finance, and military leaders. Women usually were mentioned only in passing, and then primarily as the wives or lovers of important men. Minority groups were treated, if at all, as passive objects of social customs or legislation. And, any mention of sexual orientation was simply out of the question.

Now virtually everything that has happened is considered fit for study. Books and articles tell us about the lives of ordinary people, about groups previously ignored or mentioned only in passing, and about subjects considered too trivial or commonplace to warrant examination. History "from the bottom up," once considered innovative, has become commonplace. Welcome as these innovations are, they often are encumbered by two tendencies: many are freighted down with incomprehensible prose (one of the criterion for inclusion in this volume is that articles be written in standard English), and many are produced to advance agendas the authors try to fob off as scholarship.

Traditional history is still being written. For better or worse, there *have* been men and women who have exercised great power or influence over the lives and deaths of others. They continue to fascinate. Presidents such as Franklin D. Roosevelt and Harry S. Truman had to make decisions that affected enormous numbers of people at home and abroad. Journalist Ida Tarbell, the subject of an article in this volume, influenced the way many people thought about big business through her "muckraking" articles about Standard Oil. Reformer Jacob Riis, also profiled in these pages, shocked many middle-class readers with his descriptions of how the poor lived. The Reverend Martin Luther King, Jr. provided inspiration through his oratory and presence that people of lesser gifts could not have hoped to achieve. And Margaret Sanger and Eleanor Roosevelt, though never holding official positions of power, nonetheless deeply affected the ways people perceived a number of issues.

Annual Editions: American History, Volume II, constitutes an effort to provide a balanced collection of articles that deal with great leaders and great decisions, as well as with ordinary people, at work, at leisure, and at war. Practically everyone who uses the volume will think of one or more articles he or she considers would have been preferable to the ones actually included. Some readers will wish more attention had been paid to one or another subject, others will regret the attention devoted to matters they regard as marginal. That is why we encourage teachers and students to let us know what they believe to be the strengths and weaknesses of this edition.

Annual Editions contains a number of features designed to make the volume "user friendly." These include a *topic guide* to help locate articles on specific individuals or subjects; the *table of contents extracts* that summarize each article with key concepts in boldface; and a comprehensive index. The essays are organized into six units. Each unit is preceded by an overview that provides background for informed reading of the articles, briefly introduces each one, and presents challenge questions. Please let us know if you have any suggestions for improving the format.

There will be a new edition of this volume in two years, with approximately half the readings being replaced by new ones. By completing and mailing the postage-paid article rating form included in the back of the book, you will help us judge which articles should be retained and which should be dropped. You can also help to improve the next edition by recommending (or better yet, sending along a copy of) articles that you think should be included. A number of essays included in this edition have come to our attention in this way.

Robert James Maddox
Editor

Contents

UNIT 1
Reconstruction and the Gilded Age

Seven unit articles examine the development of the United States after the Civil War. Society was changed enormously by Western expansion and technology.

The concepts in bold italics are developed in the article. For further expansion, please refer to the Topic Guide and the Index.

UNIT 2
The Emergence of Modern America

In this section, five articles review the beginnings of modern America. Key issues of this period are examined, including turn-of-the century lifestyles, politics, and military conflicts.

UNIT 3
From Progressivism to the 1920s

Six essays in this section examine American culutre in the early twentieth century. The economy began to reap the benefits of technology, women gained the right to vote, and black nationalism increased.

The concepts in bold italics are developed in the article. For further expansion, please refer to the Topic Guide and the Index.

UNIT 4
From the Great Depression to World War II

The eight selections in this unit discuss the severe economic and social trials of the Great Depression of the thirties, the slow recovery process, and the enormous impact of World War II on America's domestic and foreign social consciousness.

The concepts in bold italics are developed in the article. For further expansion, please refer to the Topic Guide and the Index.

UNIT 5
From the Cold War to 2004

The section's ten articles cover the post–World War II period and address numerous issues that include the presidency, race and sports issues, the cold war, domestic terrorism, and changing lifestyles.

The concepts in bold italics are developed in the article. For further expansion, please refer to the Topic Guide and the Index.

The concepts in bold italics are developed in the article. For further expansion, please refer to the Topic Guide and the Index.

UNIT 6
New Directions for American History

Five articles discuss the current state of American society and the role the United States plays throughout the world.

The concepts in bold italics are developed in the article. For further expansion, please refer to the Topic Guide and the Index.

Topic Guide

This topic guide suggests how the selections in this book relate to the subjects covered in your course. You may want to use the topics listed on these pages to search the Web more easily.

On the following pages a number of Web sites have been gathered specifically for this book. They are arranged to reflect the units of this *Annual Edition*. You can link to these sites by going to the DUSHKIN ONLINE support site at *http://www.dushkin.com/online/*.

ALL THE ARTICLES THAT RELATE TO EACH TOPIC ARE LISTED BELOW THE BOLD-FACED TERM.

African Americans
1. The New View of Reconstruction
2. 1871 War on Terror
4. Buffalo Soldiers
6. African Americans and the Industrial Revolution
18. Marcus Garvey and the Rise of Black Nationalism
24. African Americans and World War II
27. Baseball's *Noble* Experiment
31. The FBI Marches on the Dreamers

Anti-Semitism
14. The Fate of Leo Frank

Asians
22. Japanese Americans and the U.S. Army: A Historical Reconsideration

Atomic bomb
26. The Biggest Decision: Why We Had to Drop the Atomic Bomb

Buffalo Soldiers
4. Buffalo Soldiers

Cold war
25. Dividing the Spoils
26. The Biggest Decision: Why We Had to Drop the Atomic Bomb
28. Truman's Other War: The Battle for the American Homefront, 1950-1953
29. Women, Domesticity, and Postwar Conservatism
33. Face-Off
35. The American Century

Culture
8. Where the Other Half Lived
9. Our First Olympics
10. Lady Muckraker
13. The Ambiguous Legacies of Women's Progressivism
14. The Fate of Leo Frank
15. The Home Front
16. Evolution on Trial
17. Race Cleansing in America
18. Marcus Garvey and the Rise of Black Nationalism
19. 'Brother, Can You Spare a Dime?'
22. Japanese Americans and the U.S. Army: A Historical Reconsideration
23. American Women in a World at War
24. African Americans and World War II
27. Baseball's *Noble* Experiment
29. Women, Domesticity, and Postwar Conservatism
30. The Split-Level Years
32. The Spirit of '68
34. Dixie's Victory
37. Breaking the Global-Warming Gridlock
38. A Politics for Generation X
39. American Culture Goes Global, or Does It?
41. The Case Against Perfection

Depression, The Great
19. 'Brother, Can You Spare a Dime?'

20. A Monumental Man
21. Birth of an Entitlement: Learning from the Origins of Social Security

Diplomacy
25. Dividing the Spoils
26. The Biggest Decision: Why We Had to Drop the Atomic Bomb
28. Truman's Other War: The Battle for the American Homefront, 1950-1953
33. Face-Off
35. The American Century
36. What September 11th Really Wrought
40. The Bubble of American Supremacy

Environment
37. Breaking the Global-Warming Gridlock

Evolution
16. Evolution on Trial

Frank, Leo
14. The Fate of Leo Frank

Garvey, Marcus
18. Marcus Garvey and the Rise of Black Nationalism

Government
1. The New View of Reconstruction
2. 1871 War on Terror
11. Teddy in the Middle
15. The Home Front
20. A Monumental Man
21. Birth of an Entitlement: Learning from the Origins of Social Security
31. The FBI Marches on the Dreamers

Immigrants
8. Where the Other Half Lived
17. Race Cleansing in America

Joseph, Chief
7. The Death of Wilhautyah

Klan, Ku Klux
2. 1871 War on Terror

Korean War
28. Truman's Other War: The Battle for the American Homefront, 1950-1953

Labor
5. Undermining the Molly Maguires
6. African Americans and the Industrial Revolution
11. Teddy in the Middle
19. 'Brother, Can You Spare a Dime?'
23. American Women in a World at War
24. African Americans and World War II

World Wide Web Sites

The following World Wide Web sites have been carefully researched and selected to support the articles found in this reader. The easiest way to access these selected sites is to go to our DUSHKIN ONLINE support site at *http://www.dushkin.com/online/*.

AE: American History, Volume II, 18th Edition

The following sites were available at the time of publication. Visit our Web site—we update DUSHKIN ONLINE regularly to reflect any changes.

General Sources

American Historical Association
http://www.theaha.org

This is the logical first visitation site for someone interested in virtually any topic in American history. All affiliated societies and publications are noted, and AHA links present material related to myriad fields of history and for students with different levels of education.

Harvard's John F. Kennedy School of Government
http://www.ksg.harvard.edu/

Starting from this home page, click on a huge variety of links to information about American history, ranging from data about political parties to general debates of enduring issues.

History Net
http://www.thehistorynet.com/

Supported by the National Historical Society, this frequently updated site provides information on a wide range of topics. The articles are of excellent quality, and the site has book reviews and even special interviews.

Library of Congress
http://www.loc.gov/

Examine this Web site to learn about the extensive resource tools, library services/resources, exhibitions, and databases available through the Library of Congress in many different subfields that are related to American history.

National Archives and Records Administration
http://www.nara.gov/nara/nail.html

It is possible to access over 125,000 digital images from this National Archives and Records site. A vast array of American subjects are available.

Smithsonian Institution
http://www.si.edu/

This site provides access to the enormous resources of the Smithsonian, which holds some 140 million artifacts and specimens in its trust for "the increase and diffusion of knowledge." Here you can learn about American social, cultural, economic, and political history from a variety of viewpoints.

The White House
http://www.whitehouse.gov/

Visit the home page of the White House for direct access to information about commonly requested federal services, the White House Briefing Room, and the presidents and vice presidents. The "Virtual Library" allows you to search White House documents, listen to speeches, and view photos.

UNIT 1: Reconstruction and the Gilded Age

Anacostia Museum/Smithsonian Institution
http://www.si.edu/archives/historic/anacost.htm

This is the home page of the Center for African American History and Culture of the Smithsonian Institution. Explore its many avenues. This is expected to become a major repository of information.

American Memory
http://memory.loc.gov/ammem/ammemhome.html

American Memory is a gateway to rich primary source materials relating to the history and culture of the United States. The site offers more than 7 million digital items from more than 100 historical collections.

Gilded Age and Progressive Era Resources
http://www2.tntech.edu/history/gilprog.html

General Resources on the Gilded Age and Progressive Era including numerous links for research and further reading.

BoondocksNet.com
http://www.boondocksnet.com

Jim Zwick's site explores the often-forgotten Filipino revolt against U.S. acquisition of the Philippines after the Spanish-American War. Zwick also discusses anti-imperialist crusades within the United States during the Gilded Age.

UNIT 2: The Emergence of Modern America

The Age of Imperialism
http://www.smplanet.com/imperialism/toc.html

During the late nineteenth and early twentieth centuries, the United States pursued an aggressive policy of expansionism, extending its political and economic influence around the globe. That pivotal era in the nation's history is the subject of this interactive site. Maps and photographs are provided.

Anti-Imperialism in the United States, 1898–1935
http://boondocksnet.com/ail98-35.html

Jim Zwick created this interesting site that explores American imperialism from the Spanish-American War years to 1935. It provides valuable primary resources on a variety of related topics.

William McKinley 1843-1901
http://lcweb.loc.gov/rr/hispanic/1898/mckinley.html

Browse through this Library of Congress site for insight into the era of William McKinley, including discussion of the Spanish-American War.

American Diplomacy: Editor's Corner - If Two By Sea
http://www.unc.edu/depts/diplomat/AD_Issues/amdipl_15/edit_15.html

This essay provides a brief biography of Alfred Thayer Mahan and reviews his contributions and influence towards expansionism in American foreign policy.

www.dushkin.com/online/

Great Chicago Fire and the Web of Memory
http://www.chicagohs.org/fire/

This site, created by the Academic Technologies unit of Northwestern University and the Chicago Historical Society, is interesting and well constructed. Besides discussing the Great Chicago Fire at length, the materials provide insight into the era in which the event took place.

UNIT 3: From Progressivism to the 1920s

International Channel
http://www.i-channel.com/

Immigrants helped to create modern America. Visit this interesting site to experience "the memories, sounds, even tastes of Ellis Island. Hear immigrants describe in their own words their experiences upon entering the gateway to America."

World War I—Trenches on the Web
http://www.worldwar1.com/

Mike Lawrence's interesting site supplies extensive resources about the Great War and is the appropriate place to begin exploration of this topic as regards the American experience in World War I. There are "virtual tours" on certain topics, such as "Life on the Homefront."

World Wide Web Virtual Library
http://www.iisg.nl/~w3vl/

This site focuses on labor and business history. As an index site, this is a good place to start exploring these two vast topics.

Temperance and Prohibition
http://prohibition.history.ohio-state.edu/Contents.htm

From Ohio State University's Department of History, this Web page covers in depth inquiry into the origins and course of the American temperance movement and prohibition.

The Roaring 20's and the Great Depression
http://www.snowcrest.net/jmike/20sdep.html

An extensive anthology of Web links to sites on the Roaring 20's and the Great Depression.

UNIT 4: From the Great Depression to World War II

Japanese American Internment
http://www.jainternment.org/

This site, which focuses on the Japanese American internment during World War II, is especially useful for links to other related sites.

Works Progress Administration/Folklore Project
http://lcweb2.loc.gov/ammem/wpaintro/wpalife.html

Open this home page of the Folklore Project of the Works Progress Administration (WPA) Federal Writers' Project to gain access to thousands of documents on the life histories of ordinary Americans from all walks of life during the Great Depression.

World War II WWW Sites
http://www.besthistorysites.nte/WWWII.shtml

Visit this site as a starting point to find research links for World War II, including topics specific to the United States' participation and the impact on the country.

World War II Timeline
http://history.acusd.edu/gen/WW2Timeline/start.html

A detailed and interactive timeline covering 1917 through 1945 and includes many photographs.

Hiroshima Archive
http://www.lclark.edu/~history/HIROSHIMA/

The Hiroshima Archive was originally set up to join the on-line effort made by many people all over the world to commemorate the 50th anniversary of the atomic bombing. It is intended to serve as a research and educational guide to those who want to gain and expand their knowledge of the atomic bombing.

The Enola Gay
http://www.theenolagay.com/index.html

The offical Web site of Brigadier General Paul W. Tibbets, Jr. (Ret.) Offers a wealth of historical analysis and photographs of the events surrounding the use of atomic weapons on Japan in 1945.

UNIT 5: From the Cold War to 2004

Coldwar
http://www.cnn.com/SPECIALS/cold.war

This site presents U.S. government policies during the cold war. Navigate interactive maps, see rare archival footage online, learn more about the key players, read recently declassified documents and tour Cold War capitals through 3-D images.

The American Experience: Vietnam Online
http://www.pbs.org/wgbh/amex/vietnam/

Vietnam Online was developed to accompany Vietnam: A Television History, the award-winning television series produced by WGBH Boston.

The Federal Web Locator
http://www.infoctr.edu/fwl

Use this handy site as a launching pad for the Web sites of federal U.S. agencies, departments, and organizations. It is well organized and easy to use for informational and research purposes.

Federalism: Relationship between Local and National Governments
http://www.infidels.org/~nap/index.federalism.html

Federalism versus states' rights has always been a spirited topic of debate in American government. Visit this site for links to many articles and reports on the subject.

The Gallup Organization
http://www.gallup.com/

Open this Gallup Organization home page to access an extensive archive of public opinion poll results and special reports on a huge variety of topics related to American society, politics, and government.

STAT-USA
http://www.stat-usa.gov/stat-usa.html

This site, a service of the Department of Commerce, contains daily economic news, frequently requested statistical releases, information on export and international trade, domestic economic news and statistical series and databases.

U.S. Department of State
http://www.state.gov/

View this site for an understanding into the workings of what has become a major U.S. executive-branch department. Links explain what exactly the department does, what services it provides, what it says about U.S. interests around the world, and much more.

UNIT 6: New Directions for American History

American Studies Web
http://www.georgetown.edu/crossroads/asw/

This eclectic site provides links to a wealth of Internet resources for research in American studies, from agriculture and rural development, to history and government, to race and ethnicity.

National Center for Policy Analysis
http://www.public-policy.org/web.public-policy.org/index.php

Through this site, click onto links to read discussions of an array of topics that are of major interest in the study of American history, from regulatory policy and privatization to economy and income.

The National Network for Immigrant and Refugee Rights (NNIRR)
http://www.nnirr.org/

The NNIRR serves as a forum to share information and analysis, to educate communities and the general public, and to develop and coordinate plans of action on important immigrant and refugee issues. Visit this site and its many links to explore these issues.

STANDARDS: An International Journal of Multicultural Studies
http://www.colorado.edu/journals/standards

This fascinating site provides access to the *Standards* archives and a seemingly infinite number of links to topics of interest in the study of cultural pluralism.

Supreme Court/Legal Information Institute
http://supct.law.cornell.edu/supct/index.html

Open this site for current and historical information about the Supreme Court. The archive contains many opinions issued since May 1990 as well as a collection of nearly 600 of the most historic decisions of the Court.

We highly recommend that you review our Web site for expanded information and our other product lines. We are continually updating and adding links to our Web site in order to offer you the most usable and useful information that will support and expand the value of your Annual Editions. You can reach us at: *http://www.dushkin.com/annualeditions/.*

UNIT 1

Reconstruction and the Gilded Age

Unit Selections

Key Points to Consider

- Radical Reconstruction failed to achieve its goal of ensuring full citizenship to freed people. Could this attempt have succeeded in view of the fierce Southern resistance? How?

- Discuss the Buffalo soldiers. Why would individuals volunteer to subject themselves to such terrible conditions?

- What alternatives did mine workers have to forming secret organizations to protect their interests? Were the Molly Maguires given fair trials?

- Generally speaking, how did blacks fare during the process of industrializing? What excuses were made for such unfair treatment?

- Discuss the war between the Nez Perce and the U. S. Army. Why were the Indians doomed to lose?

 **Links: www.dushkin.com/online/**
These sites are annotated in the World Wide Web pages.

Anacostia Museum/Smithsonian Institution
http://www.si.edu/archives/historic/anacost.htm

American Memory
http://memory.loc.gov/ammem/ammemhome.html

Gilded Age and Progressive Era Resources
http://www2.tntech.edu/history/gilprog.html

BoondocksNet.com
http://www.boondocksnet.com

A struggle over who would control postwar reconstruction of the South had begun even before Lincoln was assassinated. He made it clear through speeches and actions that he intended to follow a policy of reconciliation. Southern states could resume their positions within the union by following simple procedures, and only a few high-ranking Confederate officials were prohibited from participating. Lincoln clearly hoped that his moderate approach would more quickly heal the wounds of war. Unfortunately for Freedpeople, this meant that the South would be run by essentially the same whites who had brought about succession.

A group of individuals who became known as "radical" or "extreme" Republicans opposed what they regarded as the betrayal of Freedpeople. These Republicans wanted to use the power of the federal government to ensure that former slaves enjoyed full civil and legal rights regardless of white sensibilities. In the process, they hoped to create viable Republican part in the South.

One of the great "what-ifs" in American history is: what if Lincoln had lived out his second term as president? He was a superb politician who might very well have steered his moderate reconstruction program through congress over Radical opposition. Andrew Johnson, who succeeded him, was a blundering hothead who managed to alienate practically everybody. When he tried to institute a reconstruction program similar to Lincoln's,

a bitter struggle developed that ended in Johnson's impeachment and complete victory for the Radicals.

Under Radical Reconstruction, the South was divided into five military districts and federal troops were sent to protect the rights of Freedpeople. Southern whites regarded these troops as foreign occupiers, and opposed them any way they could. The first selection in this volume, Eric Foner's "The New View of Reconstruction," analyzes the changing interpretations of this period over the years. Foner concludes that Radical Reconstruction failed to achieve its goals in the short run but provided what he calls and "enduring vision." The article "1871 War on Terror" describes efforts to crush terroristic organizations such as the Ku Klux Klan and the Knights of the White Camelia that had grown up in the South to keep blacks in subordinate positions.

The third essay in this section, "Lockwood in '84," tells the remarkable story of Belva Lockwood's presidential campaign of 1884. Running on the Equal Rights ticket, her emphasis was on women's suffrage but she took progressive stands on most of the day's issues.

There are two articles about black people, aside from the one on Reconstruction. A number of blacks, some of them freedmen, joined the army. "Buffalo Soldiers," which is what the Indians called these men, discusses those who served in the west. They

helped spearhead western expansion, and served in combat in far greater proportions than their number warranted. Author T.J. Stiles describes how these soldiers persevered in spite of having to make do with poor equipment, bad food, and the prejudice they faced when they were stationed. "African Americans and the Industrial Revolution" analyzes their role in the industrial process. During the Gilded Age, African Americans were denied many jobs in mills and factories because they were temperamentally unsuited for such work.

"The Death of Wilhautya" concerns a bloody war between the Nez Perce Indians and the United States Army that erupted after the killing of one member of the tribe. Eventually, the Indians had to surrender against overwhelming odds and one chief told his captors that he would "fight no more forever."

Mine workers in Pennsylvania led hard and dangerous lives. They worked long, back-breaking hours under constant threat of cave-ins and flooding. Their wages were kept as low as possible, often making it difficult to exist. Some miners, hoping to improve their miserable conditions, joined secret organizations that became known as "Molly Maguires." Mine operators tried to destroy these groups by any means possible, as the article "Undermining the Molly Maquires" shows. In 1876, a number of men accused of being Mollys were brought to trial. Twenty were found guilty of murder, ten of who were hanged.

The New View of Reconstruction

Whatever you were taught or thought you knew about the post-Civil War era is probably wrong in the light of recent study

Eric Foner

In the past twenty years, no period of American history has been the subject of a more thoroughgoing reevaluation than Reconstruction—the violent, dramatic, and still controversial era following the Civil War. Race relations, politics, social life, and economic change during Reconstruction have all been reinterpreted in the light of changed attitudes toward the place of blacks within American society. If historians have not yet forged a fully satisfying portrait of Reconstruction as a whole, the traditional interpretation that dominated historical writing for much of this century has irrevocably been laid to rest.

Anyone who attended high school before 1960 learned that Reconstruction was a era of unrelieved sordidness in American political and social life. The martyred Lincoln, according to this view, had planned a quick and painless readmission of the Southern states as equal members of the national family. President Andrew Johnson, his successor, attempted to carry out Lincoln's policies but was foiled by the Radical Republicans (also known as Vindictives or Jacobins). Motivated by an irrational hatred of Rebels or by ties with Northern capitalists out to plunder the South, the Radicals swept aside Johnson's lenient program and fastened black supremacy upon the defeated Confederacy. An orgy of corruption followed, presided over by unscrupulous carpetbaggers (Northerners who ventured south to reap the spoils of office), traitorous scalawags (Southern whites who cooperated with the new gov-

ernments for personal gain), and the ignorant and childlike freedmen, who were incapable of properly exercising the political power that had been thrust upon them. After much needless suffering, the white community of the South banded together to overthrow these "black" governments and restore home rule (their euphemism for white supremacy). All told, Reconstruction was just about the darkest page in the American saga.

Originating in anti-Reconstruction propaganda of Southern Democrats during the 1870s, this traditional interpretation achieved scholarly legitimacy around the turn of the century through the work of William Dunning and his students at Columbia University. It reached the larger public through films like *Birth of a Nation* and *Gone With the Wind* and that best-selling work of myth-making masquerading as history, *The Tragic Era* by Claude G. Bowers. In language as exaggerated as it was colorful, Bowers told how Andrew Johnson "fought the bravest battle for constitutional liberty and for the preservation of our institutions ever waged by an Executive" but was overwhelmed by the "poisonous propaganda" of the Radicals. Southern whites, as a result, "literally were put to the torture" by "emissaries of hate" who manipulated the "simple-minded" freedmen, inflaming the negroes' "egotism" and even inspiring "lustful assaults" by blacks upon white womanhood.

In a discipline that sometimes seems to pride itself on the rapid rise and fall of his-

torical interpretations, this traditional portrait of Reconstruction enjoyed remarkable staying power. The long reign of the old interpretation is not difficult to explain. It presented a set of easily identifiable heroes and villains. It enjoyed the imprimatur of the nation's leading scholars. And it accorded with the political and social realities of the first half of this century. This image of Reconstruction helped freeze the mind of the white South in unalterable opposition to any movement for breaching the ascendancy of the Democratic party, eliminating segregation, or readmitting disfranchised blacks to the vote.

Nevertheless, the demise of the traditional interpretation was inevitable, for it ignored the testimony of the central participant in the drama of Reconstruction—the black freedman. Furthermore, it was grounded in the conviction that blacks were unfit to share in political power. As Dunning's Columbia colleague John W. Burgess put it, "A black skin means membership in a race of men which has never of itself succeeded in subjecting passion to reason, has never, therefore, created any civilization of any kind." Once objective scholarship and modern experience rendered that assumption untenable, the entire edifice was bound to fall.

The work of "revising" the history of Reconstruction began with the writings of a handful of survivors of the era, such as John R. Lynch, who had served as a black congressman from Mississippi after the Civil War. In the 1930s white scholars like Francis Simkins and Robert Woody carried the task forward. Then, in 1935, the black historian and activist W. E. B. Du Bois produced *Black Reconstruction in America,* a monumental revaluation that closed with an irrefutable indictment of a historical profession that had sacrificed scholarly objectivity on the altar of racial bias. "One fact and one alone," he wrote, "explains the attitude of most recent writers toward Reconstruction; they cannot conceive of Negroes as men." Du Bois's work, however, was ignored by most historians.

Black initiative established as many schools as did Northern religious societies and the Freedmen's Bureau. The right to vote was not simply thrust upon them by meddling outsiders, since blacks began agitating for the suffrage as soon as they were freed.

It was not until the 1960s that the full force of the revisionist wave broke over the field. Then, in rapid succession, virtually every assumption of the traditional viewpoint was systematically dismantled. A drastically different portrait emerged to take its place. President Lincoln did not have a coherent "plan" for Reconstruction, but at the time of his assassination he had been cautiously contemplating black suffrage. Andrew Johnson was a stubborn, racist politician who lacked the ability to compromise. By isolating himself from the broad currents of public opinion that had nourished Lincoln's career, Johnson created an impasse with Congress that Lincoln would certainly have avoided, thus throwing away his political power and destroying his own plans for reconstructing the South.

The Radicals in Congress were acquitted of both vindictive motives and the charge of serving as the stalking-horses of Northern capitalism. They emerged instead as idealists in the best nineteenth-century reform tradition. Radical leaders like Charles Sumner and Thaddeus Stevens had worked for the rights of blacks long before any conceivable political ad-

vantage flowed from such a commitment. Stevens refused to sign the Pennsylvania Constitution of 1838 because it disfranchised the state's black citizens; Sumner led a fight in the 1850s to integrate Boston's public schools. Their Reconstruction policies were based on principle, not petty political advantage, for the central issue dividing Johnson and these Radical Republicans was the civil rights of freedmen. Studies of congressional policy-making, such as Eric L. McKitrick's *Andrew Johnson and Reconstruction,* also revealed that Reconstruction legislation, ranging from the Civil Rights Act of 1866 to the Fourteenth and Fifteenth Amendments, enjoyed broad support from moderate and conservative Republicans. It was not simply the work of a narrow radical faction.

Even more startling was the revised portrait of Reconstruction in the South itself. Imbued with the spirit of the civil rights movement and rejecting entirely the racial assumptions that had underpinned the traditional interpretation, these historians evaluated Reconstruction from the black point of view. Works like Joel Williamson's *After Slavery* portrayed the period as a time of extraordinary political, social, and economic progress for blacks. The establishment of public school systems, the granting of equal citizenship to blacks, the effort to restore the devastated Southern economy, the attempt to construct an interracial political democracy from the ashes of slavery, all these were commendable achievements, not the elements of Bowers's "tragic era."

Unlike earlier writers, the revisionists stressed the active role of the freedmen in shaping Reconstruction. Black initiative established as many schools as did Northern religious societies and the Freedmen's Bureau. The right to vote was not simply thrust upon them by meddling outsiders, since blacks began agitating for the suffrage as soon as they were freed. In 1865 black conventions throughout the South issued eloquent, though unheeded, appeals for equal civil and political rights.

With the advent of Radical Reconstruction in 1867, the freedmen did enjoy a real measure of political power. But black supremacy never existed. In most states blacks held only a small fraction of political offices, and even in South Carolina, where they comprised a majority of the state legislature's lower house, effective power remained in white hands. As for corruption, moral standards in both gov-

ernment and private enterprise were at low ebb throughout the nation in the postwar years—the era of Boss Tweed, the Credit Mobilier scandal, and the Whiskey Ring. Southern corruption could hardly be blamed on former slaves.

Other actors in the Reconstruction drama also came in for reevaluation. Most carpetbaggers were former Union soldiers seeking economic opportunity in the postwar South, not unscrupulous adventurers. Their motives, a typically American amalgam of humanitarianism and the pursuit of profit, were no more insidious than those of Western pioneers. Scalawags, previously seen as traitors to the white race, now emerged as "Old Line" Whig Unionists who had opposed secession in the first place or as poor whites who had long resented planters' domination of Southern life and who saw in Reconstruction a chance to recast Southern society along more democratic lines. Strongholds of Southern white Republicanism like east Tennessee and western North Carolina had been the scene of resistance to Confederate rule throughout the Civil War; now, as one scalawag newspaper put it, the choice was "between salvation at the hand of the Negro or destruction at the hand of the rebels."

At the same time, the Ku Klux Klan and kindred groups, whose campaign of violence against black and white Republicans had been minimized or excused in older writings, were portrayed as they really were. Earlier scholars had conveyed the impression that the Klan intimidated blacks mainly by dressing as ghosts and playing on the freedmen's superstitions. In fact, black fears were all too real: the Klan was a terrorist organization that beat and killed its political opponents to deprive blacks of their newly won rights. The complicity of the Democratic party and the silence of prominent whites in the face of such outrages stood as an indictment of the moral code the South had inherited from the days of slavery.

By the end of the 1960s, then, the old interpretation had been completely reversed. Southern freedmen were the heroes, the "Redeemers" who overthrew Reconstruction were the villains, and if the era was "tragic," it was because change did not go far enough. Reconstruction had been a time of real progress and its failure a lost opportunity for the South and the nation. But the legacy of Reconstruction—the Fourteenth and Fifteenth Amendments—endured to inspire future efforts for civil rights. As Kenneth Stampp wrote in *The Era of Reconstruction,* a superb summary of revisionist findings published in 1965, "if it was worth four years of civil war to save the Union, it was worth a few years of radical reconstruction to give the American Negro the ultimate promise of equal civil and political rights."

Under slavery most blacks had lived in nuclear family units, although they faced the constant threat of separation from loved ones by sale. Reconstruction provided the opportunity for blacks to solidify their preexisting family ties.

As Stampp's statement suggests, the reevaluation of the first Reconstruction was inspired in large measure by the impact of the second—the modern civil rights movement. And with the waning of that movement in recent years, writing on Reconstruction has undergone still another transformation. Instead of seeing the Civil War and its aftermath as a second American Revolution (as Charles Beard had), a regression into barbarism (as Bowers argued), or a golden opportunity squandered (as the revisionists saw it), recent writers argue that Radical Reconstruction was not really very radical. Since land was not distributed to the former slaves, the remained economically dependent upon their former owners. The planter class survived both the war and Reconstruction with its property (apart from slaves) and prestige more or less intact.

Not only changing times but also the changing concerns of historians have contributed to this latest reassessment of Reconstruction. The hallmark of the past decade's historical writing has been an emphasis upon "social history"—the evocation of the past lives of ordinary Americans—and the downplaying of strictly political events. When applied to Reconstruction, this concern with the "social" suggested that black suffrage and officeholding, once seen as the most radical departures of the Reconstruction era, were relatively insignificant.

Recent historians have focused their investigations not upon the politics of Reconstruction but upon the social and

economic aspects of the transition from slavery to freedom. Herbert Gutman's influential study of the black family during and after slavery found little change in family structure or relations between men and women resulting from emancipation. Under slavery most blacks had lived in nuclear family units, although they faced the constant threat of separation from loved ones by sale. Reconstruction provided the opportunity for blacks to solidify their preexisting family ties. Conflicts over whether black women should work in the cotton fields (planters said yes, many black families said no) and over white attempts to "apprentice" black children revealed that the autonomy of family life was a major preoccupation of the freedmen. Indeed, whether manifested in their withdrawal from churches controlled by whites, in the blossoming of black fraternal, benevolent, and self-improvement organizations, or in the demise of the slave quarters and their replacement by small tenant farms occupied by individual families, the quest for independence from white authority and control over their own day-to-day lives shaped the black response to emancipation.

The Civil War raised the decisive questions of American's national existence: the relations between local and national authority, the definition of citizenship, the balance between force and consent in generating obedience to authority.

In the post–Civil War South the surest guarantee of economic autonomy, blacks believed, was land. To the freedmen the justice of a claim to land based on their years of unrequited labor appeared self-evident. As an Alabama black convention put it, "The property which they [the planters] hold was nearly all earned by the sweat of *our* brows." As Leon Litwack showed in *Been in the Storm So Long,* a Pultizer Prize–winning account of the black response to emancipation, many freedmen in 1865 and 1866 refused to sign labor contracts, expecting the federal government to give them land. In some localities, as one Alabama

overseer reported, they "set up claims to the plantation and all on it."

In the end, of course, the vast majority of Southern blacks remained propertyless and poor. But exactly why the South, and especially its black population, suffered from dire poverty and economic retardation in the decades following the Civil War is a matter of much dispute. In *One Kind of Freedom* economists Roger Ransom and Richard Sutch indicted country merchants for monopolizing credit and charging usurious interest rates, forcing black tenants into debt and locking the South into a dependence on cotton production that impoverished the entire region. But Jonathan Wiener, in his study of postwar Alabama, argued that planters used their political power to compel blacks to remain on the plantations. Planters succeeded in stabilizing the plantation system, but only by blocking the growth of alternative enterprises, like factories, that might draw off black laborers, thus locking the region into a pattern of economic backwardness.

If the thrust of recent writing has emphasized the social and economic aspects of Reconstruction, politics has not been entirely neglected. But political studies have also reflected the postrevisionist mood summarized by C. Vann Woodward when he observed "how essentially nonrevolutionary and conservative Reconstruction really was." Recent writers, unlike their revisionist predecessors, have found little to praise in federal policy toward the emancipated blacks.

A new sensitivity to the strength of prejudice and laissez-faire ideas in the nineteenth-century North has led many historians to doubt whether the Republican party ever made a genuine commitment to racial justice in the South. The granting of black suffrage was an alternative to a long-term federal responsibility for protecting the rights of the former slaves. Once enfranchised, blacks could be left to fend for themselves. With the exception of a few Radicals like Thaddeus Stevens, nearly all Northern policy-makers and educators are criticized today for assuming that, so long as the unfettered operations of the marketplace afforded blacks the opportunity to advance through diligent labor, federal efforts to assist them in acquiring land were unnecessary.

Probably the most innovative recent writing on Reconstruction politics has centered on a broad reassessment of black Republicanism, largely undertaken by a new generation of black historians. Scholars like Thomas Holt and Nell Painter insist that Reconstruction was not simply a matter of black and white. Conflicts within the black community, no less than divisions among whites, shaped Reconstruction politics. Where revisionist scholars, both black and white, had celebrated the accomplishments of black political leaders, Holt, Painter, and others charge that they failed to address the economic plight of the black masses. Painter criticized "representative colored men," as national black leaders were called, for failing to provide ordinary freedmen with effective political leadership. Holt found that black officeholders in South Carolina most emerged from the old free mulatto class of Charleston, which shared many assumptions with prominent whites. "Basically bourgeois in their origins and orientation," he wrote, they "failed to act in the interest of black peasants."

In emphasizing the persistence from slavery of divisions between free blacks and slaves, these writers reflect the increasing concern with continuity and conservatism in Reconstruction. Their work reflects a startling extension of revisionist premises. If, as has been argued for the past twenty years, blacks were active agents rather than mere victims of manipulation, then they could not be absolved of blame for the ultimate failure of Reconstruction.

Despite the excellence of recent writings and the continual expansion of our knowledge of the period, historians of Reconstruction today face a unique dilemma. An old interpretation has been overthrown, but a coherent new synthesis has yet to take its place. The revisionists of the 1960s effectively established a series of negative points: the Reconstruction governments were not as bad as had been portrayed, black supremacy was a myth, the Radicals were not cynical manipulators of the freedmen. Yet no convincing overall portrait of the quality of political and social life emerged from their writings. More recent historians have rightly pointed to elements of continuity that spanned the nineteenth-century Southern experience, especially the survival, in modified form, of the plantation system. Nevertheless, by denying the real changes that did occur, they have failed to provide a convincing portrait of an era characterized above all by drama, turmoil, and social change.

Building upon the findings of the past twenty years of scholarship, a new portrait of Reconstruction ought to begin by viewing it not as a specific time period, bounded by the years 1865 and 1877, but as an episode in a prolonged historical process— American society's adjustment to the consequences of the Civil War and emancipation. The Civil War, of course, raised the decisive questions of America's national existence: the relations between local and national authority, the definition of citizenship, the balance between force and consent in generating obedience to authority. The war and Reconstruction, as Allan Nevins observed over fifty years ago, marked the "emergence of modern America." This was the era of the completion of the national railroad network, the creation of the modern steel industry, the conquest of the West and final subduing of the Indians, and the expansion of the mining frontier. Lincoln's America—the world of the small farm and artisan shop—gave way to a rapidly industrializing economy. The issues that galvanized postwar Northern politics—from the question of the greenback currency to the mode of paying holders of the national debt—arose from the economic changes unleased by the Civil War.

Above all, the war irrevocably abolished slavery. Since 1619, when "twenty negars" disembarked from a Dutch ship in Virginia, racial injustice had haunted American life, mocking its professed ideals even as tobacco and cotton, the products of slave labor, helped finance the nation's economic development. Now the implications of the black presence could no longer be ignored. The Civil War resolved the problem of slavery but, as the Philadelphia diarist Sydney George Fisher observed in June 1865, it opened an even more intractable problem: "What shall we do with the Negro?" Indeed, he went on, this was a problem "incapable of any solution that will satisfy both North and South."

As Fisher realized, the focal point of Reconstruction was the social revolution known as emancipation. Plantation slavery was simultaneously a system of labor, a form of racial domination, and the foundation upon which arose a distinctive ruling class within the South. Its demise threw open the most fundamental questions of economy, society, and politics. A new system of labor, social, racial, and political relations had to be created to replace slavery.

The United States was not the only nation to experience emancipation in the nineteenth century. Neither plantation slavery nor abolition were unique to the United States. But Reconstruction was. In a comparative perspective Radical Reconstruction stands as a remarkable experiment, the only effort of a society experiencing abolition to bring the former slaves within the umbrella of equal citizenship. Because the Radicals did not achieve everything they wanted, historians have lately tended to play down the stunning departure represented by black suffrage and officeholding. Former slaves, most fewer than two years removed from bondage, debated the fundamental questions of the polity: what is a republican form of government? Should the state provide equal education for all? How could political equality be reconciled with a society in which property was so unequally distributed? There was something inspiring in the way such men met the challenge of Reconstruction. "I knew nothing more than to obey my master," James K. Greene, an Alabama black politician later recalled. "But the tocsin of freedom sounded and knocked at the door and we walked out like free men and we met the exigencies as they grew up, and shouldered the responsibilities."

You never saw a people more excited on the subject of politics than are the negroes of the south," one planter observed in 1867. And there were more than a few Southern whites as well who in these years shook off the prejudices of the past to embrace the revision of a new South dedicated to the principles of equal citizenship and social justice. One ordinary South Carolinian expressed the new sense of possibility in 1868 to the Republican governor of the state: "I am sorry that I cannot write an elegant stiled letter to your excellency. But I rejoice to think that God almighty has given to the poor of S.C. a Gov. to hear to feel to protect the humble poor without distinction to race or color.... I am a native borned S.C. a poor man never owned a Negro in my life nor my father before me.... Remember the true and loyal are the poor of the whites and blacks, outside of these you can find none loyal."

Few modern scholars believe the Reconstruction governments established in the South in 1867 and 1868 fulfilled the aspirations of their humble constituents. While their achievements in such realms as education, civil rights, and the economic rebuilding of the South are now widely appreciated, historians today believe they failed to affect either the economic plight of the emancipated slave or the ongoing transformation of independent white farmers into cotton tenants. Yet their opponents did perceive the Reconstruction governments in precisely this way—as representatives of a revolution that had put the bottom rail, both racial and economic, on top. This perception helps explain the ferocity of the attacks leveled against them and the pervasiveness of violence in the post-emancipation South.

In the end neither the abolition of slavery nor Reconstruction succeeded in resolving the debate over the meaning of freedom in American life.

The spectacle of black men voting and holding office was anathema to large numbers of Southern whites. Even more disturbing, at least in the view of those who still controlled the plantation regions of the South, was the emergence of local officials, black and white, who sympathized with the plight of the black laborer. Alabama's vagrancy law was a "dead letter" in 1870, "because those who are charged with its enforcement are indebted to the vagrant vote for their offices and emoluments." Political debates over the level and incidence of taxation, the control of crops, and the resolution of contract disputes revealed that a primary issue of Reconstruction was the role of government in a plantation society. During presidential Reconstruction, and after "Redemption," with planters and their allies in control of politics, the law emerged as a means of stabilizing and promoting the plantation system. If Radical Reconstruction failed to redistribute the land of the South, the ouster of the planter class from control of politics at least ensured that the sanctions of the criminal law would not be employed to discipline the black labor force.

An understanding of this fundamental conflict over the relation between government and society helps explain the pervasive complaints concerning corruption and "extravagance" during Radical Reconstruction. Corruption there was aplenty; tax rates did rise sharply. More significant

than the rate of taxation, however, was the change in its incidence. For the first time, planters and white farmers had to pay a significant portion of their income to the government, while propertyless blacks often escaped scot-free. Several states, moreover, enacted heavy taxes on uncultivated land to discourage land speculation and force land onto the market, benefiting, it was hoped, the freedmen.

As time passed, complaints about the "extravagance" and corruption of Southern governments found a sympathetic audience among influential Northerners. The Democratic charge that universal suffrage in the South was responsible for high taxes and governmental extravagance coincided with a rising conviction among the urban middle classes of the North that city government had to be taken out of the hands of the immigrant poor and returned to the "best men"—the educated, professional, financially independent citizens unable to exert much political influence at a time of mass parties and machine politics. Increasingly the "respectable" middle classes began to retreat from the very notion of universal suffrage. The poor were not longer perceived as honest producers, the backbone of the social order; now they became the "dangerous classes," the "mob." As the historian Francis Parkman put it, too much power rested with "masses of imported ignorance and hereditary ineptitude." To Parkman the Irish of the Northern cities and the blacks of the South were equally incapable of utilizing the ballot: "Witness the municipal corruptions of New York, and the monstrosities of negro rule in South Carolina." Such attitudes helped to justify Northern inaction as, one by one, the Reconstruction regimes of the South were overthrown by political violence.

In the end, then, neither the abolition of slavery nor Reconstruction succeeded in resolving the debate over the meaning of freedom in American life. Twenty years before the American Civil War, writing about the prospect of abolition in France's colonies, Alexis de Tocqueville had written, "If the Negroes have the right to become free, the [planters] have the incontestable right not to be ruined by the

Negroes' freedom." And in the United States, as in nearly every plantation society that experienced the end of slavery, a rigid social and political dichotomy between former master and former slave, an ideology of racism, and a dependent labor force with limited economic opportunities all survived abolition. Unless one means by freedom the simple fact of not being a slave, emancipation thrust blacks into a kind of no-man's land, a partial freedom that made a mockery of the American ideal of equal citizenship.

Yet by the same token the ultimate outcome underscores the uniqueness of Reconstruction itself. Alone among the societies that abolished slavery in the nineteenth century, the United States, for a moment, offered the freedmen a measure of political control over their own destinies. However brief its sway, Reconstruction allowed scope for a remarkable political and social mobilization of the black community. It opened doors of opportunity that could never be completely closed. Reconstruction transformed the lives of Southern blacks in ways unmeasurable by statistics and unreachable by law. It raised their expectations and aspirations, redefined their status in relation to the larger society, and allowed space for the creation of institutions that enabled them to survive the repression that followed. And it established constitutional principles of civil and political equality that, while flagrantly violated after Redemption, planted the seeds of future struggle.

Certainly, in terms of the sense of possibility with which it opened, Reconstruction failed. But as Du Bois observed, it was a "splendid failure." For its animating vision—a society in which social advancement would be open to all on the basis of individual merit, not inherited caste distinctions—is as old as America itself and remains relevant to a nation still grappling with the unresolved legacy of emancipation.

Eric Foner is Professor of History at Columbia University and author of Nothing but Freedom: Emancipation and Its Legacy.

From *American Heritage*, October/November 1983, pp. 10–15. Reprinted by permission of American Heritage, Inc., a division of Forbes, Inc.

1871 War on Terror

In the aftermath of the Civil War, America's federal authorities took unprecedented action to crack down on the Ku Klux Klan.

By David Everitt

Secret cells of violent zealots target civilians in their homes and workplaces. When not carrying out terrorist acts, they conceal themselves among the general population, aided by local officials. As waves of fear spread, an American president decides the time has come to strike back.

A description of recent world events? Not necessarily. The scenario also fits another time in America's history. The campaign against Al Qaeda and its allies is not the United States' first war on terror. In the American South during the aftermath of the Civil War, a terrorist organization emerged. Cloaked in ghostly disguise, it sought to murder and maim in the dead of night as it set out to impose its ideological agenda. For several years the governmental response was ineffectual. Finally, in 1871, the U.S. Congress and President Ulysses S. Grant took action and initiated a new policy in South Carolina, where the organization was especially brazen. The government took extraordinary—some said excessive—measures to crack down on the brutal crimes of this terrorist group, the Reconstruction-era Ku Klux Klan.

Some of the issues surrounding this 19th-century war on terror are reminiscent of those we face now. Like George W. Bush's today, Grant's administration was criticized for overstepping its authority and for not understanding the true nature of the problem. In the end, the offensive that Grant launched against the Klan produced some very tangible results, but the ultimate success of his effort is still open to debate.

Terrorism thrives on great turmoil, and in the conquered and humiliated South it found an ideal breeding ground. Reconstruction upended society as white Southerners knew it, not only freeing blacks from slavery but also providing opportunity for their advancement in both business and government. Enraged by those developments, many Southern white men looked for some way to lash out at emancipated slaves and their white supporters. More than that, they hoped to restore the old order. For them, the Ku Klux Klan was the answer.

In 1868, the Klan was imported to South Carolina from Tennessee, where it had originated earlier that same year. The organization immediately demonstrated it would not tolerate former slaves exercising their right to vote. During the 1868 South Carolina election campaign, the Klan murdered eight blacks, two of them state congressmen.

The state government controlled by Republicans—the party of Abraham Lincoln—met the terrorist threat by raising a special militia and filling its ranks with black citizens. That proved to be dramatic enough to inflame the Klan, but not strong enough to defeat it.

During the 1870 election campaign, the new militia countered the Klan's intimidation tactics to some extent, and the ballot results enraged Klan members even further when the Republican governor, Robert Scott, was re-elected. The next day, South Carolina's wave of terror truly began.

South Carolina was by no means the only state plagued by Klan violence—the organization was active throughout the South—but in portions of South Carolina the acts of terror were especially alarming between the fall of 1870 and the summer of 1871. A public Klan proclamation announced that the organization's targets were "the scum of the earth, the scrapings of creation" and that they intended to do everything possible to oppose "negro rule, black bayonets, and a miserably degraded and thievish set of lawmakers." Over a nine-month period in South Carolina's York County alone, six murders were attributed to the Ku Klux Klan, while whippings and beatings might have numbered in the hundreds.

One of the most notoriously brutal cases was the murder of a black man named Tom Roundtree. The Klan shot him to death, then mutilated his body and sank it in a nearby stream. Other infamous crimes involved the black militia, an especially hated target of the Klan. In one instance, in Unionville, Klansmen lynched 10 black militiamen who had been jailed for the murder of a whiskey peddler. In another case, in the town of Yorkville, a black militia captain named Jim Williams allegedly issued a threat against whites in the area. The Klan dragged him from his house and hanged him. On his dangling body they left a card on which they had written "Jim Williams on his big muster."

The Klan cast a wide net and showed little mercy for those unlikely to be able to defend themselves. One of their whipping victims was a 69-year-old white man who had offended the Klan by acting as a Republican election officer, and another was a black preacher, incapacitated from birth by stunted arms and legs, who was charged with rabble-rousing from the pulpit. At times the Klansmen also took it upon themselves to punish what they considered domestic offenses. In an incident that would have pleased today's religiously fanatic terrorists, for example, Ku Kluxers in Spartanburg County once whipped a woman for the crime of leaving her husband.

As indefensible as the Klan's actions surely were, apologists for those acts were plentiful, and they did not necessarily come from the South.

As indefensible as the Klan's actions surely were, apologists for those acts were plentiful, and they did not necessarily come from the South. Sometimes their statements echo reactions to modern terrorism that we've heard in recent years. Certain pundits in the early 1870s, for instance, offered the terrorists-as-freedom-fighters rationalization. On the floor of the U.S. Congress, Representative S.S. Cox from New York argued that "South Carolina has been infested by the worst local government ever vouchsafed to a people." Comparing the Klan to the Carbonari, which fought for constitutional government in Italy during the early 1800s, Cox concluded, "All history shows that such societies grow by persecution and that they are the bitter fruits of tyranny." Even those in the South who criticized Klan excesses only did so because they considered them counterproductive as opposed to immoral, similar to the way some Middle Easterners today have criticized suicide bombers because they don't help the Palestinian cause, not because the acts themselves are unspeakable.

In the North, newspapers often minimized the Klan threat. A *New York Times* editorial stated that when there weren't enough real Klan atrocities to report, "the matter was put into the hands of literary gentlemen who thereupon started armed bands in all directions through the newspaper woods, dragged out newspaper negroes from newspaper homes, and, tying them up to trees of the mind, lashed their newspaper backs till blood ran down, awful to behold."

With little support for a forceful response, Governor Scott tried appeasing the South Carolina Klan. In February 1871, he disarmed York County's black militia, hoping that this would persuade the Klan to stop its raids. But the Ku Kluxers responded to that gesture as if it were a sign of weakness—they resorted to even more violence. At his wits' end, Scott requested help from Washington, and in March President Grant sent in federal troops.

The soldiers assigned to South Carolina belonged to the 7th Cavalry, Lt. Col. (Brevet Maj. Gen.) George Armstrong Custer's regiment, which had recently fought the Cheyennes on the Great Plains. The troops were headquartered in York County, the center for much of the Klan activity in the state, and they were commanded by 37-year-old Major Lewis M. Merrill. At first skeptical of the seemingly alarmist accounts of the KKK, Merrill soon became convinced of the basic truth of the allegations and would go on to play a crucial role in combating terrorism in the state.

Merrill quickly discovered that he faced great obstacles. Like terrorist organizations today, the Klan was highly compartmentalized. Klan chiefs had no direct contact with underlings, making it difficult for the Army to collect evidence against ringleaders. And even after Merrill and his men collected information on subordinates, local authorities sabotaged any effort to win a conviction in court. As Merrill later described it, "I never conceived of such a state of social disorganization being possible in any civilized community." Still, he continued to investigate in the hope that the federal government would find a way to bring the terrorists to justice.

In May 1870, Congress had passed the Enforcement Act, which had attempted to prevent the Klan from violating citizens' constitutional protections, but the law produced little result. Now, in 1871, Republicans in Congress considered passing a much stronger bill.

The Ku Klux Act, as it came to be called, targeted people who "conspire together, or go in disguise upon any public highway, or upon the premises of another" for the purpose of depriving any citizens of their legal rights. The bill authorized President Grant to dismantle those conspiracies in no uncertain terms: He could, in effect, place an area under martial law and suspend the writ of habeas corpus, which would allow authorities to imprison suspected Klansmen for extended periods of time without bringing them to court to face formal charges.

Democrats charged that the methods of enforcement amounted to tyrannical, unconstitutional powers. In rebuttal, Representative Robert B. Elliott, a black Republican from South Carolina, drew his fellow legislators' attention to more basic Constitutional protections. He pointed out that the Constitution states, "The United States shall guarantee to every State in the Union a republican form of government." States like South Carolina were denied this type of government, Elliott's argument went, as long as terrorists threatened citizens' right to vote. Strong as his case might have been, it could not overcome the congressional bickering that gridlocked the bill. What was needed was the moral authority of President Grant. The Ku Klux Act finally became law on April 20, only after Grant publicly urged Congress to ratify it.

Now, Major Merrill's efforts had a chance of making a difference. That summer, he testified before a congressional subcommittee that arrived in South Carolina to investigate the extent of Klan outrages in the state. The intelligence Merrill had gathered on whippings, beatings and murders painted a disturbing portrait for the congressmen.

'I never conceived of such a state of social disorganization being possible in any civilized community.' —Major Lewis M. Merrill

During their four-week tour of the state, the congressmen could see for themselves how desperate the situation had become. Refugees from Klan violence congregated wherever the subcommittee convened. Many of them, both white and black, had been spending their nights in the woods for months to avoid Ku Klux attacks. According to a *New York Times* report, "It was found impossible for the Committee to examine more than a small part of the crowds of whipped, maimed, or terror-stricken wretches who flocked in upon hearing of their coming."

Pressing the case for forceful action was Grant's attorney general, Amos T. Akerman. A scalawag, according to conventional Southern wisdom of the day, Akerman was a transplanted Northerner who had spent his adult life as a citizen of Georgia and was now a staunch supporter of Reconstruction. He went to South Carolina to conduct his own investigation in late September and concluded that the Klan could be smashed quickly if the government took decisive steps that would rattle rank-and-file Ku Kluxers and convince them to confess. As Klan raids continued, Akerman met with Grant in early October and helped persuade him that the time had come to activate the Ku Klux Act's enforcement measures.

On October 12, Grant ordered the South Carolina Klan to disperse and disarm in five days. The warning was ignored. On October 17, Grant proclaimed that "in my judgment the public safety especially requires that the privileges of the writ of habeas corpus be suspended." The suspension applied to all arrests made by U.S. marshals and federal troops in nine of the state's western counties.

Akerman immediately met with Merrill to assemble a list of Klansmen to be arrested, based on information gathered by the major over the previous seven months. Their strategy was to hit several towns suddenly and simultaneously, with teams of federal marshals backed up by the 7th Cavalry, in order to instill panic throughout the organization. The plan could not have worked better.

Within 10 days of Grant's proclamation, marshals and troops made 100 arrests in York and Spartanburg counties. Many more Klansmen came in on their own, and by the end of November federal officials in South Carolina had made 600 arrests in all. A large number of those were very willing to "puke," the colorful slang term in those days for confess. There were 160 confessions in York County alone, and in the process investigators learned of five murders that had previously gone unreported. The federal crackdown had such a profound effect that York's county seat had "the

look of a town in wartime recently captured by an invading army," according to a *New York Tribune* correspondent.

Louis F. Post, an aide to Merrill, contended that the mass confessions were the direct result of the suspension of habeas corpus. "For a time the prisoners were silent," he wrote. "But as hope of release died out and fears of hanging grew stronger, the weaker ones sought permission to tell Major Merrill what they knew."

Some editorialists saw grave dangers in the government's actions. Similar to some of today's critics of the war on terrorism, these people claimed that the government's aggressiveness was only making more enemies. "I shudder to think," wrote a *New York Herald* correspondent, "what the retaliation will be [from the Klan] for the imprisoning of two hundred white men and the driving from their homes of three or four hundred others."

To be precise, hundreds of South Carolinians were not driven from their homes—they fled to avoid prosecution. This was both good news and bad. True, the flight of so many Ku Kluxers disrupted the organization, but the fugitives included some of the most prominent Klan chiefs. Federal prosecutors would only be able, for the most part, to press charges against the organization's underlings. Still, Akerman believed that convictions of these men would send a strong warning to anyone considering further Klan raids.

The Ku Klux court cases began November 27, 1871, in the U.S. Circuit Court in the South Carolina capital of Columbia. The first to go on trial was farmer Robert Hayes Mitchell, an ordinary, subordinate Klansmen whose case provided an extraordinary glimpse into the inner workings of the KKK and two of its most notorious crimes.

Like other defendants who followed, Mitchell was charged with conspiracy to prevent black citizens from voting. To illustrate the nature of the conspiracy, prosecutors called on one witness to outline the elaborate series of signs and passwords that Ku Kluxers used to identify one another and maintain security. The government also presented testimony on the Klan constitution. Acquired at Merrill's instigation, the document revealed the organization's deadly oath of secrecy: Anyone breaking this oath, the constitution stated, "shall meet the fearful penalty and traitor's doom, which is death, death, death."

Specific instances of conspiracy included the murder of Captain Jim Williams of the black militia. Klan supporters maintained that the organization's raids had been provoked by militia excesses, which typically amounted to arrogant, intimidating behavior. Federal prosecutors, though, established in court that the Klan had first resorted to violence two years before the black militia was formed in 1870.

Another count of conspiracy against Mitchell involved the assault against a black man named Amzi Rainey who had offended the Klan by voting for radical Republicans. The victim's testimony dramatized the savagery of the attack. Crashing into Rainey's house around midnight, the Klan beat not only Rainey but also his wife. At one point Rainey's little daughter ran at the Klansmen, yelling, "Don't kill my pappy; please don't kill my pappy!" One of the attackers responded by firing a shot that grazed the little girl's forehead.

> ## 'In my judgement the public safety especially requires that the privileges of the writ of habeas corpus be suspended.' —U.S. Grant

In his summation for the defense, attorney Reverdy Johnson saw no point in trying to dispute the charges of Klan violence, conceding that the outrages "show that the parties engaged were brutes, insensible to the obligations of humanity and religion." Instead, he argued that the Enforcement Act of 1870 and the Ku Klux Act were unconstitutional. The argument made little impression on the jury of 10 blacks and two whites who took only 38 minutes to bring in a guilty verdict.

Through the month of December, similar verdicts followed, along with a procession of guilty pleas. In pronouncing sentences, Judge Hugh L. Bond brought a finely tuned moral voice to the proceedings, showing both leniency for unsophisticated men pressured into the Klan ranks and severity for those who exercised some degree of authority. The most common of the 58 prison sentences ranged from three to six months, while others entailed both prison time and some sort of fine.

The most severe was a combination of five years and $1,000, reserved for the likes of Klan chief John W. Mitchell, a prominent member of his community and somebody, Judge Bond asserted, who should have known better. In his sentencing, the judge stressed Mitchell's abdication of responsibility: "Knowing all this [about the Klan's activities], hearing of the ravishing, murders and whipping going on in York County, you never took any pains to inform anybody; you never went to the civil authorities and you remained a chief till they elected somebody else."

The federal crackdown did not stop there. Through 1872, Major Merrill continued to make arrests, and in April the federal court in Charleston delivered 36 more convictions. At the same time, though—as critics branded Grant a dictator—the government began to back off.

Attorney General Akerman resigned in January 1872, and though his exit was amicable on the surface, some have speculated that he was frustrated by the lack of funding for ongoing Klan prosecutions. His replacement was less concerned with Klan violence, even though a federal marshal was killed in South Carolina while enforcing the Ku Klux Act, and a prosecution witness had his throat slit. Further impeding the anti-Klan campaign was Congress' decision in 1872 to restore habeas corpus rights. By August, the federal government began pardoning convicted Ku Kluxers. The government's war on Ku Klux Klan terror came to a definitive end in 1877, when President Rutherford B. Hayes ordered the end of Reconstruction.

Looking back upon this episode, we can see that the Grant administration faced two especially difficult questions that confront us today as once again we wage a war on terror. First, how much should the government limit constitutional rights when fighting an enemy that does not respect the rights of others? By imposing federal authority on local jurisdictions and suspending the writ of habeas corpus, the Grant administration was taking unprecedented measures in peacetime to deal with a dire crisis. In 1876, five years after the first Klan prosecutions, the U.S. Supreme Court ruled that the Enforcement Act of 1870 and the Ku Klux Act were indeed unconstitutional, that they had improperly superceded the rights of the states.

The second question is: How does one know when a war on terror is truly won? Although the Klan prosecutions did not last long, some historians maintain that they accomplished their immediate goal. According to Allen W. Trelease, author of *White Terror*, "The federal government had broken the back of the Ku Klux Klan throughout most of the South." And it is true that the Klan did not rise again until after World War I, some 50 years later. But the Grant administration left larger goals unrealized. Even though the outer trappings of the Klan might have disappeared, its attitudes and the willingness to impose those attitudes through violence remained. And once Reconstruction ended and the passage of repressive Jim Crow laws began, white supremacy reigned once again throughout the South. Jim Crow would continue to rule for another 80 years, until the dawn of the modern civil rights movement.

Union forces won the Civil War against the Confederacy. President Grant's marshals and troops won the battle against the Reconstruction-era Klan. Nevertheless, the federal government failed to see its war on terror as a long-term commitment, and it failed to come up with a practical plan for rebuilding the South and bringing the Old Confederacy into the modern, fully democratic age. As a consequence, some might say that the North ultimately failed to win the peace.

From *American History*, June 2003, pages 26-28, 30-33. Copyright © 2003 Primedia Consumer Media and Magazines Inc. All rights reserved. Reprinted with permission.

Lockwood in '84

In 1884, a woman couldn't vote for the president of the United States, but that didn't stop activist lawyer Belva Lockwood from conducting a full-scale compaign for the office. She was the first woman ever to do so, and she tried again for the presidency in 1888. It's time we recognized her name.

by Jill Norgren

In 1884, Washington, D.C., attorney Belva Lockwood, candidate of the Equal Rights Party, became the first woman to run a full campaign for the presidency of the United States. She had no illusion that a woman could be elected, but there were policy issues on which she wished to speak, and, truth be told, she welcomed the notoriety. When challenged as to whether a woman was eligible to become president, she said that there was "not a thing in the Constitution" to prohibit it. She did not hesitate to confront the male establishment that barred women from voting and from professional advancement. With the spunk born of a lifelong refusal to be a passive victim of discrimination, Lockwood told a campaign reporter, "I cannot vote, but I can be voted for." Her bid for the presidency startled the country and infuriated other suffrage leaders, many of whom mistakenly clung to the idea that the Republican Party would soon sponsor a constitutional amendment in support of woman suffrage.

In the last quarter of the 19th century, Lockwood commanded attention, and not just from the columnists and satirists whom she led a merry chase. Today she is virtually unknown, lost in the shadows of the iconic suffrage leaders Elizabeth Cady Stanton and Susan B. Anthony. That's an injustice, for Belva Lockwood was a model of courageous activism and an admirable symbol of a woman's movement that increasingly invested its energies in party politics.

Lockwood was born Belva Ann Bennett in the Niagara County town of Royalton, New York, on October 24, 1830, the second daughter, and second of five children, of Lewis J. Bennett, a farmer, and Hannah Green Bennett. Belva was educated in rural schoolhouses, where she herself began to teach at the age of 14. In her first profession she found her first cause. As a female instructor, she received less than half the salary paid to the young men. The Bennetts' teenage daughter thought this treatment "odious, an indignity not to be tamely borne." She complained to the wife of a lo-

cal minister, who counseled her that such was the way of the world. But bright, opinionated, ambitious Belva Bennett would not accept that world.

From her avid reading of history, Belva imagined for herself a life different from that of her mother and her aunts—the life, in fact, of a great man. She asked her father's permission to continue her education, but he said no. She then did what she was expected to do: On November 8, 1848, she married Uriah MeNall, a promising young farmer. She threw herself into running their small farm and sawmill, wrote poetry and essays, and determined not to let marriage be the end of her individuality. She wanted to chart her own course, and tragedy gave her an opportunity to do so. In April 1853, when she was 22 and her daughter, Lura, three, Uriah McNall died.

The young widow had a second chance to go out into the world. She resumed her teaching and her education. In September 1854, she left Lura with her mother and traveled 60 miles east to study at the Genesee Wesleyan Seminary in Lima. The seminary shared a building with the newly coeducational Genesee College, which offered a more rigorous program. Belva transferred to the college (becoming its third woman student), where she took courses in science and politics. She graduated with a bachelor's degree (with honors) on June 27, 1857, and soon found a position teaching high school in the prosperous Erie Canal town of Lockport. Four years later, she took over a small school in the south-central New York town of Owego. In 1866, Belva McNall traveled to Washington and began to reinvent herself as an urban professional. She was neither flamboyant nor eccentric. Indeed, had she been a man, it would have been apparent that her life was following a conventional 19th-century course: Talented chap walks off the farm, educates himself, seeks opportunities, and makes a name. But because Belva strove to be that ambitious son of ordinary people who rises in the world on the basis of his wits and his work, she was thought a radical.

In Washington, Belva taught school and worked as a leasing agent, renting halls to lodges and organizations. She tutored herself in the workings of government and the art of lobbying by making frequent visits to Congress. In 1868 she married Ezekiel Lockwood, an elderly dentist and lay preacher who shared her reformist views. We do not know precisely when she fell in love with the law. In antebellum America the profession belonged to men, who passed on their skill by training their sons and nephews and neighbors' boys. After the Civil War a handful of women, Lockwood among them, set out to change all that. She believed from her reading of the lives of great men that "in almost every instance law has been the stepping-stone to greatness." She attended the law program of Washington's National University, graduated in 1872 (but only after she lobbied for the diploma male administrators had been pressured to withhold), and was admitted to the bar of the District of Columbia in 1873 (again, only after a struggle against sex discrimination). When the Supreme Court of the United States refused to admit her to its bar in 1876, she single-handedly lobbied Congress until, in 1879, it passed, reluctantly, "An act to relieve the legal disabilities of women." On March 3, 1879, Lockwood became the first woman admitted to the high Court bar, and, in 1880, the first woman lawyer to argue a case before the Court.

From her earliest years in Washington, Lockwood coveted a government position. She applied to be a consul officer in Ghent during the administration of Andrew Johnson, but her application was never acknowledged. In later years, she sought government posts—for women in general and for herself in particular—from other presidents. Without success. When Grover Cleveland passed over Lockwood and appointed as minister to Turkey a man thought to be a womanizer, she wrote to compliment the president on his choice: "The only danger is, that he will attempt to suppress polygamy in that country by marrying all of the women himself." A year later, in 1886, in another communication to Cleveland, she laid claim to the position of district recorder of deeds and let the president know in no uncertain terms that she had a "lien" on the job. She did not give up: In 1911 she had her name included on a list sent to President William Howard Taft of women attorneys who could fill the Supreme Court vacancy caused by the death of Justice John Marshall Harlan.

What persuaded Lockwood that she should run for the highest office in the land? Certainly, she seized the opportunity to shake a fist at conservatives who would hold women back. And she was displeased with the enthusiasm for the Republican Party shown by suffrage leaders Susan B. Anthony and Elizabeth Cady Stanton. More than that, however, campaigning would provide an opportunity for her to speak her mind, to travel, and to establish herself on the paid lecture circuit. She was not the first woman to run for president. In 1872, New York City newspaper publisher Victoria Woodhull had declared herself a presidential candidate, against Ulysses Grant and Horace Greeley. But Woodhull, cast as Mrs. Satan by the influential cartoonist Thomas Nast, had to abandon her campaign barely a month after its start: Her radical "free love" views were too much baggage for the nascent women's movement to bear, and financial misfortune forced her to suspend publication of *Woodhull & Claflin's Weekly* at the very moment she most needed a public platform.

Years later, Lockwood—and the California women who drafted her—spoke of the circumstances surrounding her August 1884 nomination, their accounts colored by ego and age. Lockwood received the nod from Marietta Stow, a San Francisco reformer who spoke for the newly formed, California-based Equal Rights Party, and from Stow's colleague, attorney Clara Foltz. Foltz later insisted that Lockwood's nomination amounted to nothing more than a lighthearted joke on her and Stow's part. But Stow's biographer, Sherilyn Bennion, has made a strong case that the nomination was, in fact, part of a serious political strategy devised by Stow to deflect attention from the rebuff given suffrage leaders that year at the Republican and Democratic conventions, and to demonstrate that "the fair sex" could create its own terms of engagement in American party politics. Women were becoming stump speakers, participants in political clubs, candidates for local office, and, in a handful of places, voters. (By 1884 the Wyoming, Utah and Washington Territories had fully enfranchised women, who in 14 states were permitted to vote in elections dealing with schools.) Marietta Stow began the Equal Rights Party because she had long been interested in matters of public policy and because readers of her newspaper, *The Women's Herald of Industry*, had expressed an interest in a "new, clean, uncorruptible party."

In July 1884 Stow urged Abigail Scott Duniway, an Oregon rights activist and newspaper editor, to accept the Equal Rights Party's nomination. But Duniway declined, believing, as Bennion writes, that "flaunting the names of women for official positions" would weaken the case for equal rights and provide "unscrupulous opponents with new pretexts and excuses for lying about them." Undiscouraged, Stow continued her search for a candidate. In August, she hit her mark.

Belva Lockwood, *Women's Herald* reader, had already begun to think of herself as a standard-bearer. On August 10 she wrote to Stow in San Francisco and asked rhetorically, and perhaps disingenuously, "Why not nominate women for important places? Is not Victoria Empress of India? Have we not among our country-women persons of as much talent and ability? Is not history full of precedents of women rulers?" The Republicans, she commented, claimed to be the party of progress yet had "little else but insult for women when [we] appear before its conventions." (She had been among those rebuffed that summer by the Republicans.) She was exasperated with the party of Lincoln and maddened by Stanton and Anthony's continuing faith in major-party politics: "It is quite time that we had our own party, our own platform, and our own nominees. We shall never have equal rights until we take them, nor respect until we command it."

Stow had her candidate! She called a party convention on August 23, read Lockwood's letter to the small group, and proposed her as the party's nominee for president of the United States, along with Clemence S. Lozier, a New York City physician, as the vice presidential nominee. Acclamation followed, and letters were sent to the two women. The dispatch to Lockwood read as follows: "Madam: We have the honor to inform you that you were nominated, at the Woman's National Equal-Rights Convention, for President of the United States. We await your letter of acceptance with breathless interest."

Lockwood later said that the letter took her "utterly by surprise," and she kept it secret for several days. On September 3, she wrote to accept the nomination for "Chief Magistrate of the United States" from the only party that "really and truly represent the interests of our whole people North, South, East, and West.... With your unanimous and cordial support ... we shall not only be able to carry the election, but to guide the Ship of State safely into port." Lockwood went on to outline a dozen platform points, and her promptness in formulating policy signaled that she (and the party) intended to be taken seriously about matters of political substance.

Forecasters in '84 were predicting another close presidential race. Four years earlier, James Garfield had defeated Winfield Hancock by just 40,000 votes (out of nine million cast), and people were again watching the critical states of New York and Indiana. The nearly even division of registered voters between the two major parties caused Democratic candidate Grover Cleveland and Republican candidate James G. Blaine to shy away from innovative platforms. Instead, the two men spent much of their time trading taunts and insults. That left the business of serious reform to the minor parties and their candidates: Benjamin Butler (National Greenback/Anti-Monopoly), John St. John (Prohibition), and Samuel Clarke Pomeroy (American Prohibition). Butler, St. John, and Pomeroy variously supported workers' rights, the abolition of child and prison labor, a graduated income tax, senatorial term limits, direct election of the president, and, of course, prohibition of the manufacture, sale, and consumption of alcohol. Lockwood joined this group of nothing-to-lose candidates, who intended to promote the public discussion of issues about which Blaine and Cleveland dared not speak.

The design of Lockwood's platform reflected her practical savvy. The platform, she said, should "take up every one of the issues of the day" but be "so brief that the newspapers would publish it and the people read it."

(She understood the art of the sound bite.) Her "grand platform of principles" expressed bold positions and comfortable compromise. She promised to promote and maintain equal political privileges for "every class of our citizens irrespective of sex, color or nationality" in order to make America "in truth what it has so long been in name, 'the land of the free and home of the brave.'" She pledged herself to the fair distribution of public offices to women as well as men, "with a scrupulous regard to civil service reform after the women are duly installed in office." She opposed the "wholesale monopoly of the judiciary" by men and said that, if elected, she would appoint a reasonable number of women as district attorneys, marshals, and federal judges, including a "competent woman to any vacancy that might occur on the United States Supreme Bench."

Lockwood's views extended well beyond women's issues. She adopted a moderate position on the contentious question of tariffs. In her statement of September 3, she placed the Equal Rights Party in the political camp that wanted to "protect and foster American industries," in sympathy with the working men and women of the country who were organized against free trade. But in the official platform statement reprinted on campaign literature, her position was modified so that the party might be identified as middle-of-the-road, supporting neither high tariffs nor free trade. Lockwood urged the extension of commercial relations with foreign countries and advocated the establishment of a "high Court of Arbitration" to which commercial and political differences could be referred. She supported citizenship for Native Americans and the allotment of tribal land. As was to be expected from an attorney who earned a substantial part of her livelihood doing pension claims work, she adopted a safe position on Civil War veterans' pensions: She argued that tariff revenues should be applied to benefits for former soldiers and their dependents; at the same time, she urged the abolition of the Pension Office, "with its complicated and technical machinery," and recommended that it be replaced with a board of three commissioners. She vowed full sympathy with temperance advocates and, in a position unique to the platform of the Equal Rights Party, called for the reform of family law: "If elected, I shall recommend in my Inaugural speech, a uniform system of laws as far as practicable for all of the States, and especially for marriage, divorce, and the limitation of contracts, and such a regulation of the laws of descent and distribution of estates as will make the wife equal with the husband in authority and right, and an equal partner in the common business."

Lockwood's position paper of September 3 was revised into the platform statement that appeared below her portrait on campaign flyers. The new version expanded on certain points, adopted some sharper rhetoric, and added several planks, including a commitment that the remaining public lands of the nation would go to the "honest yeomanry," not the railroads. Lockwood stuck to her radical positions of support for women's suffrage and the reform of domestic law, but, in a stunning retreat, her earlier promises of an equitable allotment of public positions by sex and any mention of the need for women in the judiciary were absent from the platform.

Armed with candidate and platform, the leaders and supporters of the Equal Rights Party waited to see what would happen. A great deal depended on the posture adopted by the press. Fortunately for Lockwood and the party, many of the daily newspapers controlled by men, and a number of weeklies owned by women, took an interest in the newest contender in the election of '84. A day after she accepted the nomination, *The Washington Evening Star* made her candidacy front-page news and reprinted the entire text of her acceptance letter and platform of September 3. The candidate told a *Star* reporter that she would not necessarily receive the endorsement of activist women. Indeed, leaders of the nation's two top woman suffrage associations had endorsed Blaine, and Frances Willard had united temperance women with the Prohibition Party. "You must remember," Lockwood said, "that the women are divided up into as many factions and parties as the men."

On September 5, an editorial in the *Star* praised Lockwood's letter of acceptance: "In all soberness, it can be said [it] is the best of the lot. It is short, sharp, and decisive.... It is evident that Mrs. Lockwood, if elected, will have a policy [that] commends itself to all people of common sense." Editor Crosby Noyes rued the letter's late appearance: Had it existed sooner, "the other candidates might have had the benefit of perusing it and framing their several epistles in accord with its pith and candor." Newspaper reporting elsewhere was similarly respectful.

Abigail Duniway's warning that women candidates would meet with "unpleasant prominence" and be held up "to ridicule and scorn" proved correct, but Lockwood actually encountered no greater mockery than the men in the election. She had to endure silly lies about hairpieces and sham allegations that she was divorced, but Cleveland was taunted with cries of "Ma, Ma Where's My Pa" (a reference to his out-of-wedlock child). Cartoonists for *Frank Leslie's Illustrated and Puck*, mass-circulation papers, made fun of all the candidates, including Lockwood. This was a rite of passage and badge of acceptance. *Leslie's* also ran an article on Lockwood's campaign and contemplated the entrance of women into party politics with earnest good wishes: "Woman in politics. Why not?.... Twenty years ago woman's suffrage was a mere opinion. To-day, it is another matter."

After establishing campaign headquarters at her Washington home on F Street, Lockwood wrote to friends and acquaintances in a dozen states asking that they arrange ratification meetings and get up ballots containing the names of electors (as required by the Constitution) pledged to her candidacy. This letter to a male friend in

Philadelphia was a typical appeal: "That an opportunity may not be lost for the dissemination of Equal Rights principles, cannot, and will not the Equal Rights Party of Philadelphia hold a ratification meeting for the nominee, put in nomination a Presidential Elector, and get up an Equal Rights ticket? Not that we shall succeed in the election, but we can demonstrate that a woman may under the Constitution, not only be nominated but elected. Think of it."

Closer to home, party supporters organized a ratification meeting in mid-September at Wilson's Station, Maryland. (They bypassed the District to make the point that, under federal law, neither men nor women could vote in the nation's capital.) Lockwood delivered her first speech as a candidate at this gathering of about 75 supporters and journalists, and two Lockwood-for-president electors were chosen. She did not disclose at the rally that Clemence Lozier had declined the nomination for vice president—and not until September 29 did Marietta Stow decide to run in the second spot and complete the ticket.

Throughout September the national press spread the story of the Equal Rights Party and its candidate, and letters poured in to the house on F Street. They contained "earnest inquiries" about the platform, nasty bits of character assassination, and, from one male admirer, the following poem, which so amused Lockwood that she gave it to a reporter for publication:

> O, Belva Ann!
> Fair Belva Ann!
> I know that thou art not a man;
> But I shall vote,
> Pull off my coat,
> And work for thee, fair Belva Ann.
> For I have read
> What thou hast said,
> And long I've thought upon thy plan.
> Oh no, there's none
> Beneath the sun
> Who'd rule like thee, my Belva Ann!

The letters also brought invitations to speak in cities across the East and the Midwest. In late September, Lockwood prepared to go on the stump, her expenses covered by sponsors. Many of the lectures she gave were paid appearances; indeed, she claimed to be the only candidate whose speeches the public paid to hear. She was a widowed middle-class woman (her second husband, who was more than 30 years her senior, had died in 1877), and her livelihood depended on the earnings of her legal practice. So the time she devoted to politics had to pay. When the election was over, she told reporters that she had a satisfaction denied the other candidates: She had come out of the campaign with her expenses paid and "$125 ahead."

Lockwood took to the field in October. She made at least one full circuit in October, beginning in Baltimore,

Philadelphia, and New York. Mid-month she delivered speeches in Louisville and in Cleveland, where she appeared at the Opera House before 500 people. In a loud and nasal voice, she attacked the high-tariff position of the Republicans on the grounds that it would injure American commerce, But she also assailed the free-trade policy of the Democrats, arguing that they were "willing to risk our manufacturing interests in the face of the starving hordes of pauper labor in other countries." She applauded the good that capital had done and said that "capital and labor did not, by nature, antagonize, and should not by custom."

If the people who came to hear Lockwood expected nothing but women's rights talk, they were disappointed. She and her party colleagues believed that the Equal Rights Party should not run a single-issue campaign. Of course, the platform introduced "feminist" ideas. But it also allowed Lockwood to address many other issues that preoccupied Americans. So she directed only a small part of her talk to describing how women had helped to make the country "blossom as a rose." She intended her candidacy to make history in the largest sense—by demonstrating that the Constitution did not bar women from running in elections or serving in federal elective office.

People who saw her for the first time said that her campaign photographs did not do her justice: The lady candidate had fine blue eyes, an aquiline nose, and a firm mouth, and she favored fashionable clothes. The cartoonists naturally focused on her sex, and the public had its own fun by creating dozens of Belva Lockwood Clubs, in which men meaning to disparage Lockwood paraded on city streets wearing Mother Hubbard dresses, a new cut of female clothing with an unconstructed design that freed movement and was considered improper to wear out of doors.

On November 3, the day before the election, Lockwood returned from a campaign tour of the Northwest. She had stayed "at the best hotels; had the best sleeping berths." Her last stop was Flint, Michigan, and she told a Washington reporter that 1,000 people had attended her (paid) talk there, a larger number than Ohio congressman Frank Hurd drew the following night. When asked on November 4 where she would await the election news, she replied that her house would be open throughout the evening, "the gas will be lighted," and reporters were welcome to visit. The historic first campaign by a woman for the presidency of the United States had ended, though in politics, of course, nothing is ever over.

When the ballots were tallied, Cleveland was declared the winner, with an Electoral College vote of 219 to 182. In the popular vote, he squeaked by with a margin of 23,000.

In 1884 the United States had yet to adopt the "Australian" ballot, which has the names of all candidates for office printed on a single form. The system then in effect, dating from the beginning of the Republic, required that each political party in a state issue ballots that contained the names of that party's slate and the electors pledged to them. A supporter cast his vote by depositing the ballot of his chosen party in a box. Some states required that voters sign the back of their ballot, but the overall allocation of ballots was not controlled by polling place officials, and stuffing the box was not impossible. It was also possible for officials in charge of the ballot boxes to discount or destroy ballots. And that, Lockwood claimed, is precisely what happened.

In a petition sent to Congress in January 1885, she wrote that she had run a campaign, gotten up electoral tickets in several states, and received votes in at least nine of the states, only to determine that "a large vote in Pennsylvania [was] not counted, simply dumped into the waste basket as false votes." In addition, she charged that many of the votes cast for her—totalling at least 4,711—in eight other states ("New Hampshire, 379 popular votes; New York, 1,336; Michigan, 374; Illinois, 1008; Iowa, 562; Maryland, 318; California, 734 and the entire Electoral vote of the State of Indiana") had been "fraudulently and illegally counted for the alleged majority candidate."

She asked that the members of Congress "refuse to receive the Electoral returns of the State of New York, or count them for the alleged majority candidate, for had the 1,336 votes which were polled in said state for your petitioner been counted for her, and not for the one Grover Cleveland, he would not have been awarded a majority of all the votes cast at said election in said state." (Cleveland's margin of votes in New York was 1,149). Lockwood also petitioned Congress for the electoral vote of Indiana, saying that at the last moment the electors there had switched their votes from Cleveland to her. In fact, they had not; it was all a prank by the good ol' boys of Indiana, but either she did not know this or, in the spirit of political theater, she played along with the mischief and used it to her advantage.

The electoral votes of New York (36) and Indiana (15) had been pivotal in the 1880 presidential race. With her petition and credible evidence, Lockwood—perhaps working behind the scenes with congressional Republicans—hoped to derail Cleveland's victory and keep him from becoming the first Democratic president since James Buchanan in 1856. She failed when the legislators ignored her petition, which had been referred to their Committee on Woman Suffrage. On February 11, Congress certified the election of New York governor Grover Cleveland as the 22nd president of the United States.

Subsequent interviews suggest that Lockwood was satisfied with the campaign, if not with the vote counting. The U.S. Constitution had betrayed women in the matter of suffrage, but it did not, as she said, prohibit women's speech and women's candidacies. As a celebration of the First Amendment, Lockwood's campaign was a great success. It served the interests of women (though it angered Susan B. Anthony), the candidate, and the country. Lockwood ran as an acknowledged contender and was allowed to speak her mind. American democracy was tested, and its performance did not disappoint her.

After the election, while maintaining her law practice, Lockwood embarked on the life of travel that she had long sought—and that she continued until her early eighties. Not unlike 21st-century politicians, she capitalized on the campaign by increasing her presence on the national lecture circuit; she even made at least one product endorsement (for a health tonic). She had long worked as a pension claims attorney, and, while traveling as a lecturer, she used the publicity surrounding her appearances to attract clients who needed help with applications and appeals. In 1888, the Equal Rights Party again nominated her as its presidential candidate. She ran a more modest campaign the second time around, but she still offered a broad domestic and foreign policy platform and argued that "equality of rights and privileges is but simple justice."

Lockwood always spoke proudly of her campaigns, which were important but not singular events in a life that would last 87 years. She was a woman of many talents and interests. Blocked from political office or a high-level government position because of her sex, she sought new realms after the campaigns of 1884 and 1888 where she might raise questions of public policy and advance the rights of women. Representing the Philadelphia-based Universal Peace Union, she increased her work on behalf of international peace and arbitration at meetings in the United States and Europe. She participated in an often-interlocking network of women's clubs and professional organizations. And she maintained a high profile in the women's suffrage movement, which struggled throughout the 1890s and the first two decades of the 20th century to create a winning strategy. In the spring of 1919, the House of Representatives and the Senate acted favorably on legislation to amend the Constitution to give women the right to vote; the proposed Nineteenth Amendment went out to the states in a ratification process that would not be completed until August 1920. But Belva Lockwood never got the right to vote. She died in May 1917.

Lockwood remains the only woman to have campaigned for the presidency right up to Election Day. (In 1964, Senator Margaret Chase Smith of Maine entered several Republican primaries and received 27 delegate votes; in 1972, Representative Shirley Chisholm of New York ran in a number of Democratic primaries and won 151 delegates.) In 1914 Lockwood, then 84 years old, was asked whether a woman would one day be president. The former candidate answered with levelheaded prescience and the merest echo of her former thunder: "I look to see women in the United States senate and the house of representatives. If [a woman] demonstrates that she is fitted to be president she will some day occupy the White House. It will be entirely on her own merits, however. No movement can place her there simply because she is a woman. It will come if she proves herself mentally fit for the position."

JILL NORGREN, *a former Wilson Center fellow, is professor of government and legal studies at John Jay College and the University Graduate Center, City University of New York. She is writing the first full biography of Belva Lockwood, to be published in 2003. Copyright © 2002 by Jill Norgren.*

From the *Wilson Quarterly,* August 2002, pages 12-20. Copyright © 2002 by Jill Norgren. Reprinted with permission of the author.

Buffalo Soldiers

For decades, African-American regulars were the most effective troops on the western frontier

By T. J. Stiles

On SEPTEMBER 24, 1868, MAJ. GEORGE A. FORSYTH MUST have wondered if he would live to see the next morning. He lay stretched out beside the rotting carcass of his dead horse, in the willow brush and tall grass that covered a small island in the dry bed of the Arikaree River, on the vast plains of eastern Colorado Territory. All around him lay dead and wounded men—his men. And beyond the empty riverbanks, just out of rifle shot, circled the 700 Cheyenne and Oglala warriors who had kept the major's detachment trapped on this island since the 17th.

Full-scale war with the tribes of the Great Plains had just erupted; Forsyth had taken his 50 handpicked scouts out of Fort Hays in Kansas on a march to find the enemy. But the Native Americans had found Forsyth first.

On the 17th, the Cheyenne war chief the soldiers called Roman Nose had led hundreds of fighters on a dawn charge against Forsyth's camp. Their storm of bullets and arrows laid waste to his horse herd and left many of his men dead or wounded. The major himself collapsed as a slug tore into each leg and another creased his scalp. By the 24th, repeated charges and stealthy sniping had turned half his scouts into casualties; a horrific stench now rose from the dead men and animals. The survivors, who at first had used their fallen mounts as protection, now resorted to eating the horses' decaying flesh.

The beleagured scouts saw their foes had drawn off. Then they saw why: cavalrymen... black cavalrymen.

Unknown to Forsyth, a company of cavalry was searching for him. Two of his scouts had slipped through the besieging Indians and made their way to Fort Wallace in Kansas, where they had alerted Capt. Louis H. Carpenter, an old Civil War comrade of the major's.

The next day, the beleaguered scouts on that malodorous little island noticed that the Indians had drawn off. Then they saw why: in the distance they discovered movement, which gradually took the form of mounted men... cavalrymen... black cavalrymen. They were Captain Carpenter's troopers, pounding across the dry grass. This unit went by the name of Company H, 10th Cavalry—but Forsyth's men may indeed have known them by the name that the African-American troops earned from their Indian foes: they were the buffalo soldiers.

Forsyth's fight entered Western legend as the Battle of Beecher's Island, but few remember that he was rescued so dramatically by black troops. Despite a recent wave of interest in the professional African-American soldiers of the 19th century, many writers have treated them as a footnote to the history of the frontier. In fact, black regulars took center stage in the Army's great Western drama, shouldering combat responsibilities far out of proportion to their numbers (which averaged 10 percent of the military's total strength). Over the course of three decades on the frontier, the buffalo soldiers emerged as the most professional experienced and effective troops in the service.

When Carpenter led his company into Forsyth's grim camp, only three years had passed since the end of the Civil War. Some 180,000 African-Americans had carried arms for the Union, filling out regiments, divisions, even an entire corps (the 25th, part of which occupied Richmond in the war's closing days). These were all-volunteer units, however, established for the duration of the war. Not one company in the standing Regular Army was open to African-American recruits. But on July 28, 1866, Congress provided for four Regular Army infantry regiments (the 38th, 39th, 40th and 41st) and two of cavalry (the 9th and 10th), to be composed exclusively of black enlisted men. The Army would *have* to accept African-Americans.

Almost immediately, the new black regulars found themselves in combat on the frontier. Lt. Col. George Armstrong Custer's wife, Elizabeth, described an incident in June 1867 (based on an account in one of her husband's letters), when 300 Cheyennes swept down on Fort Wallace, where Custer was in

Illustration by Arthur Shilstone

command. A squad of black infantrymen from the 38th had arrived to pick up supplies, when the white garrison spilled out to form a firing line.

Suddenly, a wagon pulled by four mules tore out to the line of battle, Elizabeth wrote. "It was filled with Negroes, standing up, all firing in the direction of the Indians. The driver lashed the mules with his blacksnake, and roared at them as they ran. When the skirmish line was reached, the colored men leaped out and began firing again. No one had ordered them to leave their picket-station, but they were determined that no soldiering should be carried on in which their valor was not proved."

Despite the brave showing, the 38th Infantry was not to last. On March 3, 1869, a new law ordained a general reduction in the Army: the 38th and 41st regiments were consolidated into the new 24th Infantry, and the 39th and 40th merged to create the 25th Infantry. Occasionally, companies from the 24th and 25th infantries served with their mounted counterparts, sometimes engaging in heavy combat. The lion's share of adventure fell to the special corps of black Seminole scouts—Indians of largely African descent (SMITHSONIAN, August 1991)—who served with the 24th Infantry under Lt. John Bullis. On the whole, however, the African-American infantry regiments missed out on much of the glory won by the black cavalry.

Throughout the frontier era, black soldiers endured nearly unbearable conditions. Indeed, they complained of receiving the worst of everything, including surplus equipment and cast-off horses; many white officers openly bemoaned their assignments and some abused their troops. Maybe worst of all was

local prejudice—and the Army did little if anything to help. In Texas, for example, when a sheriff killed a black Medal of Honor recipient, shooting him in the back, nothing was done. A Nebraskan who killed three black soldiers, including another Medal of Honor winner, also went unpunished. And it was nearly impossible for African-American soldiers to get commissions. One man from the 9th Cavalry said of the regiments at Fort Robinson, late in the century, "not a single colored soldier has been promoted from the ranks to the grade of an officer... the army is decidedly against it."

For hours they fought, pumping bullets out of the carbines so fast the barrels grew blisteringly hot.

The demands of frontier warfare, however, led to wide dispersion of most regiments, which placed tremendous importance on the leadership qualities of noncommissioned officers. That was certainly true of the 9th Cavalry, scattered across the rough Texas landscape in tiny, undermanned posts. Yet the 9th's sergeants and corporals were precisely the men whom the Army thought most unsuited to soldiering and command: in the early years they were mostly former slaves, drawn primarily from the plantation country of Louisiana and Mississippi. Often illiterate in the beginning, these officers—and their troopers—

displayed a voracious appetite for education, and they ultimately set the standard for professionalism. Desertion rates for many regiments surpassed 25 percent a year; not so among the buffalo soldiers. As the service newspaper reported, "The Ninth Cavalry astonished the Army by reporting not a single desertion for twelve months."

Illustration by Arthur Shilstone

Corporal Greaves arced his empty weapon in the air, slamming it into the body of the warrior.

Before 1867 came to a close, the 9th Cavalry's raw recruits won the respect of every armed opponent anywhere close to Texas. Christmas day found Capt. William Frohock and Company K on a patrol at the Pecos River, 75 miles east of Fort Stockton. The troopers settled for the night in empty Fort Lancaster, a long-abandoned post. Three men, privates Anderson Trimble, Edward Bowers and William Sharpe, stood guard over the horse herd as the troops stretched out to sleep.

The next day, Trimble, Bowers and Sharpe found themselves surrounded by armed men on horseback. They were lassoed and dragged to their deaths behind their assailants' horses. Meanwhile, the strangers turned to the company holed up in Fort Lancaster.

Captain Frohock had trouble making out just who was firing on his detachment (the attackers were most likely Lipans, Kickapoos and Mexican outlaws). In the flurry of shouting men, ric-

ocheting bullets, swirling dust and pounding hooves, he estimated that at least 900 opponents encircled his men. If his guess was correct, it meant that Company K—fewer than 70 troopers—faced more men than served in the entire 9th Cavalry.

The inexperienced buffalo soldiers threw down a curtain of fire from their seven-shot Spencer carbines. For hours they fought, pumping bullets out of their carbines so fast the barrels grew blisteringly hot. Finally the enemy drew off, carrying away 20 dead and scores of wounded. The buffalo soldiers had triumphed; never again would the Lipans and Kickapoos dare to attack them so directly.

For eight years, the 9th Cavalry fought numerous pitched battles against Lipans, Kickapoos, Kiowas, Comanches—and the people destined to be their most determined foes, the Apaches. Then in late 1875, Col. Edward Hatch took the regiment into the Apache homeland, the New Mexico Territory. There he assumed the role of department commander, and his men devoted themselves to battling various Apache war parties that frequently struck out on raids off the reservations.

These warriors had long since mastered mountain guerrilla warfare. Unlike the Sioux, Cheyennes, Kiowas or Comanches, who fought primarily to keep ranchers and hunters off their homelands, the Apaches had lived for centuries among Hispanic settlements, alternately raiding and trading with neighboring villages. They knew how to lay expert ambushes in the steep cliffs lining the valleys of the Southwest, how to throw off pursuers by leaving behind elaborate dummy camps, how to camouflage cuts in telegraph lines by splicing them with leather thongs.

The 9th was in the field constantly. Pvt. Henry Bush remembered being "continuously on scouting service which subjected us to great exposure, such as sleeping in rains and snows in the mountains unprotected from the elements, sometimes no sleep for two days, sometimes subsisting on the most meager diet, sometimes marches of ninety miles… in a hot scorching sun." And when they did make contact, the fighting was ferocious.

In January 1877, Capt. Charles D. Beyer learned that a party of Apaches had broken out of the San Carlos reservation in Arizona and had crossed into New Mexico. He issued orders to Lt. Henry Wright to mount six troopers and three Navajo scouts and find their trail. On a cold, clear, winter day, the detachment of buffalo soldiers clambered up through the rocky Florida Mountains, riding right up to the edge of a camp of more than 40 Apaches.

The troops immediately saw how precarious their situation was: ten men, deep in the mountains and far from help, surrounded by nearly five times their number. Even worse, they no longer carried the rapid-firing Spencer carbines, which carried seven rounds in a tubular magazine; they now used single-shot Springfields, while many Apaches wielded new multi-shot Winchesters.

Lieutenant Wright decided to brazen it out. He trotted his horse straight into the heart of the camp, followed by his tiny squad, and shouted for the Apache chiefs to meet him in council. The troopers slid off their saddles as Wright spoke to the Indians through a Navajo scout. He and his men, he said, would be happy to accept their surrender. The chiefs apparently did not laugh; as the negotiations continued, the soldiers noticed that the women and children were silently slipping away while the warriors encircled the detachment.

Suddenly Wright shouted for his men to break through the ring. At the first step forward, the Apaches shouldered their rifles. In an instant, 26-year-old Cpl. Clinton Greaves swiveled his carbine toward the closest warrior and squeezed off its single round. Leaping toward the line of warriors, he seized the barrel of his weapon and arced its wooden shoulder stock through the air, slamming it into the body of one of his foes.

Illustration by Arthur Shilstone

"When they recognized us as troops, they came out of their houses waving their towels and handkerchiefs for joy."

As this powerful trooper—"a big fine looking soldier," another trooper recalled—swung left and right, the rest of the detachment fired and reloaded madly. Lieutenant Wright shot down a nearby Apache; privates Dick Mackadoo and Richard Epps shot three more warriors as lead snapped through the air in every direction. The troopers frantically mounted and galloped through the opening Corporal Greaves had created. After a few seconds more of intense fighting, the Apaches themselves scattered to the mountain peaks for cover, intending to challenge the soldiers from afar. The troopers not only managed to get away unscathed, but left with 11 Apache horses.

Wright and his men earned nearly legendary status within the regiment for their brave stand in the Florida Mountains. But the highest recognition of all went to Corporal Greaves: on June 26,

1879, he became the second trooper in the 9th Cavalry to earn the Medal of Honor.

Soon the regiment came to grips with the leader who would prove to be its deadliest enemy of all: Victorio, chief of the Warm Springs band of Apaches. Tension had been building as the Bureau of Indian Affairs tried to shift his people to the San Carlos reservation in Arizona. After two escapes from San Carlos, Victorio and his band were permitted to remain at a reservation in their native New Mexico. Just when a measure of peace seemed to be in hand, lawmen arrived to arrest the chief for murder. In August 1879, he fled the reservation with 60 followers, soon to multiply to more than 300. The Victorio War had begun.

The men of the 9th Cavalry quickly learned how Victorio had won his reputation as a great war chief. He selected as one of his first targets the horse herd of Company E; on September 4, the Indians killed five troopers, wounded three more and rode off with 46 animals. Shortly afterward, Victorio unleashed a well-planned ambush in the canyon of the Los Animas River, leaving as many as eight buffalo soldiers dead or wounded.

After these setbacks, Col. Hatch assigned Maj. Albert B. Morrow to lead the pursuit. Morrow's hard-riding troopers repeatedly made contact with Victorio's forces, engaging in bitter but indecisive fighting. The skillful Apache would slip away over the border into Mexico, where the 9th Cavalry's scouts could not follow.

On May 13, 1880, Sgt. George Jordan of Company K learned precisely where the Apaches were. This native of Tennessee had just made camp with 25 men at a stage station, having spent a long day escorting a train of supply wagons. As the detachment prepared for a well-earned night of rest, a courier rode in with a desperate message: Victorio was headed for the settlement of Fort Tularosa.

The sergeant called his men together. "They all said they would go on as far as they could," Jordan reported. At 8 o'clock in the evening, they began a hard march for the endangered village. At about 6 the next morning, the tired troopers rode into the silent town, its women and children peering out apprehensively through shuttered windows. "When they recognized us as troops," he recalled, "they came out of their houses waving towels and handkerchiefs for joy."

Sergeant Jordan boasted more than ten years of experience in the 9th Cavalry; he knew what it meant to command a detachment, and he knew how to fight the Apaches. After a brief rest, he set his men to work building a stockade. By the end of the afternoon, they were done; the men had not slept for at least 24 hours, but they could now lead the residents inside a hastily built fort.

As the sun dipped down to the west, Sergeant Jordan stood outside the stockade talking to a civilian when a shot cracked the quiet evening. Instantly dozens of bullets spattered the ground as Jordan and his companion sprinted for the fort. Soon scores of Apache warriors charged across the dry desert floor. "[They] tried time and time again to enter our works," Jordan reported, "but we repulsed them each time, and when they finally saw that we were masters of the situation they turned their attention to the stock and tried to run it off." Head-on attacks against an entrenched foe were not the Apache way; Victorio soon pulled away. "The whole action was short but exciting while it lasted, and after it was all over the townspeople congratulated us for having repulsed a band of more than 100." Congress congratulated Jordan with the Medal of Honor.

Nine days later, a unit of Indian scouts severely shot up Victorio's camp, sending the chief flying into Mexico with Morrow's command snapping at his heels. The move set the stage for the final, decisive phase of the campaign—and shifted the burden to the rest of the buffalo soldiers: the men of the 10th Cavalry, led by Col. Benjamin Grierson, and those of the 24th and 25th infantries.

Grierson believed Victorio would reenter the United States in western Texas; to stop him, he decided to cast a net to ensnare the chief no matter which direction he turned. The key was water: only a handful of springs dotted the dry mountains southeast of El Paso. By guarding the most important water holes, and by posting a network of scouts along the Rio Grande, he could block any attempt to penetrate West Texas.

The night of July 29 found Grierson at Tenaja de los Palmos, a strategic water hole between Fort Quitman (to the west on the Rio Grande) and Eagle Springs (15 miles to the east). He had with him a half-dozen buffalo soldiers, one white officer and his 20-year-old son, Robert. Earlier that day, Grierson and his men had been met by three African-American troopers bearing a critical dispatch from the Rio Grande: the Apaches had been seen crossing the river into Texas.

It was no ordinary buffalo soldier who led the couriers; it was Lt. Henry O. Flipper, the first black graduate of West Point and an officer of the 10th Cavalry. "I rode 98 miles in 22 hours mostly at night, through a country the Indians were expected to traverse," he wrote. "I had no bad effects from the hard ride till I reached [Grierson's] tent. When I attempted to dismount, I found I was stiff and sore and fell from my horse to the ground…"

After resting, Flipper left with orders that all available troops should make haste for Grierson's position. Meanwhile the colonel and his men spent the night throwing up two stone breastworks atop the rocky ridge overlooking the water hole. Despite the desperate odds, Grierson had decided to make a stand. If he could deny Victorio access to the water in that canyon, he was certain that the Apaches would have to turn back to Mexico. The next morning, at about 4 o'clock, Lt. Leighton Finley rode in with reinforcements: a mere ten cavalrymen.

Young Robert Grierson would later scrawl in his journal a vivid account of the events that followed. Sometime after 8, as the little party finished breakfast, the scouts south of camp sent up the cry "Here come the Indians!" Then he saw them: dozens of long-haired warriors, rifles held at the ready as they nudged their horses through the canyon southeast of their position on the ridge.

As a dense cluster of Apaches rode slowly across the rough trail, the Indians heard the sound of galloping horses. Down Finley's buffalo soldiers came, snapping off shots as they thundered into the valley. "Several Indians hid in a hollow till Lt. F. passed, & then fired on his party," Robert wrote. "He had them on both sides of him & poured it into them thick & vice versa. The rifles sounded splendidly and you could hear the balls singing. Just as Lt. Finley was about to dislodge the Indians from behind a ledge, Capt. Viele's and Lt. Colladay's companies came & in the smoke and dust took F. for Indians and fired on him."

Capt. Charles Viele, Lieutenant Flipper and the troopers of Company C had just arrived from Fort Quitman. Now they fired on Finley by mistake; fortunately, both Viele and Finley pulled their men back to Grierson's breastworks. "All got back about the same time," wrote Robert, except one black trooper whose horse had been shot; after him galloped the resurgent warriors, convinced now that the battle had turned in their favor. "He got along as best he could—the Indians were nearly on him—he turned & fired his revolver & this checked them some."

Grierson ordered his men to fire. "We then let fly from our fortifications at the Indians about 300 yards off & golly!! You ought to've seen 'em turn tail & strike for the hills." In four hours of desperate fighting, the Apaches lost seven men; the 10th Cavalry, one trooper. The battle left Victorio short on food and water, and saddled with dead and wounded; he had no choice but to retreat to Mexico.

In early August, he returned and slipped past Grierson's men on his way to another strategic water hole, Rattlesnake Springs. Determined to get there first, Grierson and his men covered 65 miles in 21 hours. The buffalo soldiers outpaced their fast-moving Indian foes as Grierson led them on a parallel path, keeping to the far side of a mountain range to mask their presence from the enemy.

The 10th Cavalry won the race, arriving in the early hours of August 6. "We got there and at once took position for a fight," Flipper recalled. Grierson laid out an elaborate ambush, sending Captain Viele with companies C and G to occupy the walls of the valley above the springs. "No lights or fires were allowed and we had to eat cold suppers without coffee," Flipper continued. "If [the Apaches] once got in as far as the spring, we would have them surrounded and every vantage point occupied."

At 2 in the afternoon, the long, ragged band of Apaches rode into sight, ambling slowly through the bunchgrass and rocks and cactus on their tired horses. The Indians in the lead sensed that something was wrong and stopped their advance. When Viele saw them grow cautious, he gave orders to commence firing. The first of eight volleys of rifle fire erupted from the valley walls; Victorio's men scrambled for cover.

The master of the ambush had been ambushed himself—but the trap had been sprung too soon, and the long-range fire did little damage to the Indians. The Apaches, however, were desperate for water. Victorio rallied his men for an attack. Warriors on horseback surged across the valley floor, screaming their defiance and loosing shots at the dug-in buffalo soldiers. Just as the Apaches neared the springs, Capt. Louis H. Carpenter and Lt. Thaddeus Winfield Jones led companies H and B on a charge from one flank, crashing into the Apaches with carbines blazing. Victorio's men withdrew once again.

Over the next two hours, the firing died away to silence; Grierson knew better than to stage a pointless assault on Apaches holed up in the rocks. Then, as so often happened in battle, the unexpected occurred. At 4 o'clock a line of wagons rounded a mountain eight miles southeast of the water hole. A party of warriors emerged from the rocks and scampered onto their ponies, undoubtedly relieved to find an easy target beyond the reach of Grierson's men (and probably hoping to get some water as well).

Suddenly the Apaches pulled up short—for out of the wagons poured the buffalo soldiers of the 24th Infantry, the escort for this supply train for the 10th Cavalry. These foot soldiers unleashed a devastating fire across the valley floor. The Indians turned and fled; and within a few days they fell back to Mexico.

On October 14, 1880, Mexican troops trapped Victorio's badly reduced forces, killing the great chief in the final assault. But the victory had already been won. The Victorio War was perhaps the most difficult campaign ever waged against the Apaches. It was also one of the few Apache wars fought largely by regular troops, not Apache scouts enlisted by the Army—and those troops were largely buffalo soldiers. They out-marched, out-fought and out-generaled a foe often considered to be the hardest marching, hardest fighting, most skillful enemy in frontier history.

Over the remaining years of the frontier era, the buffalo soldiers stayed at the center of events. The 10th Cavalry, for example, played a significant role in the last major act of Indian warfare in the Southwest: the Geronimo Campaign of 1885–86. The 9th Cavalry and the 25th Infantry also joined operations against the Sioux in 1890–91.

Lieutenant Flipper, however, endured a sad sequel to the Victorio War. As the only African-American line officer in the 10th, he remained the object of special hatred by many of his fellow officers. As quartermaster at Fort Davis, Texas, in July 1881 he discovered commissary money was missing from his trunk. On December 8, 1881, a court-martial found Flipper innocent of embezzling the funds—but guilty of "conduct unbecoming an officer. (Historians believe the court-martial occurred as a result of Flipper's friendship, albeit platonic, with a white woman.) Expelled from the military, he worked as a civil engineer, and as a translator, but he failed in his unceasing efforts to clear his name. Finally, on December 13, 1976, after long campaigning by Flipper's descendants and defenders, the Army's board of corrections exonerated him, issuing an honorable discharge 36 years after his death.

As the buffalo soldiers watched the promising age of Reconstruction—the nation's first civil rights era—come crashing down into the rubble of segregation, they saw themselves as the last bastion of public service for African-Americans. "They are possessed of the notion," wrote one chaplain, "that the colored people of the whole country are more or less affected by their conduct in the Army."

In the Spanish-American War and in the Philippine insurrections, these regiments added pages to their thick record of accomplishments. Ironically, these units were largely kept out of combat in the two world wars, although African-American volunteers and draftees fought courageously in France, Italy and Germany. Yet even those who saw combat suffered severe prejudice; only a handful received awards for valor. On January 13, 1997, President Bill Clinton took a small step to rectify this injustice by awarding the Medal of Honor to seven African-Americans who had served in World War II.

In recent years, interest in the buffalo soldiers has flourished. They have been commemorated with a postage stamp, historical-reenactment groups and a 1997 cable television movie. Much of the new recognition stems from the efforts of one black officer who strongly identifies with his 19th-century predecessors. In 1982 he arrived at Fort Leavenworth, Kansas (birthplace of the 10th Cavalry), and was dismayed to find not one memorial to the buffalo soldiers' "incredible contribution to the American West." That officer was Colin Powell. In 1992, he returned to Fort Leavenworth—this time as chairman of the Joint Chiefs of Staff—to dedicate a monument by sculptor Eddie Dixon. It was a fitting tribute from a military that hesitated to accept African-Americans, learned to depend on them, and finally—under the leadership of a modern black soldier—has come to honor their memory.

T. J. Stiles, who has written several books on American history, is working on a biography of Jesse James, to be published by Alfred A. Knopf. Arthur Shilstone has illustrated numerous SMITHSONIAN *stories.*

From *Smithsonian*, December 1998, pp. 82-94. © 1998 by T. J. Stiles. Reprinted by permission.

Undermining the Molly Maguires

A series of violent crimes was plaguing Pennsylvania's coal country.
Mine owners placed the blame on a secret society of Irishmen—
and took steps to wipe it out.

by Joseph H. Bloom

ON October 27, 1873, a slightly built, bespectacled, and unshaven man calling himself James McKenna alighted from a train at the station in Port Clinton, a small community on the southern border of Pennsylvania's Schuylkill County. It was a coal-mining country, a rough part of the world suffering from the effects of what one newspaper had called a "reign of terror" orchestrated by a shadowy organization dubbed the Molly Maguires. Since 1862 the Mollies had been blamed for numerous murders, beatings, knifings, armed robberies, and incidents of arson.

The exploits of the Molly Maguires had been detailed in many colorful newspaper articles throughout the country, but that hadn't discouraged McKenna. In fact, he arrived in Schuylkill County determined to join the secret society. He wasn't sure how, but he was confident that his naturally friendly demeanor and quick wit would help him make the proper contacts.

His Irish background would help too. The Mollies were all Irish Catholics, drawn mainly from the desperately poor men who worked in the coal mines of eastern Pennsylvania. Theirs was a hard life of cave-ins, explosions, flooded mines, and long hours of back-breaking labor in the darkness, all for wages that were barely sufficient to support a family. The mine workers even had to buy

HISTORICAL SOCIETY OF SCHUYLKILL COUNTY

This man, going by the name James McKenna, arrived in eastern Pennsylvania's coal country during a time of labor unrest.

their own work tools and dynamite at the company store for elevated prices. The terrible conditions led many of the miners to join the Workingmen's Benevolent Association, a trade union that fought for better conditions in the mines. The mine owners, however, were equally determined to smash the union. The resulting conflict between workers and owners sparked the creation of the

Molly Maguires, who vowed to fight the exploitation of the workers by predominantly Protestant mine owners and supervisors.

It was in this tense atmosphere that James McKenna found himself when he stepped off the train. At first he wandered through the region's small towns, seeking out Irishmen who might have Molly Maguire connections, but he couldn't get more than a passing word from anybody. After reaching Pottsville in December 1873, he began to frequent the Sheridan House, a popular saloon run by a loquacious Irishman named "Big Pat" Dormer. McKenna soon became a popular character around the bar, entertaining customers by spinning tall tales and dancing Irish jigs. In conversation, McKenna let it be known that he was wanted for murder and counterfeiting in Buffalo, New York. He proved himself to be handy with his fists and soon gained a reputation among the rougher elements who drank at Dormer's bar. His standing was secured after the Coal & Iron Police, a private constabulary raised by the mine owners and railroad operators to help protect their interests, arrested McKenna at the bar, interrogated him, and roughed him up.

Dormer himself was impressed with McKenna, and in February 1874 took him to the neighboring town of Shenandoah to meet fellow saloon-keeper Muff

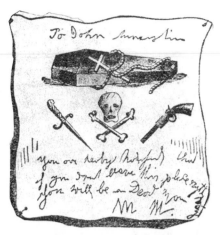

HISTORICAL SOCIETY OF SCHUYLKILL COUNTY

Individuals sometimes received coffin notices, supposedly from the Mollies.

Lawler. With Lawler's backing, McKenna got work at the Indian Ridge Shaft and later at the West Shenandoah Colliery. Lawler also took McKenna to see—or more accurately to be seen by—John "Jack" Kehoe. Jack Kehoe ran the Hibernian House saloon in Girardville, an important Molly headquarters, and was a kingpin in the organization. Without McKenna knowing how, Kehoe secretly signaled his approval of the newcomer, and McKenna soon received an invitation to a secret meeting of the Ancient Order of the Hibernians.

HISTORICAL SOCIETY OF SCHUYLKILL COUNTY

Jack Kehoe, dubbed "The King of the Molly Maguires" by prosecuting attorneys, was a leader of the Irish community in Girardville.

The A.O.H. was a nationwide fraternal organization whose membership was limited to those of Irish-Catholic descent. In the coal region, however, the A.O.H. served as the cover organization for the Molly Maguires. Although not all members of the local A.O.H. lodges were Mollies, all of the Molly Maguires eventually tried and convicted of crimes were members of the A.O.H.

Scholarly writer Francis P. Dewees summed up the era of the Molly Maguires as a "reign of blood... they held communities terror bound, and wantonly defied the law, destroyed property and sported human life."

At an A.O.H. meeting on April 14, 1874, as McKenna later related, he was "ordered to go to my knees, and take my hat off, and there was a document read to me by the Division Master, Mr. Lawler... the substance of which that I obey my superiors in everything connected with the organization, in things lawful and not otherwise. It also contained a clause that I should keep everything secret pertaining to this organization. I then kissed the Test, the same as I would a Bible in a Court of Justice." When he rose, McKenna was a confirmed member of the Molly Maguires.

Mc KENNA ROSE HIGH in the organization over the next two years, in large measure because he could read and write, accomplishments not shared by many of the brethren. He became secretary and later bodymaster (president) of the Shenandoah lodge and a trusted advisor in many matters. On one occasion, when members of the Shenandoah lodge planned to strike a blow against the mine owners by dynamiting the Ringtown bridge, a railway bridge used by coal trains, McKenna warned them that the authorities kept a close watch on the

structure. Fearing arrest, the men abandoned the plan.

Several highly publicized murders took place during McKenna's stay in the coal region, including that of Benjamin Yost, a police officer who had crossed the Mollies by arresting and beating member Thomas Duffy. In the early morning hours of July 14, 1875, three men waited in a cemetery near the end of Yost's beat in Tamaqua. As the police officer climbed a ladder to extinguish a street lamp, Hugh McGehan and James Boyle stepped forward and shot him. Yost fell mortally wounded while his attackers, along with their guide, James "Powder Keg" Kerrigan, made their escape.

HISTORICAL SOCIETY OF SCHUYLKILL COUNTY

James "Powder Keg" Kerrigan's testimony during the trials helped convict some of the accused Mollies.

The organization sometimes asked members from one lodge to carry out violent assignments in another lodge's jurisdiction, the advantage being that Mollies from outside the area would not be recognized. The plot to kill Yost was allegedly hatched in the Tamaqua tavern run by James Carroll and carried out by McGehan and Boyle of Summit Hill. After the Yost killing, two Mollies from the Laffee district, Michael J. Doyle and Edward Kelly, were commissioned to gun down Welsh mine superintendent John P. Jones of Tamaqua. The Mollies had accused the superintendent of blacklisting miners who had taken part in a strike. On September 3 Jones was shot in the back as he walked along the pipeline that led to the Lehigh and Wilkes-Barre Coal Company mine in Lansford, Carbon County.

HISTORICAL SOCIETY OF SCHUYLKILL COUNTY

James Roarity was implicated in the death of police officer Benjamin Yost. According to informer James Kerrigan, Roarity arranged for Hugh McGehan and James Boyle to commit the murder. Roarity was found guilty and was hanged in Pottsville on June 21, 1877, for his part in the police officer's murder.

In a similar fashion, Thomas Sanger, foreman of Heaton's Colliery in Raven Run near Girardville, and miner William Uren had been gunned down two days earlier as they walked along an empty street to work. Sanger died because of an alleged workplace grievance, while Uren, who boarded with the Sanger family, was slain to eliminate him as a witness.

The violence, however, was not all one-sided. The most noteworthy case of the tables being turned took place in Wiggans Patch, near Mahanoy City. Early in the morning of December 10, 1875, a group of armed and masked men burst into the home of the three men believed to be involved in the deaths of Sanger and Uren. The vigilantes killed suspected murderer Charles O'Donnell and also the pregnant wife of Charles McAllister. (McAllister was wounded but survived.) Moreover, in the frenzy and confusion, one of the attackers pistol-whipped McAllister's mother-in-

law. The true identity of the Wiggans Patch attackers was never established, but rumors blamed the attack on a group of irate valley residents trained by Captain Robert Linden of the Coal & Iron Police.

The Wiggans Patch incident came as a shock to the Molly Maguires. How had the attackers known that McAllister and O'Donnell had been involved in the Sanger and Uren killings? The organization was further shaken by a series of recent arrests, indicating that there was an informer within the Molly Maguires. On February 23, Shenandoah bodymaster Frank McAndrew warned McKenna that Jack Kehoe was laying bets that he, McKenna, was the spy among them. Instead of fleeing for his life, however, McKenna confronted Kehoe at his bar in Girardville and demanded that he call a conclave of the organization's leaders so that McKenna could defend himself. Kehoe agreed to the meeting but secretly assigned men to murder McKenna instead. Two weeks later, James McKenna disappeared from the region.

T HE FIRST OF THE MOLLY MACQUIRE trials was held in Mauch Chunk (renamed Jim Thorpe in 1954) in January 1876 and in Pottsville in May, after the Coal & Iron Police had rounded up dozens of men on charges ranging from beatings to murder. During the Pottsville trial of James Carroll, Thomas Duffy, James Roarity, Hugh McGehan, and James Boyle for the murder of Benjamin Yost, the prosecution announced a surprise witness. On May 6, 1876, an impeccably dressed, clean-shaven man strode into the courthouse, took the stand, and testified. "My name is James McParlan," he said. "I came into Schuylkill County in October 1873 under the name of James McKenna. I am a detective. I belong to the National Detective Agency commonly known as Pinkerton's Detective Force. I was sent here by Major Allan Pinkerton of Chicago, the chief. I came to discover as to who were connected with an organization known as the Molly Maguires."

Before a stunned courtroom, McParlan recounted how Yost's murder was planned in Carroll's bar. He testified that

WITH PERMISSION—PINKERTON, INC.
LIBRARY OF CONGRESS

Alan Pinkerton, head of the detective agency that bore his name, was hired by mine owners to help break up the Molly Maguires.

some time after the murder Hugh McGehan showed him the pistol he had used to kill the police officer. When defense lawyers accused the detective of being an *agent provocateur* who participated willingly in Molly outrages, McParlan responded that he was often unable to forewarn intended victims in time and was forced to appear to participate in the Mollies' plans in order to protect not just his undercover mission but very probably his life.

McParlan had been hired through the efforts of the sworn enemy of the Molly Maguires, Franklin Benjamin Gowen, president of the Philadelphia & Reading Railroad. Gowen's company held a monopoly on rail transport in and out of the southern anthracite region. Determined to forestall the rise of a strong union movement and break the Mollies, Gowen turned to Allan Pinkerton, the head of America's most famous private detective agency.

Born in Scotland, Pinkerton had come to the United States and eventually settled in Chicago, where he founded the Pinkerton National Detective Agency in 1850. While working for the Illinois

WITH PERMISSION—PINKERTON, INC.
LIBRARY OF CONGRESS

Franklin B. Gowen, president of the Philadelphia & Reading Railroad, conducted some prosecutions himself.

Central Railroad, Pinkerton met the line's vice president, George B. McClellan, who later employed him to handle intelligence for the Army of the Potomac during the Civil War. As General McClellan's intelligence chief in the Peninsula Campaign, Pinkerton substantially overstated the enemy's numbers, reinforcing the general's belief that he faced overwhelming odds. McClellan eventually lost his command, so Pinkerton returned to detective work and opened agency branches in Philadelphia and New York. He concentrated on railroad robberies and security but also became involved in helping industrialists fight labor disputes.

Gowen and Pinkerton decided that the best way to bring the Mollies to heel was to plant a trusted Pinkerton detective within the organization. Pinkerton reasoned that the man for the job would have to be an "Irishman and a Catholic, as only this class of person can find admission to the Mollie Maguires. My detective should become, to all intents and purposes, one of the order, and continue so while he remains in the case before us." Pinkerton decided that 29-year-old James McParlan was the best man for the assignment.

Born in Ulster's County Armagh in 1844, McParlan came to the United States in 1867. He made his way to Chicago, where he filled a number of billets, ranging from entertainer in a German beer garden to "preventive policeman" with a small Chicago detective agency. He joined the Pinkerton National Detective Agency in 1871 and once went undercover to expose pilferers on the streetcars of Chicago.

Pennsylvania Governor Milton J. Shapp said, "We can be proud of the men known as the Molly Maguires, because they defiantly faced allegations which attempted to make trade unionism a criminal conspiracy."

What the Irish detective lacked in experience he made up for in other ways. McParlan possessed an outgoing personality, with a good sense of humor and a knack for quickly ingratiating himself to those he met. He was an excellent boxer and an even more effective rough-and-tumble fighter, a nimble dancer of Irish jigs, a sweet-voiced tenor, a ladies' man of considerable sophistication, and a man who could drink unbelievably large quantities of whisky and retain his faculties. McParlan put these "talents" to good use during his undercover work, although the full story of McParlan's more than two years in the coal region will probably never be known. The detective, who died in 1919, never set down a full account of his adventures. Historians consider Pinkerton's own version, *The Mollie Maguires and the Detectives*, to be semi-fictional.

The only person in the coal region who knew McParlan's true identity was Captain Linden of the Coal & Iron Police. Linden was also employed by Pinkerton, and his arrests and interrogations of McParlan were orchestrated opportunities to exchange information. Whenever possible, McParlan used Linden to pass word of upcoming outrages and to

How Did They Get That Name?

Theories abound about the origin of the Molly Maguires' name, but all refer it back to Ireland. They include stories of peasants who banded together to avenge Molly Maguire, an old woman who had been evicted from her house; a tavern owner of that name who allowed a secret society to meet on her premises; and a fierce, pistol-packing woman who led her male followers on raids through the countryside. Most likely, the name came from groups of Irishmen who called themselves the Molly Maguires, and who engaged in violence against the agents of their English landlords during the eighteenth and nineteenth centuries. These men dressed in women's clothes and blackened their faces, not only as a disguise but to indicate their dedication to a mythical Molly Maguire who symbolized their struggle against injustice.

There is no evidence to suggest that the men who acted against the Pennsylvania mine owners named themselves after the Irish Molly Maguires. In 1857 Benjamin Bannan, editor of the Schuylkill County Miners' Journal, brought the name to the attention of the American public when he used it as a term for all the aspects of the Irish character that he found unsavory. He kept the name alive for several years in newspaper articles with headings such as "A Molly on the Rampage" and "Molly Beating." Franklin B. Gowen perpetuated the name during legislative hearings for rate raises for his railroad in 1871. He suggested to the committee that the area was under attack by a group of men he referred to as the Molly Maguires.

warn victims. At other times, such as in the case of the Ringtown bridge episode, he sought to scuttle or at least delay plans. McParlan reported on numerous Molly crimes by train mail sent to the head of the Pinkerton office in Philadelphia. His cover was nearly blown when a letter from the Philadelphia office arrived at the Pottsville post office ad-

LIST OF FUGITIVE MOLLIE MAGUIRES,
1879.

WILLIAM LOVE.—Murderer of Thos. Gwyther, at Girardville, Pa., August 14th, 1875. Is a miner and boatman; 26 years old; 5 ft. 9 in. high; medium build; weighs about 150 lbs.; light complexion; grey eyes; yellow hair; light mustache; has a scar from burn on left side of neck under chin, and coal marks on hands; thin and sharp features; generally dresses well. Lived at Girardville, Schuylkill Co., Pa.

THOMAS HURLEY.—Murderer of Gomer Jamas, August 14th, 1875. Is a miner; 25 years old; 5 ft. 8 in. high; well built; weighs about 160 lbs.; sandy complexion and hair; small piercing eyes; smooth face; sharp features; large hands and feet; wears black hat and dark clothes; lived at Shenandoah, Schuylkill Co., Pa.

MICHAEL DOYLE.—Murderer of Thomas Sanger and Wm. Uren, September 1st, 1875. Is a miner; 25 years old; 5 ft. 5 in. high; medium built; dark complexion; black hair and eyes; full round face and head; smooth face and boyish looking generally; wears a cap. Lived at Shenandoah.

JAMES, ALIAS FRIDAY O'DONNELL.—Murderer of Sanger and Uren, is 26 years old; 5 ft. 10½ in. high; slim built; fair complexion; smooth face; dark eyes; brown hair; generally wears a cap; dresses well; is a miner and lived at Wiggan's Patch, Pa.

JAMES McALLISTER.—Murderer of Sanger and Uren, is 27 years old; 5 ft. 8 in. high; stout built; florid complexion; full broad face, somewhat freckled; light hair and moustache; wears a cap and dark clothes, lived at Wiggan's Patch, Pa.

JOHN, ALIAS HUMPTY FLYNN.—Murderer of Thomas Devine, October 11th, 1875, and Geo. K. Smith, at Audenreid, November 5th, 1863. Is 53 years old; 5 ft. 7 or 8 in high; heavy built; sandy hair and complexion; smooth face; large nose; round shouldered and almost humpbacked. Is a miner and lived at New Philadelphia, Schuylkill Co., Pa.

JERRY KANE.—Charged with conspiracy to murder. Is 38 years old; 5 ft. 7 in. high; dark complexion; short brown hair; sharp features; sunken eyes; roman nose; coal marks on face and hands; wears black slouch hat; has coarse gruff voice. Is a miner and lived at Mount Laffee, Pa.

FRANK KEENAN.—Charged with conspiracy to murder. Is 31 years old; 5 ft. 7 in. high; dark complexion; black hair, inclined to curl and parted in the middle; sharp features; slender but compactly built; wears a cap and dark clothes. Is a miner and lived at Forrestville, Pa.

WILLIAM GAVIN.—Charged with conspiracy to murder. Is 42 year old; 5 ft. 8 in. high; sandy hair and complexion; stout built; red chin whiskers; face badly pockmarked; has but one eye; large nose; formerly lived at Big Mine Run, Pa. Is a miner. Wears a cap and dark clothes.

JOHN REAGAN.—Murderer of Patrick Burns at Tuscarora, April 15th, 1870. About 5 ft. 10 or 11 in. high; 40 years old; small goatee; stoop shouldered; dark hair, cut short; coal marks on hands and face; has a swinging walk; wears shirt collar open at the neck.

THOMAS O'NEILL.—Murderer of Patrick Burns, at Tuscarora, April 15th, 1870. About 5 ft. 9 in. high; 35 years old; light hair; very florid complexion; red moustache and think red goatee; stoop shouldered; walks with a kind of a jerk; think has some shot marks on back of neck and wounded in right thigh.

PATRICK B. GALLAGHER, ALIAS PUG NOSE PAT.—Murderer of George K. Smith, at Audenreid, November 5th, 1863. About 5 ft. 8 in. high; medium built; dark complexion and hair; latter inclined to curl; turned up nose; thick lips; wears a frown on his countenance; large coal cut across the temple; from 32 to 35 years old; has been shot in the thigh.

Information may be sent to me at either of the above offices,

ALLAN PINKERTON.

WITH PERMISSION—PINKERTON, INC.

The Pinkerton agency produced this list of Molly Maguire fugitives in 1879. Of the men on the list, only Thomas Hurley was ever apprehended. He admitted to a murder in Shenandoah, Pennsylvania, and committed suicide in a Colorado jail in 1886.

HISTORICAL SOCIETY OF SCHUYLKILL COUNTY

A photograph of Pottsville in the 1800s shows the Schuylkill County jail on the left and the courthouse—scene of some Molly Maguire trials—on the right. The jail is still operating, but the courthouse was replaced in 1889.

dressed to James McParlan instead of James McKenna.

Frustration on both sides led to violence through intimidation, beatings, industrial sabotage, and military intervention, but the founding of the United Mine Workers of America changed the lives of the miners.

The strain of undercover work took a toll of McParlan's health. He suffered from several bouts of illness but steadfastly continued his work until he learned of the Wiggans Patch incident. The detective became so incensed that he tendered his resignation in a letter to Benjamin Franklin of the Pinkerton office in Philadelphia, saying he was not "going to be accessory to the murder of women and children." Franklin immediately wrote a letter to Pinkerton: "This morning I received a report from 'Mac'

of which I sent you a copy, and in which he seems to be very much surprised at the shooting of these men; and he offers his resignation. I telegraphed 'Mac' to come here from Pottsville as I am anxious to satisfy him that we had nothing to do with what has taken place in regard to these men. Of course, I do not want 'Mac' to resign." In the end, McParlan decided to see the assignment through.

Once the arrests began, McParlan faced his final crisis. When he made his bold demand for a meeting of the organization's leaders, ostensibly to defend himself against charges of being an informer, he was actually planning a mass roundup of the Molly bosses. Unaware that Kehoe never planned to hold the meeting, McParlan notified Captain Linden by slipping an invitation to him along with those mailed to Molly leaders. When he learned that Kehoe planned to have him killed, McParlan left the region on March 7, 1876, on an early morning train bound for Philadelphia.

IN THE YEARS SINCE the accused Mollies went on trial, opinion about the organization has been divided. At the

conclusion of the court proceedings, scholarly writer Francis P. Dewees summed up the era of the Molly Maguires as "a reign of blood.... [T]hey held communities terror bound, and wantonly defied the law, destroyed property and sported human life." Other writers have characterized the Mollies as more sinned against than sinning, the victims of mine owners bent on destroying the nascent labor movement. The trials were held at a time of strong anti-Irish prejudice and were often preceded by prejudicial newspaper accounts. Labor leaders, the clergy, and hierarchy of the Catholic church, afraid of being linked with the Molly Maguires, were quick to condemn them as well. The juries in many of the trials were composed largely of German immigrants, some of whom readily confessed that their limited knowledge of English made it difficult for them to follow the proceedings. Not a single Irish American was empaneled on any of the juries. Sympathetic judges allowed Gowen, who conducted several of the prosecutions himself, to rant on endlessly about the Molly Maguires, often painting an even more sinister picture than the facts supported. As Carbon County

Judge John P. Lavelle noted in his 1994 book, *The Hard Coal Docket*, "[A]ny objective study of the… entire record of these cases must conclude that they [the Molly Maguires]… did not have fair and impartial juries. They were, therefore, denied one of the fundamental rights that William Penn guaranteed to all of Pennsylvania's citizens."

All told, 20 men were found guilty of murder and were sentenced to death. Ten of them were hanged—four at Mauch Chunk and six at Pottsville—on June 21, 1877, a date remembered as "Black Thursday." Some Molly Maguire members were probably innocent of the crimes for which they were accused. One of the more questionable convictions was that of Alexander Campbell, who was charged with masterminding the slayings of mine superintendent Morgan Powell in 1871 and John P. Jones in 1875. A prominent tavern owner and A.O.H. lodge treasurer, Campbell was never proven to be connected with the actual perpetration of any Molly Maguire crimes, but the testimony of "Powder Keg" Kerrigan, who turned state's evidence and escaped punishment, sent Campbell to the gallows.

Jack Kehoe was hanged in 1878 for the 1862 murder of mine foreman Frank W. Langdon. A century later Pennsylvania Governor Milton J. Shapp granted Kehoe a posthumous pardon, prompted by the efforts of some of Kehoe's relatives and several members of the Pennsylvania Labor History Society. The governor wrote, "…[I]t is impossible for us to imagine the plight of the 19th Century miners in Pennsylvania's anthracite region," and that it was John Kehoe's popularity among the miners that led Gowen "to fear, despise and ultimately destroy [him]." Shapp continued, "We can be proud of the men known as the Molly Maguires, because they defiantly faced allegations which attempted to make trade unionism a criminal conspiracy."

The Molly Maguire hangings ended the first wave of violence in the Pennsylvania coal regions. Labor relations throughout the United States remained turbulent, however, and the battle between mine owners and mine workers continued. Frustration on both sides led to violence through intimidation, beatings, industrial sabotage, and military intervention, but the founding of the United Mine Workers of America in 1890 ultimately changed the lives of the miners. The union advocated an eight-hour workday and opposed the compulsory buying of goods in company stores, employment for children under 14, and the use of hired gunmen to enforce company rules. Even with these regulations, coal mining remained a difficult and dangerous way to make a living, but no longer one that would have to rely on the Molly Maguires and their brand of justice.

Joseph Bloom is a full-time freelance medical writer currently living in western North Carolina.

From *American History*, August 1999, pp. 54-64. © 1999 by Primedia Consumer Media and Magazines, Inc. All rights reserved. Reprinted with permission.

African Americans and the Industrial Revolution

Joe William Trotter Jr.

Until recently, scholarship on industrialization treated Africans and African Americans as peripheral to that process. Industrialization was considered a peculiarly European or Western innovation that owed little to the rest of the world and especially to blacks in the New World. This bias was not simply one of race. It was also one of class. The masses of working-class and poor whites were also excluded from consideration of the key dynamics of technological and social change. Historians of American technology privileged the deeds of famous inventors like Eli Whitney, Samuel F. B. Morse, Thomas Edison, Cyrus McCormick, and Henry Ford. Over the past several decades, however, scholars have gradually revamped our understanding of the industrial revolution from the vantage point of the working class as well as consumers of the products of technological innovations. As such, they have also illuminated the myriad ways that African Americans both influenced and were in turn influenced by the industrial revolution.

Teachers of the industrial revolution are now able to draw upon a growing body of knowledge that treats race, class, and technology as tightly interwoven themes in African American and U.S. history. Accordingly, this essay offers a brief outline of the ways that race and technology shaped the early enslavement of Africans in the New World; the work of bondsmen and women during the antebellum era; and especially the increasing urbanization of the African American population during the industrial age. For classroom purposes, however, teachers should find this essay most useful for organizing discussions around the interplay of class, race, and technology during the late nineteenth and early twentieth centuries.

From the outset of their enslavement, Africans brought a substantial body of technological know-how to the New World. Before the advent of the international slave trade, West African societies had developed diverse trade, manufacturing, and agricultural economies. In colonial America, enslaved Africans not only lived, worked, and fought closely with whites, but shared important knowledge that enabled Europeans to survive and thrive on the southern terrain. Africans entered the low country of colonial South Carolina with knowledge of rice planting, hoeing, processing, and cooking techniques. They planted rice in the spring by creating a hole in the ground with the heel of their foot, planting the seed, and then covering it with their foot. Slaves also influenced the use of the "mortar-and-pestle" method of cleaning and processing the rice. As historian Peter Wood notes: "There was a strikingly close resemblance between the traditional West African means of pounding rice and the process used by slaves in South Carolina. Several Negroes, usually women, cleaned the grain a small amount at a time by putting it in a wooden mortar which was hollowed from the upright trunk of a pine or cypress. It was beaten with long wooden pestles which had a sharp edge at one end for removing the husks and a flat tip at the other for whitening the grains"[1]

While the technological know-how of African Americans was especially prominent in the early creation and settlement of plantations in colonial America, the advent of Eli Whitney's cotton gin during the 1790s transformed the work of bondsmen and women during the antebellum era. Manufacturers had long recognized the value of cotton, but technological obstacles precluded use of the fiber on a massive scale. The difficulty of separating the cotton fiber from its seed made the production of cotton an extremely slow, labor intensive, and costly enterprise. The fibers clung to the seed so firmly that they had to be "cut or torn away" by hand. This was particularly true for short-staple cotton, which grew in the interior, compared to long-staple sea island cotton, which grew in the low lying coastal areas of Georgia and South Carolina. The cotton gin effectively separated the fiber from the seed and fueled demand for increasing numbers of field hands to plant, cultivate, and pick cotton for national and international markets.

Cotton soon emerged at the center of southern and U.S. economic growth and stimulated the spread of the industrial revolution. Production rose from less than 300,000 bales in 1820 to over 700,000 in 1830 to over 2.0 million in 1850 and to nearly 4.5 million in 1860. Cotton dominated the nation's foreign exports, especially to England where revolutionary changes in the textile industry—i.e., new spinning and weaving machines—cheapened the production of cotton fabrics and created huge demand for raw cotton. At the same time, northern states rapidly set up their own textile mills in places like Lowell and Waltham, Massachusetts, and created their own demand for cotton.

As the demand for raw cotton escalated, the black population experienced a painful relocation from the older Chesapeake and southeast coastal regions to the Southwest. Nearly a million blacks migrated under the lash from the upper South states of Virginia and Maryland to the deep South states of Georgia, South Carolina, Alabama, Mississippi, and Louisiana. By 1860, the black population had increased to an estimated four million and nearly 60 percent lived in the deep South. More so than earlier agricultural practices, the cotton gin placed African American's labor power, rather than their technical knowledge, at the center of agricultural production.

Federal, state, and local authorities also enacted policies aimed to reinforce the separation of blacks from technical expertise. Following Nat Turner's rebellion in 1832, southern states and localities outlawed the teaching of blacks to read, write, and cipher. Since the U.S. Patent Act of 1836 required inventors to submit models showing the precise construction, design, and specifications of their innovations, literacy restrictions denied African Americans significant channels to technical knowledge as well as patents for their innovations. Moreover, following the U.S. Supreme Court's *Dred Scott* decision of 1857, the federal government ruled that bondsmen were not citizens of the republic and therefore could not receive patents for their inventions. Until then, some enslaved blacks notably Norbert Rillieux of Louisiana and Henry Blair of Maryland had received patents for sugar refining equipment and mechanical corn harvesters, respectively.

Alongside the expansion of southern plantations was the growing use of unfree black labor in rural- and urban-based industries. Southern elites regularly touted the virtues of industrial slavery for their lumber, naval stores, coal, railroad, textile, tobacco, and iron companies. In 1859 the New Orleans *Daily Picayune* predicted global success for the industrial South, based upon its low transportation costs, abundant raw materials, and slave labor: "With raw material growing within sight of the factory; with slave labor that, under all circumstances and at all times is absolutely reliable … manufactured fabrics can be produced so as to compete successfully with the world." The most prominent case of urban-industrial slavery emerged in the antebellum Chesapeake, where an estimated seven thousand blacks worked in the iron works of Maryland and Virginia.

Formed in 1836, Richmond's Tredegar Iron Works emerged as the South's leading manufacturing firm. Initially the company employed a mixed labor force of slaves and free whites. In 1847, however, when white workers walked out to protest the training and hiring of skilled slaves, the company dismissed the whites and turned to a slave labor force, except for "boss men." In the iron plants, blacks not only did the hot, heavy, and dirty tasks of cleaning the plant and lifting and hauling the ore,

they also performed the skilled jobs of puddling, heating, and rolling the iron ore into bars for market. Some two thousand bondsmen also entered "the darkest abode of man" to load and transport coal to manufacturing sites. As owners instituted boilers, steam-powered elevators, and water pumps, slave miners also operated the new equipment. More so than in the countryside, however, a small free black population supplemented the labor of urban bondsmen and women. The free black population rose from less than a hundred thousand at the turn of the century to nearly a half million by the late 1850s.

In the wake of the Civil War and Reconstruction, African Americans gradually moved off the land into the major cities of the North, South, and West. While black men had entered a variety of urban and rural industrial occupations as slaves and free blacks, they now saw their occupational horizons shrinking. As the industrial revolution expanded during the late nineteenth and early twentieth centuries, African Americans found it exceedingly difficult to move out of agricultural, personal service, and domestic jobs into the industrial sector. Employers now reversed their perception that blacks could perform profitable labor in both rural and urban industrial settings.

In 1881 a Nashville cotton manufacturer hired an all-white workforce. Blacks, these employers now claimed, were incapable of mastering work on machinery. Moreover, one employer argued that the whirring of the machines would put blacks to sleep. While blacks continued to work in the iron and tobacco industries of Richmond, one of the most industrialized cities of the South, postWar employers narrowed their range of occupations according to certain stereotypes about black character. The Richmond Chamber of Commerce declared that: "In temper he is tractable and can be easily taught … the negro in the heavier work … is a most valuable hand."

Although African Americans were largely excluded from the booming industrial sector of the late-nineteenth-century economy, they nonetheless used their newly won freedom to participate in the proliferation of mechanical innovations during the industrial era. Under the impact of emancipation, civil rights laws, and constitutional amendments, African Americans made the transition from slave to citizen and gained the right to patent their own inventions. Black domestics, farm laborers, and artisans patented a variety of implements designed to ease household, agricultural, and industrial labor. The most notable of these included Jan Matzeliger's shoe lasting machine; Elijah McCoy's numerous lubrication devices for locomotive engines for the railroads; and Granville T. Wood's electrical inventions, including a telephone transmitter. In the emerging age of Jim Crow in the aftermath of Reconstruction, black inventors faced enormous difficulties translating their technical innovations into profitable consumer products. They also found it increasingly difficult to establish their claims to authenticity against white competitors, including leading white entrepreneurs and inventors. Thomas Edison launched stiff legal challenges to the claims of Granville Wood, for example. Unlike most black inventors and entrepreneurs, however, Madame C. J. Walker transformed her hairstraightening formula for black women into a million-dollar enterprise, with sales representatives throughout the U.S.

Only the events of World War I and its aftermath brought African Americans into the industrial sector in large numbers. As European nations mobilized for war, they disrupted established patterns of immigration to the U.S. and stimulated the search for national sources of labor. In 1917, when the U.S. declared war on Germany and initiated its own mobilization of young men for war, industrialists found it even more difficult to meet their wartime labor needs and turned to southern black workers in growing numbers. By 1930 an estimated 5.1 million blacks lived in cities, an increase from about 27 percent of all blacks in 1910 to over 43 percent as the Depression got underway.

In western Pennsylvania, black steelworkers increased from less than 3 percent of the total workforce before the war to 13 percent by war's end. At the same time, the number of black workers in meatpacking firms rose from less than six thousand in 1910 to nearly thirty thousand in 1920. The meatpacking centers of Kansas City, St. Louis, and Chicago attracted the bulk of these newcomers. In Detroit, as early as May 1917, the Packard Company had 1,100 blacks on the payroll, but the Ford Company soon outdistanced other auto makers in the employment of African Americans. The number of blacks at Ford rose from only 50 in 1916 to 2,500 in 1920, 5,000 in 1923, and 10,000 in 1926. Ford also offered blacks a broader range of production and supervisory opportunities than did other companies. A reporter for the Associated Negro Press later recalled that "Back in those days [the 1920s and early 1930s] Negro Ford workers almost established class distinctions here … the men began to feel themselves a little superior to workers in other plants … 'I work for Henry Ford' was a boastful expression." In west coast cities like Seattle, one black resident, Horace R. Cayton Jr. later recalled that World War I opened up "Good jobs for negroes, in the shipyards and in many other places we had not worked before." While the textile industry continued to exclude black workers, blacks represented a large percentage of workers in southern tobacco, lumber, railroad, and coal mining industries.

Although their gains were less dramatic and less permanent than those of black men, black women also gained access to industrial jobs during the labor shortages of World War I. They not only gained employment in jobs traditionally held by white women in textiles, clothing, and food production, but glass, leather, paper, iron, and steel manufacturing as well. In the postwar years, these jobs did not entirely disappear. In Louisville, Seattle, Pittsburgh, Philadelphia, New York, and Chicago, black women continued to work in a variety of industrial jobs.

In 1922 the Women's Bureau of the U.S. Department of Labor surveyed the employment of black women in 150 plants in nine states and seventeen localities. Some 11,812 black women performed labor intensive jobs in food processing, tobacco, clothing, glass, paper, iron, and steel plants. In Chicago, the number of black women classified in manufacturing trades increased from fewer than one thousand in 1910 to over three thousand in 1920. Industrial jobs now made up 15 percent of the black female labor force, compared to less than 7 percent in 1910. One woman wrote back from Chicago to her southern home: "I am well and thankful to say I am doing well … I work in Swifts Packing Company." Prospective household employers now complained that black women wanted industrial wages: "Hundreds of jobs go begging" at domestic pay.

As the black industrial workforce expanded, African Americans faced new patterns of economic inequality. They worked in the most difficult, dangerous, dirty, and low-paying categories of industrial work. These conditions were most acute in the South. According to the Louisville Urban League (LUL), for example, black tobacco workers made between four and ten dollars per week less than their white counterparts. As the LUL put it, "It is the low wage scale … that constitutes the basis for most of our industrial troubles."

In addition to wage discrimination, black workers repeatedly complained that their jobs entailed disproportionate exposure to debilitating heat, deadly fumes, disabling injuries, and even death. In the steel industry, African Americans worked in the hottest areas of the plants. They fed the blast furnaces and performed the most tedious operations that made rails for the railroads. As one black steelworker recalled, African American men "were limited, they only did the dirty work … jobs that even Poles didn't want." In packinghouses, few blacks worked as butchers, a skilled job requiring the use of a knife. Instead, they unloaded trucks, slaughtered the animals, transported intestines, and generally cleaned the plants. Black tannery employees worked mainly in the beam houses. They placed dry hides into pits filled with lime in order to remove the hair. According to one black tannery worker, this job required rubber boots, rubber aprons, rubber gloves, "everything rubber because that lime would eat you up." For their part, coal miners reported low coal seams, excessive water, bad air and rock: "Sometimes the circulation of air or no air would be so bad you'd have to wait sometimes up to two hours before you could get back in there and load any coal … have been sick and dizzy off of that smoke many times … that deadly poison is there … It would knock you out too, make you weak as water." In New York, a black female garment worker complained that, "Over where I work in the dye factory, they expect more from a colored girl if she is to keep her job. They won't give a colored girl a break." In Philadelphia and eastern Pennsylvania, employers presumably hired black women in glass factories, "where at times bits of broken glass were flying in all directions," because of "their ability to stand the heat without suffering."

Black women carried out their jobs in addition to the work within their own households—washing, ironing, cooking, and tending children. Moreover, although large numbers of women worked in industrial jobs, most continued to work in the domestic sector. As with factory employment, certain technological changes transformed the nature of household work under the impact of the industrial revolution. The transition from open-hearth to cast-iron stoves increased the amount of housework performed by women, especially black women employed in white homes. Cooks were expected to use the new technology to prepare more complex and time-consuming meals. As technology historian Ruth Schwartz Cowan notes, "Unlike hearths, stoves had to be meticulously cleaned and coated because they were subject to rust." While a stove made "complex meals easier to prepare," they also increased the level of expectation and labor: "With a reasonably well-designed stove, a woman could bake and boil with the same fire or could bake several different items at one time." Furthermore, as the use of manufactured clothing expanded, laundry chores also increased; as flush toilets eliminated the old "slops," they added the chore of cleaning inside toilet bowls; and, as gas and oil lamps eliminated the job of candle-making, they ushered in the task of cleaning soot-covered glass globes; only the spread of mass-produced electric power during the 1920s and 1930s gradually eliminated the latter chore. In the case of black women, these processes affected their lives and labor in white households long before they affected their lives at home within their own families, where blacks faced stiff barriers in the housing market.

Black industrial workers resisted not only the strict time discipline, speed-ups, and regimentation of the industrial system, but its racially discriminatory employment, pay, and promotion policies as well. In search of higher pay, healthier conditions, and better treatment, African Americans moved from job to job; formed all black labor unions like the Brotherhood of Sleeping Car Porters and a variety of domestic and servants unions; and broke the strikes of discriminatory white labor unions in aluminum, coal mining, meatpacking, and steel industries.

In addition, black workers supplemented these strategies with a plethora of informal modes of resistance. In Atlanta, as historian Tera Hunter notes, household workers regularly supplemented their meager incomes by taking food from their employers' cupboards, taking loads of laundry home and refusing to return them, and quitting their jobs in the midst of employers' plans to lavishly entertain business and professional guests. Finally, and most importantly, black workers not only developed their own independent class-based workplace strategies for addressing economic inequality, they also forged broad community-based alliances with each other as well as black business and professional people—in churches; fraternal orders; and civil rights, nationalist, and social

service organizations like the National Association for the Advancement of Colored People, the Universal Negro Improvement Association, the National Urban League, and the black press. These efforts both reflected and promoted efforts to build the Black Metropolis—a city within the city that would serve the needs of African American families and their communities.

Before African Americans could secure their footing in the industrial workforce, they faced the onset of the Great Depression and later deindustrialization. The depression undercut the position of black workers and revealed the precarious institutional foundation of the African American community during the industrial age. While urban blacks faced extraordinary difficulties, the depression took its greatest toll on blacks in the rural South, where the collapse of cotton prices and the growing use of mechanical devices reduced the demand for farm laborers.

Neither the Republican administration of Herbert S. Hoover nor the early years of the Democratic regime of Franklin D. Roosevelt offered much hope. New Deal programs like the Agricultural Adjustment Administration hastened the exodus of blacks from the land. Large landowners gained increasing control of southern agriculture and applied new labor-saving technology. Tractors, flamethrowers, herbicides, and increasingly mechanical cotton pickers all helped to undercut the position of black agricultural labor and fueled the movement of blacks into cities. By 1950 the South had lost an estimated 1.5 million blacks as a result of war and early postwar migration. The percentage of blacks living in cities increased from less than 50 percent in 1940 to over 80 percent in 1970. Blacks were now divided almost equally between the urban North and West on the one hand, and the South on the other.

The changes of the postwar years coincided with the onset of deindustrialization. As the black urban population increased, manufacturing in the nation's central cities declined from about 66 percent of the total in 1947 to about 40 percent by the late 1960s. While African Americans would continue to rely upon their own work, familial, and community-based institutions for help, such responses were insufficient to address the mass suffering that they faced. Consequently, African Americans would deepen their political and civil rights struggles and demand greater access to government-supported social welfare and labor programs. Their campaign received its most powerful expression in the March on Washington movement of the 1940s; the modern civil rights movement of the 1950s and 1960s; and the militant Black Power movement of the late 1960s and early 1970s. These postwar changes not only revealed how the interplay of race, class, and technology would continue to shape African American and U.S. history through the last years of the twentieth century, they also revealed how the socioeconomic, technological, cultural, and political changes of the postindustrial age were deeply rooted in the era of the industrial revolution.

Joe William Trotter Jr. is Mellon Bank Professor of History and director for the Center for Africanamerican Urban Studies and the Economy (CAUSE) at Carnegie Mellon University in Pittsburgh. In addition to a new textbook on the African American experience, he is author of River Jordan: African American Urban Life in the Ohio Valley *(1998);* Coal, Class and Color: Blacks in Southern West Virginia, 1915–32 *(1990); and* Black Milwaukee: The Making of an Industrial Proletariat, 1915–45 *(1985).*

Notes

1. For the source of this and all other quotations and statistics, see Joe William Trotter Jr., *The African American Experience* (Boston: Houghton Mifflin, forthcoming 2001).

Bibliography

Cline, Darlene Clark, Wilma King, and Linda Reed, eds. *"We Specialize in the Wholly Impossible": A Reader in Black Women's History.* New York: Carson Publishers, 1995.

Cowan, Ruth Schwartz. "How We Get Our Daily Bread, or the History of Domestic Technology Revealed." *OAH Magazine of History* 12 (Winter 1998): 9–12.

———. *A Social History of American Technology.* New York: Oxford University Press, 1997.

Franklin, John Hope, and A. Moss Jr. *From Slavery to Freedom: A History of African Americans.* 7th edition. New York: McGraw Hill, 1994.

Hunter, Tera W. "African-American Women Workers' Protest in the New South." *OAH Magazine of History* 13 (Summer 1999): 52–55.

———. *To 'Joy My Freedom: Southern Black Women's Lives and Labors After the Civil War.* Cambridge: Harvard University Press, 1997.

James, Portia P. *The Real McCoy: African-American Invention and Innovation, 1619–1930.* Washington, DC: Smithsonian Institution Press, 1989.

Judd, Michael. "Lewis Latimer: African American Inventor, Poet, and Activist." *OAH Magazine of History* 12 (Winter 1998): 25–30.

Marcus, Alan I., and Howard P. Segal. *Technology in America: A Brief History.* San Diego: Harcourt, Brace, Janovich, 1989.

Norton, Mary Beth, general editor, and Pamela Gerardi, associate editor. *The American Historical Association's Guide to Historical Literature.* 3rd edition. Volume 1. New York: Oxford University Press, 1995.

Sinclair, Bruce. "Teaching About Technology and African American History." *OAH Magazine of History* 12 (Winter 1998): 14–17.

Trotter, Joe William Jr., and Earl Lewis, eds. *African Americans in the Industrial Age: A Documentary History, 1915–1945.* Boston: Northeastern University Press, 1996.

Trotter, Joe William Jr. "African American History: Origins, Development, and Current State of the Field." *OAH Magazine of History* 7 (Summer 1993): 12–18.

———. *River Jordan: African American Urban Life in the Ohio Valley.* Lexington: University Press of Kentucky, 1998.

From *OAH Magazine of History*, Fall 2000, pages 19-23. Copyright © 2000 by Organization of American Historians. Reprinted with permission.

The death of Wilhautyah

When a white settler killed a Nez
Perce warrior in 1876, the incident set
off a chain of events that led to war.

By Mark Highberger

FROM ACROSS A FREEZING Montana battlefield on October 5, 1877, Chief Joseph of the Nez Perce rode into the camp of U.S. Army Colonel Nelson Miles and surrendered his rifle. "I am tired," he said. "My heart is sick and sad. From where the sun now stands I will fight no more forever." With those words he ended the war between 750 Nez Perce—500 of them women, children, and elderly—and 2,000 soldiers, a four-month battle that had ranged across 1,200 miles. "Our chiefs are dead," Joseph told Miles. "The old men are all dead.... The little children are freezing to death."

Joseph would never again live on the land for which he had fought. The American government sent him and the 430 Nez Perce who surrendered with him to Fort Leavenworth, Kansas. Those who survived the malaria there were later moved to Indian Territory. Eventually some returned to live on the Nez Perce reservation, close to their former home. In 1885 Joseph was exiled to a reservation in Washington Territory, where he died on September 21, 1904.

The origins of the war that caused Joseph and the Nez Perce so much hardship and grief lay in the Wallowa country of northeast Oregon. For generations it had been the Nez Perce homeland, but the arrival of white settlers in the region led to violence. Settlers killed as many as 30 Nez Perce during the 1860s and '70s, yet few of the accused ever stood trial, and those who did were acquitted.

One such fatal confrontation occurred on a summer day the year before Joseph's surrender. Two settlers from the Wallowa Valley rode into a Nez Perce hunting camp searching for missing horses. When they rode out, a Nez Perce warrior named Wilhautyah (Wind Blowing) lay dead, shot by one of the settlers. The recoil from that shot started a chain of events that led to the Nez Perce War.

At the time of Wilhautyah's death, the Nez Perce were embroiled in a struggle to remain on their ancestral homeland. The roots of conflict stretched back to an 1855 treaty that gave the Wallowa country to the Nez Perce and an 1863 treaty that took it away after gold was discovered on Indian land.

Old Joseph, Chief Joseph's father and the leader of the Wallowa band, refused to sign the second treaty. His Nez Perce considered the valley their home, even as homesteaders began building cabins and planting crops there. Other Nez Perce did sign the treaty and agreed to live on the Lapwai Reservation in Idaho Territory. They were known as the treaty Nez Perce.

In 1873 President Ulysses S. Grant issued an Executive Order that divided the valley between homestead sites and an Indian reservation. Two years later, Grant gave into pressure from whites wanting to settle there and revoked the order, reopening the entire valley to settlement and sealing the fate of the Nez Perce. It was only a matter of time before they would be forced from the Wallowa Valley and onto a reservation. Unaware of what lay ahead, Indians and whites lived as reluctant neighbors until the day Alexander B. Findley noticed five of his horses were missing.

According to Union County Circuit Court records, Findley, one of the valley's first settlers. spent several days "thoroughly searching all the range my horses had run on since I had them." When on June 22, 1876, he came across a Nez Perce camp in the northern foothills, he decided his "suspicion that my horses were stolen were confirmed. I immediately returned to get assistance to search for my horses or their trail and try to recover them."

***THE TWO WHITE** men stopped and got off their horses and shot Wilhautyah.*

He got help from three men, including Wells McNall, a 21-year-old known as an Indian-hater and troublemaker. Though the men saw no horses when they returned to the camp, Findley remained convinced he had found horse thieves. "We found tracks comparing or corresponding with my horses," he said. He and McNall went on alone, following the tracks to a hunting camp containing a cache of venison. Findley "told Mr. McNall we would return home and get more help."

The next morning, however, Findley and McNall rode back to the second camp alone and watched from a distance. After about 90 minutes a Nez Perce approached from the woods, and the two white men rode down to meet him. By the time they reached the camp, three Nez Perce were there. One of them was Wilhautyah, a close friend of Chief Joseph of the Wallowa Nez Perce band. Exactly what happened next is subject to debate.

Findley said he dismounted and grabbed a Nez Perce weapon leaning against a tree, one of three hunting rifles in the Indian camp. "[I] told the Indians I believed they had stolen and we wanted them to go to the settlement until we had an understanding about the matter. They did not consent to go."

According to Findley he then put the Nez Perce rifle beside one that had been lying on the ground, and McNall laid a third rifle that had been near him beside the others. With the Indians unarmed, Findley and McNall again tried to persuade them to go to the settlement. The Nez Perce again refused, an argument erupted, and Wilhautyah and McNall ended up wrestling for McNall's rifle.

"The next thing I knew," Findley said, "McNall called on me to shoot." Then McNall's rifle fired. "About the time of the report," Findley said, "I cocked my gun and held it ready, waiting to see the result of the scuffle over the gun of McNall. Resolved not to shoot until I saw our lives were in danger." When Findley fired, it seemed to surprise him. "I had not decided to shoot when I heard the report of my gun," he said. "I was not conscious of pulling the trigger."

When recounting the story years later, Findley's son, H.R. Findley, described a different ending, saying that the fight started when Wilhautyah grabbed McNall's rifle, and the struggle lasted until a desperate McNall began cursing Findley, demanding that he shoot. "It was then that [my father] took careful aim and killed Wilhautyah," the younger Findley said. Whether the killing was accidental or deliberate, the two white men quickly left the scene. When word of the incident spread settlers feared Nez Perce retaliation. Some barricaded themselves in McNall's blockhouse-like cabin.

The next morning, the settlers persuaded McNall to ride to the county seat of Union and report the incident to County Judge E.C. Brainard. Unsure of how to handle the situation, Brainard wrote a letter to Colonel Elmer Otis, the commander of Fort Walla Walla. "More trouble in the Willowa," Brainard wrote, "one Finley and McNall accuse the Indians of stealing horses, and have managed to kill one of Joseph's band. The settlers are sufficiently alarmed to mass in the valley."

To make matters worse, three days after the killing Findley found his missing horses grazing near his home. "Blowing Wind was an honest man," said Peopeo Tholekt of the Looking Glass band of Nez Perce, "and the horses being found proved him innocent."

His killers, however, were still unpunished, and as Wallowa settlers prepared to defend themselves, John Monteith, the Indian agent at the Lapwai Reservation, met with Joseph to hear the Nez Perce version of the story. Afterwards, Monteith wrote to General Oliver Otis Howard, commander of the U.S. Army's Department of the Columbia, which had jurisdiction over the Wallowa country. Monteith's letter called the killing "willful, deliberate murder." Yet he advised Joseph to let white law determine justice. "I told him to keep his people quiet and all would end well."

Howard, a veteran officer who had lost his right arm in the Civil War, was a religious man who gained the nickname "Old Prayer Book" for his distribution of tracts and Bibles to his troops during the war. He sympathized with the Nez Perce cause and sent Major Henry Clay Wood, his assistant adjutant general, to Lapwai. As a lawyer, Wood had studied the Nez Perce case and concluded that "The nontreaty Nez Perce cannot in law be regarded as bound by the treaty of 1863." He was also critical of President Grant's revocation of the 1873 Executive Order, saying, "If not a crime, it was a blunder."

At Wood's request, 40 Nez Perce rode from Wallowa to Lapwai for a council on July 22–23. During the meetings, Joseph spoke of how among Indians, the chiefs were responsible for controlling their young men and preventing them from doing "wicked things,"

and if the chiefs did not restrain or punish unruly Indians, the chiefs were held accountable. To Joseph, then, white authorities were responsible for the killing of one "much respected by the tribe."

Joseph also cited the killing as one more claim the Nez Perce had to the land. "Since the murder had been done," Wood reported Joseph saying, "since his brother's life had been taken in Wallowa valley, his body buried there, and the earth there had drunk up his blood, the valley was more sacred to him than ever before… and that all the whites must be removed from the valley" Ollokot, Joseph's brother, added that "he did not want the whites, Findley and McNall, tried and punished for their crime, but wished them to leave that section of country that he might never see them more."

Wood told the Nez Perce that Howard had proposed that the U.S. Government appoint a commission to settle once and for all the ownership of the Wallowa country, and he asked the two Indians to let white law deal with Findley and McNall. Both Joseph and Ollokot agreed to this, and the Nez Perce returned home. Afterward, Howard wrote to Brainard to insist that the two men be tried for murder. But in August, Findley and McNall were still free.

TENSIONS GREW. Some believed the Nez Perce were preparing for war; warriors spent their days shooting arrows at targets set up near the Findley home. "Several war dances were held," H.R. Findley said, "and the beating of their drums or tom-toms could often be plainly heard from their [Findley] cabin." Yet some white settlers continued to harass the Indians by stealing livestock, and against Joseph's advice a few Nez Perce retaliated in kind.

During councils held at Indian Town, the Nez Perce summer encampment at the confluence of the valley's two rivers, Joseph and the older chiefs advised against doing anything that would give whites an excuse to force them onto a reservation. The young men, however, had lost patience with white justice. The time had come for retribution. They agreed to move slowly and avoid force for as long as possible. When the meetings ended, the Nez Perce had decided on a course of action.

On September 1, Nez Perce riders traveled through the valley, stopping at every settler's cabin and delivering the message that all whites, including Findley and McNall, were to attend a council the next day at Indian Town. Seventeen settlers showed up, but Findley and McNall stayed home. At the meeting, the Nez Perce insisted that the whites leave the valley and turn over McNall and Findley. When the settlers refused, the meeting ended with an angry agreement to meet the next day at the McNall cabin.

The next morning 60 warriors rode to the cabin, where a number of settlers waited with the Findley and McNall families. When the Nez Perce repeated their demands and the settlers again refused, Joseph warned that if they did not turn over the two men and leave the valley in one week's time the Nez Perce would drive them out and burn their houses. Then the Indians rode away. The clock started ticking toward Sunday, September 10.

After dark, a few settlers rode through the valley to warn others, and Ephraim McNall, father of Wells, traveled to Fort Walla Walla to plead with Lieutenant Albert Gallatin Forse to send troops to Wallowa. Forse refused.

Denied military assistance, McNall headed back to Wallowa, stopping along the way to recruit armed volunteers. When Forse learned about this new development he changed his mind about sending troops. On September 7 he rode out of Fort Walla Walla with a company of 48 cavalrymen to protect the Nez Perce and prevent a war.

After riding all night, 22 volunteers from the Grande Ronde Valley reached McNall's cabin on September 9 and joined with the settlers to form a force of 43 men. Because the Nez Perce had moved their main camp close to Wallowa Lake for the beginning of the salmon run, 15 men rode that way to help settlers there. The next day they moved on to a nearby ranch, where many settlers had agreed to gather.

Forse's troops had already arrived at the ranch at 1:00 A.M. on Sunday, the day of Joseph's deadline. "I found about 50 armed men," Forse noted of the gather-

ing, "also several families, who there sought protection." Later, even more families and volunteers arrived.

After leaving some militia at the cabin for protection, Forse moved his men and most of the volunteers up the valley to Alder and the home of Thomas H. Veasey, who was friendly with the Nez Perce and spoke their language. Forse and Veasey then continued on alone to meet with Joseph at his camp, seven miles away.

According to a local newspaper report, Forse and Veasey found Joseph "at the head of 100 painted warriors on the summit of a hill near his camp, drawn up in line of battle, his men divested of all their superfluous blankets, well armed and mounted on their best war steeds, all decorated with war paint and presenting a formidable appearance."

Forse was looking for a solution, not a fight, and he recognized the Nez Perce advantage. "Joseph could have fallen upon the settlers in detail, killing them and destroying their property," he said. "An enemy could not approach him without being under his fire for the distance of more than a half-mile."

Forse got down to the business of negotiating. He asked to see Joseph, whose appearance and character made an immediate impression on the lieutenant. "I thought he was the finest Indian I had ever seen not only physically but intelligently," Forse said. "He was about six feet in height, powerfully built, and strength of character written on every feature."

With Veasey interpreting, Forse "asked him if he would be satisfied if McNall and Findley were tried by the civil authorities," and "He said he would." In an attempt to avoid future trouble, Forse requested that the Nez Perce stay away from the settlers and confine themselves to the Wallowa Lake side of Hurricane Creek. Joseph agreed, and to show his good faith he and his men discharged their guns into the air. A truce had been called.

The next day Forse "sent word to McNall and Findley by two of their friends advising them to go to Union and surrender themselves." They followed his advice. Three days later, on September 14, the court released McNall after ruling he

had acted in self-defense, but Judge Brainard issued a warrant for Findley's arrest, charging him with manslaughter. After his arrest Findley was released on $250 bail.

Meanwhile, that same day Forse met again with Joseph to persuade him to send the two Nez Perce witnesses to testify at the trial. Forse offered to send along one of his noncommissioned officers as an escort. Joseph consented, but only with great reluctance. "He was afraid that whites would harm them," Forse said. Joseph might also have realized that sending witnesses would accomplish nothing.

The next day, Forse sent a corporal to escort the Nez Perce witnesses. He also sent a letter to Brainard, "requesting him to see that they were taken care of." Less than a week later, however, Brainard dismissed the charges against Findley. The two Nez Perce witnesses had refused to testify. Perhaps they feared reprisal or felt their cause was doomed anyway. Either for personal or diplomatic reasons, Findley requested that his case continue, and he faced a grand jury in October. Once again, the charges were dismissed.

Because of the missing testimony, the Nez Perce version of the events remains obscure. Battle, imprisonment, and disease later killed many in the band. Yet one eyewitness who survived, Eskawus, said years later that the Nez Perce hunting party was headed home that day when they stopped to pick up the deer they had hung in the tree.

"So Wilhautyah was told to climb the tree," Eskawus recalled, "because he was a small man, and while up the tree, unloosing the ropes, the Indians on the ground saw two white men coming at full speed. A little way off they stopped and got off their horses and shot Wilhautyah." Whatever occurred that day, Findley's and McNall's pleas of self-defense prevailed in court.

Forse and his men headed back to Fort Walla Walla on September 26, 1876. On his ride back through the valley, Forse "found everything quiet." The peace was not to last. Earlier that summer Sioux and Cheyenne warriors had wiped out troops under Lieutenant Colonel George Custer at the Battle of the Little Bighorn. The disaster put an end to the army's patience and to much of the public's sympathy for Indian rights.

CHIEF JOSEPH surrendered in 1877 with a promise, "I will fight no more forever."

To avoid future confrontations, the government had to attend to the issue of removing the Nez Perce from the Wallowa country. Howard used the Wallowa incident to press for a five-member commission to decide how to get the Nez Perce onto a reservation. On October 3, 1876, the secretary of the interior appointed General Howard, Major Wood, and three easterners, David H. Jerome of Michigan, A.C. Barstow of Rhode Island, and William Stickney of Washington, D.C., to the commission. According to Mrs. John Monteith the last three members were "excellent men... all kings of finance, but with not a speck of Indian sense, experience, or knowledge."

Joseph met with the commission at Lapwai in November and rejected its offer to buy what remained of Indian land, arguing eloquently that the Nez Perce should be allowed to stay there. But the commission's recommendation to the Department of the Interior stated, "That unless in a reasonable time Joseph consented to be removed [from Wallowa], he should be forcibly taken with his people and given lands on the reservation." Major Wood, however, refused to sign the document. Joseph, unaware of the commission's report, went with his people to their winter encampment in the Imnaha canyon.

In April and May 1877 Joseph and his brother Ollokot met three times with General Howard and others trying to convince them that although the Nez Perce did not want to fight, they had the right to stay in the Wallowa Valley. By May 14, an impatient General Howard decided that "reasonable time" was up, and he gave the Wallowa band 30 days to move to the reservation. "If you are not here in that time," he said, "I shall consider that you want to fight, and will send my soldiers to drive you on."

To avoid war, the Nez Perce were prepared to do as Howard ordered, but violence found them anyway. On their way to the reservation, with 10 days left of freedom, the five nontreaty bands came together in a gathering of about 600 Indians. The young men staged war parades and rode around simulating battle.

On June 13, two days before they were due at the reservation, a warrior named Wahlitits and two companions decided to seek revenge on a white man, Larry Ott, who had killed Wahlitits' father two years earlier. When they couldn't find Ott they waited a day then went to the cabin of a man known to be cruel to Indians and shot him. Roused by this first act of vengeance, they killed four more settlers and wounded one other. Soon other warriors joined them in a series of raids.

"For a short time we lived quietly," Joseph later said about the pre-war days. "But that could not last." One shot from a settler's rifle helped shatter a fragile peace and set the Nez Perce on the path to war.

Mark Highberger is a teacher and freelance writer from Wallowa, Oregon.

From *American History,* December 1998. © 1998 by Primedia Consumer Media and Magazines, Inc. All rights reserved. Reprinted with permission.

UNIT 2

The Emergence of Modern America

Unit Selections

8. **Where the Other Half Lived**, Verlyn Klinkenborg
9. **Our First Olympics**, Bob Fulton
10. **Lady Muckraker**, Paula A. Treckel
11. **Teddy in the Middle**, Stan Saunders
12. **The Steamer Age**, Jerry LeBlanc

Key Points to Consider

- Discuss the kinds of conditions Jacob Riis found in the slums. What combination of factors made it difficult for individuals to escape this environment?

- What practices did the Standard Oil Company follow in order to defeat competition? How did Ida Tarbell and the other muckrakers pave the way for the rise of Progressivism?

- What were the issues involved in the Pennsylvania Coal Strike of 1902? Why were Teddy Roosevelt's actions so objectionable to management?

- What advantage did steam cars have over ones that were gasoline driven? What disadvantages?

 **Links: www.dushkin.com/online/**
These sites are annotated in the World Wide Web pages.

The Age of Imperialism
http://www.smplanet.com/imperialism/toc.html

Anti-Imperialism in the United States, 1898–1935
http://boondocksnet.com/ail98-35.html

William McKinley 1843-1901
http://lcweb.loc.gov/rr/hispanic/1898/mckinley.html

American Diplomacy: Editor's Corner - If Two By Sea
http://www.unc.edu/depts/diplomat/AD_Issues/amdipl_15/edit_15.html

Great Chicago Fire and the Web of Memory
http://www.chicagohs.org/fire/

There was a great deal of ferment in the United States during the 1880s and 1890s. Rural America continued to exist, but millions of people flocked to cities in search of a better life. Often they found poor and inadequate housing, and jobs that required long, grueling hours of work at low pay. Immigrants poured into the country, where most ended up in the poorer parts of cities. The majority of these people came from Southern and Eastern Europe, and became known as the "new" immigration (previous waves had come from Ireland and Germany). Because their dress, their languages, and their customs differed so markedly from that of native-born Americans, they were seen by many as inferior peoples. Warnings about the effect of immigration are not so different today from what they were then. One of the essays in this section, "Where the Other Half Lived," shows the incredible poverty and crowded conditions some of these people had to endure.

Economic changes were vast. Small and medium sized businesses continued to exist, but corporations on a scale previously unheard of came to dominate the marketplace. Paula A. Treckel's "Lady Muckraker" tells the story of Ida Tarbell, who wrote a series of popular magazine articles detailing the seamy business practices of the Standard Oil Company. Other "muckrakers" exposed wrongdoing by other corporations, and the corruption that existed at various levels of government. These individuals helped to pave the way for the Progressive movement that will be discussed in the next unit.

Although industrial production increased dramatically, the gap between rich and poor widened steadily. Corporate leaders amassed unprecedented fortunes on which they paid no income taxes. Urban working families, on the other, often lived in unhealthy squalor even though all their members, including young children, worked in some shop or factory.

As more and more people depended solely on their jobs for income, depressions (one beginning in 1873 and another in 1893), were far more devastating than they had been in the past. Farmers did not fare well either. They had to sell what they produced on markets that fluctuated widely, but had to purchase equipment and other necessities at prices often fixed by the large companies. They also had to contend with the monopolistic practices of railroads, which charged "all the traffic would bear" for shipping and storing farm products.

Minority groups, such as Indians and blacks, continued to suffer socially and economically through good times as well as bad. The essay "Lost Bird" tells the story of a survivor of the massacre at Wounded Knee. Raised by whites, Lost Bird hovered between two cultures without finding a real place in either one.

"Our First Olympics" is about the first modern Olympic games that were held in Greece in 1896. The Frenchman who organized the event hoped they would contribute to international harmony. In contrast with the enormous hoopla that now surrounds the Olympics; the early games were neither well-attended nor widely publicized. Organized American athletic groups tended to ignore the occasion with the result that the United States sent a rag-tag contingent that nonetheless performed surprisingly well.

There was a great deal of violence between labor and management during the period. Labor was treated pretty much like any raw material used in industry—to be bought as cheaply as possible without regard for the human consequences. Workers, denied the right to form unions, often regarded going on strike as the only means to redress their grievances. "Teddy in the Middle" provides an account of a coal strike in Pennsylvania in 1902. When management and labor became deadlocked, workers voted with their feet. The prospect of fuel shortages for the coming winter emboldened President Theodore Roosevelt to intervene. His part in resolving the crisis helped define his presidency and broadened the role of the executive office.

The era also witnessed an explosion of technological advances. "The Steamer Age" tells the story of an idea whose time had seemed to come, only to have it subsequently fade. When the Stanley "Rocket" was clocked at nearly 130 miles per hour in 1906, steam-driven cars appeared to be the wave of the future. Numerous improvements in gas-powered automobiles, however, ultimately relegated the steamers to mere curiosities.

The Conscience of Place
MULBERRY BEND

Where the Other Half Lived

The photographs of Jacob Riis confronted New Yorkers with the misery of Mulberry Bend—and helped to tear it down.

By Verlyn Klinkenborg

A BLOCK BELOW CANAL STREET in lower Manhattan, just a few hundred yards from City Hall, there is a small urban oasis called Columbus Park. Early on a spring morning, the sun rises over an irregular threshold of rooftops to the east of the park—a southern spur of Chinatown— and picks out details on the courthouses and state office buildings looming over the west side of the park. Carved eagles stare impassively into the sunlight. Incised over a doorway on the Criminal Courts Building is a strangely senseless quotation from Justinian. "Justice is the firm and continuous desire to render to every man his due," it says, as though justice were mainly a matter of desire.

Beneath the sun's level rays high overhead, Columbus Park seems almost hollow somehow, and since it is open ground—open playground, to be accurate—it exposes the local topography. The land slopes downward from Bayard Street to Park Street, and downward from Mulberry to Baxter. At the north end of the park, temporary fencing surrounds an ornate shelter, the sole remnant of the park's original construction in 1897, now given over to pigeons. Plane trees lean inward around the perimeter of the asphalt ball field, where a tidy squadron of middle-aged and elderly Asian women stretches in unison, some clinging to the chain-link fence for balance. One man wields a tai chi sword to the sound of Chinese flutes from a boom box. A gull spirals down out of the sky, screeching the whole way. All around I can hear what this city calls early morning silence,

an equidistant rumble that seems to begin a few blocks away.

I watch all of this, the tai chi, the stretching, the old men who have come to sit in the cool spring sunshine, the reinforced police vans delivering suspects to the court buildings just beyond it all, and as I watch I try to remember that Columbus Park was once Mulberry Bend. Mulberry Street still crooks to the southeast here, but the Bend proper is long gone. It was the most infamous slum in 19th-century New York, an immeasurable quantity of suffering compacted into 2.76 acres. On a bright April morning, it's hard to believe the Bend ever existed. But then such misery always inspires disbelief.

The Bend was ultimately torn down and a park built on its site in 1897 after unrelenting pressure from Jacob Riis, the Danish-born journalist and social reformer. In *How the Other Half Lives*, an early landmark in reforming literature whose title became a catchphrase, Riis provides some numbers for Mulberry Bend, which he obtained from the city's Registrar of Vital Statistics. In 1888, he wrote, 5,650 people lived on Baxter and Mulberry streets between Park and Bayard. If Riis means strictly the buildings within the Bend, as he almost certainly does, then the population density there was 2,047 persons per acre, nearly all of them recent immigrants.

By itself, that's an almost meaningless figure. But think of it this way: In Manhattan today, 1,537,195 persons live on 14,720 acres, a density of slightly more than 104 per acre. (In 1890, the average

density within the built-up areas of Manhattan was about 115 per acre.) If Manhattan were peopled as thickly today as the Bend was in 1888, it would have more than 30 million inhabitants, an incomprehensible figure, the equivalent of nearly the whole of California jammed onto a single island. To put it another way, if the people who live in Manhattan today were packed as tightly as the immigrants in Mulberry Bend were, they could all live in Central Park with room to spare. But these are suppositions, imaginary numbers. The truly astonishing figure, of course, is 5,650 persons—actual human beings, every one of them—living in Mulberry Bend, among the highest population density ever recorded anywhere.

Now consider a final set of numbers: According to Riis and the city statistician, the death rate of children under five in Mulberry Bend was 140 per 1,000, roughly 1 out of 7. This is likely to be an underestimate. (Citywide, the number was just under 100 per 1,000 and falling fast.) Today, Mulberry Bend would rank between Lesotho and Tanzania in under-five mortality and worse than Haiti, Eritrea, Congo, and Bangladesh. Last year, the under-five mortality rate for the United States was 8 per 1,000, or 1 out of 125.

Numbers, even numbers as striking as these, do not do a good job of conveying horror. But when the horror is literally fleshed out, it begins to make an impression, as it did on Riis himself. After coming to America in 1870, at age 21, and enduring a vagrant existence for a few years, he found work at the *New York Tri-*

bune as a police reporter and was sent to the office at 303 Mulberry Street, a few blocks north of the Bend and across from police headquarters. Night after night, Riis visited the Bend, sometimes in police company, often not, and he reported what he saw—especially the extreme overcrowding—to the Board of Health. "It did not make much of an impression," Riis wrote in *The Making of an American*. "These things rarely do, put in mere words."

So Riis put them in pictures. With a flashgun and a handheld camera, invented just a few years earlier, Riis began to take photographs of what he found in the Bend. "From them," he wrote, "there was no appeal." They made misery demonstrable in a way that nothing else had. No political or economic or cultural theory could justify the crowding his photographs document. There was no explaining away the sense of oppression and confinement they reveal. In picture after picture you see not only the poverty and the congestion of the Bend—the stale sweatshops and beer dives and five-cent lodging houses—but the emotional and psychological consequences of people living on top of each other.

Since the mid-20th century, Riis has been considered one of the founders of documentary photography. Over the years, his photographs of Mulberry Bend and other New York slums have become a part of the city's conscience. But his approach to photography was flatly utilitarian. "I had use for it," Riis wrote of the camera, "and beyond that I never went." Printing technology at the time meant that in books and articles his pictures had to be redrawn as wood engravings, considerably reducing their impact. The actual photographs were seen only in lantern slides accompanying his lectures. What mattered was not aesthetics but what the pictures showed. Riis had a similar use for words and statistics. They were merely tools to persuade New Yorkers to witness what was right in front of their eyes.

In one of his many articles on tenement housing, Riis printed a map of the Bend drawn from overhead, a silhouette showing the proportion of open space to buildings. Looking at that map is like looking at an old-fashioned diagram of a cell, a hieroglyphic of dark and light. It's hard to know what to call the spaces depicted by the white areas on Riis's map. *Yard* is too pastoral and *air shaft* too hygienic. Riis calls them "courts" and "alleys," but even those words are too generous. What the white spaces really portray are outdoor places where only a single layer of humans could live, many of them homeless children who clustered in external stairwells and on basement steps. In the tenements of the Bend—three, four, and five stories each—families and solitary lodgers, who paid five cents apiece for floor space, crowded together in airless cubicles. "In a room not thirteen feet either way," Riis wrote of one midnight encounter, "slept twelve men and women, two or three in bunks set in a sort of alcove, the rest on the floor."

For reformers, Riis included, the trouble with the Bend wasn't merely the profits it returned to slumlords and city politicians, nor was it just the high rents that forced tenants to sublet floor space to strangers. The problem was also how to portray the Bend in a way that conveyed its contagious force, the absence of basic sanitation, of clean water and fresh air, the presence of disease, corruption, and crime, the enervation and despair. It was, for Riis, the problem of representing an unrepresentable level of defilement. The power of his silhouette map, for instance, is flawed by its white margins, which falsely imply that conditions improved across the street, when, in fact, the entire Sixth Ward was cramped and impoverished. Even the grimmest of Riis's photographs show only a few people, at most, in the back alleys and basement dives. Powerful as they are, these pictures fail to convey the simple tonnage of human flesh in those dead-end blocks.

But the problem of Mulberry Bend was also how to interpret it. On a bright spring morning in the 1880s or early 1890s, a New Yorker—curiosity aroused, perhaps, by one of Riis's articles—might have strolled over to Mulberry or Baxter Street to see for himself. What he found there would depend on his frame of mind. It might have been, as photographs suggest, a bustling streetfront crowded with people going rather shabbily about the ordinary sorts of business, much as they might in other neighborhoods. Such a New Yorker—disinclined to push through to the dark inner rooms a few flights up or to the dismal courts and alleys behind or to the dank beer dives below—might conclude that perhaps Riis had exaggerated and that perhaps all there was to see here was a people, immigrants nearly all of them, who were insufficiently virtuous or cleanly or hardworking or American. It would be possible for such a person to blame Mulberry Bend on the very people who were its victims. But when the tenements were condemned and their inhabitants moved into decent housing, particularly in Harlem, they blended imperceptibly into the fabric of the city.

Riis has been faulted for his glib descriptive use of racial and ethnic stereotypes, a convention of his time that sounds raw and coarse to us now. In his defense, he came to understand that the power of a place like Mulberry Bend was enough to corrupt its residents, no matter who they were, as it had the Irish, and then the Italians who were their successors in the Bend. No iniquity within the Bend was as great, to Riis, as the political and financial iniquity that sustained the tenements there.

But the tragedy of Mulberry Bend isn't only that it came to exist and, once in existence, to be tolerated. It was also that when the city finally tore down the Bend and at last built the park that Calvert Vaux had designed for the site, a kind of forgetfulness descended. A New Yorker coming to the newly built Mulberry Bend Park in 1897, or to its renaming in 1911, or merely to watch the sun rise on a bright spring morning in 2001, might never know that there had been such a place as the Bend. The park that stands in its place is some kind of redemption, but without memory no redemption is ever complete. And without action of the kind that Riis undertook, justice remains only a matter of desire.

From *Mother Jones*, July/August 2001, pp. 54-57. © 2001 by Foundation for National Progress. Reprinted by permission.

OUR FIRST OLYMPICS

A CENTURY AGO a tiny American team arrived in Athens drained from an awful journey and proposing to take on the champions of Europe with—among other handicaps—a discus thrower who had never seen a real discus

BY BOB FULTON

THERE WERE SURELY MOMENTS during the long journey to Greece when James Connolly was seized with foreboding, convinced this antic venture was doomed to failure. Connolly and a dozen countrymen, who constituted America's first Olympic team, certainly had cause for misgivings as they sailed toward Athens and the revival of the long-dormant Games in 1896. These thirteen competitors—an unlucky thirteen, it seemed—had received no financial support from the nation they were to represent. The general public regarded the reborn Olympics with an utter lack of interest, and even their fellow athletes didn't care; only one of the Americans was a national champion in the event he had entered.

Now, it turned out, they were due to arrive in Athens the day before the competition commenced, woefully out of shape after a wearing sixteen-day journey from Hoboken, New Jersey. Failure appeared as inevitable as the next morning's sunrise.

No one viewed the American team's plight more bleakly than Connolly, who had dropped out of Harvard to take part in the Games. The fact that he had managed to lose his wallet in Italy seemed emblematic of the whole doleful enterprise.

SEVEN HUNDRED AMERICANS will participate in the 1996 centennial Games in Atlanta, a figure that dwarfs the tiny U.S. contingent of 1896. But the contrast between the first modern Olympics and the upcoming Games transcends mere numbers, for no American team has ever encountered as much adversity as our first.

The hardships faced by the pioneers of a century ago were the result of indifference. All the prominent athletic groups in the United States turned their backs on the Olympics and, by extension, on Pierre de Coubertin, the French baron who was the driving force behind the Olympic renaissance. His grand revival barely drew a glance from an America that thought the Games a relic best left buried under the dust of the ages—especially given their checkered history.

The ancient Olympics came to an ignominious end. They had originated as a local festival in 776 B.C., but as their popularity grew, athletes journeyed to Olympia from the far margins of the known world. Increasingly elaborate prizes fomented increasingly widespread cheating. In time an avalanche of abuses buried the ideals that guided the earliest competitors. A disgusted Emperor Theodosius abolished the Games in A.D. 393.

Coubertin believed that resuscitating the Games in their old grandeur would foster international harmony. He first proposed his idea in 1892 during a lecture at the Sorbonne: "Let us export

oarsmen, runners, fencers; there is the free trade of the future. And on the day when it shall take its place among the customs of Europe, the cause of peace will have received a new and powerful support."

His vision of a multinational gathering came to fruition two years later, when the International Athletic Congress voted to hold the first modern Olympics in Greece, where the Games had been born. But while Olympic fervor burned on the Continent, American sportsmen dismissed the revival as a European creation designed for European athletes. In fact, the prestigious New York Athletic Club, which included many national track and field champions among its membership, snubbed the Games completely.

So the American presence at the first modern Olympics was utterly extemporaneous; our pioneer Olympians were spurred by personal impulse to be the representatives of a nation that didn't care whether it was represented or not.

James Connolly was a twenty-seven-year-old Harvard undergraduate when he got wind of the Games. He applied for a leave of absence from school to participate only to have a dean deny him out of hand, citing Connolly's poor academic standing. His only recourse, the dean informed him, was to resign from Harvard and then take his chances on being readmitted later. Connolly was indignant.

"I am not resigning and I am not making application to reenter," he told the dean. "But I *am* going to the Olympic Games, so I am through with Harvard right now."

Connolly never did return to school and, in fact, still held a grudge years after he had gained renown as a war correspondent for *Collier's* magazine and as the author of twenty-five novels. Offered an honorary degree by Harvard, he summarily refused it.

Robert Garrett, a twenty-year-old captain of the Princeton track team and the scion of a wealthy Baltimore banking family, learned of the revival Games from his history professor, who wholeheartedly endorsed Coubertin's efforts.

Garrett persuaded three schoolmates to accompany him—after agreeing to pay their way. His largess enabled the sprinter Francis Lane; Herbert Jamison, a middle-distance runner; and the pole vaulter Albert Tyler to carry Princeton's black and orange colors overseas (official Olympic uniforms would not be mandated until 1906).

The Boston Athletic Association sent five representatives to Greece, in no small measure because of a facetious remark uttered by the distance runner Arthur Blake three months earlier. Congratulated on winning a 1,000-yard race, Blake joked, "Oh, I am too good for Boston. I ought to go over and run the Marathon at Athens in the Olympic Games." A stockbroker named Arthur Burnham overheard him and offered to bankroll a BAA contingent. Blake was joined by Thomas Burke, the defending U.S. champion in the 440-yard run; the hurdler Thomas Curtis; Ellery Clark, a jumper; and the pole vaulter William Welles Hoyt.

Gardner Williams, a swimmer, and two marksmen, the brothers John and Sumner Paine, rounded out an American team that was really nothing more than a glorified pickup squad. After all, no trials had been held to determine the most qualified representatives, and only Burke was a national champion in his event.

Prospects for success in Athens were abysmal and declined from there when the star-crossed competitors began their odyssey on March 20 aboard the tramp steamer *Fulda*. The ship was ill equipped to carry passengers, but it was cheap. With little room to exercise, the athletes were reckoning on the benefits of two weeks' worth of workouts in Athens prior to the start of the Olympics.

But when the *Fulda* docked in Naples, twelve dreary days later, on April 1, they discovered to their horror that the Games were scheduled to begin on April 6, not April 18 as they had supposed; the Greeks observed the Julian calendar, not the Gregorian. Time was running out.

After crossing Italy by train, the team sailed to Patras, a Greek port on the Ionian Sea. The weary Americans disembarked and immediately boarded a train for a ten-hour trip to Athens. They arrived on April 5 utterly dispirited.

An official reception in the capital, while hospitable, served only to deplete the team further. Curtis recalled: "We were met with a procession, with bands blaring before and behind, and were marched on foot for what seemed miles to the Hôtel de Ville. Here speech after speech was made in Greek, presumably very flattering to us, but of course entirely unintelligible. We were given large bumpers of the white-resin wine of Greece and told by our advisors that it would be a gross breach of etiquette if we did not drain these off in response to the various toasts. As soon as this ceremony was over, we were again placed at the head of a procession and marched to our hotel. I could not help feeling that so much marching, combined with several noggins of resinous wine, would tell on us in the contests the following day."

Fortunately Curtis proved a poor prophet. Only two finals were held on the opening day, and the wrung-out, hung-over Americans won them both.

Connolly gained a landmark victory—and acclaim as the first Olympic champion since the fourth-century athlete Varastades—with a leap of 44 feet 11 3/4 inches in the triple jump. In a matter of hours he had completed a stunning metamorphosis from unknown to celebrity.

THE JUDGES PRESENTED CONNOLLY WITH A tangible link to his predecessors. "The olive crown that was awarded the victors," wrote the New York *Herald's* correspondent, "will be made from material furnished from the same grove from which were taken the leaves and sprigs that formed the crowns of victory more than 15 centuries ago."

Connolly also received a diploma and a medal—a *silver* medal. Although Olympic records list gold, silver, and bronze recipients back to 1896, gold medals were not actually given champions until the 1908 London Games (for clarity's sake, winners have been referred to throughout this article as gold medalists). Runners-up were awarded bronze medals and diplomas.

Connolly's historic victory in the triple jump notwithstanding, the opening-day highlight was unquestionably Robert Garrett's performance with the discus. Garrett had never even seen a real discus before his arrival in Athens—the event was still all but unknown in the United States—but "having noticed on the program

the throwing of the discus, [he] decided in youthful fashion to have a try at it merely for the sake of competing in an event that belonged to antiquity.... "

Unable to locate a genuine discus with which to practice at Princeton, Garrett commissioned a local blacksmith to forge one, patterned on a description he unearthed in the works of the second-century Greek writer Lucian: "A lump of brass, circular and not unlike a small shield." The finished product weighed twenty pounds. Discouraged by his inability to throw this monster any distance at all, Garrett abandoned his plan to compete in the discus throw.

He reconsidered only after making a fortuitous discovery in Athens. While strolling to the Panathenaic Stadium, Garrett happened upon a discarded discus, picked it up, and was astonished to find that it weighed less than five pounds. After several experimental throws, he decided to enter the event after all.

It seemed a reckless choice. He was up against Panagiotis Paraskevopoulos, the reigning Greek champion, the prohibitive favorite whose countrymen called him a "discus demigod."

"Garrett entered the arena unknown and unheralded," said the *Herald*. "His hair was not as dark or curly as his antagonist's, nor his nose as straight. He was scantily clad and looked hungry. The Athenians gazed with pity."

ENTERING AN OLYMPIC EVENT, as Sumner Paine demonstrated by joining (and winning) one on a whim, was simple proposition in 1896: Just show up.

Soon they were gazing with wonder. "We all held our breath as he carefully prepared for the last throw," recalled Albert Tyler, Garrett's Princeton classmate. "By this time he had caught the knack … and had complete confidence in himself. He put all his energy into the last cast, and as the discus flew through the air the vast concourse of people were silent as if the structure were empty. When it struck, there was a tremendous burst of applause from all sides." The spindly American had spun the discus 7½ inches beyond Paraskevopoulos's best toss to snatch the gold medal from his adversary. Although the distance was modest by modern standards—95 feet 7½ inches (the existing Olympic record is 225 feet 9 inches)—it was a "throw considered something phenomenal," the *Herald* reported.

Garrett humbled another Greek star the next day. He heaved the shot put 36 feet 9¾ inches to dethrone Miltiades Gouskos before an estimated hundred thousand spectators. "Even Garrett was hailed with enthusiasm when he defeated Gouskos," wrote the *Herald* reporter, "although the Greeks were surprised and disappointed by the downfall of their champion."

Garrett's victories doubtless surprised those back home too. "Captain Robert Garrett was up to a year ago little known as an athlete, even at Princeton," noted the New York *Herald*. "In his freshman year young Garrett showed some ability in the weights and jumps and was taken on the track team largely because of his promise to make an athlete with training. George Goldie, the trainer, took him in hand, trained him, especially in putting in the shot, and has now succeeded in putting him very close to the first rank of college athletes."

Of world-class athletes, for that matter. Garrett won four medals at the revival Olympics—a total eclipsed only by the German gymnast Hermann Weingartner's seven—and added two more at the Paris Games four years later.

Thomas Burke joined Garrett in the winner's circle on the second day, having coasted to victory in the 400-meter run. Then Ellery Clark attempted the long jump.

Like Connolly, Clark had requested a leave of absence from Harvard to participate in the Games; unlike Connolly, he received permission, because of his superior grades. But after fouling on his first two jumps, Clark lamented ever having petitioned his dean for time off. "I was little short of agony," he wrote later. "I shall never forget my feelings as I stood at the end of the path for my third—and last—try. Five thousand miles, I reflected, I had come; and was it to end in this? Three fouls and then five thousand miles back again, with that for my memory of the Games."

He gathered himself, ran, leaped—and touched the ground 20 feet 10 inches later to claim the championship. He and his Boston Athletic Association teammates burst forth with their distinctive victory cheer, "B-A-A, rah, rah, rah." While most of the startled Greeks considered this outburst "barbaric," some spectators found the display of enthusiasm refreshing; King George, a frequent visitor to the stadium, asked the BAA members to repeat their cheer on several occasions. Even discounting royal requests, the Bostonians' shouts were heard regularly in Athens: Of the twelve track and field events, BAA athletes won half.

After posting victories on the second day, Clark and Burke returned to claim additional honors. Clark followed his gold-medal performance in the long jump with a winning leap of 5 feet 11¼ inches in the high jump. Burke, fresh off his 400-meter success, captured the 100-meter championship in 12.0 seconds, aided by a "crouch" start then foreign to the Europeans. Curtis collected a gold medal with a 17.6-second effort in the 110-meter hurdles, and Hoyt soared 10 feet 10 inches to win the pole vault.

Not all the U.S. victories came in track. The Paine brothers had traveled to Athens independently of the American team and thus been spared the claustrophobic miseries of the *Fulda*. Sumner was working at a Paris art gallery when John passed through en route to Athens and persuaded his brother to accompany him. Sumner did more than tag along; he entered the free-pistol event on a whim and won. He also finished second in the military-revolver competition—to John.

Entering an Olympic event, as Sumner Paine demonstrated, was a simple proposition in 1896: Just show up. An Oxford student named John Boland, for instance, traveled to the Olympics as a spectator, then impulsively entered the tennis competition and wound up winning gold medals in the singles and doubles competitions.

Conversely, one American athlete underwent a transformation from competitor to spectator in Greece—quite unintentionally. Williams, a champion swimmer accustomed to the tepid water of indoor pools, was not prepared for the 100-meter freestyle event, held in the frigid Bay of Zea. Curtis described his teammate's all-too-brief performance: "… as he poised with the others on the edge of the float, waiting for the gun, his spirit thrilled with patriotism and determination. At the crack of the pistol, the contestants dived head first into the water. In a split second his head reappeared. 'Jesu Christo! I'm freezing!' he cried. With that shriek of astonished frenzy he lashed back to the float. For him the Olympics were over."

The fifty-five-degree water temperatures fazed even the hardiest of participants. "The icy water almost cut into our stomachs," said Alfréd Hajós of Hungary, the champion, who later entered—and won—the 1,500-meter freestyle, having this time taken the precaution of smearing a layer of grease over his body as insulation.

Swimming, as it turned out, was the only sport U.S. athletes entered but did not win. Indeed, the ad hoc team captured more gold medals than any other nation in the showcase sport of track and field; it won nine of the twelve events and demoralized several Greek champions. Overall, the United States claimed eleven gold medals to outstrip more established European rivals, such as Greece (ten), Germany (seven), France (five), and Great Britain (three).

ADMITTEDLY, THE QUALITY OF THE COMPETITION was watered down; a multitude of elite athletes—not just U.S. champions—spurned Coubertin's revival, which accounts for the mediocre winning times and distances. In fact, not a single world record fell in Athens. Casper Whitney of *Harper's* declared Spiridon Louis's climactic victory in the marathon "the only remarkable performance at the Games."

Maybe so (although Panagiotis Paraskevopoulos probably wouldn't have agreed), but that shouldn't diminish the achievements of America's first Olympians. These intrepid pioneers who weathered adversity en route to Greece and surpassed every expectation once they got there could celebrate not only victories but a pre-eminent role in a momentous event—the rebirth of the Olympic Games.

"Nothing could equal this first revival," Clark wrote afterward. "The flavor of the Athenian soil—the feeling of helping to bridge the gap between the old and the new—the indefinable poetic charm of knowing one's self thus linked with the past, a successor to the great heroic figures of olden times. There is but one first time in everything, and that first time was gloriously, and in a manner ever to be remembered, the privilege of the American team of 1896."

Bob Fulton is the author of The Summer Olympics: A Treasury of Legends and Lore, *recently published by Diamond Communications, South Bend, Indiana.*

From *American Heritage,* July/August 1996, pages 53-54, 56, 58, 60. Reprinted by permission of American Heritage, Inc., a division of Forbes, Inc.

Lady Muckraker

Investigative reporter Ida Tarbell probed into the excesses of big business, but she faced her biggest challenge when she took on the Standard Oil Company and the formidable John D. Rockefeller.

by Paula A. Treckel

THE LION AND THE MOUSE made its Broadway debut on Saturday, November 25, 1905. The play told the tale of "the richest and the ablest and the hardest and the most unscrupulous" millionaire in America, John Burkett Ryder, and his confrontation with Miss Shirley Rossmore, a young woman of "clear moral intensity." The story opened with Miss Rossmore's father, a judge, accused of accepting securities from Ryder in exchange for making judicial decisions in the millionaire's favor. To prove her father's innocence, Miss Rossmore—the "mouse" to Ryder's "lion"—set out to expose the millionaire's criminal activities.

Unlikely as it may appear, the plot of this Broadway melodrama was snatched from the headlines of the day. It was loosely based on the story of Ida M. Tarbell and her investigation of millionaire John D. Rockefeller and his Standard Oil Company monopoly. Although it lacked the Broadway play's love story and happy ending, Tarbell's investigation of how Rockefeller achieved domination of the oil industry had more than its share of intrigue, crime, and corruption. Tarbell used her sense of moral outrage, passion for justice, and historian's eye for detail to reveal the inner workings of Rockefeller's business empire to the world. Her work helped lead to the prosecution of Standard Oil by the United States government and the company's subsequent dismantling in 1911.

Ida Minerva Tarbell was born on November 5, 1857, in the frontier town of Hatch Hollow, Pennsylvania, one of the rough and rowdy oil boomtowns of the region. Her father, Franklin Tarbell, hoped to make his fortune in the young industry by manufacturing tanks to hold the black gold taken from beneath the Pennsylvania hills. As a child, Ida saw how boom and bust cycles swept through the dirty, oil-slick communities that dotted the countryside and witnessed the horrors of accidents—fires and explosions—that plagued the industry.

In 1872, suddenly and without warning, the region's railroads—the link necessary to bring the oil to market—doubled their shipping rates, deeply cutting the independent producers' profits. Then word leaked out that the railroads had favored a mysterious Cleveland-based outfit called the South Improvement Company by giving it rebates, in direct violation of federal law. Young Ida watched as her father and his friends crusaded against this menace to their livelihood. Violence swept the oil fields of western Pennsylvania as vigilantes destroyed the South Improvement Company's oil cars and burned out the men who joined or sold out to that organization. "It was my first experience in revolution," Tarbell recalled. She learned "it was your privilege and duty to fight injustice."

The force behind the threatened takeover of the region's oil production was John D. Rockefeller, a man who had risen from humble beginning to become one of the nation's wealthiest and most powerful industrialists. Born in upstate New York in 1839, Rockefeller was the son of con artist William Avery Rockefeller and his long-suffering wife, Eliza. The family's poverty soon taught John the importance of saving and investing money and fired his dreams of becoming wealthy. "Some day, sometime, when I am a man, I want to be worth a-hundred-thousand-dollars," he confided to a friend. "And I'm going to be, too—some day." The somber boy found spiritual comfort in the Baptist church, which instilled in him the values of self-reliance and self-improvement and the belief that hard work would be rewarded both on earth and in heaven. Throughout his life John turned to his church for practical lessons in living.

When the Rockefeller family moved to Cleveland Ohio, 16-year old John sought work to help support his family. "I did not go to any small establishments," he recalled. "I did not guess what I would be, but I was after something big." During a meeting with Henry B. Tuttle, partner in a produce-shipping firm, Rockefeller boldly stated, "I understand bookkeeping, and I'd like to get work."

"We'll give you a chance," Tuttle said, and he hired the boy to handle the company's books, thereby launching one of the most successful careers in American business.

The Ida M. Tarbell Collection, Special Collections,
Pelletier Library, Allegheny College, Meadville, Pennsylvania

Ida Tarbell works at home at her desk made neat for the photographer. She wrote hundreds of articles dealing with politics, public figures, and social issues.

John worked hard and invested his clerk's salary in local grain and livestock businesses. By age 18 he had made enough money to start his own produce business with Englishman Maurice Clark. When the Civil War dramatically increased the price of commodities, the young Rockefeller invested his profits in a local oil refinery. Refineries bought crude oil from the oil producers and processed it into products such as kerosene. Cleveland was then the center of the refining industry because it was close to the oil-rich fields of western Pennsylvania, and its location on Lake Erie provided an easy means of shipping the valuable commodities it produced. Over time John D. Rockefeller purchased several more refineries in the area; in 1870 he incorporated his holdings as Standard Oil.

As America's industry boomed in the years following the Civil War and railroads became an ever-more important force, Rockefeller used every advantage—legal and illegal—that the market allowed. One tactic was to secure reduced rates from railroads by guaranteeing them volume shipments on a regular basis. When other companies refused to join forces with Rock-

efeller or agree to control the production and price of oil, he drove them out of business. Ida Tarbell saw for herself the effect of Rockefeller's machinations when he formed an alliance between three of the most powerful railroads and a handful of oil refiners, called it the South Improvement Company, and used it as a tool to gain further dominance. Using such tactics, Standard Oil's 409 companies gained control of 90 percent of the nation's oil refining industry by 1881.

In addition to buying refineries, Rockefeller sought control of the oil fields themselves. He built his own transportation network of pipelines and tankers, and marketed his products both at home and abroad. Rockefeller's efforts produced added benefits as well. He introduced cutting-edge technology and efficiency to the oil industry. And as the cost of processing petroleum dropped, so too did prices for fuel oil and lighting products.

While John D. Rockefeller was ruthlessly cornering the nation's oil market, Ida Tarbell was attending college in western Pennsylvania. From an early age she had planned to become an independent, professional woman. "I would never marry," she pledged. "It would interfere with my plan; it would fetter my freedom." In 1876 she enrolled as a freshman at Allegheny College in Meadville, Pennsylvania. She was the only woman in her class. Following her graduation in 1880, Tarbell taught for a year before joining the staff of the Meadville, Pennsylvania, *Chautauqua Assembly Herald,* a publication of the Chautauqua Assembly's Literary and Scientific Circle.

During her six years at the *Chautauquan,* Tarbell learned the art and craft of journalism. She started out as a researcher and eventually assumed the duties, if not the title, of managing editor. Nevertheless, Tarbell longed for more. In church one Sunday, a visiting minister thundered, "You're dying of respectability!" at his complaisant congregation and spurred Tarbell to action. In 1889 she decided to try supporting herself with her own pen. The young journalist left the *Chautauquan* and headed for France.

Tarbell was ready for a new beginning. In Paris she made friendships that lasted a lifetime and reinvented herself as a historian, researching the life of French Revolutionary heroine Madame Manon Phlipon de Roland. To support herself, Tarbell wrote articles on French life for American news syndicates. One story, "The Paving of the Streets of Paris by Monsieur Alphand," piqued the interest of editor Samuel Sidney McClure, founder of *McClure's Magazine.* McClure had emigrated from Ireland in 1866, and in 1884 he had established one of the earliest U. S. newspaper syndicates. A dynamic, energetic man—Rudyard Kipling described him as a "cyclone in a frock coat"—McClure launched his magazine in 1893 to campaign for solutions to the pressing problems of the day. He was always looking for fresh, talented writers to join his staff. On a trip to Paris in the summer of 1892, he bounded up the stairs of Ida Tarbell's apartment building and into her life, changing it forever.

McClure asked Tarbell if she would come to New York to work at his magazine. Reluctant to give up her hard-earned independence, she agreed only to submit occasional articles to *McClure's* while she completed her biography of Madame Roland. But by 1894, Tarbell was unable to financially support herself, and she returned to the United States with her unfinished Madame Roland manuscript and joined the staff of *McClure's* in New York.

Ida Tarbell returned to a nation still reeling from the panic caused by the stock market crash of 1893. More than 15,000 businesses had failed, and at least one third of all manufacturing workers had lost their jobs. Midwestern farmers also suffered as they faced rising interest rates and falling crop prices. Tarbell's own family's financial distress clouded her homecoming. Her father had become an independent oil producer just as Standard Oil forced an increase in the price of the region's crude oil. Refiners were reluctant to buy crude from small, independent producers like Franklin Tarbell, and he had to mortgage the family's Titusville home to pay his debts. One of his friends committed suicide when his own business failed.

The nation as a whole was changing, evolving from a largely agrarian economy into a more industrial one. With the change came abuses—not just the great concentration of wealth in the hands of a few industrialists such as Andrew Carnegie and Rockefeller, but also urban corruption, boss politics, and child labor. The Progressive Movement emerged in response to these issues and prompted Congress to pass the Sherman Anti-Trust Act in 1890, making it illegal to monopolize or restrain trade through unfair collaborations or conspiracies. The law was vague, however, and authorities had difficulty enforcing it against America's powerful industrialists.

At *McClure's* a team of journalists—Tarbell, Lincoln Steffens, William Allen White, and Ray Stannard Baker—reflected Progressive concerns in their articles about some of the era's excesses. Yet not everyone approved of this new breed of journalism. Although he knew and befriended many of the magazine's writers, including Tarbell, President Theodore Roosevelt publicly complained that these journalists focused only upon society's evils. "In Bunyan's *Pilgrim's Progress*," he said, "you may recall the description of the Man with the Muckrake, the man who could look no way but downward with the muck-rake in his hands; who was offered a celestial crown for his muck-rake, but who would neither look up nor regard the crown he was offered, but continued to rake to himself the filth of the floor." The president's comments gave a name to the new generation of investigative journalists, with Ida Tarbell the foremost "Lady Muckraker" of her time.

McClure's January 1903 issue epitomized the work of the muckrakers. Lincoln Steffens contributed an article about political corruption in Minneapolis, part of his "Shame of the Cities" series. Ray Stannard Baker wrote about corruption and violence in the labor union movement in a piece called "The Right to Work." The issue also included an installment in a series by Ida Tarbell on "The History of Standard Oil," one of the most important exposés of the twentieth century.

The proliferation of industrial trusts interested *McClure's* staff members. They decided the best way to approach the subject would be to tell "the story of a typical trust to illustrate how and why the clan grew," recalled Tarbell. "How about the greatest of them all—the Standard Oil Company?" Tarbell decided she wanted to tackle the project, and she traveled to Europe where Sam McClure and his family were vacationing while he recovered from exhaustion. Tarbell expected to stay only a week while she pitched her idea to the publisher, but he asked her to join them in their travels. Finally, after visiting Switzerland and Italy, McClure approved Tarbell's story idea. She later admitted, "It had been a strong thread weaving itself into the pattern of my life from childhood on." Tarbell later explained to critics who charged that her work was motivated by personal concerns, "We were undertaking what we regarded as a legitimate piece of historical work. We were neither apologists nor critics, only journalists intent on discovering what had gone into the making of this most perfect of all monopolies."

The Ida M. Tarbell Collection, Special Collections, Pelletier Library, Allegheny College, Meadville, Pennsylvania

The July 1903 issue of *McClure's* contained an installment of Tarbell's series on Rockefeller and the Standard Oil Company.

Tarbell had no shortage of material to draw upon. Congress had been investigating Standard Oil almost continually since the company's creation in 1870 when it was suspected of receiving rebates from railroads and violating free trade. In the years since, government investigators had generated volumes of testimony, a massive collection of documentary evidence, as well as countless newspaper and magazine articles. These resources provided Tarbell with the foundation for her work, although at first she found the sheer mass of material at her disposal overwhelming. "The task confronting me is such a monstrous one that I am staggering a bit under it," she lamented. Aided by a young, eager assistant, John Siddall, she spent a year researching her subject before *McClure's* announced the series to readers.

Initially Tarbell was going to write the story in three parts—in the end she wrote 19. Dissecting the inner workings of Standard Oil with the precision of a surgeon wielding a scalpel, she exposed espionage and industrial terrorism. In one example, Tarbell detailed the testimony of Mrs. Butts, whose oil company had a regular customer in New Orleans. A Standard Oil representative approached the customer and "made a contract with him to pay him $10,000 a year for five years to stop handling the independent oil and take Standard Oil." Tarbell also told of a young office boy in a Standard Oil plant who was told to destroy some company papers when the name of his Sunday school teacher, an independent oil refiner, caught his eye. The records contained information, collected by railroad freight clerks in Standard Oil's pay, about his teacher's oil shipments. Armed with such inside knowledge, the great trust could act against its competition by sidetracking rail cars, interfering with or destroying rivals' shipments, or pressuring buyers to cancel orders. By showing how the corporation worked in collusion with the railroads and carefully explaining its elaborate system of rebates and "drawbacks," Tarbell meticulously built her case against the great monopoly.

Rockefeller himself refused to meet with the woman he privately called "Miss Tarbarrel," and he met her series with stony silence. One day, while strolling in the grounds of his Cleveland home, a friend asked Rockefeller why he did not respond to Tarbell's charges. "Not a word!" he interrupted. "Not a word about that misguided woman." The he pointed to a worm on the ground nearby. "If I step on that worm I will call attention to it," Rockefeller said. "If I ignore it, it will disappear."

Tarbell understood Rockefeller's need for silence. "His self-control has been masterful," she said; "he knows, nobody better, that to answer is to invite discussion, to answer is to call attention to the facts in the case." This, she was confident, he would not do. She also never feared that Rockefeller would take steps to silence her. "What had we to be afraid of?" she declared.

The journalist's curiosity got the best of her, however, when John Siddall learned that Rockefeller planned to give a talk in October 1903 to the Sunday school at the Euclid Avenue Baptist Church in Cleveland. She could not resist the opportunity to get a peek at the man. On that crisp October morning, Tarbell and Siddall arrived early at the church and awaited Rockefeller's entrance. Tarbell vividly recalled the moment when she first saw him: "We were sitting meekly at one side when I was suddenly aware of a striking figure standing in the doorway. There was an awful age in his face—the oldest man I had ever seen, I thought, but what power!" She recalled that his voice was "Clear and utterly sincere. He meant what he was saying. He

was on his own ground talking about dividends, dividends of righteousness." When the talk ended, Tarbell and Siddall slipped out to get a good seat in the gallery, from where they could see the Rockefeller pew. Tarbell noted, "It was plain that he, and not the minister, was the pivot on which that audience swung."

Tarbell's findings strengthened the United States government's case against Standard Oil. Following publication of her series, President Roosevelt decided to make an example of the great oil trust. On November 15, 1906, the government charged the Standard Oil Company of New Jersey and its 70 affiliates with violating the Sherman Anti-Trust Act. The company and its trustees were eventually found guilty of creating a monopoly, conspiring to restrain and control interstate commerce through the use of railroad rebates and drawbacks, controlling pipelines, conducting industrial espionage, and illegally eliminating competition from the marketplace. Following a series of appeals, the Supreme Court upheld the original decision against Standard Oil in May of 1911, and the mighty monopoly was broken up. Rockefeller retained stock in Standard Oil of New Jersey and the 33 independent subsidiaries created by the Supreme Court's decision. Ironically, the break-up of the trust made Rockefeller the world's richest man with a net worth of $900 million in 1913. And by the time of his death at age 98 on May 23, 1937, John D. Rockefeller was more widely known as "the world's greatest philanthropist" than the great "Lion" of the industrial age.

In addition to prompting the government's suit against Standard Oil, Ida Tarbell's series, published in two volumes as *The History of the Standard Oil Company* in 1904, contributed to the passage of new laws to protect competition in the marketplace. In 1914 the government established the Federal Trade Commission to oversee business activities.

Despite an illustrious career—in 1922 the *New York Times* included her as one of the "Twelve Greatest Living American Women"—Ida Tarbell never equaled *The History of Standard Oil*. Historian and Rockefeller biographer Allan Nevins declared, "It was the best piece of business history that America had yet produced." Before Tarbell's death on January 6, 1944, a young history professor asked her, "If you could rewrite your book today, what would you change?"

"Not one word, young man," she proudly replied, "Not one word."

Paula A. Treckel is a professor of history at Allegheny College, Meadville, Pennsylvania. She is the author of To Comfort the Heart: Women in Seventeenth Century America, *and is currently writing a history of American weddings.*

From *American History Illustrated*, June 2001, pp. 38-44. © 2001 by Primedia Consumer Media and Magazines, Inc. All rights reserved. Reprinted with permission.

Teddy in the Middle

By Stan Saunders

A coal strike in eastern Pennsylvania pitted management against mine workers. With winter coming and no settlement in sight, President Theodore Roosevelt decided to intervene and use his "bully pulpit" to end the deadlock before it brought the nation to its knees. It proved to be a turning point in his presidency.

George F. Baer, president of the Philadelphia and Reading Railway Company, was furious as he descended from his elegant horsedrawn carriage on the morning of October 3, 1902, to meet with President Theodore Roosevelt.

For years Baer and the five other coal operators who accompanied him—railroad presidents who owned northeastern coal mines—had fought to prevent official recognition of the United Mine Workers of America (UMWA). Now Roosevelt had undone all their work by inviting the union's leader, John Mitchell, to this meeting in Washington, D.C. The invitation implied *de facto* recognition and seriously jeopardized the mine owners' efforts to squelch the union and its leader.

The owners had been forced into this situation because a coal strike in northeastern Pennsylvania threatened to deprive the country of one of its most important energy sources, anthracite coal, just as winter approached. Roosevelt, anxious about the situation's political repercussions, had arranged the meeting to find a way out of the impasse. It was the first time that a president of the United States had invited representatives of both capital and labor to meet with him on equal terms.

Delighted with the invitation, Mitchell was determined to create a favorable impression on Roosevelt. While the mine owners arrived in expensive carriages, Mitchell and three of his union aides took a streetcar to the meeting. Thirty-two-year-old Mitchell, who had led the UMWA since 1899, projected an air of sobriety with his conservative clothes, clean-shaven face, and a reversed white collar

that made him look like a clergyman. Mitchell had begun working in the mines when he was 12, and it was only in the last five years that he had left manual labor behind to work for the union.

Coal had powered America's industry during the nineteenth century, and by 1900 it was a vital part of the nation's economy, supplying energy for businesses, the transportation network, and millions of American homes. Anthracite coal—harder and of better quality than the bituminous variety—had become the dominant commercial and domestic fuel of the northeastern United States, largely because of Pennsylvania's rich anthracite coalfields. Wealthy coal companies controlled mainly by railroad interests operated these fields. The miners there labored under dangerous conditions, usually working 12 hours a day, six days a week, for miserable wages. "My lamp is my sun, and all my days are nights," were the words of a traditional miners' song.

Union efforts to improve working conditions in the late nineteenth century often led to confrontations with management and sometimes violence. As railroad companies consolidated ownership of coalfields, miners realized they needed one dominant union of their own, and in 1890 they formed the UMWA. In the decade following, the union's membership steadily increased, as the American economy's expanding industrialization led to ever-increasing demands for coal.

Mitchell's first test as head of the UMWA came in 1900. He possessed well-honed political instincts and believed the time was right to strike for higher wages and better conditions. Not only was the nation experiencing an economic upturn, but President William McKinley was also running for re-election against William Jennings Bryan, a candidate who was urging workers to take political action. The Republicans realized a strike could hurt their chances in November, so Senator Mark Hanna of Ohio, McKinley's closest political advisor, and financier John Pierpont Morgan spearheaded an effort to persuade the coal operators to give miners the 10-percent pay raise they demanded. It would be a small price to pay, they argued, to deny Bryan the presidency. The coal operators agreed to the pay hike, but they refused to recognize the UMWA.

Mitchell and the UMWA hailed the settlement as a victory, while the operators vowed never again to let political pressure interfere with their efforts to crush the union. Mitchell continued to try to win miners another pay raise, a shorter workday, fairer weighing of the coal they dug, and recognition of the UMWA. The operators refused to give in to any of the union's demands, and in the spring of 1902 more than 125,000 anthracite miners, union and non-union, walked off the job. An additional 18,000 bituminous workers struck in sympathy with their fellow miners.

Despite facing a winter without sufficient supplies of anthracite coal, many Americans supported the strike because Mitchell consistently rejected violence and expressed his willingness to negotiate with the owners at any time. The coal operators lost public support by absolutely refusing to consider arbitration. Their inflammatory statements did not help matters. In July 1902 George Baer received a letter from a man in Wilkes-Barre, Pennsylvania, who said it was Baer's religious duty to end the strike as soon as possible. Baer replied with a heated letter, saying that, "the rights and interests of the laboring men will be protected and cared for—not by the labor agitators, but by the Christian men to whom God in His infinite wisdom has given the control of the property interests of the country." When Baer's letter became public, many newspapers condemned the arrogance of his remarks while the religious press were infuriated.

The strike dragged on into autumn and coal supplies began to dwindle. Something had to be done before winter arrived, and many people began looking to the White House for a solution.

One of Roosevelt's sons is said to have commented, "Father always wanted to be the bride at every wedding, and the corpse at every funeral."

PRESIDENT THEODORE ROOSEVELT was anxious to find a role in the growing crisis. He was not a man who was comfortable sitting on the sidelines. As one of his sons is said to have commented, "Father always wanted to be the bride at every wedding, and the corpse at every funeral." Roosevelt had become president in September 1901 after anarchist

Leon Czolgosz assassinated William McKinley, and he was still growing into the position. "Every day or two," an editorial in the *Detroit Press* said, "he rattles the dry bones of precedent and causes sedate Senators and heads of departments to look over their spectacles in consternation."

One of those precedent-rattling moves was Roosevelt's decision early in 1902 to have the justice department file suit against the Northern Securities Company. The giant holding company controlled a large number of western railroads, and the government's suit charged it with violating the Sherman Anti-Trust Act, legislation designed to prevent trusts and monopolies from creating restraints on trade or commerce and reducing competition. Such "trust-busting" was generally popular with the American public, but it was bitterly opposed by much of the business community, particularly by J.P. Morgan, who had bought out the companies of Andrew Carnegie and others the previous year to form the gigantic United States Steel Corporation.

Trust busting was one thing. Stepping into the middle of an ongoing labor dispute, however, would be a very different role for Roosevelt. In the past, U.S. presidents had sent in federal troops to maintain public order during strikes. Rutherford Hayes did so during the 1877 railroad strike, but only after the strike spread to 14 states, and nine governors requested federal assistance. Grover Cleveland carried this precedent even further during the Pullman Strike of 1894, when he had U.S. attorney general Richard Olney obtain an injunction from the federal court in Chicago to prevent the American Railroad Union from "compelling or inducing by threats, intimidation, persuasion, force or violence, railway employees to refuse or fail to perform their duties." Armed with this ruling, Cleveland sent in federal troops to break up the strike. But those presidential actions came in response to specific threats to public order, a factor largely absent from the 1902 anthracite strike.

Roosevelt was concerned about winter coal shortages, but he also worried about how the strike could affect the Republican Party in November's midterm elections. Roosevelt would not run for election for another two years, but his party could be badly hurt in the meantime. In a letter to Senator Hanna, Roosevelt lamented that, "we have no earthly responsibility for it, but the public at large will visit upon our heads responsibility for the shortage in coal." So once again Hanna tried to end this strike, just as he had in 1900. This time the coal operators refused to settle.

Roosevelt suffered a personal setback in September as he campaigned for Republican candidates in Pittsfield, Massachusetts. A trolley car slammed into his carriage, throwing him to the ground and killing Secret Service agent William Craig. Roosevelt escaped with only a scraped face and bruised leg, and he continued his speaking tour. During the next few weeks, however, his leg developed a painful abscess that began to swell, and the president underwent two operations to drain the leg to avoid blood poisoning. For the next several weeks, he would be confined to a wheelchair.

By the beginning of October, newspapers were reporting empty coal bins in hospitals and schools, and prices for anthracite coal in some areas had risen from $5 a ton to more than $30. At the urging of Massachusetts governor Winthrop Murray Crane—who shared the president's concerns about coal shortages and their effect on the Republican vote—Roosevelt decided to invite both sides of the coal dispute to a meeting in Washington.

The White House was undergoing renovations, so Roosevelt held the meeting in his temporary quarters at 22 Jackson Place in Lafayette Square. On October 3, the participants waited uneasily in the meeting room just before 11:00 A.M. Shortly after the hour, President Roosevelt briskly wheeled himself in to begin the proceedings. Waiting for him were Mitchell and his aides Thomas D. Nicholls, Thomas Duffy, and John Fahy, as well as coal operators Baer; William H. Truesdale, president of the Delaware, Lackawanna, and Western Railroad; Eben B. Thomas, chairman of the Erie Railroad Company; Thomas Fowler of the New York, Ontario, & Western; David Willcox, vice president and general counsel of the Delaware and Hudson Railroad; and John Markle, representing independent mine owners. Roosevelt immediately disclaimed any legal or constitutional right or duty to intervene in the strike, but then asked both sides to consider the third party in this struggle, the public. He appealed to the operators and miners alike to work together and avoid a devastating shortage of coal. "I appeal to your patriotism," Roosevelt concluded, "to the spirit that sinks personal considerations and makes individual sacrifices for the general good."

Mitchell deftly seized the moment. He responded to the president's plea and agreed with the seriousness of the situation. The miners would be more than willing, he said, to have the president name an arbitration board whose decisions would be binding on all parties. At this point, Roosevelt called a recess until three o'clock that afternoon so both sides could consider the proposal.

When the meeting reconvened, George Baer—a self-made man who had started work at the age of 13 as a printer's apprentice in a Somerset, Pennsylvania, newspaper office and gone on to become the newspaper's owner—began speaking. He used a tone of "studied insolence," as Roosevelt recounted. Baer attacked the actions of the union, described unremitting violence against innocents in the coalfields, and decried the strikers' lack of respect for basic property rights. Baer fixed his eyes on the president, who listened grimly from his wheelchair, and requested that the administration proceed against the UMWA. "The Constitution of the United States requires the president, when requested by the governor, to suppress domestic violence," declared Baer, although Pennsylvania's governor had not requested assistance. Roosevelt controlled his temper with difficulty. "If it wasn't for the high office I hold," he said later, speaking of Baer, "I would have taken him by the seat of the breeches and the nape of the neck and chucked him out of that window."

The operators flatly refused to deal with Mitchell, and by 5:00 P.M. the union's president was walking despondently through the streets of Washington. "Well, I have tried and failed," Roosevelt wrote to Senator Hanna after the meeting. "I feel downhearted over the result because of the great misery ahead for the mass of our people."

"I knew that this action would form an evil precedent, and that it was one which I should take most reluctantly," declared Roosevelt.

On October 8, five days after the unsuccessful meeting, Roosevelt appealed to Mitchell to have his men return to work immediately. The president said he would appoint a commission and do everything possible to persuade the operators to accept the results of the commission's report. But as the coal companies would not agree to binding arbitration, Mitchell declined this offer.

Roosevelt was now forced to consider a last-resort idea to get mining operations resumed. He would send federal troops to take possession of the coalfields. "I only wanted a method of getting the army in, and then I would run the situation as I thought it ought to be run," Roosevelt later wrote to Governor Crane. "I knew that this action would form an evil precedent, and that it was one which I should take most reluctantly."

Roosevelt's idea rested on shaky constitutional ground. Under Article IV, Section 4 of the Constitution, the president could send troops into a state "on Application of the Legislature, or of the Executive (when the Legislature cannot be convened) against domestic Violence." But what little violence there had been in Pennsylvania's coalfields was certainly not beyond the capabilities of state forces. By sending in the troops to run the mines, Roosevelt declared, he would dispossess "the operators and run the mines as a receiver" until the commission reported its decision to him. This threat was a useful stick with which to prod the coal operators, and this may have been his primary intention. "Theodore was sometimes a bit of a bluffer occasionally, and at the same time he had the nerve to go on," his secretary of war Elihu Root reflected years later.

Root volunteered to meet unofficially with J.P. Morgan and see if the financier would use his influence with the operators to persuade them to accept the proposed commission's findings. Root spent October 11 aboard Morgan's yacht, *Corsair*, where he found the businessman weary of the strike's bad publicity and eager to end it. Later, after discreet discussions between the coal operators and Morgan, the operators agreed to binding arbitration, but they insisted that the commission should consist of a military engineer, a civilian mining engineer, a federal judge from eastern Pennsylvania, a mining operator, and "a man of prominence, eminent as a sociologist."

Both Mitchell and the operators claimed victory, but Roosevelt ended up as the strike's greatest beneficary.

Mitchell met with Roosevelt on October 15 and objected to the commission's lack of union representation. The union leader said the UMWA would accept arbitration if the commission added two more members, to be selected by the president. Mitchell urged Roosevelt to appoint a high Roman Catholic ecclesiastic, as many of the miners were Catholic, and the president suggested Bishop John Spalding of Peoria, Illinois. For the other member, Roosevelt nominated Edgar E. Clark, leader of the Railway Conductors Union.

That evening, Robert Bacon and George Perkins, two junior partners from Morgan's firm, arrived in the capital to negotiate with Roosevelt on behalf of the coal operators. After hearing the president's proposal of the two additional commission members, Bacon and Perkins contacted the coal operators. The operators decided they might reluctantly allow a Catholic prelate to become a member of the commission, but they would never permit a labor leader to join.

Roosevelt believed the operators were displaying a pigheaded stupidity that threatened public safety. They "grew more and more hysterical, and not merely admitted but insisted that failure to agree would result in violence and possible social war," he recorded later. The meeting then took an abrupt turn into "ludicrous comedy," as Roosevelt put it, when "Bacon finally happened to mention that they would not object at all to my exercising any latitude I chose in appointments under the headings that they had given." The operators were not objecting to the substance of labor representation, but the form. In other words, they would accept a labor leader, just as long as he wasn't called a labor leader. Roosevelt then proposed that E. E. Clark be put into the "eminent sociologist" slot. After consultation with the operators, Bacon and Perkins accepted the president's proposals. Roosevelt later noted, "I shall never forget the mixture of relief and amusement felt when I thoroughly grasped the fact that while they would heroically submit to anarchy rather than have Tweedledum, yet if I would call it Tweedledee they would accept it with rapture; it gave me an illuminating glimpse into one corner of the mighty brains of these 'captains of industry'."

Yet the operators were shrewder then the president had indicated. As Roosevelt biographer H.W. Brands pointed out, they held out to the end to get the best terms possible. When Roosevelt's army takeover plan forced them to accept arbitration, the owners at least made sure that the union received no formal recognition. The UMWA would not win this vital point from the coal companies for another 13 years.

The coal miners returned to work on October 23, 1902. Five months later the Anthracite Coal Strike Commission re-

TEDDY TURNS 100

It may seem to us today that the teddy bear has always been a staple of childhood. But in fact the cuddly toy didn't make an appearance until 1902, with President Theofore Roosevelt helping spur its creation.

In November 1902, the president traveled to Mississippi to hunt bear, with little success. Roosevelt's guide finally captured and tethered a female bear that had been fighting with the hunting dogs, and he invited the president to shoot it. Roosevelt refused and told the guide to put the animal "out of its misery." The dead bear was taken to the Smithsonian Institution for study purposes, and its pelt is still stored there.

Back in Washington, D.C., political cartoonist Clifford Barryman heard about the incident and drew a cartoon about it. He changed the adult bear to a wide-eyed cub and portrayed Roosevelt turning away from the creature with his rifle lowered. Titled "Drawing the Line in Mississippi—probably a reference to a boundary dispute between Mississippi and Louisiana that was before the U.S. Supreme Court at that time—it appeared in the *Washington Post* on November 16, 1902, and caused an immediate sensation among readers who loved the cub.

The fervor didn't go unnoticed by entrepreneurs. According to Alisa Litwin, Berryman's famous cartoon inspired great-grandparents, Morris and Rose Michtom of Brooklyn, New York, to create a stuffed bear in honor of the president's actions. The Michtoms named their creation "Teddy's Bear" and placed it in the window of their candy and stationery store. Teddy's Bear was such an enormous hit with customers that the Michtoms started the first teddy bear manufacturing company in the United States.

Around the same time, Richard Steiff was working for his aunt Margarete Steiff's stuffed toy business in Germany. Richard often visited the Stuttgart Zoo to sketch animals, particularly the bear cubs. The Steiff firm made a prototype of the toy bear based on Richard's designs, and a few months later, at the Leipzig Toy Fair in March 1903, Steiff introduced its first bear—Bear55PB. European buyers showed little interest, but an American toy buyer, aware of the growing interest in Teddy's Bears in the States, ordered 3,000.

The passion for Teddy's Bears continued to spread in the United States. In 1904 Roosevelt used a little bear as the mascot for his successful presidential campaign. By 1906 "teddy bear" had become the accepted term worldwide, and manufacturers in the U.S. and Germany were turning out millions.

The nation's century-long love affair with the teddy bear shows no signs of fading, and teddy bears haven't lost hold on the Roosevelt family either. Tweed Roosevelt, the 26th president's great grandson, represents the German boy company Steiff at teddy bear shows. He oftens points out that the teddy bear must be the most popolar presendential memento ever produced.

—Marianne Clay

leased its decision. It awarded the miners a pay increase of 10 percent and fixed some of the coal weighing abuses, but did not award recognition to the union, a concession beyond the scope of its powers. Both Mitchell and the operators claimed victory, but Roosevelt ended up as the strike's greatest beneficiary. Accounts of his decisive leadership during the crisis enhanced his popularity and probably played a role in Republican gains in the midterm elections of 1902 and in his smashing re-election bid two years later. He also had established precedents that broadened the expected role of the executive office during labor strife.

The anthracite strike also allowed Roosevelt to move out of McKinley's shadow. He later declared that this period was the decisive turning point of his presidency. "The mere force of events had made me strike absolutely my own note by October 1902, when I settled the coal strike and started the trust-control campaign." It was the true beginning of the Roosevelt era.

Stan Saunders is a technical and marketing writer in the Los Angeles area. He holds a master's degree in history.

From *American History,* February 2003, pages 42-48. Copyright © 2003 Primedia Consumer Media and Magazines, Inc. All rights reserved. Reprinted with permission.

THE STEAMER AGE

WHEN AN ODDLY-SHAPED STANLEY RACER WAS CLOCKED AT MORE THAN 2 MILES PER MINUTE IN 1906, IT LOOKED AS THOUGH STEAM-POWERED AUTOMOBILES REPRESENTED THE WAVE OF THE FUTURE.

BY JERRY LEBLANC

IT WAS "The battle for the Crown Trophy and the unchallenged title of Speed King of the World" according to a newspaper dispatch describing the scene at Ormond Beach, Florida, in January 1906, when the greatest new automotive inventions—still called horseless carriages by many—assembled for a series of races designed to test their power and efficiency. Thousands of spectators lined the 500-foot-wide, 23-mile-long stretch of hard-packed white sand that formed an excellent natural racetrack at the edge of the surf.

Many of those on hand speculated that someone was going to try to break the world land-speed record. Rumors even circulated about a speed of two-miles-a-minute, an incredible mark achieved up to then only by the fastest railroad engines on special all-out runs. Not even the fledgling aeroplanes could approach that speed. If such a record were to be broken by an automobile, the fans wanted to be able to tell their grandchildren that they watched it happen.

Automobile makers, who had been struggling to demonstrate the new invention's superiority over horse-drawn wagons, wanted desperately to break the speed record. Whether a steam-powered vehicle succeeded in doing so would be a factor in the future of the auto industry.

Understandably then, all the great automobile makers of Europe were represented at this American Automobile Association-sponsored competition. The participants' names were impressive: Mercedes, Fiat, Maxwell, Napier, Daimler, Darracq. And competing drivers included now-famous auto makers Henry Ford, Louis Chevrolet, and Vincenzo Lancia.

A flimsy-looking, thirty-horsepower Stanley Steamer, which fans, ignoring its posted name—the Rocket—dubbed "the Flying Teapot," was the surprise of the meet. Its laurels already secure from previous competition, the red Stanley Steamer rolled out onto the beach, building up power. A special 1,600-pound racing model, it was said by re-porters to resemble an upside-down canoe, a rather apt description.* With a rear-mounted, two-cylinder engine, a boiler 30 inches in diameter and 18 inches deep, the "Rocket" rode on 34-inch wire wheels that looked more suited to a bicycle.

At noon on the 26th, the skies were clearing after an overcast morning, and the sand was wet and hard. Fred Marriott, the Rocket's driver, buckled the strap o his helmet and adjusted his goggles as he prepared for an unscheduled, timed, solo run. The 33-year-old Marriott, a dark-haired, good-looking man with a heavy moustache and a confident manner, worked as a mechanic for the Stanley Company in Boston. Now, positioned two miles behind the measured mile, he waited for the steam pressure to build toward its maximum capacity of nine hundred pounds.

---

* The wood and canvas body of the racer had come from the Robertson Canoe Factory of Auburndale, Massachusetts, so its design did owe its inspiration to the ancient Indian craft

Steam car drivers usually approached the starting line and then let the throttle out full blast. So, as Marriott neared the starting line, the crowd got to its feet, cheering and shouting, "Here she comes!" Just then, Marriott pulled the throttle wide open, and the vehicle shot ahead with a frightening surge, its front wheels raised with the momentum. A comet-like tail of steam rose in its wake, and the noise swelled into a shriek that drowned out the sound of the surf.

Since the Rocket had no windshield, the driver felt the full force of the air on his face. "My eyes felt as though they were melting, even under my wind glasses," Marriott said later. "I gripped the tiller like the last thread of life … My ears were stricken numb … Toward the end it seemed as though the top of my head would be taken away."

It was over in a flash. The red blur streaked by the grandstand as straight as a bullet and, after a brief hush, a murmur arose as the crowd awaited the official timekeepers' report. The Rocket had no speedometer, but timers consulted their stopwatches in head-shaking amazement and announced a new world record—127.7 miles an hour. Faster than two miles a minute!

The crowd roared and tossed hats up into the air. And on the beach, standing stiffly proper at six-feet tall, the neatly bearded Francis Edgar Stanley, inventor of the incredible machine, tipped his cap in acknowledgement. But it was the driver who received the greatest fanfare. "The feat has dimmed all the other records … and stamped Marriott as the greatest driver of an automobile in the world," an impressed reporter wrote. "This is not only an automobile record but is also the fastest official time ever recorded for a contrivance driven by a human being," another publication noted.

The press reports of the day were ecstatic. "The time is almost inconceivable, but those who saw the flying streak of a cigar-shaped machine fly past them would believe it even less," enthused one paper. Said another: "It was a horrible, indescribable sight … everyone expecting that each succeeding second would see the end of the daring chauffeur." The Louisville *Courier Journal* headlined, "Auto's Frightful Speed Made Spectators Shudder!" and one journalist wrote: "No whir of any death plunge was like that stream of steam and the shriek of the air through the flying steel steed. It sounded like the strike of a death-dealing storm."

Marriott and F. E. Stanley saw more promise than fear in the Steamer's speed,

however. Stanley felt that with a few minor design changes the vehicle could do much better. Amid all the accolades, he vowed to return to the annual event the following year to break the record just set.

Speed. Safety. Reliability. These were the watchwords of the image-conscious makers of the Stanley Steamer from the time the Stanley twins—F. E. and his brother Freelan Oscar, or F. O.—started their auto business. The brothers were conservative New Englanders originally involved in the making of photographic plates. They moved their Stanley Dry Plate Company from Lewiston, Maine, to Newton, Massachusetts, in 1888, and sold the business to Eastman Kodak in late 1903.

Their interest in automobiles was said to have begun in 1896, when the brothers attended a fair in Brockton, Massachusetts, where a Frenchman exhibiting a steam-powered automobile ran into mechanical difficulty and could not follow through on his boast that the machine could be driven all around the fairground track. F. E., after examining the faulty vehicle, immediately decided that he could do better.

In 1897, as he worked on building his first automobile, F. E.—exasperated by the undependability of the horse and buggy—sold his last horse. He wrote to his wife, Augusta, in June of that year that "I am all out of horses and shall not own a horse again until I have seen the outcome of the motor carriage business."

A month later, F. E. provided Augusta with some details of his creation. "I am making all the plans," he wrote, "and it will weigh 350 pounds and will be four inches wider and five inches taller than our best buggy was. It will cost me about $500 and will be finished the 1st of September or soon after you get home. It will not be afraid of a steam roller and will have no bad habits …"

The Stanleys' first ride in the invention, completed as promised in September 1897, was a memorable event. F. O. recalled that they "went out our alley way on to Maple Street, and turned … A horse hitched to a produce wagon … heard the car coming, turned his head around, took a look, gave a snort and jumped so quickly that he broke the Wiffle tree …" The Stanleys paid the two-dollar damage bill for repairs to the runaway horse's harness.

Throughout their careers, the two men also paid numerous fines for speeding, as the press duly reported. Raymond Stanley, F. E.'s son, often told the story of how, on

one occasion, "F. E. came over a hill and was stopped by a policeman for an on-the-spot five-dollar fine. 'I may as well give you ten,' Stanley said, 'because my son will be coming over that hill any minute.'"

By the time automobiles converged on Boston in the Fall of 1898 for the first national exhibition of motor vehicles, the Stanley motorcar had undergone improvements that included a new body, engine, and tires. On November 9, the autos participating in the exhibition gathered at the Charles River Park velodrome track, where an eighty-foot-long wooden ramp had been built with a grade sufficient to test the cars' climbing abilities.

The Stanley twins, wearing identical derbies, their beards trimmed alike, drove triumphantly around the track, demonstrating their vehicle's trouble-free operation. The little Steamer then easily conquered the hill, exhibiting a clear superiority over all the other autos tested.

"Following this spin around the track, people flocked around the car and besieged both Stanleys with questions," Raymond recalled. "Most wanted to know how soon they could get a Stanley Steamer and how much it would cost." After collecting one hundred car orders, the twins decided to form a company and manufacture the vehicles.

In February 1899, the Stanleys were visited by John Brisben Walker, publisher of *The Cosmopolitan* magazine, who wanted to buy an interest in their company. Undeterred by their refusal, Walker offered in April to buy them out completely. Hoping to put an end to Walker's entreaties, the brothers set their asking price at $250,000. Much to their surprise, Walker accepted their terms. With Amzi Lorenzo Barber as his partner, Walker renamed the enterprise the Locomobile Company of America.

As part of the agreement, the Stanleys agreed to help promote the steam cars. To that end, F. O. and his wife, Flora, set out on August 16, 1899 to drive a 4.5-horsepower, Stanley-designed Locomobile up an eight-mile dirt road to the top of Mount Washington, the highest peak in New England. The total trip time, including a stop to refill the water tank, was two hours and forty minutes—twice as fast as the best time for horses.

The Stanley invention gained additional attention when F. E., driving his own personal car, raced the Kingfield, Maine, express train in a 14-mile challenge over hilly terrain—and won by ten seconds. The feat was headlined in the *Boston Post* and became a legend in the Kingfield area, where the Stanley twins were born.

The brothers' publicity efforts for the Locomobile Company climaxed in 1899 when E.O. visited the White House in Washington, D.C., and presented his engraved card to President William McKinley "I've heard of you, Mr. Stanley," the president said. "You recently invented a steam-propelled horseless carriage, did you not?" "Yes, Mr. President," F. O. replied, "and I have called to inquire if you will do me the favor of witnessing a demonstration of my invention, at your convenience, and perhaps take a short ride in it."

Warily, the president asked: "Are you quite sure the contraption is safe? You know, as Chief Executive, I must refrain from taking unnecessary risks." Assured that there was not the slightest danger, McKinley became the first U.S. president to ride in an automobile. Stanley commented that the "news that the President has recognized horseless carriages as a new mode of travel will stimulate interest in the further development of these machines. I venture to predict that within a few years they will be a commonplace means of transportation."

But McKinley apparently did not enjoy his Steamer ride very much. He is said to have later told a friend that throughout the jaunt he "expected every minute to be blown to bits," or that the vehicle would get out of control and run away with him and its inventor. "Stanley's over-optimistic, I think, when he says those things will some day replace horses," McKinley is said to have remarked.

By 1900, more than 1,600 steam cars were operating in America, compared to only 900 gas-powered vehicles. A *McClure's Magazine* advertisement for the Locomobile boasted that the $600 auto ran at a speed of forty miles an hour. But competitions, not ads, kept the steamer car's reputation growing. In 1902, the Stanley brothers bought their patents back from Walker and organized the Stanley Motor Carriage Company.

At the turn of the century, steam was clearly the preferred means of powering automobiles. It required a rather simple mechanism. Water, kept in a 24-gallon tank under the frame, was pumped into a drum-shaped, fire-tube boiler under the hood. A kerosene burner turned the water into steam, building up hundreds of pounds of pressure quickly, easily, and safely. The steam then drove a two-cylinder engine that was directly connected to turn the rear axle.

The simplicity of the steam car made it particularly attractive. The absence of moving parts made it simple to operate and extremely quiet. "Control," said the promotional literature, "is … the only thing the steam car driver has to think of—and this rests in a single small lever on the steering wheel."

Salesmen peddling gas-powered vehicles warned potential customers that Stanley Steamers required a good deal of technical knowledge and were liable to blow up, thus posing a danger to all aboard. In reality, no case of a Steamer blowing up was ever reported; gas vehicles, however, possessed a crank starter known to have broken many a wrist.

By 1906, despite increasing competition with gas-powered cars, the Stanley Steamer seemed to have its future secured, thanks to the world speed record set that year by Marriott in the Rocket. And at the 1907 Ormond Beach race, the Stanley Steamer promised to establish another, even faster time. But fewer competitors showed up that year. Not wishing to be embarrassed once again by the Rocket, most European automobile makers stayed home.

The 1907 Stanley entry was an improved model of the Rocket—16 feet long and 3 feet wide at its widest point, with a steam pressure of 1,300 pounds, 400 pounds more than the 1906 model's capacity. When it rolled out on January 25 for what promised to be its definitive speed run, the sands were particularly hard-packed and driver Marriott noticed at once that the track surface was risky. "There were rough spots and places where the sea water had gathered in pools after the tide dropped and had left impressions," he later recalled. "I didn't think too much of these dips at the time, but I did know they could be dangerous to a car skimming over them at high speed. Anyway, I gave the signal to go ahead with the timing run."

With its throttle open all the way, the Rocket's speed grew to a breakneck pace. Every spectator was on his feet, eyes peeled. Then something happened. "About one third of the way," Marriott remembered, "the car took a slight dip in one of those shallow spots and we took to the air. People who saw it said I went up about fifteen to eighteen feet and came down on the sand more than a hundred feet from where the Rocket hit again and blew up."

Reports of the accident stated that the vehicle flew into the air, twisted, crashed, and broke in two. The Steamer was buried upside down in the sand, and some auto parts, including the boiler, were strewn along the beach. The driver's section of the car was thrown clear of the boiler, and the unconscious Marriott landed face-down in the water.

A doctor rushed to the scene to examine Marriott, who suffered four cracked ribs, a broken breastbone, and a cut through his left cheek. His right eye had popped from its socket and had to be spooned back into place. As the injured driver was carried away, a hush fell over the spectators who mingled around the ruins of the racer.

Augusta May Stanley recorded the day's events in her diary "Truly," she wrote, "this is Black Friday. I can hardly write I am in such a nervous condition. And it is all so dreadful. Oh! Why did we come down to this horrible place … The car was dashed to atoms—and Fred inside!"

Fortunately, Marriott recovered quickly. A month after the accident, he was healthy enough to serve as a judge in another auto competition. But after the crash, the Stanley Steamer never made a racing comeback; Mrs. Stanley would not allow it. "That was the last time we raced," Marriott said. "The Stanleys would never build another racer; they said it was risky." In fact, the Stanley brothers, shocked by what had happened, especially at the near loss of life, turned completely away from racing and most other types of promotion for their vehicles.

Not until 1910, when legendary race driver Barney Oldfield took the wheel of a powerful Blitzen Benz, was the land speed record set by Marriott in the Rocket broken with a new mark of 131.7 miles an hour. By 1913, the supremacy of the gas-powered automobile was established, the invention of the automatic self-starter having eliminated the unpopular and dangerous crank. Now, even the least mechanically inclined person could master the starter without fear. With other improvements to gas-powered vehicles, Henry Ford created the high demand that led to automobile mass-production.

Although it was not known at the time, steam as a power source for automobiles was on its way out as soon as it began. Marriott's 1907 accident probably hastened its demise. Not only did it add to the public perception of danger in the Stanley Steamer's design, it caused the brothers, who did not believe in advertising, to lose interest in promoting their vehicles through racing. And when salesmen for gas-powered vehicles concocted rumors about the shortcomings, danger, and complexity of the Steamer, the Stanleys failed to counter with accurate information. By 1917, F. E. and F. O. had removed themselves from the business, and in 1924, the Stanley Motor Carriage Company ceased production.

On July 31, 1918, F. E., the Steamer's primary inventor, was involved in an automobile accident in Massachusetts and died in an ambulance on his way to the hospital. His brother lived to the age of 91, passing away on October 2, 1940.

Marriott, who entered only a few races after the Ormond incident, maintained his connection with the Stanley interests until 1919, two years after the brothers themselves had left the business. Borrowing money from F. O. Stanley, he opened a garage that, during its early years, catered to all those who owned Stanley vehicles around the world. He died in 1956 at the age of 83.

While it is true that the Rocket's 1906 speed has been eclipsed many times since then by more powerful engines, the record still stands for vehicles in the weight and horsepower class of "the Flying Teapot." Quite simply, there never was another car like it.

Jerry LeBlanc is a scientific, environmental, and travel writer whose latest book is titled Guide to Java and Bali.

From *American History,* July/August 1996, pages 18-20, 64-66. Copyright © 1996 Primedia Consumer Media and Magazines Inc. All rights reserved. Reprinted with permission.

UNIT 3

From Progressivism to the 1920s

Unit Selections

Key Points to Consider

- Why does the author of the essay on Women's Progressivism claim that the legacies of the movement were "ambiguous?"

- What factors were at work in the trial and ultimate lynching of Leo Frank? That he was Jewish was obvious, but what else did he represent that seemed so threatening?

- Why did the question of evolution seem so important to people at the time? Why does the issue continue to stir up controversy?

- Discuss the eugenics movement. Why did it seem attractive to many people at the time? What dangers did it present?

- Marcus Garvey's movement failed in the end. Why did it appeal to so many African Americans?

 **Links: www.dushkin.com/online/**
These sites are annotated in the World Wide Web pages.

International Channel
http://www.i-channel.com/

World War I—Trenches on the Web
http://www.worldwar1.com/

World Wide Web Virtual Library
http://www.iisg.nl/~w3vl/

Temperance and Prohibition
http://prohibition.history.ohio-state.edu/Contents.htm

The Roaring 20's and the Great Depression
http://www.snowcrest.net/jmike/20sdep.html

Unlike most reform movements that emerge during periods of economic crises, Progressivism developed during a time of relative prosperity—at least for the middle class. Industrialization, the growth of cities with their miserable slums, and the rising tide of immigration, disturbed many Americans. In addition to Ida Tarbell's exposé of Standard Oil, mentioned in the previous unit, other "muckrakers" published books and articles that revealed the seamier side of American life. One focused on the terrible working conditions in the meat-packing industry, another on corruption and cronyism in the Senate, still another on the "boss-ism" and "machine politics" he found in a number of cities. The popularity of muckraking in newspapers, journals, and books showed that many segments of the public were receptive to such exposures.

The Progressive movement generally was led by white, educated, middle or upper-middle class men and women. They were not radicals, though their opponents often called them that, and they had no wish to destroy the capitalist system. Instead they wanted to reform it to eliminate corruption, to make it function more efficiently, and to provide what we would call a "safety net" for the less fortunate. The reforms they proposed were modest ones such as replacing political appointees with trained experts, having senators elected directly by the people, and conducting referenda on important issues. The movement arose on local levels, percolated upward to state governments, then into the national arena.

Teddy Roosevelt as president had responded to progressive sentiment through actions such as his "trust busting." He did not seek a third term in 1908, and anointed William Howard Taft as the Republican candidate for the presidency. Taft won the election but managed to alienate both progressives and conservatives during his tenure of office. By 1912, progressivism ran strongly enough that the Democratic party nominated Woodrow Wilson, who had compiled an impressive record as a reform governor in the state of New Jersey. Roosevelt, now counting himself a full-blown progressive, bolted the Republican Party when Taft won renomination and formed the Progressive or "Bull Moose" Party. Roosevelt was still popular, but he managed only to split Republican support with the result that Woodrow Wilson won the election with just 42 percent of the popular vote.

Those progressives who held or competed for political offices were almost exclusively white males. Women had not yet been granted the right to vote, let alone be elected to positions in government, and the prevailing racism ensured that blacks would be excluded from the power structure. "Jim Crow" laws in the South had virtually pushed blacks out of the political arena altogether. Yet members of both groups were attracted to progressivism. Blacks, at least as much as whites, wanted to change the power structures that kept them down. Female progressives shared these goals as well. "The Ambiguous Legacies of Women's Progressivism" points out that, contrary to what one might think, the movement did not always serve to liberate women.

Anti-Semitism was a fact of life during this era and beyond. "The Fate of Leo Frank" describes how a Northern Jew was convicted in 1913 for the murder of a little girl, and later removed from jail and lynched. He was almost certainly innocent, yet the things he represented enraged those who persecuted him. Leonard Dinnerstein examines what has been called "one of the most shocking frame-ups ever perpetrated by American law-and-order officials."

Woodrow Wilson compiled a fairly impressive progressive record during his first administration. Whether he would have continued along this course can never be known. Unfortunately, war broke out in Europe in 1914, and during the following years the United States became embroiled in disputes over its rights as a neutral power. Although he did not use the phrase himself, Wilson's supporters during the elections of 1916 boasted that he had "kept us out of war." This was not to last. When Germany resorted to unrestricted submarine warfare and American ships were sunk, Wilson believed he had no choice but to ask Congress for a declaration of war in April 1917.

America's entry into World War I or "The Great War," as people at the time called it, to a great degree stifled the progressive impulse. Furthering the war effort seemed more important than experimenting with this or that reform, and the perceived threat of espionage or sabotage by German agents brought about drastic curtailments of civil liberties. "The Home Front" examines the impact of mobilization, government propaganda, and the drive for "national unity" on the society. The question, according to author Ronald Schaffer, was whether "the United States Government could be strong enough to defend the nation without destroying American freedoms." This issue is very much with us today in the wake of the war on Iraq.

After numerous crusades against inequities at home and the consequences of waging war abroad, the American people in 1920 yearned to return to what Republican presidential candidate Warren G. Harding referred to as "normalcy." Harding was elected in a landslide. Following a recession brought about by postwar reconversion, prosperity returned again although not equally shared by all. The genial Harding presided over this economic boom and was an extremely popular president at the time of his death in 1923. He was succeeded by his vice president, Calvin Coolidge, who also was disinclined to make any waves.

There are three selections in this unit about the 1920s. "Evolution on Trial" focuses on the notorious "Scopes trial." John Scopes, a public school teacher, had agreed to challenge Tennessee's laws against teaching the theory of evolution. When William Jennings Bryan and Clarence Darrow agreed to participate in the trial, it was guaranteed to become a media extravaganza. "Race Cleansing in America" discusses the eugenics movement, which peaked during the 1920s. Its proponents advocated measures such as compulsory sterilization of women and restrictive immigration laws, which were supposed to help eliminate crime, alcoholism, and other social ills. The final essay, "Marcus Garvey and the Rise of Black Nationalism," discusses the man who founded the United Negro Improvement Association. The movement peaked during the 1920s; then floundered over charges of fraud and other financial misdeeds. Whatever the truth of these charges, Garvey was able to "tap successfully the ambitions and emotions of people whose lives were held down by class, economics, and racism."

The Ambiguous Legacies of Women's Progressivism

Robyn Muncy

Most undergraduates come into my classroom convinced that men have so dominated American political life that they are responsible for all the good and evil in America's public past. The history of progressive reform usually persuades them otherwise. Students discover that black and white women, by the hundreds of thousands—even millions—threw themselves into progressive reform, helping to chart the direction of public policy and American values for the century to come. When they learn this, students want to believe that such activism and power must have tended unambiguously to liberate women. My job is to explain that this is not altogether the case.

The truth is that female progressive activism left a complicated legacy to twentieth-century American women. First, women reformers generally failed to overcome (and white activists often worked to sustain) racial divisions in American life. Second, black and white female progressives changed "the place" of American women in many important senses, especially in winning admittance to the polls and the policymaking table. Third, despite carving out significant public space for women, female progressives—mostly white in this case—embedded in public policy the notion that motherhood and economic independence were incompatible. Women reformers thus empowered successive generations of women in some ways while continuing to deny them the multiplicity of roles open to men.

Most women's activism took place through the many local, regional, and national organizations that women formed around 1900. The sheer number of women participating in these associations boggles the late-twentieth-century mind and suggests an engaged, cohesive female citizenry well before the achievement of women's suffrage. For instance, two hundred local white women's clubs joined together in 1890 to form the General Federation of Women's Clubs (GFWC), which by 1920 claimed over a million members. Along with the National Mothers' Congress (NMC), formed in 1897, the GFWC became a vehicle for moderate white women's political activism. In

similar fashion, one hundred middle-class black women's clubs created the National Association of Colored Women (NACW) in 1896, and by 1914 this group claimed fifty thousand members in one thousand local clubs. Jewish women organized the National Council of Jewish Women in 1893, and black Baptist women founded the Woman's Convention of the National Baptist Convention in 1900. That organization alone embraced over one million members (1).

Although gender and race segregation were the rule among civic organizations early in this century, there were exceptions. Some women participated in gender-integrated groups like the National Child Labor Committee, which targeted child labor as an urgent public problem, and some women helped to found such gender- and race-integrated groups as the National Association for the Advancement of Colored People and the National Urban League. One of the most important progressive organizations, the National Consumers League (NCL), was ostensibly a gender-integrated group, though white women dominated it throughout the period, and thousands of women—overwhelmingly white—invigorated the Progressive party of 1912 (2).

In these organizations, women pursued an agenda that set them squarely in the social justice wing of progressivism. They aimed to ameliorate the worst suffering caused by rapid industrialization, immigration, and urbanization without forsaking capitalism altogether. To do so, they strove to make government at all levels more responsible for the social and economic welfare of citizens, and though many hoped ultimately to improve the lives of America's entire working class or the whole community of color, most women reformers found that they were especially effective when they spoke specifically to the needs of women and children. Their agendas ran the gamut from antilynching campaigns to the prohibition of alcohol, from maximum hours laws to women's suffrage, from improved educational opportunities for African-American children to the

The mansion of the late Chicago businessman Charles Hull served as the original home of Jane Addams's famous social settlement. This photo-to of Hull House was taken around 1893. (Courtesy of the Jane Addams Memorial Collection, Special Collections, The University Library, The University of Illinois at Chicago, Negative 146.)

abolition of prostitution. A brief article can glimpse only a tiny portion of their work.

One example, the campaign for protective labor legislation, reveals some of the complex meanings of women's progressivism. Although many working-class women believed the solution to workplace problems lay in unionization, some accepted the middle-class preference for legislation as the surest route to job-related improvements. Thus, both groups—organized, for instance, in the National Women's Trade Union League—lobbied their states for guarantees of factory safety, maximum hours laws, and less often, minimum wage provisions as well. Many states passed such laws and even hired women as factory inspectors to enforce them.

These legislative successes were threatened in 1905, when the U.S. Supreme Court handed down its famous *Lochner* decision. In it, the Court struck down a New York law that regulated the hours of bakers, an overwhelmingly male group. The Court ruled that states could interfere in the freedom of contract only if long hours constituted a clear health risk either to the workers themselves or to the general public.

Women reformers would not see their protective laws undone. Indeed, their determination to sustain protective labor legislation led to their participation in a second case, *Muller v. Oregon*. In 1903, Oregon passed a law that limited the hours of women in industrial work to ten per day. Two years later, the state prepared a case against laundry owner Curt Muller for violation of the law. Muller took the case to the U.S. Supreme Court, where he expected the reasoning in *Lochner* to strike down Oregon's law. The NCL, with the fiery Florence Kelley at its head, took up Oregon's fight, leading the charge for protective legislation for women workers.

Kelley, who had fought for and implemented a similar law in Illinois, hired Louis Brandeis to argue against Muller. Kelley's colleague, Josephine Goldmark, aided Brandeis in preparing a precedent-setting brief. Providing over one hundred pages of evidence that showed that women workers were hurt by long hours in ways that men were not, the brief argued that women

workers warranted the state's interference in freedom of contract even when men did not. In 1908, the Supreme Court accepted their arguments, concluding that "woman's physical structure and the performance of maternal functions place her at a disadvantage in the struggle for subsistence" (3).

Women reformers thus won a progressive end—government intervention in the economy on behalf of workers—by perpetuating an older belief in male/female difference and moreover inscribing that difference into law. In this crusade, activist women, mostly middle-class and white, gained public power for themselves while at the same time cementing in public policy a view of working women as peculiarly vulnerable workers. This image of working women, while justifying legislation that genuinely helped many, made it impossible for women to compete effectively with men in many sectors of the labor market. This law created a complicated bequest to later generations of American women. Moreover, these maximum hours laws, antecedents of the Fair Labor Standards Act of 1938, also supported racial difference, not explicitly as in the case of gender, but implicitly, by omitting from coverage the occupations in which African-American women were heavily represented: agricultural labor and domestic service.

Another campaign rooted in a belief in the difference between women and men was the movement for mothers' pensions. Mothers' pensions were public stipends paid to mothers—usually widows—who found themselves without male support. The purpose of these payments was to allow impoverished mothers to remain at home with their children rather than having to put them in an orphanage or neglect them while working for wages. Led especially by the NMC and the GFWC, white activists lobbied their state governments for such programs and won them in virtually every state by the mid 1920s. These programs, unfortunately poorly funded and often unjustly administered, set the precedent for Aid to Dependent Children, a federal program enacted as part of the Social Security Act in 1935 during Franklin Roosevelt's New Deal (4).

African-American women reformers, seeing that social workers often reserved mothers' pensions for white women, lobbied for their extension to qualified African-American women. Simultaneously however, they promoted day care services as an alternative response to mothers' need to work for pay. These services revealed not only black women's suspicion of government programs—based in part on the disenfranchisement of African-American men and spread of Jim Crow laws in the early twentieth century—but also their greater acceptance of working mothers. Poor wages for men were so endemic to African-American communities that black reformers could not so easily envision a world in which mothers were spared paid labor, and so they were more ready than white women to create institutions that allowed women to be both good mothers and good workers (5).

In both black and white neighborhoods, day care services were often provided by other, multifaceted progressive women's institutions. Indeed, the quintessential progressive women's institutions were social settlements and neighborhood unions. Social settlements first appeared in the United States in the 1880s. They were places where middle-class women and

To counter the claim that suffragists deserted their families or disrespected motherhood, suffragists often took their children on parade with them, as some did in this 1912 demonstration in New York City. (Library of Congress, Division of Prints and Photographs.)

men lived in the midst of working-class, largely immigrant neighborhoods. Their purpose was to bridge the gap between the classes. By the turn of the century, settlements existed in most sizable cities. Educated women took the lead in the establishment of settlement communities. Once acquainted with their working-class neighbors, these middle-class women created social services that they believed their neighbors needed. Much of the time, settlement residents piloted local health services, educational series, or recreational programs and then lobbied their municipal, county, or state government to provide permanent funding and oversight. In this way, settlement residents became leaders in progressive reform.

The most famous social settlement was Hull House in Chicago. Founded in 1889 by Jane Addams and Ellen Gates Starr, Hull House set the standard for the hundreds of settlements that subsequently opened in cities all over the country. Beginning with a day nursery (considered a regrettable, stop-gap measure by the white reformers) and evening classes and clubs for its immigrant neighbors, Hull House eventually housed seventy middle-class residents, a library for the neighborhood, a community theater, a gym, playground, labor museum, many classrooms and clubhouses for adults and children, and a coffee house. It offered a visiting nurse and employment counseling to the neighborhood, as well as a meeting ground for unions and political groups. It was a vital hub of neighborhood life and provided the initiative and/or support for much progressive legislation, including protective legislation for women workers and children, women's suffrage, workers' compensation programs, increased funding for public education, and the creation of the U.S. Children's Bureau.

Besides women's suffrage, the Children's Bureau may have been progressive women's most significant national achievement. The idea for a federal agency devoted to child welfare is usually credited to Lillian Wald, founder and head resident of the Henry Street Settlement in New York City. Herself a visiting nurse, Wald joined Jane Addams in creating a female reform network that stretched across the country by 1903. That year Wald first proposed that the U.S. government create a bu-

reau to collect information and propose legislation of benefit to the country's children. In 1912, Congress finally rewarded the women's lobbying efforts by establishing the Children's Bureau in the U.S. Department of Labor.

Addams immediately argued that a woman should head the new agency and proposed in particular Julia Lathrop, a long-time resident of Hull House. To everyone's surprise, President William Howard Taft accepted the recommendation, and Lathrop became the first woman ever to head a federal agency. She quickly hired other women to staff the bureau, which became a female beachhead in the federal government for decades to come. In 1921, Lathrop and her staff drafted and won from Congress the first piece of federal social/welfare legislation: the Sheppard-Towner Maternity and Infancy Act, which sent public health nurses into nearly every corner of America to teach pregnant women how best to care for themselves and their newborns. This set another precedent for New Deal programs (6).

Although African-American women also founded social settlements, as did some interracial groups, more typical of black women's institution building was the neighborhood union. Such entities differed from social settlements mainly in that few reformers actually lived in them, reflecting in part the tendency of black women reformers to be married while their white counterparts often remained unmarried. Many of these progressive institutions called themselves missions, community centers, institutional churches, or even schools, but like settlements, they provided meeting places and services for those living nearby, and they joined the middle and working classes in local political crusades (7).

The most famous such center was the Neighborhood Union in Atlanta. Founded in 1908 by Lugenia Burns Hope, the union provided day care services, health care and health education, and playgrounds. It sponsored clubs and classes for children and adults alike, and organized lobbying campaigns to obtain greater funding for the education of African-American children, as well as improved street lights and sanitation in black neighborhoods. Members urged public relief for the unemployed. The Neighborhood Union's appeals for governmental support remind us that even though black women had less hope for a positive response from government officials than white women, they did not—even in this hour of miserable race relations—give up entirely on obtaining government resources (8).

Just as social settlements and neighborhood unions were usually race-segregated, so were organizations that fought for women's suffrage. Ratification of the Nineteenth Amendment in 1920 stood as a monumental victory for women progressives; it is one of the signal achievements of progressive reform. But even that fight to expand democracy was marked by racial division and hierarchy. Hoping to win support from white southerners, leaders in the North refused to admit black women's clubs to the National American Woman Suffrage Association, which, with two million members in 1917, was the largest suffrage organization in U.S. history. In response, black women formed their own suffrage associations—like the Equal Suffrage League founded by Ida Wells-Barnett in Chicago—or fought for enfranchisement through multi-issue groups like the

The history of these women reformers moreover reveals some of the ways that race has shaped women's experience and political agendas in the past, and it embodies the ways that racism has crippled democracy and betrayed democratic movements in the United States. It reminds us that the renewed political life we might create in the twenty-first century, if it is to fulfill the promise of democracy, must strive to overcome the racial hierarchy that progressives—and all of their successors—failed to defeat.

Lugenia Burns Hope founded the Neighborhood Union in Atlanta. While white progressives in the South usually pursued policies that assured white dominance, Hope's activism reminds us that southern African Americans were also progressives. (Courtesy of the National Park Service, Mary McLeod Bethune Council House National Historic Site, Washington DC.)

NACW or the black Baptist Women's Convention (9). Complicating black women's struggle for suffrage was their simultaneous fight for the re-enfranchisement of African-American men in the South, whose right to vote was eroding in the face of brutal violence, literacy tests, and poll taxes. When the women's suffrage amendment passed, no state could deny suffrage on the basis of sex, but the same measures that disenfranchised black men in the South also prevented most black women from approaching the polls. Thus, not until the Voting Rights Act of 1965 did women's suffrage achieve a complete victory.

Black and white women were integral to progressivism. No history of progressive reform could possibly be complete without discussing the campaign for women's suffrage, the work of neighborhood unions, or the struggle for protective legislation.

These efforts by millions of American women suggest several conclusions. This history illuminates the source of sometimes contradictory views of women embedded in public policy and personal identities since the Progressive Era: while most American women received the vote by 1920, imparting a new parity with men in public life, the same period produced legislation that construed women primarily as mothers rather than as workers and as more vulnerable, weaker workers than men. This ambiguous legacy has reverberated through the twentieth century.

END NOTES

1. Karen J. Blair, *Clubwoman as Feminist. True Womanhood Redefined, 1868–1914* (New York: Holmes and Meier, 1980); Evelyn Brooks Higginbotham, *Righteous Discontent. The Women's Movement in the Black Baptist Church* (Cambridge: Harvard University Press, 1993), 8; and Stephanie Shaw, "Black Club Women and the Creation of the National Association of Colored Women," *Journal of Women's History 3* (Fall 1991): 10–25.

2. Dorothy Salem, *To Better Our World: Black Women in Organized Reform, 1890–1920* (Brooklyn: Carlson, 1990), 45–46, 100–14, 146–96, 274; Kathryn Kish Sklar, "The Historical Foundations of Women's Power in the Creation of the American Welfare State, 1830–1930," in *Mothers of a New World: Maternalist Politics and the Origins of Welfare States*, ed. Seth Koven and Sonya Michel (New York: Routledge, 1993), 43–93; and Robyn Muncy, "'Women Demand Recognition': Women Candidates in Colorado's Election of 1912," in *We Have Come to Stay: American Women and Political Parties, 1880–1960*, ed. Melanie Gustafson, Kristie Miller, and Elisabeth Israels Perry (Albuquerque: University of New Mexico Press, 1999), 45–54.

3. Muller v. Oregon, 208 U.S. 412; Nancy Woloch, *Muller v. Oregon: A Brief History with Documents* (Boston: Bedford Books, 1996); Sybil Lipschultz, "Social Feminism and Legal Discourse," *Yale Journal of Law and Feminism 2* (Fall 1989): 131–60; and Kathryn Kish Sklar, "Hull House in the 1890s: A Community of Women Reformers," *Signs* 10 (Summer 1985): 658–77.

4. Molly Ladd-Taylor, *Mother-Work: Women, Child Welfare, and the State, 1890–1930* (Urbana: University of Illinois Press, 1994), 135–66; and Theda Skócpol, *Protecting Soldiers and Mothers: The Political Origins of Social Policy in the United States* (Cambridge: Belknap Press of Harvard University, 1992), 424–79.

5. Linda Gordon, "Black and White Visions of Welfare: Women's Welfare Activism: 1890–1945," *Journal of American History 78* (September 1991): 559–90; Eileen Boris, "The Power of Motherhood: Black and White Activist Women Redefine the 'Political,'" *Yale Journal of Law and Feminism 2* (Fall 1989): 25–49.

6. Robyn Muncy, *Creating a Female Dominion in American Reform, 1890–1935* (New York: Oxford University Press, 1991).

7. Salem, *To Better Our World;* and Elisabeth Lasch-Quinn, *Black Neighbors: Race and the Limits of Reform in the American Settlement House Movement, 1890–1945* (Chapel Hill: University of North Carolina Press, 1993).
8. Jacqueline Anne Rouse, *Lugenia Burns Hope: Black Southern Reformer* (Athens: University of Georgia Press, 1989).
9. Rosalyn Terborg-Penn, "Discrimination Against Afro-American Women in the Woman's Movement, 1830–1920," in *The Afro-American Woman: Struggles and Images*, ed. Sharon Harley and Rosalyn Terborg-Penn (Port Washington, NY: National University Publications, 1978); and Higginbotham, *Righteous Discontent, 226*.

BIBLIOGRAPHY

In addition to the works cited in the endnotes, the following sources are helpful for studying women's activism in the Progressive Era.

Boris, Eileen. *Home to Work: Motherhood and the Politics of Industrial Homework in the United States*. New York: Cambridge University Press, 1994.

Cott, Nancy F. *The Grounding of Modern Feminism*. New Haven: Yale University Press, 1987.

Crocker, Ruth Hutchinson. *Social Work and Social Order: The Settlement Movement in Two Industrial Cities, 1889–1930*. Urbana: University of Illinois, 1992.

Goodwin, Joanne L. *Gender and the Politics of Welfare Reform: Mothers' Pensions in Chicago, 1911–4929*. Chicago: University of Chicago Press, 1997.

Gordon, Linda. *Pitied But Not Entitled: Single Mothers and the History of Welfare, 1890–1935*. New York: Maxwell MacMillan International, 1994.

Hewitt, Nancy A. and Suzanne Lebsock, eds. *Visible Women: New Essays on American Activism*. Urbana: University of Illinois Press, 1993.

Knupfer, Anne Meis. *Toward a Tenderer Humanity and a Nobler Womanhood: African American Women's Clubs in Turn-of-the-Century Chicago*. New York: New York University Press, 1996.

Neverdon-Morton, Cynthia. *Afro-American Women of the South and the Advancement of the Race, 1895–1925*. Knoxville: University of Tennessee Press, 1989.

Scott, Anne Firor. *Natural Allies: Women's Associations in American History*. Urbana: University of Illinois Press, 1991.

Robyn Muncy is an associate professor of history at the University of Maryland. She is the author of Creating a Female Dominion in American Reform, 1880–1935 *(1991) and coauthor with Sonya Michel of* Engendering America: A Documentary History, 1865–The Present *(1999).*

From *OAH Magazine of History*, Spring 1999, pp. 15-19. © 1999 by the Organization of American Historians. Reprinted by permission.

The Fate of Leo Frank

He was a Northerner. He was an industrialist. He was a Jew.
And a young girl was murdered in his factory.

By Leonard Dinnerstein

COURTESY OF THE ATLANTA HISTORY CENTER

Leo M. Frank, manager and co-owner of National Pencil Company (above), was accused of the murder of Mary Phagan.

On December 23, 1983, the lead editorial in the Atlanta *Constitution* began, "Leo Frank has been lynched a second time." The first lynching had occurred almost seventy years earlier, when Leo Frank, convicted murderer of a thirteen-year-old girl, had been taken from prison by a band of vigilantes and hanged from a tree in the girl's hometown of Marietta, Georgia. The lynching was perhaps unique, for Frank was not black but a Jew. Frank also is widely considered to

have been innocent of his crime. Thus the second "lynching" was the refusal of Georgia's Board of Pardons and Paroles to exonerate him posthumously.

Frank's trial, in July and August 1913, has been called "one of the most shocking frame-ups ever perpetrated by American law-and-order officials." The case became, at the time, a cause célèbre in which the injustices created by industrialism, urban growth in Atlanta, and

fervent anti-Semitism all seemed to conspire to wreck one man.

Until the discovery of Mary Phagan's body in the basement of Atlanta's National Pencil Company factory, Leo Frank led a relatively serene life. Born in Cuero, Texas, in 1884, he was soon taken by his parents to Brooklyn, New York. He attended the local public schools, the Pratt Institute, and Cornell University. After graduation he accepted the offer of an uncle, Moses Frank, to

COURTESY OF THE ATLANTA HISTORY CENTER

Mary Phagan, found dead in the factory's basement.

help establish a pencil factory in Atlanta and become both co-owner and manager of the plant. He married Lucille Selig, a native Atlantan, in 1910, and in 1912 he was elected president of the local chapter of the national Jewish fraternity B'nai B'rith. Then, on the afternoon of April 26, 1913, Mary Phagan, an employee, stopped by Frank's factory to collect her week's wages on her way to see the Confederate Memorial day parade and was murdered.

Hugh Dorsey built a case around Frank's alleged perversions. Four weeks after the murder the grand jury granted the indictment he sought.

A night watchman discovered the girls' body in the factory basement early the next morning. Sawdust and grime so covered her that when the police came they could not tell whether she was white or black. Her eyes were bruised, her cheeks cut. An autopsy would reveal that her murderer had choked her with a piece of her own underdrawers and broken her skull. The watchman, Newt Lee, sum-

moned the police; they suspected that he might have committed the murder, and they arrested him. After inspecting the scene, the officers went to Frank's home and took him to the morgue to see the body. The sight of the corpse unsettled him, and he appeared nervous. He remembered having paid the girl her wages the previous day but could not confirm that she had then left the factory. The police would find no one who would admit to having seen her alive any later.

A number of unsolved murders had taken place in Atlanta during the previous eighteen months, and the police were under pressure to find the culprit. Early newspaper reports erroneously suggested that Mary Phagan had been raped, and crowds of people were soon milling about the police station, anxious to get their hands on whoever had committed the crime. Frank's uneasy behavior and the public's hunger for justice made him a prime suspect. He was arrested two days later.

Shortly thereafter some factory employees told a coroner's jury, convened to determine the cause of death and suggest possible suspects for investigation, that Frank had "indulged in familiarities with the women in his employ." And the proprietress of a "rooming house" signed an affidavit swearing that on the day of the murder Frank had telephoned her repeatedly, seeking a room for himself and a young girl. Both these charges were later proved false (many witnesses recanted their accusations later), but newspapers headlined them, fueling talk of Jewish men seeking Gentile girls for their pleasure. The solicitor general, Hugh Dorsey, built a case for the prosecution around Frank's alleged perversions. Four weeks after the murder the grand jury granted the indictment Dorsey sought.

Unknown to the members of the grand jury, however, another suspect had also been arrested. He was Jim Conley, a black janitor at the factory who had been seen washing blood off a shirt there. He admitted having written two notes found near her body. They read: "Mam that negro hire down here did this i went to make water and he push me down that

hole a long tall negro black that hoo it was long sleam tall negro i wright while play with me" and "he said he wood love me land dab n play like the night witch did it but that long tall black negro did buy his slef."

At first almost all investigators assumed that the author of these items had committed the crime. But Conley claimed to have written them as Frank dictated the words, first the day before the murder occurred, then, according to Conley's second affidavit, on the day of the crime.

Conley ultimately signed four affidavits, changing and elaborating his tale each time. Originally he said he had been called to Frank's office the day before the murder and asked to write phrases like "dear mother" and "a long, tall, black negro did this by himself;" and he claimed to have heard Frank mumble something like "Why should I hang?" But the newspapers found the idea of Frank's having prepared for an apparent crime of passion by asking a black janitor to write notes about it utterly ridiculous. So Harry Scott, the chief detective, said he then "pointed out things in [Conley's] story that were improbable and told him he must do better than that." Another lengthy interrogation led to the second affidavit. It stated that Frank had dictated the notes just after the murder and that Conley had removed the dead body from a room opposite Frank's office, on the second floor, and taken it by elevator to the basement. (Later evidence showed that the elevator had not been in operation from before the time of the girl's death until after her body was discovered.) A third affidavit spelled out in greater detail the steps Conley had allegedly taken in assisting Frank with the disposal of the dead girl. The Atlanta *Georgian* had already protested after the janitor's second statement that with Conley's "first affidavit repudiated and worthless it will be practically impossible to get any court to accept a second one." But Atlantans had been so conditioned to believe Frank guilty that few protested the inconsistencies in the janitor's tale.

Among those who questioned the prosecution's case against Frank were the members of the grand jury that had originally indicted him. They wanted Dorsey to reconvene them so that they could charge Conley instead. Dorsey refused, so the jury foreman did it on his own. It was the first time an Atlanta grand jury had ever considered a criminal case against the wishes of the solicitor general. Then Dorsey came back before the group and pleaded with them not to indict the black man. Exactly what he told them was not made public, but the next day the Atlanta *Constitution* reported that "the solicitor did not win his point without a difficult fight. He went in with a mass of evidence showing why the indictment of the negro would injure the state's case against Frank and stayed with the grand jurors for nearly an hour and a half."

It is difficult to say why the grand jury ultimately supported Dorsey. Perhaps they accepted the Atlanta *Georgian*'s explanation: "That the authorities have very important evidence that has not yet been disclosed to the public is certain." Or, given Southern values, they may have assumed that no attorney would base his case on the word of a black man "unless the evidence was overwhelming." In any case, the solicitor prevailed and prepared to go to trial.

T he trial began on July 28, 1913, and brought forth large and ugly-tempered crowds. The heinous nature of the crime, rumors of sexual misdeeds, newspaper reports of "very important evidence that has not yet been disclosed," the solicitor general's supreme confidence, and anti-Semitism (a Georgia woman had written that "this is the first time a Jew has ever been in any serious trouble in Atlanta, and see how ready every one is to believe the worst of him") combined to create an electric tension in the city. Gossip about Frank had been widespread, and many Georgians wondered if an unbiased jury would be possible. But jury selection was swift, and in an atmosphere punctuated by spontaneous applause for the prosecuting attorney and shouts of "Hang the Jew" from throngs outside the courthouse, the proceedings unfolded.

Solicitor Dorsey opened his presentation by trying to establish where and when the crime had occurred. He elicited testimony from several witnesses about blood spots on the floor and strands of hair on a lathe that Mary Phagan had allegedly fallen against in the room opposite Frank's office. (The state biologist had specifically informed the prosecution that the hair was not Mary Phagan's, and many witnesses testified that the bloodstains could have been merely paint spots; Dorsey ignored them.)

COURTESY OF THE ATLANTA HISTORY CENTER

Frank's wife, Lucille Selig Frank, sits close by him during the murder trial.

The heart of the state's case, however, revolved around Jim Conley's narrative. Although his story had gone through several revisions during the previous weeks—all of them published in the newspapers—his courtroom account mesmerized the spectators. Conley told how he had served as a lookout in the past when Frank "entertained" women in the factory (no such women ever appeared at the trial), how after an agreed-upon signal he would lock or unlock the front door or go up to the superintendent's office for further instruction. He claimed that on the fatal day Frank had summoned him to his office, and when he arrived there, he had found his boss "standing up there at the top of the steps and shivering and trembling and rubbing his hands.... He had a little rope in his hands.... His eyes were large and they looked right funny.... His face was red. Yes, he had a cord in his hands.... After I got up to the top of the steps, he asked me 'Did you see that little girl who passed here just a while ago?' and I told him I saw one.... 'Well... I wanted to be with the little girl and she refused me, and I struck her and... she fell and hit her head against something, and I don't know how bad she got hurt. Of course you know I ain't built like other men.' The reason he said that was, I had seen him in a position I haven't seen any other man that has got children." Conley did not explain that last sentence; instead he went on to detail how Frank had offered, but never given him, money to dispose of the body. He said Frank had then asked him if he could write and, when he said yes, had dictated the murder notes.

When Dorsey concluded his presentation, *Frost's Magazine* of Atlanta, which had previously made no editorial comment about the case, condemned both the solicitor and Atlanta's chief detective for misleading the public into thinking that the state had sufficient evidence to warrant an accusation against Frank. "We cannot conceive," the commentary read, "that at the close of the prosecution, before the defense has presented one single witness, that it could be possible for any juryman to vote for the conviction of Leo M. Frank."

Frank had retained two of the South's best-known attorneys to defend him: Luther Z. Rosser, an expert at cross-examination, and Reuben R. Arnold, a prominent criminal lawyer. Despite their brilliant reputations, they failed to display their forensic talents when they were most needed. Rosser and Arnold cross-examined Conley for a total of sixteen hours on three consecutive days and could not shake his basic tale. He continually claimed to have forgotten anything that tended to weaken the case against Frank, and some observers thought Conley had been carefully coached by the solicitor general and his subordinates. The murder and disposal of the body would have taken at least fifty minutes to accomplish as the janitor described them, yet witnesses corroborated "Frank's recollection of his whereabouts for all but eighteen minutes of that time. Furthermore, much of Conley's narrative depended on his having removed the body to the basement via the elevator, but floor markings, the absence of blood in the elevator, and other incontrovertible evidence proved that he hadn't. Why Frank's attorneys failed to exploit these facts, and why they also failed to request a change of venue before the trial began, has never been explained. But their inability to break Conley undermined their client's case. A reporter who attended every session of the hearings later observed, "I heard Conley's evidence entire, and was impressed powerfully with the idea that the negro was repeating something he had seen.… Conley's story was told with a wealth of infinitesimal detail that I firmly believe to be beyond the capacity of his mind, or a far more intelligent one, to construct from his imagination."

> *One juror had allegedly been overheard to say, "I am glad they indicted the God damn Jew. They ought to take him out and lynch him."*

Rosser and Arnold's biggest error was probably their attempt to delete from the record Conley's discussion of times he had "watched for" Frank. For a day the two men got the janitor to talk about Frank's alleged relationships with other women, hoping to poke holes in the testimony; then they tried to get the whole discussion stricken. Even one of Dorsey's assistants agreed this information should not have been allowed into the record but added that once Conley had been examined and cross-examined on the subject, it was wrong to try to expunge. "By asking that the testimony be eliminated," the Atlanta *Constitution* noted, the defense "virtually admit their failure to break down Conley."

It did not matter thereafter that witnesses came in to attest to Frank's good character and his whereabouts before, during, and after the murder. It also made little difference that Frank's explanation of his activities on the day of the murder carried, according to the *Constitution*, "the ring of truth in every sentence."

Conley's narrative absolutely dominated the four-week trial.

In their summations Arnold and Rosser accused the police and solicitor general of having fabricated the evidence. Arnold stated that "if Frank hadn't been a Jew, there would never have been any prosecution against him," and he likened the entire case to the Dreyfus affair in France: "the savagry [*sic*] and venom is… the same."

But once again Dorsey emerged the winner. The *Constitution* described his closing argument as "one of the most wonderful efforts ever made at the Georgia bar." The solicitor reviewed the evidence, praised his opponents as "two of the ablest lawyers in the country," and then reemphasized how these men could not break Conley's basic narrative. He went on to state that although he had never mentioned the word *Jew*, once it was introduced he would use it. The Jews "rise to heights sublime," he asserted, "but they also sink to the lowest depths of degradation." He noted that Judas Iscariot, too, had been considered an honorable man before he disgraced himself. The bells of a nearby Catholic church rang, just as the solicitor was finishing. Each time Dorsey proclaimed the word *guilty* the bells chimed, and they "cut like a chill to the hearts of many who shivered involuntarily" in the courtroom.

The jury took less than four hours to find Frank guilty, and the judge, fearing mob violence, asked the defense to keep their client out of court during sentencing. Rosser and Arnold agreed. Solicitor Dorsey requested that they promise not to use Frank's absence as a basis for future appeals—even though barring a defendant from his own sentencing might constitute a denial of his right to due process of law—and the two defense attorneys assented.

Frank's attorneys kept their word and ignored the issue in their appeals for a new trial. According to state law, appeals in a capital case could be based only on errors in law and had to be heard first by the original trial judge. Rosser and Arnold based their appeal on more than 115 points, including the alleged influence of the public on the jury, the admissibility of Conley's testimony about Frank's al-

leged sexual activities, and affidavits from people who swore that two of the jurors were anti-Semitic. (One had allegedly been overheard to say, "I am glad they indicted the God damn Jew. They ought to take him out and lynch him. And if I get on that jury I'd hang that Jew sure.") Dorsey and his associates countered with affidavits from the jurors swearing that public demonstrations had not affected their deliberations. In his ruling, Leonard Roan, the trial judge, upheld the verdict and commented that although he was "not thoroughly convinced that Frank is guilty or innocent. The jury was convinced."

The next appeal, to the Georgia Supreme Court, centered on Roan's doubt of Frank's guilt, but the justices went along with the earlier decision. This court concluded that only the trial judge could decide whether the behavior of the spectators had prevented a fair trial and whether the jurors had been partial. The judges also ruled Conley's testimony relevant and admissible and dismissed Roan's personal expression of doubt.

At this point Frank replaced his counsel. The new attorneys did not feel bound by their predecessors' promise to Dorsey, and they pressed the argument that Frank had been denied due process by being absented from his sentencing. But the state supreme court responded that "it would be trifling with the court to… now come in and… include matters which were or ought to have been included in the motion for a new trial."

The new attorneys went on to try to get the United States Supreme Court to issue a writ of habeas corpus, on the ground that the mob had forced Frank to absent himself from the court at the time of his sentencing, and thus he was being held illegally. The Court agreed to hear arguments on that question and, after two months, rejected the plea by a vote of 7-2.

Justice Mahlon Pitney explained that errors in law, no matter how serious, could not legally be reviewed in a request for a writ of habeas corpus but only in a petition for a writ of error. And Frank's contention of having been denied due process "was waived by his failure to raise the objection in due season...." In a celebrated dissent, Justices Oliver Wendell Holmes and Charles Evans Hughes concluded, "Mob law does not become due process of law by securing the assent of a terrorized jury."

It is difficult for those not well versed in the law to follow the legal reasoning behind such procedural and constitutional questions, especially when judges are not even considering disputes in testimony or blatantly expressed prejudices. Thus many people assumed that the Court was reconfirming the certainty of Frank's guilt. Afterward his attorneys sought commutation to life imprisonment rather than a complete pardon because they concluded that after all the judicial setbacks they would have a better chance with the governor that way.

Once the case came before him, Gov. John M. Slaton moved with dispatch. He listened to oral presentations from both sides, read the records, and then visited the pencil factory to familiarize himself with the scene of the crime. Since the two sides differed in their arguments on where the murder had actually taken place—the metal-lathe room on the second floor versus the factory basement—and whether the elevator had been used, the governor paid particular attention to those parts of the building. Besides the voluminous public records, Slaton received a personal letter written by the trial judge recommending commutation, a secret communication from one of Hugh Dorsey's law partners stating that Jim Conley's attorney believed his own client was guilty, and a note from a federal prisoner indicating that he had seen Conley struggling with Mary on the day of the murder.

For twelve days Slaton wrestled with the materials. On the last day he worked well into the night, and at 2:00 A.M., on June 21, 1915, he went up to his bedroom to inform his wife. "Have you reached a decision?" she asked.

"Yes," he replied, "... it may mean my death or worse, but I have ordered the sentence commuted."

Mrs. Slaton then kissed her husband and confessed, "I would rather be the widow of a brave and honorable man than the wife of a coward."

A ten-thousand-word statement accompanied the governor's announcement. Slaton appeared thoroughly conversant with even the minutiae of the case. He saw inconsistencies in Conley's narrative and zeroed in on them. The first significant discrepancy dealt with the factory elevator. Conley had admitted defecating at the bottom of the shaft on the morning before the murder. When police and others arrived the next day, the feces remained. Not until someone moved the elevator from the second floor was the excrement mashed, causing a foul odor. Therefore, Slaton concluded, the elevator could not have been used to carry Mary Phagan's body to the basement. Furthermore, according to scientific tests, no bloodstains appeared on the lathe or on the second floor—where the prosecution had contended that the murder had taken place—or in the elevator. But Mary's mouth, nostrils, and fingernails had been full of sawdust and grime similar to that in the basement, not on the second floor.

Other details also incriminated Conley. The murder notes found near the body had been written on order pads whose numerical sequence corresponded with those stored in the basement and not at all with those in Frank's office. Another major discrepancy that Slaton noticed concerned the strand of hair found on the metal lathe. Since the state biologist had determined that it could not have come from Mary's head, testimony from Dorsey's witness that "it looked like her hair" had to be dismissed.

Although most of Marietta knew who the killers were, a coroner's jury concluded that Frank had been lynched by persons unknown.

Privately Slaton told friends that he believed Frank was innocent, and he claimed that he would have pardoned him except that he had been asked only for a commutation and he assumed the truth would come out shortly anyway, after which the very people clamoring for Frank's death would be demanding his release. Slaton's announcement of the commutation sent thousands of Atlantans to the streets, where they burned Frank and the governor in effigy; hundreds of others marched toward Slaton's mansion, where state troopers prevented them from lynching him.

A wave of anti-Semitic demonstrations followed. Many Georgians assumed that the governor's "dastardly" actions resulted from Jewish pressures upon him. Atlanta Jews feared for their lives, and many fled the city. Responding to these actions a few days later, Slaton declared: "Two thousand years ago another Governor washed his hands of a case and turned over a Jew to a mob. For two thousand years that Governor's name has been accursed. If today another Jew were lying in his grave because I had failed to do my duty I would all through life find his blood on my hands and would consider myself an assassin through cowardice."

But the mob would not be thwarted. A fellow inmate at the state prison farm cut Frank's throat. While he was recovering in the hospital infirmary, a band of twenty-five men, characterized by their peers as "sober, intelligent, of established good name and character—good American citizens," stormed the prison farm, kidnapped Frank, and drove him 175 miles through the night to Marietta, Mary Phagan's hometown, where, on the morning of August 17, 1915, they hanged him from an oak tree. Although most of the people in Marietta knew who the killers were, a coroner's jury concluded that Frank had been lynched by persons unknown. The Pittsburgh *Gazette* restated that finding: "What the coroner's jury really meant was that Frank 'came to his death by hanging at the hands of persons whom the jury wishes to remain unknown.'"

Many of Frank's friends and later defenders attributed the hanging to unbridled mob passions, but the explanation cannot suffice. "The very best people," a local judge opined at the time, had allowed the Frank case to go through all the courts, letting the judicial process take its course. Then, after every request

71

for a new trial had been turned down, the governor had outrageously stepped in. "I believe in law and order," the judge said. "I would not help lynch anybody. But I believe Frank has had his just deserts."

Obviously, much more than just a wish to carry out the court's decision motivated Frank's killers. The man symbolized all that Georgians resented. He was the Northerner in the South, the urban industrialist who had come to transform an agrarian society, a Jew whose ancestors had killed the Savior and whose co-religionists rejected the truth of Christianity. Thus, despite the fact that the state used a black man as its key witness, something that would have been unthinkable had the accused been a Southern white Christian, Atlantans could easily believe the worst about this particular defendant.

Over the years scores of people have wondered why many Georgians were loath to suspect that a black man might have committed the murder. The answer may have come from the pastor of the Baptist church that Mary Phagan's family attended. In 1942 the Reverend L. O. Bricker wrote: "My own feelings, upon the arrest of the old negro night-watchman, were to the effect that this one old negro would be poor atonement for the life of this little girl. But, when on the next day, the police arrested a Jew, and a Yankee Jew at that, all of the inborn prejudice against the Jews rose up in a feeling of satisfaction, that here would be a victim worthy to pay for the crime."

As time passed, people no longer remembered the specific facts of the case, but they told the story of Mary Phagan and Leo Frank to their children and grandchildren. As with all folktales, some details were embellished, others were dropped; however, as the first three verses of "The Ballad of Mary Phagan" unfold, no listener can have any difficulty knowing what happened:

Little Mary Phagan
She left her home one day;
She went to the pencil-factory
To see the big parade.

She left her home at eleven,
She kissed her mother good-by;

Not one time did the poor child think
That she was a-going to die.

Leo Frank he met her
With a brutish heart, we know;
He smiled and said, "Little Mary,
You won't go home no more."

People have argued the Frank case again and again, but usually without specific knowledge, falling back on hearsay to support their positions. However, in 1982 a dramatic incident put the case back in the public spotlight. Alonzo Mann, who had been a fourteen-year-old office boy in the Atlanta pencil factory in 1913, swore that he had come into the building on the day of the murder and witnessed Jim Conley carrying Mary Phagan's body toward the steps leading to the basement. The janitor had warned him, "If you ever mention this, I'll kill you." Lonnie Mann ran home and told his mother what he had seen and she advised him to "not get involved." He obeyed her but eventually began telling his tale to friends. Finally, in 1982, two enterprising reporters filed the story in the Nashville *Tennessean*.

Mann's revelations stimulated a renewed effort to achieve a posthumous pardon for Leo Frank. Newspapers editorialized on the need to clear his name, public-opinion polls showed a majority in Georgia willing to support a pardon, and the governor of the state announced in December 1983 that he believed in Frank's innocence. But three days before Christmas the Board of Pardons and Paroles denied the request. It asserted that Mann's affidavit had provided "no new evidence to the case," that it did not matter whether Conley had carried the body to the basement or taken it via the elevator, and that "there are [so] many inconsistencies" in the various accounts of what had happened that "it is impossible to decide conclusively the guilt or innocence of Leo M. Frank."

Once again a storm broke as editorials and individuals excoriated the Board of Pardons and Paroles. The *Tennessean* said that "the board turned its back on the chance to right an egregious wrong."

The *Tennessean*, and others that were so certain about what the board should have done, had the advantage of hind-

sight. While this historian believes there is no question that Frank was an innocent man, the fact is that his case was much more complex than those who have read about it afterward recognize. One should not dismiss the impact of Jim Conley's performance on the witness stand or the electrifying effects of the innuendoes and charges in the courtroom that Frank might have engaged in improper sexual activities with the young people who worked in the pencil factory. Aside from the defendant's partisans, most people who heard the evidence or read about it in the newspapers during the summer of 1913 accepted its truthfulness. No reporter who attended the proceedings daily ever wrote of Frank's innocence. Long after the trial ended, O. B. Keeler and Herbert Asbury, newspapermen who covered the case, still regarded him as guilty; Harold Ross, another writer and later the founding editor of *The New Yorker*, stated merely that the "evidence did not prove [Frank] guilty beyond that 'reasonable doubt' required by law."

Another factor is the ineptitude of Frank's counsel. They failed to expose the inaccuracies in Conley's testimony, and they blundered by asking him to discuss occasions when Frank had allegedly entertained young women. This opened the door for a great deal of titillating but irrelevant material and allowed Dorsey to bring in witnesses to corroborate Conley's accusation. The defense attorneys demonstrated their limitations once more by ignoring relevant constitutional questions in their original appeal to the Georgia Supreme Court. Thus a reinvestigation of the case in the 1950s led one observer to write that "the defense of Leo Frank was one of the most ill-conducted in the history of Georgia jurisprudence."

Still another consideration is the environment in which the trial took place. Today judicial standards have been tightened, and it is unlikely that any court proceedings would be conducted in so hostile an atmosphere as that in which Frank met his doom. But that does not necessarily outweigh the effect of the witnesses' testimony and the subsequent cross-examinations. To be sure, many of the jurors feared going against popular opinion, but perhaps they might have reached an identical judgment in a hermetically sealed chamber.

There is no reason to doubt that Alonzo Mann's affidavit is accurate. Had he ignored his mother's advice and gone to the police with his information right away, Conley would surely have been arrested, the police and district attorney would not have concentrated their efforts on finding Frank guilty, and the crime would most likely have been quickly solved. But by the time the trial began, in July 1913, Mann's testimony might hardly have even seemed important.

When reviewing the case, one need not be so one-sided as to ignore the very real gut reactions that Atlantans had to Mary Phagan's murder, the trial, and Leo Frank. Prejudice did exist in Atlanta, some people did lie at the trial, and anti-Semitism did contribute to the verdict.

There were also contradictions in the case that people could not understand. Rational persons believed Conley's tale, and there is no denying that the janitor made a tremendously good impression on the stand. A reporter listening to him wrote that "if so much as 5 per cent" of his story was true, it would suffice to convict Frank.

The struggle to exonerate Leo Frank continued, and in March 1986 the state Board of Pardons and Paroles reversed itself and granted a pardon. It had been granted, said the accompanying document, "in recognition of the state's failure to protect the person of Leo Frank and thereby preserve his opportunity of continued legal appeal of his conviction, and in recognition of the state's failure to bring his killers to justice, and as an effort to heal old wounds."

Not, that is, because Frank was innocent.

In the late 1980s a Georgia citizen, firmly convinced of Frank's guilt, vehemently underscored the point in a letter to the Marietta *Daily Journal:* "The pardon expressly does not relieve Mr. Frank of his conviction or of his guilt. Rather, it simply restored to him his civil rights, permitting him to vote and serve on juries, activities which, presumably, at this date are meaningless."

Meaningless they may be. Still, Leo Frank's unquiet spirit continues to vex the conscience of many Georgians eighty-one years after he died on an oak tree in Marietta.

Leonard Dinnerstein is a professor of history and the director of Judaic Studies at the University of Arizona. His books include The Leonard Frank Case *(available in paperback from the University of Georgia Press),* America and the Survivors of the Holocaust, *and* Antisemitism in America.

From *American Heritage*, October 1996, pp. 99–102, 105–109. © 1996 by Forbes, Inc. Reprinted by permission of *American Heritage* magazine, a division of Forbes, Inc.

The Home Front

Ronald Schaffer

By the time the United States entered World War I, the belligerent powers were approaching total warfare, pitting their entire societies against one another. American leaders believed their country must do the same; yet the obstacles to mobilizing a united American society were formidable. This essay discusses the ways by which the United States government sought to overcome those obstacles, particularly how it attempted to unify the home front and to convert the nation's economy for war. It considers the interaction between government and elements of the society it sought to mobilize, examines the effectiveness of mobilization, and looks at precedents the war created for later emergencies.

Unity was a crucial requirement for success. Yet America in 1917 was far from unified. Race riots, lynchings, and increasing segregation characterized its racial system. Decades of business consolidation and industrial violence had left the nation's middle class citizens wary both of radical labor organizations and of the economic and political power of large corporations. With millions of Americans connected by ancestry to the warring nations, ethnic conflict threatened to tear the United States apart once it joined the Allies. And ominous signs were appearing that American women might divide over the war. Women had been prominent in the prewar peace movement. The first woman elected to congress voted against entering the war, and militant women suffragists had begun to picket the White House, publicizing the gaps between government slogans about making the world safe for democracy and a political system in which millions of women could not vote.[1]

There were other threats to unity on the eve of war. Although some Americans—particularly those with ancestral ties to the Allies—were willing and perhaps even eager to fight the Central Powers, other intellectuals and religious organizations strenuously opposed intervention. Pacifism, isolationism, antimilitarism, and apathy were so widespread that in the fall of 1916, President Woodrow Wilson ran for reelection with the slogan "He Kept Us Out of War."

To develop the support needed to mobilize America, the United States government followed several approaches. It directed massive propaganda at the American people and imprisoned those who openly challenged its war policies. Yet it often used a softer method, what one of its leaders called "engines of indirection", [2] to encourage rather than compel Americans to pay for the war, conserve scarce resources, and participate in home front activities. It offered rewards to those who cooperated and withheld benefits from those who declined to go along. The result was a wartime welfare state that benefitted millions of Americans, especially those with the power, resources, and organization needed to induce the federal government to respond to their needs. In the America of 1917–1918 self-sacrifice, idealism and patriotism existed side by side with efforts to reap private gain from the war, with government management of interest groups, and with efforts by those groups to manipulate the government that sought to control them.

Foremost among the wartime propaganda agencies was the Committee on Public Information (CPI), headed by the journalist and social reformer George Creel. This committee sought to meld all Americans into what its director called "one white-hot mass … with fraternity, devotion, and deathless determination" to support an Allied victory. It deluged the country with press releases and pamphlets, newspaper and magazine advertisements, and organized scores of pageants and parades. The CPI had educators explain to students the official reasons for fighting, stimulate their patriotism, and enhance their admiration for American and Allied armed forces. It told immigrants in their own languages why they owed it to America to assist it against its enemies. To those who could not read, the committee communicated with billboards, posters, motion pictures, and an army of patriotic speakers.

Although Creel's committee sometimes allowed its audience to know that the government was addressing them, it frequently followed an indirect or covert approach. It set up front organizations, such as the American Alliance for Labor and Democracy, led by conservative labor union leader Samuel Gompers, that opposed radicalism and pacifism among workers. Its own name was a euphemism, suggesting that it conveyed, not propaganda, but simply information. The head of the committee's film division observed that one of the CPI's objectives was to spread "telling propaganda which at the same time would not be obvious propaganda, but will have the effect we desire to create."

Among the CPI's great variety of messages, certain themes appeared repeatedly. One was the notion that the enemies were vicious, subhuman monsters who had committed unspeakable atrocities and were preparing to bring horror and devastation to America. Thus one wartime poster showed lower Manhattan in flames, a decapitated Statue of Liberty, and enemy warplanes hovering overhead. Another depicted Germany as a spike-helmeted slobbering ape-like creature standing on the American shore. A second theme was the crusade motif, that America was engaged in a holy war to avenge those atrocities, safe-guard democracy and assure lasting peace. Third, there was the theme that Americans of all classes, national origins, occupations, and genders must stand together to support that crusade.

Like other warring nations, the United States used forceful methods, along with exhortation, to control the way its people felt. Although President Wilson expressed concern that war would deeply curtail American freedoms, his administration rarely hesitated to crack down on dissenters. With the authority of legislation, such as the Espionage Act of 1917 and the Sedition Act of 1918, it denied the mails to publications it believed would embarrass or hamper it in the prosecution of the war. It jailed members of a radical labor organization, the Industrial Workers of the World, that threatened to disrupt production of war materials. It imprisoned a former Socialist candidate for president, Eugene V. Debs, and hundreds of other persons for statements that government prosecutors claimed would interfere with the government's war programs. At times, the, administration also stifled dissent subtly and indirectly, as when the CPI urged editors to censor themselves or face penalties, without specifying what would cause the government to silence their publications.

In its efforts to clamp down on pacifists, radicals and persons too friendly to the enemy, the federal government allied itself with state and private groups. It sponsored a quarter million volunteer members of the American Protective League, who sought to root out opponents of war. State governments authorized councils of defense that not only assisted mobilization in positive ways but also attacked persons the councils considered pro-German, antiwar, or too favorable toward social reform. Other groups, some of them nameless organizations, or just mobs, joined in the repression of alleged internal enemies.

While many Americans felt intense exhilaration and national pride during this war, a large number experienced it as a time of terror. People spied on one another; intimidated those who seemed slow to purchase government war bonds or to join the military; forced suspected pro-Germans to kiss the American flag or painted them yellow; threatened; tortured; and, in two cases, murdered those who seemed to oppose the war. Citizens and governments attacked the country's German American subculture, suppressed German music, threatened German American religious sects, forbade the speaking and teaching of the German language, and sought to remove words of German origin from American speech, turning "frankfurters" into "liberty sausages" and "dachshunds" into "liberty dogs".

Some of these actions were an outgrowth of the patriotism that led Americans to volunteer spontaneously for military service, to enter war industries, to roll bandages or become Red Cross nurses, to join local home defense leagues, and to buy government bonds. Some were responses to government propaganda that encouraged suspicion of strangers or reactions to fear of sabotage at home or to the loss or potential loss of loved ones overseas. Repressive activities on the home front sometimes grew from long-standing ethnic conflicts, were ways of settling old scores, or represented efforts to secure political power under the guise of patriotism or to use the war to secure economic advantages. Much of the war hysteria grew from a community of interest between the United States Government and those who used the war for their own purposes. This interplay of public and private interests similarly characterized the mobilization of the economy.

The experience of other belligerents and early breakdowns in American economic systems showed that conversion for total war would be difficult and made clear that there had to be some kind of centralized control of economic mobilization. But who would do it? The armed forces lacked the capacity; yet to give them enough power to control the economy would be to emulate Germany. People called it "Prussianization." Large industrial and financial corporations might have the skills and organization to run a war economy, but many citizens thought they had too much power to begin with. Although some government regulatory agencies had developed before the war, there was as yet no large civil service to guide mobilization, and the notion of creating a war bureaucracy troubled businessmen and other Americans who believed in limited government.

The solution, which responded both to fears of excessive government regulation and of expanded corporate influence, was an improvised administrative apparatus, staffed largely by volunteer "dollar-a-year" persons on leave from their companies, designed to self-destruct once the war ended. When the national transportation system collapsed in the winter of 1917–1918 the U.S. government created a Railroad Administration to coordinate and manage the important lines. Actual running of the railroad system was assigned to former private railroad executives under temporary government direction. Volunteer food industry executives ran the Food Administration. Staffed with thousands of American women, the FA promoted food production and conservation and saw that food supplies were sent where the government considered them most needed. Such people were unlikely to perpetuate a government food bureaucracy.

The leading economic mobilization agency was the War Industries Board (WIB), which arranged for American industries to supply Allied and American armed forces and civilians with industrial products. Like most other economic mobilization agencies, it was dominated by volunteers from American businesses. Its powers evolved gradually. The Wilson administration, reflecting prewar public distrust of the power of big business, continued to keep those powers in check, leaving the board's legal authority vague and permitting the War Department to retain substantial control over military procurement.

The WIB typified the operations of the wartime welfare state. It often used an indirect approach, inducing companies to produce voluntarily what the government wanted them to provide. Together with cooperating businesses that supplied materials needed for production and with government agencies that regulated labor supplies, fuel and transportation, it developed a priority system, the essential mechanism for regulating wartime businesses. If a company chose to produce essential items it received high priorities for what it needed. If it decided to make items deemed nonessential, its priorities dropped to the bottom of the list.

Many businessmen contributed to the war with pride and patriotism. Also, they were offered tangible incentives for converting to war work, such as the priorities that enabled them to keep their companies operating. The fact that the people who negotiated with them for the government were executives from their own industries rather than uninformed bureaucrats was bound to reassure them. And finally they had the incentive of substantial profit, particularly for companies that sold something the government badly needed. In the steel industry, for instance, prices were set high enough for inefficient producers to make money. For efficient producers, the returns were awe inspiring. An excess profits tax was supposed to recapture some of these returns but ways were found to limit its effects.

For certain business leaders the war government provided special incentives. Executives of leading companies were allowed to set priorities for their own industries because only they knew enough about those industries to assess priority requests. These corporate leaders really ran much of industrial mobilization in the government's name. For one group of businessmen the wartime system of business self-regulation, cooperation, and government sanctioned profitability offered a model for the future. These men wanted to replace competitive capitalism with a permanent welfare state for business.

The war brought benefits to other groups that served America at home. Emerging professions gained recognition for wartime activities—psychiatrists, for example, for treating victims of battle stress, and psychologists for testing the mental capacity of recruits. Intellectuals, in a country that rarely paid attention to them and often scorned them, found opportunities to serve their nation by writing propaganda or lecturing on the war. Wheat farmers benefitted from government price supports. Conservative, prowar labor unions won government endorsement for collective bargaining and improved wages, hours, and working conditions by arguing that these benefits would increase productivity at a time when labor shortages hindered mobilization. Housing reformers developed model towns for workers near shipyards and war factories.

A number of the wartime programs helped advance reforms of special interest to women. Suffragists drew a variety of arguments from the war for granting women the right to vote—for example, women should be rewarded for their patriotic service on the home front, and that in a "war to make the world safe for democracy," it was absurd to deny women the vote. Advocates of temperance, including many women, successfully argued against producing alcoholic beverages that took grain supplies needed to make bread for soldiers and civilians. A government sponsored program to close brothels near army camps and provide troops with healthy sports and clean entertainment as a substitute for sex, also appealed to women in the vice reform movement.

War also brought economic benefits to women and their families. Labor shortages enabled more than one million women to find work in arms factories and in other occupations previously closed to them. It created what amounted to a system of "mothers pensions". To sustain families whose male wage earners were in uniform and to free the troops from some anxiety over their families' financial conditions, the federal government arranged for service personnel to buy cheap life and disability insurance. It withheld money from the pay of enlisted men, sending it to their dependents along with direct government allowances for wives and children. It also aided war widows and orphans.

Yet not all groups were strong enough and influential enough to secure rewards from the war welfare state. Some African American leaders, such as the scholar and editor W. E. B. Du Bois, encouraged blacks to support the war on the ground that fighting for democracy abroad would advance racial equality at home. African Americans did make certain wartime gains, but in ways limited by the existing color line. For instance, they were allowed to fight for their country, but were segregated and shunted mainly into noncombatant roles requiring physical labor. By threatening that color line, the war may have made racial conflict even more intense. The prospect of trained and armed black soldiers returning home after living in France, a less racist society, troubled many white Americans. The allotments and allowances the federal government sent to female dependents of black troops disturbed the prewar racial equilibrium by making those women less willing to accept low-wage jobs[3]. Wartime demand for labor drew African Americans, who were already migrating from the rural South, to the cities and to the North where they competed for jobs and living space with white workers. That competition helped set off an explosion of race riots during and just after the war. Such events left Du Bois and other blacks deeply dissatisfied by the "war to make the world safe for democracy."

How well did the American home front achieve the American government's objectives? If the measure is unity of thought and behavior, the answer is well enough. There was general support for the war by the time of the Armistice, although continuing resistance to the draft suggests that some Americans had not been welded into "one white-hot mass" in support of victory[4]. If the criterion is production and delivery of war materials, the results were also mixed. By 1918, more than one-fifth of the nation's Gross National Product reflected war spending[5]. Yet the GNP as a whole rose by less than four percent from 1916 through 1918. Although the country spent some seven billion dollars for ordnance, American forces in Europe commonly used French artillery and projectiles. Aircraft manufacturers consumed millions of dollars, but produced only sixteen thousand planes during 1917–1918, far fewer than government projections. As David Lloyd George, the British prime minister noted, "one of the inexplicable paradoxes of history" was that "the greatest machine-producing nation on earth failed to turn out the mechanism of war after 18 months of sweating and toiling and hustling...." Still, it might be argued that the fighting ended too soon for the United States to reach full war production.

The most important contribution America made to the defeat of its enemies was its armed forces, or more exactly, the notion of what those armed forces could do if the war continued. To German leaders, the prospect that a huge American army would soon join the doughboys already fighting alongside the Allies, made an early armistice seem prudent. By helping to motivate those troops to volunteer or accept conscription, by supporting them morally once they were in uniform, by helping to pay for them and to arm, clothe, feed and equip them, the home front did much to make that armistice possible.

The World War I home front provided important precedents for future crises. To fight the Great Depression, the Hoover and Roosevelt administrations employed wartime ideas, like business self-regulation, publicity campaigns like those used in wartime, and restyled wartime agencies, such as the National Recovery Administration. Finally, the Wilson administration's efforts to create unity on the home front left a problematic legacy for civil liberties in future wars, raising the question of whether the United States Government could be strong enough to defend the nation without destroying American freedoms.

Ronald Schaffer is an emeritus professor of history at California State University, Northridge, where he taught from 1965 through 1999. He previously taught at Columbia University and Indiana University. His publications include America in the Great War: The Rise of the War Welfare State *(1991);* Wings of Judgment: American Bombing in World War II *(1989); and* The United States in World War I: A Selected Bibliography *(1978).*

Notes

1. This article is based chiefly on Ronald Schaffer, *America in the Great War: The Rise of the War Welfare State* (New York: Oxford University Press, 1991). For other accounts of the home front in World War I see David M. Kennedy, *Over Here: The First World War and American Society* (New York: Oxford University Press, 1980), and Robert H. Zieger, *America's Great War: World War I and the American Experience* (Lanham, MD: Rowman & Littlefield Publishers, Inc., 2000).

2. Herbert Hoover quoted in George H. Nash, *The Life of Herbert Hoover*, vol. 3, *Master of Emergencies, 1917–1918* (New York: W.W. Norton & Company), 15.

3. For the effects of federal payments to dependents of black troops see K. Walter Hickel, "War, Region, and Social Welfare: Federal Aid to Servicemen's Dependents in the South, 1917–1921," *Journal of American History* 87 (March 2001): 1362–91.

4. Jeanette Keith, "The Politics of Southern Draft Resistance, 1917–1918: Class, Race and Conscription in the Rural South," *Journal of American History* 87 (March 2001): 1335–61.

5. For the war component of GNP, see Paul A. C. Koistinen, *Mobilizing for Modem War: The Political Economy of American Warfare, 1865–1919* (Lawrence, KS: University Press of Kansas, 1997), 265.

From *OAH Magazine of History*, October 2002, pages 20-24. Copyright © 2002 by Organization of American Historians. Reprinted with permission.

Evolution on Trial

In 1925 science teacher John Scopes agreed to challenge Tennessee's new anti-evolution law in court. The resulting legal battle pitted two of the country's premier orators against each other and treated newspaper readers worldwide to what Baltimore Sun columnist H.L. Mencken called a "genuinely fabulous" show.

by J. Kingston Pierce

Travelers wandering through Dayton, Tennessee, in mid-July 1925 might have been excused for thinking that the tiny hill town was holding a carnival or perhaps a religious revival. The street leading to the local courthouse was busy with vendors peddling sandwiches, watermelon, calico, and books on biology. Evangelists had erected an open-air tabernacle, and nearby buildings were covered with posters exhorting people to "read your Bible" and avoid eternal damnation.

If there was a consistent theme to the garish exhibits and most of the gossip in Dayton it was, of all things, *monkeys*. Monkey jokes were faddish. Monkey toys and souvenirs were ubiquitous. A soda fountain advertised something called a "monkey fizz," and the town's butcher shop featured a sign reading, "We handle all kinds of meat except monkey."

As comical as this scene sounds, its background was anything but amusing. Sixty-six years after Charles Darwin published his controversial *Origin of Species*, the debate he'd engendered over humankind's evolution from primates had suddenly reached a fever pitch in this hamlet on the Tennessee River. Efforts to enforce a new state statute against the teaching of evolution in public schools had precipitated the arrest of Dayton educator John T. Scopes. His subsequent prosecution drew international press attention as well as the involvement of the American Civil Liberties Union (ACLU). It also attracted two headliners of that era--Chicago criminal attorney Clarence Darrow and former presidential candidate William Jennings Bryan—to act as opposing counsel.

Bryan characterized the coming courtroom battle as a "duel to the death"—one that would pit religious fundamentalists against others who trusted in scientific conclusions, and would finally determine the right of citizens to dictate the curricula of the schools their tax dollars supported. The case rapidly took on a farcical edge, however, as attorneys shouted at each other and outsiders strove to capitalize on the extraordinary publicity surrounding this litigation. (At one point, for instance, a black man with a cone-shaped head who worked New York's Coney Island sideshows as Zip, the "humanoid ape," was offered to the defense as the "missing link" necessary to prove Darwin's scientific claims.) The "Scopes Monkey Trial," as history would come to know it, also included a personal dimension, becoming a hard-fought contest not just between rival ideas, but between Bryan and Darrow, former allies whose political differences had turned them into fierce adversaries.

Crusades to purge Darwinism from American public education began as early as 1917 and were most successful in the South, where Fundamentalists controlled the big Protestant denominations. In 1923, the Oklahoma Legislature passed a bill banning the use of all school texts that included evolutionist instruction. Later that same year, the Florida Legislature approved a joint resolution declaring it "improper and subversive for any teacher in a public school to teach Atheism or Agnosticism, or to teach as true, Darwinism, or any other hypothesis that links man in blood relationship to any other form of life."

To Fundamentalists, for whom literal interpretation of the Bible was central to their faith, there was no room for compromise between the story of God's unilateral creation of man and Darwin's eons-long development of the species. Moreover, these critics deemed evolutionist theories a threat not only to the belief in God but to the very structure of a Christian society. "To hell with science if it is going to damn souls," was how one Fundamentalist framed the debate.

John Washington Butler couldn't have agreed more. In January 1925, this second-term member of the Tennessee House of Representatives introduced a bill that would make it unlawful for teachers working in schools financed wholly or in part by the state to "teach any theory that denies the story of the divine creation of man as taught in the Bible." Violation of the statute would constitute a misdemeanor punishable by a fine of not less than $100 or more than $500 for each offense.

Butler's bill flummoxed government observers but delighted its predominately Baptist backers, and it sailed through the Tennessee House on a lopsided 71 to 5 vote. It went on to the state Senate, where objections were more numerous, and where one member tried to kill the legislation by proposing an amendment to also "prohibit the teaching that the earth is round." Yet senators ultimately sanctioned the measure 24 to 6. As the story goes, many Tennessee lawmakers thought they were safe in voting for this "absurd" bill because Governor Austin Peay, a well-recognized progressive, was bound to veto it. However, Peay—in a prickly political trade-off that won him the support of rural representatives he needed in order to pass educational and infrastructural reforms—signed the Butler Act into law. As he did so, though, he noted that he had no intention of enforcing it. "Probably," the governor said in a special message to his Legislature, "the law will never be applied."

Peay's prediction might have come true, had not the ACLU chosen to make the statute a *cause célèbre*. Worried that other states would follow Tennessee's lead, the ACLU agreed in late April 1925 to guarantee legal and financial assistance to any teacher who would test the law.

John Scopes wasn't the obvious candidate. A gawky, 24-year-old Illinois native, he was still new to his job as a general science teacher and football coach at Rhea County Central High School. Yet his views on evolution were unequivocal. "I don't see how a teacher can teach biology without teaching evolution," Scopes insisted, adding that the state-approved science textbook included lessons in evolution. And he was a vocal supporter of academic freedom and freedom of thought. Yet Scopes was reluctant to participate in the ACLU's efforts until talked into it by Dayton neighbors who hoped that a prominent local trial would stimulate prosperity in their sleepy southeastern Tennessee town.

On May 7, Scopes was officially arrested for violating Tennessee's anti-evolution statute. Less than a week later, William Jennings Bryan accepted an invitation from the World's Christian Fundamentals Association to assist in Scopes' prosecution.

No one who knew the 65-year-old Bryan well should have been surprised by his involvement in the case. Bryan had been trained in the law before being elected as a congressman from Nebraska, and he made three spirited but unsuccessful runs at the presidency on the Democratic ticket. He had served as secretary of state during President Woodrow Wilson's first term but had spent the last decade writing and lecturing more often about theology than politics. With the same silver tongue he'd once used to excoriate Republican office seekers and decry U.S. involvement in World War I, Bryan had since promoted religious ethics over man's exaltation of science. "It is better

to trust in the Rock of Ages than to know the ages of the rocks," Bryan pronounced; "It is better for one to know that he is close to the Heavenly Father than to know how far the stars in the heavens are apart." Ever the rural populist— "the Great Commoner"—Bryan saw religion as the crucial backbone of agrarian America, and he reserved special enmity for accommodationists who struggled to reconcile Christianity and evolution. Such modernism, he wrote, "permits one to believe in a God, but puts the creative act so far away that reverence for the Creator is likely to be lost."

Bryan's role elevated the Scopes trial from a backwoods event into a national story. Clarence Darrow's agreement to act in the teacher's defense guaranteed the story would be sensational. A courtroom firebrand and a political and social reformer, the 68-year-old Darrow was still riding high from his success of the year before, when his eloquent insanity defense of Chicago teenagers Nathan Leopold and Richard Loeb, who had kidnapped and murdered a younger neighbor, had won them life imprisonment instead of the electric chair. The ACLU would have preferred a less controversial and more religiously conservative counsel than Darrow, an agnostic who characterized Christianity as a "slave religion" that encouraged complacency and acquiescence toward injustices. According to biographer Kevin Tierney, the Chicago attorney "believed that religion was a sanctifier of bigotry, of narrowness, of ignorance and the status quo." The ACLU feared that with Darrow taking part, the case would, to quote Scopes, "become a carnival and any possible dignity in the fight for liberties would be lost." In the end, Darrow took part in the Dayton trial only after offering his services free of charge—"for the first, the last, and the only time in my life," the attorney later remarked.

After spending the previous Friday impaneling a jury (most members of which turned out to be churchgoing farmers), all parties gathered for the start of the real legal drama on Monday, July 13, 1925. Approximately 600 spectators—including newspaper and radio reporters, along with a substantial percentage of Dayton's 1,700 residents—elbowed their way into the Eighteenth Tennessee Circuit Court. Presiding was Judge John T. Raulston, who liked to call himself "jest a reg'lar mountin'er jedge." The crowded courtroom made the week's stifling heat even more unbearable. Advocates on both sides of the case quickly resorted to shirtsleeves. The prosecution included Bryan, Circuit Attorney General Arthur Thomas Stewart, and Bryan's son, William Jennings Bryan, Jr., a Los Angeles lawyer. For the defense were Darrow, New York lawyer and co-counsel Dudley Field Malone, ACLU attorney Arthur Garfield Hays, and Scopes' local lawyer, John Randolph Neal.

The prosecution's strategy was straightforward. It wasn't interested in debating the value or wisdom of the Butler Law, only in proving that John Scopes had broken it. "While I am perfectly willing to go into the question of evolution," Bryan had told an acquaintance, "I am not sure that it is involved. The right of the people speaking through the legislature, to control the schools which they create and support is the real issue as I see it." With this direction in mind, Bryan and his fellow attorneys took two days to call four witnesses. All of them confirmed that Scopes had lectured his biology classes on evolution, with two students adding that these lessons hadn't seemed to hurt them. The prosecution then rested its case.

Scopes' defense was more problematic. Once a plea of innocence had been lodged, Darrow moved to quash the indictment against his client by arguing that the Butler Law was a "foolish, mischievous, and wicked act … as brazen and bold an attempt to destroy liberty as ever was seen in the Middle Ages." Neal went on to point out how the Tennessee constitution held that "no preference shall be given, by law, to any religious establishment or mode of worship." Since the anti-evolution law gave preference to the Bible over other religious books, he concluded, it was thus unconstitutional. Raulston rejected these challenges.

From the outset, defense attorneys focused their arguments on issues related to religion and the influences of a fundamentalist morality. Early in the proceedings, Darrow objected to the fact that Judge Raulston's court opened, as was customary, with a prayer, saying that it could prejudice the jury against his client. The judge overruled Darrow's objection. Later the defense examined the first of what were to be 12 expert witnesses—scientists and clergymen both—to show that the Butler Law was unreasonable and represented an improper exercise of Tennessee's authority over education. When the state took exception, however, Raulston declared such testimony inadmissible (though he allowed affidavits to be entered into the record for appeal purposes).

With the defense's entire case resting on those 12 experts, veteran courtroom watchers figured that this decision effectively ended the trial. "All that remains of the great case of the State of Tennessee against the infidel Scopes is the formal business of bumping off the defendant … " harrumphed journalist H.L. Mencken after the sixth day of litigation. "[T]he main battle is over, with Genesis completely triumphant." So sure were they of a swift summation that Mencken and others in the press corps simply packed their bags and left town. Yet Darrow had a surprise up his sleeve. When the court reconvened on Monday, July 20, the ACLU's Arthur Hays rose to summon one more witness—William Jennings Bryan. "Hell is going to pop now," attorney Malone whispered to John Scopes.

Calling Bryan was a highly unusual move, but an extremely popular one. Throughout the trial, the politician-cum-preacher had been the toast of Dayton. Admirers greeted Bryan wherever he went and sat through long, humid hours in court just for the opportunity to hear him speak. He'd generally been silent, listening calmly, cooling himself with a fan that he'd received from a local funeral home, and saving his voice for an hour-and-a-half-long closing argument that he hoped would be "the mountain peak of my life's effort." But Bryan didn't put up a fight when asked to testify. In fact, he agreed with some enthusiasm, convinced—as he always had been—of his righteous cause.

Judge Raulston, concerned that the crowd massing to watch this clash of legal titans would prove injurious to the courthouse, ordered that the trial reconvene on the adjacent lawn. There, while slouched back in his chair and pulling now and then on his signature suspenders, Darrow examined Bryan for almost two hours, all but ignoring the specific case against Scopes while he did his best to demonstrate that Fundamentalism—and Bryan, as its representative—were both open to ridicule.

Darrow wanted to know if Bryan really believed, as the Bible asserted, that a whale had swallowed Jonah. Did he believe that Adam and Eve were the first humans on the planet? That all languages dated back to the Tower of Babel? "I accept the Bible absolutely," Bryan stated. As Darrow continued his verbal assault, however, it became clear that Bryan's acceptance of the Bible was not as literal as his followers believed. "[S]ome of the Bible is given illustratively," he observed at one point. "For instance: 'Ye are the salt of the earth.' I would not insist that man was actually salt, or that he had flesh of salt, but it is used in the sense of salt as saving God's people." Similarly, when discussing the creation, Bryan conceded that the six days described in the Bible were probably not literal days but periods of time lasting many years.

With this examination dragging on, the two men's tempers became frayed, and humorous banter gave way to insults and fists shaken in anger. Fundamentalists in the audience listened with increasing discomfort as their champion questioned Biblical "truths," and Bryan slowly came to realize that he had stepped into a trap. The sort of faith he represented could not adequately be presented or justly parsed in a court of law. His only recourse was to impugn Darrow's motives for quizzing him, as he sought to do in this exchange:

BRYAN: Your Honor, I think I can shorten this testimony. The only purpose Mr. Darrow has is to slur at the Bible, but I will answer his questions … and I have no objection in the world. I want the world to know that this man, who does not believe in God, is trying to use a court in Tennessee—

DARROW: I object to that.

BRYAN: —to slur at it, and, while it will require time I am willing to take it.

DARROW: I object to your statement. I am examining you on your fool ideas that no intelligent Christian on earth believes.

It was a bleak moment in what had been Bryan's brilliant career. He hoped to regain control of events and the trust of his followers the next day by putting Darrow on the stand. But Attorney General Stewart, who'd opposed Bryan's cross-examination, blocked him and instead convinced the judge to expunge Bryan's testimony from the record.

Before the jury was called to the courtroom the following day, Darrow addressed Judge Raulston. "I think to save time," he declared, "we will ask the court to bring in the jury and instruct the jury to find the defendant guilty." This final ploy by Darrow would ensure that the defense could appeal the case to a higher court that might overturn the Butler Law. The defense also waived its right to a final address, which, under Tennessee law, deprived the prosecution of a closing statement. Bryan would not get an opportunity to make his last grandiloquent speech.

The jury conferred for only nine minutes before returning a verdict of guilty. Yet Bryan's public embarrassment in Dayton would become legend—one that the prosecutor could never overcome, for he died in his sleep five days after the trial ended.

Following the trial, the school board offered to renew Scopes' contract for another year providing he complied with the anti-evolution law. But a group of scientists arranged a scholarship so he could attend graduate school, and Scopes began his studies at the University of Chicago in September. Mencken's *Baltimore Sun* agreed to pay the $100 fine Judge Raulston levied against Scopes. On appeal, the Tennessee Supreme Court ruled that the jury, rather than the judge, should have determined Scopes' fine, but it upheld the Butler Law's constitutionality. Darrow had hoped to take the matter all the way to the U.S. Supreme Court. Any chance of that, though, was foreclosed when Tennessee's chief justice nullified Scopes' indictment and threw what he called "this bizarre case" out of the courts.

Not until April 1967—42 years after the Butler Law was passed, and 12 years after *Inherit the Wind*, a play based on the Scopes Monkey Trial, became a Broadway hit—did the Tennessee Legislature repeal the anti-evolution law.

Since then, a series of court decisions has barred creationists' efforts to have their beliefs taught in public schools. Yet 75 years after the Scopes trial, debate over evolution still continues to simmer as states and education boards struggle with the subject that pits science against religion.

From *American History*, Vol. 25, No. 3, August 2000, pages 26-34. Copyright © 2000 Primedia Consumer Media and Magazines Inc. All rights reserved. Reprinted with permission.

RACE CLEANSING
IN AMERICA

A nationwide gene-purity movement promoted methods that eventually were adopted by the Third Reich and everyone from John D. Rockfeller to W.E.B. Du Bois supported it.

by Peter Quinn

Carrie Buck was in her third year at the State Colony for Epileptics and Feeble-Minded in Lynchburg, Virginia, when the U.S. Supreme Court affirmed the state's right to sterilize her. Seventeen at the time she had been institutionalized, the child of a feeble-minded mother and the mother to an illegitimate daughter of her own, Buck had refused to submit to sterilization, and the case had finally made its way to the nation's highest court. Writing for a lopsided eight-to-one majority (which included Justices Louis Brandeis and Harlan Fiske Stone as well as Chief Justice William Howard Taft), Justice Oliver Wendell Holmes left no doubt about either the overall legality of the procedure or its appropriateness for Miss Buck.

"It is better for all the world," Justice Holmes asserted in *Buck v. Bell*, "if instead of waiting to execute degenerate offspring for crime, or to let them starve for their imbecility, society can prevent those who are manifestly unfit from continuing their kind. The principle that sustains compulsory vaccination is broad enough to cover cutting the Fallopian tubes." In the case of Carrie Buck, her mother, and her daughter, the requirement of sterilization was glaringly self-apparent. "Three generations of imbeciles," Holmes concluded, "are enough."

None of the justices who decided Buck's fate ever saw or met her. They relied in part on the expert opinion of Dr. Harry Hamilton Laughlin to help them make up their minds. Though Laughlin had never met her either, a report had been sent to him at the Eugenics Record Office, in Cold Spring Harbor, New York. After reviewing the documentation, including a score on the Stanford-Binet test that purportedly showed Buck had the intellectual capacities of a nine-year-old, Laughlin concluded that she was part of the "shiftless, ignorant and worthless class of anti-social whites of the South" whose promiscuity offered "a typical picture of the low-grade moron."

Laughlin passed over the possibility that Buck's supposed imbecility might be the sullen withdrawal of an abused, frightened girl with little formal education, who had been given away by her mother at the age of four. He almost certainly had no knowledge that she had been raped and impregnated by a friend of her foster parents and sent away to have her baby in the confines of an institution so there would be no public scandal. For Laughlin, the notion that Buck's "feeble-mindedness" could be anything but hereditary was "exceptionally remote."

Buck had been made a test case of Virginia's compulsory sterilization law, which was in good measure based on a "model" statute Laughlin himself had drafted, and he believed that if the Supreme Court upheld Buck's sterilization, it would lead to the widespread passage of similar legislation in other states. Once this happened, the eugenics movement would have a potent weapon against those who, in his own words, "through inherent defects and weakness are an economic and moral burden ... and a constant source of danger to the national and racial life."

Rendered in May 1927, *Buck v. Bell*'s judicial endorsement of compulsory sterilization proved the landmark victory many eugenicists had sought. Several states acted quickly to pass new or revised sterilization laws. By 1932, 28 states had such legislation in place. The annual average of forced sterilizations increased tenfold, from 230 to almost 2,300, and one year reached nearly 4,000. By the 1970s, when compulsory sterilization had largely ceased, more than 60,000 Americans had been subjected to the procedure and eugenics had had a long life in America as a pervasive public force.

Eugenics—the theory as well as the word (which means "wellborn")—originated with Francis Galton, a cousin of Charles Darwin. Inspired by Darwin's theory of natural selection, Galton's study of the family backgrounds of prominent members of British society led him to the conclusion that achievement and heredity were clearly linked. He declared in his 1869 book *Hereditary Genius: An Inquiry Into Its Laws and Consequences*: "It is in the most unqualified manner that I object to pretensions of natural equality." A wise and enlightened state, in Galton's view, would encourage "the more suitable races or strains of blood" to propagate and increase their numbers before they were overwhelmed by the prolific mating habits of the pauper classes.

Galton's beliefs were mirrored in the work of Cesare Lombroso, an Italian physician who warned of the "atavistic being who reproduces in his person the ferocious instincts of primitive humanity and the inferior animals." (Robert Louis Stevenson made Lombroso's theory the basis of his novel *Dr. Jekyll and Mr. Hyde*.) Lombroso wrote: "There exists, it is true, a group of criminals, born for evil, against whom all social cures break as against a rock—a fact which compels us to eliminate them completely, even by death."

In 1874 Richard Dugdale, a wealthy English expatriate social reformer, made a tour of upstate New York jails. Acquainted with Lombroso's notion of hereditary criminality, he focused in particular on a jail in which six inmates were related and found that they shared a family tree perennially abloom with social deviates. He called them the "Jukes," and gave the pseudonym to his book.

Dugdale insisted that human behavior was influenced by several factors, environment among them, but it was the portrait of a self-perpetuating clan of reprobates that the public focused on and embraced. He said he found among the 700 Juke descendants 181 prostitutes ("harlotry may become a hereditary characteristic," he speculated), 42 beggars, 70 felons, and 7 murderers. The Jukes became a staple of eugenic literature, a spur to similar case studies, and a symbol of all those whose poverty and aberrancy were seen as expressions of the ineluctable dictates of biology. A decade after *The Jukes* appeared, the eminent German biologist August Weismann added to the notion of eugenic predestination his theory of a hereditary "germ plasm," an embedded legacy that dictated individual physical, mental, and moral traits and was the collective basis of rigidly distinct race differences.

By the beginning of the twentieth century, several forces had joined together to give the eugenics movement new power and prominence, foremost among them the growing concern over the quality and quantity of the country's newest immigrants. By the 1890s a large—and, to many old-stock Americans, alarming—wave of foreigners was arriving. Between 1898 and 1907, annual immigration more than quintupled, from 225,000 to 1,300,000, and its primary source was no longer Northern Europe but Italians, Slavs, and Jews from southern and eastern Europe.

Along with the alarm over hordes of foreign defectives swarming into America was a growing perception of a fecund stratum of feeble-minded whose numbers, if left unchecked, would fatally weaken the germ plasm of the country's Anglo-Saxon majority. These feeble-minded were often said to have formidable procreative power: "weak minds in strong, oversexed bodies."

It wasn't long before the presumptions of eugenics about the unfit and the growing threat they posed began to find their way into law. With the enthusiastic endorsement of President Theodore Roosevelt, a true believer in the threat posed by "weaker stocks," Congress voted in 1903 to bar the entry of persons with any history of epilepsy or insanity. Four years later, the restriction was expanded to include imbeciles, the feeble-minded, and those with tuberculosis. Connecticut became the first of several states to forbid marriage by those "epileptic, imbecilic or feeble-minded," but such laws proved hard to enforce. A far more feasible method of controlling reproduction by those deemed unfit was the development of surgical sterilization.

In 1897 A. J. Ochsner, chief surgeon at St. Mary's Hospital and Augustana Hospital in Chicago, published a paper entitled "Surgical Treatment of Habitual Criminals" that would have widespread impact. He described performing vasectomies and wrote that with the physical elimination of "all habitual criminals from the possibility of having children," crime would decrease significantly. A similar treatment "could reasonably be suggested for chronic inebriates, imbeciles, perverts and paupers."

Other doctors took up the cause of compulsory sterilization. In 1907 Indiana became the first state to authorize its use on criminals, idiots, rapists, and imbeciles housed in state-run institutions and judged by a medical panel to be "unimprovable." In a few years, 15 states had followed suit. Yet despite this legislative success, implementation was blocked in some states by gubernatorial veto and in others by the state courts. Only in California, where fear of "race-suicide" was fueled by anxieties over Asian immigration, did legislation result in a significant program of eugenic sterilization.

"WE HAVE BEEN INVADED," WROTE DR. HAISELDEN, "OUR STREETS ARE INFESTED WITH AN ARMY OF THE UNFIT."

Beyond sterilization, another Chicago surgeon, Harry Haiselden, provoked a storm of controversy in 1915 by actively publicizing his practice of killing defective newborns by leaving them untreated. He even produced the first pro-eugenics propaganda film, *The Black Stork*, a silent movie that remained in circulation for the next 30 years. In his campaign for eugenics, Dr. Haiselden left no doubt that the foremost danger lay in what he termed "lives of no value." He told the mother of a baby he let die that had it lived, it would have been "an imbecile and possibly criminal." He drew an equally bleak picture of American society at large. "We have been invaded," he wrote. "Our streets are infested with an Army of the Unfit—a dangerous, vicious army of death and dread...."

Shrill as this sounded, Haiselden's was no voice in the wilderness. HALF WITS PERIL MANY proclaimed a front-page headline of Hearst's Chicago *American* in November 1915. Look around, Haiselden admonished at the end of his autobiography, at the "horrid semi-humans drag themselves along all of our streets" and then ask, "What are you going to do about it?"

The American eugenics movement was diffuse and decentralized, encompassing a wide variety of interests. At a popular level, social hygienists and health enthusiasts emphasized staying physically fit and finding an equally fit marriage partner. The "beautiful baby" contests held at state fairs and amusement parks were one manifestation of the interest in "good breeding." Articles on mate selection and the science of the "wellborn child" frequently ran in newspapers and magazines. At a more elite level, the hard-core disciples of Galton's beliefs saw the need for a forceful and focused agenda of legislative action. The founding of the Eugenics Record Office (ERO) in 1910 provided the adherents of that agenda with a coordination and direction previously lacking.

Charles Davenport, a Harvard-trained biologist and the founder of the ERO, first obtained funding from the Carnegie Institute in 1904 to establish a Station for Experimental Evolution at Cold Spring Harbor, New York. Davenport was convinced by Mendel's laws of heredity that behavior and moral traits were passed on in the same way as eye color, and he published a book-length study in 1919 titled *Naval Officers: Their Heredity and Development*, in which he identified a single recessive gene as responsible for "thalassophilia"—love of the sea— to explain why naval careers seemed to run in certain families.

Seeking to start a second institution at Cold Spring devoted solely to eugenics, Davenport found a sympathetic supporter in Mary Williamson Harriman, widow of the railroad magnate E. H. Harriman. She remained a financial mainstay of the ERO until 1917, when the Carnegie Institute assumed responsibility for annual operating expenses. These twin sources of funding were indicative of the generous support the eugenics movement would receive from some of America's wealthiest families and foundations. The Philadelphia soap millionaire Samuel Fels was a regular contributor, and John D. Rockefeller was the ERO's second-largest supporter.

Subsequently, the Rockefeller Foundation expanded this commitment on an international scale. Beginning in the 1920s, the foundation backed the research of German eugenicists and helped establish the Kaiser Wilhelm Institute for Anthropology, Eugenics and Human Heredity, in Berlin. The Russell Sage Foundation funded research on the feeble-minded and endorsed eugenic solutions, particularly for "feeble-minded girls of child bearing age." In Michigan, Dr. John Harvey Kellogg, brother of the cereal manufacturer, organized America's First Race Betterment Conference in Battle Creek, in 1914, and set up a special school for "eugenic education." Charles Brush, a Cleveland millionaire and one of the founders of the Brush

Electric Company, created his own eugenic organization, and Dr. Clarence Gamble, heir to the Gamble soap fortune, started more than 20 sterilization clinics and was a force in the eugenics movement until the middle of the century.

At the ERO, Davenport set out to build a network of fieldworkers to compile an index of eugenic information on American families. This included not just medical facts but such traits as "liveliness, moribundity, lack of foresight, rebelliousness, trustworthiness, irritability, missile throwing, popularity, radicalness, conservativeness, nomadism." His hope was to create a clearinghouse that could give advice to individuals and communities on preventing reproduction by defectives, encourage research, and propagate "eugenic truths." Early on, Davenport made a decision crucial to the future of the ERO. He offered the job of superintendent to Harry Laughlin, a biology teacher in Iowa with whom he had been corresponding for several years.

Laughlin envisioned a day when every sort of defective would be barred from entry into the United States. He also hoped to help bring about a new social order "wherein selection for parenthood will not be held a natural right of every individual; but will be a prize highly sought and allotted to the best individuals of proven blood, and those individuals who are not deemed worthy and are by society denied the right to perpetrate their own traits in subsequent generations will be held in pity by their fellows." Laughlin would play a significant part in turning eugenic theory into legislative reality.

One of Laughlin's first assignments with the ERO was to assist the American Breeder's Association (ABA). The first formal eugenics group in the United States, with a self-proclaimed mission to "emphasize the value of superior blood and the menace to society of inferior blood," the ABA included among its original members Alexander Graham Bell, Luther Burbank, Vernon L. Kellogg, and the Stanford University president David Starr Jordan. In 1913 Laughlin wrote a report for the ABA that concluded that "approximately 10% of our population, primarily through inherent defect and weakness, are an economic and moral burden on the 90% and a constant source of danger to the national and racial life." He recommended an aggressive policy of involuntary sterilization and began drafting a model law to provide state legislatures with a working example of how to proceed.

Laughlin found a highly effective ally in Henry H. Goddard. Among the first American social scientists to use intelligence testing, Goddard was looking for the causes of retardation and mental defectiveness, and his search led him to a family in the Piney Woods of New Jersey that would function, in Stephen Jay Gould's words, "as a primal myth of the eugenics movement for several decades."

The family consisted of two bloodlines living in close proximity, each descended from the same Quaker progenitor who left home to fight in the American Revolu-

In 1990 the Human Genome Project set out to map the basic genetic makeup of our species. Celera Genomics, a private, for-profit corporation, eventually challenged the international nonprofit undertaking represented by the Genome Project and began its own effort. In June 2000, the Genome Project and Celera made a joint public announcement that they had successfully mapped about 90 percent of the genome, with the rest to be completed shortly.

Those involved with the Genome Project reject any connection with the all-encompassing biological determinism that was at the core of hard-line eugenics. While they hope to produce significant therapies for genetically influenced or controlled diseases, they deny any wish to revisit the kind of reductionism that seeks the roots of every human quality or quirk in a single gene or a set of them.

Nonetheless, some skeptics question the purposes and consequences of the final sequences of human DNA. In a collection of essays titled *It Ain't Necessarily So: The Dream of the Human Genome and Other Illusions*, published last year, Richard Lewontin, the Alexander Agassiz Research Professor at Harvard, writes: "The scientist writing about the Genome Project explicitly reject an absolute genetic determinism, but they seem to be writing more to acknowledge theoretical possibilities than out of conviction. If we take seriously the proposition that the internal and external codetermine the organism, we cannot really believe that the sequence of the human genome is the grail that will reveal to us what it is to be human, that it will change our philosophical view of ourselves, that it will show how life works."

Whatever future medical breakthroughs the Genome Project may or may not produce, it is already laying to rest the eugenic belief in distinctly separate races defined by fundamental genetic differences. Our species is such a recent evolutionary phenomenon that we haven't had time to develop into distinct biological groups in any significant way. The genes responsible for our external differences of skin color and hair texture represent about .01 percent of each individual's total genetic makeup. The bulk of the 30,000 or so genes of the human genome are proving to be strikingly alike. In the words of Dr. Eric Lander, a genome expert at the Whitehead Institute, in Cambridge, Massachusetts, "There is no scientific evidence to support substantial differences between groups, and the tremendous burden of proof goes to anyone who wants to assert those differences."

Though humans will undoubtedly continue to be divided by culture and environment, it seems that when all is said and done, we really are one big family. Whether we'll ever manage to be one big *happy* family remains to be seen.—*P.Q.*

---

tion. Before returning to the fold, marrying an upright woman, and settling down as a prosperous farmer, the wayward soldier sired an illegitimate son with a feeble-minded tavern wench in a nearby settlement. Two hereditary roads diverged in those Piney Woods, both of which Goddard gathered under the pseudonym of the Kallikaks (*kallos* is the Greek for "beauty"; *kakos*, for "bad"). One led to generations of solid, hardworking citizens; the other, to a morass of felony, harlotry, and idiocy. Published in 1912, *The Kallikak Family* was widely quoted. It would be another 70 years before the photographs in the book, which displayed the imbecilic, almost demonic faces of the defective branch of the family, were exposed as having been heavily doctored to create the desired effect.

The spreading influence of eugenics not only drew on a conservative fear of lower-class behavior, and on the enthusiasm of middle-class progressives seeking scientific answers to the dislocations inflicted by industrialization and urbanization, but also attracted support from those even more radically opposed to the status quo. For the birth-control crusader Margaret Sanger, eugenics was "the great biological interpretation of the human race" that provided "the most adequate and thorough avenue to the solution of racial, political and social problems." The African-American writer and philosopher W. E. B. Du Bois even accepted the need for "the fit" of each race to increase their numbers, while vehemently rejecting the notions of white supremacy spouted by many eugeni-

cists. African-Americans must learn, he wrote, "that among human beings, as among vegetables, quality and not mere quantity count."

The aftermath of American participation in World War I provided an ideal environment for the movement. The postwar hysteria over alien radicals and the resurgence of the racist, antiforeign Ku Klux Klan signaled a wider willingness to curtail dramatically the influx of new immigrants. Madison Grant's *The Passing of the Great Race*, published in 1916, had sounded a call to arms against "the maudlin sentimentalism" that left America's borders open to the riffraff of Europe and that was "sweeping the nation toward a racial abyss."

When, in 1921 the House Committee on Immigration and Naturalization took up the issue of postwar controls on foreign entry into the United States, Chairman Albert Johnson called only one scientific expert, Harry Laughlin. Laughlin was charged with making a statistical survey of the impact of recent immigration. His findings, published by Congress, repeated what was by now a familiar refrain: "...the recent immigrants (largely from Southern and Eastern Europe) as a whole, present a higher percentage of inborn socially inadequate qualities than do older stocks." In 1921 Congress took the historic step of imposing a quota system on immigration that was based on national origin and limited annual arrivals from Europe to 3 percent of those Americans who had claimed a specific country as their place of origin in 1910.

That same year, the Second International Congress on Eugenics was held in New York City, at the American Museum of Natural History, home to the recently established Galton Society—the inner circle of the movement—and a center of eugenic fervor. In his opening address, Henry Fairfield Osborn, a professor at Columbia University and president of the museum, insisted that the battle "to maintain the predominance of our race" had still to be won. He warned that America must learn from the example of "national decadence and decline which undermined the great republics of Greece and Rome" and reject "the appeals of false humanitarianism." As chairman of the Exhibits Committee at the conference, Harry Laughlin prepared elaborate displays on the genetic toxicity of the unfit. He displayed this skill again when Congress revisited its immigration restrictions imposed in 1921. In the months preceding passage of the Immigration Act of 1924, members of Congress and visitors walking the halls of the Capitol passed charts and posters that made clear the looming threat to the nation's germ plasm.

This new immigration act proved a collective triumph for the eugenics movement. It shifted the base year for determining national quotas from 1910 to 1890, cutting allowable immigration from Eastern and Southern Europe by 80 percent. Yet the supporters of eugenic reform weren't about to rest now; they switched their focus to a state-by-state campaign to institute compulsory sterilization. Virginia provided the decisive battleground. In 1924, the same year as it tightened the state's antimiscegenation law (Georgia and Alabama soon followed suit), the Virginia legislature enacted a compulsory sterilization statute based on Laughlin's model law. Three years later, shortly after upholding the constitutionality of Carrie Buck's sterilization, Justice Holmes said he felt he "was getting near to the first principle of real reform."

NAZI MEASURES DROVE SOME IN THE U.S. TO RECONSIDER THEIR OWN SUPPORT OF EUGENICS, BUT THE MOVEMENT DIDN'T COLLAPSE.

By the end of the 1920s, the imposition of racially based immigration controls, the growing use of compulsory sterilization, and the widespread ban on interracial marriage gave American eugenicists the right to brag that they had made their nation the world's most advanced eugenic state. German eugenicists in particular had long been aware of the progress of their American counterparts. The National Socialist Physician League head Gerhard Wagner praised America's eugenic policies and pointed to them as a model for Germany to follow. It wasn't long in happening. As a first order of business, the new National Socialist regime put in place sweeping eugenic legislation that demonstrated a comprehensive commitment to racial hygiene. Now it was the turn of Americans to look with a mixture of admiration and envy at what was occurring in Germany.

Marie Kopp, an observer for the American Committee on Maternal Health, reported that the Nazi system of Hereditary Health Courts, which were charged with seeking out the unfit and compelling their sterilization, not only was administered "in entire fairness" but was "formulated after careful study of the California experiment." The ERO's *Eugenical News* also commented on the resemblance between the German and American programs, boasting that "the text of the German statute reads almost like the 'American model sterilization Law.'" In 1936, upon being awarded an honorary degree by the University of Heidelberg for his devotion to the cause of racial biology, Harry Laughlin thanked the university for reaffirming the "common understanding of German and American scientists of the nature of eugenics." In Virginia, Dr. J. H. Bell, superintendent of the State Colony for Epileptics and Feeble-Minded and the physician who had severed Carrie Buck's fallopian tubes, lauded Nazi Germany's "elimination of the unfit."

The Nazis went on to compel the sterilization of upward of 375,000 people. Their measures drove some in the United States to reconsider their own support of eugenics, especially its compulsory and racist aspects. But the movement didn't instantly collapse. As late as 1942, a sterilization bill based on the German law was introduced before the New Jersey legislature.

In October 1939 Hitler gave the order to begin the systematic killing of the retarded and mentally ill, an act of mass murder that proved prelude to a far larger holocaust. As extreme as it was, the theory behind the destruction of the mentally ill was not exclusive to a small band of Nazi fanatics. Eugenic euthanasia had been widely discussed for years, both in and out of Germany. In America, as early as the turn of the century, Dr. William Duncan McKim had suggested a state-run program to weed out the mentally defective by inflicting a "gentle, painless death" with carbonic acid gas. The eminent physician G. Frank Lydston, a professor of surgery at the University of Illinois and of criminal anthropology at the Kent School of Law in Chicago, had advocated use of the gas chamber "to kill properly the convicted murderer and the driveling idiot."

In the South, where eugenics had often been advanced as part of a progressivist program of reform, the superintendent of the Alabama Insane Hospitals warned his fellow doctors in 1936 that if compulsory sterilization wasn't employed broadly enough, "euthanasia may become a necessity." The year before, Alexis Carrel, inventor of the iron lung and winner of a Nobel Prize in Physiology or Medicine, wrote that the insane should be "humanely and economically disposed of in small euthanasia institutions supplied with proper gases." Even after America entered the war against Nazi Germany, Dr. Foster Kennedy, a professor of neurology at Cornell Medical College, espoused the notion that retarded children age five and older—"Nature's mistakes"—be put to death. He cited Justice Holmes's reasoning in *Buck v. Bell* as providing a legal basis.

Madison Grant's *The Passing of the Great Race*, which Hitler is said to have read and admired, called for putting aside a "sentimental belief in the sanctity of human life." Grant envisioned a massive eugenic cleansing that would solve once and for all the problem of the unfit and their offspring: "In mankind it would not be a matter of great difficulty to secure a general consensus of public opinion as to the least desirable, let us say, ten per cent of the community. When this unemployed and unemployable human residuum has been eliminated together with the great mass of crime, poverty, alcoholism and feeblemindedness associated therewith it would be easy to consider the advisability of further restricting perpetuation of the then remaining least valuable types. By this method mankind might ultimately become sufficiently intelligent to choose deliberately the most vital and intellectual strains to carry on the race."

During World War II, the number of compulsory sterilizations in the United States dropped significantly. The cause was not so much revulsion at Nazi medical practices as a shortage of civilian doctors. The immigration quotas stayed in place. Joining the chorus of those who opposed any exemptions was the Chamber of Commerce of New York State, which had issued a report in 1934 demanding "no exceptional admission for Jews who are refugees from persecution in Germany." The report had been written by Harry Laughlin. In the scientific community, however, the currents of genetic research and medical advances were sweeping away the crude presumptions of eugenics.

Dr. Abraham Myerson, a tireless campaigner against eugenic sterilization, published a study showing that cases in which mental disabilities had a genetic component tended to occur proportionally in all socioeconomic groups. In 1934 he chaired a committee of the American Neurological Association that attacked the whole notion of "racial degeneracy." Hereditary feeble-mindedness was shown in many instances to be the incidental result of birth trauma, inadequate nutrition, untreated learning disabilities, infant neglect, or abuse, often enough the consequences of poverty rather than the cause. In 1938 the Carnegie Institute expressed grave doubts to Harry Laughlin about the scientific worth of the ERO. Laughlin resigned the next year. The ERO closed its doors on the last day of 1939.

The eventual unwinding of America's eugenics experiment came too late for Carrie Buck. In 1979 the director of the hospital in which she had been sterilized more than half a century earlier searched her out. He was led to Buck by her sister, who had also been sterilized. (As with many other victims of compulsory sterilization, Buck's sister had been told at the time that the procedure was an appendectomy). It was transparently clear that neither Buck nor her sister was feebleminded or imbecilic. Further investigation showed that the baby Carrie Buck had given birth to—Justice Holmes's third-generation imbecile—had been a child of normal intelligence. Like thousands of women and men involuntarily stripped of their capacity to have children, Carrie Buck had not committed any offense against the laws of nature. Her crime was for the ancient one of being poor and powerless.

Peter Quinn, author of the Civil War-era novel Banished Children of Eve, *is at work on a book about the eugenics movement.*

From *American Heritage*, Vol. 54, No. 1, February/March 2003, pages 35-43. Reprinted by permission of American Heritage, Inc., a division of Forbes, Inc.

Marcus Garvey

and the Rise of Black Nationalism

"[Garveyism] was able to tap successfully into the ambitions and emotions of the downtrodden, the beaten, the hopeless—people whose lives were held down by class, economics, and racism."

BY ELWOOD D. WATSON

MARCUS MOSIAH GARVEY'S campaign to promote the virtues of self-pride, self-motivation, self-sufficiency, and other progressive attributes to his brethren of African descent and the fiercely independent segregationist legacy he promoted are still being felt by a largely integrationist U.S. During the 1990s, there was a remarkable reawakening of Garvey's philosophy. Young black men and women began to become increasingly acquainted with the literature of their ancestors and contemporaries. Moreover, black writers are enjoying a renewed interest of nationalism among an eager contemporary public (including a small niche of suburban white youth) that had not been seen since the 1960s. Various entertainers and intellectuals have made a valiant effort to analyze and reexamine the legacy of Garvey, in addition to other early- and mid-20th-century black nationalists.

The years following World War I were filled with disillusionment for American blacks. U.S. involvement in that war encouraged a new wave of African-American migration out of the South. As northern industries supplied the needs of the Allies and with European immigration closed off, the nation had a demand for both skilled and un-skilled labor. Black hopes raised by these opportunities were dashed as relations between the races worsened in the 1920s. After the Supreme Court declared municipal segregation ordinances unconstitutional in 1917, restricted residential covenants were drawn up by many white real estate agents. These discriminatory practices carried over into the labor force, where African-American workers were given the more menial, lower-paid, or arduous jobs.

In 1917, Garvey had opened the New York Division of the United Negro Improvement Association (UNIA), which he had founded in his native Jamaica three years earlier in order to establish "a Universal Confraternity among the race," promote "the spirit of race pride and love," create "Agencies in the principal countries of the world for the protection of all Negroes irrespective of nationality," and conduct "a world-wide commercial and industrial intercourse." By the mid 1920s, the UNIA had more than 700 branches in 38 states in every section of the country (including the Deep South) and another 200 branches in the West Indies and Central and South America. In 1918, Garvey established his newspaper, the *Negro World*, which, by the early 1920s, had a weekly circula-tion of more that 50,000 and was read as far away as Africa.

In 1919, Garvey purchased an auditorium on 138th Street in Harlem, New York's largest black neighborhood, renamed it Liberty Hall, and held nightly meetings where his great eloquence transformed listeners into followers. Within a few years, he could address his fellow blacks in Liberty Halls in Philadelphia, Pittsburgh, Cleveland, Detroit, Cincinnati, Chicago, and Los Angeles. It was also during 1919 that he organized the Black Star Line of Ships, financed by the donations of his followers. Within a year, the line raised $610,000, owned three ships, and began to carry out its ultimately unsuccessful scheme of transporting passengers and cargo between the U.S., the West Indies, and Africa.

THE RISE OF GARVEYISM

Garveyism and the UNIA combined the various elements of black nationalism—religious, cultural, economic, and territorial—into a distinctive blend of philosophy and agenda. Fundamental to this viewpoint was the emotive power of blackness. Garvey was a zealot who advocated self-economic determination and African redemption. Garveyism proclaimed and promoted the coming revitalization of people of color around the world and exalted the power of the black race.

The UNIA spread rapidly throughout many urban American cities, particularly New York and Chicago. Its Pan-African elements, earthy aura, gut-wrenching rhetoric, and relentless message of self-love enraptured many Americans of African descent. The message of Garveyism its followers espoused was simple and direct: Although slavery, past and current racial discrimination, and other forms of injustice had contributed to the desolate conditions of many African-Americans, no one but blacks acting on their own behalf and out of conviction of their intrinsic worth could ameliorate those misfortunes. The movement argued that it was an insult to God for any person to view himself or herself as inferior.

Garveyism could not have come along at a more pivotal time. Colonialism was solidifying throughout Africa. In the U.S., the continuation of black codes, race riots, Jim Crow laws, lynchings, abject poverty, and other social indignities continued to plague a sizable portion of the African-American population. Since race relations varied from place to place, this limited the contact that people of different cultures had with one another and rigidly defined the level at which Garveyism could succeed. Nonetheless, the politics of race was the cornerstone of the movement.

Garveyism advocated racial separation, rejecting the goals of assimilation and integration. The movement was driven by spellbinding oratory and rhetoric designed to awaken the fires of black nationalism. The ideology attracted attention because it managed to put into language the powerful phrases and secret thoughts of the African-American world. By the 1920s, the UNIA and followers of Garvey began to emerge in many northern, urban African-American communities, appealing in particular to the working class. The movement possessed a strong resemblance to Islam, which also advocated economic empowerment, self-sufficiency, strict dietary laws, self-discipline, and, perhaps most important, a love for oneself.

Garveyism gained wide acceptance among many African-Americans because it stood for economic independence and self-sufficiency, yet avoided endorsing either capitalism or socialism. Two of Garvey's business enterprises—the Black Star Line of Ships and the Negro Factories Corporation—were more cooperative than corporate forms of white business enterprise. Both existed for the purpose of mitigating the plight of Africans as well as those spread around the globe by the black diaspora. Garvey felt that, by attempting to do this, the circumstances of the black man all over the world would improve dramatically.

This ability to understand the needs and desires of his fellow blacks was the primary reason for his rapid accession to a position of power and influence. When Garvey assured his followers that man "is master of his own destiny, and architect of his own fate" and enjoined them to "take yourselves out of the mire and hitch your hopes to the stars; yes, rise as high as the very stars themselves," he was preaching a traditional doctrine deeply rooted in 19th-century American ideology and carefully inculcated in the freedmen during the years of Reconstruction and after. When Garvey shouted his slogan, "Up, you mighty race," he was enunciating a credo which, however radical a racial doctrine, was appealingly familiar. He transformed black educator Booker T. Washington's philosophy of individual mobility into a mechanism designed to increase worldwide consciousness, unity, and power of the race.

Garvey was similarly astute in understanding the importance of religion in black culture and incorporating many of its elements in his movement. He regularly employed a religious vocabulary and frequently cast himself in the role of Jesus. Most importantly, Garvey incorporated elaborate religious liturgy and zeal into his sermons. Hymns were sung, prayers recited, and offerings received, just as in church. However, his penchant for pomp and ceremony; wearing gaudy uniforms and robes; bestowing such titles as Knight Commander of the Nile upon his lieutenants; and creating such groups as the blue-clad African Legion, the Black Cross Nurses, marching bands, choristers, and other uniformed, military-style auxiliaries brought him enormous ridicule in some quarters as a "clown" and a "charlatan" who led big parades of ignorant people down a misguided path of failure.

Garvey's racial ideology was conservative in its message. His deep suspicion of the white working class made it difficult for him to cooperate with labor unions or the political left. The underlying message to African-Americans was simple: Open your own churches, schools, stores, banks, hospitals, hotels, cab companies, and universities—in short, "do things for yourself." Garveyism provided an economic antidote to blacks frustrated with second-class status and citizenship, especially the urban poor, working class, and angriest African-Americans.

The most important element of Garveyism, though, was its emphasis on a return to Africa, the expulsion of all European powers from the African continent, and the belief that, once a strong independent African nation was established, African-Americans would gain power and prestige. Although Garvey was practical enough to realize that it wasn't feasible for all people of African descent to return to Africa, at least in the physical sense, he viewed himself and his organization as representing the struggle for African liberation: "The thoughtful and industrious of our race want to go back to Africa, because we realize it will be our only hope of permanent existence. We do not want all the Negroes in Africa. Some are no good here and naturally will be no good there. The no-good Negro will naturally die in fifty years. The Negro who is wrangling about and fighting for social equality will naturally pass away in fifty years, and yield his place to the progressive Negro who wants a society and country of his own."

Garvey had no tolerance or respect for those blacks he felt were tools of whites or content to remain second-class citizens mired in the injustices of racism, segregation, discrimination, lynchings, and other atrocities. He was well-aware that men and women who reveled in self-pity and self-contempt were useless to themselves, as well as their children, families, community, and race. Perhaps out of frustration at being unable to garner the support of many of the African-American bourgeoisie, he began to relentlessly echo the message of Africa today! Africa now! Africa forever! to the black underclass.

Garvey viewed the UNIA as the epitome of the black liberation struggle. In a speech delivered at a convention in 1920, he made evident his determination to develop an African empire free of European habitation and domination. He spoke at length of the great increase of the power and numbers of people of African heritage and of the grand attempt to cleanse the motherland from European domination.

At the height of Garveyism's membership, Garvey had formed branches of the UNIA all over the world. These branches held themselves in readiness for a convention on a grand scale that would unite people of African races around the globe. Plans for the convention included the drafting of grievances and a declaration of rights, the election of international officers, and the discussion of special reports on political and economic aspects of the African problem.

The convention took place during the entire month of August, 1920, at New York's Madison Square Garden. The spectacle was a Pan-Africanist's haven. More than 25,000 delegates from various regions of Africa, Brazil, Colombia, Haiti, Panama, and the West Indies—as well as Canada, England, and France—attended. Garvey captivated the audience by announcing that the Negro would no longer suffer the indignities that had been thrust upon him. In his speeches, he would frequently refer movingly to African-American soldiers who, upon returning home after World War I, were beaten or lynched in their uniforms in the South.

Garvey argued that other ethnic groups did not hesitate to claim a homeland; consequently, displaced Africans should not relent from claiming one. If Europe was for the Europeans, Africa should belong to Africans and their 400,000,000 descendants. At succeeding

conventions between 1920 and 1922, Garvey and other leaders, many of them officers of the UNIA, actively demanded that all whites who were living in Africa evacuate the continent.

As a consequence, many whites in Africa began to demand that their governments investigate Garvey. The already less than admirable feelings they harbored toward him were further strained by this direct ultimatum. Threats of expulsion from Africa hurled at white imperialists by the UNIA naturally alarmed the Western world, despite the fact that such a threat was chimerical. French and British colonial authorities in Africa successfully suppressed the *Negro World*. To possess any Garveyite publication became a serious offense that could result in imprisonment. Liberia, which the UNIA had planned to use as the center for the upcoming Negro National State, suddenly withdrew support for the Garvey movement because of pressure from the U.S.

THE MOVEMENT'S DOWNFALL

Garvey paid a heavy price for underestimating the formidable power of his foes—black as well as white. Many of his opponents were leading black intellectuals, who resented his global audacity and popularity. They and a number of journalists began to demand an investigation of his ventures, including an audit of UNIA businesses. Garvey ignored them. Instead, he concentrated his energy on demonstrating the moral and philosophical views of his movement.

George W. Harris, editor of the *Harlem News*; William Pickens and Robert W. Bagnal of the National Association for the Advancement of Colored People (NAACP); and Robert S. Abbott, editor and publisher of the *Chicago Defender*, were just a few of the influential blacks who called for his arrest. Charles Johnson, a prominent African-American leader and member of the National Urban League, described Garvey as a "dynamic, blundering, temerarious visionary and a trickster." Johnson further denounced Garvey's ideals as unrealistic, his financial exploits as unsound, and his great plan for the eventual redemption of Af-

rica as unreasonably visionary. The National Urban League essentially saw Garveyism as a therapeutic, spiritual, "touchy-feely" movement that offered disenfranchised, fringe individuals a superficial, psychological, delusionary empowerment that would eventually prove more harm than good.

One of Garvey's most formidable opponents and chief rival, W.E.B. Du Bois, made a serious effort to undermine both him and the UNIA. Du Bois, arguably the most influential African-American leader of his era, founded the NAACP and served as editor of the *Crisis*, the organization's newspaper. Initially, the two men enjoyed cordial relations. From 1920 on, however, Du Bois started to aim editorials in the *Crisis* directly at Garvey and the UNIA.

By 1922, an erstwhile staunch supporter and UNIA insider, E. Eterald Brown, began to levy suspicion about Garvey: "I next turn my attention to the Universal Negro Improvement Association. This has grown from the simple improvement association to a full fledged 'Back to Africa' movement. As it is such now, known as Garveyism.... Garveyism aims to free Africa from European domination and to hand it over to Negroes for the establishment of a Negro republic. Let me only say this in reference to the aim that it can only be accomplished by force of arms, and to this Garvey has not proved his seriousness of purpose by even beginning to make the most elementary preparations for this invasion of Africa." The article, laced with ambiguity, both complimented and condemned Garvey's efforts as founder of the UNIA. Intentionally or not, Brown started wheels turning against Garvey. Opponents of Garveyism wasted no time in denouncing, discrediting, and destroying the black nationalist leader.

Among liberals, Garvey was quick to earn the enmity of socialists. A. Philip Randolph and Chandler Owen, joint editors of a leftist magazine titled *Messenger*, were among the more vocal critics of Garveyism. For a considerable time, Garvey and Randolph, despite profound differences in their racial and political attitudes, maintained a cordial relationship. The two men would often attend conferences to speak on the other's behalf.

As the UNIA expanded, though, relations between Garvey and Randolph became radically strained. Garvey's glorification of African-American capitalism was in direct opposition to the Randolph-Owen belief in democratic socialism. Other aspects of Garveyism earned their disapproval as well. In a series of articles in the *Messenger*, the editors attacked Garvey's African "schemes" as being based on unsound reasoning. They also charged Garvey with irresponsibly promoting white racism against blacks as well as fostering nativism between West Indians and African-Americans. By 1923, the critiques in the *Messenger* had begun to exhibit anti-Caribbean overtones.

This response was the result of Garvey's June, 1922, symbiotic meeting in a closed-door session with Georgia white supremacist and Ku Klux Klan member Edward Young Clarke. After the meeting, Garvey was quoted as saying about the discussion, "I was speaking to a man who was brutally a white man and he was speaking to a man who was brutally Negro."

After Garvey extended his "olive branch" to the Klan, Randolph and Own announced that they would launch a campaign that would culminate in his deportation from America. The *Messenger* adopted the slogan "Garvey Must Go." In 1920, the two socialists formed the Friends of Negro Freedom, a civil rights organization that included a few NAACP officials. Their goal was to get rid of Garvey "by any means necessary!"

In 1923, eight leaders of the "Garvey Must Go" campaign, led by Owen as secretary, wrote the U.S. Attorney General, urging the government to speed up its prosecution of Garvey for mail fraud. Signatures on the enclosed petition included those of prominent African-American leaders. After he was convicted and imprisoned, Garvey's foes forcefully advocated the destruction of the UNIA, closing of the *Negro World*, dismantilization of the Black Star Line of Ships, and a complete denunciation of Garveyism. The UNIA entered bankruptcy. After serving a two-year prison sentence, Garvey was pardoned by Pres. Calvin Coolidge and deported to Jamaica.

In 1928, he journeyed to England, where he unsuccessfully attempted to start a Garveyite chapter. He died in London in 1940, ironically without ever stepping foot on the African continent. As its enemies had foreseen, with the removal of the founding father of Garveyism from America, the movement suffered a severe setback, one from which it was never able to recover.

Yet, despite his shortcomings, it would be unfair and unwise to say that Marcus Garvey did not accomplish anything. Quite the contrary, in addition to rehabilitating the color black, he rejuvenated the large masses of the African diaspora and instilled in them a consciousness of their African-American heritage. This in itself was a mammoth task in the face of the centuries of humiliation and degradation that people of African descent, particularly in America, had endured. Garveyism proved to be a very important beginning that

helped set the agenda for future black nationalists.

Garveyism made such a great impact on working-class blacks in the 1920s because it elevated all things African and diminished all things Eurocentric, while retaining the colorless mores of white-dominated society. For every white organization, Garveyism offered an African-American counterpart—from a black shipping fleet to a black Christ. Everything of virtue was linked to blackness. Out of Garveyism came the phrase "Black is beautiful."

The larger significance of Garveyism lies in the fact that it was able to tap successfully into the ambitions and emotions of the downtrodden, the beaten, the hopeless—people whose lives were held down by class, economics, and racism. It told them that they were the descendants of great kings and queens and to say with boldness, "I am somebody!" and feel good about it.

Even after Garvey's imprisonment and deportation, the movement, no matter how minimal, was able to espouse this message. Du Bois and other rivals commended both Garvey and Garveyism after his death. Black organizations adopted much of their philosophy from Garveyism. Prominent among them were Father Divine's peace movement in the 1930s and the Nation of Islam. His message lives on in a segment of America in the 21st century.

Elwood D. Watson is assistant professor of history, East Tennessee State University, Johnson City.

From *USA Today* magazine, November 2000, pp. 64–66. © 2000 by the Society for the Advancement of Education. Reprinted by permission.

UNIT 4

From the Great Depression to World War II

Unit Selections

Key Points to Consider

- Discuss the personality and character of Franklin D. Roosevelt. What made him such an effective president?

- Why did the United States place people of Japanese descent into internment camps but not those who came from German or Italian stock? Why did some Japanese Americans willingly join the armed forces while other did not?

- Consider the experiences of both women and African Americans during World War II. Which were similar, which were different?

- What were the outstanding issues discussed at the Potsdam Conference? How were they resolved? What impact did the settlements made there have on the future of Europe?

- Analyze the situation President Truman faced at the time the atomic bombs were dropped on Japan. What alternatives did he have, and how were they likely to have turned out?

 **Links: www.dushkin.com/online/**
These sites are annotated in the World Wide Web pages.

Japanese American Internment
http://www.jainternment.org/
Works Progress Administration/Folklore Project
http://lcweb2.loc.gov/ammem/wpaintro/wpalife.html
World War II WWW Sites
http://www.besthistorysites.nte/WWWII.shtml
World War II Timeline
http://history.acusd.edu/gen/WW2Timeline/start.html
Hiroshima Archive
http://www.lclark.edu/~history/HIROSHIMA/
The Enola Gay
http://www.theenolagay.com/index.html

Republicans like to proclaim the prosperity of the 1920s as a "New Era." Business was booming, and more people than ever before had surplus money to spend. Some groups, such as farmers, did not truly share in the affluence but even many of them were purchasing automobiles, radios, and the sundry other consumer goods pouring off assembly lines. When people ran out of things to buy and had money left over—they dabbled in the stock market. As stock prices rose dramatically, a kind of speculative mania developed in the latter half of the decade. In the past most people bought stocks as investments. That is, they wanted to receive income from the dividends that reliable companies would pay over the years. Speculators had no interest in the long run; they bought stocks on the assumption that they would make money when they sold on the market—in a matter of months or even weeks. Rumors abounded, some of them true, about individuals who had earned fortunes "playing" the market.

By the end of the 1920s the stock market prices had soared to unprecedented heights. As long as people were confident that they would continue to rise, they did. There were a few voices warning that stocks were overpriced, but they were denounced as doomsayers. Besides, had not the highly regarded President Herbert Hoover predicted that "we are on the verge of a wave of never ending prosperity?" No one can say why this confidence began to falter when it did and not months earlier or later, but on October 24, 1929 the market crashed. "Black Thursday" set off an avalanche of selling as holders dumped their shares at whatever price they could get, thereby driving prices even lower. Some large banks tried to shore up confidence by having representatives appear at the stock exchange where they ostentatiously made large purchase orders. Despite such efforts, prices continued to tumble in the following months.

President Herbert Hoover tried to restore confidence by assuring the public that what had happened was merely a glitch, a necessary readjustment of a market that had gotten out of hand. The economy of America was sound, he claimed, and there was no reason business should not go on as usual. His reassurances met with increasing disbelief as time went on. Businessmen as well as stockholders were worried about the future. In order to protect themselves they laid off workers, cut back on inventory, and put off previous plans to expand or to introduce new products. But their actions, however much sense they made for an individual firm, had the collective result of making the situation worse. "Brother, Can You Spare a Dime" provides a close-up view of the pathetic lives led by those who fell prey to the widespread unemployment.

Hoover endorsed more federal programs than had any of his predecessors to combat the depression, but they failed to stop the downward slide. Just as people tend to credit an incumbent when times are good, they also blame him things go sour. Hoover became the most widely detested man in America: trousers with patches on them were scoffingly referred to as "Hoover" pants and in every city the collection of shacks and shanties in which homeless people lived were called "Hoovervilles." In the presidential election of 1932, the discredited Hoover lost by a landslide to Democrat candidate Franklin D. Roosevelt. Although Roosevelt had compiled an impressive record as governor of New York State, his greatest asset in the election was that he was not Hoover.

Roosevelt assumed the presidency without any grand design for ending the depression. Unlike Hoover, however, he was willing to act boldly and on a large scale. His "first 100 days" in office resulted in passage of an unprecedented number of bills designed to promote recovery and to restore confidence. "A Monumental Man" provides a portrait of Roosevelt as president: his appearance, his confidence, his ability to persuade people that he cared about them.

Some of Roosevelt's reforms were intended to be temporary measures to get the economy going again. "Pump priming," to use a popular phrase, consisted of pouring money into various projects in order to provide recipients with the money necessary to purchase consumer goods. This newly-created demand, FDR hoped, would stimulate businesses to hire more workers and to build up inventory. Once the process became self-generating the props could be removed and deficit spending eliminated.

Other New Deal legislation was intended to provide permanent structural changes to prevent a recurrence of depression and to provide a safety net for the unemployed and the aged. "Birth of an Entitlement: Learning from the Origins of Social Security" provides a somewhat jaundiced view of one such effort.

Roosevelt's "New Deal" mitigated the effects of the depression but did not end it. That came with the onset of war in Europe and America's preparedness program. Unlike Woodrow Wilson, Roosevelt made no effort to remain neutral when conflict engulfed Europe and Asia. He believed the United States ought to cooperate with other nations to stop aggression, but had to contend with a congress and public that was deeply influenced by those who thought the United States should remain aloof.

After war broke out, Roosevelt took decidedly unneutral steps when he transferred 50 overage destroyers to Great Britain and later pushed through congress a "Lend Lease" program providing aid for those nations fighting the Axis Powers. Alarmed at Japan's attempt to conquer China, Roosevelt tried to use economic pressure to get Japan to back off. His efforts only stiffened the will of Japanese hard liners who planned and carried out the raid on Pearl Harbor on December 7, 1941

Pearl Harbor and Germany's declaration of war against the United States a few days later united Americans in their determination to win this global war. For the next six months the Japanese ran rampant as they inflicted a string of defeats against British and American forces in the Pacific. The British suffered a humiliating defeat at Singapore, and though American forces fought with greater determination in the Philippines they too had to surrender. The tide of Japanese expansion was halted during the summer of 1942 by the naval battles at the Coral Sea and at Midway. The United States launched its first offensive operations on Guadalcanal in the Solomon Islands. Though much bitter fighting remained, American military and industrial might ensured Japan's ultimate defeat.

Hatred towards the Japanese who had mounted the "sneak attack" on Pearl Harbor extended to those who resided in the United States. Americans who were quite willing to believe there were "good" Germans who had been bamboozled by their Nazi leaders, despised all Japanese as inherently treacherous and savage. Long-standing racism against the Japanese who resided on the west coast crystallized during the months after Pearl. Although not a single case of espionage or sabotage was ever proven, rumors spread that Japanese agents were busily trying to undermine the war effort. In "Japanese Americans and the U.S. Army: A Historical Reconsideration," author James C. McNaughton discusses the forcible relocation of Japanese-Americans in the name of national security. He also provides an account of those of Japanese descent who fought in the U.S. army and those who refused to do so.

Some 14 million men and women served in the armed forces during World War II. To help make up labor shortages on the home front millions of women took jobs previously held almost exclusively by men. Their experiences were mixed; they experienced discrimination in the workplace, and often felt conflicted between their jobs and taking care of their children. "American Women in a World at War" shows that many of them gained a greater sense of self, and took pride that they could do most jobs as well or better than men.

One of the most common themes in wartime propaganda was that the United States was fighting for freedom as opposed to tyranny. Black Americans were dismayed to learn that such rhetoric did not apply to their own positions within the society. "African Americans and World War II" describes how racial discrimination continued to be a fact of life both at home and in the armed forces. When black units such as the Tuskegee Airmen got into combat they performed superbly.

United States ground forces did not get into the war against Germany until they landed in North Africa in late 1942. They then participated in campaigns in Sicily and Italy, and the cross-channel invasion of France in June 1944. After initial stalemate, Allied forces broke out of the beachheads and began moving across France. Although there were setbacks such as what became known as the "Battle of the Bulge," Anglo-American-Canadians eventually penetrated the German border and beyond. Germany was caught in a huge vise as massive Soviet armies closed in on the Eastern Front. Hitler committed suicide in his Berlin bunker and Germany surrendered in early May 1945.

Harry S. Truman had assumed the presidency when Roosevelt died in April. Determined to carry out his predecessor's goals, Truman met with British Prime Minister Winston Churchill and Soviet leader Joseph Stalin in a conference held outside Berlin in July 1945. Michael Beschloss's "Dividing the Spoils" shows how the decisions made there helped to shape the future of Europe.

Meanwhile, American forces in the Pacific were steadily advancing toward the Japanese homeland. Capture of the Mariana Islands enabled the United States to mount massive air attacks against Japanese cities, and naval actions progressively strangled their war machine. Some historians have argued that President Harry S. Truman could have attained a Japanese surrender by the summer of 1945 if only he had assured them that they could retain their sacred emperor. That is incorrect. The Japanese will to resist still ran strong, as the bloody battles of Iwo Jima and Okinawa during the first half of 1945 had shown. Indeed, Japanese generals claimed that they welcomed an invasion of the home islands, where they would inflict such staggering casualties that the United States would settle for a negotiated peace instead of unconditional surrender. "The Biggest Decision: Why We had to Drop the Bomb" shows that Truman used atomic weapons to end a bloody war that would have been far bloodier if an invasion had been necessary.

'Brother, Can You Spare a Dime?'

1930–1940: Making do and trying to forget reality during the Depression

By Henry Allen
Washington Post Staff Writer

It's not like you go out on your porch and see the Depression standing there like King Kong. Most neighborhoods, things look pretty normal, not that different from before the Crash. Paint peels on houses. Cars get old, break down. Nothing you'd notice right away. Kids play with their Buck Rogers ray guns. You go to the movies on Dish Night—you like the Fiesta Ware, very modernistic, red and blue.

Definitely, you read in the papers how in Chicago unemployment hit 50 percent, and men were fighting over a barrel of garbage; or in the Dust Bowl, farmers saying they'll lynch judges who foreclose on their property. That kind of thing. It's terrible.

But most places you don't see it. Roosevelt can say: "I see one-third of a nation ill-housed, ill-clad, ill-nourished." That leaves two-thirds where you don't see the hobo jungles, people lined up for government cheese.

You feel what isn't there: It's like on Sunday afternoon, the quiet. You don't hear carpenters driving nails, you don't hear rivet hammers going in the city.

Fewer cars in town, just the stoplights rocking in the wind. You don't hear as many whistles: factory, railroad. You don't hear as many babies crying. People are afraid to have them.

Down the block there's a man you don't see outside his house on workdays. He doesn't want the neighbors to know he's out of work again. Smoking cigarettes, looking out the window, waiting for "Amos 'n' Andy" to come on the radio.

He was a sales manager for a train wheel company, back when the railroads were buying 1,300 locomotives a year. In 1932, they don't buy any. The company lets him go.

He takes a job selling insurance. Insurance companies know you can sell policies to your family, your friends. When you can't sell any more, they let you go.

He sells vacuums, the encyclopedias, door to door. He ends up spending all day at the movies. He won't let his wife apply for relief. He's too proud. His son quits high school—he's out West building a national park for the Civilian Conservation Corps, $30 a month. He sends most of it home so his mother can get her teeth fixed. And put dimes in the chain letters she mails out.

People write songs about tramps—"Brother, Can You Spare a Dime?"—but you don't see them unless they come to your back door; people say they make a chalk mark on your fence if

DOROTHEA LANGE/FARM SECURITY ADMINISTRATION COLLECTION; LIBRARY OF CONGRESS

Dorothea Lange's photograph of a migrant farm worker and her child has come to symbolize the wrenching poverty that characterized much of the decade.

© UNITED PRESS INTERNATIONAL/Corbis, Inc.

In 1932, in the depths of the Depression, President Hoover called out troops to roust impoverished World War I veterans—"Bonus Marchers"—from their camp in Washington, D.C. Their burning shanties blackened the skies around the Capitol.

you're good for a handout. You've never found the mark but they keep coming. You wonder how they survive.

One guy's feet are coming out of his shoes but he's got a new tweed overcoat.

You say: "Glad to see you got a warm coat."

He says: "I got it raking leaves for an undertaker. They're good for clothes."

You see the Depression in the papers, the magazines and newsreels: heads getting busted during strikes, dust storms burying cows, Reds parading through Wall Street with their fists in the air, shouting "bread, bread," or Huey Long, the Louisiana Kingfish himself, flapping his arms and shouting about "every man a king," Roosevelt looking over plans for electric power dams in the Tennessee Valley, his cigarette holder pointing up—the columnists say "at a jaunty angle." And the lines: in front of soup kitchens, relief offices, banks that are failing. And cute stuff: Kids hang a sign that says "Depression" on a snowman and throw snowballs at it.

THEN YOU'RE LOOKING AT BLOOD AND BULLET holes from gangster shootouts, a girl drinking a glass of beer at the end of Prohibition, kids jitterbugging to Benny Goodman or Count Basie. Bathing beauties, bathing beauties, bathing beauties, and the glamour girls of cafe society—Brenda Diana Duff Frazier, the debutante of the year, smiling from her table at El Morocco or the Rainbow Room. No Depression there.

The Yankees win the pennant. Jesse Owens makes the Olympic team. Soldiers goose-step in front of Hitler or Mussolini or Stalin. Hemingway in the Spanish Civil War, glamorous in that manly way that took over from everybody wanting to look like boys in the 1920s, including the women.

In the new styles, women have waists and busts again. They aren't supposed to look bored anymore, either. You don't get a job, relief, whatever, looking bored. Hemlines go back down. People say hemlines go up and down with the stock market, but that's hooey. The idea is to look more mature. Women's hats, though—feathers, veils, flowers. You read how a woman in a New York tearoom put a bread basket on her head and nobody knew the difference.

From the Crash until Roosevelt took office in 1933, everybody tried to keep living the way they had been living. It didn't work. Things had to change. Now Fortune magazine says the Flaming Youth of the 1920s are gone and we've got "a generation that will not stick its neck out. It keeps its shirt on, its pants buttoned, its chin up, and its mouth shut."

If you're older, during those good years you felt like a self-made man, so now when you're cleaning out your desk, boarding up your store, you feel like a self-ruined man.

THE PREACHERS AND BUSINESSMEN ALL HAVE SOMEthing to blame: moral breakdown, a natural cycle, the Wall Street short-sellers, the installment plan, high tariffs, low tariffs, the British, the Russians. That didn't use to be the American way, to blame anybody but yourself. Lot of things have changed.

Your father's job was to build towns, raise wheat. Your job is to buy things. A poster shows a guy with a lunch bucket and

a paycheck, his wife smiling at him. The words say: "When You BUY an AUTOMOBILE You GIVE 3 MONTHS WORK to Someone Which Allows Him to BUY OTHER PRODUCTS."

If you ain't got the mazuma to spend, you don't count.

You hear a husband and wife arguing.

"Why don't you fix cars?" the wife asks. "Every time I go downtown I see a new garage, everybody's car is breaking down."

"I'm not a car mechanic. I'm a machinist," the husband says.

"It's money," she says.

"That's the sad part," he says. "Back when we got married, I had a trade. I'm a machinist. Then they bring in the efficiency experts with their clipboards, timing every move I make. They turn me from a machinist into a machine. I say, what the hell, it's still good money. Then they take away the money. What a mug I was to think we were on Easy Street. What have I got left?"

"You've got a wife and kids wearing cardboard in the bottoms of their shoes," she says.

"Take in a show," he says.

People think you get away from the Depression in the movies, but Hollywood knows there's hard times and unrest, and they don't just show it in the newsreels.

When Mickey Mouse first came along in "Steamboat Willie" he was a mean little pest, and now Walt Disney is making him the common man, a hero like the common man in the murals the government artists paint in post offices. The little guy as hero. That's a change, all right.

In the "Thin Man" movies, they make William Powell a pal with every working stiff in the city—he stops to gas with the iceman, the news butcher, the local pickpocket before he goes off to drink martinis someplace with white telephones and Myrna Loy sliding around in a bathrobe suitable for a coronation. Witty as hell. You walk out of the theater wanting to not give a damn like that.

She says: "I read you were shot five times in the tabloids."

He says: "It's not true. He didn't come near my tabloids."

Here's the power of the movies: You read that John Dillinger and his gang pretend to be a movie company on location in front of a bank in Sioux Falls, S.D. The whole city gawks while inside, the pretend actors clean out the bank.

The FBI guns Dillinger down outside a movie theater in Chicago. You hear the coroner sent part of his anatomy to the Smithsonian Institution in Washington, it was that big.

YOU HEAR A LOT OF STORIES: YOU HEAR ABOUT A smart guy, out of work. He starts an employment agency and takes the first job he was supposed to fill.

The stories about stockbrokers jumping out windows on Black Tuesday, Oct. 29, 1929: the suicide rate was higher right before the Crash than after it, but nobody wants to hear it.

Everybody's brother-in-law knows a banker who works as a caddie at his old country club.

In 1931, Cameroon, in West Africa, sent New York City a check for $3.77 to help the starving. Immigrants are going back to Europe by the shipload. Makes you feel bad.

When Roosevelt closed all the banks in 1933, you hear about one lucky woman who overdrew her account the day before.

In Deming, N.M., the Southern Pacific yard dicks drive so many hobos off the trains, the town has to hire a constable to drive them back on. On the Grand Concourse in the Bronx they have a poorhouse for the rich, the Andrew Freedman home, a mansion, so when the rich lose their money they don't have to live like the poor.

Eleanor Roosevelt is out visiting the poor and she sees a boy hiding a pet rabbit. His sister says: "He thinks we are not going to eat it. But we are."

Babies go hungry while farmers in Iowa dump their milk trying to get the price up to where they can keep producing milk so babies won't go hungry.

Herbert Hoover himself believes that "many persons left their jobs for the more profitable one of selling apples."

The apple story is enough to make you think the Reds are right.

In 1930, right after the Crash, Washington State has a bumper crop of apples. Too many to sell. So instead of dumping them, they give them to vendors on credit.

Next thing, men are lined up in Wall Street, wearing homburgs and selling apples, 5 cents apiece. There are so many of them they start cutting prices on each other. At the same time, the growers get greedy—raise the prices and don't cull the rotten ones. Pretty soon, you can't make any money in the apple business, and it's all over.

The feeling is: damned if you do, damned if you don't. Like playing the Irish Sweepstakes. Lots of gambling now: bingo, punchboards, slot machines, the numbers.

SOME PEOPLE SAY COMMUNISM WILL SAVE US. GUYS in black hats and leather jackets at the union meetings. They know how to organize, they know what they think, but you wonder if they could sell apples any better than anybody else. People are scared of the Reds. A witness tells the House Un-American Activities Committee that out in Hollywood, Shirley Temple is "a stooge of the Reds" for sending money to the Spanish Loyalists. A little girl!

They say J. Edgar Hoover and the FBI will save us from the Reds, the Nazi spies, the gangsters. The kids love him, running around in their Junior G-Man badges.

They say Roosevelt will save us. He comes on the radio in the Fireside Chats, not like Father Coughlin yelling about Reds and Jews. Just talking. "My friends," he says. Like he knows you know he knows how you feel. He doesn't have it all figured out like the Reds or Huey Long. He'll try anything until the Supreme Court knocks it down. The problem is, things don't get much better. He said in 1932:

"The only thing we have to fear is fear itself." He's still right.

And science will save us. You go to the world's fairs in Chicago and New York and learn how technocrats will build things out of plastic and beryllium bronze, the World of Tomorrow. Diesel trains. Television.

No class struggle because science solved all the problems. You never have to sweat out a toothache. Modern management. All you need is brains, not courage. You wonder, though: Is that the American way?

What you know for sure is, whoever's running things right now, it isn't you.

First it was the trusts and the railroads that took control of your life, then Wall Street and advertising, and now it's Roosevelt's Brain Trust and the alphabet agencies—NRA, PWA, WPA, CCC, CWA. They prove everything with numbers and polls; 37 percent of housewives spend 22 percent more hours blah blah…

Everything's scientific. You don't just get married, you go to college and take a course in "modern marriage." Half the babies in the country are born in hospitals. A mother isn't supposed to feed her baby with her own milk. It doesn't have enough of the vitamins they've discovered now. Science turns into a fashion. White tile and stainless steel, waitresses wearing white uniforms. Progress.

ONE DAY THE OUT-OF-WORK SALESMAN AND HIS wife down the block are gone. Not a word of goodbye.

The machinist gets a job in an airplane factory, making bombers.

When your nephew comes to the breakfast table, he swings his leg over the back of the chair, like Clark Gable in "It Happened One Night." Or Mickey Rooney in the Andy Hardy movies with Judy Garland.

Men don't wear tops on their bathing suits anymore.

Girls wear saddle shoes and apron dresses. They drink Cokes in drugstores. The soda jerk thinks they all have a crush on him, his white paper hat cocked to one side.

If you want to show your social consciousness, you don't have a "cleaning woman" anymore, you have a "cleaning lady."

How is vaudeville going to stand up to movies and radio? What will Milton Berle do for a living?

Modern furniture gets crazier. You see a picture of a bedroom in Hollywood with these reading chairs only Ming the Merciless could be comfortable in, and a laminated wood bed you could put on a Mayan funeral barge, everything tapered—table legs, lamps, vases.

You hear stories that Roosevelt, the British and the Jews are trying to get us into a war.

Huey Long gets shot dead in Baton Rouge.

There's a feeling you hardly notice after a while—a shabby feeling, dust and phone wires, a cold spring wind, things exposed…

From the *Washington Post National Weekly Edition*, October 25, 1999, pp. 10–11. © 1999 by The Washington Post. Reprinted by permission.

A Monumental Man

FDR's chiseled features defined an American epoch

By Gerald Parshall

Franklin Roosevelt made no small plans—except for his own commemoration. The first Roosevelt memorial, now all but forgotten, was installed outside the National Archives building in 1965. A marble slab about the size of Roosevelt's desk, it was scaled to its subject's wishes. The new Roosevelt memorial now being completed in Washington is scaled to its subject's significance: Some 4,500 tons of granite went into it. Designer Lawrence Halprin laid out a wall that meanders over 7.5 acres, forming four outdoor rooms, each devoted to one of FDR's terms in the White House and each open on one side to a stunning vista of the Tidal Basin. Waterfalls, reflecting pools, and sculptures are set along what is likely to become one of the most popular walks in the nation's capital. The entry building contains a photograph of FDR in his wheelchair and a replica of the chair itself. The memorial's time line includes these words: "1921, STRICKEN WITH POLIOMYELITIS—HE NEVER AGAIN WALKED UNAIDED." But because no statue depicts him in his wheelchair, the dedication ceremony on May 2 faces a threatened protest by the disabled. Controversy often surrounded Roosevelt in life; his spirit should feel right at home.

THE POWER OF HIS SMILE

Today, we carry the face of Franklin Roosevelt in our pockets and purses—it is stamped on more than 18 billion dimes. From 1933 to 1945, Americans carried it in their hearts. It was stamped on their consciousness, looking out from every newspaper and newsreel, FDR's smile as bright as the headlight on a steam locomotive. Roosevelt's portrait hung in bus stations, in barber shops, in kitchens, in parlors, in Dust Bowl shacks—and in Winston Churchill's bedchamber in wartime London. It was the face of hope and freedom for the masses. Even among the "economic royalists," the haters of "that man in the White House," the portrait could stir emotion—as a dartboard.

In 1911, when the 28-year-old Roosevelt was newly elected to the New York Senate, the *New York Times* found him "a young man with the finely chiseled face of a Roman patrician" who "could make a fortune on the stage and set the matinee girl's heart throbbing with subtle and happy emotion." Tammany Hall Democrats, however, weren't swooning. They noted the freshman's habit of tossing his head back and peering down his nose (on which he wore pince-nez like Theodore Roosevelt, a fifth cousin) and read in it a squire's disdain for grubby city boys. The quirk persisted but acquired a new meaning decades later, when FDR wrestled with unprecedented domestic and foreign crises. His upturned chin and eyes, along with his cigarette holder, itself tilted toward the heavens, became symbols of indomitable determination to triumph over adversity—his own and the country's.

It was, indeed, the face of a great actor, a living sculpture continuously reshaped by the artist. The knowing twinkle. The arched eyebrow. The eloquent grimace. Roosevelt was a master of misdirection. He could lie without blinking, disarm enemies with infectious bonhomie, and make a bore feel like the most fascinating fellow on Earth. Officials with rival agendas often came away from the Oval Office equally sure that they alone had the president's ear. "Never let your left hand know what your right is doing," FDR once confided to a cabinet member. Idealism and duplicity fused behind his smile, buttressing one another like the two sides of a Roosevelt dime.

THE WARMTH OF HIS WORDS

He was one of the greatest orators of his time but suffered from stage fright. While he waited on the dais, Franklin Roosevelt fidgeted, shuffled the pages of his speech, chain-smoked, and doused the butterflies in his stomach with gulps of water. At last, they let him start—"My friends...." In a New York minute, his nervousness was gone and the audience under his spell. His voice—languid one moment, theatrical the next—dripped with Groton, Harvard, and centuries of blue blood. Yet no president has ever communicated better with ordinary people.

THE SPLENDOR OF HIS STRIDE

At the 1936 Democratic National Convention, Franklin Roosevelt fell down as he moved across the podium to address the delegates. He was quickly pulled up again, his withered legs bruised but unbroken. No newspaper stories or radio reports mentioned this incident—and for good reason. It hadn't happened. America was in denial. Prejudice against "cripples" was widespread. The nation wanted no reminders that it was following a man who could not walk.

From the earliest days of the polio that ravaged his legs in 1921, denial had been Roosevelt's way of coping. He spoke of his infirmity with no one, not even with members of his family. For seven years, almost every day, he took his crutches, tried—and failed—to reach the end of his Hyde Park driveway. He could not walk. But how he ran. Campaigning animatedly from open cars and the rear platform of trains, he was elected governor of New York twice and president of the United States four times. No crutches were seen and no wheelchair. His steel leg braces were painted black to blend with his socks; he wore extra long trousers. The Secret Service built ramps all over Washington, D.C., to give his limousine close access to his destinations. FDR jerkily "walked" the final distance by holding on to one of his sons with his left arm and supporting his right side with a cane. Newsreel cameras stopped; press photographers took a breather. If an amateur was spotted attempting to get a picture, the Secret Service swiftly closed in and exposed the film.

"FDR's splendid deception," historian Hugh Gallagher dubbed the little conspiracy in his book of that title. It worked so well that most Americans never knew of Roosevelt's disability, or they repressed what they did know. Such was the national amnesia, cartoonists even drew him jumping. FDR dropped the ruse for only one group. Military amputee wards were filled with men brooding about what fate had done to their futures. A high official sometimes came calling. The severely wounded GIs recognized the visitor immediately—no face was more famous—and his arrival brought an exhilarating revelation. Down the aisles came the nemesis of Hitler and Hirohito, his wheelchair in full view and looking like a royal chariot.

THE MAINSPRING OF HIS MIND

When the British monarch visited America in 1939, Franklin Roosevelt greeted him with unaccustomed familiarity. He served him hot dogs at a Hyde Park picnic and addressed him not as "your majesty" but as "George." "Why don't my ministers talk to me as the president did tonight?" an enchanted George VI remarked to a member of his entourage. "I felt exactly as though a father were giving me his most careful and wise advice." It was Roosevelt's genius to treat kings like commoners and commoners like kings. And both loved him for it.

His monumental self-assurance was bred in the bone. His mother, Sara, had reared him, her only child, to believe he had a fixed place in the center of the cosmos like other Roosevelts.

ATLANTA CHANCE—FRANKLIN D. ROOSEVELT LIBRARY

Revisionist. FDR rewrote his speeches until they sang.

A Roosevelt speech sounded spontaneous, straight from the heart, effortless—effects that took much effort to achieve. Some speeches went through a dozen drafts, with speech writers laboring at the big table in the Cabinet Room until 3 a.m. Roosevelt then revised mercilessly—shortening sentences, substituting words with fewer syllables, polishing similes—until his own muscular style emerged. Sometimes, he wrote a speech entirely by himself. He used a yellow legal pad to draft his first inaugural address, which rang with one of the most effective buck-up lines in history: "The only thing we have to fear is fear itself." He dictated to his secretary most of the Pearl Harbor message he delivered to Congress. He edited himself, changing "a date which will live in world history" to "a date which will live in infamy."

Roosevelt held two press conferences a week right in the Oval Office. Relaxed and jocular, he gently decreed what could and could not be printed. He talked to reporters, John Dos Passos remembered, in a fatherly voice "like the voice of a principal in a first-rate boy's school." Likewise, Roosevelt's "fireside chats" on the radio reverberated with paternal intimacy. He had a flair for homely analogies, such as equating Lend-Lease aid to Britian with loaning your neighbor a garden hose to put out a house fire. Who wouldn't do that? Speaking into the microphone, he gestured and smiled as if the audience would somehow sense what it could not see. Millions shushed the children and turned up the radio. They ached for leadership and "Doctor New Deal"—soon to become "Doctor Win the War"—was making a house call.

She—and the example set by cousin Theodore—imparted another formative lesson: Privileged people have a duty to do good. Noblesse oblige, Christianity, and the golden rule made up the moral core of the aristocrat who became both the Democrat of the century and the democrat of the century.

Critics called him a socialist and a "traitor to his class." History would call him the savior of capitalism, the pragmatist who saved free enterprise from very possibly disappearing into the abyss and taking democracy with it. It seemed evident to him that only government could curb or cushion the worst excesses of industrialism. But, at bottom, he was less a thinker than a doer. Luckily, like gardeners and governesses, intellectuals could be hired. Roosevelt hired a brain trust and pumped it for ideas to which he applied this test: Will it work? If one program belly-flopped, he cheerfully tried another. "A second-class intellect," Justice Oliver Wendell Holmes pegged him. "But a first-class temperament."

For all his amiability, FDR knew with Machiavelli that self-seekers abound this side of paradise. Navigating perilous domestic and foreign waters by dead reckoning, he often felt compelled to be a shameless schemer. He hid his intentions, manipulated people, set aides to contrary tasks—all to keep control of the game in trustworthy hands (his own). Charm and high purposes palliated the pure ether of his arrogance. Franklin Roosevelt was hip-deep in the muck of politics and power, but his eyes were always on the stars.

From *U.S. News & World Report*, April 28, 1997, pp. 59-61, 64. © 1997 by U.S. News & World Report, L.P. Reprinted by permission.

BIRTH OF AN ENTITLEMENT

LEARNING FROM THE ORIGINS OF SOCIAL SECURITY

BY CAROLYN WEAVER

When a Social Security advisory council appointed by Health and Human Services Secretary Donna Shalala decides to issue a final report with three reform options, one of which would privatize half the retirement program, and when a Republican presidential candidate not only discusses Social Security privatization but also makes it a key element of his campaign, you know that business is definitely not as usual. In a remarkable turn of events, proposals that once were ignored or denounced as efforts to "smash and destroy" Social Security are being explored as possibly the only real means of saving Social Security. The ongoing support of middle-aged and younger people is clearly threatened by the woefully poor rates of return the program now offers. Numerous proposals circulating on Capitol Hill would move toward a system of true saving, where a portion of a worker's taxes would go directly into a personal retirement account that the worker owns, invests, and earns interest on.

As the idea of privatizing a portion of Social Security gains currency, a debate with the old guard is intensifying over what constitutes "radical" reform. This debate has a certain back-to-the-future quality to it. Far from being universally embraced when first considered, Social Security was bitterly contested in the 1930s and was, at the time, the radical alternative. With real reform now in the wind, it is worth remembering just how close this nation came to maintaining a basically private system of retirement pensions.

FDR's compulsory old-age pension program was nearly stricken from his grander "economic security bill" in the House Ways and Means Committee and again on the House floor, where an amendment to strike the program mustered a third of the votes cast. After this rocky start, the legislation moved to the Senate where an amendment was offered to permit companies to contract out of the public program if they could provide comparable pensions to their employees. Leading to more controversy in the Finance Committee and on the Senate floor than did any other, this amendment was killed in committee by a tie vote, then went on to be approved in the Senate by a wide margin and to stalemate House and Senate conferees.

> FAR FROM BEING UNIVERSALLY EMBRACED WHEN FIRST CONSIDERED, SOCIAL SECURITY WAS BITTERLY CONTESTED IN THE 1930S AND WAS, AT THE TIME, THE RADICAL ALTERNATIVE. IT IS WORTH REMEMBERING HOW CLOSE THIS NATION CAME TO MAINTAINING A BASICALLY PRIVATE SYSTEM OF RETIREMENT PENSIONS.

No doubt the idea that Social Security lacked broad bipartisan support is at odds with many people's understanding of the birth of this mighty program. It is true that the Social Security Act moved through Congress quickly. Introduced on January 17 and signed into law on August 14, 1935, this landmark expansion of the role of the federal government wended its way through Congress and was adopted largely intact in just seven months.

However, what we know as Social Security—the old-age pension program—was just a piece of the Social Security Act that ushered in the modern welfare state. Many now-familiar programs got their start, or at least a federal boost, then too. Federal grants for aid to dependent children (now the AFDC program), aid to the elderly and to the blind (later merged with aid to the disabled into a single program of Supplemental Security Income), and maternal and child health services, to name a few, plus a tax-offset arrangement for unemployment compensation, were all contained in the original Social Security Act.

To appreciate the widespread and bipartisan resistance to Social Security, it is important to recognize the distinction that was made at the time between the problem of *preventing* poverty in old age and the problem of *alleviating* poverty among the elderly poor—a distinction that some find difficult to grasp today. Prevention was seen as a problem of retirement-income planning, of personal saving and continued employment, that could and should be addressed through voluntary arrangements—by individuals and families working together with employers, trade unions, fraternal organizations, and financial institutions.

Alleviation ultimately came to be seen as a problem demanding at least some government intervention at the state or local level.

In the first three decades of this century, many states debated means-tested public assistance for the elderly poor and several states passed laws enabling counties to collect and dispense funds for this purpose. No one, however, introduced legislation to get the federal government involved in poverty relief for the elderly poor—let alone involved in the direct provision of retirement pensions for working Americans.

Advocates of social insurance worked hard to blur the distinction between prevention and alleviation, and between insurance and welfare, in the redistributive programs they promoted. They met with a decided lack of success. In historian Arthur Schlesinger's words, "While the friends of social security were arguing out the details of the program, other Americans were regarding the whole idea with consternation, if not with horror." Samuel Gompers, leader of the American Federation of Labor for nearly half a century, put his feelings succinctly in 1917. "Compulsory social insurance," he said, "is in its essence undemocratic."

The public was not naive about the political difficulties of controlling public income-transfer programs. The federal government had long provided pensions and other special programs for veterans, and the generosity and cost of these programs had been a subject of continuous controversy. In 1920, the federal government set up a retirement program for its own employees, spending on which quickly outstripped original projections. And, of course, two or three decades' worth of experience with state and local pension funds for teachers, firemen, and other public employee groups revealed the inevitable pressures to increase benefits, defer tax costs, and shift burdens to future generations. Overexpansion, severe underfunding, and even cutbacks in benefits were not unheard of. In some ways, the political risks attached to long-term benefit promises by government were better understood in the 1920s than they have been since—or at least until very recently.

With the onset of the Great Depression in 1929 and the election of Franklin Roosevelt in 1932, the political landscape began to shift. Old-age assistance programs cropped up in many states, but were strained severely by burgeoning numbers of poor people and shrinking local tax bases. Pressures mounted—especially in the larger, more industrialized states—for federal assistance and a redistribution of tax costs. In 1934, a bill to provide federal matching funds to states operating old-age assistance programs received unanimous approval in both the House Labor Committee and the Senate Finance Committee, revealing broad, bipartisan support for public assistance for the elderly poor.

In a masterful political ploy, however, FDR refused to support the bill and it died at the end of the session. FDR's strategy, clear to all observers at the time, was to take the substantial momentum behind federal assistance for the poor—especially the elderly poor—and leverage it into support for his Social Security Act, a comprehensive legislative program whose heart was the compulsory, government-administered pension program.

Across party lines, members of Congress recognized and complained that they were being put in the position of voting for everything or being labeled as opposed to "social security." As Abraham Epstein, an early proponent of social insurance, described the dilemma for members of Congress, "Their choice was 'all-or-none,' [so] they voted for all and left it to the Supreme Court to separate the good from the bad." (Interestingly, the terms *pension, annuity,* and *insurance* appeared nowhere in the original Social Security Act because of the concern that a compulsory pension program would be found unconstitutional.)

FDR was well aware of the battle to be waged over compulsory old-age pensions. When his Committee on Economic Security submitted its comprehensive legislative package to Congress in 1935, the Great Depression had been raging for six years. The Depression wreaked havoc on everyone—nearly 20 million Americans were on direct relief from the government—but it hit the aged especially hard. Yet not a single bill had been introduced into either chamber of Congress to establish a compulsory old-age pension program. FDR's social-insurance proposal was the first of its kind, even though social insurance had emerged in Europe nearly a half-century earlier, had spread widely among industrial nations, and had been a topic of debate in the United States for more than two decades.

The battle for Social Security began in earnest in the Senate when Sen. Bennett Clark (D-Mo.) offered an amendment to allow companies with private pensions to opt out of the public program. Under the amendment, any company could contract out of the public program if it had a pension plan that offered benefits at least as generous as the federal program, provided that the plan was available to all employees, that premiums were deposited with an insurance company or approved trustee, that employee contributions plus interest were refunded to the government in the event an employee's job was terminated, and that the company was willing to subject its books to federal scrutiny. Employees of companies that contracted out would have their choice of the public or private plan. (Those familiar with modern social security systems will recognize the concept of company-wide contracting out from systems in the United Kingdom and in Japan.)

While the Clark amendment conceded a great deal to Social Security proponents—it accepted, for instance, the premise of compulsory participation and left companies exposed to substantial federal regulation—it nevertheless would have given workers some degree of choice and given employers the right to compete with the government in providing retirement pensions. Individual choice and competition in supply would help ensure maximum value for workers' tax "contributions," protect workers' non-contractual rights to future benefits, and provide a much-needed check on the use of Social Security for the purposes of income redistribution.

According to University of Chicago economist Paul Douglas, a leading figure in the social-insurance movement and later a U.S. senator, the fight over the Clark amendment was "the most vigorous" of the debates surrounding the economic security bill. And little wonder: In less than 10 sentences, the amendment cut through the "insurance" rhetoric and exposed the redistributive underpinnings of Social Security.

Clark and his supporters argued that the amendment would preserve competition in the supply of pensions and allow freedom of choice for workers, while ensuring the nation's elderly a level of protection at least as generous as the federal program. Why stifle the development of private pensions, they reasoned, that potentially could provide higher benefits for retirees while building good will with workers? Company pension plans were spreading rapidly among large companies in the 1920s, having first emerged in the 1880s, and coverage was destined to expand as the tax and business environment improved.

It was in 1926, for example, that the basic features of the tax code pertaining to pensions were established, effectively eliminating the double taxation that penalized ordinary savings. (The favorable tax treatment of employer-sponsored pensions did not extend to individual retirement savings until much later—individual retirement accounts and Keogh plans are creatures of the 1960s and 1970s.)

But critics recognized that the Clark amendment, if passed, would put the federal government in the position of regulating and competing with private pension plans rather than monopolizing its own. That competition would have profound implications for the ability to use Social Security for purposes of income redistribution. As Sen. Robert LaFollette (Prog-Wisc.) put it, "If we shall adopt this amendment, the government … would be inviting and encouraging competition with its own plan which ultimately would undermine and destroy it."

The critics' key argument was that contracting out would leave the public program at a great disadvantage. The feds' benefit formula, weighted in favor of those near retirement (and with lower earnings), would attract people who were relatively more costly to "insure," thus making the government program more expensive, if not prohibitively so. Critics reasoned that firms with relatively young workers would establish or maintain pension plans, choosing to contract out of the public plan (at a savings). Firms with older workers would discontinue or fail to establish plans, allowing their workers to gain retirement protection through the government (also at a savings). Said Sen. Robert Wagner (D-N.Y.), one of the bill's sponsors, "I am firmly convinced that if this amendment were adopted we should find the government holding the bag for older men … while industries would take care of only the younger men *who earned every bit of annuity they received*" (italics added).

COMPULSORY GOVERNMENT-CONTROLLED RETIREMENT SAVINGS IS HARD TO DEFEND IN A WORLD WITH MODERN FINANCIAL MARKETS, A MATURE PRIVATE PENSION SYSTEM, AND EXTENSIVE EXPERIENCE WITH IRAS, 401(K) PLANS, AND OTHER SELF-DIRECTED INVESTMENT PLANS.

Undoubtedly the critics were right. In a competitive setting and in the absence of coercion, workers would be compensated whether in the form of wages, pensions, or some other form of benefit or payment—in relation to the value of their output. There would be little room for anything unearned. But, as proponents of the Clark amendment reasoned, if the purpose of the new program was to provide pensions based on earnings and contributions, not to redistribute income, the private sector was perfectly capable of performing this function. Unearned benefits, not competition, were the source of the problem.

FDR and his allies went to some lengths to kill the Clark amendment, including threatening to veto the entire bill—and thus to block all federal assistance for the poor—if the amendment were passed. Such efforts didn't work, at least initially: The Clark amendment was passed by the Senate (where Democrats held a 44-vote margin) by a vote of 51 to 35. Paul Douglas later acknowledged that, "In view of all the safeguards, it seemed to the majority of the Senate and to a goodly section of the public that there was really no legitimate objection against granting such an exemption." The Senate then approved the economic security bill as amended by a vote of 77–6. The House had already approved the legislation—without the Clark amendment—by a vote of 372–33.

When the House and Senate bills reached conference early in July 1935, negotiators spent a couple of weeks resolving all matters of disagreement in the various welfare programs, the unemployment compensation program, and the compulsory old-age pension program, with the exception of one—the Clark amendment. The House strongly opposed the amendment on the grounds that it would ruin the federal program and could, by resulting in different tax treatment of employers who had and had not contracted out, render the federal program unconstitutional. The Senate refused to budge. On July 16, conferees returned their reports to their respective houses, seeking approval on all issues except the Clark Amendment and seeking further instructions. Both houses responded with instructions to adhere to their positions.

Negotiations dragged on for several more weeks until the conferees decided that a further delay of the entire economic security bill—over a single amendment to a single program—could not be justified. They dropped the Clark amendment with the understanding that a special joint legislative committee would be formed to prepare an amendment, for consideration during the next session of Congress, that embodied the essence of the Clark amendment without raising the constitutional complications.

This, of course, was a major victory for FDR and his allies. The House and Senate accepted the conference report on August 8 and 9, respectively, and the president signed the Social Security Act into law on August 14. The Clark amendment was never reconsidered.

Just five years later, Social Security's income-transfer machinery began churning out checks to elderly people who had paid taxes for at most three years and to people who had paid no taxes at all (elderly spouses and widows, young widows with children, and children of retired or deceased workers). Financed on a quasi-pay-as-you-go basis, the program grew in size and scope in the decades that followed, delivering lifetime annuities to a broader and broader segment of the population at a fraction of the true cost—and piling up larger and larger liabilities to be met by younger generations. Worries about the political risks attached to the government's long-term benefit promises seemed to evaporate.

It was not until the 1970s that reality began to pinch. This is when Social Security first began running gaping long-term deficits and when, as a "mature" pay-as-you-go system, its ability to produce large windfall gains to retirees was fast disappearing. Nothing's been quite the same since.

Today, middle-aged and younger workers, who face the prospect of potentially large wealth losses under the system, naturally seek the right to save privately for retirement, both to reap the gains of investing in higher yielding real capital and to secure their rights to future income. Neither steeped in the traditions of New Deal programs nor beneficiaries of the windfalls those programs delivered in decades past, these workers question the value of Social Security as a retirement savings vehicle in the next century and seek new solutions to the age-old problem of retirement income security. In this case, the best new solutions lie in some old ideas.

When Congress takes up the issue of Social Security reform, it can aim much higher than proponents of the Clark amendment were able to in the 1930s. With modern financial markets, a mature private pension system, and extensive experience with IRAs, 401(k) plans, and other self-directed investment plans, there is no reason to be limited by the idea of company-wide contracting out. Giving individual workers the right to fund and control the investment of their own retirement accounts is now a viable alternative that demands consideration—whether on a limited basis, as envisioned in the legislation introduced by Senators Kerrey (D-Neb.) and Simpson (R-Wyo.), or on a large-scale basis, as under the system adopted in Chile over a decade ago.

Carolyn Weaver is resident scholar and director of Social Security and Pension Studies at the American Enterprise Institute, and was a member of the 1995–1996 Social Security Advisory Council. She has written widely on the economics, politics, and history of Social Security.

Reprinted with permission from the May 1996 issue of *Reason* Magazine. Copyright © 1996 by Reason Foundation, 3415 S. Sepulveda Blvd., Suite 400, Los Angeles, CA 90034. www.reason.com

Japanese Americans and the U.S. Army: A Historical Reconsideration

"The complex history of Japanese Americans and the U.S. Army shows that there is still plenty of room for fresh interpretations. This history can teach us important lessons about the obligations of citizenship and the varieties of valor, topics that will never go out of style."

By James C. McNaughton

A dramatic painting hangs in many Army offices, one of a well-known series of historical lithographs. *Go For Broke* depicts a platoon of Japanese-American soldiers in the Vosges Mountains battling a German tank at close range with rifles and bazookas in October 1944. The phrase "Go For Broke" was the motto of the famous 442d Regimental Combat Team.[1]

This unit and its predecessor, the 100th Infantry Battalion (Separate), hold a special place in the Army's memory. The battalion's lineage and that of the 442d Infantry are preserved by today's 100th Battalion, 442d Infantry, a unit in the U.S. Army Reserve. Both the battalion and the regiment, of which the battalion became a part in 1944, were composed of Japanese Americans from Hawaii and the West Coast who called themselves *Nisei,* the Japanese word for "second-generation." About 22,000 Nisei served in the U.S. Army during World War II. Their valor in Italy and France was unsurpassed as they battled the Germans and simultaneously fought for acceptance as loyal Americans.

The proud history of these units has been celebrated in countless books, ceremonies, films, and public monuments.[2] Two Nisei veterans, Spark Matsunaga and Daniel K. Inouye, went on to represent Hawaii in both houses of Congress.

In 1999 a Japanese-American officer, General Eric K. Shinseki, became chief of staff of the Army. Finally, after Congress in the mid-1990s directed the secretary of the Army to review the award records of Asian Americans in World War II for possible upgrade to the Medal of Honor, President Bill Clinton in June 2000 awarded new Medals of Honor to 22 Asian Americans, 20 Nisei and 2 from other Asian-American groups.[3]

Taken as a whole, these powerful memories evoke a compelling storyline that has changed little since the war: how the Nisei overcame prejudice through heroic military service to achieve national recognition. More than fifty years later, new interpretations are moving beyond this basic storyline. Today multiple viewpoints coexist, sometimes in uneasy balance, reflecting evolving perspectives on World War II. Patriotic narratives and memoirs have now been followed by academic works from the emerging field of Asian-American studies. As the Nisei have begun passing from the scene, scholars and community activists are focusing more on the Japanese-American internment camps than on battlefield valor, stimulated in large measure by the successful redress movement of the 1980s.[4] Yet these new approaches have done little to displace the continual outpouring of publications and commemo-

rations that honor Nisei veterans. The new studies seem reluctant to address military service, as if the continued need to honor surviving veterans might preclude more critical treatment. Hence two storylines now coexist side by side: military service and the internment camps.

Several recent books indicate that scholars may now be more willing to move beyond the celebratory to address issues of Nisei military service in a critical fashion. One result has been to put the U.S. Army in the spotlight once again. The Army played two apparently contradictory roles in the history of Japanese Americans during this period. First, in 1942 the Western Defense Command removed some 110,000 persons of Japanese birth or ancestry from the West Coast, citing "military necessity." Second, in 1943 the War Department called for Nisei volunteers for a segregated regimental combat team, and this was followed in early 1944 by the renewed application of selective service laws to the Nisei. The new books shed light on both episodes and show there is more to the heroic story in the painting than is commonly realized.

Relocation: A Military Necessity?

The Army's removal of all persons of Japanese descent from the West Coast to so-called "war relocation centers" was a

Japanese Americans in San Francisco report for processing under the Army's civilian relocation order, 25 April 1942.

Photo by Dorothea Lange, National Archives photo

watershed in the history of Japanese Americans. On 19 February 1942 President Franklin Roosevelt signed Executive Order 9066 giving military commanders the authority to designate "military areas" from which "any or all persons may be excluded." The commander of the Western Defense Command proceeded over the next six months to remove from the entire West Coast all Japanese immigrants and their American-born children to ten internment camps. Once established, the camps were administered by the War Relocation Authority, but the Army continued to provide security forces.[5]

The decision to evacuate has been studied in great detail. Morton Grodzins of the University of Chicago completed a thorough scholarly examination of the decision-making process and its political context just seven years after the evacuation began. In 1959 Stetson Conn of the Office of the Chief of Military History completed the first study of the decision that was based on War Department records. Grodzins's essay and Conn's careful account have remained the foundation of all subsequent scholarship on the topic.[6] Since 11 September 2001 renewed attention has been given to the evacuation as a potentially dangerous precedent for the detention of suspect groups without due process in time of war.[7] Because the government cited "military necessity" for its rationale, Conn and more recent scholars have focused on the actions of several of the Army's senior leaders—particularly Assistant Secretary of War John J. McCloy; Provost Marshal General Maj. Gen. Allen W. Gullion, who was responsible for internal security; and the commanding general of the Western Defense Command, Lt. Gen. John L. DeWitt. The staff judge advocate who oversaw the evacuation, Col. Karl R. Bendetsen, is often singled out for special opprobrium.[8]

A new book usefully supplements Conn's essay and for the first time places the commander in chief under the microscope: Greg Robinson, *By Order of the President: FDR and the Internment of Japanese Americans* (Cambridge, Mass., 2001). Robinson begins not on 7 December 1941 but decades earlier in Roosevelt's long public career. He carefully documents Roosevelt's attitudes towards Japan and the Japanese, beginning with the Russo-Japanese War in 1904–05 and his years as assistant secretary of the Navy (1913–20), when American naval strategists became concerned about Japanese naval power. Robinson concludes that Roosevelt and the military "seem to have perceived Japanese Americans not only as aliens but as appendages of Japan." This was not so much wrong as simply outdated. In 1920 the census found that only 27 percent of persons of Japanese descent on the West Coast were native born, most of them still minors. With relatively few exceptions their parents had not been permitted to become naturalized citizens because they were not considered "free white person(s)" or "aliens of African nativity or persons of African descent" as required under U.S. law. They were thus deemed "aliens ineligible for citizenship." California and a dozen other states prohibited such aliens from owning land.[9] By 1940, however, the citizen Nisei had grown to 64 percent of the West Coast Japanese American community and about 75 percent in Hawaii.[10]

The Japanese attack in December 1941 on American forward-deployed forces in Hawaii and the Philippines plunged America into global war. Longstanding suspicion by white Americans of the Japanese community in Hawaii made it an easy target of blame for the disaster. In California public officials urged the War Department to take action to prevent a similar disaster on the West Coast. Solid intelligence about any real threat was difficult to come by in an atmosphere rife with rumor and exaggeration. Military intelligence and the Federal Bureau of Investigation downplayed any threat. However, as Robinson points out, "the President was willingly misled…. He was prepared to believe the worst, and expected the worst, from them." After several weeks of pubic pressure and intense discussions among high-ranking officials from the War Department, Justice Department, and state of California, Secretary of War Henry L. Stimson asked the president to decide whether to remove from the West Coast all Japanese Americans, citizens as well as aliens, as he recommended. In a telephone conversation on 11 February 1942, the president "was very vigorous about it" and told Stimson to "go ahead on the line that I [Stimson] had myself thought the best."[11]

Armed with an executive order and a subsequent act of Congress, the Western Defense Command in 1942 removed, by its own count, 109,427 persons of Japanese ancestry from the West Coast. The initial plan was to disperse them throughout the rest of the country, but this was blocked by several Rocky Mountain governors who refused to accept any unless they were kept under tight control.[12]

Over the next few months the tide turned in the Pacific with naval victories in the Coral Sea and at Midway. But the die was cast for evacuation. No one had cause to reassess the decision, either in Washington or the Western Defense Command, which was also responsible for the defense of Alaska, now an active theater of war. Robinson laments that "Roosevelt displayed a shocking unconcern for the negative effects and ramifications of the policy as it developed," while conceding "the enormous demands made on him by the war."

The Supreme Court initially upheld the constitutionality of the evacuation. Most Japanese immigrants were subjects of the emperor, it is true, as technically were many of their American-born children who held dual citizenship. But most of the immigrants had lived in the United States for more than twenty years, owing to the fact that immigration from Japan had been severely restricted in 1907–08 and completely halted in 1924. As Chief Justice William H. Rehnquist emphasizes in his popular study, *All the Laws But One: Civil Liberties in Wartime* (New York,

1998), the U.S. Constitution afforded the government the right to intern enemy aliens in time of war.[13] Rehnquist generally applauds the Supreme Court's reluctance to overturn government actions in time of war. In this case he only expresses doubts about the right of the government to evacuate and incarcerate American citizens based on race alone. He suggests that the Army should have required "far more substantial findings to justify this sort of discrimination, even in wartime."

Beyond the issue of its constitutionality, was the evacuation truly necessary, or even good policy? Scholars have long questioned the "military necessity" justification, pointing out the glaring discrepancy between the handling of Japanese-Americans on the West Coast and in Hawaii, where persons of Japanese ancestry approached 40 percent of the population. In Hawaii, which was certainly at greater risk, shipping was simply not available to remove Japanese Americans, who in any event made up a large proportion of the territory's work force. Instead Army officials opted for cooperation and strict surveillance, which worked well throughout the war.

Robinson documents Roosevelt's lack of interest in Japanese Americans once the evacuation had been set in motion. Not until late 1944, after the strategic situation had markedly improved, the president had won reelection to a fourth term, and the Supreme Court was poised to begin releasing detainees, did Roosevelt agree to close the camps and permit Japanese Americans to return to the West Coast.

Robinson's perspective as a presidential scholar helps us see this tragic episode in a new light and to understand the various patterns in national decision making it exemplifies. First, the decision was fundamentally political in nature, not military. Conn concluded that the Army carried out the evacuation "because the Secretary of War and his principal civilian assistant [McCloy] in this matter themselves thought it necessary to carry it out."[14] The evidence suggests that Roosevelt and his civilian assistants were more concerned about public morale on the West Coast and the need to appear decisive than they were about any threat posed by the Japanese-American

community. The Army was called upon to provide the justification of "military necessity" for a political decision that had already been made on other grounds.

Second, the decision was a product of a specific moment in the war. If the decision had been delayed by even a few months, as it was for Hawaii, the result might have been very different. Finally, once Stimson had obtained Roosevelt's blessing, it was next to impossible to reopen the question. Policy drifted for the next two years, as lower-level officials wrestled with the complications of its implementation. Top-level decisions develop a momentum that make them difficult to alter or reverse unless something dramatic elevates the underlying issue to senior policy levels again. Robinson, in *By Order of the President*, laments Roosevelt's subsequent disengagement, saying his "decision to maintain public silence on the internment policy was perhaps his most crucial and damaging act of injustice toward Japanese Americans during 1942." Indeed, "the President's direct involvement in internment policy after 1942 was restricted in large part to its political defense."

Robinson's craftsmanlike study puts the evacuation in the context of the messy way the Roosevelt Administration made policy during the darkest hours of the war. "Roosevelt failed to transcend the prejudice around him in his direction of public policy," Robinson concludes. "He also deserves censure for not providing moral and constitutional leadership." That is not the same thing as to say his actions had no basis, only that Robinson wishes he had decided differently.

The claim of "military necessity" has remained a lightning rod for those determined to prove that no such necessity existed and that the claim was not even supported at the time by competent intelligence or law enforcement officials. It has likewise been a rallying point for those who insist that the Roosevelt Administration was fully justified, or at least had reasonable cause to suspect the Japanese community.

David D. Lowman's book, *MAGIC: The Untold Story of U.S. Intelligence and the Evacuation of Japanese Residents from the West Coast during WW II* (Athena Press, 2001) has reasserted the latter view. Lowman, who died in 1999, was a career intelligence officer with the National Security Agency. He spent his retirement years battling the redress movement for Japanese Americans, writing newspaper opinion pieces, and testifying before congressional committees to defend "our wartime leaders, ... some of the finest men to have ever served our nation," who, he asserted, "were all branded by the Commission [on Wartime Relocation and Internment of Civilians] and now by the U.S. Congress and the country they served as racists and political opportunists." His book, completed in 1989 but only published a dozen years later, argues forcefully that scholars who dismiss the military necessity of the evacuation have ignored the MAGIC evidence that pointed to extensive Japanese plans for espionage before Pearl Harbor.[15]

Lowman's book reproduces and summarizes selected MAGIC messages, intercepted cables between Tokyo and its embassies and consulates in the United States in 1940–41, together with other non-MAGIC intelligence reports about Japanese Americans. (The Department of Defense first published the MAGIC intercepts in a five-volume set of decoded and translated messages, The "MAGIC" Background of Pearl Harbor [Washington, D.C., 1978].) Lowman provides an overview of American signals intelligence before and during the war and describes the work of the U.S. Army Signal Intelligence Service and the Navy cryptographers working for OP-20-G within the Office of Naval Communications.

Japanese diplomatic messages gave indications that Japan was trying to build an espionage network in Hawaii and on the West Coast. On 30 January 1941 Japanese Foreign Minister Yosuke Matsuoka directed his nation's diplomatic assets in the United States to engage in stepped-up espionage using labor unions, anti-Semitic groups, Communists, African Americans, and individuals of foreign extraction other than Japanese. He also called for the use of Japanese nationals and the American-born Nisei but warned that "if there is any slip in this phase, our people in the U.S. will be subjected to considerable persecution, and the utmost caution must be exercised." A few months later the Japanese consulate in Los Angeles boasted, "We shall maintain connection with our second generations who are at present in the (U.S.) Army, to keep us informed of various developments in the Army. We also have connections with our second generations working in airplane plants for intelligence purposes." Subsequent messages from the consulates in Los Angeles, San Francisco, Seattle, and Honolulu reported defense contracts for aircraft, ship movements, and the like.

Lowman claims these messages prove that military necessity indeed existed and that it provided sufficient justification for the mass evacuation of all persons of Japanese descent from the West Coast. MAGIC and other intelligence, he asserts, revealed "the specter of subversive nets up and down the West Coast, controlled by the Japanese government, utilizing large numbers of local Japanese residents, and designed to operate in a wartime environment." He admits that the claim of military necessity may have been vulnerable to criticism during the war, but he explains that "the most important reason for the evacuation, MAGIC, couldn't be put into the [Western Defense Command's] report." However, his reading of the evidence is too simplistic.

Lowman fervently believes that the raw intercepts speak for themselves and trump other sources of intelligence on the Japanese American community.[16] However the messages speak more of intentions than results. One critic, retired Army Lt. Col. John A. Herzig, pointed out that "newspaper articles which appeared a few days before the date of the intercepts show a remarkable resemblance to the cables sent to Tokyo."[17] The U.S. government was fully aware of the legitimate connections between Japan and some of its emigrants in the United States, and immediately after 7 December 1941 authorities arrested thousands of Japanese aliens who had been too close to the Japanese government. But Lowman has no interest in such nuances. He dismisses his critics as lacking expertise in the arcana of signals intelligence and being highly biased. Herzig, he tells his readers, "was married to a Japanese-American."

Few historians have paid much attention to Lowman's charges since he first raised them in the 1980s. Joseph E. Persico in Roosevelt's Secret War: FDR and World War II Espionage (New York, 2001) describes MAGIC in connection with the Pearl Harbor attack, but not with internment. Rather, he states that "FDR had convincing information from [William J.] Donovan's COI [Office of Coordinator of Information], John Franklin Carter's ring, the FBI, and Army intelligence that Japanese Americans and Japanese aliens posed no threat to American security." He ascribes Roosevelt's decision instead to "the President's sincere and ingrained fear of internal subversion, however unfounded."

Roosevelt's most thorough biographer, Kenneth S. Davis, describes a similar cold-blooded calculus. The decision, he asserts, "was further eased by the fact that it involved no political risk, whereas a contrary decision would loose a storm of criticism of the administration."[18] Greg Robinson relegates the impact of MAGIC on the evacuation decision to a footnote and there concludes that "the MAGIC excerpts do not reveal conclusive evidence of any espionage activities by Japanese Americans." William Rehnquist, however, argues that the MAGIC intercepts do give some support to the view that "first generation American citizens of Japanese descent were more likely than the citizenry as a whole to include potential spies or saboteurs."[19]

Lowman claims that traditional historians have found no traces of MAGIC in documents that were not the direct product of this intelligence source because the secret was so closely guarded. While I do not find this persuasive, historians may be too quick to dismiss MAGIC out of hand. A more useful approach would be to examine these messages in light of how national decision-makers actually use intelligence during crises. The evidence for any threat from Japanese Americans was mixed and indirect. The hints contained in MAGIC, if decision-makers paid them any heed at all, were not by themselves sufficient to justify the mass evacuation and incarceration of over 100,000 civilians. However, the trickle of ambiguous messages may have contributed to Roosevelt and Stimson's fears.

President Clinton awards the Medal of Honor to Senator Inouye and twenty–one other Asian Americans at a White House ceremony, 21 June 2000.

Courtesy of the Clinton Presidential Materials Project, Natonal Archives and Records Administration

Lowman extols the evacuation as "a legitimate wartime measure" that had minimal impact on the evacuees, and he includes wartime propaganda pictures to demonstrate how well the internees were treated. He sees no need to delve into the well-documented history of anti-Japanese prejudice, as he is convinced that "the motivating force behind the evacuation was the intelligence being fed on an almost daily basis to the President and his key advisers." The explanation seems clear to him: "It was because of MAGIC that the U.S. government decided in early 1942 to evacuate all persons of Japanese ancestry from the West Coast of the United States."

Lowman's book swings from history to politics as he pours out more than fifty pages of polemical interpretation of the movement for Japanese-American redress in the 1980s. He focuses his attack on the work of the Commission on Wartime Relocation and Internment of Civilians, created by a 1980 statute, which held hearings and issued a report, *Personal Justice Denied*.[20] Lowman accuses the commissioners and their staff of first being ignorant of MAGIC and then denying its influence. Five years after the commission issued its final report, Congress passed the Civil Liberties Act of 1988, which President Ronald Reagan signed into law. This act called for an of-

ficial government apology and a $20,000 payment to each surviving internee. Lowman is critical of what he considers the commission's creation of a politicized official history containing a "hodgepodge of dishonest research and shocking disinformation."

Lowman's book rehashes old arguments and gives a tortured reading of the available intelligence sources. He errs in giving absolute primacy to communications intelligence, no matter how ambiguous. His polemics should be viewed as symptomatic of the lingering bitterness stemming from Pearl Harbor and the emotions raised by apologies and compensation.

Military Service or Resistance

The internment story must be balanced by an account of the Nisei's outstanding military service, which led to ultimate acceptance of this group by mainstream America as the nation's "model minority." The inspiring story of the 100th Battalion and the 442d Regimental Combat Team has been retold many times. One historian recently commented that rather than being the "forgotten heroes" of World War II, the Nisei soldiers "are probably the most remembered, almost forgotten heroes of the war."[21]

In recent years, however, another story has emerged that runs counter to

the familiar version, that of the small but significant number of Nisei from the internment camps who resisted the draft. Their story reminds us that the issue of Nisei military service is more complex than is usually presented.

The history of the Nisei soldiers did not begin on 7 December 1941. A few Japanese immigrants had served in the Spanish-American War and more than a thousand Japanese Americans entered the Army during World War I. Between the wars, however, few, if any, Nisei served on active duty until the Selective Service Act of 1940 mandated that American men be subject to induction in such a way that "there shall be no discrimination against any person on account of race or color." From the fall of 1940 until December 1941 about 5,000 Nisei were inducted into the U.S. Army. Most Nisei draftees in Hawaii were assigned to two Hawaii National Guard regiments, the 298th and 299th Infantry. West Coast Nisei were scattered throughout various units and training centers in California and Washington. After the Japanese attack on Pearl Harbor, most Nisei soldiers on the mainland were discharged or transferred to inland posts. Selective Service stopped accepting Nisei in early 1942 and subsequently reclassified them IV-C on the ground that they were "not acceptable to the armed forces because of nationality or ancestry." When the 27th Infantry Division arrived to help secure the Hawaiian Islands in the spring of 1942, all Hawaiian Nisei draftees who had been assigned to the 298th and 299th Infantry were sent to the mainland, organized into the 100th Infantry Battalion, and shipped to Camp McCoy, Wisconsin. Of the several hundred left behind on Hawaii, most went into 1399th Engineer Construction Battalion. The Military Intelligence Service took others as translators and interpreters.[22]

In the fall of 1942 Assistant Secretary McCloy persuaded the General Staff to form an all-Nisei combat unit. The call for volunteers, announced in January 1943, was greeted with great enthusiasm in Hawaii, where 10,000 Nisei volunteered, a key moment in the historical memory of Nisei military service. Less remembered is the low turnout in the internment camps on the mainland, where the call for volunteers was complicated by the War Relocation Authority's decision to administer a loyalty questionnaire to all individuals for a "leave clearance" program designed to release selected individuals from the camps for military service, schooling, or civilian employment.[23]

In late September 1943 the 100th Infantry Battalion was committed to battle with the 34th Infantry Division near Avellino, Italy, north of Salerno. Meanwhile the 442d Regimental Combat Team, formed from the new volunteers, trained at Camp Shelby, Mississippi, for fifteen months before deploying to Italy in May 1944, where it joined Fifth Army for the Rome-Arno campaign. But this is not the whole story of Nisei manpower. In the winter of 1943–44 the 100th Infantry Battalion suffered an individual replacement crisis when it took heavy casualties at Monte Cassino and Anzio. Because it was a segregated unit, the battalion required a separate stovepipe replacement stream. For this the Army drew hundreds of replacements from the 442d, which was still training at Camp Shelby.[24]

By January 1944 the War Department decided it had to resume applying Selective Service laws to the Nisei to keep these units at full strength.[25] Conscription brought to the surface the contradic-

tions inherent in compelling young men to serve at a time when many of their families remained behind barbed wire. The Japanese American Citizens League wholeheartedly supported the resumption of Selective Service, but in the camps the move was met with scattered protests and bitterness. More than 300 Nisei resisted induction and landed in jail. They were sometimes called the "No-No Boys," for answering "no" to two questions on the loyalty questionnaire: "Are you willing to serve in the armed forces of the United States on combat duty, wherever ordered?" (Some responded yes, but only if their civil rights were restored) and "Will you … foreswear any form of allegiance or obedience to the Japanese emperor?" (Some thought this was a trick question, because they had never offered any allegiance to the emperor.)[26]

The "No-No Boys" were controversial within their communities, much as Vietnam-era "draft dodgers" were to a later generation. They have remained so to this day, for they contradict the public perception of Nisei willingness to prove their loyalty by volunteering for military service. Their story has finally been told in detail by Eric L. Muller, a law professor at the University of North Carolina at Chapel Hill. Muller's book, *Free to Die for Their Country: The Story of the Japanese American Draft Resisters in World War II* (Chicago, 2001), is the first full treatment of this sensitive story.[27] Muller's tightly focused work is based on careful legal research, supplemented by oral histories with eleven of the resisters.

Muller briefly covers the familiar story of the evacuation and internment, followed by the formation of the 442d. His story really begins when the War Department announced the resumption of Selective Service for the Nisei on 20 January 1944. Soon afterward came the orders to individual Nisei to report for their induction physicals. Responses were divided. Most young men chose to comply without incident, although many did so with mixed feelings.

The strongest organized resistance sprang up at Heart Mountain, Wyoming, where a few activists organized the Fair Play Committee and issued a manifesto declaring, "We would gladly sacrifice

our lives to protect and uphold the principles and ideals of our country as set forth in the Constitution and the Bill of Rights.…But have we been given such freedom, such liberty, such justice, such protection? NO!!" Camp administrators, Japanese-American community leaders, and the Justice Department came down on them hard.

In May 1944 a federal grand jury in Cheyenne, Wyoming, indicted seven Fair Play Committee leaders and a sympathetic Nisei newspaper editor for conspiring to counsel, aid, and abet young men to evade the draft. Soon 63 Nisei resisters from Heart Mountain were in jail. Others were arrested from the other camps, and their number eventually grew to 315 from all camps and Hawaii. Muller details the various cases as they progressed through the court system. In all 263 Nisei were convicted and most were sentenced to three years in federal prison. Only one federal judge demurred, Louis B. Goodman of the U.S. District Court for the Northern District of California. Goodman dismissed the indictments of 27 Nisei, declaring, "It is *shocking to the conscience* that an American citizen be confined on the ground of disloyalty, and then, while so under duress and restraint, be compelled to serve in the armed forces, or be prosecuted for not yielding to such compulsion."

With this lone exception, hundreds of Nisei draft resisters were sent to federal penitentiaries. President Harry Truman pardoned these Nisei in December 1947, along with several thousand other Americans convicted of violating the Selective Service Act. In a country and an ethnic community that honored their returning war heroes, the Nisei draft resisters were a scorned minority within a minority and were ostracized by the Japanese-American community. Muller unfortunately does not explore their postwar experiences, which have been portrayed by the novelist John Okada, himself a Nisei veteran, in his novel, *No-No Boy* (which Muller curiously does not cite).[28]

Muller instead follows the legal twists and turns as the cases moved through the courts. He reluctantly draws the conclusion that the law and the constitution supported Selective Service. His reluctance marks the views of a generation now three decades removed from any form of military conscription. "I struggled to match my sense of moral outrage with a corresponding conviction that the law was on their side." He regrets that "America would not extend the option of loyal protest" to the Nisei. "Through the force of criminal sanction, it demanded that these young Japanese Americans prove their patriotism through unquestioning obedience to authority, ironically a trait more Japanese than American."

Muller does not place the Nisei in the broader context of the 50,000 conscientious objectors during World War II, many of whom served in non-combat assignments. Another 5,000 men were jailed for resisting the draft. But he gives readers an opportunity to see in a new light the choice of those Nisei who did serve. They did so not blindly or automatically, but in full knowledge that their country had not given their parents a fair shake.

On balance the Japanese American Citizens League had the better side of the argument. Rather than insist on full restoration of civil rights before they would serve, most Nisei looked to the future. Their pragmatic strategy was to use military service to effect positive changes, rather than holding back and demanding their rights as a precondition for service. As President Truman told returning 442d veterans in 1946, "You fought not only the enemy, you fought prejudice—and you won."[29] The story of the Nisei draft resisters in no way diminishes the valor of the Nisei who served. On the contrary, it places their choice in stark relief. No less a figure than Senator Inouye declares in the Foreword to Muller's book: "In this climate of hate, I believe that it took just as much courage and valor and patriotism to stand up to our government and say 'you are wrong.' I am glad that there were some who had the courage to express some of the feelings that we who volunteered harbored deep in our souls."[30]

Honors and History

Nisei valor is often measured by the thousands of military awards they received. In 2001 Lee and Sam Allen of Athena Press, David Lowman's publishers, attacked an exhibit in the Smithsonian Institution's National Museum of American History on the ground that these statistics were inflated.[31] The exhibit, *A More Perfect Union: Japanese Americans and the U.S. Constitution*, opened in 1987 to mark the bicentennial of the U.S. Constitution. The Smithsonian had developed the exhibit in cooperation with Asian-American scholars and the Japanese-American community to tell the story of the wartime Japanese-American evacuation, internment, and military service. It has long been controversial, although it has not drawn as much criticism as the Smithsonian's 1995 exhibit on the *Enola Gay*.[32]

The exhibit's section on Nisei military service presents commonly cited statistics about the casualties suffered by and the medals awarded to Japanese American soldiers. The Allens do not dispute the bravery or valor of the Nisei but challenge what they call "the gratuitous embellishment of military achievements."[33] Beyond the statistics, they consider the exhibit yet one more example of official history giving a revisionist view of the American past in favor of a privileged minority group. In an August 2002 press release Lee Allen, a retired Army lieutenant colonel, comments that "the politically correct notion that race was the main motivation [for the evacuation], which the Smithsonian with its poor scholarship buys into, results from denying, ignoring, exaggerating and fabricating important facts."[34]

When the museum's staff reviewed the statistics, they discovered that reliable sources from the immediate postwar period reported substantially lower numbers. For example, the exhibit claimed 9,486 Purple Hearts, but a regimental history published in 1946 estimated the total to be less than half that amount. In consequence the museum promised to correct the numbers.[35]

The Allens' attack on the Smithsonian exhibit and Lowman's polemical book in the end shed little new light on the evacuation and Nisei military service. Instead they exploit weaknesses in others' scholarship for their own questionable ends. They do remind us, however, that although the Army often differentiates between "history" and "heritage" activities, heritage must be based on sound history.

The subject of Japanese Americans and the U.S. Army is still an area of controversy and on-going scholarship. Old controversies die hard or get recycled endlessly on the internet. These questions burn brightest in the thoughts of those who were most affected as well as those who still fervently insist that the evacuation was based on military necessity and deny that racial prejudice had anything to do with it. However, Greg Robinson's policy-oriented study of presidential decision-making shows that sound scholarship can still contribute new insights. Eric Muller's legal study of the Nisei draft resisters takes nothing away from the valor of those who chose differently and fought for their country. If anything, it helps us appreciate all the more the civic courage of those who volunteered when others refused. The complex history of Japanese Americans and the U.S. Army shows that there is still plenty of room for fresh interpretations. This history can teach us important lessons about the obligations of citizenship and the varieties of valor, topics that will never go out of style.

Dr. James C. McNaughton is the command historian for U.S. Army, Pacific. He holds a doctorate in history from the Johns Hopkins University and is a retired U.S. Army Reserve lieutenant colonel. He directed the research team for the Asian-American Medal of Honor review. The Center of Military History hopes to publish his book-length manuscript, "Loyal Linguists: Japanese Americans in the Military Intelligence Service."

Notes

1. H. Charles McBarron, *Go For Broke*, lithograph, 1978, U.S. Army Center of Military History.
2. For some works since the 1980s see Thelma Chang, *"I Can Never Forget": Men of the 100th/442nd* (Honolulu, 1991); Lyn Crost, *Honor by Fire: Japanese Americans at War in Europe and the Pacific* (Novato, Calif., 1994); Masayo Umezawa Duus, *Unlikely Liberators: The Men of the 100th and 442nd*, trans. Peter Duus (Honolulu, 1987); and Chester Tanaka, *Go for Broke: A Pictorial History of the Japanese American 100th Infantry Battalion and the 442d Regimental Combat Team* (Richmond, Calif., 1982). Recent documentary films include *Beyond Barbed Wire* (Mac and Ava, 1997); *Forgotten Valor* (Lane Nishikawa, 2001);

Uncommon Courage: Patriotism and Civil Liberties (Bridge Media, 2001); and *A Tradition of Honor* (Go For Broke Educational Foundation, 2002).

3. "A Last Battle Won for 22 Asian Americans Given Medal of Honor," *Washington Post*, 22 Jun 2000; James C. McNaughton, Kristen E. Edwards, and Jay M. Price, "'Incontestable Proof Will Be Exacted': Historians, Asian Americans, and the Medal of Honor," *The Public Historian* 24 (Fall 2002): 11–33.

4. Recent surveys include Sucheng Chan, *Asian Americans: An Interpretive History* (Boston, 1991); Harry H. L. Kitano and Roger Daniels, *Asian Americans: Emerging Minorities*, 3d ed. (Upper Saddle River, N.J., 2001); and Ronald T. Takaki, *Strangers from a Different Shore: A History of Asian Americans*, rev. ed. (Boston, 1998). For useful bibliographic essays, see Paul R. Spickard, *Japanese Americans: The Formation and Transformations of an Ethnic Group* (New York, 1996), 177–85; and Gary Y. Okihiro, *Teaching Asian American History* (Washington, D.C., 1997).

5. The government labeled the camps "war relocation centers" and referred to them publicly as concentration camps. However, since 1945 "concentration camp" has carried the connotation of the Nazi death camps. "Internment camp" usually refers to the separate camps established by the Department of Justice for enemy aliens, not citizens, but for convenience I have used the term to include the ten camps operated by the War Relocation Authority.

6. Morton Grodzins, *Americans Betrayed: Politics and the Japanese Evacuation* (Chicago, 1949); Stetson Conn, "The Decision to Evacuate the Japanese from the Pacific Coast," in Kent Roberts Greenfield, ed., *Command Decisions* (New York, 1959), pp. 88–109. A later version appeared as a chapter entitled "Japanese Evacuation from the West Coast" in Stetson Conn, Rose C. Engelman, and Byron Fairchild, *Guarding the United States and Its Outposts* (Washington, D.C., 1964), 115–49. For a convenient summary see Roger Daniels, *Prisoners Without Trial: Japanese Americans in World War II* (New York, 1993). Grodzins made substantial use of the Western Defense Command's published report on the evacuation and on congressional and Justice Department sources.

7. For example, Sam Tanenhaus, "Outside In," *New Republic* 225 (8 Oct 2001): 22.

8. For example, Michi Weglyn labeled Colonel Bendetsen "the Army architect-to-be of the racial uprooting." See Michi Weglyn, *Years of Infamy: The Untold Story of America's Concentration Camps* (New York, 1976), p. 43. Bendetsen would serve as assistant secretary of the Army in 1950–1952. Recent studies of the camps include Daniels, *Prisoners Without Trial*, and Lawson Fusao Inada, ed., *Only What We Could Carry: The Japanese American Internment Experience* (Berkeley, Calif, 2000). David Guterson's award-winning novel, *Snow Falling on Cedars* (New York, 1994), and its 1999 film adaptation brought the story to a new generation.

9. Takaki, *Strangers from a Different Shore*, pp. 203–09; Bradford Smith, *Americans from Japan*, reprint ed. (1948, Westport, Conn., 1974), pp.148–49; "Alien Land Laws," in Brian Niiya, ed., *Encyclopedia of Japanese American History: An A-to-Z Reference from 1868 to the Present*, updated ed. (New York, 2001), pp. 111–12. Congress had initially limited eligibility for naturalization in 1790 to any "free white person" meeting certain qualifications and extended to "aliens of African nativity and persons of African descent" in 1870. See *U.S. Statutes at Large*, 1: 103, 16: 256. However, the undisputed right to citizenship of permanent resident alien veterans of World War I without regard to race was granted by the Lea-Nye Act of 1935. See Frank F. Chuman, *The Bamboo People: The Law and Japanese-Americans* (Del Mar, Calif, 1976); *U.S. Statutes*, 49: 397–98. The McCarran-Walter Act of 1952 lifted the bars to naturalization of immigrants from Japan and to further immigration from that country.

10. West Coast Nisei population: Western Defense Command, *Final Report: Japanese Evacuation from the West Coast*, 1942 (Washington, D.C., 1943), pp. 84, 402. The narrative portions of this report should be used with caution. Hawaii Nisei population: Thomas D. Murphy, *Ambassadors in Arms: The Story of Hawaii's 100th Battalion* (Honolulu, 1954), p. 1.

11. Conn, Engelman, and Fairchild, *Guarding the United States*, pp. 131–32, quoting Stimson's diary.

12. Executive Order 9066, 19 Feb 1942, printed in War Department Bulletin 10, 28 Feb 1942; Public Law 503, 77th Congress, approved 21 Mar 1942, printed in *US. Statutes*, 56: 173. The evacuation figures are in Western Defense Command, *Final Report*, p. 362. The evacuees included 259 persons from Arizona.

13. See also William H. Rehnquist, "When the Laws Were Silent," *American Heritage* 49 (October 1998): 76–89.

14. Conn, Engelman, and Fairchild, *Guarding the United States*, p. 147.

15. David D. Lowman, *MAGIC: The Untold Story of U.S. Intelligence and the Evacuation of Japanese Residents from the West Coast During WW II* (n.p., 2001); David D. Lowman, "MAGIC and the Japanese Internments," *Baltimore Sun*, 24 Jun 1983; Testimony of David D. Lowman, 27 Jun 1984, in *Japanese-American and Aleutian Wartime Relocation: Hearings before the Subcommittee on Administrative Law and Governmental Relations of the Committee on the Judiciary, House of Representatives, Ninety-Eighth Congress, Second Session, on H.R. 3387, H.R. 4110, and H.R. 4322* (Washington, D.C., 1985), pp. 430–548; testimony of David D. Lowman, 16 Aug 1984, in *Recommendations of the Commission on Wartime Internment and Relocation of Citizens: Hearings before the Subcommittee on Civil Service, Post Office, and General Services of the Committee on Governmental Affairs, United States Senate, Ninety-Eighth Congress, Second Session, on S. 2116* (Washington, D.C., 1986), pp. 310–50.

16. Another possible problem which Lowman does not consider is mistranslation. See Keiichiro Komatsu, *Origins of the Pacific War and the Importance of 'MAGIC'* (New York, 1999), pp. 247–88.

17. John A. Herzig, "Japanese Americans and MAGIC," *Amerasia Journal* 11 (Fall/Winter 1984): 56.

18. Kenneth S. Davis, *FDR: The War President, 1940–1943* (New York, 2000), p. 425. Davis follows James MacGregor Burns, *Roosevelt: The Soldier of Freedom* (New York, 1970), 213–17.

19. William H. Rehnquist, *All the Laws But One: Civil Liberties in Wartime* (New York, 1998), pp. 208–09, with quoted words on p. 208.

20. The commission's findings were given in *Personal Justice Denied: Report of the Commission on Wartime Relocation and Internment of Civilians*, 2 vols. (Washington, D.C., 1982–83).

21. T. Fujitani, "*Go For Broke*, the Movie: Japanese American Soldiers in U.S. National, Military, and Racial Discourses," in T. Fujitani, Geoffrey M. White, and Lisa Yoneyama, eds., *Perilous Memories: The Asia-Pacific War(s)* (Durham, N.C., 2001), p. 239. See also T. Fujitani, "The Reischauer Memo: Mr. Moto, Hirohito, and Japanese American Soldiers," *Critical Asian Studies* 33 (September 2001): 379–402.

22. "World War I Veterans," *Encyclopedia of Japanese American History*, p. 413; Brian McAllister Linn, *Guardians of Empire: The U.S. Army and the Pacific, 1902–1940* (Chapel Hill, N.C., 1997), pp. 149–57; Ted T. Tsukiyama, "Gero Iwai," *Secret Valor: M.I.S. Personnel, World War II, Pacific Theater, pre*

Pearl Harbor to Sept. 8, 1951: 50th Anniversary Reunion, July 8–10, 1993 (Honolulu, 1993); Murphy, *Ambassadors in Arms*, pp. 39–74; Tamotsu Shibutani, *The Derelicts of Company K: A Sociological Study of Demoralization* (Berkeley, Calif, 1978), p. 49; U.S. Selective Service System, *Special Groups*, Special Monograph No. 10, 2 vols. (Washington, D.C., 1953), 1: 113–42, quotations on pp. 74, 117–18.

23. Duus, *Unlikely Liberators*, pp. 50–71. The best study of the Army's decision to organize a Japanese-American combat unit is in Murphy, *Ambassadors in Arms*, pp. 104–12. Only 1,256 Nisei in the internment camps, or roughly 5 percent of the 23,606 interned Nisei of draft age, volunteered by 23 March 1943. See Duus, *Unlikely Liberators*, p. 70.

24. Murphy, *Ambassadors in Arms*, pp. 123–84; Martin Blumenson, *Salerno to Cassino*, U.S. Army in World War II (Washington, D.C., 1969), pp. 161–62; Crost, *Honor by Fire*, pp. 115, 137.

25. Selective Service rules were later amended to allow the enlistment of selected aliens, mostly those who had been born in Japan but brought to America at an early age and were otherwise indistinguishable from Nisei. About forty Japanese aliens served in the U.S. military during the war. See Duus, *Unlikely Liberators*, p. 231.

26. *Personal Justice Denied*, 1; 191–92; Daniels, *Prisoners Without Trial*, p, 69.

27. The story of Nisei draft resistance is also described in the documentary film *Conscience and the Constitution* that was written, directed, and produced by Frank Abe in 2000. The most widely read book on Japanese-American history, Bill Hosokawa, *Nisei: The Quiet Americans* (New York, 1969), significantly makes no mention of the draft resisters.

28. John Okada, *No-No Boy* (Rutland, Vt., 1957).

29. Quoted in Ronald Takaki, *Double Victory: A Multicultural History of America in World War II* (Boston, 2000), p. 165. The Japanese American Citizens League's approach was similar to the "Double V" campaign by African Americans during the war.

30. Few works treat the Asian American military experience after World War II. Two exceptions are Toshio Whelchel, *From Pearl Harbor to Saigon: Japanese American Soldiers and the Vietnam War* (New York, 1999), and Carina A. del Rosario, ed., *A Different Battle: Stories of Asian Pacific American Veterans* (Seattle, 1999). See also "Asian Americans in the U.S. Military," in the *Asian American Almanac: A Reference Work on Asians in the United States* (Detroit, 1995), pp. 371–402.

31. Typescript, Lee Allen and Sam Allen, "Critique of the Smithsonian Institution's Exhibition, 'A More Perfect Union: Japanese Americans and the U.S. Constitution,'" 9 May 2001, copy in *Army History* files, CMH. An unpaginated copy of the document is posted on web at http://www.athenapressinc.com/smithsonian/critique.html. An online version of the Smithsonian exhibit can be found at http://americanhistory.si.edu/perfectunion/experience/index.html.

32. I. Michael Heyman, "Smithsonian Perspectives," *Smithsonian* 26 (September 1995): 6.

33. Typescript, Allen and Allen, "Critique of the Smithsonian Exhibition," p. 4.

34. Press release, Athena Press, 16 August 2002, copy in *Army History* files, CMH. The press release is posted at http://www.athenapressinc.com/smithsonian/press_release.html.

35. Information and Education Section, Mediterranean Theater of Operations, United States Army, *The Story of the 442nd Combat Team*, p. 44 (n.p., 1945); Orville C. Shirey, *Americans: The Story of the 442d Combat Team* (Washington, D.C., 1946), p.l0l; Marc Pachter, Acting Director, National Museum of American History, letter to Rep. Chris Cannon, 12 Jul 2002, copy in *Army History* files, CMH. The letter is posted at http://www.athenapressinc.com/smithsonian/response.html. The author assisted museum staff with obtaining more accurate numbers.

Article from *Army History*, Summer/Fall 2003, pages 5-15. Reprinted with approval of the author (Public Domain material).

American Women in a World at War

Judy Barrett Litoff and David C. Smith

Early in 1943, Max Lerner, the well-known author and journalist, writing for the New York newspaper *PM*, predicted that "when the classic work on the history of women comes to be written, the biggest force for change in their lives will turned out to have been war." With the renewed interest in American women's history that has occurred over the last quarter century, most historians interested in women and World War II have addressed the implication of Lerner's statement by asking the question "Did World War II serve as a major force for change in the lives of American women?" Our reading of approximately thirty thousand letters written by more than fifteen hundred women representing a broad cross-section of the wartime population has led us to conclude that the events of World War II did indeed have a dramatic and far-reaching effect on the lives of American women.

For more than a decade, we have been engaged in a nationwide effort to locate, collect, and publish the wartime correspondence of American women. Our search began in the late 1980s as we were making the final revisions for a book, *Miss You: The World War II Letters of Barbara Woodall Taylor and Charles E. Taylor* (1990), which was based on thousands of pages of correspondence between a young war bride and her soldier husband. We found the Taylors' letters to be extremely powerful documents, chronicling a grand story of romance, making do, and "growing up" during wartime.

We were convinced that Taylor's story was similar to those of other women during the war. But how could we be sure? While conducting the research for *Miss You*, we learned that the letters written by men in combat had often been carefully preserved by loved ones, donated to military and university archives, and made into many books. But what had happened to the billions of letters written by American women? No one seemed to have an adequate answer to this question.

During the early stages of our search for the missing letters, many of our colleagues and friends discouraged us from taking on this challenge because of the perceived wisdom that few, if any, letters written by American women had survived the vicissitudes of the war and the postwar years. After all, it was well known that men in combat were under orders not to keep personal materials such as diaries and letters. Moreover, we were repeatedly warned that should we locate letters written by women, they would include little, if any, significant commentary because of strict wartime censorship regulations. Others discounted our effort, arguing that women's letters would contain only trivial bits of information about the war years. Yet the historical detective in each of us was not persuaded by these arguments.

In the spring of 1988, we intensified our search for women's wartime correspondence by devising a brief author's query requesting information from anyone who had knowledge about letters written by American women during the Second World War. We sent the query to every daily newspaper in the United States—about fifteen hundred newspapers in all—and requested that the query be printed on the letters-to-the-editor page. Much to our delight, newspapers throughout the United States complied. Very shortly thereafter, wartime letters from across the United States began to pour into our offices. We soon realized that we had struck a gold mine of information.

We supplemented our author's query to the nation's newspapers with more than five hundred letters of inquiry to magazines and newsletters specializing in issues of concern to women, World War II veterans, and minorities. We wrote letters about our search to every state historical society and to dozens of research and university libraries. In an effort to locate the correspondence of African American women, we solicited the advice of prominent black historians, surveyed archives specializing in African American history, and sent out a special appeal to five hundred predominately black churches around the nation. In total, we have written more than twenty five hundred letters of inquiry. We often wonder if this might qualify us for inclusion in the *Guinness Book of World Records*.

Today, some thirty thousand letters and seven books later, we can state, without question, that the perceived wisdom about women's wartime correspondence was wrong. The thirty thousand letters we have collected were written by more than fifteen hundred women representing diverse social, economic, ethnic, and geographic circumstances from all fifty states. We have collected letters written by grade-school dropouts, but we also have letters composed by college graduates. Our archive includes letters by women from rural and smalltown America, as well as large metropolitan areas. The letters of sweethearts, wives, mothers, stepmothers, mothers-in-law, grandmothers, daughters, sisters, aunts, nieces, the "girl next door," and just plain friends of men in the military have been donated to us. Moreover, we have letters written by representatives of the four hundred thousand pioneering women who joined one of the women's branches of the army, navy, marines, and coast guards, as well as from those extraordinary women who flew military aircraft of all types for the Women Air Force Service Pilots (WASPs). In addition, we have powerful letters written by women who served overseas with the American Red Cross and the Army and Navy Nurse Corps.

Many of the women who have donated materials to our archive have included the note that they doubt there is anything of value in their letters because they were careful to follow the dictates of strict wartime censorship regulations. Others have apologized for the allegedly cheery, upbeat quality of their letters, noting that they did not want to cause the recipients, who were often family members, undue worry and stress. Yet these same letter collections contain commentary about the stresses of balancing a war job with raising young children alone, the difficulties of "making do" on meager allotment checks, the fear of losing a loved one to battle, the challenges of performing emergency surgery in evacuation hospitals near the front lines, what it was like to provide aid and comfort for returning prisoners of war who had been incarcerated by the Japanese, and the caring for the survivors of German concentration camps. We have come to realize that what is most extraordinary about the letters in our archive is how *much*—rather than how *little*—frank and detailed discussion they contain.

These letters are honest accounts, written "at the scene" and "from the heart" for a limited audience and with little idea that historians such as ourselves would one day be interested in their content. They offer perceptive insights, untempered by the successive events of the past fifty years, into heretofore unexplored but fundamental aspects of the war. Indeed, they provide us with the first significant opportunity to incorporate the actual wartime voices of American women into our accounts of the Second World War.

One of the most striking themes expressed in the letters is the new sense of self experienced by wartime women. Whether the writer was a stepmother from rural South Dakota reassuring her recently departed stepson that "you've always been a model son whether you're my blood or not" or a Mexican American migrant worker from Kansas discussing with her combat-decorated sweetheart whether she should go to Denver in search of a new job, the challenges of the war necessitated that women develop a new sense of who they were and of their capabilities.

Young war wives frequently wrote of how they were becoming more self-reliant individuals as they traveled across the country to distant places to be with their husbands, learned how to live on meager allotment checks, coped with raising young children alone, grappled with worry, loneliness, and despair, and shared their experiences with what *The New York Times* described as those "wandering members of [that] huge unorganized club" of war brides.

Early in 1945, war bride Frances Zulauf wrote to her husband in the Army AirForce and discussed how the events of the war had contributed to her growing sense of self:

> Personally, I think there's no doubt that this sacrifice we're making will force us to be bigger, more tolerant, better citizens than we would have been otherwise. If it hadn't been for all this upset in my life, I would still be a rattle brained… spoiled 'little' girl in college, having dates and playing most of my way thru school…. I'm learning—in this pause in my life—just what I want for happiness later on—so much different than what I wanted two years ago.

With more than 16 million men serving in the military, the need for new war workers was unprecedented. Responding to this need, some 6.5 million women entered the workforce, increasing the female labor force by more than 50 percent. In fact, Rosie the Riveter became a national heroine. In their letters to loved ones, women expressed pride in their war work and often commented, with enthusiasm, about the new sense of responsibility and independence they were achieving.

Polly Crow, a young mother living with her parents in Louisville, Kentucky, for the duration, explained in a June 1944 letter to her army husband why she wanted a war job. She also highlighted the advantages of swing shift work for working mothers:

> I'm thinking seriously of going to work in some defense plant… on the swing shift so I can be at home during the day with Bill [their young son] as he needs me… . Of course, I'd much rather have an office job but I couldn't be with Bill whereas I could if I worked at nite which I have decided is the best plan as I cain't save anything by not working and I want to have something for us when you get home.

After securing a job at the Jefferson Boat and Machine Company in nearby Anderson, Indiana, Polly Crow wrote a letter in which she proudly proclaimed, "You are now the husband of a career woman—just call me your little Ship Yard Babe!" Her letters describe the "grand and glorious feeling" of opening her own checking account for the first time, gas rationing, the challenges of automobile maintenance, and what it was like to join a union. Late in 1944, upon learning that the work of building landing ship tanks at the shipyard would be completed within the next few months, she wrote a letter in which she bemoaned the fact that "my greatly enjoyed working career will [soon] come to an end."

Women welders, including the women's welding champion, of Ingalls Shipbuilding Corporation in Pascagoula, Mississippi, ca. 1943 (NARA NWDNS-86-WWT-85-35).

Betty Bleakmore, a nineteen-year-old blueprint supervisor at Douglas Aircraft Company in Tulsa, Oklahoma, wrote to her sweetheart and husband-to-be, a marine corps pilot, and reported that she was responsible for keeping "all [blue]prints up to date so that the [workers] in the factory can build the planes perfectly for people like you to fly." She then continued: "Imagine, [me], little Betty, the youngest in her department with seventeen people older than her… under her. Of course, I too, have higher ups to report to—but I am the big fish in my own little pond—and I love it."

In the fall of 1945, with the war finally over, Edith Speert, a supervisor at a federally funded day care center in Cleveland, Ohio, took the opportunity to tell her husband that she had received a great deal of satisfaction from her war work. On 21 October 1945, she commented:

Last night [we] were talking about some of the adjustments we'll have to make to our husbands' return. I must admit I'm not exactly the same girl you left—I'm twice as independent as I used to be and to top it off, I sometimes think I've becomes "hard as nails"—hardly anyone can evoke any sympathy from me.

Three weeks later, she reiterated:

Sweetie, I want to make sure I make myself clear about how I've changed. I want you to know *now* that you are not married to a girl that's interested solely in a home—I shall definitely have to work all my life—I get emotional satisfaction out of working and I don't doubt that many a night you will cook the supper while I'm at a meeting. Also dearest—I shall never wash and iron—there are laundries for that! Do you think you'll be able to bear living with me?

World War II also brought about significant changes in the lives of farm women as 6 million agricultural workers departed from rural America to don military uniforms or seek more lucrative work in war industries. The crucial role played by American women in the planting and harvesting of the nation's wartime crops is demonstrated by the fact that the proportion of women engaged in agricultural work increased from 8 percent in 1940 to 22.4 percent in 1945. Of particular significance were the 3 million women who came "to the rescue of the nation's crops" and joined the federal Women's Land Army. One young farm woman wrote to a friend in the service and proudly announced, "I'm quite the farmer, Jack. You should see me—I ride the horse after the cows, drive hay trucks, and yesterday I even learned to drive the tractor."

The correspondence of the four hundred thousand American women who exchanged their civilian clothes for military uniforms is replete with examples of how their wartime experiences opened up new, and heretofore, unimaginable opportunities for women. In choosing to support the war effort by joining one of the newly created women's branches of the military, these trailblazers challenged fundamental assumptions about the "proper" role of women in American society. For many women in uniform, World War II was *the* defining event in their lives.

The letters of women in uniform contain telling accounts of the courage of African American women as they combated racism at home and fascism abroad; the agony and isolation experienced by the only Jewish servicewoman at her duty station; glimpses of the stress and strain that lesbians in the military encountered; the blossoming of heterosexual love in the face of battle; establishing Red Cross clubs in remote areas around the world; dodging "buzz bombs" in England; helping to perform emergency surgery in evacuation hospitals near the front; and the intense camaraderie that women in uniform shared as they faced new and challenging responsibilities for the sake of the war effort.

Entrance into the military presented many new job opportunities for women. Although a large percentage of women in uniform performed traditional "women's jobs," such as administrative and clerical work, many other employment possibilities existed, especially in the field of aviation where women served as metalsmiths, aircraft mechanics, parachute-riggers, air traffic controllers, link trainer instructors, and flight orderlies.

One of the most unusual and exciting of the new jobs for women was that of ferrying military aircraft of all types throughout the United States for the WASPs, a quasi-military organization affiliated with the Army Air Forces. From September 1942 until December 1944, when the WASPs were disbanded after not being accorded full military status, approximately one thousand women had the distinction of flying military aircraft throughout the United States. The WASPs gloried in their work, and their wartime letters are filled with details of their love of flying. In a 24 April 1943 letter to her mother, Marion Stegeman of Athens, Georgia, recounted her joy of flying:

> The gods must envy me! This is just too, *too* good to be true. (By now you realize I had a good day as regards flying. Nothing is such a gauge to the spirits as how well or how poorly one has flown.) … I'm far too happy. The law of compensation must be waiting to catch up with me somewhere. Oh, god, how I love it! Honestly, Mother, you haven't *lived* until you get way *up* there—all alone—just you and that big, beautiful plane humming under your control.

While uniformed women from the United States did not participate in organized combat during World War II, they were regularly assigned to postings that brought them up to or near the front lines of battle. Army nurse June Wandrey served in North Africa, Sicily, Italy, France, and Germany, where her work as a combat surgical nurse brought her close to the front lines of action. Writing from "Poor Sicily" in August 1943, she bluntly informed her parents:

> We were so close to the [front] lines we could see our artillery fire and also that of the Germans…. Working in the shock wards, giving transfusions, was a rewarding, but sad experience. Many wounded soldiers' faces still haunt my memory. I recall one eighteen year old who had just been brought in from the ambulance to the shock ward. I went to him immediately. He looked up at me trustingly, sighed and asked, "How am I doing, Nurse?" I was standing at the head of the litter. I put my hands around his face, kissed his forehead and said, "You are doing just fine soldier." He smiled sweetly and said, "I was just checking up." Then he died. Many of us shed tears in private. Otherwise, we try to be cheerful and reassuring.

Army nurses assisgned to a field holspital arrive in France on 12 August 1944. (National Archives)

By the time of the 6 June 1944 D-Day invasion of France, almost two million American troops were stationed in England. To help provide for these service personnel, the American Red Cross opened service clubs and operated one hundred and fifty clubmobiles throughout Great Britain where Red Cross "doughnut girls" distributed coffee and doughnuts to the troops.

Four days after D-Day, on 10 June 1944, army nurses and Red Cross hospital workers arrived in France to set up field and evacuation hospitals. Army nurse Ruth Hess arrived in France in late June 1944. In a long retrospective letter, written to friends and colleagues at the Louisville, Kentucky, General Hospital, Hess described her first days as a combat nurse in Europe:

> We embarked by way of a small landing craft with our pants rolled up—wading onto the beach a short distance…. We marched up those high cliffs… about a mile and a half under full packs, hot as 'blue blazes'—till finally a jeep… picked us up and took us to our area…. For nine days we never stopped [working]. 880 patients operated; small debridement of gun shot and shrapnel wounds, numerous amputations, fractures galore, perforated guts, livers, spleens, kidneys, lungs, … everything imaginable…. It's really been an experience…. At nite—those d——d German planes make rounds and tuck us all into a fox hole—ack ack in the field right beside us, machine guns all around—whiz—there goes a bullet—it really doesn't spare you—you're too busy—but these patients need a rest from that sort of stuff.

As the Second World War drew to a close in the late summer of 1945, letter writers both at home and abroad turned their attention to the larger meaning of the conflict and how the experience of four years of total war had changed their lives. Writing from Snoqualmie Falls, Washington, on 14 August 1945, war wife Rose McClain spoke for many women when she expressed the hope that World War II would mark "the end of war for all time," and "that our children will learn, the kindness, patience, honesty, and the depth of love and trust we have learned, from all of this, without the tragedy of war."

From her duty station in the Southwest Pacific, Jane Warren, a member of the Women's Army Corps, forthrightly asserted in a letter, "You know, Mother, my life has really changed. I've learned in these past two years that I can really do things and make a difference as a woman.... I truly think that this war and opportunity it has provided for women like me (and women at home in the war effort) is going to make a profound difference in the way a lot of women think and do after the war is over."

Writing to her parents from Germany in late August 1945, army nurse Marjorie LaPalme explained how the experience of war had dramatically transformed her life:

One thing is sure—we will never be the naïve innocents we were… none of us …. It was a wonderful experience—no doubt the greatest of my entire life. I am sure nothing can surpass the comradeship and friendship we shared with so many wonderful men and women from all over our country—the good and the bad, suffering death and destruction falling from the skies, but perhaps most of all I will remember the quiet courage of common, ordinary people.

The lives of American women were dramatically changed by the experience of war. The war transformed the way women thought about themselves and the world in which they lived, expanding their horizons and affording them a clearer sense of their capabilities.

Although the postwar decade witnessed a renewed interest in motherhood and the family, which resulted in a return to a more conventional way of life for many women—what Betty Friedan would label as "the feminine mystique"—the immense changes wrought by World War II were not forgotten. A generation later, these changes provided the foundation for the rejuvenation of the contemporary women's movement. Indeed, the legacy of World War II inspired a new generation of women—the daughters of our World War II foremothers—to demand greater equality for women in the workplace and in society at large.

Life would never be the same for the women who lived through World War II. With fortitude and ingenuity, they had surmounted the challenges posed by total war. As the women of the wartime generation are quick to acknowledge, "We knew that if we could overcome the trials and

tribulations of the war years, we could do anything." What better legacy to leave to us as we face the challenges and the opportunities of the twenty-first century.

Suggestions for Further Reading

Campbell, D' Ann. *Women at War With America: Private Lives in a Patriotic Era* (Cambridge: Harvard University Press, 1984).

Earley, Charity Adams. *One Woman's Army: A Black Officer Remembers the WAC* (College Station: Texas A & M University Press, 1989).

Goosen, Rachel Waltner. *Women Against the Good War: Conscientious Objection and Gender on the American Home Front, 1941-1947* (Chapel Hill: University of North Carolina Press, 1997).

Hartmann, Susan M. *The Home Front and Beyond: American Women in the 1940s* (Boston: Twayne, 1982).

Kaminski, Theresa. *Prisoners in Paradise: American Women in the Wartime South Pacific* (Lawrence: University Press of Kansas, 2000).

Litoff, Judy Barrett ed. *Dear Poppa: The World War II Berman Family Letters* (St. Paul: Minnesota Historical Society Press, 1997).

Litoff, Judy Barrett and David C. Smith, eds. *American Women in a World at War: Contemporary Accounts from World War II* (Wilmington: Scholarly Resources, 1997).

Litoff, Judy Barrett and David C. Smith. *Miss You: The World War II Letters of Barbara Wooddall Taylor and Charles E. Taylor* (Athens: University of Georgia Press, 1990).

Litoff, Judy Barrett and David C. Smith, eds. *Since You Went Away: World War II Letters from American Women on the Home Front* (New York: Oxford University Press, 1991).

Litoff, Judy Barrett and David C. Smith, eds. "'To the Rescue of the Crops:' The Women's Land Army during World War II", *Prologue* 25 (Winter 1993): 347-60.

Litoff, Judy Barrett and David C. Smith, eds. *We're In This War Too: World War II Letters from American Women in Uniform* (New York: Oxford University Press, 1994).

Litoff, Judy Barrett and David C. Smith, eds. *What Kind of World Do We Want? American Women Plan for Peace* (Wilmington: Scholarly Resources, 2000).

Poulos, Paula Nassen ed. *A Woman's War Too: U.S. Women in the Military in World War II* (Washington, DC: National Archives and Records Administration, 1996).

Putney, Martha S. *When the Nation Was In Need: Blacks in the Women's Army Corps During World War II* (Metuchen, NJ: Scarecrow Press, 1992).

Judy Barrett Litoff, Professor of History at Bryant College in Smithfield, Rhode Island, is the author or coauthor of ten books on U.S. women's history. She and David C. Smith, Professor of History Emeritus at the University of Maine, have coauthored six books and dozens of articles on U.S. women and World War II.

From *OAH Magazine of History*, Spring 2002, pages 7-12. Copyright © 2002 by Organization of American Historians. Reprinted with permission.

African Americans and World War II

Andrew E. Kersten

Thirty years ago, it was commonplace to refer to the era of World War II as the "forgotten years of the Negro revolution"[1]. Beginning in the late 1960s, however, scholars started to focus attention on the black experience during the early 1940s, examining both the battle and homefronts. At first, historians concluded that this period constituted a watershed in history. They maintained that African American men and women made major advances as workers and military personnel and that communities across the United States witnessed a dramatic rise in black social activism and political participation. Over time, however, historians have tempered their enthusiasm for this interpretation. Social, economic, and political gains were often lost in the postwar period, something which contributed to the disillusionment and upheaval of the 1960s. Still, there is no denying the importance of the war years. Accompanying the global conflict were transformations in employment, geography I and social status that permanently affected not only African Americans but all Americans in general. Thus the Second World War may not be a watershed, but it was an unprecedented era in which African Americans sought a "Double V," a victory over fascism abroad and apartheid at home.

A central component to the Double V was the quest to eradicate job discrimination, particularly in the defense industries. When the Second World War began with the German invasion of Poland in 1939, President Franklin D. Roosevelt began in earnest to put the country on a war footing. For the average American, the results of the defense preparedness program were dramatic and beneficial. By the time of the Pearl Harbor attack in late 1941, conversion to war production was occurring nationwide. Gigantic factories such as the one at Willow Run near Detroit were built, and American workers as well as businessmen profited from the increased economic activity. Unemployment rapidly decreased from 8,120,000 persons in 1940 to 5,560,000 in 1941 to 2,660,000 in 1942. Moreover, union membership rose from roughly 8 million in 1940 to 10 million in 1941[2].

But not all felt the return of prosperity equally. Some Americans, blacks in particular, were left behind as the economy geared up for war. Since the 1920s, African Americans had suffered from high rates of unemployment. 1920 was a high water mark for black employment in American industry. The Great Depression however, had wiped out these advances. Despite the New Deal's assistance, black and other minority workers languished through the lean and stagnant years of Roosevelt's first two terms. As the United States prepared for war at the end of FDR's second term, they were again left out in the cold[3].

As American industry converted to war production, African Americans demanded equal treatment in obtaining the new jobs. At first, that was not forthcoming. Less than six months after the bombing of Pearl Harbor, a little over half—144,583 out of 282,245—prospective war-related job openings were reserved for whites only. Moreover, blatant job discrimination was not merely a southern phenomenon. In Texas, African Americans were barred from over 9,000 out of the 17,435 openings (52 percent) for defense jobs. In, Michigan the figure was 22,042 out of 26,904 (82 percent); in Ohio, 29,242 out of 34,861 (84 percent); and in Indiana, 9,331 out of 9,979 (94 percent)[4]. Even before the Japanese attack on Hawaii, civil rights leaders and organizations sought to end discrimination in employment and the military. In January 1941, one black leader, A. Philip Randolph, president of the Brotherhood of Sleeping Car Porters, announced that if the Roosevelt administration did not take action against discrimination in the defense program he would parade one hundred thousand African Americans down Pennsylvania Avenue in Washington, D.C., on 1 July 1941. Through that winter and spring, Roosevelt and his advisors negotiated with Randolph without result. Finally, on 25 June 1941—six days before the scheduled protest march—FDR issued Executive Order 8802 banning employment discrimination because of race, creed, color, or national origin for employers with defense contracts, labor unions, and civilian agencies of the federal government. To enforce the policy, FDR set up an executive agency, the Fair Employment Practice Committee (FEPC), that accomplished much during the war. With no more than one hundred and twenty officials, the FEPC exposed prejudice in the war industries and broke some racial barriers, processing over twelve thousand complaints of discrimination and settling nearly five thousand to its satisfaction. The committee also vigorously pursued an educational campaign in order to create more harmonious industrial relations between white and minority workers. Above all, the FEPC influenced the course of civil rights reform as it became a postwar model for city, state, and federal efforts against employment discrimination[5].

Despite its successes, the Fair Employment Practice Committee did not rid American society of job bias. At most, it opened some new opportunities where there previously had been none. Nevertheless, African American workers rushed to fill these new employment openings, often moving from their homes in the South to cities in the Midwest, North, and West. During the war, the black population of San Francisco increased by over five hundred percent. In the Willow Run area near Detroit, the percentage growth of African Americans was nearly ten times that of whites[6]. These job seekers were at times frustrated by discrimination and yet often with the assistance of the FEPC and civil rights organizations, such as the National Association for the Advancement of Colored People (NAACP) and the National Urban League, African Americans found war jobs. In addition to well paying defense jobs, black migrants, especially to northern and western cities, found it possible to escape the oppressions brought by Jim Crow. Marion Clark, daughter of John Clark, head of the St. Louis Urban League, provides an illustrative example. In 1942, Marion moved to Chicago. Describing the city in a letter home, she wrote, "it is fun, as you agree, to be able to breathe the freeer air of Chicago"[7]. Northern and some western cities offered other amenities that African Americans found welcoming. Housing in cities such as Chicago and New York was much better than that of the rural South. Blacks also had access to superior health care and to foods higher in nutrition. As a result, during the war, the black mortality rates dropped considerably and the birthrate rose. Generally speaking, the four hundred thousand African Americans who moved out of the South during the war created significantly better lives for themselves.

To improve their new lives, many African Americans joined civil rights groups such as the NAACP, the Urban League, and the newly formed Congress of Racial Equality (CORE). These groups were dedicated to the Double V. Not only did they attempt to create new employment opportunities, but they challenged racism and segregation in public accommodations, housing, and education. In many ways, these activists laid the groundwork for the modern civil rights movement. Although housing in northern ghettos was often an improvement, there was not enough to meet the needs of southern black migrants. City governments responded to the crisis slowly. Eventually the Roosevelt administration sought to alleviate the situation.

For instance in 1942, the federal government in cooperation with Detroit's city government built the Sojourner Truth Housing Project to relieve overcrowding in the black ghettos. Pressure from a white "improvement association" caused a reversal in policy, resulting in the exclusion of blacks in the project. Vigorous objections from civil rights activists caused another quick about-face. Yet as blacks attempted to move into the housing, whites formed a picket line, burned crosses, and used violence to turn the residents away. In the end, federal officials held firm, but the Sojourner Truth Housing controversy demonstrated not only how desperate the housing situation was but also how tense race relations were in America. During the war, there were dozens of incidents of racial violence. The war's worst riot happened again in Detroit, one year after the violence at the Sojourner Truth homes. On 22 June 1943, at Belle Isle Park, Detroit's main recreational area, fights broke out between white and black men. As news of the fights and rumors of murder and rape spread, so did the conflict, which lasted four days. By the time federal troops had restored order on 24 June, twenty-five African Americans and nine whites were dead, nearly seven hundred were injured, and two million dollars worth of property had been destroyed[9].

The wartime race riots as well as employment discrimination and segregation greatly lowered black morale for the war. At no point were African Americans as a group disloyal. Nevertheless, as a federal official wrote in 1942, the lack of racial equality in the United States had given rise to "a sickly, negative attitude toward national goals"[8]. In its extreme form, disaffection with the war effort resulted in draft resisters who refused to fight "the white man's war." More commonly, cynicism produced scathing editorials and newspaper articles condemning the hypocrisy of American democracy. Some of President Roosevelt's White House advisors pressured him to indict black editors for sedition. FDR refused to sanction such an action. Instead his administration began to collect information on black morale. A 1942 Office of War Information report detailed the widespread discontent. One Cincinnati housemaid told investigators that to her it did not matter if Hitler won the war. "It couldn't be any worse for colored people—it may and it may not. It ain't so good now," she commented[10]. The Federal Bureau of Investigation also conducted its own investigation. In its RACON (racial conditions in America) report, the FBI concluded that although most African Americans supported the war, racism undercut the government's efforts to build a unified nation in wartime. Nevertheless, the bureau noted that while cynicism was found in nearly every black community, so was the strong desire to aid the war effort. In fact, other federal officials close to the situation had discovered the same "positive attitude toward racial aims and aspirations"[11].

While one goal of the Double V campaign was to conquer employment discrimination another was to eradicate discrimination in the armed services. Like the fight for fair employment, the battle to end racism and preju-

Captain Andrew D. Turner, who in a few minutes will be escorting heavy bombers en route to enemy targets, signals to the chief of his ground crew before taking off from a base in Italy in September 1944. (National Archives, Records of the Office of War Information)

dice in the military began before formal American entry into the Second World War. At the start of the war, there were minimal opportunities for African Americans in the military. Although blacks had served valiantly in all American conflicts from the Revolution to the First World War, the War Department systematically discriminated against them. In 1939, African American participation in the army was at a nadir. There were only 3,640 black soldiers, five of whom were officers (three of them were chaplains). All were segregated into four units under white command. The navy was even worse. African Americans could only enlist to work in the galleys. The Coast Guard's racial policies were slightly more enlightened and were far more liberal than the marines and the Army Air Corps, which prior to the Second World War did not allow any blacks to serve.

African Americans took great pride in their past service in American wars and were angry at their exclusion from the military preparedness program. Initially, Rayford W. Logan, black historian, World War I veteran, and leader of the Committee for the Participation of Negroes in National Defense, led the charge to break the racial barriers in the military. The committee's major success was the inclusion of nondiscrimination language in the 1940 Selective Service Act which required that draftees be taken and trained regardless of race. To open more avenues in the military, on 27 September 1940, Walter White, executive secretary of the NAACP, T. Arnold Hill of the National Urban League, and A. Philip Randolph met with President Roosevelt. They brought a list of seven demands: that black officers and men be assigned on the basis of merit, not race; that more black officers be trained; that African Americans be allowed to serve in the Army Air Corps; that blacks be allowed to participate in the selective service process; that black women be permitted to serve as nurses; and that "existing units of the army and units to be established should be required to accept and

select officers and enlisted personnel without regard to race"[12]. Although Roosevelt seemed receptive to these ideas, he later signed policy statements which reaffirmed segregation in the military and established a racial quota system to limit black participation in the military to nine percent, roughly the African American proportion in the general population.

FDR's actions sparked a flurry of protests. To pacify black leaders and to encourage blacks to vote for the Democratic Party in the November elections, Roosevelt made some concessions such as forming an all-black Army Air Corps unit, promoting Colonel Benjamin O. Davies to the rank of general (making him the first African American to hold that rank), and appointing Colonel Campbell C. Johnson as Negro Advisor to the Selective Service Director and William H. Hastie, dean of Howard Law School, as civilian aide to the Secretary of War. Following Roosevelt's appointments came moderate improvement in the armed services for black Americans. In 1941, an Army Air Force training base was established at the Tuskegee Institute. Although still segregated, African Americans were accepted into regular service in the navy and the marines. Moreover, the number of black servicemen in the army rose dramatically, from 98,000 in late 1941 to 468,000 in late 1942. Still, serious problems remained. The army never met its promised quota of becoming nine percent African American. At most, only five percent of the total number of G.I.s were black. Moreover, over eighty percent were stationed in the United States. The was partly due to requests of Allied governments such as Australia that the War Department not send African American troops so as to not upset local whites. Moreover, African Americans were not shipped overseas, because ranking officials in the military believed them to be inferior soldiers. African American soldiers were also largely confined to the Corps of Engineers and the Quartermaster Corps. Working conditions for black servicemen on the homefront were at times horrible. Nothing demonstrated this more than what happened on 17 July 1944 at Port Chicago in San Francisco Bay. Two hundred and fifty black stevedores were killed when two ammunition-carrying ships they were loading exploded. The survivors were sent to Vallejo where they were asked to stow munitions in similar dangerous conditions. Initially almost two hundred and sixty refused to accept this assignment. In the end, all but fifty returned to work. The navy court-martialed the protestors, handing down sentences of fifteen years hard labor and dishonorable discharge[13]. The Port Chicago incident, as it became known, was the most extreme case of hazardous duty, but even basic training was often treacherous. Across the nation, black soldiers encountered not only segregation and discrimination but also racially motivated violence. Racial tensions on and off base were high and clashes between whites and black were altogether too common. In a scathing report to his superiors in the War Department, Civilian Aide Hastie summarized these problems. His protests fell on largely deaf ears, and he later resigned.

Despite the obvious handicaps to military service, African American men and women made considerable contributions to the victory over the Axis powers. General Dwight D. Eisenhower publicly praised the 99th Fighter Squadron which had trained at Tuskegee as well as the engineer and antiaircraft ground units stationed in Italy. Perhaps black soldiers' greatest achievement came in December 1944 when Nazi forces launched a last-ditch offensive at the Ardennes. In the Battle of the Bulge, the American army was caught desperately short of infantry replacements. To fill the voids in the American lines, General Eisenhower sent in black platoons which were partially integrated into regular units. Thus reinforced, the Americans defeated the Germans. Moreover, after the Battle of the Bulge, all branches of the military began instituting integration policies. The navy, including its Women's Accepted for Voluntary Emergency Service (WAVES), was first and followed shortly thereafter by the air force and the army.

By helping defeat the Axis, black Americans realized one-half of their Double V. The remaining half—a victory over discrimination and segregation in American life—remained elusive. And yet, blacks made remarkable strides in four short, war-torn years. With the federal government's assistance, African Americans attacked employment discrimination and achieved some positive results. Civil rights organizations such as the NAACP were reinvigorated. Moreover, African American communities across the nation became healthier and more socially and politically dynamic. Perhaps the greatest achievements came in the military, which continued after the war to break down barriers to not only African Americans but to women and minorities generally. V-J Day may have marked the end of the military conflict, but it did not signal an end to the struggle for civil rights on the homefront. Indeed, these efforts became the basis for a postwar civil rights movement which has continued for more than fifty years.

Notes

1. Richard Dalfiume, "The 'Forgotten Years' of the Negro Revolution," *Journal of American History* 55 (1968): 90-106 and Neil A. Wynn, "War and Racial Progress: The African American Experience During World War II," *Peace and Change* 20 (July 1995): 348-63.
2. United States Bureau of the Census, *Historical Statistics of the United States: Colonial Times to 1957* (Washington, DC: Government Printing Office, 1960), 98, 446, 466.
3. "Out in the Cold," *Crisis* (July 1940): 209.
4. Andrew E. Kersten, *Race, Jobs, and the War: The FEPC in the Midwest, 1941-46* (Urbana: University of Illinois Press, 2000), 37.
5. Ibid., 1-3.
6. Allan M. Winkler, *Home Front U.S.A.: America During World War II*, 2d ed. (Wheeling, IL: Harlan Davidson, 2000), 67
and Neil A. Wynn, *The Afro-American and the Second World War* (New York: Holmes and Meier, 1993), 62.
7. Letter, Marion Clark to John Clark, 22 November 1942, St. Louis Urban League Papers, series 1, box 9, Washington University Archives.
8. Cornelius L. Golightly, "Negro Higher Education and Democratic Negro Morale," *Journal of Negro Education* 11 (July 1942): 324.
9. Thomas J. Sugrue, "Crabgrass-Roots Politics: Race, Rights, and the Reaction against Liberalism in the Urban North, 1940-1964," *Journal of American History* 82 (Sept. 1995): 551-578.
10. Office of War Information, "Negroes and the War: A Study in Baltimore and Cincinnati, July 21, 1942," appendix D, vi, Franklin D. Roosevelt Presidential Library, Presidential Office Files, OF 4245G, box 7.
11. Golightly, "Negro Higher Education and Democratic Negro Morale," 324.
12. Quoted in Wynn, *The Afro-American and the Second World War*, 23.
13. After the war, the convictions were set aside.

Suggestions for Further Reading

Buchanan, A. Russell. *Black Americans in World War II*. Santa Barbara: Clio Books, 1977.

Cripps, Thomas. *Making Movies Black: The Hollywood Message Movie from World War II to the Civil Rights Era*. New York: Oxford University Press, 1993.

Dalfiume, Richard M. "The 'Forgotten Years' of the Negro Revolution." *Journal of American History* 55 (1968) 90-106.

———. *Desegregation of the United States Armed Forces: Fighting on Two Fronts, 1939-1953*. Columbia: University of Missouri Press, 1969.

Finkle, Lee. *Forum for Protest: The Black Press During World War II*. New Jersey: Fairleigh Dickinson University Press, 1975.

Hill, Robert A. *The FBI's RACON: Racial Conditions in the United States During World War II*. Boston: Northeastern University Press, 1995.

Jakeman, Robert J. *The Divided Skies: Establishing Segregated Flight Training at Tuskegee, Alabama, 1934-1942*. Birmingham: University of Alabama Press, 1992.

Kersten, Andrew E. *Race, Jobs, and the War: The FEPC in the Midwest, 1941-46*. Urbana: University of Illinois Press, 2000.

Myrdal, Gunnar. *An American Dilemma: The Negro Problem and Modern Democracy*. New York: Harper and Brothers, 1944.

Washburn, Patrick. *A Question of Sedition: The Federal Government's Investigation of the Black Press During World War II*. New York: Oxford University Press, 1986.

Weaver, Robert C. *Negro Labor: A National Problem*. New York: Harcourt, Brace, and Company, 1946.

Wynn, Neil A. *The Afro-American and the Second World War*. New York: Homes and Meier, 1993.

Andrew E. Kersten received his B.A. in History at the University of Wisconsin-Madison and his M.A. and Ph.D at the University of Cincinnati. Since 1997, he has taught in the History Department at the University of Wisconsin-Green Bay. Kersten has published in the *Queen City Heritage*, the *Michigan Historical Review*, the *Missouri Historical Review* and several anthologies and encyclopedias. He is the author of *Race, Jobs, and the War: The FEPC in the Midwest, 1941-1946* (2000) and the coeditor of *Politics and Progress: The State and American Society since 1865* (2001). Currently, he is writing a history of the American Federation of Labor during World War II.

From *OAH Magazine of History*, Spring 2002, pages 13-17. Copyright © 2002 by Organization of American Historians. Reprinted with permission.

DIVIDING THE SPOILS

*In a new book, historian Michael Beschloss re-creates the 1945
Potsdam Conference at which Harry Truman found his
presidential voice and determined the shape of postwar Europe*

Adapted from *The Conquerors* by Michael Beschloss

IN EARLY FEBRUARY OF 1945, when the defeat of Germany was finally a foregone conclusion, President Franklin Delano Roosevelt, Prime Minister Winston Churchill and Premier Joseph Stalin met in the Crimean city of Yalta, on the Black Sea, to consider the future of Europe and set the stage for a later meeting at Germany's Potsdam, whose name would become synonymous with statecraft of the highest order.

At Yalta, the leaders of the "Big Three" confirmed they would accept nothing less than Germany's unconditional surrender; demand that Germany pay reparations to the victors; and divide the defeated nation into four zones, occupied, respectively, by the United States, Britain, France and the Soviet Union. FDR, whose resolute authority was crucial to forging the accords, would not live to see the war's end. On April 12, less than three weeks before Hitler committed suicide and Germany surrendered, FDR died in Warm Springs, Georgia. Vice President Harry S. Truman, who had little experience in foreign affairs, was sworn in as President.

In *The Conquerors: Roosevelt, Truman and the Destruction of Hitler's Germany 1941-1945* (just published by Simon & Schuster), historian Michael Beschloss draws on recently opened U.S. and Soviet documents to describe the diplomatic maneuvers. Beschloss, the author of six other books, believes that Roosevelt and Truman had to wrestle with a central question: "Did they presume that Germans, humiliated by their defeat, would soon turn to another Adolf Hitler—or had they fought World War II with the belief that German history could be diverted in the direction of a lasting democracy?" A similar question confronts the U.S.

administration today as it contemplates an Iraq after Saddam Hussein.

The following excerpt from Beschloss' book portrays an increasingly self-confident Truman sparring with Stalin and Churchill at Potsdam, site of the 17-day conference held in July and August to refine the Yalta plans.

TRUMAN HAD NEVER met Churchill before Potsdam. He wrote in his diary that when the Prime Minister called on him at his villa on Monday morning, July 16, Churchill "gave me a lot of hooey about how great my country is and how he loved Roosevelt and how he intended to love me." As Truman recalled in 1954, "I liked him from the start.... I think he was surprised and pleased when he met me. Of course, he had been informed of what an inadequate chief of state he had to deal with. But I think he changed his mind."

Truman was told that Stalin would be late reaching Potsdam. With time on his hands, the President decided to tour Berlin. Conquerors like Genghis Khan and Julius Caesar, whom Truman had read about so voraciously as a boy, staged vast pageants in which they viewed their vanquished lands on horseback. Had Franklin Roosevelt achieved his dream of touring a conquered Berlin, he would almost certainly have arrived in Hitler's capital with theater and ceremony.

But Truman was more modest. Along with his new Secretary of State James Byrnes and Chief of Staff William Leahy, he simply climbed into the backseat of his Chrysler convertible and had his driver start up the autobahn. Along the roadside he saw "a long, never-ending procession" of men, women and children, "all staring straight ahead." Ejected from their homes by the Russians, they were "carrying what they could of their belongings to nowhere in particular."

The sight of defeated Germans and their victims reminded Truman of his Confederate grandmother and her family after the Civil War: "Forced off the farm by Yankee laws," they had wandered for weeks "along the hot Missouri roads until they found a safe place to stay." He thought of the "millions of people who were like her in Europe now."

Touring Berlin's ruins, the new President smelled the stench of rotting corpses and saw the blackened Reichstag, Germany's parliament building. "It is a terrible thing," he said of the bleak scene, but "they have brought it on themselves." He imagined what a victorious Hitler might have done to Washington, D.C. He felt "thankful" that Americans had been "spared the devastation."

The car pulled up at Hitler's chancellery, near his underground bunker. Truman refused to go in, saying that he wouldn't want any of "those unfortunate people" to think he was "gloating over them." But he muttered acidly to Byrnes that he wasn't sure the Germans had "learned anything" from the Nazis' miserable end.

Truman returned to his villa that evening deeply depressed. He wrote to his wife, Bess: "This is a hell of a place—ruined, dirty, smelly, forlorn people, bedraggled hangdog look about them. You never saw as completely ruined a city." In his diary, he wrote that the "absolute ruin" of Berlin was "Hitler's folly. He overreached himself by trying to take in too much territory. He had no morals and his people backed him up."

On Tuesday, July 17, at noon, the President was working in his study when, "I looked up from the desk and there stood Stalin in the doorway.... We had lunch, talked socially, put on a real show drinking toasts to everyone, then had pictures made in the backyard. I can deal with Stalin. He is honest, but smart as hell."

Over lunch, Byrnes, who had joined them, asked Stalin how he thought Hitler had died. The Marshal speculated that the Führer was still alive—"in Spain or Argentina." Stalin may have been putting forward the idea of a living Hitler in order to license harsher measures against Germany or, as the historian Alonzo Hamby notes, to deflect attention from his own aggressive ambitions.

Truman told Stalin that he was "very anxious to get the German setup in operation" so that the Allied Control Council could "govern" Germany "as a whole."

THE FIRST FORMAL conference session was at 5:00 P.M. July 17 at the Cecilienhof Palace, built in 1917. To demonstrate their equality, in a great-power minuet, Truman, Stalin and Churchill entered simultaneously through separate doors.

Seated with his allies at a burgundy-draped round table, Truman recalled the tragedy of Versailles in 1919, when the treaty's vindictive exactions left Germans impoverished and bitter, and, many believed, opened the way for Hitler's rise. This time, he said, any final German peace conference should be "prepared beforehand by the victor powers." He proposed that the groundwork be laid by a Council of Foreign Ministers, composed of the Big Three—the United States, Britain and Russia—plus France and China.

Stalin complained that the French were U.S. lackeys and that the Chinese should not be involved in "European problems." Truman and Churchill compromised by excluding the Chinese. Stalin joked that if foreign ministers were to do the work, "we will have nothing to do." Truman said, "I don't want to discuss. I want to decide." He hoped they could start early tomorrow morning. To Truman, Churchill jovially promised to "obey your orders."

Stalin said that since Churchill was in "such an obedient mood," he wished to know whether the British would "share the German fleet with us." Churchill said that perhaps the armada should be destroyed. Weapons of war were horrible things. "Let's divide it," Stalin suggested. "If Mr. Churchill wishes, he can sink his share."

On Wednesday afternoon, July 18, Churchill noted that his partners kept using the word "Germany." He asked them, "What is now the meaning of 'Germany'? Is it to be understood in the same sense as before the war?"

Debate on postwar Germany's borders began. At Yalta, six months before, Stalin, Roosevelt and Churchill had agreed that a line drawn after World War I would be Poland's eastern border with the Soviet Union. The three leaders had also decided that Poland should be compensated with "substantial" German territory to its west.

Stalin felt that Poland deserved all of Germany east of the Oder and Neisse Rivers. This would force millions of Germans westward and strip Germany of some of its richest farmland. As far as Stalin was concerned, this was a fait accompli: "Germany is what she has become after the war," he announced.

But Truman refused to consider the matter settled: "Why not say Germany as she was *before* the war, in 1937?" he asked. Stalin replied, "As she *is*—in 1945." Truman reminded Stalin that Germany had "lost everything in 1945," and that at Yalta, the Big Three had agreed to defer such questions until there was a final peace conference on Germany. Impatient, Truman wrote in his diary, "I'm not going to stay around this terrible place all summer just to listen to speeches. I'll go home to the Senate for that."

ON FRIDAY, JULY 20, Truman joined Generals Dwight Eisenhower and Omar Bradley to watch the official raising of the Stars and Stripes over the American sector of Berlin. Speaking without notes, Truman told the crowd of American soldiers, "We are not fighting for conquest. There is not one piece of territory or one thing of a monetary nature that we want out of this war."

Exactly one year had passed since German Army Col. Claus von Stauffenberg had tried and failed to kill Hitler. If any of the Americans remembered the anniversary, they did not mention it in public. At a moment when they were trying to establish collective guilt for Hitler's horrors, they did not wish to confuse the issue by reminding the world that some Germans had risked their lives, however belatedly and for whatever reasons, to stop the Führer.

The next day, Saturday, July 21, Secretary of War Henry Stimson brought the President an urgent message. The plutonium implosion bomb tested in Alamogordo, New Mexico, five days earlier had been "successful beyond the most optimistic expectations of everyone," Stimson said. Truman told his aide that the news gave him "an entirely new feeling of confidence." He knew that if the United States were sole possessor of a successful atomic bomb, it would be poised to end the Japanese war fast, without Soviet or British help, and exercise American will on the postwar world. That afternoon, Truman complained to Stalin that the Poles had been effectively assigned a zone of Germany "without consultation with us." Were the three leaders going to "give away Germany piecemeal"? Truman warned Stalin that it would be hard to agree on reparations—monetary and other payments by the defeated Germany to the Allied victors—"if Germany is divided up before the peace conference."

Stalin replied, "We are concerned about reparations, but we will take that risk." He insisted that giving German land to Poland should be no problem because no Germans were left in the region. "Of course not," Leahy whispered to Truman. "The Bolshies have killed all of them!"

Churchill noted that "two or three million Germans remain" in the area Stalin wanted to give Poland. Removing the area from Germany would remove a quarter of Germany's farmland, "from which German food and reparations must come."

"France wants the Saar and the Ruhr," said Truman. "What will be left?" Churchill warned that if Germany lacked sufficient food, "we may be confronted with conditions like those in the German concentration camps— even on a vaster scale." Stalin said, "Let the Germans buy more bread from Poland!"

Churchill demanded that the food supply of all Germany, according to its 1937 borders, be available to all Germans, "irrespective of the zones of occupation." He complained that Poland was already selling German coal to Sweden, while the British people faced "a bitter, fireless winter, worse than that experienced during the war."

Stalin retorted that the coal was being mined by Polish labor. As for the Germans, "we have little sympathy for these scoundrels and war criminals," he said.

Churchill noted that Stalin had earlier said that "past bitterness" should not "color our decisions." Stalin reminded him that "the less industry we leave in Germany, the more markets there will be for your goods."

Truman warned that he could not approve eastern Germany's removal from "contributing to the economy of the whole of Germany." He later wrote Bess: "Russia and Poland have gobbled up a big hunk of Germany and want Britain and us to agree. I have flatly refused."

Churchill attributed the President's new boldness to the bracing news from Alamogordo. "When he got to the meeting after having read this report, he was a changed man," the Prime Minister said to Stimson. "He told the Russians just where they got on and off and generally bossed the whole meeting."

AS THE SOLE PROPRIETOR of the atomic bomb, President Truman had just become the most powerful man on earth. And possibly the most homesick. Even before the success at Alamogordo, he had longed to get back to America and his wife. Still smoldering over Stalin's defense of his "Bolsheviki land grab," Truman wanted his counterparts to approve a plan that would punish the Germans, quash their ability to start another global war and still feed and warm all Europeans. Now, with the atomic weapon in his arsenal, Truman asked James Byrnes to put on pressure to wind the Potsdam meeting up fast. Truman knew that the new Secretary of State felt he should be President instead of Truman, but the President believed that if Byrnes could be made to defer to his authority, he would be a tough diplomatic bargainer and a powerful Congressional champion for Truman's postwar programs.

Born Catholic in Charleston, South Carolina, in 1882, Byrnes had become a Senator in 1930. An early Roosevelt supporter, he was one of the President's Senate stalwarts and helped Roosevelt push through the Lend-Lease Act and other aid to Britain. Roosevelt repaid him with a seat on the Supreme Court, where Byrnes predictably felt chained and miserable. After Pearl Harbor, FDR took him off the court to be his chief war mobilizer. Given the sobriquet "assistant President" by the press, which annoyed Roosevelt, Byrnes had harnessed American business behind the war effort.

Suspecting that Roosevelt might not serve out a fourth term and eager to be his successor, Byrnes schemed in 1944 to become Vice President. Roosevelt admired Byrnes but was wary of his brains, wiliness and gumption. With customary duplicity, Roosevelt told Byrnes in July 1944 that he was "the most qualified man in the whole outfit," adding: "You must not get out of the race [for Vice President]. If you stay in, you are sure to win."

Told by others that Roosevelt was really for Truman or Supreme Court Justice William O. Douglas, Byrnes had forced a showdown with the President in a telephone call to Hyde Park. As Roosevelt spoke, Byrnes took shorthand notes to protect himself in case the President later distorted what he said. Roosevelt insisted he was not pushing for Truman or Douglas: "Jimmy, that is all wrong…. I told you I would have no preference…. Will you go on and run? After all, Jimmy, you're close to me personally…. I hardly know Truman."

After Truman's nomination, Byrnes was furious at Roosevelt's "hypocrisy" but still hoped that Roosevelt would appoint him to succeed Cordell Hull as Secretary of State. Nervous about Byrnes' willfulness, Roosevelt opted instead for the docile Edward Reilly Stettinius.

To salve Byrnes' wounded pride, Roosevelt took him to Yalta, but when Byrnes realized that he was being kept out of vital meetings, he complained, "I did not come along for the ride." Roosevelt caved in. When Stalin spotted Byrnes at the conference table, he thought him "the most honest-looking horse thief he had ever met."

Returning to Washington, Byrnes dutifully held a press conference praising the Yalta agreements. Then he quit government, assuring Roosevelt that he was "not mad at anybody" about the vice presidency. After Truman became President, overimpressed by Byrnes' presence at Yalta and mindful of his prestige in the Senate, he appointed Byrnes to his secret "Interim Committee" on how a successful atomic bomb should be used. Exhilarated by the new weapon, Byrnes advised the President that it "might well put us in a position to dictate our own terms at the end of the war." When Truman began preparing for the conference, he tapped Byrnes to be his Secretary of State. He was sworn in on July 3, only two weeks before leaving for Potsdam.

Monday, July 23: Byrnes expressed Truman's concerns about reparations to Soviet Foreign Minister Vyacheslav Molotov. Byrnes suggested that each power take reparations from its own zone and that the British and Americans would be inclined to give their share to victims of the Nazis. Molotov volunteered to reduce Soviet demands by 20 percent, if they could claim a portion of spoils from the industrially rich Ruhr.

On Wednesday, July 25, Stalin told Truman and Churchill that "if the Ruhr remains a part of Germany, it must supply the whole of Germany."

The Americans blanched. Charles Bohlen (the President's Russian interpreter) of the U.S. delegation privately warned that Stalin would use such leverage to "paralyze the German economy" and push the defeated nation "toward communism."

THE POTSDAM CONFERENCE recessed on July 25 while Churchill returned to London to await announcement of the results of the British election.

Truman flew to Frankfurt to visit Eisenhower at the former headquarters of I. G. Farben, one of the German war-making enterprises investigated by Senator Truman during the war. "The big towns like Frankfurt and Darmstadt were destroyed," Truman wrote his mother and sister Mary, "but the small ones are intact. It is awful to see what the bombs did to the towns, railroads and bridges. To think that millions of Russians, Poles, English and Americans were slaughtered all for the folly of one crazy egotist by the name of Hitler. I hope it won't happen again."

In London, Churchill learned that despite his triumphant role in ending the European war, British voters, focused now on domestic problems, had turned out the Conservative Party and the new Prime Minister would be Clement Attlee. Churchill's aides complained of the En-

glish people's "ingratitude," but Churchill, though despondent, replied paternally, "I wouldn't call it that. They have had a very hard time."

Saturday, July 28: Molotov reminded Byrnes that it had been agreed at Yalta that the Soviets should take "as much reparations as possible from Germany." Byrnes parried that things had changed: German devastation was greater than originally thought. He pointed out that the Soviets had already given Poland a large and valuable chunk of German land.

On Sunday, July 29, Truman wrote his wife that if he could make a "reasonably sound" deal on reparations and the Polish-German border, he could "wind up this brawl" and head home.

Sunday, July 29: Molotov conveyed to Byrnes that the Soviets wanted a percentage of German wealth from the other zones as well as $2 billion of industrial equipment from the Ruhr. Byrnes did not want to put a specific dollar amount on any reparations and instead offered a percentage of equipment from the Ruhr, which the Soviets would barter for with supplies from their own zone. On Monday afternoon, July 30, Byrnes relayed to Molotov that the United States would go along with giving some German territory to Poland temporarily and would grant diplomatic recognition to Romania, Hungary, Bulgaria and Finland. But having made two concessions, Byrnes would not yield to Stalin's demand for a dollar amount.

That night, Truman wrote in his diary that the talks were at an "impasse." He wrote Bess, "The whole difficulty is reparations. Of course, the Russians are naturally looters and they have been thoroughly looted by the Germans over and over again and you can hardly blame them for their attitude. The thing I have to watch is to keep our skirts clean and make no other commitments."

Tuesday July 31: Byrnes told Molotov that the American proposals on diplomatic recognition of Eastern Europe, German land for Poland, and German reparations were all one package and couldn't be granted piecemeal. Stalin argued that because the Soviet Union had suffered such heavy losses of equipment during the war, he needed more reparations.

That evening, Truman secretly scrawled out formal approval for the first atomic bomb to be dropped on Japan. Three days after learning of the successful Alamogordo test, the President had quietly told Stalin that the United States now had an unusually destructive new weapon. Truman did not know that Soviet intelligence had already briefed Stalin on the Manhattan Project and the test. Stalin simply replied to Truman that he hoped the Americans would use the weapon well against Japan. Now Truman specified that the thunderous event should unfold only after he and his party were safely gone from Potsdam: "Release when ready but not sooner than August 2."

ON WEDNESDAY AFTERNOON, August 1, while discussing German assets abroad, Stalin made a fateful suggestion. To Truman and Britain's new Labour Prime Minister,

Clement Attlee, who had taken Churchill's place at Potsdam, Stalin proposed that the Soviet Union "regard the whole of western Germany as falling within your sphere and eastern Germany as within ours."

Truman asked whether Stalin meant to establish a "line" down Europe, "running from the Baltic to the Adriatic."

Stalin said yes. "As to the German investments in Europe, they remain with us, and the rest with you." Truman asked, "Does this apply only to German investments in Europe or in other countries as well?"

"Let me put it more specifically," said Stalin. "The German investments in Romania, Bulgaria, Hungary and Finland go to us, and all the rest to you.... In all other countries—South America, Canada and the like—all this is yours." Stalin went on, "We are not fighting Great Britain or the United States."

They moved on to war crimes. No doubt suspicious that the United States would try to curry favor with the Germans—especially big German capitalists—Stalin complained that the Americans were unwilling to publish long lists of German war criminals: "Aren't we going to act against *any* German industrialists? I think we should." As one example, Stalin mentioned the Krupp dynasty, long known for making German arms: "If they will not do, let's name others."

Truman said, "I don't like any of them!" His colleagues laughed. The President argued that if they mentioned some names but omitted others, "people may think that we have no intention of putting those others on trial."

As at Yalta, Stalin tweaked the British by mentioning Hitler's old underling Rudolf Hess, still imprisoned in the Tower of London: "It is surprising that Hess is in Britain, all provided for, and is not being put on trial."

Ernest Bevin, the new British Foreign Secretary, replied, "If there is any doubt about Hess, I will give an understanding that Hess will be handed over—and we will also be sending a bill for his keep!"

Stalin said he would be satisfied by listing "just three names" of German war criminals. Briefed on Stalin's view that Hitler might still be alive, Attlee suggested that they start with Hitler. Stalin said they did not have Hitler "at our disposition," but he would be willing to name him. The Big Three finally agreed to publish a list of top German war criminals within a month.

THAT EVENING AT 10:40, Truman, Stalin and Attlee signed the Potsdam Declaration. "The German people," it said, "have begun to atone for the terrible crimes committed under the leadership of those whom, in the hour of their success, they openly approved and blindly obeyed."

The victors did not wish to "destroy or enslave" the Germans, but to help them "prepare for the eventual reconstruction of their life on a peaceful and democratic basis." Allied policies toward the Germans would be uniform, "so far as is practicable."

During occupation, "Germany shall be treated as a single economic unit." Each occupying power would take reparations from its own zones. Beyond that, the Soviets would take 15 percent of industrial equipment that was "unnecessary for the German peace economy," in exchange for food, coal and other goods. They would also receive an additional 10 percent for free. The Council of Foreign Ministers would draft a peace treaty "to be accepted by the government of Germany when a government adequate for that purpose is established."

After the document was signed by all three leaders, Truman pronounced the conference "adjourned until our next meeting, which I hope will be in Washington." Stalin smiled and said, "God willing!"

Truman wrote his mother, "You never saw such pigheaded people as are the Russians. I hope I never have to hold another conference with them. But of course I will."

He was wrong. Because of the deepening Cold War, Truman never saw Stalin again.

MONDAY, AUGUST 6, Truman was recrossing the Atlantic aboard the *Augusta* when he was handed a message over luncheon. An atomic bomb had been dropped on Hiroshima and was "successful in all respects." The war against Japan would soon be won. The President said, "This is the greatest thing in history." After a second report, declaring "complete success," Truman leapt to his feet and told Byrnes, "It's time for us to get home!"

THREE DAYS LATER, on Thursday, August 9, the United States closed its victory over Japan with a second atomic bomb, dropped, under existing orders, on Nagasaki. Emperor Hirohito secretly decided to "bear the unbearable" and meet the Allies' demand for unconditional surrender.

But Truman did not know that yet. That evening, he addressed Americans by radio on his European trip: "I have just returned from Berlin, the city from which the Germans intended to rule the world." He reported that Hitler's capital was now a "ghost city.... How glad I am to be home again—and how grateful to Almighty God that this land of ours has been spared!"

He reported that the declaration signed at Potsdam was "intended to eliminate Naziism, armaments, war industries, the German General Staff and all its military tradition." It hoped to "rebuild democracy by control of German education, by reorganizing local government and the judiciary, by encouraging free speech, free press, freedom of religion and the right of labor to organize." German industry would be "decentralized in order to do away with concentration of economic power in cartels and monopolies." Germans would be granted no higher standard of living than their former victims.

Truman said that the wartime allies were resolved to "do what we can to make Germany over into a decent nation" and "eventually work its way" back into the "civilized world."

Truman's speech largely obscured the unresolved questions and harsh compromises that were the legacy of Potsdam. The Soviets would get reparations, but the victors had still to agree on specifics or exact terms. Germany would be treated as an "economic whole," but in each zone, the commander would have paramount authority. The defeated nation would not be partitioned; the shift of land to Poland was merely "provisional."

As the American diplomat and scholar W. R. Smyser wrote in 1999, at Potsdam "each side paid what it had to pay to get what it wanted most." Stalin got almost one quarter of pre-World War II German territory for Poland. Britain and America, by demanding that each victor seize reparations from its own zone, spared postwar Germany the staggering reparations and debt that in the 1920s had brought inflation, unemployment and Hitler. They had also prepared a means to protect western Germany from Soviet encroachment.

Assistant Secretary of War John McCloy knew that if Soviet-American relations deteriorated, the slash between the Soviet and Western zones would become much more than an abstraction. He wrote in his diary, "We are drifting toward a line down the middle of Germany."

In the wake of Potsdam, Germany and Europe were divided for almost half a century as the Soviet Union and the West were engaged in a bitter cold war. In October 1990, after the tearing down of the Berlin Wall, East and West Germany were reunited. Chancellor Kohl promised the world's leaders that "in the future, only peace will emanate from German soil." Today, no longer trapped behind the ugly wall, the Cecilienhof Palace is a museum. Its chief attraction is the round oak table at which Truman, Stalin and Churchill once sat to decide the fate of the world.

From *Smithsonian,* December 2002, pages 111-120; adapted from and reprinted by the permission of Simon © Schuster Adult Publishing Group from *The Conquerors,* by Michael Beschloss. Copyright © 2002 by Michael Beschloss.

The Biggest Decision: Why We Had to Drop the Atomic Bomb

Robert James Maddox

On the morning of August 6, 1945, the American B-29 Enola Gay dropped an atomic bomb on the Japanese city of Hiroshima. Three days later another B-29, *Bock's Car*, released one over Nagasaki. Both caused enormous casualties and physical destruction. These two cataclysmic events have preyed upon the American conscience ever since. The furor over the Smithsonian Institution's *Enola Gay* exhibit and over the mushroom-cloud postage stamp last autumn are merely the most obvious examples. Harry S. Truman and other officials claimed that the bombs caused Japan to surrender, thereby avoiding a bloody invasion. Critics have accused them of at best failing to explore alternatives, at worst of using the bombs primarily to make the Soviet Union "manage-able" rather than to defeat a Japan they knew already was on the verge of capitulation.

By any rational calculation Japan was a beaten nation by the summer of 1945. Conventional bombing had reduced many of its cities to rubble, blockade had strangled its importation of vitally needed materials, and its navy had sustained such heavy losses as to be powerless to interfere with the invasion everyone knew was coming. By late June advancing American forces had completed the conquest of Okinawa, which lay only 350 miles from the southernmost Japanese home island of Kyushu. They now stood poised for the final onslaught.

> *Okinawa provided a preview of what an invasion of the home islands would entail. Rational calculations did not determine Japan's position.*

Rational calculations did not determine Japan's position. Although a peace faction within the government wished to end the war—provided certain conditions were met—militants were prepared to fight on regardless of consequences. They claimed to welcome an invasion of the home islands, promising to inflict such hideous casualties that the United States would retreat from its announced policy of unconditional surrender. The militarists held effective power over the government and were capable of defying the emperor, as they had in the past, on the ground that his civilian advisers were misleading him.

Okinawa provided a preview of what invasion of the home islands would entail. Since April 1 the Japanese had fought with a ferocity that mocked any notion that their will to resist was eroding. They had inflicted nearly 50,000 casualties on the invaders, many resulting from the first large-scale use of kamikazes. They also had dispatched the superbattleship *Yamato* on a suicide mission to Okinawa, where, after attacking American ships offshore, it was to plunge ashore to become a huge, doomed steel fortress. *Yamato* was sunk shortly after leaving port, but its mission symbolized Japan's willingness to sacrifice everything in an apparently hopeless cause.

The Japanese could be expected to defend their sacred homeland with even greater fervor, and kamikazes flying at short range promised to be even more devastating than at Okinawa. The Japanese had more than 2,000,000 troops in the home islands, were training millions of irregulars, and for some time had been conserving aircraft that might have been used to protect Japanese cities against American bombers.

Reports from Tokyo indicated that Japan meant to fight the war to a finish. On June 8 an imperial conference adopted "The Fundamental Policy to Be Followed Henceforth in the Conduct of the

War," which pledged to "prosecute the war to the bitter end in order to uphold the national polity, protect the imperial land, and accomplish the objectives for which we went to war." Truman had no reason to believe that the proclamation meant anything other than what it said.

Against this background, while fighting on Okinawa still continued, the President had his naval chief of staff, Adm. William D. Leahy, notify the Joint Chiefs of Staff (JCS) and the Secretaries of War and Navy that a meeting would be held at the White House on June 18. The night before the conference Truman wrote in his diary that "I have to decide Japanese strategy—shall we invade Japan proper or shall we bomb and blockade? That is my hardest decision to date. But I'll make it when I have all the facts."

Truman met with the chiefs at three-thirty in the afternoon. Present were Army Chief of Staff Gen. George C. Marshall, Army Air Force's Gen. Ira C. Eaker (sitting in for the Army Air Force's chief of staff, Henry H. Arnold, who was on an inspection tour of installations in the Pacific), Navy Chief of Staff Adm. Ernest J. King, Leahy (also a member of the JCS), Secretary of the Navy James Forrestal, Secretary of War Henry L. Stimson, and Assistant Secretary of War John J. McCloy. Truman opened the meeting, then asked Marshall for his views. Marshall was the dominant figure on the JCS. He was Truman's most trusted military adviser, as he had been President Franklin D. Roosevelt's.

Marshall reported that the chiefs, supported by the Pacific commanders Gen. Douglas MacArthur and Adm. Chester W. Nimitz, agreed that an invasion of Kyushu "appears to be the least costly worthwhile operation following Okinawa." Lodgment in Kyushu, he said, was necessary to make blockade and bombardment more effective and to serve as a staging area for the invasion of Japan's main island of Honshu. The chiefs recommended a target date of November 1 for the first phase, code-named Olympic, because delay would give the Japanese more time to prepare and because bad weather might postpone the

invasion "and hence the end of the war" for up to six months. Marshall said that in his opinion, Olympic was "the only course to pursue." The chiefs also proposed that Operation Cornet be launched against Honshu on March 1, 1946.

Leahy's memorandum calling the meeting had asked for casualty projections which that invasion might be expected to produce. Marshall stated that campaigns in the Pacific had been so diverse "it is considered wrong" to make total estimates. All he would say was that casualties during the first thirty days on Kyushu should not exceed those sustained in taking Luzon in the Philippines—31,000 men killed, wounded, or missing in action. "It is a grim fact," Marshall said, "that there is not an easy, bloodless way to victory in war." Leahy estimated a higher casualty rate similar to Okinawa, and King guessed somewhere in between.

King and Eaker, speaking for the Navy and the Army Air Forces respectively, endorsed Marshall's proposals. King said that he had become convinced that Kyushu was "the key to the success of any siege operations." He recommended that "we should do Kyushu now" and begin preparations for invading Honshu. Eaker "agreed completely" with Marshall. He said he had just received a message from Arnold also expressing "complete agreement." Air Force plans called for the use of forty groups of heavy bombers, which "could not be deployed without the use of airfields on Kyushu." Stimson and Forrestal concurred.

Truman summed up. He considered "the Kyushu plan all right from the military standpoint" and directed the chiefs to "go ahead with it." He said he "had hoped that there was a possibility of preventing an Okinawa from one end of Japan to the other," but "he was clear on the situation now" and was "quite sure" the chiefs should proceed with the plan. Just before the meeting adjourned, McCloy raised the possibility of avoiding an invasion by warning the Japanese that the United States would employ atomic weapons if there were no surrender. The ensuing discussion was inconclusive be-

cause the first test was a month away and no one could be sure the weapons would work.

In his memoirs Truman claimed that using atomic bombs prevented an invasion that would have cost 500,000 American lives. Other officials mentioned the same or even higher figures. Critics have assailed such statements as gross exaggerations designed to forestall scrutiny of Truman's real motives. They have given wide publicity to a report prepared by the Joint War Plans Committee (JWPC) for the chiefs' meeting with Truman. The committee estimated that the invasion of Kyushu, followed by that of Honshu, as the chiefs proposed, would cost approximately 40,000 dead, 150,000 wounded, and 3,500 missing in action for a total of 193,500 casualties.

That those responsible for a decision should exaggerate the consequences of alternatives is commonplace. Some who cite the JWPC report profess to see more sinister motives, insisting that such "low" casualty projections call into question the very idea that atomic bombs were used to avoid heavy losses. By discrediting that justification as a cover-up, they seek to bolster their contention that the bombs really were used to permit the employment of "atomic diplomacy" against the Soviet Union.

Myth holds that several of Truman's top military advisers begged him not to use the bomb. In fact, there is no persuasive evidence that any of them did.

The notion that 193,500 anticipated casualties were too insignificant to have caused Truman to resort to atomic bombs might seem bizarre to anyone other than an academic, but let it pass. Those who have cited the JWPC report in countless op-ed pieces in newspapers and in magazine articles have created a myth by omitting key considerations: First, the report itself is studded with qualifications that casualties "are not subject to accurate estimate" and that the projection "is admittedly only an educated guess." Second, the figures never were conveyed to Truman. They were excised at high military echelons, which is why Marshall cited only estimates for the first thirty days on Kyushu. And indeed, subsequent Japanese troop build-ups on Kyushu rendered the JWPC estimates totally irrelevant by the time the first atomic bomb was dropped.

Another myth that has attained wide attention is that at least several of Truman's top military advisers later informed him that using atomic bombs against Japan would be militarily unnecessary or immoral, or both. There is no persuasive evidence that any of them did so. None of the Joint Chiefs ever made such a claim, although one inventive author has tried to make it appear that Leahy did by braiding together several unrelated passages from the admiral's memoirs. Actually, two days after Hiroshima, Truman told aides that Leahy had "said up to the last that it wouldn't go off."

Neither MacArthur nor Nimitz ever communicated to Truman any change of mind about the need for invasion or expressed reservations about using the bombs. When first informed about their imminent use only days before Hiroshima, MacArthur responded with a lecture on the future of atomic warfare and even after Hiroshima strongly recommended that the invasion go forward. Nimitz, from whose jurisdiction the atomic strikes would be launched, was notified in early 1945. "This sounds fine," he told the courier, "but this is only February. Can't we get one sooner?" Nimitz later would join Air Force generals Carl D. Spaatz, Nathan Twining, and Curtis LeMay in recommending that a third bomb be dropped on Tokyo.

Only Dwight D. Eisenhower later claimed to have remonstrated against the use of the bomb. In his *Crusade in Europe*, published in 1948, he wrote that when Secretary Stimson informed him during the Potsdam Conference of plans to use the bomb, he replied that he hoped "we would never have to use such a thing against any enemy," because he did not want the United States to be the first to use such a weapon. He added, "My

views were merely personal and immediate reactions; they were not based on any analysis of the subject."

Eisenhower's recollections grew more colorful as the years went on. A later account of his meeting with Stimson had it taking place at Ike's headquarters in Frankfurt on the very day news arrived of the successful atomic test in New Mexico. "We'd had a nice evening at headquarters in Germany," he remembered. Then, after dinner, "Stimson got this cable saying that the bomb had been perfected and was ready to be dropped. The cable was in code… 'the lamb is born' or some damn thing like that." In this version Eisenhower claimed to have protested vehemently that "the Japanese were ready to surrender and it wasn't necessary to hit them with that awful thing." "Well," Eisenhower concluded, "the old gentleman got furious."

The best that can be said about Eisenhower's memory is that it had become flawed by the passage of time. Stimson was in Potsdam and Eisenhower in Frankfurt on July 16, when word came of the successful test. Aside from a brief conversation at a flag-raising ceremony in Berlin on July 20, the only other time they met was at Ike's headquarters on July 27. By then orders already had been sent to the Pacific to use the bombs if Japan had not yet surrendered. Notes made by one of Stimson's aides indicate that there was a discussion of atomic bombs, but there is no mention of any protest on Eisenhower's part. Even if there had been, two factors must be kept in mind. Eisenhower had commanded Allied forces in Europe, and his opinion on how close Japan was to surrender would have carried no special weight. More important, Stimson left for home immediately after the meeting and could not have personally conveyed Ike's sentiments to the President, who did not return to Washington until after Hiroshima.

On July 8 the Combined Intelligence Committee submitted to the American and British Combined Chiefs of Staff a report entitled "Estimate of the Enemy Situation." The committee predicted that as Japan's position continued to deteriorate, it might "make a serious effort to

use the USSR [then a neutral] as a mediator in ending the war." Tokyo also would put out "intermittent peace feelers" to "weaken the determination of the United Nations to fight to the bitter end, or to create inter-allied dissension." While the Japanese people would be willing to make large concessions to end the war, "For a surrender to be acceptable to the Japanese army, it would be necessary for the military leaders to believe that it would not entail discrediting warrior tradition and that it would permit the ultimate resurgence of a military Japan."

Small wonder that American officials remained unimpressed when Japan proceeded to do exactly what the committee predicted. On July 12 Japanese Foreign Minister Shigenori Togo instructed Ambassador Naotaki Sato in Moscow to inform the Soviets that the emperor wished to send a personal envoy, Prince Fuminaro Konoye, in an attempt "to restore peace with all possible speed." Although he realized Konoye could not reach Moscow before the Soviet leader Joseph Stalin and Foreign Minister V. M. Molotov left to attend a Big Three meeting scheduled to begin in Potsdam on the fifteenth, Togo sought to have negotiations begin as soon as they returned.

American officials had long since been able to read Japanese diplomatic traffic through a process known as the MAGIC intercepts. Army intelligence (G-2) prepared for General Marshall its interpretation of Togo's message the next day. The report listed several possible constructions, the most probable being that the Japanese "governing clique" was making a coordinated effort to "stave off defeat" through Soviet intervention and an "appeal to war weariness in the United States." The report added that Undersecretary of State Joseph C. Grew, who had spent ten years in Japan as ambassador, "agrees with these conclusions."

Some have claimed that Togo's overture to the Soviet Union, together with attempts by some minor Japanese officials in Switzerland and other neutral countries to get peace talks started through the Office of Strategic Services (OSS), constituted clear evidence that the Japanese were near surrender. Their sole prerequisite was retention of their sacred emperor, whose unique cultural/religious status within the Japanese polity they would not compromise. If only the United States had extended assurances about the emperor, according to this view, much bloodshed and the atomic bombs would have been unnecessary.

A careful reading of the MAGIC intercepts of subsequent exchanges between Togo and Sato provides no evidence that retention of the emperor was the sole obstacle to peace. What they show instead is that the Japanese Foreign Office was trying to cut a deal through the Soviet Union that would have permitted Japan to retain its political system and its prewar empire intact. Even the most lenient American official could not have countenanced such a settlement.

Togo on July 17 informed Sato that "we are not asking the Russians' mediation in *anything like unconditional surrender* [emphasis added]." During the following weeks Sato pleaded with his superiors to abandon hope of Soviet intercession and to approach the United States directly to find out what peace terms would be offered. "There is… no alternative but immediate unconditional surrender," he cabled on July 31, and he bluntly informed Togo that "your way of looking at things and the actual situation in the Eastern Area may be seen to be absolutely contradictory." The Foreign Ministry ignored his pleas and continued to seek Soviet help even after Hiroshima.

"Peace feelers" by Japanese officials abroad seemed no more promising from the American point of view. Although several of the consular personnel and military attachés engaged in these activities claimed important connections at home, none produced verification. Had the Japanese government sought only an assurance about the emperor, all it had to do was grant one of these men authority to begin talks through the OSS. Its failure to do so led American officials to assume that those involved were either well-meaning individuals acting alone or that they were being orchestrated by Tokyo. Grew characterized such "peace feelers" as "familiar weapons of psychological warfare" designed to "divide the Allies."

Some American officials, such as Stimson and Grew, nonetheless wanted to signal the Japanese that they might retain the emperorship in the form of a constitutional monarchy. Such an assurance might remove the last stumbling block to surrender, if not when it was issued, then later. Only an imperial rescript would bring about an orderly surrender, they argued, without which Japanese forces would fight to the last man regardless of what the government in Tokyo did. Besides, the emperor could serve as a stabilizing factor during the transition to peacetime.

There were many arguments against an American initiative. Some opposed retaining such an undemocratic institution on principle and because they feared it might later serve as a rallying point for future militarism. Should that happen, as one assistant Secretary of State put it, "those lives already spent will have been sacrificed in vain, and lives will be lost again in the future." Japanese hard-liners were certain to exploit an overture as evidence that losses sustained at Okinawa had weakened American resolve and to argue that continued resistance would bring further concessions. Stalin, who earlier had told an American envoy that he favored abolishing the emperorship because the ineffectual Hirohito might be succeeded by "an energetic and vigorous figure who could cause trouble," was just as certain to interpret it as a treacherous effort to end the war before the Soviets could share in the spoils.

There were domestic considerations as well. Roosevelt had announced the unconditional surrender policy in early 1943, and it since had become a slogan of the war. He also had advocated that peoples everywhere should have the right to choose their own form of government, and Truman had publicly pledged to carry out his predecessor's legacies. For him to have formally *guaranteed* continuance of the emperorship, as opposed to merely accepting it on American terms pending free elections, as he later did, would have constituted a blatant repudiation of his own promises.

Nor was that all. Regardless of the emperor's actual role in Japanese aggression, which is still debated, much wartime propaganda had encouraged Americans to regard Hirohito as no less a war criminal than Adolf Hitler or Benito Mussolini. Although Truman said on several occasions that he had no objection to retaining the emperor, he understandably refused to make the first move. The ultimatum he issued from Potsdam on July 26 did not refer specifically to the emperorship. All it said was that occupation forces would be removed after "a peaceful and responsible" government had been established according to the "freely expressed will of the Japanese people." When the Japanese rejected the ultimatum rather than at last inquire whether they might retain the emperor, Truman permitted the plans for using the bombs to go forward.

Reliance on MAGIC intercepts and the "peace feelers" to gauge how near Japan was to surrender is misleading in any case. The army, not the Foreign Office, controlled the situation. Intercepts of Japanese military communications, designated ULTRA, provided no reason to believe the army was even considering surrender. Japanese Imperial Headquarters had correctly guessed that the next operation after Okinawa would be Kyushu and was making every effort to bolster its defenses there.

General Marshall reported on July 24 that there were "approximately 500,000 troops in Kyushu" and that more were on the way. ULTRA identified new units arriving almost daily. MacArthur's G-2 reported on July 29 that "this threatening development, if not checked, may grow to a point where we attack on a ratio of one (1) to one (1) which is not the recipe for victory." By the time the first atomic bomb fell, ULTRA indicated that there were 560,000 troops in southern Kyushu (the actual figure was closer to 900,000), and projections for November 1 placed the number at 680,000. A report, for medical purposes, of July 31 estimated that total battle and non-battle casualties might run as high as 394,859 *for the Kyushu operation alone*. This figure did not include those men expected to be killed outright, for obviously they would require no medical attention. Marshall regarded Japanese defenses as so formidable that even after Hiroshima he asked MacArthur to consider alternate landing sites and began contemplating the use of atomic bombs as tactical weapons to support the invasion.

> *By late July the casualty projection of 31,000 that Marshall had given Truman at the June 18 strategy meeting had become meaningless.*

The thirty-day casualty projection of 31,000 Marshall had given Truman at the June 18 strategy meeting had become meaningless. It had been based on the assumption that the Japanese had about 350,000 defenders in Kyushu and that naval and air interdiction would preclude significant reinforcement. But the Japanese buildup since that time meant that the defenders would have nearly twice the number of troops available by "X-day" than earlier assumed. The assertion that apprehensions about casualties are insufficient to explain Truman's use of the bombs, therefore, cannot be taken seriously. On the contrary, as Winston Churchill wrote after a conversation with him at Potsdam, Truman was tormented by "the terrible responsibilities that rested upon him in regard to the unlimited effusions of American blood."

Some historians have argued that while the first bomb *might* have been required to achieve Japanese surrender, dropping the second constituted a needless barbarism. The record shows otherwise. American officials believed more than one bomb would be necessary because they assumed Japanese hard-liners would minimize the first explosion or attempt to explain it away as some sort of natural catastrophe, precisely what they did. The Japanese minister of war, for instance, at first refused even to admit that the Hiroshima bomb was atomic. A few hours after Nagasaki he told the cabinet that "the Americans appeared to have one hundred atomic bombs... they could drop three per day. The next target might well be Tokyo."

Even after both bombs had fallen and Russia entered the war, Japanese militants insisted on such lenient peace terms that moderates knew there was no sense even transmitting them to the United States. Hirohito had to intervene personally on two occasions during the next few days to induce hard-liners to abandon their conditions and to accept the American stipulation that the emperor's authority "shall be subject to the Supreme Commander of the Allied Powers." That the militarists would have accepted such a settlement before the bombs is farfetched, to say the least.

Some writers have argued that the cumulative effects of battlefield defeats, conventional bombing, and naval blockade already had defeated Japan. Even without extending assurances about the emperor, all the United States had to do was wait. The most frequently cited basis for this contention is the *United States Strategic Bombing Survey,* published in 1946, which stated that Japan would have surrendered by November 1 "even if the atomic bombs had not been dropped, even if Russia had not entered the war, and even if no invasion had been planned or contemplated." Recent scholarship by the historian Robert P. Newman and others has demonstrated that the survey was "cooked" by those who prepared it to arrive at such a conclusion. No matter. This or any other document based on information available only after the war ended is irrelevant with regard to what Truman could have known at the time.

What often goes unremarked is that when the bombs were dropped, fighting was still going on in the Philippines, China, and elsewhere. Every day that the war continued thousands of prisoners of war had to live and die in abysmal conditions, and there were rumors that the Japanese intended to slaughter them if the homeland was invaded. Truman was Commander in Chief of the American armed forces, and he had a duty to the men under his command not shared by those sitting in moral judgment decades later. Available evidence points to the conclusion that he acted for the reason he said he did: to end a bloody war that would have become far bloodier had invasion proved necessary. One can only imagine what would have happened if tens of thousands of American boys had died or been wounded on Japanese soil and then it had become known that Truman had chosen not to use weapons that might have ended the war months sooner.

Robert James Maddox teaches American history at Pennsylvania State University. His Weapons for Victory: Hiroshima Fifty Years Later *is published by the University of Missouri Press (1995).*

From *American Heritage*, May/June 1995, pp. 70-74, 76-77 © 1995 by Forbes, Inc. Reprinted by permission of *American Heritage* magazine, a division of Forbes, Inc.

UNIT 5

From the Cold War to 2004

Unit Selections

Key Points to Consider

- Discuss the short and long fun effects of permitting Jackie Robinson to play major league baseball? Why was he such an excellent choice to break the race barrier?

- The conflict in Korea was a limited war. Why did it have such important consequences at the time and later?

- What was "The Spirit of '68?" Does John Judis make a convincing case for his claims about the impact the 1960s had on American culture?

- Why did J. Edgar Hoover find Reverend Martin Luther King so dangerous? What did he do to destroy King's reputation? What does this tell us about Hoover?

- Analyze "The American Century." Why did the Vietnam War cause such dislocation at home and call into question American goals abroad?

- Discuss the article on 9/11. How valid has it turned out to be?

 **Links: www.dushkin.com/online/**
These sites are annotated in the World Wide Web pages.

Coldwar
http://www.cnn.com/SPECIALS/cold.war

The American Experience: Vietnam Online
http://www.pbs.org/wgbh/amex/vietnam/

The Federal Web Locator
http://www.infoctr.edu/fwl

Federalism: Relationship between Local and National Governments
http://www.infidels.org/~nap/index.federalism.html

The Gallup Organization
http://www.gallup.com/

STAT-USA
http://www.stat-usa.gov/stat-usa.html

U.S. Department of State
http://www.state.gov/

President Franklin D. Roosevelt sought to build a working relationship with Soviet leader Josef Stalin throughout World War II. Roosevelt believed that the wartime collaboration had to continue if a lasting peace were to be achieved. At the Yalta Conference of February 1945, a series of agreements were made that FDR hoped would provide the basis for continued cooperation. Subsequent disputes over interpretation of these agreements, particularly with regard to Poland, raised doubts in Roosevelt's mind that Stalin was acting in good faith. Roosevelt died on April 12, 1945, and there is no doubt that he was moving toward a "tougher" position during the last weeks of his life.

His successor, Harry S. Truman, assumed the presidency with little knowledge of Roosevelt's thinking. Truman had not been part of the administration's inner circle and had to rely on discussions with the advisers he inherited and his own reading of messages passed between FDR and the Soviets. Aside from an ugly encounter with Soviet Foreign Minister V. M. Molotov at the White House only eleven days after Roosevelt's death, Truman attempted to carry out what he believed were Roosevelt's intentions: be firm with the Soviets, but continue to seek accommodation. He came to believe that Molotov was trying to sabotage U.S.-Soviet relations and that the best way to reach agreements was to negotiate directly with Stalin. He did this at the Potsdam Conference during the summer of 1945, and left the talks believing that Stalin was a hard bargainer but one who could be trusted.

Events during the late summer and early autumn eroded Truman's hopes that the Soviets genuinely wanted to get along. Disputes over Poland and other Eastern European countries, the treatment of postwar Germany, and a host of other issues finally persuaded Truman that it was time to stop "babying" the Soviets. A militant public speech by Stalin, which one American referred to as the "declaration of World War III," appeared to confirm this view. Increasingly hostile relations led to what became known as the "Cold War," during which each side increasingly came to regard the other as an enemy rather than merely an adversary.

Meanwhile the United States had to cope with the problems of reconversion to a peacetime economy. Demobilization of the armed forces proved especially vexing as the public clamored to have service men and women, stationed virtually all over the world, brought home and discharged as quickly as possible. When the administration seemed to be moving too slowly, the threat "no boats, no votes" became popular. Race riots, labor strife, and inflation also marred the postwar period.

There was social ferment as well. Many blacks had served in the armed forces or worked in defense industries, presumably to win a war for freedom and justice. Yet they had encountered segregation in the military and unequal treatment in civilian jobs. Professional sports at that time was kept "lily white,"—an affront to the principles for which the war had been fought. "Baseball's Noble Experiment" describes how Brooklyn Dodger president Branch Rickey maneuvered to break down the color line in baseball. Jackie Robinson, a former army officer, was chosen to be the test case as much for his mental toughness as for his physical skills. Robinson proved more than equal to the challenge. Despite the taunts of opponents, fans, and even some of his own teammates, he carved out a distinguished career and opened the doors for other black players.

A series of events during the late 1940s escalated the Cold War into a global conflict. Soviet conduct in Eastern and Southern Europe, and its first test explosion of an atomic bomb heightened the sense of peril. Revelations of domestic spying for the "Reds," and the Chinese Communist victory over our ally Chiang Kai-Shek seemed to confirm the notion that "they" were everywhere. Then, in 1950, a scant five years after the end of World War I, the United States found itself at war again. The North Korean invasion of the South in June of that year appeared to American leaders as a Soviet-inspired probe to test Western resolve. Failure to halt aggression there, many believed, would embolden the Soviets to strike elsewhere just as Hitler had done in the 1930s. "Truman's Other War" shows how this conflict "provided the foundation upon which the entire Cold War military and defense apparatus was built."

Domestically, the 1950s offered a mixed bag. Social critics denounced the conformity of those who plodded up the corporate latter, purchased tract homes that all looked alike, or who had no greater ambition than to sit in front of their television sets every night. A conservative reaction against the New Deal, which had begun during World War II, grew stronger. "Women, Domesticity, and Postwar Conservatism" describes how some white middle and upper class women became "militant anti-Communist crusaders." "The Split-Level Years" provides a sketch of the decade that witnessed the emergence to stardom of Marilyn Monroe, Howdy Doody, and James Dean.

The period from the mid-1960s to the early 1970s was a turbulent era. Blacks and their allies mounted increasing protests against the pervasive racism in this country. They used a variety of tactics such as sit-ins at lunch counters and in buses, and organizing marches in various cities. "The FBI Marches" details the FBIs harassment of the Reverend Martin Luther King, Jr., one of the great civil rights leaders. Protests grew beyond the cause the civil rights. Opposition against the Vietnam War often spilled over into violence, many young people denounced the beliefs of their elders, and drug use skyrocketed. John B. Judis, in "The Spirit of '68," claims that during the 1960s the United States changed from a culture based on work, sacrifice, and deferred gratification to one that emphasized "consumption, lifestyle, and quality of life." He sees this passage as the result of what he calls "consumer capitalism."

Few predicted that the Soviet Union, which once had seemed so formidable, would collapse like a wet paper sack in 1991. John Lewis Gaddis, in "Face Off," provides a chronological survey of how the Cold War developed and finally came to an end. Michael Barone's "The American Century" plays off a famous 1941 editorial of the same name written by publisher Henry Luce. Victory in World War II and American leadership in the Cold War appeared to validate this prophecy. Then, as the Vietnam War dragged on and domestic problems mounted, "the elites lost confidence in America and the American people lost confidence in the elites." The nation appeared to regain its confidence in the last third of the century Barone's essay was written before the devastating terrorist attacks on the World Trade Center buildings. "What September 11th Really Wrought" examines the impact of this tragedy on the American people and government.

One often hears the phrase "culture wars" used today. It is a kind of catchall term that can be applied to matters such as education and attitudes toward gun control and abortion, to name just a few. Johsua Zeitz's "Victory" explores the impact of the South on popular culture, which far exceeds the stale telling of "redneck" jokes. Demographic and social changes, he argues, have resulted in an enormous Southern influence on sports, popular entertainment and religion.

Baseball's *Noble* Experiment

When former Negro Leaguer Jackie Robinson took his place in the Brooklyn Dodgers' starting lineup on April 15, 1947, he initiated a major change not only in sports, but in American society as a whole.

by William Kashatus

On August 28, 1945, Jackie Robinson, the star shortstop of the Negro Leagues' Kansas City Monarchs, arrived at the executive offices of the Brooklyn Dodgers Baseball Club. Invited on the pretense that Branch Rickey, since 1942 a part owner of the club as well as its president and general manager, was seeking top black talent in order to create a Negro League team of his own, Robinson approached the meeting with great reluctance. Deep down he wanted to break the color barrier that existed in professional baseball, not discuss the possibility of playing for yet another all-black team. Little did he realize that Rickey shared his dream.

A shrewd, talkative man who had dedicated his life to baseball, the 64-year-old Rickey was secretly plotting a sweeping revolution within the national pastime. He believed that integration of the major leagues would be good for the country as well as for the game. Financial gain was only part of his motive—it was also a matter of moral principle. Rickey, a devout Methodist, disdained the bigoted attitudes of the white baseball establishment.

Greeting Robinson with a vigorous handshake, Rickey wasted no time in revealing his true intentions. "The truth is," he confessed, "I'm interested in you as a candidate for the Brooklyn Dodgers. I think you can play in the major leagues. How do you feel about it?"

The young ball player was speechless. He had taught himself to be cynical toward all baseball-club owners, especially white ones, in order to prevent any personal disillusionment.

"What about it? You think you can play for Montreal?" demanded the stocky beetle-browed executive.

Robinson, awestruck, managed to say "yes." He knew that the Montreal Royals was the Dodgers' top minor-league team and that if he made good there, he had an excellent chance to crack the majors. "I just want to be treated fairly" he added. "You will not be treated fairly!" Rickey snapped. " 'Nigger' will be a compliment!"

For the next three hours, Rickey interrogated the star shortstop. With great dramatic flair, he role-played every conceivable scenario that would confront the first player to break baseball's color barrier: first he was a bigoted sportswriter who only wrote lies about Robinson's performance; next he was a Southern hotel manager refusing room and board; then, a racist major leaguer looking for a fight; and after that a waiter throwing Robinson out of a "for whites only" diner. In every scenario, Rickey cursed Robinson and threatened him, verbally degrading him in every way imaginable. The Dodger general manager's performance was so convincing, Robinson later said, that "I found myself chain-gripping my fingers behind my back."

When he was through, Rickey told Robinson that he knew he was "a fine ballplayer. But what I need," he added, "is more than a great player. I need a man that will take abuse and insults for his race. And what I don't know is whether you have the guts!"

Robinson struggled to keep his temper. He was insulted by the implication that he was a coward. "Mr. Rickey," he retorted, "do you want a Negro who's afraid to fight back?"

"No!" Rickey barked, "I want a ballplayer with guts enough *not* to fight back. We can't *fight* our way through this. There's virtually nobody on our side. No owners, no umpires, virtually no newspapermen. And I'm afraid that many fans will be hostile too. They'll taunt you and goad you. They'll do anything to make you react. They'll try to provoke a race riot in the ball park."

As he listened, Robinson became transfixed by the Dodger president. He felt his sincerity his deep, quiet strength, and his sense of moral justice. "We can only win," concluded Rickey, "if we can convince the world that I'm doing this because you're a great ballplayer and a fine gentleman. You will symbolize a crucial cause. One incident, just one incident, can set it back twenty years."

"Mr. Rickey," Robinson finally said, "I think I can play ball in Montreal. I think I can play ball in Brooklyn.... If you want to take this gamble, I will promise you there will be no incident."

The agreement was sealed by a handshake. Jackie Robinson and Branch Rickey had launched a noble experiment to integrate major-league baseball. Two years later, in 1947, when Robinson actually broke the color barrier, winning rookie-of-the-year honors with the Dodgers, he raised the hopes and expectations of millions of black Americans who believed that deeply rooted patterns of discrimination could be changed.

In 1945, segregation was the most distinguishing characteristic of American race relations. More than half of the nation's 15 million African Americans still lived in the South, amidst a society that sanctioned the principle of "equal but separate." A rigid system of state and local ordinances enforced strict separation of the races in schools, restaurants, movie theaters, and even restrooms. For blacks, these so-called "Jim Crow laws"[1] meant inferior public schools, health care, and public lodging, as well as discriminatory voter registration procedures that kept many of them disenfranchised.

For the nearly one million African Americans who had served in the armed forces during World War II, the contradiction inherent in their fight against totalitarianism abroad while enduring segregation at home was insufferable. No longer willing to knuckle under to Jim Crow this young generation of black Americans was determined to secure full political and social equality. Many migrated to Northern cities, where they found better jobs, better schooling, and freedom from landlord control. Together with their white allies, these Northern blacks would lay the foundations of the momentous civil rights campaign of the 1950s and '60s. And Jackie Robinson became their hero.

To be sure, Robinson's challenge to baseball's whites-only policy was a formidable one. Blacks had been expelled from the major leagues when segregation was established by the 1896 Supreme Court ruling in *Plessy v. Ferguson*.[2] Racist attitudes were reinforced by the significant numbers of white Southerners who played in the majors, as well as by the extensive minor-league system that existed in the South. When blacks established their own Negro Leagues, white journalists, as well as historians, ignored them.

Despite the periodic efforts of some white club owners to circumvent the racist policies and sign exceptional Negro Leaguers, the majors continued to bar blacks through the end of World War II. Baseball Commissioner Judge Kenesaw Mountain Landis ensured the sport's segregationist policies by thwarting all efforts to sign blacks, while publicly stating that "There is no rule, formal or informal, or any understanding—unwritten, subterranean, or sub-anything—against the hiring of Negro players by the teams of organized baseball." Not until Landis died in 1944, however, did baseball open the door for integration..

The new commissioner, Albert "Happy" Chandler, was adamant in defending the "freedom of blacks," especially those who served in the war, to "make it in major league baseball." Chandler's support for integration earned for him the open hos-

BASEBALL HALL OF FAME LIBRARY

A versatile athlete, Robinson earned varsity letters in four sports, including track (above, left), while a student at the University of California at Los Angeles.

tility of the owners of 15 of the 16 major-league clubs, the exception being the Dodgers and Branch Rickey.

Publicly, Rickey never revealed his intentions of breaking the color barrier. Instead, he announced to the baseball world that he was going to organize a team to be known as the "Brown Dodgers" or the "Brown Bombers" as part of a new all-black "United States League." His scouts combed baseball leagues across the country, as well as in Cuba, Mexico, Puerto Rico, and Venezuela, for black prospects. What Rickey really wanted to find was a talented, college-educated ballplayer who would be able to contradict the popular myth of black ignorance. His search narrowed to Jack Roosevelt Robinson, then an infielder for the Kansas City Monarchs.

Born on January 31, 1919, in Cairo, Georgia, Jackie was the grandson of a slave and the fifth child of a sharecropper who deserted his family. Raised by his mother in a white, middle-class neighborhood in Pasadena, California, Jackie and his brothers and sister were verbally ridiculed and frequently pelted with rocks by local children. Rather than endure the humiliation, the boys formed a gang and began to return fire

What saved the young Jackie from more serious trouble and even crime was his exceptional athletic ability. Robinson's high school career was distinguished by remarkable success in football, baseball, basketball, and track. His versatility earned him

With Rachel's Support

When Jackie Robinson met with Branch Rickey in August 1945, the Dodgers' general manager asked him if he had a girlfriend, and was pleased when Jackie told him that he was engaged to be married. As he had made abundantly clear to Robinson that day, Rickey was aware that the first black player in the major leagues would face a terrible ordeal, and he clearly believed that he should not face it alone.

In her recent book, *Jackie Robinson: An Intimate Portrait,* Rachel Robinson writes that it was at the start of the '47 season that she and Jackie first realized "how important we were to black America and how much we symbolized its hunger for opportunity and its determination to make dreams long deferred possible." If Jackie failed to make the grade as a player, or if the pressures became so great that he decided to pull out of Rickey's "noble experiment," the hopes of all the nation's blacks would be done enormous, if not irreparable harm. It was a tremendous burden to have to bear, and it belonged not only to Jackie, but also to his family.

Rachel Isum had met her future husband in 1940 while they were both students at UCLA, where she earned a degree in nursing. Engaged in 1941, they endured long separations during World War II, and in 1945, as Jackie traveled with the Kansas City Monarchs. Finally, in February 1946—just before Jackie was due to report to Daytona Beach, Florida, to try to earn a place with the Montreal Royals—they were married. Both Jackie and Rachel had known racial bigotry and discrimination in Southern California, where they grew up, but they

realized that they would face something much more difficult in the institutionalized segregation of the 1940s South. During that first trip to Florida, they experienced repeated humiliations that were, according to Rachel, "merely a foreshadowing of trials to come." As the Royals played exhibition games in other Florida cities, Jackie got a taste of how many Americans viewed his presence in professional baseball.

Following spring training, Jackie joined the Royals in Montreal, where the couple found a much more receptive environment. Although Jackie still faced racism during road trips, the Robinsons' year in Canada was fondly remembered as a respite that helped them prepare for the real test that came when he moved on to the Dodgers in 1947.

As players and fans in cities around the National League tormented Jackie, Rachel was forced to sit "through name calling, jeers, and vicious baiting in a furious silence." For his part, the Dodgers' rookie infielder, who had promised Rickey that he would turn the other cheek, "found that the most powerful form of retaliation against prejudice was his excellent play." But after the '48 season, Robinson called off his deal with Rickey. He would no longer submit quietly to insults, discrimination, and abuses. Able at last to release some of the pent-up pressure and emotion, Robinson became a more confident player; in 1949, he won the National League batting championship with a .349 average and received a trophy ironically named for Kenesaw Mountain Landis, the man who tried to keep blacks out of baseball.

an athletic scholarship, first to Pasadena Junior College and later to the University of California at Los Angeles, where he earned varsity letters in four different sports and All American honors in football.

Drafted into the Army in the spring of 1942, Robinson applied to be admitted to Officers' Candidate School, but was denied admission because of his race. His application was eventually approved, however, thanks to the help of boxing champion Joe Louis, who was stationed with Jackie at Fort Riley, Kansas. Commissioned a second lieutenant, Robinson continued during the next few years to defy discriminatory practices within the military. When, in July 1944, he refused to move to the rear of a military bus at Fort Hood, Texas, Robinson was charged with insubordination and court-martialed. But the case against him was weak—the Army had recently issued orders against such segregation—and a good lawyer won his acquittal. Although he received an honorable discharge in November 1944, Robinson's time in the military had left him feeling vulnerable and uncertain about the future.

Shortly after his discharge, the Kansas City Monarchs, one of the most talented of baseball's Negro League teams, offered Robinson a contract for four hundred dollars a month. While with the Monarchs, Robinson established himself as a fine defensive shortstop with impressive base stealing and hitting abilities. But he hated barnstorming through the South, with its Jim

Crow restaurants and hotels, and frequently allowed his temper to get the better of him.

Some teammates thought Jackie too impatient with the segregationist treatment of blacks. Others admired him for his determination to take a stand against racism. Yet Robinson never saw himself as a crusader for civil rights as much as an athlete who had grown disillusioned with his chosen career. "When I look back at what I had to go through," he recalled years later, "I can only marvel at the many black players who stuck it out for years in the Jim Crow leagues because they had nowhere to go. The black press, some liberal sportswriters and even a few politicians were banging away at those Jim Crow barriers in baseball, but I never expected the walls to come tumbling down in my lifetime. I began to wonder why I should dedicate my life to a career where the boundaries of progress were set by racial discrimination."

There were indications, however, that the tide was turning in favor of integration. On April 16, 1945, Robinson was invited along with two other Negro League stars—Marvin Williams of the Philadelphia Stars and the Cleveland Buckeyes' Sam Jethroe—to tryout for the Boston Red Sox. Manager Joe Cronin was especially impressed with the Monarchs' shortstop, but still passed on the opportunity to sign him. Nevertheless, the tryout brought Robinson to the attention of Clyde Sukeforth, the chief scout of the Brooklyn Dodgers. Convinced of Robinson's exceptional playing ability and personal determination, Sukeforth set the stage for the memorable August meeting between Robinson and Rickey.

Robinson had no illusions about the purpose of his agreement with the Dodgers. He realized that Rickey's altruism was tempered by a profit motive, and yet he admired the moral courage of the Dodger president. "Mr. Rickey knew that achieving racial equality in baseball would be terribly difficult," Robinson remembered. "There would be deep resentment, determined opposition and perhaps even racial violence. But he was convinced that he was morally right and he shrewdly sensed that making the game a truly national one would have healthy financial results." Rickey was absolutely correct on both counts.

The Dodgers' October 23, 1945, announcement that Robinson had signed a contract for six hundred dollars a month[3] to play for their top minor-league club at Montreal was greeted with great hostility by baseball's white establishment. Rickey was accused of being "a carpetbagger who, under the guise of helping, is in truth using the Negro for his own self-interest." Criticism even came from the Negro League owners who feared, not without reason, that Robinson's signing would lead to declining fan interest in their clubs. The Monarchs were especially angered by the signing and went so far as to threaten a lawsuit against the Dodgers for tampering with a player who was already under contract.

By mid-November the criticism became so hostile that Rickey's own family pleaded with him to abandon his crusade for fear that it would destroy his health. The Dodger president refused, speaking only of the excitement and competitive advantage that black players would bring to Brooklyn baseball, while downplaying the moral significance he attached to integration. "The greatest untapped reservoir of raw material in the history of the game is the black race," he contended. "The Negroes will make us winners for years to come and for that I will happily bear being called a 'bleeding heart' and a 'do-gooder' and all that humanitarian rot."

Robinson's first test came during the 1946 preseason, even before he debuted with the Montreal Royals. Rickey named Mississippian Clay Hopper, who had worked for him since 1929, to manage the Royals. There were reports, probably true, that Hopper begged Rickey to reconsider giving him this assignment. But Rickey's careful handling of Robinson's jump to the big leagues would seem to suggest that he believed that having a Southerner at the helm of the Montreal club would head off some dissension among the players and that he trusted Hopper to handle any situations that might arise.

Throughout the '46 season, Robinson endured racist remarks from fans and opposing players and humiliating treatment in the South. By season's end, the constant pressure and abuse had taken its toll—his hair began to gray, he suffered with chronic stomach trouble, and some thought he was on the brink of a nervous breakdown. Finding himself unable to eat or sleep, he went to a doctor, who concluded that he was suffering from stress. "You're not having a nervous breakdown," the physician told him. "You're under a lot of stress. Stay home and don't read any

BASEBALL HALL OF FAME LIBRARY

By the 1948 season, Robinson was no longer the only black player in the majors. African Americans brought up by Rickey that year included catcher Roy Campanella, (right) who would be voted the National League's Most Valuable Player three times.

newspapers, and don't go to the ballpark for a week." Jackie, his wife Rachel remembered, stayed home for one day. The problem, she said, came from his "not being able to fight back." It was, as Rickey had warned him, "the cross that you must bear."

Despite the tension and distractions, Robinson managed to hit for an impressive .349 average and led the Montreal Royals to victory over the Louisville Colonels in the Little World Series. After the final game in that championship series, grateful Royals fans hoisted Robinson onto their shoulders and carried him to the locker room. Hopper shook his shortstop's hand and said: "You're a real ballplayer and a gentleman. It's been wonderful having you on the team." Robinson had made his first convert.

Because Robinson's success with Montreal had been so impressive, Rickey assumed that all the Dodgers would demand his promotion to the majors for the 1947 season. "After all," he reasoned, "Robinson could mean a pennant, and ball players are not averse to cashing World Series checks."

To promote and protect his young black star, Rickey made some additional moves. First, in order to avoid Jim Crow restrictions, he held spring training in Havana, Cuba, instead of Florida. Next, he moved Robinson, an experienced shortstop and second baseman, to first base, where he would be spared physical contact with opposing players who might try to injure him deliberately.

Finally, Rickey scheduled a seven-game series between the Dodgers and the Royals in order to showcase Robinson's talent. "I want you to be a whirling demon against the Dodgers in this series," Rickey told Robinson. "You have to be so good that the Dodger players themselves are going to want you on their club.... I want you to hit that ball. I want you to get on base and run wild. Steal their pants off. Be the most conspicuous player on the field. The newspapermen from New York will send good stories back about you and help mold favorable public opinion."

Robinson more than obliged, batting .625 and stealing seven bases in the series. But instead of helping him, the performance served only to alienate him from his future teammates, many of whom were Southerners. Alabamian Dixie Walker drafted a petition stating that the players who signed would prefer to be traded than to play with a black teammate. While the team was playing exhibition games in Panama, Walker proceeded to gather signatures from Dodger teammates. Harold "Pee Wee" Reese, although a Kentuckian, refused to sign. It was a tremendously courageous act on his part because, as the team's shortstop, Reese had more to lose than any other Dodger. "If he can take my job," Reese insisted, "he's entitled to it."

When Dodger manager Leo Durocher learned of the petition, he was furious. He had asked Rickey to bring Robinson up to Brooklyn during the previous year's pennant drive. At a late-night team meeting, according to Harold Parrott, the Dodger road secretary, Durocher told Walker and the other petitioners that "I don't care if the guy is yellow or black, or if he has stripes like a zebra. I'm the manager of this team and I say he plays. What's more, I say he can make us all rich.... An' if any of you can't use the money, I'll see that you're traded."[4]

The rebellion squelched, Rickey announced on April 10, 1947, that Jackie Robinson had officially been signed to play first base for the Brooklyn Dodgers. The noble experiment was in full swing.

O f all the major-league cities, Brooklyn, with its ethnically diverse and racially mixed neighborhoods, was just the place to break the color barrier. Despite their reputation as "perennial losers"—since the franchise's establishment in 1883, no Brooklyn team had won a World Series—the Dodgers enjoyed an enduring love affair with their fans. This warm affinity was fostered, in part, by their cramped but colorful ballpark, Ebbets Field, located in the Flatbush section of Brooklyn. The double-decked grandstand stood only along the foul lines, allowing the fans a special intimacy with the players. "If you were in a box seat," said broadcaster Red Barber, "you were so close you were practically an infielder." Aside from the patchwork collection of local advertisements in left field; the large, black scoreboard in right; and the tone-deaf "Dodger Symphony Band" that roamed the grandstand, nothing came between the Dodgers and their die-hard fans.

When Robinson made his first appearance as a Dodger on April 15, 1947, more than 26,000 fans packed Ebbets Field; reportedly some 14,000 of those were African Americans. The afternoon was cold and rainy and Robinson went hitless. Nonetheless, the sight of a black man on a major-league diamond during a regular season game moved the crowd so deeply that they cheered the Dodgers on to a 5–3 victory over the Boston Braves. Every move the 28-year-old rookie made

BASEBALL HALL OF FAME LIBRARY

After his baseball career ended, Robinson became even more deeply involved in the Civil Rights Movement, supporting the work of leaders such as Dr. Martin Luther King, Jr., (left). Jackie and his family took part in the 1963 March on Washington that featured King's stirring "I Have a Dream" speech.

seemed to be greeted with the chant: "Jackie! Jackie! Jackie!" It seemed as if baseball had finally shed its three-quarters of a century of hypocrisy to become truly deserving of the title "national pastime."

When the Philadelphia Phillies arrived in Brooklyn a week later, however, all hopes that integration would come peaceably were shattered. In one of the lowest moments ever in baseball history the Phillies, led by their Southern manager, Ben Chapman, launched a tirade of racial epithets during the pre-game batting practice. And the jeering did not let up throughout the entire three-game series.

Two weeks later, when the Dodgers traveled to the so-called "City of Brotherly Love," Chapman and his Phillies picked up where they had left off, warning the Dodger players that they would contract diseases if they touched Robinson and indulging in even more personal racial slurs. Robinson's less-than-stellar hitting in the series only added to the Phillies' contention that he did not belong in the majors and was a ploy to attract blacks to Dodger games and make more money for Rickey.

After the second game of the series, angry Dodger fans launched a full-scale protest with the National League's president, Ford Frick, who responded by ordering Chapman and the Phillies to stop their verbal assault immediately. In fact, Chapman probably would have lost his job over the incident, if Robinson had not agreed to pose with him for a conciliatory newspaper photograph. Under duress, the Phillies' manager agreed to stand next to the Dodger rookie. "Ben extended his hand," Harold Parrott recalled, "smiling broadly as if they had been buddy-buddy for a lifetime. Robinson reached out and grasped it. The flicker of a smile crept across his face as the photographer snapped away getting several shots."

Years later Robinson admitted that the incessant abuse during those games with the Phillies almost led him to the breaking point. As he described it: "For one wild and rage-crazed minute I thought, 'To hell with Mr. Rickey's noble experiment. It's clear that it won't succeed.... What a glorious, cleansing thing it would be to let go.' To hell with the image of the patient black freak I was supposed to create. I could throw down my bat, stride over to the Phillies dugout, grab one of those white sons of bitches and smash his teeth in with my despised black fist. Then I could walk away from it and I'd never become a sports star. But my son could tell his son some day what his daddy could have been if he hadn't been too much of a man."

The experience with the Phillies revealed the shocking severity of the racism that existed in baseball. At the same time, however, Robinson's tremendous restraint in the face of such ugly prejudice served to rally his teammates around him and the cause of integration. Eddie Stanky one of those who had signed the petition against Robinson joining the team, became so angered by the Phillies' relentless abuse that he challenged them to "yell at somebody who can answer back." Soon after, before a game in Cincinnati, the Reds' players taunted Pee Wee Reese about playing with a black teammate. The Dodger shortstop walked over to Robinson and, in a firm show of support, placed his arm around the first baseman's shoulders.

As the season unfolded, Dodger support for Robinson strengthened in response to the admirable way he handled all the adversity. Opposing pitchers threw at his head and ribs, while infielders would spit in his face if he was involved in a close play on the base paths. And the hate mail was unending. But through it all, Robinson persevered. He even managed to keep a sense of humor. Before one game in Cincinnati, when the Dodgers learned that their first baseman's life had been threatened, one teammate suggested that all the players wear Robinson's uniform number "42" on their backs to confuse the assailant. "Okay with me," responded the rookie. "Paint your faces black and run pigeon-toed too!"

Even the white baseball establishment began to embrace the Dodger infielder. In May of 1947, when Ford Frick learned of the St. Louis Cardinals' intention to instigate a league-wide strike by walking off the ball diamond in a scheduled game against the integrated Dodgers, he vowed to suspend the ringleaders if they carried out their plan. "... I don't care if I wreck the National League for five years," he declared. "This is the United States of America, and one citizen has as much right to play as another. The National League will go down the line with Robinson whatever the consequence." The conspiracy died on the spot.

When the season ended, the *Sporting News,* which had gone on record earlier as opposing the integration of baseball because "There is not a single Negro player with major league possibilities," named Robinson the National League's "Rookie of the Year" for his impressive performance that season—29 stolen bases, 12 home runs, 42 successful bunt hits, and a .297 batting average.

Those efforts helped the Dodgers to capture a pennant, and on September 23, jubilant Brooklyn fans cheered their first baseman with a "Jackie Robinson Day" at Ebbets Field. In addition to a new car and other gifts, Robinson received tributes for his contribution to racial equality. Song-and-dance man Bill "Bojangles" Robinson, one of the guest speakers, told the

BASEBALL HALL OF FAME LIBRARY

Jackie Robinson's death in October 1972 deeply affected African Americans and baseball fans across the country. As his funeral cortege made its way to his final resting place in Cypress Hills Cemetery in Brooklyn, the camera captured one mourner, shown in the foreground, offering Robinson a black-power salute.

crowd: "I'm 69 years old but never thought I'd live to see the day when I'd stand face-to-face with Ty Cobb in Technicolor."

The Dodgers forced the New York Yankees to a seventh and deciding game in the World Series. And when all was said and done, no amount of hate mail or verbal and psychological abuse could tarnish the indisputable fact that Jackie Robinson was an exceptional baseball player. He belonged in the major leagues.

Robinson's greatest accomplishment, however, was the inspiration that he provided for other African Americans, both in and out of baseball. Thousands of blacks came to watch him play, setting new attendance records in such cities as Chicago and Pittsburgh. Even in St. Louis, Cincinnati, and Philadelphia, where the opposing teams were the most hostile toward the Dodger rookie, black fans would arrive on chartered buses called "Jackie Robinson Specials," having traveled hundreds of miles just to see him play.

Ed Charles, a black youngster from the Deep South who went on to play in the major leagues himself, remembered the thrill of seeing his childhood hero for the first time. "I sat in the segregated section of the ball park and watched Jackie," he said. "And I finally believed what I read in the papers—that one of us had made it. When the game was over we kids followed Jackie to the train station. When the train pulled out, we ran down the tracks listening for the sounds as far as we could. And when we couldn't hear it any longer, we stopped and put our ears to the track so we could feel the vibrations of that train carrying Jackie Robinson. We wanted to be part of him as long as we could."

Indeed, Robinson had jolted the national consciousness in a profound way. Until 1947 all of baseball's heroes had been white men. Suddenly there was a black baseball star who could hit, bunt, steal, and field with the best of them. His style of play was nothing new in the Negro Leagues, but in the white majors, it was innovative and exciting. Robinson made things happen on the base paths. If he got on first, he stole second. If he could not steal third, he would distract the pitcher by dancing off second in order to advance. And then he would steal home. The name of the game was to score runs without a hit, something quite different from the "power hitting" strategy that had characterized major-league baseball. During the next decade, this new style of play would become known as "Dodger Baseball."

Before the '47 season was over, Branch Rickey had signed 16 additional Negro Leaguers, including catcher and future three-time "Most Valuable Player" Roy Campanella; pitcher Don Newcombe, who in 1956 would win 27 games; and second baseman Jim Gilham, like Robinson always a threat to steal a base. Together with Robinson and such white stars as Pee Wee Reese, Edwin "Duke" Snider, Gil Hodges, and Carl Erskine, these men would form the nucleus of a team that would capture six pennants and, at long last, in 1955, a world championship, before the Dodgers left Brooklyn for the West Coast at the end of the 1957 season. By 1959, every team in major-league baseball was integrated, one of every five players being of African-American descent.

When Rickey talked of trading Robinson to the New York Giants after the '56 season, the pioneering ballplayer chose to retire at the age of 38. His career totals, which included 1,518 hits, more than 200 stolen bases, and a lifetime batting average of .311, earned him a place in the National Baseball Hall of Fame in 1962, the first African American so honored. He continued to fight actively for civil rights long after his baseball career had ended, supporting Dr. Martin Luther King, Jr., and his call for the peaceful integration of American society.

Despite his tremendous accomplishments on and off the baseball field, Jackie Robinson, with characteristic humility never gave himself much credit. A year before his untimely death in 1972, he reflected on his struggle to break baseball's color barrier. "I was proud," Robinson admitted, "yet I was uneasy. Proud to be in the hurricane eye of a significant breakthrough and to be used to prove that a sport can't be called 'national' if blacks are barred from it. But uneasy because I knew that I was still a black man in a white world. And so I continue to ask myself 'what have I really done for my people?'"

The answer was evident to everyone but him; for by appealing to the moral conscience of the nation, Jackie Robinson had given a young generation of blacks a chance at the "American Dream" and in the process taught many white Americans to respect others regardless of the color of their skin.

Notes

1. Originally used in connection with legislation enacted in Southern states during the nineteenth century to separate the races on public transportation, the term "Jim Crow law" eventually applied to all statutes that enforced segregation.
2. The 1896 decision of the Supreme Court in *Plessy v. Ferguson* upheld a Louisiana law that required railroads in that state to provide "equal but separate accommodations for the white and colored races." It was this "equal but separate" doctrine that made the discriminatory practices of this century legal in the United States. The Court essentially reversed itself in its 1954 *Brown v. Board of Education of Topeka, Kansas* decision, effectively ending legal segregation.
3. Robinson also received a bonus of $3,500.
4. Walker, one of a handful of players who asked to be traded, eventually went to the Pittsburgh Pirates, but not until after the '47 season. Durocher, himself, was suspended from baseball before the '47 season and never had the opportunity to manage Robinson.

William Kashatus is a school teacher and freelance writer who lives in Philadelphia.

From *American History*, March/April 1997, pages 32-37, 56-57. Copyright © 1997 by Primedia Consumer Media and Magazines Inc. All rights reserved. Reprinted with permission.

Truman's Other War: The Battle for the American Homefront, 1950–1953

Paul G. Pierpaoli Jr.

For decades after the guns fell silent, the Korean War remained a faintly distant conflict in popular memory. Even scholars largely ignored the war until the 1980s rekindled interest in this crucial episode in American and world history. Sandwiched as it was between World War II (the "Good War") and the agony of Vietnam (the "Bad War") Korea became known simply as the Forgotten War. When the Korean conflict ended in an armistice in July 1953, most Americans wanted nothing more than a return to normalcy. They wanted to like Ike and focus on the American Dream. So they bought television sets, went to college in record numbers, ogled Detroit's bigfinned behemoths, moved en masse to suburbia, and gyrated themselves into the era of rock and roll. But they also forgot the sacrifice and slaughter that had taken place on the Korean Peninsula, and quickly pushed aside the scourge of McCarthyism, which the war had unleashed.

To be sure, the Korean War was an unpopular war here at home. It was the first war that the United States did not win; thus, our nation's collective amnesia is not at all surprising. But the scholarship of the war, generated mostly since the early 1980s, paints a very different picture. Korea was a pivotal turning point in modern American history. Indeed, it unleashed far greater consequences than its better-known successor of Vietnam, and in fact it laid much of the groundwork for America's struggle in Indochina. Remembering Korea, especially the changes it wrought on the homefront, is the principle endeavor of this article[1].

Prior to 25 June 1950, President Harry S. Truman had no notion of fighting a major land war in Asia or, for that matter, engaging the nation in a vast and exorbitant Cold War rearmament program. In his January 1949 inaugural address, the president—always a rather staunch fiscal conservative—had promised to balance the budget, decrease the national debt, keep inflation at bay, and implement his Fair Deal program, an ambitious social welfare plan that sought to address an array of problems from public housing and health care to civil rights. To accomplish this, Truman cast his lot with those who sought to keep national security and defense spending to a bare minimum. He also sought to provide America's allies with protection from the perceived Russian threat by using the strength of the U.S. economy as a bulwark against Communism. Thus, initiatives such as the Marshall Plan, the International Monetary Fund, and the General Agreement on Tariffs and Trade (GATT) would emphasize economic—rather than military—containment of the Soviet Union.

In other words, Truman's hope was to focus on domestic issues by building upon New Deal-style reform, focusing on modest civil rights initiatives such as his 1948 order to desegregate the armed forces, and combating the growing perception of a Communist menace at home. However, beginning in 1949 a convergence of domestic and international events conspired against Truman's best intentions. Even before the sudden outbreak of war in Korea, the president had begun to realize that more would have to be done to defend against Communist advances abroad. Nevertheless, it took the blunt force of Korea to push the Truman administration into action[2].

Between the winter of 1949 and 1950, the domestic and international atmosphere changed dramatically, and not necessarily for the better. Early in 1949 Dean Acheson replaced retiring Secretary of State George C. Marshall. More hawkish and less willing to capitulate to Truman's domestic priorities than his predecessor, Acheson began an almost immediate and sustained effort to build up U.S. military forces at home and abroad, arguing that the United States was incapable of defending itself and its allies against an all-out Soviet offensive. By mid 1949, in fact, Truman was coming under increased pressure even from within his own administration to spend more on defense.

> Throughout 1951 and 1952, Truman would contend with growing criticism of his handling of the economy and homefront, some of which went so far as to accuse him of socialism and outright despotism.

Then, coming in rapid and relentless procession beginning in September 1949 was a series of events that shook the nation and the Truman administration. In September the Soviets surprised the world and obliterated the U.S. atomic monopoly by exploding their first A-bomb. Then came the October Communist victory in the Chinese Civil War, which was quickly followed by the permanent division of Germany.

January 1950 brought more setbacks. First, the Soviet Union began a boycott of the United Nations to protest its nonrecognition of the new People's Republic of China (PRC). Next came the February 1950 alliance of friendship and mutual assistance between the Soviet Union and China. At about the same time, Alger Hiss was convicted of perjury in the infamous Whittaker Chambers-Alger Hiss spy Case; Ethel and Julius Rosenberg awaited execution for espionage; and Senator Joseph R. McCarthy began his four-year-long anti-Communist witch hunt at a speaking engagement in Wheeling, West Virginia.

Thus, by early spring 1950 two things had become clear. First, President Truman's Fair Deal was on the ropes, for the deteriorating international and domestic political scenes were going to require a further de-emphasis of domestic imperatives. Second, Senator McCarthy's groundless and vituperative accusations of internal communist subversion were about to poison the well of foreign policy bipartisanship and, in the process, make Truman's job of governing ever more difficult.

In April 1950 President Truman first viewed the seminal blueprint for waging the Cold War: NSC-68, a joint effort of the Departments of State and Defense, as well as the National Security Council. Using particularly baleful and alarming language, NSC-68 argued that the United States was losing the initiative in the Cold War, that the nation was woefully ill-prepared to defend itself and its allies against Communist advances, and that the administration must embark upon and complete a massive conventional and nuclear build-up by 1954, which it described as the year of maximum danger. Taken aback by its conclusions and prescriptions—not to mention its likely astronomical costs—Truman demurred and insisted that the actual costs of the plan be calculated before he took any action on it. In the meantime NSC-68 was shelved, until hell broke loose on the Korean peninsula that June[3].

When North Korea unexpectedly lashed out and attacked South Korea on 25 June 1950, the Truman administration wasted little time in deciding to respond, with force, to the Communist aggression. Fearing a larger Communist conspiracy, which might have included a simultaneous attack against Western Europe, Japan, or other U.S. strongholds, and determined that there would be "no more Munichs," Truman committed American troops to the Korean struggle. He also began, quite fatefully perhaps, to rearm the nation along the lines prescribed in NSC-68. Thus, America's new military rearmament program would be targeted not so much at Korea, but at the long haul and massive build-up envisioned in NSC-68. What America was to witness during the three years of the war was actually a mobilization within a mobilization: rearmament for the immediate needs of the Korean War and, more critically, a long-term rearmament earmarked to contain Communism in every corner of the world. The United States was now on its way to constructing a permanent national security state and defense economy, if not an incipient "garrison state." With this construction, of course, came the destruction of Truman's Fair Deal.

The monetary and psychological costs of this massive military defense effort would prove to be enormous. By the end of 1951, the annual defense budget had nearly quadrupled to $50 billion from a pre-war low of $13.5 billion. As a result, the economy began to overheat, and Americans began to chafe under mounting government controls on everything from prices and wages to raw materials. During the first five months of the war, high inflation and growing shortages periodically lashed at the United States economy. Budget deficits began to pile up ominously, and the Truman administration tried its best to provide for the troops and allay Americans' concerns by encouraging voluntary controls on prices, wages, production, and hoarding. The administration also raised corporate and income taxes and tightened credit. For a time these methods worked, and Truman enjoyed the support of a majority of Americans—including many Republicans—until disaster struck in late November 1950[4].

The unexpected and vicious Chinese intervention in Korea caused military as well as economic havoc. Just as inflation and shortages had begun to ease in the mid fall of 1950, a new round of panic-buying and hoarding stoked the flames of inflation after the military reversals in the Korean theater. The Truman administration, fearing a far wider war, dramatically accelerated the rearmament effort, which further fanned the inflation firestorm. Republicans and even some Democrats began to question and publicly criticize the president's handling of the war and the homefront. Americans began to panic and as Christmas 1950 approached a pall of defeatism and doom descended. An editorial in *Life* magazine, surrounded by a giddy blitz of Christmas ads, warned darkly that "the news is of disaster; World War III moves ever closer...our leaders are frightened, befuddled, and caught in a great and inexcusable failure to marshal the strength of America"[5].

The Chinese intervention resulted in Truman's decision to augment significantly U.S. military aid to NATO countries, including the placement of large troop deployments in Europe.

This move raised the eyebrows and ire of his political and ideological foes, most notably the conservative and isolationist wings of the Republican party. It also provided Senator McCarthy with more cannon fodder, which he aimed with deadly accuracy at the Truman administration. McCarthyism was now fully unleashed on an American populace that felt quantifiably more vulnerable and frightened than ever before. Quite naturally, as McCarthy's star rose, Truman's popularity sank[6].

Yet Truman's political afflictions were perhaps the least of his problems in December 1950. He now faced the dangerous prospect of a full-scale war with China and, perhaps, a confrontation with the Soviet Union. In addition, he had to search for a way to rally the American people around an unpopular, undeclared, and limited war; stabilize an economy poised at a meltdown; and mobilize even faster an industrial and defense establishment that was already near the breaking point. Such were the challenges and vicissitudes of limited war in the nuclear age. By December, the Korean War had become "Truman's War," and he alone would come to shoulder the enormous burden of governing a people and political process that had become breathless with fear and rife with criticism and chicanery.

On 16 December 1950, President Truman declared a state of national emergency and began to set in place a series of powerful mobilization agencies. Using the presidential war powers granted to him by Congress in the Defense Production Act of September 1950, Truman sought to mobilize the nation for war and control the economy in a fashion not seen since World War II. To help him in this herculean task, he named Charles E. Wilson, president of General Electric and former World War II mobilization executive, to head the new Office of Defense Mobilization, a "super mobilization agency" to oversee every aspect of civilian and military mobilization during the Korean War. In these circumstances, Wilson's authority was powerful indeed; he became a virtual mobilization czar, and the press was quick to dub his position as a "co-presidency"[7].

By late January 1951, with American-led United Nations troops still fighting desperately to wrest away the military gains made by the Chinese and North Koreans, the Truman administration had created some nineteen separate mobilization agencies to control virtually every aspect of the economy. Included among these were the Office of Price Stabilization, which administered prices for almost all consumer products, and the Wage Stabilization Board, which controlled wages for all hourly employees and which some months later would create a Salary Stabilization Board to control all salaries as well. This level of economic control, designed principally to lower inflation and spur industrial production, was an unprecedented foray into government regulation of the economy at a time in which no war had been officially declared. The Korean mobilization thus challenged America's age-old devotion to antimilitarism and antistatism. Throughout the remainder of his term in office, Truman would contend with growing criticism of his handling of the economy and homefront, some of which went so far as to accuse him of socialism and outright despotism.

Although mobilizing people and resources for this unpopular war with vague and changing goals was never simple or easy, two periods stand out as true tests of Truman's resolve and ability as a leader: the winter and spring of 1951, and the spring and summer of 1952. In February 1951 organized labor precipitated a long-running feud with Truman's chief mobilizer Charles E. Wilson. Angered at what they believed to be their exclusion from the decision-making process on mobilization issues, and dissatisfied with the controls placed upon worker's wages, labor leaders walked out of wage negotiation sessions, resigned their positions on the Wage Stabilization Board, and effectively boycotted the entire mobilization program until late April. Labor's boycott frustrated and angered the Truman administration heretofore considered labor's ally, and threatened to disrupt defense production and economic stabilization just as mobilization efforts were moving into high gear. After weeks of tense negotiation and bitter repudiation and criticism from its critics, the Truman administration finally resolved the crisis in late April, but not before the presdent had lost even more support for his handling of the war effort.

Then, of course, came what was surely one of the biggest crises of the entire war: Truman's decision to fire Douglas MacArthur on 11 April 1951. Although MacArthur had clearly undermined his commander-in-chief, had engaged in essentially insubordinate behavior, and had made repeated strategic and tactical blunders in prosecuting the war, Truman was mercilessly lambasted by the press and excoriated by his opponents for dismissing the vain-glorious war hero. McCarthyites, conservative Republicans, and other foes of Truman used the MacArthur dismissal to launch a fresh barrage of abuse at the president, who nonetheless stood firm by his decision. Be that as it may, the crisis further crippled Truman's ability to respond to changing circumstances on and off the battlefield and, of course, his approval ratings were by then in a virtual free-fall.

The Korean War engendered yet another major crisis in the spring of 1952, when some 600,000 steel workers threatened to strike. In an attempt to avert a work stoppage, which he believed would imperil the nation's war and rearmament effort, Truman ordered a government take-over of the affected steel companies. Amidst cries of dictatorship from Truman's detractors, and a stony silence even from many of his supporters, the Supreme Court deliberated on the constitutionality of the president's seizure order. In June, the Court dealt Truman a crippling blow by ruling his action unconstitutional. Truman then reversed his order, which marked the beginning of a fifty-three-day steel strike. Although the strike was not as devastating as Truman had feared, the entire incident led many to believe that the exigencies of the war were damaging the American system, empowering the executive branch with too much authority, and leading to the imposition of a spartan garrison state. The steel crisis also resulted in the resignation of head mobilizer Charles E. Wilson. From that point on, the best Truman could do was to fight a rearguard battle on the mobilization and stabilization fronts.

Clearly, America's homefront during the Korean War reflected a house divided. It engendered bitter rhetoric and partisan infighting, encouraged the continued antics of Senator McCarthy and his minions, fostered a poisonous atmosphere of paranoia and fear, and created two separate constitutional crises: the MacArthur Affair and the Steel Crisis. Despite the turbulence of these three years, however, it must be said that the Truman administration did an admirable job of keeping the ship of state on a relatively straight course, especially when one considers that the ship was navigating in completely uncharted waters.

So what, then, were the important legacies of this ferocious and bloody war? Why is it important to study this period? First, the Korean War provided the foundation upon which the entire Cold War military and defense apparatus was built. The nation girded itself to fight a protracted—perhaps indefinite—war to contain Communism around the world, an effort that would last for forty years. Second, the Korea conflict institutionalized permanently large defense budgets, which had been hitherto anathema. In the process, the federal government was granted sweeping power as it controlled more and more of the nation's resources and as its bureaucracies ballooned ever larger. At the same time, cyclical and growing budget deficits and mounting debt became the norm rather than the exception. Third, as a result of all of this government-sponsored economic activity, America's industrial base became badly skewed. The older industrial areas of the Northeast and Midwest suffered a decades-long decline as new areas of industrialization sprang up in the South and West, which came to be dominated by defense-related firms. The nation's population and economic power bases thus began to shift further south and west, which in turn resulted in a realignment of political power. Finally, the Korean War unseated the Democratic party's nearly uninterrupted hold on power in Washington, one that went all the way back to 1932. In 1952 Americans elected a Republican president for the first time since 1928, and turned over control of the House and Senate to the Republicans as well. In an important, if ironic way, Korea helped to rehabilitate a Republican party that had been forced to carry the heavy cross of the Great Depression on its back for nearly a generation[8].

To be sure, the Korean War was devastating for the Korean people, both in the North and the South. Both nations' villages, cities, infrastructure, and agriculture were left in utter ruin. Casualties for all Koreans were estimated at 3 million. The United States lost upwards of 34,000 of its soldiers in the struggle in just three years—a fatality rate far greater in relative terms than that of the Vietnam War. Moreover and tragically, Korea set the stage for another bloody war on another artificially divided Asian peninsula, this time in Indochina. Remembering this conflict is important, not only because of the many lives it cut short, but because our nation today, fifty years after the war began, still bears the deep scars of the Korean War.

Notes

1. The literature on the Korean War is rather extensive, and the military aspects of the war have gained the most attention from historians and writers. Much of the work in this regard is excellent, but as in so many instances, the quality is disparate. For our purposes here, I recommend the following overviews of the non-military aspects of the Korean War: Michael J. Hogan, *A Cross of Iron: Harry S. Truman and the Origins of the National Security State, 1945-1954* (New York: Cambridge University Press, 1998); Burton I. Kaufman, *The Korean War: Challenges in Crisis, Credibility, and Command* (New York: McGraw-Hill, 1997); Paul G. Pierpaoli Jr., *Truman and Korea: The Political Culture of the Early Cold War* (Columbia: University of Missouri Press, 1999); and Gary W. Reichard, *Politics as Usual: The Age of Truman and Eisenhower* (Arlington Heights, IL: Harlan Davidson, 1988).
2. Much of the information contained herein and throughout this article comes from my recently published book, *Truman and Korea*, the first in-depth, scholarly treatment of the homefront and political culture of the Korean War era (see above for full citation).
3. See "NSC-68: United States Objectives and Programs for National Security," *Foreign Relations of the United States*, vol. 1 (Washington, DC: Government Printing Office, 1977), 237-92; Ernest R. May, ed., *American Cold War Strategy: Interpreting NSC-68* (Boston: Bedford/St. Martin's Press, 1993); Samuel F. Wells Jr., "Sounding the Tocsin: NSC-68 and the Soviet Threat," *International Security* 4 (Fall 1979): 116-58; and Pierpaoli, *Truman and Korea*, 25-27.
4. See Paul G. Pierpaoli Jr., "Mobilizing for the Cold War: The Korean Conflict and the Birth of the National Security State, June-December 1950," *Essays in Economic and Business History* 12 (June 1994): 106-17.
5. *Life* (11 December 1950): 46.
6. For the corrosive effects of McCarthyism at mis time, see Thomas C. Reeves, *The Life and Times of Joe McCarthy: A Biography* (Lanham, MD: Madison Books, 1997); Stephen J. Whitfield, *The Culture of the Cold War* (Baltimore: Johns Hopkins University Press, 1991); and Richard M. Fried, *Nightmare in Red: The McCarthy Era in Perspective* (New York: Oxford University Press, 1990).
7. *Business Week* (23 December 1950): 19.
8. For an extended analysis of these important shifts and trends, see my *Truman and Korea*. See also Ann Markusen, et al., *The Rise of the Gunbelt: The Military Remapping of Industrial America* (New York: Oxford University Press, 1991), which provides an excellent study of the shifting of America's industrial and population centers after World War II.

Dr. Paul G. Pierpaoli Jr. is the assistant to the president and a professor of history at the Virginia Military Institute. He is the author of numerous scholarly articles and has recently published *Truman and Korea: The Political Culture of the Early Cold War (1999)*, a book that analyzes the American homefront during the war. He is also an assistant editor of the *Journal of Military History* and is an associate editor of *The Encyclopedia of the Korean War*, released in June 2000 by ABC-CLIO.

From *OAH Magazine of History*, Spring 2000, pages 15-19. Copyright © 2000 by Organization of American Historians. Reprinted with permission.

Women, Domesticity, and Postwar Conservatism

"If social conservatism is not a distinguishing mark of the New Right, what is unique about the New Right is the visible presence of women." —Rebecca Klatch[1]

"McCarthyism got its power from the willingness of the men (few women here) who ran the nation's main public and private institutions to condone serious violations of civil liberties in order to eradicate what they believed was the far more serious danger of Communism." —Ellen Schrecker[2]

Michelle Nickerson

Throughout the past two decades, the American histori-cal community has witnessed a renaissance in the study of postwar conservatism. We have come along way since Alan Brinkley declared the field to be "something of an or-phan in historical scholarship"[3]. Recent works document-ing the right-wing takeover of the Republican Party in the 1960s and studies of conservative intellectual and grass-roots movements show us that conservatives actively shaped, rather than merely reacted to, history[4]. Neverthe-less, the growing subfield of conservative history has its own orphans to contend with, namely women and gender. The largest body of scholarship on women, gender, and the postwar right focuses on antifeminism. Jane DeHart and Donald Mathew's work on Equal Rights Amendment bat-tles, Rebecca Klatch's study of women in the New Right, and Kristin Luker's work on the abortion wars challenge the assumption that conservatism is a male movement. They have also shown the extent to which gender issues drove the New Right agenda[5]. But what about the Old Right? What role did women and gender play in McCarthyism and Goldwaterism? As the above quotations from Rebecca Klatch and Ellen Schrecker suggest, women of the Old Right have been invisible to historians. It is time, however, to address this issue of invisibility and finally answer the question: Did women and gender play important roles or did they not?

A case study of the conservative movement in Los Ange-les and its suburbs suggests that yes, women were impor-tant actors in the postwar conservative ascendancy. If we look below the surface of formal politics, especially in the conservative stronghold of southern California, we see a very feminine world of grassroots activism. Southern Cali-fornia women show us that postwar gender norms created room for a highly effective female sphere of activism. They also demonstrate that the 1950s revival of domesticity had a politically radicalizing effect on many women. Groups of predominantly white, middle-, and upper-class wives and mothers took advantage of their privileged social circum-stances to become militant anticommunist crusaders. By measuring the reach of their political activism and evaluat-ing its impact, we see that women's clubs were important incubators of McCarthyism and that housewife activists played a critical role in mobilizing the grassroots base of the conservative movement.

The organizational infrastructure of housewife activism was laid decades before the postwar era. Ideological and institutional antecedents include early twentieth-century women's patriotic societies and Republican clubs, as well as the World War II era isolationist "mother's movement"[6]. These groups carved out a female political niche that was conducive to the values, responsibilities, and schedules of traditional homemakers, yet removed from the unladylike world of partisan politics. However, the Cold War gave women even more reasons to become political, especially in Los Angeles. As the power centers of American conservatism shifted from the Northeast to points west and south during the 1950s, southern California became the face of the Old Right. The region's military-industrial economy created fertile ground for a prodefense, free enterprise, "get-the-government-off-our-backs" brand of conservatism. Wary of Hollywood Communists in their backyards, many conservative Californians felt that they should become more proactive about fighting the "enemy within." This was where right-wing women entered the political landscape. Loyalty oath controversies and textbook investigations in California, covered in alarming detail by the Hearst newspapers, convinced many mothers that they needed to be more vigilant when it came to education policy. Consequently, a subculture of housewife activists flourished over the 1950s. Women left their imprint on the Old Right in two important ways: They brought McCarthyism to "Main Street America" by becoming vigilante "Red" hunters in local politics and they expanded the base of the grass roots movement by becoming evangelizers of patriotism.

Conservative women's groups found new life in the early 1950s partly because new role models presented themselves, namely J. Edgar Hoover, Joseph McCarthy, and the House Un-American Activities Committee. Though housewife investigators date back to the first Red Scare, they became more common and formidable during the Cold War[7]. In southern California, women formed study groups, letter-writing networks, and patriotic clubs that coordinated efforts to identify and eradicate subversion. From Orange County to the San Fernando Valley, from Hollywood to Pasadena, women activists gathered in living rooms, church meeting halls, and clubhouses to research and report on Communist Front activity[8]. They monitored political developments in Washington, Sacramento, and their own communities. The American Public Relations Forum is a useful example. The Forum was a Catholic women's anticommunist study club founded by Stephanie Williams, a San Fernando Valley housewife. Williams started the organization because she and her friends wanted to get out of the house and fight communism. "We are wives and mothers," she announced at the group's founding meeting, "who are vitally interested in what is happening in our country"[9]. 1952 saw the establishment of the American Public Relations Forum and a battery of other conservative women's groups because that was the year that anticommunist lecturer Florence Fowler Lyons started her campaign against the United Nations Educational, Scientific, and Cultural Organization (UNESCO). "Stalking through every phase of American life today," warned Lyons in one of her speeches, "is a stark, grinning," crimson clad Pied Piper called UNESCO. He's piping a tune he calls 'peace,' … I warn you—if you do not stop his march through the streets and schoolrooms of America … this nation will die, and you and you alone will be to blame"[10]. The American Public Relations Forum, joined by the Los

Angeles Women's Breakfast Club, the Keep America Committee, the Women's Republican Study Club and others, lined up at school board meetings to demand that teachers stop using UNESCO manuals. They argued that UNESCO inculcated schoolchildren with internationalist ideas and principles of one-worldism—goals that were in line with communist ideology[11]. They attacked UNESCO as a foreign, antinationalist program that threatened local control of schools and independent thinking. In early 1953, the board capitulated to this pressure and voted to ban UNESCO from all of the city's classrooms[12].

The UNESCO controversy was one of many instances in which women proved able to influence local policy-making by raising the specter of communism. These and other episodes involving housewife activists illustrate how McCarthyism trickled down to the everyday lives of Americans. One of the major reasons that women felt compelled to do this work was because men, as the family breadwinners, simply did not have enough time to do it. As Marie Koenig, the public relations officer for American Public Relations Forum explained, "Men don't have time to be … doing the things that we women do … to sit and write letters … when they get home at night they don't want to run around to meetings"[13]. J. Edgar Hoover, director of the Federal Bureau of Investigation, also reinforced this idea. As he explained in *Masters of Deceit: The Story of Communism in America and How to Fight It* (1958), "in a country with over 170,000,000 inhabitants there are fewer than 6,200 agents of the FBI. Hence, all of these agents are not available for the investigation of subversive activities. We need the help of *all* loyal Americans"[14]. But time was not the only issue. Since the early twentieth-century fight for suffrage, women had been crafting feminine political roles and rhetoric premised on their differences from men. The postwar revival of domesticity created new opportunities for women to leverage gender norms in politics. The heightened concerns over brainwashing, mind control, and indoctrination invited conservative women to become political right where they were: in PTA meetings, church groups, and their homes. Postwar domesticity also breathed new life into notions of women's moral superiority. The threat of "Godless" communism gave women a mandate to become more assertive in their roles as the upholders of spiritual and civic virtues. As a result, housewife activists often saw themselves as crusaders and developed a reputation for their militancy and patriotic fervor. They held the nation to a stricter ideological litmus test.

Some of the most widely regarded intellects of the conservative movement recognized the gender distinction that historians have failed to notice. Russell Kirk, in *The Intelligent Woman's Guide to Conservatism* (1957), declared that "women are the conservative sex." Taking a moment to pay homage to their virtue, he wrote: "Women's attachment to hard realities has something to do with their social principles and their realization of the need for genuine security has something to do with it; and so has their practical understanding of the worth of the family and the community;

and so has their instinctive knowledge that society is not a 'machine for living,' but rather a spiritual thing, founded upon love"[15].

Less enchanted political observers also commented on the gendered patterns of political ideology in Cold War America. In 1954, a group of pollsters published *Communism, Conformity and Civil Liberties*, a survey of 6,000 people, which concluded that American women tended to be less tolerant of communists, socialists, and atheists than men. The investigators suggested that this was because women were more concerned about the Communist menace[16]. All this evidence suggests that if historians want a better sense of who comprised the social base of McCarthyism, housewife activism would be a good place to start looking. However, the question still remains, how did McCarthyite housewives help conservatism become a powerful movement?

In addition to vigilance, according to J. Edgar Hoover, the war over hearts and minds required an extra dose of civic spirit and volunteerism. As he wrote in *Masters of Deceit*: "We, as a people, have not been sufficiently articulate, and forceful in expressing pride in our traditions and ideals. In our homes and our schools we need to learn how to 'let freedom ring' … Most Americans believe that our light of freedom is a shining light. As Americans we should stand up, speak of it, and let the world see this light, rather than conceal it"[17].

Housewife activists proved especially willing to step up to this challenge and they found creative ways to instill love of country. They preached "Americanism" as a cross between ideology and religion, often invoking the nation's "Christian heritage" as a counterpoint to communism's atheism[18]. One result of women's patriotic evangelism was a stronger a sense of solidarity and community in the California Right.

Patriotic bookstores, most of which were created and staffed by women, were some of the earliest signs of conservatism's growing strength in Los Angeles. The first, Poor Richard's Book Shop on Hollywood Boulevard, opened in May 1960. Florence and Frank Ranuzzi of nearby Los Feliz started Poor Richard's because they believed "education, not agitation" was needed to reverse "the socialistic trend our country was taking"[19]. Because Frank earned the family's income through his insurance agency, Florence worked as the full-time, unpaid manager of the shop[20]. She kept the shelves stocked with the books exposing the communist threat, like Whittaker Chambers's, *Witness* and Stanton Evans, *Revolt on Campus!* The Ranuzzis also printed bumper stickers, like "I am Proud to be an American" and "Socialism, Cancer of Liberty, Never Worked"[21]. Conservative study groups patronized Poor Richard's because Florence kept copies of pending bills and legislative hearings available. The store became so big and popular that the Ranuzzis started a mail order business and shipped all over the country. On weekends, Florence turned Poor Richard's into a conservative salon. Adults and teens would sit at a big captain's table and listen to her lecture about communism. "If somebody started an argument … she'd grab this book [and] that book," remembers her daughter, "[and] she'd say read it for yourself"[22]. Since Florence, like many mothers, was particularly concerned about the indoctrination of youths, she also supplied school libraries with books free of charge. In 1963, she sent seventy-three copies of *Communist America—Must it Be?* to a school in Nebraska[23].

The success of Poor Richard's inspired other conservative women to start bookstores. More than fifty housewives staffed the Main Street Americanism Center in South Pasadena, which opened in 1961[24]. "It had a big round oak table," remembers founder Jane Crosby, it was cozy … so pretty, and so patriotic looking." In addition to selling books, the center rented out audio-visual materials and sold copies of the John Birch Society's *American Opinion* magazine[25]. In the San Fernando Valley, a group called Women for America, Inc., established the Betsy Ross Book Shop[26]. Six months after Betsy Ross's grand opening, William F. Buckley Jr. came from New York to make a donation and guest appearance[27]. By 1965, twenty different patriotic bookstores had opened for business in the greater Los Angeles area[28].

The bookstores, like the anticommunist study clubs and investigative committees, illustrate the extent to which postwar domesticity had an impact on the conservative movement. Out of the political limelight, housewife activists transformed the domestic sphere into the grassroots sphere. They revise our understanding of women, gender, and postwar conservatism in three ways. First, they show us that domesticity did not necessarily render women apolitical. These "kitchen table activists," to borrow an expression from historian Lisa McGirr, were not the cloistered, depressed, valium-popping housewives of Betty Friedan's *Feminine Mystique*. Second, they demonstrate how women can develop a militantly conservative worldview out of their own experiences. Housewife activists were not foot soldiers to their husbands or slaves to patriarchy. Lastly, women of the Old Right strike an important balance in the history of gender and postwar conservatism. Though the scholarly work on antifeminism is sophisticated and enlightening, it reinforces the misconception that conservative women are reactionary and backward looking. Antifeminism loses some of its "backlash," in other words, when we introduce women of the Old Right and women of the prewar Right. We see that in addition to the Stop ERA and right-to-life movements, a long tradition of women's conservatism has been brought to bear on United States political history.

Notes

1. Rebecca Klatch, "The Two Worlds of Women of the New Right," in *Women, Politics and Change*, ed. Louise A. Tilly and Patricia Gurin (New York: Russell Sage Foundation, 1990), 529-52.
2. Ellen Schrecker, *Many Are the Crimes: McCarthyism in America* (Boston: Little, Brown and Co., 1998), xi.

3. Alan Brinkley, "AHR Forum: The Problem of American Conservatism," *American Historical Review* 99 (1994): 409-429.

4. For more on the rise of the right, see Jerome L. Himmelstein, *To the Right: The Transformation of American Conservatism* (Berkeley, CA: University of California Press, 1990), Sara Diamond, *Roads to Dominion: Right-wing Movements and Political Power in the United States* (New York: Guilford Press, 1995), and Mary C. Brennan, *Turning Right in the Sixties: The Conservative Capture of the GOP* (Chapel Hill, NC: University of North Carolina Press, 1995). Recent works on the right-wing ascendancy in California also contribute to this literature, including Kurt Schuparra, *The Triumph of the Right: The Rise of the California Conservative Movement, 1945-1966* (Armonk, NY: M.E. Sharpe, 1998) and Matthew W. Dallek, *The Right Moment: Ronald Reagan's First Victory and the Decisive Turning Point in American Politics* (New York: Free Press, 2000). For more on the postwar right-wing intellectuals, see George H. Nash, *The Conservative Intellectual Movement in America, Since 1945* (New York: Basic Books, 1976). William B. Hixon's *Search for the American Right Wing: An Analysis of the Social Science Record, 1955-1987* (Princeton, NJ: Princeton University Press, 1992) ambitiously investigates the intellectual and scholarly currents that have informed the study of postwar conservatism. Lisa McGirr's *Suburban Warriors: The Origins of the New American Right* (Princeton, NJ: Princeton University Press, 2001), which focuses on Orange County, California, shows how the grassroots right helped bring conservatives to power in the early 1960s.

5. Donald G. Mathews and Jane Sherron De Hart, *Sex, Gender, and the Politics of ERA: A State and a Nation* (New York: Oxford University Press, 1990); Rebecca Klatch, *Women of the New Right* (Philadelphia: Temple University Press, 1987); Kristin Luker, *Abortion and the Politics of Motherhood* (Berkeley, CA: University of California Press, 1984). See also Faye D. Ginsburg, *Contested Lives: The Abortion Debate in an American Community* (Berkeley, CA: University of California Press, 1989).

6. For more on women's patriotic organizations see Kirsten Delegard, "Women Patriots: Female Activism and the Politics of American Anti-Radicalism, 1919-1935" (Ph.D. diss., Duke University, 1999) and Francesca Morgan, "'Home and Country': Women, Nation, and the Daughters of the American Revolution, 1890-1939" (Ph.D. diss., Columbia University, 1998). For more on Republican women's activism see Catherine Rymph, "Forward and Right: The Shaping of Republican Women's Activism: 1920-1967" (Ph.D diss., University of Iowa, 1998). For more on the isolationist war mothers movement see Glen Jeansomme, *Women of the Far Right: The Mother's Movement and World War II* (Chicago: University of Chicago Press, 1996) and Laura McEnaney, "He-Men and Christian Mothers: The America First Movement and the Gendered Meanings of Patriotism and Isolationism," *Diplomatic History* 18 (Winter 1994): 47-57.

7. Delegard,4-5. Delegard shows that one of the most notorious women blacklisters, Lucia Ramsey Maxwell, came out of the first Red Scare. Maxwell's *Spider Web Chart*, released in 1924, connected a list of women's reform organizations, in one column, to a list of socialist and communist organizations, in another. Maxwell was a Daughter of the American Revolution.

8. For more on women and the political culture of postwar suburbia, see Sylvie Murray, *The Progreevise Housewife: Community Activism in Suburban Queens, 1945-1965*, (Philadelphia: University of Pennsylvania Press, 2003).

9. Community Relations Committee, Notes on American Public Relations Forum-Meeting Friday Evening, 2 May 1952 [Los Angeles: Community , Relations Committee], 1, CRC. The Community Relations Committee was a Los Angeles Jewish Defense organization, affiliated with the Jewish Community Federation, that monitored anti-Semitic and right-wing activity in southern California. CRC spies recorded the minutes of several APRF meetings in 1952. The Community Relations Committee collection at the Urban Archives, California State University, Northridge, [hereafter CRC].

10. Florence Fowler Lyons, "The Menace in UNESCO," 15 November 1952, Encinitas, CA. (Program sponsored by San Dieguito Veterans Committee).

11. George Piness, "Report on American Public Relations Forum, 6 June 1952" [Los Angeles: Community Relations Committee, 1952],1; Glen Adams Warren, "The UNESCO Controversy in Los Angeles, 1951-1953: A Case Study of the, Influence of Right-Wing Groups on Urban Affairs" (Ph.D. diss., University of Southern California, 1970), 48, 56.

12. "Los Angeles Bans UNESCO Program," *New York Times* 21 January 1953.

13. Marie Koenig, interview with author, tape recording, Pasadena, California, 5 April 2001.

14. J. Edgar Hoover, *Masters of Deceit: The Story of Communism in America and How to Fight It* (New York: Henry Holt and Company, 1958), 310.

15. Russell Kirk, *The Intelligent Woman's Guide to Conservatism* (New York: The Devin-Adair Company, 1957), 8.

16. Samuel A. Stouffer, *Communism, Conformity, and Civil Liberties: A Cross-section of the Nation Speaks Its Mind* (Garden City, N.Y.: Doubleday & Company, Inc., 1955), 131-51.

17. Hoover, 334.

18. Helen Courtois, "Christian Women of America Are You Crackpots?" [leaflet distributed by the Keep America Committee] October 1950, Hoover Institution, Stanford University.

19. Florence Ranuzzi, "Greetings from Poor Richards Bookshop," (letter to friends of the book shop), ca. 1964.

20. Florence Ranuzzi, interview by author, tape recording, Tehachapi, California, 11 February 2001.

21. Poor Richard's Book Shop, Los Angeles, Calif. (mail order catalogue), 1962.

22. Mary Cunningham, interview by author, tape recording, Tehachapi, California, 12 February 2001.

23. D. Cortney to Poor Richard's Book Shop, 25 February 1963, Sunol, Nebraska.

24. Dee Dickson, "Americanism Center Sets Up Shop," *Los Angeles Herald Express*, 18 December 1961, CRC.

25. *Standard Daily Journal* 20 January and 8 February 1965.

26. Dee Dickson, "They'll Fight the Reds Through Books," *Los Angeles Herald Express* 20 January 1961.

27. Mrs. Carleton Young, President, Women for America, Inc., to William F. Buckley Jr., 31 December 1962, Los Angeles.

28. Project Alert, "Visit the Book Store in Your Area," (leaflet distributed anticommunism rally), December 1961.

MICHELLE NICKERSON is a Ph.D. candidate in the American Studies program at Yale University and is finishing her dissertation, "Domestic Threats: Women, Gender and Conservatism in Cold War Los Angeles, 1945-1966." She has delivered papers and written essays about the role of right-wing women activists and the importance of gender to the postwar conservative ascendancy.

From *OAH Magazine of History*, January 2003, pages 17-21. Copyright © 2003 by Organization of American Historians. Reprinted with permission.

The Split-Level Years

*1950–1960: Elvis, Howdy Doody time, McDonald's
and the rumblings of rebellion*

By Henry Allen
Washington Post Staff Writer

Smell it, smell it all, smell the sour cities you leave behind in bosomy cars that smell of dusty sunlight and thump over Eisenhower's concrete interstate highways whose joints ooze tar that smells like industrial licorice till you arrive in a suburb smelling of insecticide and freshly cut grass outside identical houses full of the scents of postwar America: baked air hovering over the TV set; the mucilage on stickers for your art-appreciation course—"Mona Lisa," "American Gothic"…; the cozy stink of cigarette smoke freshened by Air-Wick deodorizer amid sweet pine paneling whose knots watch over you like the loving eyes of Disney forest creatures.

How sweet and new it all is, this incense of mid-century, this strange sense of coziness and infinite possibility at the same time.

Don't worry, Ike seems to say as he smiles and hits another tee shot. You light another Camel, knowing that "It's a psychological fact: pleasure helps your disposition: For more pure pleasure—have a CAMEL."

There's a cartoon fullness to things. Everybody is somebody. Everything is possible. Hence a cushiony give in the national psyche, a pleasant ache that feels like nostalgia dispensed by a spray can. You believe in the future, be it a perfect marriage, racial integration, commuting via your personal autogiro, Formica countertops, or a day coming soon when everybody will be sincere and

mature. ("Sincerity" and "maturity" are major virtues.)

Ignore the viruses of dread that float through family rooms: the hydrogen bomb erupting from the South Pacific like a cancerous jellyfish the size of God; or the evil Sen. Joseph McCarthy and the evil Commies he never catches one of, not one, though he does manage to strew the land with damaged lives and the liberal tic of anti-anti-communism; or Sputnik, the first satellite, built by Russian slave labor, no doubt, while our top scientists were developing the Princess phone, 3-D movies and boomerang-shaped coffee tables.

Ignore Marilyn Monroe saying: What good is it being Marilyn Monroe? Why can't I just be an ordinary woman?… Oh, why do things have to work out so rotten? And ignore the Korean War, which is nothing but ugly except for the embroidered silk dragon jackets the soldiers bring back. Ignore the newspaper pictures of racists with faces like wet-combed hand-grenades, screaming at Martin Luther King's boycotters and schoolchildren who will overcome… people whose isolation and invisibility in this white society are incalculable.…

Progress will take care of everything.

Amid the Ford Country Squire station wagons and slate roofs, wealthier homeowners boast that neighborhood covenants still keep out Jews and Negroes. They offer you highballs and cigarettes. They show you black-and-white photo-

graphs of themselves waving from the rail of the Queen Elizabeth. They turn on lights till their houses blaze like cruise ships. What lonely darkness are they keeping off? Do they know their time has gone?

Meanwhile, AMID THE TRACT housing and developments, the genius of William Levitt and Henry Kaiser creates the loneliness of growing up in your own bedroom, in your own house where the green grass grows all around. It takes some getting used to, but do you really want to go back to the apartment with three kids to a bedroom and Nana mumbling over the cabbage? You know your future is here. You wish you knew what it held.

"Children, your father's home!" Mom yells.

A father's Florsheim Imperials are heard. A Dobbs center-dent fedora is seen, with a jaunty trout-fly feather on the grosgrain band. Dad exudes the tired authority of cigarette smoke and Arrid underarm deodorant cream. His knuckles whiten on a Christmas-present attaché case.

"Can't you kids get up off your duffs and do something instead of sitting there watching…"

"Hey, Dad's home."

"…'Howdy Doody,' a little children's show?"

"There's nothing else on, Dad."

Dad shouts over his shoulder: "Doris! You have any chores for these kids?"

"No, hon, everything's hunky-dory. You hungry?"

"Hell, yes, I'm hungry."

"Be dinner soon's I do the limas."

Sighing as if he has made a huge decision, Dad walks into the kitchen. He cracks ice for a drink. "The kids," he says. "It's like I'm not even here."

"Well, it's like I always am," she says. "They're scared of you, but they take me for granted."

"Make you a drink?"

"Not too big, now."

His face struggles toward some home truth, but doesn't find it. "Aw, Doris," he says. "Turn off the stove and let's go to the Roma for veal scaloppine. Please. Just the two of us."

"I have to drop Tommy at Boy Scouts, and then Kitty Kennard is doing her slide show at L'Esprit Francais. Forgive me?"

Doris and Tom Sr. are only trying to live by what their parents taught them—manliness, graciousness, a day's work, good posture—and pass it on to their children. The problem is, they don't quite believe it themselves, anymore, but they have to teach their kids something.

Should they really confess their emptiness and bad faith instead? Should the children feel betrayed by parents who are only trying to do the best they know how?

HOW SQUALID. LETS LEAVE ALL this behind. It's a symptom, not a cause, a failure where success is what you see on "Ozzie & Harriet" and all the other shows about breakfast-nook families where no one is taken for granted and everyone says hello.

Hi, Rick. Hi, Pop. Hi, Dave. Good morning, Mom.

Dad's a bit of a bumbler, and what won't those darn kids think of next! Nevertheless, perfection is attainable. How smug one feels to know this. How inadequate one feels to know one hasn't attained it yet, oneself, but one can put on a long-playing record of the perfect Ella Fitzgerald singing the Jerome Kern songbook perfectly.

Some of the young folks seem to have a hard time adjusting.

If I could have just one day when I wasn't all confused.... If I felt I belonged someplace.
—James Dean as the anguished son in "Rebel Without a Cause"

Be part of progress like everybody else—the everybody you see on television and in Life magazine. Here's the equation: If you're just like everybody, then you're somebody.

The way to be somebody is to buy something that makes you like everybody else who's bought the same thing—Ford owners reading their Ford Times, Parliament smokers joined in aromatic sophistication. Remember: Consumption is a moral good. Madison Avenue admen are cultural heroes, with cool slang like 'Let's run it up the flagpole and see who salutes.'

Look at all the college kids stuffing themselves into phone booths and Volkswagens. And a lovely girl whose picture appears in Life next to the comment: "She has forgotten all about emancipation and equality. To belong is her happiness." And Mary Ann Cuff, a regular among the teen dancers who appear on Dick Clark's "American Bandstand": "What it is we all want is to get married and live on the same street in new houses. We'll call it Bandstand Avenue."

Ignore the hipsters and intellectuals sneering at Bandstand Avenue, and at the triumphalism of tailfins, Time magazine and pointy bras whose tips sort of crinkle under sweaters. Fun can be made of bomb shelters stocked with Franco-American canned spaghetti and Reader's Digest Condensed Books.

J.D. Salinger can appeal to adolescent self-righteousness by railing against phonies in "The Catcher in the Rye." Scorn can be heaped on Ray Kroc, who runs those new McDonald's drive-ins; he writes a memo: "We cannot trust some people who are non-conformist. The organization cannot trust the individual, the individual must trust the organization."

And certainly critics can make a living by attacking the men in the gray flannel suits, the organization men, the lonely crowd of ulcer-proud hidden persuaders bringing us ads where women in crinoline-fluffed shirtwaists invite us to

buy into the carefree new patio-perfect world of hyper-power Torqueflite Cyclamatic Teletouch Whatever that gives you more pleasure. (Repeat thru fade-out: MORE PLEASURE! MORE PLEASURE! MORE PLEASURE!)

WHICH DOES NOT MEAN SEX, boys and girls. Sex is for Europeans, people in movies (off-screen) and juvenile delinquents. White people believe that colored people have sex lives of unimaginable ecstasy and variety. Italian kids drive surly Mercurys to the Jersey Shore, spread blankets and neck in Ace-combed 1953 look-at-me majesty beneath the outraged stares of moms in bathing suits with little skirts... prefiguring the erotic insolence of Elvis, Marilyn, James Dean, and the secret subtext of Annette on "The Mickey Mouse Club."

Otherwise, sex, the lonely vandal, is safe in the stewardship of middle-class women who manage the courtship rituals of dating, going steady, pinning and engagement, and aren't very interested in sex anyway, according to the Kinsey Report on Women. Life magazine sums it up: "Woman is the placid gender, the female guppy swimming all unconcerned and wishing she could get a few minutes off to herself, while the male guppy pursues her with his unrelenting courtship.... Half or more of all women... seldom dream or daydream about sex; they consider the human body to be, if anything, rather repulsive."

Maybe men make cracks about women's driving and spending, and they want dinner served on time, but Life has learned that the unrelenting guppy is becoming "the new American domesticated male" who is "baby tender, dishwasher, cook, repairman.... Some even go to baby-care classes, learn to wrap a neat diaper and to bubble Junior deftly. With father available as sitter, wives can have their hair done, shop, go to club meetings." Lawn mowing gives him "a sense of power and a gadget to tinker with."

What happened to the red-blooded, can-do, all-American male? And female?

Well, sexed women and powerful men are a threat. We don't need them now. Passion has been replaced by love, adventure by fun. If you want sex, watch Elvis Presley on "The Ed Sullivan Show," even if Ed refuses to show the King below the waist. Or go to a movie with Marilyn Monroe or Ava Gardner. If you want male brooding and rage, go see Marlon Brando or Montgomery Clift, the prince of loneliness. The great thing about the '50s is that rebels can fling their grenades of anger and irony into the cafes of the conformists, safe in the knowledge that they can't really change anything. The '50s are an irresistible force still in search of an immovable object.

So pay no attention to that slouching bohemian with sunglasses black as telephones and a tremor induced by his benzedrine inhaler. He says he wants to get back to Europe, "where they really know how to live, where they don't have these hang-ups."

"Europe?" asks the astonished corporate executive who helped liberate Europe from the Nazis only a decade or so ago. "You can't even drink the water in Europe."

"You drink wine, man," says the bohemian. "You drink wine."

Don't worry about snooty intellectuals, either. For a moment, a Columbia University professor named Charles Van Doren is a national celebrity on a big-money TV quiz show called "Twenty-One." He appears on the cover of Time. He seems to be the answer to the old American question: "If you're so smart, why aren't you rich?"

Then it turns out the producers are slipping him the answers to keep him on the show. Van Doren is disgraced, treated like a traitor for lying on television. Well, intellectuals. It just goes to show you. They're all homos or Commies anyway.

And don't worry about the alienation of the modern jazz that lures college boys to the big city for a taste of hip, and the self-loathing notion that "white cats don't swing."

Don't worry about rock-and-roll, which sounds like a national anthem for the republic of vandalism and anarchy, which it is. Rock may drive the young folk to drugs and groin-thrusting madness, it may cause riots in the streets and insurrection in the schools, which it does—but it can't last, it's just a fad.

Ignore the sly joke of Frankie Lymon and the Teenagers singing "No, no, no, no, no, I'm not a juvenile delinquent" to suburban kids who actually think JDs are cool in their rumbles fought with bicycle chains and switchblade knives. So cool that Leonard Bernstein, Mr. Music Appreciation Class himself, will write "West Side Story," a musical that puts romantic love and gang wars together in a climactic switchblade duel.

Forget about civil rights workers heading south, where they're known as "Northern agitators." And the revival of pinko folk singers like Pete Seeger and the Weavers. And marijuana in Harvard Square. And Hugh Hefner proposing in Playboy magazine that we should think of sex as fun, like a game of picnic badminton where nobody tries too hard to win.

"There's a place for us," the cast sings at the end of "West Side Story," to reassure us that, despite the tragedy of Tony and Maria, the promise of progress is intact. "Someday, somewhere, we'll find a new way of living."

There are no VA mortgages for veterans of gang wars, but America will find a way to get them into little Cape Cod starter homes sooner than you think. Haircuts, briefcases, Peter Pan blouses, Formica, Bisquick and pole lamps while the whole family sits in front of the television to sing along with Mitch:

I'm looking over a four-leaf clover...
How could it be otherwise?

From the *Washington Post National Weekly Edition,* November 8, 1999, pp. 9–10. © 1999 by The Washington Post. Reprinted by permission.

The FBI Marches on the Dreamer

After the March on Washington, the FBI launched a vicious campaign to utterly discredit Martin Luther King Jr.

by Richard Gid Powers

A nation that could rarely agree on anything found itself in rare agreement about the March on Washington. Martin Luther King Jr.'s vision of racial harmony represented a noble goal for America, and King himself was the moral embodiment of that dream. Everyone, it seemed, could agree on that.

Well—almost everyone.

The March on Washington touched off an explosion at the FBI. When the dust had settled and discipline had been re-established, the Bureau embarked on a campaign to utterly discredit King, to destroy him personally and as a public figure. It was a war that the Bureau would continue to wage against King as long as he lived. It would continue, obsessively, almost maniacally, even after King was dead.

Right after the March, William C. Sullivan, head of the Bureau's powerful Division Five, its Domestic Intelligence Division, set down his reflections on the March in an August 30 memo:

> Personally, I believe in the light of King's powerful demagogic speech yesterday he stands head and shoulders over all other Negro leaders put together when it comes to influencing great masses of Negroes. We must mark him now, if we have not done so before, as the most dangerous Negro of the future in this nation from the standpoint of communism, the Negro, and national security…. [I]t may be unrealistic to limit ourselves as we have been doing to legalistic proofs or definitely conclusive evidence that would stand up in testimony in court or before Congressional Committees that the Communist party, USA, does wield substantial influence over Negroes which one day could become decisive.

The March produced a radical change in the Bureau's tactics toward King. For the past two years the FBI had been watching King with mounting hostility. After the March the Bureau shifted from a hostile—but relatively passive—surveillance of King to an aggressive—at times violently aggressive—campaign to destroy him.

King's biographer, David J. Garrow, has demonstrated rather conclusively that the origin of the Bureau's suspicion of King was its discovery in January 1962 that a wealthy New York businessman named Stanley Levison had emerged as King's closest adviser. And Levison, according to the Bureau's most trusted informants in the American Communist Party, code-named "Solo" (Jack and Morris Childs), had been until about 1954 the American Communist Party's most important financier. Then he had apparently dropped out of the party. Now the Bureau learned that it had been shortly after Levison's supposed separation from the party when he had befriended King. The Bureau's conclusion—based on circumstantial logic rather than hard evidence—was that Levison represented an ambitious and apparently successful Communist plan to gain control over the Civil Rights Movement and its most prominent spokesman, Martin Luther King.

The Bureau's hostility toward King had been exacerbated by King's criticism of the FBI's performance in the field of civil rights. When the Bureau's overtures to King were ignored—perhaps due to staff incompetence in his Southern Christian Leadership Conference (SCLC) office—King's failure to respond was interpreted by the Bureau as evidence of his insincerity and proof that he held a deep-seated hostility toward the Bureau, sentiments the FBI habitually regarded as evidence of even more deep-seated subversive tendencies.

When the Bureau installed wiretaps in King's office, these taps provided absolutely no evidence that Levison's interest in King was other than a shared commitment to the civil rights movement. They did, however, provide the FBI with its first inkling of King's promiscuous sexual activities, which would later be amply augmented by surveillance bugs installed in his hotel rooms.

Given the Bureau's concerns over King's association with Levison and Jack O'Dell, another SCLC staff member with a Communist history, Sullivan had Division Five produce a report on Communist infiltration of the Civil Rights Movement, with particular attention to its likely role in the upcoming March. Sullivan's August 23 report concluded that "there has been an obvious failure of the Communist Party of the United States to appreciably infiltrate, influence, or control large numbers of American Negroes in this country." Although the report played it safe by saying "time alone will tell" whether future efforts by the party to exploit blacks would be as unsuccessful as those in the past, Sullivan's conclusion was that Communist infiltration of the Civil Rights Movement was negligible and need be of no further concern to the Bureau or the country.

FBI Director J. Edgar Hoover was baffled. Sullivan's latest report contradicted the steady stream of information he had been sending Hoover about Communist influences on King. Hoover fired the report back at Sullivan with the handwritten comment that "this memo reminds me vividly of those I received when Castro took over Cuba. You contended then that Castro and his cohorts were not communists and not influenced by communists. Time alone proved you wrong. I for one can't ignore the memos re [deletion, presumably Levison and O'Dell] as having only an infinitesimal effect on the efforts to exploit the American Negro by the Communists."

Sullivan later explained to a Senate committee that the August 23 report precipitated a crisis between him and Hoover: "This [memorandum] set me at odds with Hoover.... A few months went by before he would speak to me. Everything was conducted by exchange of written communications. It was evident that we had to change our ways or we would all be out on the street."

Following the August 23 report, whenever Domestic Intelligence sent Hoover anything on King and Levison (or for that manner, anything on Communist activities), Hoover would ridicule it with comments like "just infinitesimal!" (on a report on Communist plans for participating in the March) or "I assume CP functionary claims are all frivolous" (on a report on Communist plans to hold follow-up rallies after the March to advance "the cause of socialism in the United States").

At this point Sullivan evidently panicked. Instead of holding to what he felt was an accurate assessment of the declining fortunes of the American Communists, his memo to Hoover after the March retracted everything he had said on August 23: "The Director is correct. We were completely wrong about believing the evidence was not sufficient to determine some years ago that Fidel Castro was not a communist or under communist influence. On investigating and writing about communism and the American Negro, we had better remember this and profit by the lesson it should teach us."

Then he issued his denunciation of King as "the most dangerous Negro of the future" and concluded that "we

greatly regret that the memorandum did not measure up to what the director has a right to expect from our analysis."

Sullivan followed this memo with a recommendation on September 16, 1963, calling for "increased coverage of communist influence on the Negro." And he now proposed something new: "We are stressing the urgent need for imaginative and aggressive tactics to be utilized through our Counterintelligence Program—these designed to neutralize or disrupt the Party's activities in the Negro field."

Stripped of euphemisms, Sullivan was proposing unleashing on Martin Luther King the aggressive and disruptive techniques the Bureau had been using against foreign intelligence agents and Communists.

After he retracted his August 23 memorandum Sullivan tried to prove the strength of his latest set of convictions by becoming the most aggressive advocate of the Bureau's new campaign to discredit King within the government, to disrupt and neutralize his movement and to destroy him professionally and personally.

When Hoover finally adopted Sullivan's revised conclusion as Bureau policy, he pointed to the March on Washington as the most graphic illustration of the Communist Party's influence over King and his movement. In a letter to the Special Agents in Charge in the field, Hoover wrote:

> The history of the Communist Party, USA (CPUSA) is replete with its attempts to exploit, influence and recruit the Negro. The March on Washington, August 28, 1963, was a striking example as party leaders early put into motion efforts to accrue gains for the CPUSA from the March. The presence at the March of around 200 Party members, ranging from several national functionaries headed by CPUSA General Secretary Gus Hall to many rank-and-file members, is clear indication of the party's favorite target (the Negro) today. All indications are that the March was not the "end of the line:" and that the party will step up its efforts to exploit racial unrest and in every possible way claim credit for itself relating to any "gains" achieved by the Negro.

On December 23, FBI executives, including Sullivan, F.S. Baumgardner, three other headquarters officials and two agents from Atlanta, met to draw up plans against King. During the nine-hour session at FBI headquarters, they considered 21 proposals, including one that focused on ways of turning King's wife against him. The conclusion of the meeting was that the Bureau would gather information about King to use "at an opportune time in a counterintelligence move to discredit him.... We will, at the proper time when it can be done without embarrassment to the Bureau, expose King as an opportunist who is not a sincere person but is exploiting the racial situation for personal gain."

Two weeks later Sullivan was even contemplating what the post-Martin Luther King world would be like if the Bureau's plans succeeded:

> It should be clear to all of us that Martin Luther King must, at some propitious point in the future, be revealed to the

people of this country and to his Negro followers as being what he actually is—a fraud, demagogue and scoundrel. When the true facts concerning his activities are presented, such should be enough, if handled properly, to take him off his pedestal and to reduce him completely in influence. When this is done, and it can be and will be done, obviously much confusion will reign, particularly among the Negro people.... The Negroes will be left without a national leader of sufficiently compelling personality to steer them in the proper direction. This is what could happen, but need not happen if the right kind of national Negro leader could at this time be gradually developed so as to overshadow Dr. King and be in the position to assume the role of the leadership of the Negro people when King has been completely discredited.

Over the next four years, that is, for the rest of King's life, there would be about 25 separate illegal attempts by the FBI to discredit King. These ranged from efforts to keep universities from awarding him honorary degrees, interfering with the publication of his writings, to attempting to disrupt his relationships with religious leaders, to leaking the tapes of some 16 microphone recordings of King's private activities in hotel and motel rooms to congressional figures and the media.

During 1964, Hoover's hatred of King broke out into the open. King complained about the FBI's performance in civil rights cases, and Hoover responded with increasing fury, questioning King's facts and sincerity. Finally, at a press conference with the Washington women's press corps on November 18, Hoover called King "the most notorious liar in the country," rebuffing efforts by FBI publicity chief Cartha "Deke" DeLoach to have the phrase taken off the record. King responded with a press release that in effect called Hoover senile.

Two days later, on November 20, 1964, Hoover lashed out in an internal memo to the Bureau's number three man, Deputy Associate Director Alan Belmont: "I can't understand why we are unable to get the true facts before the public. We can't even get our accomplishments published. We are never taking the aggressive, but above lies [i.e., King's charges against the Bureau and Hoover] remain unanswered."

Later that same day—and it would be reasonable to surmise it was in response to Hoover's outburst—Sullivan slipped a piece of untraceable unwatermarked paper into an old, also untraceable, typewriter, and composed and crudely typed a letter to King:

King, look into your heart. You know, you are a complete fraud and a greater liability to all of us Negroes. White people in this country have enough frauds of their own but I am sure they don't have one at this time that is anywhere near your equal. You are no clergyman and you know it. I repeat that you are a colossal fraud and an evil, vicious one at that....

King, like all frauds your end is approaching. You could have been our greatest leader.... But you are done. Your honorary degrees, your Nobel Prize (what a grim farce) and other awards will not save you. King, I repeat you are done....

The American public, the church organizations that have been helping—Protestants, Catholics and Jews will know you for what you are—an evil beast. So will others who have backed you. You are done.

King, there is only one thing left for you to do. You know what it is. You have just 34 days in which to do (this exact number has been selected for a specific reason, it has definite practical significance). You are done. There is but one way out for you. You better take it before your filthy fraudulent self is bared to the nation.

When he had finished typing, Sullivan placed the note in a package containing a reel of tape. Earlier that day, Sullivan had had the FBI labs prepare a composite tape of the most salacious episodes recorded by microphones hidden in King's hotel. The tape contained bawdy conversations between King and his friends, sexual conversations between King and several different female sexual partners, and sounds—mattress creaking, groans and cries—associated with sexual intercourse. The next morning Sullivan handed the package to an agent, told him to fly to Miami, and mail the package to King at his Atlanta SCLC office.

The package was opened, as it happened, by King's wife Coretta. She often received recordings of King's speeches, and assumed that this was another. She listened to part of it, quickly recognizing that this was something different, and then she read the threatening note. She called King. Then she, King, Ralph Abernathy, Andrew Young and Joseph Lowery listened to it all. They immediately realized that the source had to be the FBI. Some of King's friends thought the purpose had been to blackmail King into declining the Nobel Prize. Others thought the tapes were intended to goad Coretta into divorcing King. A third theory, and the most plausible, was that Sullivan was trying to put the thought of suicide in King's mind. "They are out to break me," King said. "They are out to get me, harass me, break my spirit."

He was right. The FBI was trying to destroy him, cruelly using "the content of his character" against him. And even after King's death, the Bureau continued its assault on his name and memory. Whenever there were calls to honor the fallen civil rights leader, Hoover was sure to counter with an unsolicited missive alluding to King's character flaws and his associations with Communists.

The March on Washington had set the FBI marching, too—marching against the dreamer and his dream.

From *American History*, August 2003, pages 43-44, 46-47. Copyright © 2003 Primedia Consumer Media and Magazines Inc. All rights reserved. Reprinted with permission.

The Spirit of '68

What really caused the Sixties.

By John B. Judis

This year Bob Dylan's album *Time Out of Mind* won the Grammy for best popular record, and teenagers in my local video store were waiting in line to rent *Don't Look Back*, D.A. Pennebaker's 1967 documentary about the irreverent Dylan. The National Organization for Women, the Consumer Federation of America, the Environmental Defense Fund, and other organizations from the Sixties are still influential in American politics. On the other hand, a host of grumpy social critics and cultural commissars, from Robert Bork and William Bennett to John Leo and Hilton Kramer, have continued to make a career out of denouncing that climactic period of American politics and culture. According to these critics, the 'Vietnam syndrome" ruined our foreign policy, and the spirit of permissiveness and "anything goes" corrupted our schools and youth and destroyed the nuclear family. "The revolt was against the entire American culture," Bork declared recently.

Why all the fuss? As a political era—one characterized by utopian social experiments, political upheaval, and dramatic reform—the Sixties ended sometime during Richard Nixon's presidency. But the era left an indelible mark on the decades that followed. It vastly expanded the scope of what citizens expect from their government—from clean air and water to safe workplaces, reliable products, and medical coverage in their old age. It also signaled a change in what Americans wanted out of their lives. During the Sixties, Americans began to worry about

the "quality of life" and about their "life-style" rather than simply about "making a living." The Sixties unleashed conflicts within these new areas of concern—over affirmative action, abortion, homosexuality, drugs, rock lyrics, air pollution, endangered species, toxic waste dumps, and automobile safety. And the era raised questions about the purpose of America and its foreign policy that are still being debated. The Sixties have preoccupied late-twentieth-century America almost as much as the Civil War preoccupied late-nineteenth- century America.

The difficulty in understanding the Sixties lies partly in the sheer diversity of people, events, and institutions that defined it—from John Kennedy's New Frontier to the Weatherman "Days of Rage," from the Black Panther Party to the Ford Foundation, from Betty Friedan and Ralph Nader to Barry Goldwater and George Wallace. Many of the books and articles that purport to be about the Sixties focus on one aspect of the era to the exclusion of the others. Todd Gitlin's excellent book, for instance, has only a passing reference to Nader and to the Sierra Club's David Brower but multiple references to Carl Oglesby, Huey Newton, and Staughton Lynd.

The nature of the Sixties has also been clouded by conservative jeremiads. Much of what disturbs the critics of the Sixties—from the spread of pornography to the denigration of the work ethic—was not the product of radical agitators but of tectonic shifts in American capitalism.

Many of those who complain most vociferously about the Sixties' counterculture, such as House Speaker Newt Gingrich, are themselves products of the period. They no longer carry signs, as Gingrich once did, proclaiming the right of campus magazines to publish nude pictures, but, even as they denounce the Sixties, they echo the decade's themes and vocabulary in articulating their own political objectives. Unable to come to terms with their own past, they sow confusion about one of the most important periods in our history.

Like most periods described by the name of a decade, the Sixties don't strictly conform to their allotted time span. You could make a good case that the Sixties began in December 1955, when Rosa Parks refused to give up her seat in a segregated Montgomery, Alabama, bus, and only ended in 1973 or 1974, when the New Left lost its fervor. You could also make a case for dividing the Sixties into two periods. The first period—running from 1955 to 1965—spans the rise of the Southern civil rights movement and of Martin Luther King, the founding of Students for a Democratic Society (SDS) in 1960, the passage of the civil rights bills and Medicare, and the initiation of the War on Poverty. The second period begins with the escalation of the war and the ghetto riots and goes through the rise of the black power and militant antiwar movements, the growth of the counterculture, the rapid development of environmental, consumer, and women's movements, and the major legislative achievements of Nixon's first term.

On the most visible level—the level at which most books about the period have dwelled—there is a pronounced shift in mood during the escalation of the war and the onset of the riots in the mid-'60s. The antiwar and black movements became violent and apocalyptic, and the country itself seemed on the verge of disintegration. But the sharp difference in tone between the two periods obscures important continuities. Most of the major movements that began in the Sixties—the consumer and environmental movements, the modern women's movement—started in the early years of the decade. And the roots of the counterculture go back well into the 1950s, if not before. These movements, as well as the counterculture, took root in Europe, too. In the United States, the simultaneous presence of massive antiwar demonstrations, riots, and demands for black power merely lent those movements and the counterculture a frenzy and an urgency that they might otherwise not have possessed.

The first period of the Sixties looks exactly like a belated continuation of the Progressive era and the New Deal. Just as in earlier periods of reform, political change was precipitated by an economic downturn. Successive recessions in 1958 and 1960 helped Democrats increase their margin in Congress and helped put Kennedy in the White House. In 1964, Johnson, benefiting from a buoyant economy and an impolitic opponent, Barry Goldwater, identified with Southern segregationists and with a trigger-happy foreign policy, won a landslide victory, and liberal Democrats gained control of Congress for the first time since 1936.

Just as before, reform was aided by an alliance of popular movements, elite organizations, and pragmatic business leaders. By the early '60s, the Southern civil rights movement enjoyed enormous support in the North, financial backing from the Ford Foundation and the Rockefeller Brothers Fund, and editorial support from the major media. Business leaders, encouraged by prosperity after having endured four recessions in a decade, accepted Johnson and the administration's major legislative initiatives with equanimity. They didn't oppose Medicare (only the American Medical Association lobbied against it), and they actively backed the Great Society and War on Poverty programs, which they saw, correctly, as creating demand for new private investment. When Johnson appointed a National Commission on Technology, Automation, and Economic Progress, the nation's most powerful businessmen joined labor and civil rights leaders in recommending a guaranteed annual income and a massive job-training program.

The spirit of the early '60s—epitomized in Johnson's vision of the Great Society—was one of heady, liberal optimism. Many of the key leaders of the period, including Martin Luther King Jr., George McGovern, Hubert Humphrey, and Walter Mondale, were raised on the Protestant Social Gospel's millennial faith in the creation of a Kingdom of God in America. The political-economic premise of this optimism, enunciated in Galbraith's *The Affluent Society* and in Michael Harrington's *The Other America*, was that American industry, which was becoming highly automated, was capable of producing great abundance, but archaic political and economic arrangements were preventing many Americans from enjoying its fruits. The goal of such programs as Medicare and the War on Poverty was to allow the poor, the aged, and the disadvantaged to share in this abundance.

This first phase of the Sixties was also marked by signs of a looming redefinition of politics that would differentiate it from early reform epochs. During the Progressive era and the New Deal, politics pivoted primarily on conflicts among different sectors of business and between business and labor. The great battles of the first five decades of the twentieth century had been over the trusts, the tariff, the banking system, the abolition of child labor, and government regulation of collective bargaining. No legislative struggle attracted so many lobbyists, was fought as fiercely, and had as much impact on presidential politics as the Taft-Hartley labor bill in 1947.

In the early '60s, new issues that didn't fit easily within this pattern began to emerge. Americans became concerned not merely with obtaining lower prices for goods but with government overseeing the safety, reliability, and quality of goods. President Kennedy announced a consumer bill of rights in 1962. That same year, over the strong objection of the clothing industry, Congress passed landmark legislation requiring flame-resistant fabrics in children's clothing. In 1964, Assistant Secretary of Labor Daniel P. Moynihan hired a young Harvard Law graduate, Ralph Nader, to research auto safety. Two years later, amidst the furor created by Nader's work, Congress passed the National Traffic and Motor Vehicle Safety Act.

In the early '60s, Americans also became concerned about the environment—not merely as a source of renewable resources or as a wildlife preserve but as the natural setting for human life. In 1962, Rachel Carson's *Silent Spring* became a best-seller. Congress passed its first Clean Air Act in 1963 and its first Clean Water Act in 1965. During the early '60s, American women also began to stir as a political force in their own right. In 1963, Betty Friedan published *The Feminine Mystique*, and, three years later, she and other feminists formed the National Organization for Women. While the older women's movement had focused on suffrage, the new movement reached into the workplace and the home and even into the private lives of men and women.

The new concerns about work, consumption, and personal life were part of a fundamental change in American culture that began to manifest itself clearly in the early '60s. During the nineteenth and early twentieth centuries, Americans had still adhered to the Protestant work ethic introduced by seventeenth-century English emigrants to America and memorialized in Benjamin Franklin's *Autobiography*. They viewed idleness and leisure as sinful and saw life and work as unpleasant prerequisites to a heavenly reward. By the early '60s, Americans had begun to abandon this harsh view for an ethic of the good life. They wanted to discover a "lifestyle" that suited them.

They worried about the "quality of life," including the kinds of foods they ate, the clothes they wore, and the cars they drove.

This change was not the work of sinful agitators but reflected deep-seated changes that had taken place in American capitalism over the century. In the nineteenth century and early twentieth century, economic growth, and the growth of the working class itself, was driven by the expansion of steel, railroads, machine tools, and other "capital goods" industries. Workers' consumption was held down in order to free up funds that could be used to invest in these new capital goods. To prevent recurrent economic crises, American industrialists were always on the lookout—in China, among other places—for new outlets for investment in railroads and other capital goods. But, as the historian Martin J. Sklar has demonstrated, sometime around the 1920s, the dynamic of economic growth changed. The growth of capital goods industries became, ironically, a threat to prosperity.

It happened because American industry, like American agriculture, became too successful for its own good. The introduction of electricity and the assembly line made the modern factory so productive that it could now increase its output without increasing its overall number of employees. During the '20s, manufacturing output grew 64 percent, but the number of workers in capital goods industries fell by twelve percent. Expanding the production of capital goods no longer required the sacrifice of workers' consumption. By the same token, it imperiled prosperity by encouraging the production of more goods than those producing them—the workers—could purchase and consume.

During the '20s, Edward Filene and other far-seeing businessmen understood that the fulcrum of the economy had shifted from production to consumption and that, to avoid depressions, employers would have to pay higher wages and induce their workers, through advertising, to spend money on consumer goods. Filene advocated a different kind of "industrial democracy" centered on workers' freedom to consume. After World War II, businesses adopted Filene's ethic

and his strategy. They paid higher wages and devoted growing parts of their budgets to advertising, which was aimed at convincing Americans to spend rather than to save. Advertising budgets doubled between 1951 and 1962. Businesses and banks also introduced the installment plan and consumer loans and, later, credit cards as inducements to buy rather than to save.

In search of profit, businesses also invaded the family and home. They sold leisure and entertainment on a massive scale; they produced not merely clothes but fashion; they processed exotic foods and established fast-food chains; they sold physical and psychological health; they filled the home with appliances and gadgets. They convinced Americans that they should care about more than just having food on the table, a house to live in, and clothes on their backs. They encouraged the idea that Americans could remake themselves—that they could create their own "look," their own personality. They encouraged the idea that sex was not merely a means to procreate but a source of pleasure and visual excitement.

The origins of the counterculture lay at the interstices of this new American culture of leisure and consumption that business helped to promote. The counterculture was a product of the new culture at the same time as it represented a critique of and a counter to it. It rejected Filene's suggestion that workers seek their freedom entirely in consumption rather than work. It held out for meaningful work, but not as defined by the nineteenth or early twentieth centuries. In 1960, when Paul Goodman, writing in *Growing' Up Absurd*, complained that "there are not enough worthy jobs in our economy for average boys and adolescents to grow up toward," he was not complaining about the lack of jobs at General Motors or on Wall Street.

The counterculture also rejected TV dinners and cars with tail fins that the advertisers urged Americans to buy, but it did so on behalf of more discriminating standards of its own. The critique of consumerism—articulated in the '50s by Vance Packard's *The Waste Makers* and

The Hidden Persuaders—led directly to the formation of the modern consumer and environmental movements. And the rejection of sex symbols and stereotypes did not lead to a celebration of abstinence but to a wider exploration into sexual pleasure and to a reevaluation of homosexuality and heterosexuality. In the early '60s, all these concerns became the subjects not merely of books and small artistic cults, but of political manifestos and platforms and embryonic social movements.

The movements initially took root among college students and recent college graduates. Students who entered college in 1960 had been born after the Depression—they had been, in the words of SDS's Port Huron Statement, "bred in at least modest comfort." Living in a time of unprecedented prosperity, they could afford not to worry about whether they would be able to get a job. They were raised to think about the "quality of life" rather than the iron law of wages, even to scorn some elements of what was then called "materialism." By 1960, they had become a major social group, capable on their own of disrupting society and upsetting its politics.

The New Left movements of the early '60s attacked the new economy, but they, too, implicitly used the new standards and ideals it had fostered. SDS's Port Huron Statement condemned the "idolatrous worship of things" but called for "finding a meaning in life that is personally authentic"—a formulation that would have made no sense to an industrial worker in 1909. In Berkeley, the Free Speech Movement of 1964—aimed at reclaiming the rights of students to distribute political literature on campus— gave way the next year to the Filthy Speech Movement, aimed at defending students against literary and sexual censorship. Over the next decade, these two movements—political and cultural— would develop in tandem.

The second period of the Sixties began with the Watts riot and Lyndon Johnson's escalation of the Vietnam War in 1965. These events signified and helped to precipitate a darker, more frenzied and violent period of protest. By escalating the war, Johnson broke a campaign promise not to send "our American boys to do the fighting for Asian boys." The war's escalation also threw into question the purpose of American foreign policy. Students who entered college in the Sixties had been imbued with the idea that America's mission was to create a democratic world after its own image. But, in Vietnam, the United States was backing a corrupt dictatorship, which, at our urging, had ignored the 1954 Geneva agreements to hold elections in Vietnam. The seeming contradiction between U.S. intervention and American ideals, Johnson's dishonesty and betrayal, and the rising list of casualties on both sides of the war inspired a growing rage against Johnson and the government. The antiwar movement split into a moderate wing that sought a negotiated withdrawal and a violent pro-North Vietnamese wing that threatened to bring the war home." As the conviction grew that U.S. intervention was not an unfortunate blunder but reflected the priorities of American capitalism and its power elite, antiwar militants began to see the United States itself as the enemy. SDS, the leading student organization, imagined itself by 1969 to be the vanguard of a violent revolution *against* the United States.

The first ghetto riots took place in the summer of 1964 and then grew in size and strength over the next three summers. In the Watts riot of 1965, 1,072 people were injured, 34 were killed, 977 buildings were damaged, and 4,000 people were arrested. In July 1967, there were 103 disorders, including five full-scale riots. In Detroit, 43 people were killed, and 7,200 were arrested. 700 buildings were burned, and 412 were totally destroyed. The riots were spontaneous. but they were invariably triggered by black perceptions of unequal treatment, particularly at the hands of white police officers.

At the same time that the riots began, Martin Luther King Jr. attempted to take the civil rights movement northward to Chicago. Contrary to the fantasies of his current conservative admirers, King never saw political and civil equality as

ends in themselves but as part of a longer struggle for full social and economic equality. King wanted to desegregate housing in the North (which was the key to de facto school segregation), improve city services for blacks, and gain higher wages and better jobs for blacks. He failed abysmally in Chicago. The combination of the ghetto riots and King's failure contributed to the radicalization of the black movement. By 1968, when King was assassinated in Memphis while trying to support striking black garbagemen, many in the black movement had turned toward insurrectionary violence. It saw the Northern ghettos as Third World colonies that had to be liberated from their white imperialist oppressors.

Both the radical antiwar and the black power movements espoused what they called "revolutionary politics." They saw themselves in the tradition of Marx, Lenin, Mao, Fanon, Castro, and even Stalin, but, by the late '60s, they had become unwitting participants in a much older American tradition of Protestant millennialism. As historian William G. McLoughlin argued in *Revivals, Awakenings and Reform*, the Sixties were part of a religious revival comparable to the great awakenings of the mid-eighteenth and early nineteenth centuries. At such times, the seeming discord between ideal and reality has inspired intense self-examination, the proliferation of new sects and schisms, and alternating visions of doom and salvation. While the first phase of the Sixties saw the revival of the post-millennial Protestant Social Gospel—the view that the world would end after the millennium—the second phase saw "pre-millennial" visions of the apocalypse and Armageddon occurring before the millennium.

The emergence of this pre-millennial vision was provoked by the war's escalation and the combination of rage and guilt (guilt at complicity in the slaughter of seeming innocents) that it inspired; the repeated visions of violence and destruction in Vietnam and in American cities, which reinforced an image of change as conflagration; the assassinations of John and Robert Kennedy and of Martin Luther King, Jr., and Malcolm X; the Republican advances in 1966 and Nixon's election in November 1968,

which discouraged New Left activists who had believed they could achieve majority support for their revolutionary aspirations; and the apparent success of the North Vietnamese in the war and the onset of China's Cultural Revolution, which suggested that revolution in the United States would occur only after a global revolution against American imperialism had succeeded.

The New Left of the late '60s dreamed not of America's salvation but of its destruction. If socialism or the "good life" were to come to the United States, it would be only after Armageddon—after a victorious armed struggle that would lay waste to the United States. The Panthers referred to the United States as "Babylon." When the Weatherman group took over SDS in 1969, it changed the name of SDS's newspaper, *New Left Notes*, to *Fire*. The new revolutionaries steeled themselves for a life of sacrifice and eventually death in the service of world revolution. Huey Newton, the cofounder of the Panther Party, described its program as "revolutionary suicide." Hal Jacobs, a Weatherman sympathizer, wrote in the movement magazine *Leviathan:* "Perhaps the best we can hope for is that in the course of the struggle we can develop human social relations among ourselves, while being engulfed by death and destruction."

The vision of Weatherman or the Panthers perfectly matched that of the Millerites—the precursors of today's Seventh Day Adventists. They were preparing themselves to be saved in the face of an imminent Armageddon. Even their organization resembled that of earlier Christian sects. The Weatherman group abandoned any pretense of building a mass movement. Instead, it sought to establish "revolutionary Marxist-Leninist-Maoist collective formations" that, through "criticism—self-criticism," would convert its members to true revolutionaries. Under Weatherman leadership, SDS, which at one point boasted 100,000 members, dwindled to several hundred aspiring visible saints.

During the late '60s, many of the people in the New Left, myself included, got caught up in the debate over class struggle, imperialism, racism, and revolution as if it were a genuine discussion based on reasonable, if debatable, assessments of world conditions. But others sensed that something was deeply wrong. In his 1968 campaign as the Democratic anti-war candidate, Eugene McCarthy continually frustrated his own followers by counseling calm and "reasoned judgment." Said McCarthy, "It is not a time for storming the walls, but for beginning a long march." Paul Goodman, whose writings had inspired the New Left, realized by 1969 that the political movement had turned unworldly even while it pretended to speak of world revolution:

If we start from the premise that the young are in a religious crisis, that they doubt there is really a nature of things and they are sure there is no world for themselves, many details of their present behavior become clearer. Alienation is a powerful motivation, of unrest, fantasy and feckless action. It can lead… to religious innovation, new sacraments to give life meaning. But it is a poor basis for politics, including revolutionary politics.

At the time, however, these voices were largely ignored. The question wasn't whether it made any sense at all to talk of revolution, but when the revolution would come and who would be on what side of the barricades.

This turn toward violence and revolutionary fantasy alienated many Americans and led to the rise of Ronald Reagan in California and George Wallace's surprising showing in the 1968 presidential election. That year, Richard Nixon ran a subtle "law and order" campaign to exploit the unpopularity of the antiwar and black protesters. Yet these movements still wielded enormous influence over the nation's political and legislative agenda. By the early '70s, they had helped force the Nixon administration to withdraw from Vietnam and had provoked Congress and the administration into pouring money into cities and adopting a strategy of affirmative action in hiring and federal contracts. During Nixon's first term, spending on Johnson's Great Society programs and on welfare and Food Stamps

dramatically increased, while spending on the military went down.

There were two reasons for the movements' remarkable success. First, the movements were large and unruly enough to pose a constant threat of disruption. The major riots stopped by 1969, but the threat of riots persisted—both in actual fact and in the rhetoric and behavior of the black activists. In the summer of 1970 alone, city officials reported that black and Chicano militants made over 500 attacks on police, resulting in the deaths of 20 policemen. The antiwar movement also became increasingly violent. During the fall semester in 1970, 140 bombings occurred; at Rutgers, classes had to be vacated 175 times because of bomb threats.

Second, these movements had either the support or sympathy of policy elites. Some members of the foreign policy elite, acting partly out of conviction and partly out of fear of further disruption, favored immediate negotiation with the North Vietnamese and later unilateral withdrawal from Vietnam. By 1968, these included *The New York Times* editorial board and prominent members of the Council on Foreign Relations. Foundations and policy groups responded to the antiwar movement and to the riots and the black power movement the same way elite organizations in the early 1900s had responded to the threat of socialist revolution. They sought to tame the militants by helping them achieve their more reasonable objectives.

The Ford Foundation, the wealthiest and most powerful of all the foundations, with assets four times that of the Rockefeller Foundation, was particularly important. In 1966, Henry Ford and foundation board chairman John McCloy desirous that the foundation play a more active role in national affairs, brought in former Kennedy national security adviser McGeorge Bundy as the new president. Bundy threw the foundation into the struggle for racial equality. He helped new groups get off the ground, including La Raza and the Mexican-American Legal Defense Fund. But he also embroiled the foundation in controversy. Money that Ford gave to the Congress of Racial Equality in Cleveland went to funding a voter registration drive that helped elect Democrat Carl

Stokes as Cleveland's first black mayor—in seeming violation of the foundation's nonpartisan status. In New York, Bundy sold New York City Mayor John Lindsay on a plan for community control of schools that put local blacks in charge of their own schools, which ended up pitting the city's blacks against the predominantly Jewish teachers' union.

While the late '60s are remembered mainly for the violent antiwar and black power movements, their most enduring legacy was the establishment of the environmental, consumer, and women's movements. By the early '70s, the National Organization for Women had 200 local chapters and had been joined in effort by the National Women's Political Caucus, the National Association for the Repeal of Abortion Laws, and hundreds of small local and national women's organizations. The movement enjoyed remarkable success. In 1972, the year Ms. magazine was founded, Congress approved the Equal Rights Amendment to the Constitution, strengthened and broadened the scope of the Equal Employment Opportunity Commission, and included a provision in the new Higher Education Act ensuring equal treatment of men and women.

The consumer and environmental movements enjoyed equally spectacular success. Organizations like the Sierra Club, Wilderness Society, and the Audubon Society expanded their purview and quadrupled their membership from 1960 to 1969. They were also joined by new groups, including Environmental Action, the Environmental Defense Fund, and Friends of the Earth. The Consumer Federation of America, a coalition of 140 state and local groups, was founded in 1967, and Consumers Union, which had published a magazine since 1936, moved its office to Washington in 1969. These groups got the Nixon administration and Congress to adopt a raft of reforms from establishing the Environmental Protection Agency and the Consumer Product Safety Commission to major amendments to the Clean Air and Clean Water acts.

The key individual behind these movements was Nader. He used his fame and income from *Unsafe at Any Speed*—his best-selling book about auto safety—and his successful battle with General Motors to help build a consumer movement. Nader started hiring young lawyers called "Nader's Raiders" in 1968 and founded his first campus-based Public Interest Research Group in 1970. By the mid-'70s, he had founded eight new organizations, including the Center for Responsive Law, Congress Watch, and the Health Research Group, which played an important role in getting Congress to pass a mass of new legislation, including the Wholesome Poultry Products Act, the Natural Gas Pipeline Safety Act, and the Occupational Safety and Health Act.

If Nader was the key individual, the key institution was once more the Ford Foundation. The foundation stepped in when the Audubon Society, worried about its own contributors, balked at funding the Environmental Defense Fund, the first public interest law firm designed to force business and government to comply with the new environmental laws. Ford also gave generous grants to the Sierra Club Legal Defense Fund and to the Los Angeles-based Center for Law in the Public Interest. By 1972, Ford was providing 86 percent of the grants to groups practicing consumer and environmental public interest law.

Unlike the later antiwar and civil rights movements, the environmental and consumer movements enjoyed enormous popular support. Republican and Democratic politicians vied to sponsor environmental and consumer legislation. In 1970, Nixon and Edmund Muskie, who was planning to run for president in 1972, got into a bidding war for the movements support, with each championing successively tougher revisions to the Clean Air Act. Businesses might have fought environmental and consumer legislation, but, in these years, they were restrained by a combination of complacency and defensiveness. From February 1961 to September 1969, the United States enjoyed the longest consecutive boom on record. The economy grew by 4.5 percent a year, compared to 3.2 percent in the '50s. Secure in their standing, only 50 corporations had registered lobbyists stationed in Washington in the early '60s.

In the mid-'60s, as the country's mood darkened, the public's opinion of business began to fall precipitously, but, as David Vogel recounts in *Fluctuating Fortunes*, business's initial response was to stress corporate social responsibility and to accommodate the demands of the consumer and environmental movements. While the auto and tobacco companies took umbrage at regulations targeted at them, business as a whole thought it could adapt the new environmental and consumer legislation to its own ends just as it had done earlier with the Interstate Commerce Commission and the Federal Trade Commission. A Fortune survey in February 1970 found 53 percent of Fortune 500 executives in favor of a national regulatory agency and 57 percent believing that the federal government should "step up regulatory activities." In a spirit of social responsibility, 85 percent of the executives thought that the environment should be protected even if that meant "reducing profits."

In the second phase of the Sixties, the counterculture spread from Berkeley, Madison, Ann Arbor, and Cambridge to almost every high school and college in America. Teenagers from pampered suburban homes who had never read Allen Ginsberg or Nelson Algren nevertheless denounced the "rat race" and the "neon wilderness." In extensive polls and interviews conducted from 1968 to 1974, Daniel Yankelovich saw steadily growing "acceptance of sexual freedom," rejection of "materialism," opposition to the laws against marijuana, and questioning of "such traditional American views as putting duty before pleasure [and] saving money regularly."

Like the other movements of the Sixties, the counterculture had its theorists, and its own millennial vision, which propounded a utopian version of consumer capitalism. Sociologist Theodore Roszak, ecologist Murray Bookchin, Yale Law School professor Charles Reich, and other post-millennialists foresaw a transformation in human nature and human arrangements that would subordinate work to play and science to art. The instrument of change would not be a political movement but the change

in consciousness that had already begun among college students. Reich saw the essence of change in the new "freedom of choosing a lifestyle." Work would become an "erotic experience, or a play experience."

Reich attributed the new counterculture to capitalism—what he called the "machine." As capitalism became capable of producing more goods than it could sell, it was forced to devise ways to expand people's needs and wants. It had to transform people themselves, moving them from the work ethic of "Consciousness II" to the lifestyle ethic of "Consciousness III," where a human being could "develop the aesthetic and spiritual side of his nature."

Reich, Roszak, and other spokesmen for the counterculture did not exalt idleness but artistic expression. They didn't promote pornography but eroticism. Most of what their current critics like Bork and Kramer lay at their door was attributable to consumer capitalism rather than the counterculture. And, while much of their vision of the future appears daffy, they—in contrast to their latter-day critics—realized that America had turned a corner. What they didn't understand was exactly where it was headed.

As a political era, the Sixties came to a close around 1973. In January 1973, Nixon signed a peace accord with North Vietnam, which not only put an end to the antiwar movement but, in doing so, removed a major source of political mobilization and energy. In 1969, the booming war economy also began a six-year slowdown. This slowdown, aggravated by the energy crisis of 1973, put a damper on the counterculture. Students became focused on preparing for jobs and careers rather than discovering the meaning of life.

The downturn of the early '70s, combined with a wave of strikes that began in 1969 and with growing competition from Japan and Western Europe, made American business leaders lose their tolerance for new government intervention. They began to push hard to limit new consumer and environmental regulations. They began hiring lobbyists and establishing corporate offices in Washington and funding policy groups and think tanks, and by the mid-'70s, many business leaders were beginning to look fondly upon Republican conservatives who combined their opposition to the social movements of the Sixties with support for business's agenda of "deregulation." By 1978, these two groups were setting the nation's political and legislative agenda, even with Democrats in control of the White House and Congress.

What, then, is the legacy of the Sixties? It endures, for one thing, in Bill Clinton's passionate commitment to racial reconciliation and in Al Gore's ardent environmentalism. It also could be found in Clinton's mistaken belief after November 1992 that he could fashion a "new beginning," including a wildly ambitious health care plan. But the era also endures ironically in its most bitter opponents—Gingrich, Dick Armey, Phil Gramm, and many of the leaders of the religious right. Gingrich and Armey's fantastic belief that they had led a "revolution" in November 1994 was straight out of the late '60s. So, too, is Gingrich's futurism and his insistence that Americans should have the highest "range of choices of lifestyle." Within the religious right, Weatherman has been reincarnated as Operation Rescue, and the commu-

nards of the Sixties have become the home-schoolers of the 1990s.

The Sixties clearly bequeathed political conflicts that continue to seethe but also made lasting contributions that cannot easily be undone. Medicare and the environmental and consumer legislation of Nixon's first term have withstood furious attacks from conservatives and business. While the issues of urban poverty and decay that King addressed in the last years of his life remain unsettled, the premises of the Civil Rights Act of 1964 and the Voting Rights Act of 1965 are no longer open to question.

The Sixties enlarged the scope of politics by adding new issues and constituencies to the traditional mix created by business and labor, and they changed the way politics was conducted. A proliferation of new movements, interests, and interest groups—some of them funded door-to-door and others through the mail—shifted the struggle to change the country from the halls of Congress to the media and even to time streets. By the 1980s, business lobbyists were employing "grassroots" techniques developed by shaggy protesters from the Sixties.

Perhaps most important of all, America passed irreversibly during the Sixties

from a culture of toil, sacrifice, saving, and abstinence to a culture of consumption, lifestyle, and quality of life The agent of this change was not the counterculture but consumer capitalism, to which the counterculture, like the religious right, is a reaction. This new stage of capitalism has opened to the average American possibilities of education, leisure, and personal fulfillment that had been reserved in the past for the upper classes. It has also, of course, exalted consumption over production, razed redwoods, turned shorelines into boardwalks, flooded cyberspace with spam, used sex to sell detergents, and helped to transform many American teenagers into television zombies. If our cultural commissars would understand this distinction between the culture of capitalism and the counterculture, perhaps they would waste less of our time blaming the radicals of the Sixties for all of today's problems and turn their attention to the real causes.

This article draws from JOHN B. JUDIS's book on twentieth-century American politics, *The Paradox of American Democracy* (Pantheon Books, 2000).

From *The New Republic,* August 31, 1998, pp. 20–27. Copyright © 1998 by The New Republic. Reprinted by permission.

Face-Off

East-West tension defined the Cold War, but its legacy is the victory of hope over fear

By John Lewis Gaddis

The Cold War began to end 10 years ago, not with any great decision grandly proclaimed but with a hapless official spokesman fumbling his lines. On Nov. 9, 1989, Gunter Schabowski, Berlin district secretary for the ruling East German Communist Party, was *supposed* to announce a decision by his bosses to allow a limited and controlled flow of East Germans through the Berlin Wall, to take effect the next day. This concession would, they hoped, relieve the pressures on the German Democratic Republic that had been mounting throughout the summer and fall, as Mikhail Gorbachev made it increasingly clear that the Soviet Union would no longer prop up its fellow Marxist-Leninist regimes in Eastern Europe. Schabowski slipped up on a detail, however, telling a televised press conference that the new rules were to take effect "immediately, without delay."

Within hours, excited East Berliners had overwhelmed the border guards, forced open the crossing points, and surged into West Berlin, forbidden territory for as long as most of them could remember. Soon they were dancing on top of the wall, chipping away at it with hammers and crowbars, and then quite literally toppling it with bulldozers and backhoes. The very symbol of a continent divided for almost half a century—indeed of a world so divided—came tumbling down, almost overnight.

Nobody on either side had anticipated this: The wall had seemed as permanent a fixture of the Berlin landscape as the Cold War had appeared to be within the post-World War II international system. That such a forbidding structure proved so fragile surprised everyone. But even then, few who witnessed the wall's collapse would have guessed what was soon to come:

that the division of Germany would disappear within a year, or that in just over two years the Soviet Union itself would cease to exist.

Today we take for granted what astonished us then: We assume, far more easily than we should, that the process that began with the opening of the Berlin Wall and ended with the Soviet Union's essentially peaceful breakup could *only* have happened in the way that it did. History works like that: Our view of the past is so much clearer than our vision of the future that we tend to forget that the past once had a future, and that it was just as opaque to those who lived through it as our own future is for us today. My college students were between 8 and 11 years old when the Berlin Wall came down. They've known only a pitifully weak Russia that cannot keep its borders secure, its military intact, its economy afloat, or its prime ministers in office. How, they wonder, could such a country have ever caused Americans and their allies to fear for their future?

I suggest, as an answer, a short time-machine trip. Set the dial first for November 1989, the anniversary we're commemorating, to get a sense of the unexpectedness of what happened and of the euphoria it produced. Then go back in 10-year intervals from that event. A very different picture emerges.

November 1979: Jimmy Carter is in his third year as president of the United States, and the mood is anything but euphoric. The American Embassy staff has just been taken hostage in Tehran, following the overthrow of a longtime friend, the shah of Iran. In Nicaragua, the Sandinistas have deposed the Somoza regime, an even older ally. The Soviet Union

The East-West Divide

The Cold War dominated politics for 40 years

MARCH 1946. Former British Prime Minister Winston Churchill warns the world, during a speech in Fulton, Mo., that an "iron curtain" is descending across Europe.

APRIL 1948. Start of Marshall Plan, a U.S.-sponsored economic program to aid 16 European nations ravaged by World War II.

JUNE 1948. Soviet troops block all road, rail, and water traffic between West Berlin and the West. U.S., Britain, and France airlift 2.3 million tons of food and supplies to the city for 15 months.

APRIL 1949. North Atlantic Treaty Organization (NATO) sets up common defense alliance to counter-weigh Soviet forces in Eastern Europe.

AUGUST 1949. Soviet Union tests its first atomic bomb.

OCTOBER 1949. China turns Communist under Mao Zedong's leadership.

JUNE 1950. North Korean troops invade South Korea. U.S. and 16 other United Nations countries fight alongside South Korea until July 1953 armistice.

JUNE 1953. Soviet troops quell anti-Communist revolts in East Germany.

MAY 1955. Warsaw Pact signed by Soviet Union and seven Eastern European countries to ensure unified command against NATO.

NOVEMBER 1956. Soviet tanks crush national rebellion against communism in Hungary. Thousands flee to the West.

MAY 1960. American U-2 reconnaissance plane shot down over Sverdlovsk, Russia. Pilot Francis Gary Powers survives and in August is sentenced to 10 years' confinement in U.S.S.R. In 1962 Powers is exchanged for Soviet spy Rudolf Abel.

APRIL 1961. U.S.-sponsored invasion of Cuba by 1,500 Cuban exiles opposed to Fidel Castro fails at Bay of Pigs. Between 1962 and 1965, Cuba releases captured prisoners in exchange for $53 million worth of food and medicine.

APRIL 1961. Soviet cosmonaut Yuri Gagarin gains worldwide fame as first man to travel in space aboard the Vostok 1 spacecraft.

AUGUST 1961. East Germany erects Berlin Wall to stem increasing flight of its citizens to the West.

OCTOBER 1962. President John Kennedy orders naval blockade of Cuba to prevent Soviet shipments of nuclear missiles. Threat of nuclear war recedes when Soviet Premier Nikita Khrushchev halts work on launch sites and removes missiles already in Cuba.

AUGUST 1963. Nuclear Test-Ban Treaty prohibits nuclear-weapons tests in the atmosphere, underwater, and in space.

AUGUST 1964. Congress authorizes expansion of U.S. involvement in Vietnam after North Vietnamese torpedo boats attack two American destroyers.

AUGUST 1968.. Troops from the Soviet Union, East Germany, Poland, Hungary, and Bulgaria invade Czechoslovakia to prevent political reforms.

FEBRUARY 1972. President Richard Nixon reopens severed ties with China during 10-day official visit.

MAY 1972. SALT I agreements curtail Soviet and U.S. nuclear-arms race by limiting antiballistic missile systems.

APRIL 1975. Vietnam War ends as Communist North Vietnamese forces occupy Saigon without resistance.

DECEMBER 1979. Soviet Army invades Afghanistan on Christmas Day. Soviets suffer 60,000 casualties in nine-year war against Afghan guerrillas.

SEPTEMBER 1980. Independent trade union, Solidarity, founded in Poland under Lech Walesa.

MARCH 1985. Mikhail Gorbachev launches economic and political restructuring program dubbed "perestroika."

NOVEMBER 1989. Fall of Berlin Wall. East German government opens the country's borders with West Germany.

OCTOBER 1990. East and West Germany reunify under NATO auspices and with Soviet approval.

DECEMBER 1991. Soviet reformer Gorbachev resigns from office. The Soviet Union collapses, ending 74 years of Soviet communism.

under Leonid Brezhnev has deployed a new generation of SS-20 missiles aimed at European targets and is openly encouraging Marxist revolutions in what Carter's national-security adviser, Zbigniew Brzezinski, has called an "arc of crisis" running from Southern Africa to Southeast Asia. The Russians are on the verge of invading Afghanistan and are threatening to crack down on Poland, where the Solidarity trade union movement is only beginning to test its capacity for resistance. Still reeling from defeat in Vietnam, the disruptions of Watergate, and a continuing energy crisis, Americans are confronting the prospect of double-digit inflation and unemployment. Détente is dying, if not dead, and a highly visible Committee on the Present Danger has been insisting that if nothing is done to reverse these trends, the credibility of the United States as a superpower will not survive. Ronald Reagan has announced his intention to run for the presidency, precisely with a view to restoring it.

Flashpoints. *East Berlin, 1953: Workers clash with riot police. Prague, 1968: Soviet tanks crush Czechoslovakia's hopes for reform.*

November 1969: The United States is mired in an unwinnable war in Southeast Asia. Although Richard Nixon's new administration has promised gradually to withdraw American troops, some 500,000 remain in Vietnam—most disillusioned about their mission, many demoralized and on drugs, and some even challenging the authority of their officers. The Air Force is secretly bombing enemy sanctuaries in Cambodia, while at home antiwar protests have mounted to such an extent that Nixon has had to ask the "silent majority" of Americans to help him avoid national humiliation. The Soviet Union has overtaken the United States in the production and deployment of intercontinental ballistic missiles, thereby ending an American superiority in strategic weaponry that had prevailed since the beginning of the Cold War. In striking contrast to the Americans' failure in Vietnam, the Soviet Union has crushed Alexander Dubcek's reform movement in Czechoslovakia and has threatened to respond similarly to such experiments elsewhere. China, still in the throes of Chairman Mao Zedong's Great Cultural Revolution, is preparing for nuclear war—not with the United States, as one might have expected, but with its erstwhile ideological ally. How would the Americans react, a Soviet diplomat has discreetly inquired in Washington, if the Russians were to launch a pre-emptive strike against the Chinese?

November 1959: Soviet space achievements—the first ICBM, the first artificial Earth satellite—have caused a crisis of confidence in the United States, where an aging Dwight Eisenhower is presiding over a country seriously worried about its apparent inferiority in science and technology. The Soviet leader is the ebulliently bumptious Nikita Khrushchev, who is claiming to be turning out rockets "like sausages," capable of devastating any point on the face of the Earth. He has challenged the exposed position of the United States and its allies in West Berlin, has exploited growing anti-American sentiment in the Middle East, and has just returned from a highly publicized

visit to the United States, where he repeated his frequent prediction that America's grandchildren would live under communism. Just to the south, a young guerrilla fighter and occasional baseball player named Fidel Castro has come to power in Cuba—with the result that the former playground for American gangsters and vacationers already seems well along the path that Khrushchev has laid out.

November 1949: Joseph Stalin is alive and in command inside the Kremlin, while Harry S. Truman is president of the United States. The Soviet Union has consolidated its post-World War II sphere of influence in Eastern Europe, forcing the United States to respond with the Truman Doctrine, the Marshall Plan, and most recently the North Atlantic Treaty Organization—an unprecedented peacetime commitment to the defense of an increasingly desperate Western Europe. The Russians have just exploded their first atomic bomb, several years earlier than expected, and Truman is under pressure to respond by building thermonuclear weapons with a thousand times the destructive power of the device the Americans had dropped, only four years before, on Hiroshima. Mao has proclaimed the People's Republic of China and will soon depart for Moscow to forge a Sino-Soviet alliance, thereby confirming communist control over most of the Eurasian continent. Allegations of espionage within the United States are creating an atmosphere of near hysteria, which Sen. Joseph McCarthy will soon exploit and which his critics will name for him. Meanwhile, George Orwell has published *1984*, a profoundly pessimistic vision of survival in an apparently endless Cold War.

What this brief trip through time suggests is that for anyone living in November of 1949, 1959, 1969, or 1979, the Cold War's outcome would not have been at all clear. If anything, it looked as though the Soviet Union and its allies might win: There was a remarkable gap between what people *thought* was happening and what we now know to have happened. Fears outweighed hopes for so long that when the latter actually prevailed it was a completely unexpected development.

It's now the historians' task to explain this triumph of hopes over fears. It helps to have partial access to Soviet, Eastern European, and Chinese archives. Before the Cold War ended, the American public had more than enough information from Western sources to expose the shortcomings of the United States and its allies, but historians could only hint at those that may have existed on the other side. We now know much more, and what emerges is a pattern of brutality, shortsightedness, inefficiency, vulnerability, and mistrust within the Marxist-Leninist world that dates back to the earliest days of the Cold War.

Just as important, though, is our knowledge of how the Cold War turned out. The view from inside any historical event is bound to be limited—and the Cold War was an unusually protracted event. We have a better sense now of where it's going to fit within the long sweep of history. And we can see, more clearly, why so much of what the West feared never came to pass.

A list of such fears, for an American at the end of 1949, might well have included the following: that, as Orwell's novel suggested, authoritarianism could be the wave of the future; that, as the Marshall Plan and NATO implied, Europe was in danger of becoming a Soviet sphere of influence; that, as Mao's

Setting the Record Straight

Archives slowly yielding their secrets

There is much we still don't know—and may never know—about the Cold War. But once-secret documents are providing a glimpse into key events and showing that some of what we do know—or think we know—is wrong. Among the findings:

• Moscow secretly deployed 100 nuclear warheads in Cuba during the 1962 missile crisis, making the era's most dangerous standoff even scarier in retrospect.

• President Eisenhower in 1957 gave U.S. military commanders *advance* permission to use nuclear weapons if they were in danger of being overwhelmed by a Soviet attack and could not reach him.

East-bloc archives have provided the most important new revelations, showing that communism wasn't a monolith:

• Stalin reluctantly approved North Korea's June 1950 attack on the South (Kim Il Sung pestered him with 48 telegrams), believing the United States would not respond militarily. Stalin may have been motivated more by intramural competition with Mao Zedong, newly victorious in China, than by the global struggle with the United States. U.S. officials thought the attack was a Soviet foray that had to be met head on, a misjudgement that led to America's rearmament and eventual involvement in Vietnam.

In many other instances, Moscow's clients called the tune (or tried to), says Christian Ostermann, director of the Woodrow Wilson Center's Cold War International History Project:

• East German leader Walter Ulbricht was the driving force behind the Berlin Wall, not a hesistant Soviet Premier Nikita Khrushchev.

• Former Polish leader Wojciech Jaruzelski has long maintained he imposed martial law in 1981 to forestall a Soviet invasion. A Soviet general's diary indicates the opposite: Jaruzelski pleaded fruitlessly for Moscow to intervene, fearing he could not handle the challenge posed by Solidarity alone.

But the communist threat was no chimera:

The U.S. Venona code-breaking project and KGB archives belatedly removed any doubt that dozens of Moscow spies penetrated the U.S. government and the scientific community. While not every U.S. communist in the '30s and '40s was a spy, the U.S. party actively helped the Soviet Union. But Joe McCarthy isn't vindicated. By the time he began sounding off on the issue, Moscow had already cut ties to U.S. Communists. "What is vindicated is the much broader and more general… anticommunism of the postwar period," says historian John Haynes.

Also vindicated: fears about KGB dirty tricks. *The Sword and the Shield,* a new book based on secret KGB archives, details how Moscow tried to smear U.S. leaders ranging from Martin Luther King Jr. to President Reagan, obsessed over famous Soviet dissidents and planned sabotage in America and Europe.

—*Warren P. Strobel*

victory seemed to indicate, international communism was a coordinated, monolithic movement; that, as the Soviet atomic bomb appeared to show, a new and far more devastating world war loomed on the horizon; that, as the spy cases revealed, the nation's most closely held secrets were transparent to the enemy. Today, half a century later, we can see how each of these fears became hopes, and then accomplishments, and then the means by which the West prevailed in the Cold War.

Authoritarianism. It was not at all unreasonable in 1949 to have feared the eventual triumph of authoritarianism: Democracy and capitalism had hardly enhanced their reputation during the 1930s, and the United States and Great Britain had defeated Nazi Germany in World War II only by collaborating with Stalin's Soviet Union. There were plenty of people who, during those difficult years of Depression and war, saw at least a short-term denial of liberties as a necessary evil and found a certain allure in a vision of socialism they hoped would overcome the shortcomings of capitalism. But as postwar economic recovery

proceeded, it began to reward lateral rather than hierarchical forms of organization: Only the decentralized, largely spontaneous market system could make the millions of decisions required each day if the supply and demand of goods and services was to be kept in balance. And with freedoms so obviously suppressed in the authoritarian East even as they flourished in the democratic West, it became increasingly hard to see how coercion could ever lead to equity. It was no coincidence, then, that as the Cold War neared its end, democracies were replacing, rather than succumbing to, dictatorships. Or that the first modern examples of what Marx understood a proletarian revolution to be—a spontaneous mass movement led by workers and intellectuals, aimed at achieving liberty and justice—occurred only in Eastern Europe in 1989 and in the Soviet Union in 1991.

Spheres of influence. We can now see, as a consequence, that the spheres of influence the United States and the Soviet Union maintained in Europe were always asymmetrical: The first existed by invitation, the second by imposition. Stalin may well have expected the Europeans to welcome him as a liberator at the end of World War II, but when that did not happen—largely because his regime's reputation preceded its armies—he could establish his authority only by imposing it. But that caused the Europeans beyond his reach to invite the Americans to remain as a counterweight. Europe was divided, as a result, but there was dissimilarity in the division: Washington's sphere of influence arose by consent; Moscow's by denying it. That distinction made all the difference in how the Cold War came out, because it allowed the NATO countries to legitimize the American presence through free elections that repeatedly ratified it. No such opportunities existed within the Warsaw Pact: hence the ease with which it fell apart in 1989–90 when the only glue that had kept it together—Moscow's determination to use force—itself dissolved.

Confrontation. *The Soviet Union closed all land routes from the West to Berlin in 1948. Britain and the United States responded with a massive airlift.*

International communism. The consolidation of Soviet authority in Eastern Europe, together with Mao's victory in China, caused many Americans in 1949 to worry that the Kremlin commanded not only the traditional resources of a great state but also the subversive capabilities of a purposefully expansionist ideology. If Marxism-Leninism continued to advance as it had since the end of World War II, then the Western democracies could find themselves surrounded by hostile communist states. What happened instead, though, was that as communists took over states, the states took over the communists. Quarrels over how to align a common ideology with dissimilar national interests led first the Yugoslavs, and then the Chinese, and then the Poles, Hungarians, and Czechs, to challenge Moscow's authority. By the 1970s the American diplomat W. Averell Harriman could point out, with total accuracy, that it was the *Soviet Union* that now found itself surrounded by hostile communist states. And by the end of the 1980s, so little was left of the international communist movement that it was difficult to remember why the West had ever feared it in the first place.

The bomb. The Soviet atomic bomb also alarmed the West in 1949, but its effect over the long run was to make war with the United States not more likely but less so. The single most important characteristic of the Cold War—the reason we attach the adjective to the noun—is that it went on for so long with such high levels of tension without ever producing a direct military clash between its major antagonists. The obvious explanation is nuclear weapons, which expanded the potential arena of mili-

tary conflict to such an extent that the superpowers had no way of fighting each other with any assurance of keeping their own territories insulated from the resulting violence. Since wars had mostly arisen, in the past, over the *protection* of territory, this was a fundamental change in the way nations thought about, and used, military force. The Cold War may well be remembered as the point at which the costs of hot wars, at least among the great powers, became too exorbitant, the benefits too problematic, and the issues that had always before provoked such wars too insignificant. The fact that the Soviet Union collapsed with its military power intact is as eloquent an indication as one might want of such power's ultimate irrelevance.

Espionage. Even the spies look less sinister now than they did in 1949, despite the fact that we now know there were more of them than anyone then suspected. For the Cold War also changed our thinking about secrecy. Whereas the idea in the past had been to *conceal* information from enemies, a paradoxical side effect of ICBMs was the reconnaissance satellite, from which very little could be concealed. The Americans and the Russians soon saw the benefits of this new technology and agreed tacitly to tolerate it: Neither side made any effort to shoot down such spies in space, as a well-known spy in the sky, U-2 pilot Francis Gary Powers, had been shot down over the Soviet Union in 1960. The strategic arms limitation agreements of the 1970s could hardly have worked without overhead surveillance. But if transparency made sense when it came to the arms race, might it have at earlier stages of the Cold War? We know little, as yet, about how Stalin used the information his spies provided. There is reason to suspect, though, that on balance it reassured him by minimizing the possibility of surprise, just as reconnaissance satellites did for a subsequent generation of Cold War leaders. If that is the case, then some future historian may well revise what we think of the spies as well, finding that even in those deep fears there was some hope.

United at last. *Doing what was for more than 40 years unthinkable, East Berliners used crowbars and sledgehammers to tear down the wall on Nov. 9, 1989.*

The world has spent the past half-century having its worst fears not confirmed. That is a big difference from the way in which it spent the first half of this century, when the opposite happened. No one could have anticipated, in 1900, that the next five decades would see unprecedented violence, including two world wars, a nearly successful effort to wipe out an entire people, and the invention of the most lethal form of military technology in human history.

But it is equally the case that few people at the beginning of 1950 could have imagined that the five decades to follow would witness great-power peace—that, although the world was hardly free from violence and injustice during the second half of the 20th century, the record was decidedly preferable to that of the first half. Fears did become hopes, although it took us a while to begin to realize what was happening. With the dancing feet, and then the hammers and crowbars, and then the bulldozers and backhoes at the Berlin Wall, however, a certain amount of progress in human affairs became difficult to deny.

John Lewis Gaddis is Robert A. Lovett professor of history at Yale University. His most recent book is We Now Know: Rethinking Cold War History.

From *U.S. News & World Report,* October 18, 1999, pp. 38–45. © 1999 by U.S. News & World Report, L.P. Reprinted by permission.

Dixie's Victory

The old confederacy got only as far north as Pennsylvania, but its great-grandchildren have captured America's culture. Joshua Zeitz looks at sports, entertainment, and religion to show how.

Joshua Zeitz

About 60 years ago, in July 1942, a 35-year-old coal miner from East Kentucky named Jim Hammittee packed up his belongings and traveled with his wife to Detroit, where he found work in a roller-bearing plant. "When I first came there, we only planned to stay till the war was over and then we's moving back South," he later recalled. "But by the time the war's over in 1945, we had pretty well adjusted and accepted that way of life as the way we wanted to live. So we settled down...." The Hammittees raised three children in the Detroit suburbs. Except for trips to visit friends and kin, they never returned to their native South.

Jim Hammittee and his family were part of a demographic revolution that changed America. Between 1910 and 1970 more than 11 million Southerners pulled up stakes and settled in the North, mostly in the industrial Northeast and Midwest, and in Western boom states like California and Washington. Meanwhile, another internal migration caused the almost overnight transformation of the South's traditional rural landscape. In just two decades between 1940 and 1960, roughly 9 million Southern farmers, well over half the region's total agricultural force, left the cotton patches of the Mississippi Delta and the wheat fields of the Southern plains for cities like Houston, Dallas, Richmond, and Atlanta.

These two migrations, from South to North and from farm to city, amounted to a major turning point in American cultural history. They're why jazz and the blues graduated from being regional "race music" to being the stuff of PBS documentaries and college courses. They're why white Manhattanites travel to Harlem to eat "soul food" at the landmark restaurant Sylvia's and why the whole nation is involved in a never-ending debate about the varieties of barbecue. They're why Southern folk music has become "American roots" music. They help explain why Wal-Mart, once just a small Southern chain, represents American consumer culture in Argentina and Brazil, China and South Korea.

In the mid-twentieth century the arrival of Southern rural traditions in the urban marketplace created a new breed of Southland culture that exploded onto the national scene. At the same time, the millions of white Southerners planting new roots in the North introduced the rest of the country to their conservative religious and political culture and to once-regional pastimes like stock car racing and country music. The consequences have been revolutionary.

Surprisingly, though, while the effects of the black Southern migration have garnered considerable academic attention, only recently have historians considered the importance of that other stream of Southern country migrants. The significance of their travels is apparent everywhere. NASCAR ranks as one of the most popular and lucrative spectator sports nationwide, claiming some 40 million fans, staging races from Chicago to Phoenix, and recently closing a $2.8 billion television deal with NBC and Fox. And recording industry executives have long ceased to laugh at what Northern sophisticates once ridiculed as "hillbilly" music. With the sole exception of rock music, annual country music sales over the past decade have rivaled or outstripped all other genres, including pop, rap, hip hop, R&B, and jazz. At the same time, mainline Christian churches in every region find themselves steadily eclipsed by their fundamentalist and charismatic competitors, which formerly bore a distinctly Southern profile and were widely regarded as dying. More and more, it appears, Southern culture has become *American* culture.

It is one of history's ironies that white Southern culture never stood a chance of becoming nationally ascendant until the Old South itself became a relic. And that didn't occur until quite recently. Although the former Confederate states were hardly immune to economic and social changes after the Civil War, the region's fundamental social and economic landscape remained remarkably much the same in the 1920s as it had been in the 1860s. Southern boosters like the brash young journalist Henry Grady were heralding the emergence of a "New South" as early as 1886, but the historian Jack Temple Kirby reminds us that this vision was largely predicated on "hyperbole and fraud." Well into the twentieth century "the region remained rural and poor."

All of this changed with the coming of the New Deal and World War II. Federal subsidy programs initiated in the 1930s helped spur crop reductions and land consolidations that forced millions of tenant farmers off the land, while technological innovations in the 1940s and 1950s—chemical pesticides, fertilizers, the mechanical cotton picker—swiftly transformed Southern agriculture from a labor-intensive endeavor to a capital-intensive one. These structural developments, in addition to a massive infusion of federal defense and research dollars during World War II and the early Cold War, helped thrust the South into the modern age.

In 1920 the population of nearly every Southern state was at least two thirds rural, a figure all the more remarkable when we remember that the U.S. Census qualified towns of just 2,500 as urban. By 1960 everything had changed. Industrial work had outstripped farming for more than a decade, and in eight Southern states a majority of citizens now lived in urban areas, where they were swiftly closing regional gaps in education and income. In short, the South finally started to resemble the rest of the country. Paradoxically, it was at just this historical moment that Southland culture matured and circulated nationally.

Why then? Pete Daniels, a leading student of that culture, has written that "having worked outdoors in harmony with the seasons most of their lives," many white and black migrants "resented confining hourly jobs that demanded discipline and regularity. Each day they faced the whip, chair, and pistol of corporate management that punished them for displaying any residue of wildness. They chafed at punching a time clock and at other constraints that challenged their will, and they longed for escape, if not retribution." One means of escape—and retribution—was stock car racing, a sport that had evolved from outlaw origins during the Depression into a wildly popular industry by the early 1950s.

Early racers were, strictly speaking, not stock car racers at all. They were professional "trippers," drivers in the liquor racket who used expensively souped-up automobiles to outrun revenue agents. Trippers drove every variety of car, but they generally preferred 1939 and 1940 Fords, with easily available spare parts that could be modified for greater speed and better suspension, and with generous trunk space to accommodate their cargo. Trippers tended to be mountain folk and thus had had to master the blind curves and nonexistent shoulders of old hill country roads. Dexterity and speed were imperative; losing the race meant prison.

Many trippers took to racing for sport and occasionally for prize money in their spare time. Some early NASCAR greats like Junior Johnson and the Flock brothers—Bob and Fonty—got their start hauling home brewed whiskey for their parents and only gradually found themselves drawn to the racetrack. Even as his competitive racing star ascended in the 1950s, Johnson faithfully plied his talents for the family business. He was arrested in 1956, served 11 months for liquor trafficking, and returned to the track in 1959 in time to participate in a fierce NASCAR run at Charlotte, North Carolina, where he drove another contestant into a wall.

Informal car racing flourished in the 1940s, when war production gave Southerners unprecedented capital to put into cars and wagers. Tim Flock, an early NASCAR Grand National champion and younger brother to Bob and Fonty, insisted that modern stock car racing was inaugurated immediately after the war in a "cow pasture right outside Atlanta, Georgia," where drivers competed for cash prizes that could total as much as $20,000. For the most part these early races were rowdy affairs, their fans notorious for boozing, womanizing, and supremely proficient cursing.

It took a visionary to realize the commercial potential of stock car racing in a modernizing South. William Getty France, a service station owner in Daytona Beach, Florida, and an occasional participant in so-called outlaw races, understood the appeal this raffish new sport held for the country migrants in their newfound factories. On December 14, 1947, he convened a summit of three dozen leading mechanics and racers to form a sanctioning body for stock car competitions. Thus was born the National Association for Stock Car Auto Racing (NASCAR). "Big Bill" France became the organization's first president.

From its inception NASCAR embodied the split personality of postwar Southland culture: at once urban and market oriented, yet still close to its rural, precommercial roots. Locked at first in tough competition with four other sanctioning organizations, France's NASCAR sponsored standard races featuring modified cars, but it also launched a 150-mile contest at Charlotte whose participants were allowed to drive only automobiles that were "strictly stock"—that is, wholly unenhanced. The ploy was a great success with many fans, who enjoyed seeing professionals race the same cars an ordinary consumer could own. It was an even bigger hit with the car companies; they quickly recognized the marketing potential in NASCAR and invested accordingly. Keeping his eye on commercial strategy, France also enforced stern discipline. Even such driving legends as Tim Flock, Lee Petty, and Red Byron found they could pay a high price, in cumulative points lost, if they participated in unsanctioned races or otherwise bucked Big Bill's authority.

Yet if NASCAR was big business, its success was intimately related to its self-styled reputation as a place of last refuge for Southerners who missed the wild pulse of old country ways. So NASCAR promoted its drivers as cowboys on wheels, drinkers, skirt chasers and partygoers, whose much-publicized (and often exaggerated) debauches offered spectators to behave just as raucously—or at least to dream of it. Drivers like Curtis Turner gave NASCAR fans plenty of legend to revel in. Decked out in his trademark silk suits, Turner partied with movie stars and burned through enormous sums of money—$6,000 a month, according to some sources. His fellow driver Smokey Yunick remembered spending "a lot of time with Curtis, drinking, chasing women, racing, raising hell, teaching people how to turn around in the middle of the road at 60 miles an hour, putting cars in swimming pools."

Over the years, as its fans climbed the socioeconomic ladder, NASCAR angled for a more respectable image. In the 1950s it banned women from the pit, thus drawing to a premature close the racing careers of drivers like Sara Christian, Louise Smith, and Ethel Flock Mobley. As the organization steadily moved North, where millions of white transplants demonstrated as much enthusiasm for the sport as their Southern cousins, it began to look less like itself. By 1960 the Southern circuit had eight paved courses; in the 1970s officials introduced organized prayer services at the start of races. In time the tracks came to resemble big-city sports arenas. At Darlington, South Carolina, spectators who can afford $500 tickets are now ushered off to the Azalea Terrace; others vie for even more expensive chairs in the President's Suite or the Fourth Turn Club. In perhaps the most conspicuous example of NASCAR's self-reformation, drivers are now fined $10,000 for fighting.

If skeptics had any lingering doubt about NASCAR's stature as a national pastime, the coverage of this year's Daytona 500 put the issue to rest. On February 17, NBC bumped its coverage of the Winter Olympics in Utah in favor of the race at Daytona Beach. The decision reflected NASCAR's immense profitability to its sponsor networks. In 2001 NBC's stock car ratings jumped 34 percent over the previous year; among men earning $75,000 and more, a phenomenal 74 percent. NASCAR is no longer a Southern phenomenon.

Writing in the mid-1990s, Peter Applebome, a former Atlanta bureau chief for *The New York Times*, affirmed that country music had become "white America's music of choice," and Nashville, the capital of country, "the Tin Pan Alley of the nineties." What was once a marginal form of entertainment is today the staple of more radio stations—2,600, to be precise—than any other kind of music. Seventy million Americans tune into country and help drive what has become a two-billion-dollar industry. Country superstar Garth Brooks has sold more than 60 million records, making him second only to the Beatles in total U.S. sales.

Unlike stock car racing, country music was a highly lucrative industry as early as the 1920s, when advances in recording and radio helped capture and institutionalize the "hillbilly" sounds rural Southerners had invented, and reinvented, over the better part of two centuries. Bill C. Malone, the leading historian of country music, has written that the South prior to World War II was sufficiently conservative to encourage "the preservation of older values and institutions," particularly a rich "folk culture." Yet that folk culture, at least in its musical form, was always a "vigorous hybrid."

The mix contained evangelical hymns and camp songs (first dubbed "gospel" music in 1875), African-American song styles—most notably the blues—outpourings of New York City's Tin Pan Alley, whose professionals produced a variety of music wide enough to satisfy both Northern urbanites and Southern country folk. Most regional troubadours probably

didn't realize that such Southern favorites as "Old Dan Tucker," "Listen to the Mockingbird," and "Cotton-Eyed Joe" had been written by Northern minstrel troupes, or that sturdy American tunes like "Flop-Eared Mule," "Fire on the Mountain," and "Leather Breeches" had been born in Britain. Anthropologists in the 1920s were astounded to find "maverick" remnants of sixteenth century English verse alive and fully integrated into regional music in the Southern Appalachians. In some cases whole songs, like the haunting ballad "Barbara Allen," remained intact. Yet even these enthusiastic and knowledgeable students never appreciated the dynamic evolution of Southern country music. It was neither entirely authentic nor invented.

Thanks to technology—the phonograph and the radio—country music matured after World War I. At first record companies weren't interested in rural sounds. But early radio producers were, and in the twenties radio fast outpaced the phonograph as a source of popular home entertainment. Between 1920—the first year of commercial broadcasting—and 1930, annual sales of radios jumped from $60 million to $842 million. At the close of the 1920s more than 12 million American households owned radio sets.

Because most stations then could reach only local audiences, their selection of music tended to be more democratic than the recording industry's. Small stations carried local country talent from the beginning, and in 1922 the Atlanta *Journal's* radio station, WSB, became the first high-power outlet to feature what Americans soon called "hillbilly music," and for the first time millions of listeners heard authentic country talent like "Fiddlin' John" Carson.

Following quickly on the heels of WSB's coup, WBAP in Fort Worth invented the first-ever broadcast "barn dance," a live country-music and talk program that proved immensely popular with Southern listeners. By the late 1920s WLS (Chicago) and WMS (Nashville) had perfected the form with "National Barn Dance" and "Grand Ole Opry," two mainstays of American radio culture: "Barn Dance" ran for a quarter-century, and the "Opry" is with us still. By the 1940s "Grand Ole Opry" was perhaps the most admired radio show in the United States, with a cast of songsters and comedians that included Roy Acuff, Bill Monroe, Minnie Pearl, and "Uncle Dave" Macon. Like its Chicago counterpart, the "Opry" purveyed rural folk culture with an urban, commercial twist. After the 1920s that combination, more than anything else, would define the otherwise eclectic and diffuse art form that was country music.

The early success of hillbilly radio spurred the recording industry into action. While it's not clear who the first country recording artist was, good money is on the duo of Alexander Campbell ("Eck") Robertson, a fiddle player from Amarillo, Texas, and Henry Gilland, of Altus, Oklahoma, who on impulse traveled together to New York in June 1922 to cut a few tracks for Victor. The seminal moment in country recording came several years later, in August 1927, when a professional talent scout and producer, Ralph Peer, discovered and recorded modern country's first two sensations, the Carter Family and Jimmie Rodgers.

Originally comprising Alvin Pleasant ("A.P.") Carter, his wife, Sara, and his sister-in-law Maybelle, the Carters remained popular long after their joint singing career ended in the 1940s. Together they recorded over 300 songs for various labels. Their repertoire of new and traditional material, their trademark three-part harmony, and Maybelle's unique thumb-brush method on lead guitar gained a wide following throughout the South. Long after hillbilly music had gone mainstream and invaded the North, so-called Carter Family songs, like "Keep on the Sunny Side" and "The Wabash Cannonball," remained standard titles in the catalogues.

While the Carters gave the fledgling industry a down-home, family aura, Jimmie Rodgers, a native of Meridian, Mississippi, cultivated a somewhat different image as country music's "singing brakeman." He was the genre's first self-styled rambling balladeer. In truth Rodgers's railroad days were short lived: He developed tuberculosis, which, coupled with his hard-living ways, drove him to an early grave in 1933. But in his few years of productive fame, his appealing blend of old and new music, his distinctive yodeling style, and his Western affectations brought him a level of renown unprecedented among country artists.

In the 1930s and early 1940s the evolving style that the Carters and Rodgers helped create became a national sensation, urged along by two unrelated phenomena: electrification and World War II.

Musicians and guitar makers had experimented with electrifying string instruments as early as the 1920s. The electric guitar made its country-music debut in Texas in 1934, and new models manufactured by Gibson, Rickenbacker, Bigsby, and Fender soon made it widely accessible to small-time musicians. In turn, electrification helped spur the decade's "honky-tonk" sound, as small roadside bars throughout the Southwest featured a new form of country music that was both electrified and more rhythmic (so that customers could dance to it) than the usual hillbilly fare. These modern features helped make country more accessible to non-Southerners; World War II accelerated the process exponentially.

Since U.S. Army training camps were disproportionately located in Southern states, millions of Northern GIs heard their first licks of hillbilly music while sojourning in Dixie. Ferlin Husky, a popular country performer during the 1950s, recalled serving in the merchant marine with "lots of boys ... who had never really heard country music before, and it was interesting to see how fast they acquired a taste for it." So fast, it seems, that by 1945 GIs stationed in Munich, Germany, were debating the relative talents of Frank Sinatra and Roy Acuff. Well into the postwar period, the armed forces would continue to anchor the nation's country-music obsession. In 1960 some 65 percent of all country record sales took place at base PX's.

At the same time, war production catalyzed an exodus of Southern whites, and they took their music with them. In the 1950s the ABC Music Corporation, Chicago's largest jukebox supplier, reported that of its 12 city routes, 2 were dominated by country music. The city's largest record store, Hudson-Ross, found that in neighborhoods where Southern transplants were heavily concentrated, 30 percent of its sales volume was country and western. The trend had prompted *Billboard* to run headlines like HILLBILLY TUNES GAIN POPULARITY IN

BALTIMORE, and HILLBILLY TUNES SCORE BIG HIT IN MOST DETROIT JUKES.

Country was also making considerable headway in California, thanks to the influx of Dust Bowl migrants during the 1930s and defense-industry workers in the 1940s. By 1945 a music writer in the state's East Bay region could report, "It hasn't been so many years since Hillbilly and Western programs were a real scarcity out here.... Boy, OH BOY, it's a different story now! Turn the dial just any hour of the day and you'll get a good old time program of OUR KIND of music." Even in so unlikely a place as New York City, the country sound was coming into its own. In 1947 "Grand Ole Opry" staged a two-night performance at Carnegie Hall and grossed $9,000.

Already enjoying a national profile, country music continued to evolve in the 1950s and 1960s in much the same way it had originally ambled onto the airwaves and 78s in the 1920s: by melding tradition and commercialism. As home to the "Opry," Nashville attracted considerable recording talent. In the 1950s the city gave birth to what was termed the "Nashville sound" or the Chet Atkins Compromise, a highly electrified pop-country blend, made wildly popular by rising talents like Atkins, Elvis Presley, Johnny Cash, Jim Reeves, and Patsy Cline, the cowgirl sensation who always felt most comfortable with country music and never quite reconciled herself to performing pop hits like "Walking After Midnight," "I Fall to Pieces," and" Crazy. " The 1960s and 1970s saw this formula tempered but essentially left intact as country music—now electrified and rhythmic and spread to the North and West—set out to conquer television. Two of the first and most successful experiments in country television were "The Wilburn Brothers Show," which helped propel Loretta Lynn to stardom, and "The Porter Wagoner Show," which in 1967 provided a national stage for a young, blonde country-pop hopeful named Dolly Parton. As always, the music was in flux, but the country style remained so distinct and recognizable that many listeners confused new creations like "Tennessee Stud," "The Long Black Veil," and "The Battle of New Orleans" with traditional folk music.

Since the 1970s country stars from Willie Nelson, Kris Kristofferson, and Kenny Rogers to Garth Brooks and Lyle Lovett have continued to merge old and new aesthetics in a way that appeals to an immense national audience. Like NASCAR, country music triumphed at the moment when the South itself began to modernize demographically and economically, so its ascendance is a mark of both Dixie's triumph and its metamorphosis.

The South's cultural conquest has also had powerful religious implications. In his classic 1931 work *Only Yesterday: An Informal History of the Nineteen Twenties*, Frederick Lewis Allen recalled the famous 1925 Scopes monkey trial as a turning point for American religion. "Theoretically, Fundamentalism had won," Allen observed, noting that a local court in Dayton, Tennessee, had essentially upheld a state law enjoining public schools from teaching Charles Darwin's theory of evolution. "Yet really Fundamentalism had lost ... and the slow drift away from Fundamentalism certainly continued." Allen's book sold more than a million copies and became "the font at which most subsequent writers about the decade initially drank," according to the historian Roderick Nash. Echoing Allen's insight on the topic, scholars and journalists like Mark Sullivan, author of the 1935 bestseller *Our Times: The United States, 1900-1925*, concluded that the "Scopes trial marked the end of the age of *Amen* and the beginning of the age of *Oh Yeah!*" Allen and Sullivan would have been astonished by what the next 70 years would reveal. The evangelical Christians hadn't been defeated; they were simply regrouping. From their base in the South they have brought conservative Christianity to the rest of the country.

Over the past several decades, mainline Christian groups—most notably those affiliated with the United Methodist Church, the Presbyterian Church (U.S.A.), the Episcopal Church, the Evangelical Lutheran Church in America, and the United Church of Christ—have seen their memberships fall off precipitously, while evangelical, charismatic, and fundamentalist sects have emerged as an almost equal force within America's splintered Christian community. Today roughly 50 million Americans are affiliated with mainline churches, while 45 million others identify themselves as evangelicals. The battle that began in a small Tennessee courtroom is far from over.

All evangelicals share a commitment to the doctrine of salvation, to personal conversion experiences, to the authority of Scripture, and to missionary work to spread the gospel. Fundamentalism first emerged at the turn of the last century as a particular strain of evangelicalism. It was a reaction to liberalism, particularly in the leading Christian denominations, which were trying to reconcile the Bible with modern science and social activism.

Fundamentalists championed biblical inerrancy and the literal reading of Scripture. They also believed in dispensational premillennialism, a doctrine that prophesied Christ's imminent return to earth. They were deeply scornful of their liberal counterparts, particularly adherents of the activist Social Gospel movement, who tended to believe in postmillennialism, the idea that Christ's Second Coming would only follow a 1,000-year era of peace. They also argued incessantly with Pentecostals, another group of conservative evangelicals who shared many of the fundamentalists' convictions but who also believed that the Holy Spirit could bestow special gifts upon the saved—for instance, glossolalia, the ability to speak in tongues.

Though most nonevangelicals see little distinction among the various conservative factions, a wide gulf persists between Pentecostals and other "charismatic" sects, on one hand, and strict fundamentalists, on the other. This is the source of the lasting animosity between two modern-day leaders of the Christian right—Pat Robertson, who professes to speak in tongues, and Jerry Falwell, who once joked that glossolalia was just a symptom of indigestion.

In the early 1900s conservative theologians in the South pretty much ruled the Baptist, Pentecostal, and Presbyterian denominations in their region. But in the North there was a real fight, with the leading churches split almost evenly between liberals and fundamentalists. Greatly concerned after World War I by the apparent harbingers of moral and cultural decay—labor strife, loosening sexual mores, modernist art and literature—the

conservatives went on the offensive. In 1919 they formed the World Christian Fundamentals Association and, under the direction of leaders like William Bell Riley of Minneapolis and J. Gresham Machen of Princeton, undertook to purge liberals from the Northern churches.

The battle came to a head in 1925, when a group of local boosters in Dayton, Tennessee, persuaded a young high school science teacher, John Scopes, to violate the state's anti-evolution law. They merely wanted to draw attention to their economically depressed crossroads town. Instead, what followed was a sensational trial that pitted the famous lawyer Clarence Darrow, a committed civil libertarian and an almost fanatical atheist, against William Jennings Bryan, the famously eloquent former congressman from Nebraska who had thrice failed to attain the Presidency but who remained a hero to the rural, fundamentalist South. The trial's climax came when Darrow called his adversary to the stand as a biblical expert and Bryan admitted that some Scriptural language might be more allegorical than literal.

Although the trial was technically a win for the prosecution, Northern liberals declared it a great victory for their cause. Bryan, they said, had unintentionally exposed fundamentalism for the inchoate drivel it was, while Darrow had established the modern North's supremacy over the backward, hyperreligious South. Fundamentalism receded in the Northern denominations and became essentially a regional phenomenon. But the conservatives were far from licked. In the decades following the trial they chartered missions, publishing houses, and radio stations; they founded 70 Bible institutions nationwide, including Bryan College in Dayton but also Moody Bible Institute in Chicago and Riley's Northwestern Bible Training School in Minneapolis. In the 1940s they began to reappear in public life.

In the West, areas like Orange County, California, which had long been home to pockets of Pentecostal and fundamentalist activity, witnessed an explosion of conservative Christian activity during the massive influx of Southern migrants that began with World War II. In Northern California's East Bay area, mainline churches formed an umbrella group, the United Ministry, to organize religious worship for tens of thousands of new defense workers, almost a quarter of whom came from Dixie. The United Ministry found its efforts largely ignored; only about 2 percent of migrant families attended the services. Instead, new defense workers set up their own evangelical and fundamentalist churches, many of them in storefronts or private homes. By 1945 area residents could listen to radio sermons by C. L. Hunter of Texas, the "Cowboy Evangelist," or Bebe Patten of Tennessee, the "Girl Evangelist."

In the Midwest many Southern transplants also found their new local Baptist churches at once unsatisfyingly staid and yet liberal in the interpretation of the Bible, and so they began establishing their own fundamentalist churches. Although in 1894 the (liberal) Northern Baptist and (fundamentalist) Southern Baptist Conventions had signed the Fortress Monroe agreement, a mutual pledge not to step across the Mason-Dixon line, by the late 1940s the Northern Baptists found themselves on the defensive. So many Dixieland transplants were organizing fundamentalist churches that in 1949 the SBC voted to abrogate Fortress Monroe. In response, the NBC became ABC: The Northern Baptist Convention changed its name to the American Baptist Convention and pledged retaliation. But the momentum was with the South. In the 1950s and 1960s the Southern Baptists were the swiftest-growing denomination in Ohio. By 1971 they had registered 169 churches in Michigan, 230 in Indiana, 380 in Ohio, and 893 in Illinois. In Ohio and Michigan the American Baptists and Southern Baptists enjoyed almost equal numbers.

The rise of evangelical Christianity in the North and West has reinvigorated politics. On the whole, Pentecostals and fundamentalists assume more conservative positions on social issues, like abortion and the separation of church and state, than do mainline Protestants, Catholics, and Jews. Scholars have recently suggested that much of the postwar conservative movement's strength, particularly in California, grew out of this relatively new infusion of fundamentalism. It is precisely this religious migration that accounts for the rise of Rep. Gary Condit, a socially conservative Democrat, born in Oklahoma, the son of a Baptist minister, a transplant to the West Coast, and once a local favorite in his heavily evangelical district.

The importance of the great white migration has not gone unnoticed, though often enough liberal writers like John Eagerton, the Nashville author of *The Americanization of Dixie: The Southernization of America*, have been quick to castigate Southern migrants for "exporting" the "vices" of their region "without importing values." Or, as Peter Applebome argued more recently, "at a time when a Democratic president like Bill Clinton is coming out for school prayer, going along with sweeping Republican legislation shredding welfare and taking his cues from a consultant, Dick Morris, who formerly worked for Southern archconservatives like Jesse Helms and Trent Lott, when race is a fractious national obsession … when the Supreme Court is acting as if Jefferson Davis were chief justice … in times such as these, to understand America, you have to understand the South."

Despite his tone of aggrievement, Applebome's point is sound: Southern culture today enjoys far more national influence than it has at any time since a Virginian was given command of the Continental Army.

In 1971, in the first stages of a short-lived country-music phase, the folk singer Joan Baez helped popularize Robbie Robertson's wistful composition "The Night They Drove Old Dixie Down." The song was recorded by many others, including Bob Dylan and the Band. Its title is revealing enough, but the final verse, uttered by a former Confederate, Virgil Caine, is more poignant still: "Like my father before me I will work the land / Like my brother above me who took a rebel stand / He was just 18, proud and brave, but a Yankee laid him in his grave / I swear by the mud below my feet, you can't raise a Caine back up when he's in defeat." In truth the Virgil Caines of the world stopped working the land several decades ago. They moved to Nashville, Atlanta, Chicago, and Los Angeles. They went to work in factories and offices. They took their culture, their music, and their religion with them, and they have changed America.

From *American Heritage*, August/September 2002, pages 46, 48-55. Reprinted by permission of American Heritage, Inc., a division of Forbes, Inc.

The American Century

From movies to microchips to military might, Uncle Sam has left his mark around the world

By Michael Barone

On Dec. 8, 1941, the day after the attack on Pearl Harbor, Franklin D. Roosevelt stood before Congress and called for a declaration of war. "The American people in their righteous might," the president proclaimed, "will win through to absolute victory."

Absolute victory: No compromise, no deals with the enemy. *Righteous might:* Not just a strong America—a virtuous one. *The American people:* A people united, not just the military, or a few elected leaders.

With those 13 words, FDR sketched a history of the 20th century that, if exceedingly short, was also disarmingly accurate. In February 1941, Henry Luce, in his famous "American Century" editorial in *Life*, called on Americans to "accept wholeheartedly our duty and our opportunity as the most powerful and vital nation in the world…to exert upon the world the full import of our interests."

And so we have. The most riveting story of the 20th century is the rise of totalitarianism and its defeat at the hands of America. But there are other stories, other chapters. Luce could have no way of knowing it when he penned his editorial, but Americans literally took him at his word, thrusting upon the world the full import of their interests and energies over the course of these hundred years. At the dawn of a new millennium now, one may look back at the old and find it impossible not to recognize an indelible American imprint in virtually every area of human endeavor—in science and medicine, business and industry, arts and

letters—it has been Uncle Sam's century. Over the years, America has been criticized by friend and foe for a dominance both real and perceived. But there is no gainsaying the fact that, if nations were people, Uncle Sam would be the man of the century.

The American legacy is impressive—but it is one no one could have predicted at the dawn of the now departing century. A hundred years ago, America was the largest of the great powers. Its economy had surged ahead of those in Europe. For all of America's sweep and swagger, however, Britain was the dominant world power, with the largest empire and Navy, rivaled only by Germany, with its huge Army and strength in science.

America, for many reasons, was unwilling and unready to inherit the mantle of leadership. The United States was united in name only, the wounds of the Civil War still far from healed. Though wages in the North were twice those in the South, few Southerners deigned to cross the Mason-Dixon line. On both sides of the divide, racial segregation was the order of the day. On the borders, meanwhile, immigrants were pouring in—17 million between 1890 and 1914. The new arrivals gave cold comfort to America's elites. The Poles, Jews, Italians, they feared, couldn't possibly become *true* Americans.

Happily, the elites were wrong—dead wrong. Before too long, an America that had been "a nation of loosely connected islands," as historian Robert Wiebe called it, was becoming a more cohesive

U.S. POPULATION:
 1900: 75,994,575
 2000: 273,482,000*

MEDIAN AGE:
 1900: 22.9
 2000: 35.7

URBAN VS RURAL:
 1900: 40% urban, 60% rural
 2000: 75% urban, 25% rural

BIRTHRATE:
 1900: 32.3 births per thousand
 2000: 14.2 births per thousand

IMMIGRANT POPULATION:
 1900: 14.7 percent
 2000: 7.9 percent

BIGGEST SOURCE OF IMMIGRANTS:
 1900: Austria-Hungary
 2000: Mexico

* ESTIMATE FOR 2000 OR MOST RECENT STATISTIC AVAILABLE

and unified whole. The building blocks of the civic life we take for granted today soon began falling into place. The medical profession standardized the curricula of the nation's medical schools. The practice of law, once open to anyone, was limited to those who had passed state bar exams. Teachers worked from a common curriculum that emphasized English and civics. Education became a transforming engine. The number of kids enrolled in high schools quadrupled from 1890 to 1910. At more rarefied levels, dozens of great research universities were formed.

NUMBER OF MILLIONAIRES:
1900: 3,000
2000: 3.5 million

AVERAGE INCOME:
1900: $8,620[*] a year
2000: $23,812 a year

DEATHS FROM INDUSTRIAL ACCIDENTS:
1900: 35,000 a year
2000: 6,100 a year

AVERAGE WORK WEEK
1900: 60 hours
2000: 44 hours

[*]ALL MONEY COMPARISONS ARE IN 1999 DOLLARS

A new order. The way America worked changed, too. Businesses were transformed from buccaneering, seat-of-the-pants outfits run by ragged eccentrics into professionally managed organizations. Factories were increasingly run according to the precepts of "scientific" management. The concept was pioneered by Frederick W. Taylor. His time-and-motion studies reduced each task to single steps, allowing managers to maximize production, even by unskilled laborers. Suddenly, the chaotic and unstable economy of the 19th century was a thing of the past.

Nowhere was change so pronounced as in the military. "We are a great nation," Theodore Roosevelt said in 1898, "and we are compelled, whether we will or not, to face the responsibilities that must be faced by all great nations." This was not just rhetoric. In February 1898, as Americans protested Spain's suppression of a revolt in Cuba, Assistant Secretary of the Navy Roosevelt ordered the Pacific fleet to stand ready to attack the Philippines if war came. It did, and before American forces could roust the Spaniards from Cuba, Admiral Dewey sailed into Manila Harbor and destroyed the Spanish fleet. To the surprise and delight of TR, the "splendid little war" sparked enthusiasm among Southerners and Northerners alike. Americans were suddenly possessed of a swaggering new confidence: They could project power far beyond their borders to achieve good ends.

That confidence swelled when Roosevelt, as president, won a treaty to let America build the Panama Canal. American engineers succeeded where the French had failed, bridging jungles and mountains with an elaborate system of interlocking channels; at the same time, Dr. Walter Reed conquered yellow fever. The lesson, taught in textbooks for years after, was simple—and breathtaking: American expertise could make the world a better place.

But the world was an increasingly perilous place, too. No sooner had the Panama Canal opened, in August 1914, than Europe was plunged into war—which leveraged its own kind of change. President Wilson nationalized the railroads and the shipyards. Newspapers were censored. War critics were jailed. In the meantime, Wilson raised a military of nearly 3 million men, and Americans took pride in helping to win "the war to end wars."

After, America boomed economically. But still it declined to take up the mantle of Britain, now exhausted by wartime costs and slaughter. At home Americans disagreed furiously about Prohibition and, in the Scopes trial of 1925, science and religion. Mass immigration was ended in 1924, but the melting pot kept bubbling. Millions of workers bought cars and fled the teeming tenements on new highways. For a brief, shining moment, Americans seemed freed from the workaday worries of the rest of the world.

So they were thoroughly unprepared for the shocks of the second third of the century—worldwide depression and the rise of totalitarianism. Between 1929 and 1933, the nation's economy shrank by nearly half; 1 in 4 workers was unemployed. Abroad, the wounds of World War I festered, the result, Lenin's Soviet Russia in 1918, Mussolini's Fascist Italy in 1922, Hitler's Nazi Germany in 1933.

Instead of dividing the nation, however, these shocks forged new bonds of common purpose. Popular culture helped. Despite the Depression, radio ownership doubled between 1929 and 1932. Americans went mad for movies. In 1930, in a country of 130 million people, movie attendance hit 90 million a week. The big screen created the strongest popular culture since Dickens and defined for the world a characteristic American style—breezy, friendly, open, optimistic.

All the way. But war clouds soon gathered again. The Sudetenland, Austria, Czechoslovakia—Nazi belligerence knew no bounds. Most Americans, however, were unmoved. It would require another president named Roosevelt to change that. In June 1940, as France surrendered to Hitler and Britain prepared for invasion, FDR started selling arms to Britain and boosted defense spending. Facing re-election, he took the politically risky steps of supporting a military draft, then dispatched 50 destroyers to Britain. Americans supported the moves, and Roosevelt was re-elected. Almost immediately, he won more aid for Britain. After Nazi forces attacked the Soviet Union in the summer of 1941, Roosevelt sent arms to Moscow and blocked oil sales to Japan. Again, Americans applauded: If it required war to stop totalitarianism, so be it.

Then came Pearl Harbor. "We are all in it together—all the way," FDR said in his fireside chat, two days later. "Every single man, woman, and child is a partner in the most tremendous undertaking in our American history." Roosevelt built his war effort on cooperation between big government, big business, big labor. America became "the arsenal of democracy," its industrial might churning out the awesome tools of victory: 7,333 ships, 299,000 aircraft, 634,000 jeeps, 88,000 tanks. The top-secret Manhattan Project, which cost $2 billion—the nation's total economic production in 1940 was $99 billion—produced the atomic bomb. The result was victory over Germany and Japan, confirming America's status as the world's dominant military and economic power.

Just as the first World War had, the war against the Axis powers wrought extraordinary change at home. Americans got used to working productively, and even creatively, in large organizations. Big business, big labor, and big government—with occasional friction—produced a bounteous economy, not another depression. Postwar America's "organization men" and "conformists" produced the baby boom, the habits of the bur-

cause of Joe Stalin, "an iron curtain" had fallen across Eastern Europe.

Americans responded boldly. The Truman Doctrine promised to protect all "free peoples of the world." The Marshall Plan provided vast economic aid to Europe. The NATO treaty of April 1949 was America's first peacetime military alliance. In June 1950, Truman sent troops to Korea to stop the Communist invasion. Defense spending increased, and stayed high for years. America was engaged in a "long, twilight struggle," John Kennedy said. And her people paid for it with high taxes for defense and foreign aid, a military draft, air-raid drills, and listening to Soviet threats of nuclear war over Berlin and Cuba. All that is taken for granted today, but in historic perspective it was extraordinary. "Only a society with enormous confidence in its achievements and in its future," as Henry Kissinger wrote later, "could have mustered the dedication and the resources to strive for a world order in which defeated enemies would be conciliated, stricken allies restored, and adversaries converted."

Doubts set in. It didn't last. Halfway around the globe, a commitment that started with just a few hundred Pentagon advisers escalated into a war with more than half a million American troops—a war that could not be won. Aides to Presidents Kennedy and Johnson had devised a military strategy in Vietnam that was incapable of working. Defense Secretary Robert McNamara scornfully dubbed it, "the social scientists' war."

It was a war many affluent Americans did not find important enough to draft their sons for. McNamara's draft system allowed college students to avoid service. Antiwar movements on elite campuses produced a generation of academics and professionals who regarded the United States and the Communists as morally equivalent. By 1968, many of the planners and supporters of the Vietnam War saw it as deeply immoral. They no longer believed, as the Roosevelts did, in American exceptionalism—the belief that this country was uniquely strong and uniquely good.

In other ways, the postwar system was breaking down. Congress had passed civil rights laws in response to the nonviolent movement led by Martin

Luther King Jr. But black protesters called for violence in response to white oppression.

Big government produced not only war and riots, but also stagflation—high inflation and low economic growth. Big businesses grew less supple and creative, turning out gas guzzlers with "planned obsolescence." Big labor unions stagnated, then lost membership. And the cultural unity of postwar America was splintering. Families with two television sets and several radios no longer watched the same shows and listened to the same music. The universal popular culture of midcentury soon gave way to rival countercultures, many hostile to old values. Starting in the late 1960s, birth rates fell and divorce and births to unwed mothers rose: "the great disruption," as Francis Fukuyama calls it. Crime and welfare dependency tripled from 1965 to 1975.

As the elites lost confidence in America, the American people lost confidence in the elites. Richard Nixon's rhetorical appeals to "the silent majority" rallied only some Americans, and his cool pursuit of geopolitical advantage, the opening to China, and withdrawal from Vietnam failed to engage Americans' yearning for moral purpose, even before his own moral authority was destroyed by Watergate.

Foreign policy elites increasingly saw American strength as malevolent, and were pleased to see it reduced. This was symbolized by the 1977 treaty to relinquish the Panama Canal. Elites, guilty about how America obtained the canal, saw this as necessary to prevent violence in Panama. But most voters still felt pride in this great American achievement, and opposition to the treaty energized Ronald Reagan's nearly successful challenge of President Gerald Ford in 1976.

American pride sank even lower when Iran refused to release 52 Americans held hostage in the U.S. Embassy in November 1979. Under international law, this was an act of war. But for months President Jimmy Carter refused to use force and tried to negotiate, and his half-hearted seven-helicopter rescue attempt in April 1980 failed. Each Carter policy was approved in the polls. But in the end, voters wanted results. Carter

geoning middle class reflected in the new universal culture of 1950s television. Church membership reached new highs. Crime fell to record lows. Confidence in major institutions surged. Americans were bound together by common experiences—the comprehensive high school, the military draft, large corporations, suburbia.

This was also Cold War America. In March 1946, Winston Churchill, now out of office, went to Fulton, Mo., with Harry Truman and proclaimed that, be-

ADULTS COMPLETING HIGH SCHOOL:
1900: 15 percent
2000: 83 percent

HOMES WITH ELECTRICITY:
1900: 8 percent
2000: 99.9 percent

PRICE OF A STAMP:
1900: 59 cents*
2000: 33 cents

FEDERAL BUDGET OUTLAY:
1900: $10.3 billion*
2000: $1.7 trillion

DEFENSE EXPENDITURES:
1900: $4 billion*
2000: $268 billion

NATIONAL DEBT:
1900: $24.8 billion*
2000: $5 trillion

PER CAPITA NATIONAL DEBT:
1900: $325*
2000: $23,276

VOTER TURNOUT:
1900: 73.7 percent
2000: 48.9 percent

BOOKS PUBLISHED
1900: 6,536
2000: 65,800

AVERAGE SIZE OF HOUSEHOLD:
1900: 4.76 persons
2000: 2.62 persons

BEER CONSUMPTION:
1900: 58.8 gallons per adult
2000: 31.6 gallons per adult

NUMBER OF BISON:
1900: 400
2000: 200,000

* MONEY COMPARISONS ARE IN 1999 DOLLARS

LIFE EXPECTANCY FOR MEN:
1900: 46.3 years
2000: 73.6 years

LIFE EXPECTANCY FOR WOMEN:
1900: 48.3 years
2000: 79.7 years

MOST POPULAR SONG:
1900: "Good-Bye Dolly Gray"
2000: "Believe"

DEATHS IN CHILDBIRTH:
1900: 9 per thousand
2000: 0.1 per thousand

CANCER DEATHS:
1900: 64 per 100,000
2000: 200 per 100,000

DIVORCED MEN:
1900: 0.3 percent
2000: 8.2 percent

DIVORCED WOMEN:
1900: 0.5 percent
2000: 10.3 percent

star. He shared most Americans' pride in their country and rejected the guilt complex of the elites. His tax cuts led to two decades of solid economic growth and low inflation, interrupted by recession briefly in 1990–91. Complacent corporate executives were ousted by leveraged buyouts and directors seeking more profits. Big corporations were challenged by tiny start-ups: IBM was replaced as the major high-tech firm by Microsoft. American computers and high-tech—the latest manifestation of 20th-century Americans' scientific and technological expertise—led the world. The peacetime expansions of the 1980s and 1990s produced 40 million new jobs, while the sputtering economies of Europe and Asia produced virtually none. Ordinary Americans' incomes surged and widespread stock ownership resulted in a stock market boom and real gains in wealth for the masses.

Unmatched prowess. Abroad Reagan, despite scorn from the elites, pursued an assertive policy like Harry Truman's. He increased defense spending, sent American troops to Grenada, and supported anti-Communist forces in Central America and Afghanistan. The defense buildup and Reagan's Strategic Defense Initiative convinced Soviet leaders that they could never match the economic and technological prowess of the United States.

Like the two Roosevelts, Reagan insisted on proclaiming the superiority of the American system. In London in 1983, he predicted the demise of the Soviet Union. In Berlin in 1987, he demanded, "Mr. Gorbachev, tear down this wall." By October 1989 the wall was history. The Soviet empire soon followed.

Today, at century's end, America is unquestionably the world's dominant military, economic, and cultural superpower. This has been the work of the American people. The 76 million of 1900 are now the 273 million of 2000. The descendants of the immigrants who choked the slums in 1900 are now firmly

interwoven into the American fabric. The descendants of the blacks who were excluded by segregation in 1900 now have full civil rights and are surging into the middle classes and upper ranks of society. The new immigrants from Latin America and East Asia who have arrived since the 1965 immigration reform are progressing as their counterparts did a century ago.

The American traditions of excellence fostered by the elite of the first third of the century and the characteristic American openness depicted in the popular culture of the second third of the century gave the American people the strength and the confidence to forge ahead in the last third of the century when so many in the elite lost confidence in their country. Sharing with Ronald Reagan the belief that this country is "a city on a hill," they have won through to absolute victory over totalitarianism, as Franklin Roosevelt promised, and have made this the American century that Henry Luce envisioned.

was beaten soundly by Reagan, whose threats to use force resulted in the hostages' release just as he was sworn into office.

Reagan embodied the characteristic American style of the 1930s and 1940s movies in which he himself had been a

From *U.S. News & World Report*, December 27, 1999, pp. 38-46. © 1999 by U.S. News & World Report L.P. Reprinted by permission.

What September 11th really wrought

America is getting back to normal after September 11th, partisan bickering and all. But the attacks may change politics in ways its politicians have not yet grasped

WASHINGTON, DC

IN ONE of the greatest political speeches, his second inaugural address, Abraham Lincoln argued that the civil war then raging was remaking American society despite the expectations and wishes of its leaders. "Neither party," he said, "expected for the war the magnitude or duration which it has already attained. Each looked for an easier triumph, and a result less fundamental and astounding."

Lincoln's equating of the difficulties of war with its consequences is telling. The civil war was momentous because it was traumatic. In contrast, the war against the Taliban has been "an easier triumph". Will it bring about "a result less fundamental"?

The war in Afghanistan, of course, is only the beginning of the war against terror. No one knows how further attacks—by or against America—would affect the country. But already some changes are clear. September 11th ended what Charles Krauthammer, a columnist, mocked as a decade-long "holiday from history", when headlines were dominated by O.J. Simpson, Monica Lewinsky and Gary Condit (and, lest Britons feel smug, by Princess Diana). The new seriousness has shocked people out of that sense of fantasy.

More important, September 11th changed the non-trivial features of the 1990s, too. Back then, business, technology and communications mattered, but politics did not. Local issues meant more than national ones. Bill Gates and Jack Welch ranked as heroes, but government officials, from the president down, were villains, or near it.

In different ways, all these features were predicated on peace and prosperity. The prosperity was eroding even before September 11th, with the bursting of the dotcom bubble. The peace ended that day. As a result, personal insecurity was added to the mix. At a time when almost every indicator of well-being shows a "damn-the-terrorists" self-confidence, one measure points the other way. An increasing number of people say they think the future for their children got worse after September 11th. Americans used to believe that their mainland, at least, was invulnerable to outside attack, and felt secure accordingly. They no longer do.

The implications are profound. Politics will now become more important again, since the more people feel insecure, the more they will turn to the government for defence. This is a point that goes back to Thomas Hobbes (because the life of man is "nasty, brutish and short", people band together and create governments for self-protection). The most noticeable change to have occurred in America after September 11th is therefore not so surprising; a sharp rise in the level of public trust in the institutions of government.

In the mid-1960s, two-thirds of Americans said they trusted the federal government to do the right thing most or all of time—the highest rate in the world. By the mid-1990s, that figure had fallen to 20%, the lowest in any democracy. On September 11th, the figure more or less doubled overnight (see chart on next page).

The scale of the change has been, to use Lincoln's term, astounding. The new trustfulness is felt on all sides, by Republicans and Democrats alike. Good opinions of the president, Congress, previously unknown cabinet officials and almost every institution of government have soared. Except in the case of the president himself, the rise in approval has been much larger than on any recent comparable occasion. "We're still too close to it, probably, to understand it all," the vice-president, Dick Cheney, told the *Washington Post* in late October. Still, he concluded, "it has altered the way the American people think about their government, and the role we have in society and overseas."

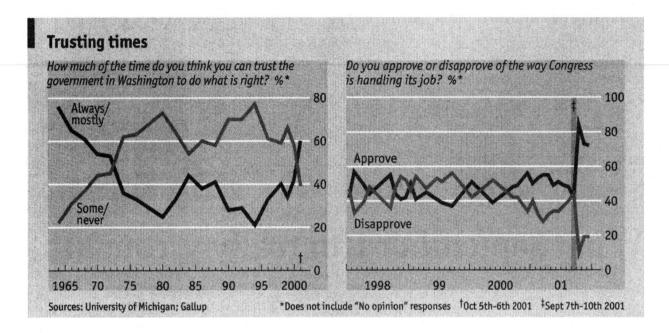

Trusting times

How much of the time do you think you can trust the government in Washington to do what is right? %*

Always/mostly

Some/never

1965 70 75 80 85 90 95 2000

Do you approve or disapprove of the way Congress is handling its job? %*

Approve

Disapprove

1998 99 2000 01

Sources: University of Michigan; Gallup   *Does not include "No opinion" responses   †Oct 5th–6th 2001   ‡Sept 7th–10th 2001

The persistence of trustfulness

The question is whether this level of trust will be sustained. If it were, it would affect America profoundly. In "The Confidence Gap" (1987), Bill Schneider and Seymour Martin Lipset argued that declining trust in government was the driving force of American politics in the 1970s and 1980s. It made Ronald Reagan's presidency possible, and Mr Schneider has argued since that it encouraged others, notably Newt Gingrich, to give history a shove in the right direction by pruning back the functions of the state still further. If this nation-defining trend were reversed, it would presumably make possible a new round of government activism, comparable to one that took place during the cold war.

In the immediate aftermath of September 11th, such an interpretation seemed plausible. President George Bush won a large increase in federal spending to rebuild New York, compensate the families of victims and bail out airlines. He set up a new office of homeland security, the first such executive expansion for a decade, and agreed that the federal government should assume responsibility for airport security. John Ashcroft, the attorney-general, obtained expanded powers to monitor and detain terrorist suspects. The anthrax attacks ensured that the public health system would play a larger role against bioterrorism.

Yet, four months later, politics as normal is back. The parties are bickering about tax cuts. Both sides are preparing to fight the 2002 elections on the economy, health care and education, issues that have dominated the agenda for years. Neither side expects the war to dampen partisan feelings. It is as if the attacks and the change in public sentiments never happened. Why?

For one thing, as Mr Schneider points out, opinion polls held at moments of crisis should always be taken with a pinch of salt. Respondents interpret questions about trust in government as "Who do you support, your representatives or Osama bin Laden?" (Mr Bush's personal approval rating is boosted by the same phenomenon.) Moreover, the fact that the big rise in trust took place right after September 11th—before the successes in Afghanistan—shows that it was driven not by popular acclaim for policies, but by a threatened nation rallying round the flag. As long as the sense of crisis remains, so will the level of trust. But, all things being equal, the two things are likely to fall in tandem. Already, the immediacy of the crisis is ebbing.

There is also evidence in the polls of public ambivalence towards government. When the Gallup organisation asked people whether they thought the government solved more problems than it created, it found the highest-ever proportion of respondents saying yes. But that was still only 42%, slightly smaller than the share which thinks the government creates more problems than it solves. When they asked people to rate the honesty of various professions, only a quarter gave members of Congress high marks, barely more than in 2000 (and far below the 90% rating for firemen and 84% for nurses in 2001). Even now, a narrow majority of Americans say they want a smaller government, providing fewer services. So, despite increased support for government at a general level, concerns about specific inefficiency or intrusiveness remain strong.

When all is said, the default setting for American politics is turned to "distrust", and only the biggest upheavals—civil war, depression, world war—can alter it profoundly. In his recent book, "The Strange Death of American Liberalism" (Yale, 2001), H. W. Brands argues that the expansion in the powers of government after the second world war was a historical anomaly. In the 1950s and 1960s, Americans defined themselves in opposition to the Soviet Union and its allies, and the occasional embarrassments of the comparison (America's treatment of blacks at home, for instance) drove politicians to enact the civil-rights legislation which expanded the federal government in the 1960s. When the ideological period of confrontation ceased and was replaced, with the start of détente, by traditional balance-of-power diplomacy, American politics began to revert to its distrustful mean, and the long slide in support for government began—exacerbated by defeat in Vietnam, Watergate and all the rest.

181

The war against terror, of course, is also a struggle of ideas rather than a territorial conflict. But this has never meant that it will have the same government-expanding effect as the cold war because, in one respect, it is quite different. Americans do not define themselves in contrast to terrorism in the same way as they did in opposition to communism. Mr bin Ladin's ideas seem too medieval and outlandish for direct comparison. Hence America's "asymmetric" conflict with small groups of terrorists is unlikely to have the same nation-defining quality as did the decades-long conflict between democratic and communist systems. The current high level of trust, therefore, is unlikely to be sustained. That, at least, is the politicians' view.

So far, all the examples of increased government activity have been in the area of national security itself or in sub-sectors of it (the airlines, for example). There is little evidence that the impetus to expand government is being carried beyond this. It is true that some mooted privatisations, of the Postal Service and of water-treatment plants around New Orleans, have been postponed. But these examples are few and far between, and would perhaps have happened anyway. It is also possible that, as recession takes its toll on local tax revenues, cities and states will be looking to save money over the next few years. If so, that would increase the pressure to privatise and shrink the role of the state.

Unchanging ways

Some Democrats had hoped that increased trust in government would translate into increased support for new entitlement programmes. The opposite seems to have happened. The "patients' bill of rights" (limiting the immunity of health maintenance organisations from being sued) had been high on the Democrats' agenda for this session of Congress. It is now dead. Debate may yet resume on a proposal to make prescription drugs available to old people through the government-funded Medicare system. But don't hold your breath: the proposal is costly, and federal dollars are more likely to go on defence. Gun sales have risen slightly, too, and new gun-control measures look unlikely. Paradoxically, then, one of the first effects of an attack that increased trust in government has been to destroy the most imminent proposals for increasing government's scope.

More broadly, if you compare domestic politics, the economy and foreign policy now with what they were like on September 10th, the striking thing is how little has changed, not how much. At home, politicians are reverting to partisan type, which could be significant: few things will do more to reduce trust in government than a year's worth of bickering.

On the economy, the terrorist attacks have not had the impact that was first feared. They did not cause the slowdown, of course (which had begun months before), nor did the response to them single-handedly destroy the federal budget surplus, which started to shrink in the summer. And although they may have deepened both, they do not seem likely to prolong the recession further than it would run anyway, at least if recent indicators are to be believed (the budget deficit is another matter).

On foreign policy, initial expectations of change have also been dashed. Europeans and many Democrats had hoped the war in Afghanistan would turn the Bush administration towards greater multilaterialism. That has not happened. Although Colin Powell, the secretary of state, cobbled together an impressive anti-terrorist alliance, in Afghanistan itself the allied contribution was confined to providing air bases, overflight rights and British and Australian special forces. The war was conducted from day to day by Americans and Afghans, not by the wider coalition.

Subsequently, America has not engaged in the nation-building operations in Afghanistan, though it will provide the lion's share of money for rebuilding. And the administration has made good on its promise, made before September 11th, to withdraw from two arms-control treaties, abrogating the anti-ballistic missile (ABM) treaty and killing off the protocol to enforce the biological weapons convention.

This does not mean the administration has become hawkishly more unilateralist (remember that it has also been drawn back into diplomatic attempts to resolve disputes between the Palestinians and Israel and between India and Pakistan). Rather, the president and his men seem to be taking the high level of public support they now enjoy as a mandate for continuing with the foreign policy they had embarked upon anyway.

Shifts in the subsoil

In short, if you look at the immediate impact on America's current agenda, it seems modest. There is little support for a significant expansion in the scope of government (though, of course, plenty of argument over reordering priorities between, say, defence and social programmes). There are few signs that politicians think anything new is afoot. And the continuities of domestic, economic and foreign affairs seem more striking than the disruptions. So is the rising trust in government much ado about nothing?

Not quite. As Lincoln implied, wars change countries in ways that politicians do not necessarily expect or understand. They can set in motion events beyond anyone's control, for example raising expectations of government which demand to be met, or cause trouble if denied. Their impact is inherently unpredictable.

So it is worth asking whether American politicians may be misreading the signs of change. After all, less traumatic events than September 11th have changed the course of politics. The Oklahoma City bombing, for example, weakened Mr Gingrich's anti-government revolution by showing federal employees as objects of sympathy. Has September 11th affected the subsoil of politics in such a way as to support bigger changes in future?

The answer is yes—or, at least, there are candidates for such changes. First, the attack seems to have altered the balance in America between security and civil liberties. Americans have acquiesced in Mr Ashcroft's plans to boost the surveillance powers of law-enforcement officials and to make counter-terrorism the focus of the Justice Department. This is potentially a far-reaching change, confirming Alexander Hamilton's view that "to be more safe, [people] at length become willing to run the risk of being less free."

Second, the extremes of the political spectrum are likely to become less influential within the parties. The terrorist attacks cast a cloud of suspicion over all forms of religious certainty, and the fumbled response of the religious right has led many to disengage from politics altogether. On the left, the outpouring of patriotism, and the renewed focus on what holds Americans together, is likely to erode the influence of those who see the country largely as a coalition of ethnic subgroups and hyphenated-Americans. By eroding the influence of the two extremes—the most viscerally pro- and anti-government groups—September 11th may make incremental political change easier.

Third, the attacks may have the effect of explaining to Americans why they need to engage with the rest of the world on a sustained basis. So far, foreign policy has hardly changed, and the doctrine of seeking national security through military might

understandably prevails. Yet the attacks on New York and Washington also showed that not even the world's largest defence budget can buy insulation from the world's demons any more. That, too, could have profound significance.

In short, this is a moment when American politics and the country's place in the world could be recast. The political class does not see it that way, and the eventual outcome will depend partly on the president. Franklin Roosevelt used the Depression to change Americans' relationship to their government. Harry Truman used the second world war to change their relationship with the rest of the world. It is not yet clear whether George Bush will be able to use the terrorist attacks to shape a comparable historic shift. But it is possible.

From *The Economist,* January 12, 2002, pp. 23–25. © 2002 by The Economist, Ltd. Distributed by the New York Times Special Features. Reprinted by permission.

UNIT 6

New Directions for American History

Unit Selections

Key Points to Consider

- Is global warming a genuine threat, or merely a case of crying wolf? If it is a threat, what should we be doing about it?

- Consider the article "American Culture Goes Global, or Does It?" Does the author make a convincing case for his theme? Is it likely to make any differences in what others think of us?

- President Bush's foreign policies to a great extent have been unilateral, while only lip service has been paid to the notion of collective security. Will this be, as author George Soros claims, counterproductive in the long run?

- Genetic engineering raises the apparently attractive prospect of being able to help determine the kind of children we have. What are the dangers involved?

 **Links: www.dushkin.com/online/**
These sites are annotated in the World Wide Web pages.

The breakup of the Soviet Union and the end of the Cold War could only be welcomed by those who feared a great power confrontation might mean all-out nuclear conflict. One scholar proclaimed that the collapse of Communism as a viable way of organizing society (only a few small Communist states remain and China is Communist in name only) in effect signaled "the end of history." By that he meant that liberal democracy has remained as the only political system with universal appeal. Not so, argued another scholar. He predicted that the "clash of cultures" would engender ongoing struggles in the post-Cold War era. At the time of this writing, the United States is enmeshed in a war against Iraq, the ostensible goals are to bring democracy to that unfortunate nation and to counter terrorism. George Soros, in "The Bubble of American Supremacy" charges that President George W. Bush's response to September 11 marks a "discontinuity" in American foreign policy. Soros argues that the United States should pursue its interests within the framework of collective security rather than to act unilaterally.

Critics have posited a number of reasons for what appears to be a rising tide of anti-Americanism around the globe. Some focus on various American foreign policies, past and present, which they claim have placed the United States in the position of being perceived as an international bully. Others stress cultural factors. They point to the exportation of American "institutions" such as Coca-Cola, MacDonald's, and Wal-Mart, as well as films and music. "American Culture Goes Global, or Does It?" presents a different view. Author Richard Pells argues that such a charge is simplistic, and claims that American culture has "never felt all that foreign to foreigners."

Environmentalists have long warned that, in addition to other degradations, global warming presents a clear and potentially disastrous threat to the planet. Others have criticized these people as doomsayers who wildly exaggerate the danger. "Breaking the Global-Warming Gridlock" argues that the debate over this issue has focused on the wrong issues and distracts our attention from what needs to be done. Its authors propose that instead of merely continuing the argument, we focus on the political and social conditions that cause people "to behave in environmentally disruptive ways."

Two essays focus on domestic matters. Young adults today differ in many respects from their parents and grandparents with regard to their allegiance to political parties, their concept of "patriotism, and a host of other matters. "A Politics for Generation X" examines these differences, and speculates on whether their at-

titudes and goals will prevail in the future. The last article in this unit, "The Case Against Perfection" examines the case for genetic engineering. Though the prospects appear dazzling, Michael J. Sandel warns of genetic arms races to produce what he calls "designer children" and "bionic athletes."

Breaking the

Global-Warming

GRIDLOCK

Both sides on the issue of greenhouse gases frame their arguments in terms of science, but each new scientific finding only raises new questions—dooming the debate to be a pointless spiral. It's time, the authors argue, for a radically new approach: if we took practical steps to reduce our vulnerability to today's weather, we would go a long way toward solving the problem of tomorrow's climate

by
DANIEL SAREWITZ
and ROGER PIELKE JR.

IN THE LAST WEEK OF OCTOBER, 1998, hurricane Mitch stalled over Central America, dumping between three and six feet of rain within forty-eight hours, killing more than 10,000 people in landslides and floods, triggering a cholera epidemic, and virtually wiping out the economies of Honduras and Nicaragua. Several days later some 1,500 delegates, accompanied by thousands of advocates and media representatives, met in Buenos Aires at the fourth Conference of the Parties to the United Nations Framework Convention on Climate Change. Many at the conference pointed to Hurricane Mitch as a harbinger of the catastrophes that await us if we do not act immediately to reduce emissions of carbon dioxide and other so-called greenhouse gases. The delegates passed a resolution of "solidarity with Central America" in which they expressed concern "that global warming may be contributing to the worsening of weather"

and urged "governments,… and society in general, to continue their efforts to find permanent solutions to the factors which cause or may cause climate events." Children wandering bereft in the streets of Tegucigalpa became unwitting symbols of global warming.

But if Hurricane Mitch was a public-relations gift to environmentalists, it was also a stark demonstration of the failure of our current approach to protecting the environment. Disasters like Mitch are a present and historical reality, and they will become more common and more deadly regardless of global warming. Underlying the havoc in Central America were poverty, poor land-use practices, a degraded local environment, and inadequate emergency preparedness—conditions that will not be alleviated by reducing greenhouse-gas emissions.

At the heart of this dispiriting state of affairs is a vitriolic debate between those who advocate action to reduce global

warming and those who oppose it. The controversy is informed by strong scientific evidence that the earth's surface has warmed over the past century. But the controversy, and the science, focus on the wrong issues, and distract attention from what needs to be done. The enormous scientific, political, and financial resources now aimed at the problem of global warming create the perfect conditions for international and domestic political gridlock, but they can have little effect on the root causes of global environmental degradation, or on the human suffering that so often accompanies it. Our goal is to move beyond the gridlock and stake out some common ground for political dialogue and effective action.

FRAMING THE ISSUE

In politics everything depends on how an issue is framed: the terms of debate, the allocation of power and resources, the potential courses of action. The issue of global warming has been framed by a single question: Does the carbon dioxide emitted by industrialized societies threaten the earth's climate? On one side are the doomsayers, who foretell environmental disaster unless carbon-dioxide emissions are immediately reduced. On the other side are the cornucopians, who blindly insist that society can continue to pump billions of tons of greenhouse gases into the atmosphere with no ill effect, and that any effort to reduce emissions will stall the engines of industrialism that protect us from a Hobbesian wilderness. From our perspective, each group is operating within a frame that has little to do with the practical problem of how to protect the global environment in a world of six billion people (and counting). To understand why global-warming policy is a comprehensive and dangerous failure, therefore, we must begin with a look at how the issue came to be framed in this way. Two converging trends are implicated: the evolution of scientific research on the earth's climate, and the maturation of the modern environmental movement.

Since the beginning of the Industrial Revolution the combustion of fossil fuels—coal, oil, natural gas—has powered economic growth and also emitted great quantities of carbon dioxide and other greenhouse gases. More than a century ago the Swedish chemist Svante Arrhenius and the American geologist T. C. Chamberlin independently recognized that industrialization could lead to rising levels of carbon dioxide in the atmosphere, which might in turn raise the atmosphere's temperature by trapping solar radiation that would otherwise be reflected back into space—a "greenhouse effect" gone out of control. In the late 1950s the geophysicist Roger Revelle, arguing that the world was making itself the subject of a giant "geophysical experiment," worked to establish permanent stations for monitoring carbon-dioxide levels in the atmosphere. Monitoring documented what theory had predicted: atmospheric carbon dioxide was increasing.

In the United States the first high-level government mention of global warming was buried deep within a 1965 White House report on the nation's environmental problems. Throughout the 1960s and 1970s global warming—at that time typically referred to as "inadvertent modification of the atmosphere," and today embraced by the term "climate change"—remained an intriguing hypothesis that caught the attention of a few scientists but generated little concern among the public or environmentalists. Indeed, some climate researchers saw evidence for global cooling and a future ice age. In any case, the threat of nuclear war was sufficiently urgent, plausible, and horrific to crowd global warming off the catastrophe agenda.

Continued research, however, fortified the theory that fossil-fuel combustion could contribute to global warming. In 1977 the nonpartisan National Academy of Sciences issued a study called *Energy and Climate*, which carefully suggested that the possibility of global warming "should lead neither to panic nor to complacency." Rather, the study continued, it should "engender a lively sense of urgency in getting on with the work of illuminating the issues that have been identified and resolving the scientific uncertainties that remain." As is typical with National Academy studies, the primary recommendation was for more research.

In the early 1980s the carbon-dioxide problem received its first sustained attention in Congress, in the form of hearings organized by Representative Al Gore, who had become concerned about global warming when he took a college course with Roger Revelle, twelve years earlier. In 1983 the Environmental Protection Agency released a report detailing some of the possible threats posed by the anthropogenic, or human-caused, emission of carbon dioxide, but the Reagan Administration decisively downplayed the document. Two years later a prestigious international scientific conference in Villach, Austria, concluded that climate change deserved the attention of policymakers worldwide. The following year, at a Senate fact-finding hearing stimulated by the conference, Robert Watson, a climate scientist at NASA, testified, "Global warming is inevitable. It is only a question of the magnitude and the timing."

At that point global warming was only beginning to insinuate itself into the public consciousness. The defining event came in June of 1988, when another NASA climate scientist, James Hansen, told Congress with "ninety-nine percent confidence" that "the greenhouse effect has been detected, and it is changing our climate now." Hansen's proclamation made the front pages of major newspapers, ignited a firestorm of public debate, and elevated the carbon-dioxide problem to pre-eminence on the environmental agenda, where it remains to this day. Nothing had so galvanized the environmental community since the original Earth Day, eighteen years before.

Historically, the conservation and environmental movements have been rooted in values that celebrate the intrinsic worth of unspoiled landscape and propagate the idea that the human spirit is sustained through communion with nature. More than fifty years ago Aldo Leopold, perhaps the most important environmental voice of the twentieth century, wrote, "We face the question whether a still higher 'standard of living' is worth its cost in things natural, wild, and free. For us of the minority,... the chance to find a pasque-flower is a right as inalienable as free speech." But when global warming appeared, environmentalists thought they had found a justification better than inalienable rights—they had found facts and rationality, and they fell head over heels in love with science.

Of course, modern environmentalists were already in the habit of calling on science to help advance their agenda. In 1967, for example, the Environmental Defense Fund was founded with the aim of using science to support environmental protection through litigation. But global warming was, and is, different. It exists as an environmental issue only because of science. People can't directly sense global warming, the way they can see a clear-cut forest or feel the sting of urban smog in their throats. It is not a discrete event, like an oil spill or a nuclear accident. Global warming is so abstract that scientists argue over how they would know if they actually observed it. Scientists go to great lengths to measure and derive something called the "global average temperature" at the earth's surface, and the total rise in this temperature over the past century—an increase of about six tenths of a degree Celsius as of 1998—does suggest warming. But people and ecosystems experience local and regional temperatures, not the global average. Furthermore, most of the possible effects of global warming are not apparent in the present; rather, scientists predict that they will occur decades or even centuries hence. Nor is it likely that scientists will ever be able to attribute any isolated event—a hurricane, a heat wave—to global warming.

A central tenet of environmentalism is that less human interference in nature is better than more. The imagination of the environmental community was ignited not by the observation that greenhouse-gas concentrations were increasing but by the scientific conclusion that the increase was caused by human beings. The Environmental Defense Fund, perhaps because of its explicitly scientific bent, was one of the first advocacy groups to make this connection. As early as 1984 its senior scientist, Michael Oppenheimer, wrote on the op-ed page of *The New York Times*,

> With unusual unanimity, scientists testified at a recent Senate hearing that using the atmosphere as a garbage dump is about to catch up with us on a global scale.... Carbon dioxide emissions from fossil fuel combustion and other "greenhouse" gases are throwing a blanket over the Earth.... The sea level will rise as land ice melts and the ocean expands. Beaches will erode while wetlands will largely disappear.... Imagine life in a sweltering, smoggy New York without Long Island's beaches and you have glimpsed the world left to future generations.

Preserving tropical jungles and wetlands, protecting air and water quality, slowing global population growth—goals that had all been justified for independent reasons, often by independent organizations—could now be linked to a single fact, anthropogenic carbon-dioxide emissions, and advanced along a single political front, the effort to reduce

those emissions. Protecting forests, for example, could help fight global warming because forests act as "sinks" that absorb carbon dioxide. Air pollution could be addressed in part by promoting the same clean-energy sources that would reduce carbon-dioxide emissions. Population growth needed to be controlled in order to reduce demand for fossil-fuel combustion. And the environmental community could reinvigorate its energy-conservation agenda, which had flagged since the early 1980s, when the effects of the second Arab oil shock wore off. Senator Timothy Wirth, of Colorado, spelled out the strategy in 1988: "What we've got to do in energy conservation is try to ride the global warming issue. Even if the theory of global warming is wrong, to have approached global warming as if it is real means energy conservation, so we will be doing the right thing anyway in terms of economic policy and environmental policy." A broad array of environmental groups and think tanks, including the Environmental Defense Fund, the Sierra Club, Greenpeace, the World Resources Institute, and the Union of Concerned Scientists, made reductions in carbon-dioxide emissions central to their agendas.

The moral problem seemed clear: human beings were causing the increase of carbon dioxide in the atmosphere. But the moral problem existed only because of a scientific fact—a fact that not only provided justification for doing many of the things that environmentalists wanted to do anyway but also dictated the overriding course of action: reduce carbon-dioxide emissions. Thus science was used to rationalize the moral imperative, unify the environmental agenda, and determine the political solution.

RESEARCH AS POLICY

THE summer of 1988 was stultifyingly hot even by Washington, D.C., standards, and the Mississippi River basin was suffering a catastrophic drought. Hansen's proclamation that the greenhouse effect was "changing our climate now" generated a level of public concern sufficient to catch the attention of many politicians. George Bush, who promised to be "the environmental President" and

to counter "the greenhouse effect with the White House effect," was elected that November. Despite his campaign rhetoric, the new President was unprepared to offer policies that would curtail fossil-fuel production and consumption or impose economic costs for uncertain political gains. Bush's advisers recognized that support for scientific research offered the best solution politically, because it would give the appearance of action with minimal political risk.

With little debate the Republican Administration and the Democratic Congress in 1990 created the U.S. Global Change Research Program. The program's annual budget reached $1 billion in 1991 and $1.8 billion in 1995, making it one of the largest science initiatives ever undertaken by the U.S. government. Its goal, according to Bush Administration documents, was "to establish the scientific basis for national and international policymaking related to natural and human-induced changes in the global Earth system." A central scientific objective was to "support national and international policymaking by developing the ability to predict the nature and consequences of changes in the Earth system, particularly climate change." A decade and more than $16 billion later, scientific research remains the principal U.S. policy response to climate change.

Meanwhile, the marriage of environmentalism and science gave forth issue: diplomatic efforts to craft a global strategy to reduce carbon-dioxide emissions. Scientists, environmentalists, and government officials, in an attempt to replicate the apparently successful international response to stratospheric-ozone depletion that was mounted in the mid-1980s, created an institutional structure aimed at formalizing the connection between science and political action. The Intergovernmental Panel on Climate Change was established through the United Nations, to provide snapshots of the evolving state of scientific understanding. The IPCC issued major assessments in 1990 and 1996; a third is due early next year. These assessments provide the basis for action under a complementary mechanism, the United Nations Framework Convention on Climate Change. Signed by 154 nations at the

1992 "Earth Summit" in Rio de Janeiro, the convention calls for voluntary reductions in carbon-dioxide emissions. It came into force as an international treaty in March of 1994, and has been ratified by 181 nations. Signatories continue to meet in periodic Conferences of the Parties, of which the most significant to date occurred in Kyoto in 1997, when binding emissions reductions for industrialized countries were proposed under an agreement called the Kyoto Protocol.

The IPCC defines climate change as any sort of change in the earth's climate, no matter what the cause. But the Framework Convention restricts its definition to changes that result from the anthropogenic emission of greenhouse gases. This restriction has profound implications for the framing of the issue. It makes all action under the convention hostage to the ability of scientists not just to document global warming but to attribute it to human causes. An apparently simple question, Are we causing global warming or aren't we?, has become the obsessional focus of science—and of policy.

Finally, if the reduction of carbon-dioxide emissions is an organizing principle for environmentalists, scientists, and environmental-policy makers, it is also an organizing principle for all those whose interests might be threatened by such a reduction. It's easy to be glib about who they might be—greedy oil and coal companies, the rapacious logging industry, recalcitrant automobile manufacturers, corrupt foreign dictatorships—and easy as well to document the excesses and absurdities propagated by some representatives of these groups. Consider, for example, the Greening Earth Society, which "promotes the optimistic scientific view that CO_2 is beneficial to humankind and all of nature," and happens to be funded by a coalition of coal-burning utility companies. One of the society's 1999 press releases reported that "there will only be sufficient food for the world's projected population in 2050 if atmospheric concentrations of carbon dioxide are permitted to increase, unchecked." Of course, neither side of the debate has a lock on excess or distortion. The point is simply that the climate-change problem has been framed in a

way that catalyzes a determined and powerful opposition.

THE PROBLEM WITH PREDICTIONS

WHEN anthropogenic carbon-dioxide emissions became the defining fact for global environmentalism, scientific uncertainty about the causes and consequences of global warming emerged as the apparent central obstacle to action. As we have seen, the Bush Administration justified its huge climate-research initiative explicitly in terms of the need to reduce uncertainty before taking action. Al Gore, by then a senator, agreed, explaining that "more research and better research and better targeted research is absolutely essential if we are going to eliminate the remaining areas of uncertainty and build the broader and stronger political consensus necessary for the unprecedented actions required to address this problem." Thus did a Republican Administration and a Democratic Congress—one side looking for reasons to do nothing, the other seeking justification for action—converge on the need for more research.

How certain do we need to be before we take action? The answer depends, of course, on where our interests lie. Environmentalists can tolerate a good deal more uncertainty on this issue than can, say, the executives of utility or automobile companies. Science is unlikely to overcome such a divergence in interests. After all, science is not a fact or even a set of facts; rather, it is a process of inquiry that generates more questions than answers. The rise in anthropogenic greenhouse-gas emissions, once it was scientifically established, simply pointed to other questions. How rapidly might carbon-dioxide levels rise in the future? How might climate respond to this rise? What might be the effects of that response? Such questions are inestimably complex, their answers infinitely contestable and always uncertain, their implications for human action highly dependent on values and interests.

Having wedded themselves to science, environmentalists must now cleave to it through thick and thin. When research results do not support their cause,

or are simply uncertain, they cannot resort to values-based arguments, because their political opponents can portray such arguments as an opportunistic abandonment of rationality. Environmentalists have tried to get out of this bind by invoking the "precautionary principle"—a dandified version of "better safe than sorry"—to advance the idea that action in the presence of uncertainty is justified if potential harm is great. Thus uncertainty itself becomes an argument for action. But nothing is gained by this tactic either, because just as attitudes toward uncertainty are rooted in individual values and interests, so are attitudes toward potential harm.

Charged by the Framework Convention to search for proof of harm, scientists have turned to computer models of the atmosphere and the oceans, called general circulation models, or GCMs. Carbon-dioxide levels and atmospheric temperatures are measures of the physical state of the atmosphere. GCMs, in contrast, are mathematical representations that scientists use to try to understand past climate conditions and predict future ones. With GCMs scientists seek to explore how climate might respond under different influences—for example, different rates of carbon-dioxide increase. GCMs have calculated global average temperatures for the past century that closely match actual surface-temperature records; this gives climate modelers some confidence that they understand how climate behaves.

Computer models are a bit like Aladdin's lamp—what comes out is very seductive, but few are privy to what goes on inside. Even the most complex models, however, have one crucial quality that non-experts can easily understand: their accuracy can be fully evaluated only after seeing what happens in the real world over time. In other words, predictions of how climate will behave in the future cannot be proved accurate today. There are other fundamental problems with relying on GCMs. The ability of many models to reproduce temperature records may in part reflect the fact that the scientists who designed them already "knew the answer." As John Firor, a former director of the National Center for Atmospheric Research, has observed, climate models "are made by humans who tend to shape or use their models in ways that mirror their own notion of what a desirable outcome would be." Although various models can reproduce past temperature records, and yield similar predictions of future temperatures, they are unable to replicate other observed aspects of climate, such as cloud behavior and atmospheric temperature, and they diverge widely in predicting specific regional climate phenomena, such as precipitation and the frequency of extreme weather events. Moreover, it is simply not possible to know far in advance if the models agree on future temperature because they are similarly right or similarly wrong.

In spite of such pitfalls, a fundamental assumption of both U.S. climate policy and the UN Framework Convention is that increasingly sophisticated models, run on faster computers and supported by more data, will yield predictions that can resolve political disputes and guide action. The promise of better predictions is irresistible to champions of carbon-dioxide reduction, who, after all, must base their advocacy on the claim that anthropogenic greenhouse-gas emissions will be harmful in the future. But regardless of the sophistication of such predictions, new findings will almost inevitably be accompanied by new uncertainties—that's the nature of science—and may therefore act to fuel, rather than to quench, political debate. Our own prediction is that increasingly complex mathematical models that delve ever more deeply into the intricacies and the uncertainties of climate will only hinder political action.

An example of how more scientific research fuels political debate came in 1998, when a group of prominent researchers released the results of a model analyzing carbon-dioxide absorption in North America. Their controversial findings, published in the prestigious journal *Science*, suggested that the amount of carbon dioxide absorbed by U.S. forests might be greater than the amount emitted by the nation's fossil-fuel combustion. This conclusion has two astonishing implications. First, the United States—the world's most profligate energy consumer—may not be directly contributing to rising atmospheric levels of carbon dioxide. Second, the atmosphere seems to be benefiting from young forests in the eastern United States that are particularly efficient at absorbing carbon dioxide. But these young forests exist only because old-growth forests were clearcut in the eighteenth and nineteenth centuries to make way for farms that were later abandoned in favor of larger, more efficient midwestern farms. In other words, the possibility that the United States is a net carbon-dioxide sink does not reflect efforts to protect the environment; on the contrary, it reflects a history of deforestation and development.

Needless to say, these results quickly made their way into the political arena. At a hearing of the House Resources Committee, Representative John E. Peterson, of Pennsylvania, a Republican, asserted, "There are recent studies that show that in the Northeast, where we have continued to cut timber, and have a regenerating, younger forest, that the greenhouse gases are less when they leave the forest.... So a young, growing, vibrant forest is a whole lot better for clean air than an old dying forest." George Frampton, the director of the White House Council on Environmental Quality, countered, "The science on this needs a lot of work... we need more money for scientific research to undergird that point of view." How quickly the tables can turn: here was a conservative politician wielding (albeit with limited coherence) the latest scientific results to justify logging old-growth forests in the name of battling global warming, while a Clinton Administration official backpedaled in the manner more typically adopted by opponents of action on climate change—invoking the need for more research.

That's a problem with science—it can turn around and bite you. An even more surprising result has recently emerged from the study of Antarctic glaciers. A strong argument in favor of carbon-dioxide reduction has been the possibility that if temperatures rise owing to greenhouse-gas emissions, glaciers will melt, the sea level will rise, and populous coastal zones all over the world will be inundated. The West Antarctic Ice Sheet has been a subject of particular concern, both because of evidence that it is now retreating and because of geologic studies showing that it underwent catastrophic collapse at least once in the past million years or so. "Behind the reasoned scientific estimates," Greenpeace warns, "lies the possibility of... the potential catastrophe of a six metre rise in sea level." But recent research from Antarctica shows that this ice sheet has been melting for thousands of years. Sea-level rise is a problem, but anthropogenic global warming is not the only culprit, and reducing emissions cannot be the only solution.

To make matters more difficult, some phenomena, especially those involving human behavior, are intrinsically unpredictable. Any calculation of future anthropogenic global warming must include an estimate of rates of fossil-fuel combustion in the coming decades. This means that scientists must be able to predict not only the amounts of coal, oil, and natural gas that will be consumed but also changes in the mixture of fossil fuels and other energy sources, such as nuclear, hydro-electric, and solar. These predictions rest on interdependent factors that include energy policies and prices, rates of economic growth, patterns of industrialization and technological innovation, changes in population, and even wars and other geopolitical events. Scientists have no history of being able to predict any of these things. For example, their inability to issue accurate population projections is "one of the best-kept secrets of demography," according to Joel Cohen, the director of the Laboratory of Populations at Rockefeller University. "Most professional demographers no longer believe they can predict precisely the future growth rate, size, composition and spatial distribution of populations," Cohen has observed.

Predicting the human influence on climate also requires an understanding of how climate behaved "normally," before there was any such influence. But what are normal climate patterns? In the absence of human influence, how stationary is climate? To answer such questions, researchers must document and explain the behavior of the pre-industrial climate, and they must also determine how the climate would have behaved over the past two centuries had human beings not been changing the composition of the atmosphere. However, despite the billions spent so far on climate research, Kevin Trenberth, a senior scientist at the National Center for Atmospheric Research, told the *Chicago Tribune* last year, "This may be a shock to many people who assume that we do know adequately what's going on with the climate, but we don't." The National Academy of Sciences reported last year that "deficiencies in the accuracy, quality, and continuity of the [climate] records... place serious limitations on the confidence" of research results.

If the normal climate is non-stationary, then the task of identifying the human fingerprint in global climate change becomes immeasurably more difficult. And the idea of a naturally stationary climate may well be chimerical. Climate has changed often and dramatically in the recent past. In the 1940s and 1950s, for example, the East Coast was hammered by a spate of powerful hurricanes, whereas in the 1970s and 1980s hurricanes were much less common. What may appear to be "abnormal" hurricane activity in recent years is abnormal only in relation to this previous quiet period. As far as the ancient climate goes, paleoclimatologists have found evidence of rapid change, even over periods as short as several years. Numerous influences could account for these changes. Ash spewed high into the atmosphere by large volcanoes can reflect solar radiation back into space and result in short-term cooling, as occurred after the 1991 eruption of Mount Pinatubo. Variations in the energy emitted by the sun also affect climate, in ways that are not yet fully understood. Global ocean currents, which move huge volumes of warm and cold water around the world and have a profound influence on climate, can speed up, slow down, and maybe even die out over very short periods of time—perhaps less than a decade. Were the Gulf Stream to shut down, the climate of Great Britain could come to resemble that of Labrador.

Finally, human beings have been changing the surface of the earth for millennia. Scientists increasingly realize that deforestation, agriculture, irrigation, urbanization, and other human activities can lead to major changes in climate on a regional or perhaps even a global scale. Thomas Stohlgren, of the U.S. Geological Survey, has written, "The effects of land use practices on regional climate may overshadow larger-scale temperature changes commonly associated with observed increases in carbon dioxide." The idea that climate may constantly be changing for a variety of reasons does not itself undercut the possibility that anthropogenic carbon dioxide could seriously affect the global climate, but it does confound scientific efforts to predict the consequences of carbon-dioxide emissions.

THE OTHER 80 PERCENT

IF predicting how climate will change is difficult and uncertain, predicting how society will be affected by a changing climate—especially at the local, regional, and national levels, where decision-making takes place—is immeasurably more so. And predicting the impact on climate of reducing carbon-dioxide emissions is so uncertain as to be meaningless. What we do know about climate change suggests that there will be winners and losers, with some areas and nations potentially benefiting from, say, longer growing seasons or more rain, and others suffering from more flooding or drought. But politicians have no way to accurately calibrate the effects—human and economic—of global warming, or the benefits of reducing carbon-dioxide emissions.

Imagine yourself a leading policymaker in a poor, overpopulated, undernourished nation with severe environmental problems. What would it take to get you worried about global warming? You would need to know not just that global warming would make the conditions in your country worse but also that any of the scarce resources you applied to reducing carbon-dioxide emissions would lead to more benefits than if they were applied in another area, such as industrial development or housing construction. Such knowledge is simply unavailable. But you do know that investing in industrial development or better housing would lead to concrete political, economic, and social benefits.

More specifically, suppose that many people in your country live in shacks on a river's floodplain. Floodplains are created and sustained by repeated flooding, so floods are certain to occur in the future, regardless of global warming. Given a choice between building new houses away from the floodplain and converting power plants from cheap local coal to costlier imported fuels, what would you do? New houses would ensure that lives and homes would be saved; a new power plant would reduce carbon-dioxide emissions but leave people vulnerable to floods. In the developing world the carbon-dioxide problem pales alongside immediate environmental and developmental problems. The *China Daily* reported during the 1997 Kyoto Conference:

> The United States... and other nations made the irresponsible demand.... that the developing countries should make commitments to limiting greenhouse gas emissions.... As a developing country, China has 60 million poverty-stricken people and China's per capita gas emissions are only one-seventh of the average amount of more developed countries. Ending poverty and developing the economy must still top the agenda of [the] Chinese government.

For the most part, the perspectives of those in the developing world—about 80 percent of the planet's population—have been left outside the frame of the climate-change discussion. This is hardly surprising, considering that the frame was defined mainly by environmentalists and scientists in affluent nations. Developing nations, meanwhile, have quite reasonably refused to agree to the targets for carbon-dioxide reduction set under the Kyoto Protocol. The result may feel like a moral victory to some environmentalists, who reason that industrialized countries, which caused the problem to begin with, should shoulder the primary responsibility for solving it. But the victory is hollow, because most future emissions increases will come from the developing world. In affluent nations almost everyone already owns a full complement of energy-consuming devices. Beyond a certain point increases in income do not result in proportional increases in energy consumption; people simply trade in the old model for a new and perhaps more efficient one. If present trends continue, emissions from the developing world are likely to exceed those from the industrialized nations within the next decade or so.

Twelve years after carbon dioxide became the central obsession of global environmental science and politics, we face the following two realities:

First, atmospheric carbon-dioxide levels will continue to increase. The Kyoto Protocol, which represents the world's best attempt to confront the issue, calls for industrialized nations to reduce their emissions below 1990 levels by the end of this decade. Political and technical realities suggest that not even this modest goal will be achieved. To date, although eighty-four nations have signed the Kyoto Protocol, only twenty-two nations—half of them islands, and none of them major carbon-dioxide emitters—have ratified it. The United States Senate, by a vote of 95-0 in July of 1997, indicated that it would not ratify any climate treaty that lacked provisions requiring developing nations to reduce their emissions. The only nations likely to achieve the emissions commitments set under Kyoto are those, like Russia and Ukraine, whose economies are in ruins. And even successful implementation of the treaty would not halt the progressive increase in global carbon-dioxide emissions.

Second, even if greenhouse-gas emissions could somehow be rolled back to pre-industrial levels, the impacts of climate on society and the environment would continue to increase. Climate affects the world not just through phenomena such as hurricanes and droughts but also because of societal and environmental vulnerability to such phenomena. The horrific toll of Hurricane Mitch reflected not an unprecedented climatic event but a level of exposure typical in developing countries where dense and rapidly increasing populations live in environmentally degraded conditions. Similar conditions underlay more-recent disasters in Venezuela and Mozambique.

If these observations are correct, and we believe they are essentially indisputable, then framing the problem of global warming in terms of carbon-dioxide reduction is a political, environmental, and social dead end. We are not suggesting that humanity can with impunity emit billions of tons of carbon dioxide into the atmosphere each year, or that reducing those emissions is not a good idea. Nor are we making the nihilistic point that since climate undergoes changes for a variety of reasons, there is no need to worry about additional changes imposed by human beings. Rather, we are arguing that environmentalists and scientists, in focusing their own, increasingly congruent interests on carbon-dioxide emissions, have framed the problem of global environmental protection in a way that can offer no realistic prospect of a solution.

REDRAWING THE FRAME

LOCAL weather is the day-to-day manifestation of global climate. Weather is what we experience, and lately there has been plenty to experience. In recent decades human, economic, and environmental losses from disasters related to weather have increased dramatically. Insurance-industry data show that insured losses from weather have been rising steadily. A 1999 study by the German firm Munich Reinsurance Company compared the 1960s with the 1990s and concluded that "the number of great natural catastrophes increased by a factor of three, with economic losses—taking into account the effects of inflation—increasing by a factor of more than eight and insured losses by a factor of no less than sixteen." And yet scientists have been unable to observe a global increase in the number or the severity of extreme weather events. In 1996 the IPCC concluded, "There is no evidence that extreme weather events, or climate variability, has increased, in a global sense, through the 20th century, although data and analyses are poor and not comprehensive."

What has unequivocally increased is society's vulnerability to weather. At the beginning of the twentieth century the earth's population was about 1.6 billion people; today it is about six billion peo-

ple. Almost four times as many people are exposed to weather today as were a century ago. And this increase has, of course, been accompanied by enormous increases in economic activity, development, infrastructure, and interdependence. In the past fifty years, for example, Florida's population rose fivefold; 80 percent of this burgeoning population lives within twenty miles of the coast. The great Miami hurricane of 1926 made landfall over a small, relatively poor community and caused about $76 million worth of damage (in inflation-adjusted dollars). Today a storm of similar magnitude would strike a sprawling, affluent metropolitan area of two million people, and could cause more than $80 billion worth of damage. The increase in vulnerability is far more dramatic in the developing world, where in an average year tens of thousands of people die in weather-related disasters. According to the *World Disasters Report 1999*, 80 million people were made homeless by weather-related disasters from 1988 to 1997. As the population and vulnerability of the developing world continue to rise, such numbers will continue to rise as well, with or without global warming.

Environmental vulnerability is also on the rise. The connections between weather impacts and environmental quality are immediate and obvious—much more so than the connections between global warming and environmental quality. Deforestation, the destruction of wetlands, and the development of fragile coastlines can greatly magnify flooding; floods, in turn, can mobilize toxic chemicals in soil and storage facilities and cause devastating pollution of water sources and harm to wildlife. Poor agricultural, forest-management, and grazing practices can exacerbate the effects of drought, amplify soil erosion, and promote the spread of wildfires. Damage to the environment due to deforestation directly contributed to the devastation wrought by Hurricane Mitch, as denuded hillsides washed away in catastrophic landslides, and excessive development along unmanaged floodplains put large numbers of people in harm's way.

Our view of climate and the environment draws on people's direct experience and speaks to widely shared values. It therefore has an emotional and moral impact that can translate into action. This view is framed by four precepts. First, the impacts of weather and climate are a serious threat to human welfare in the present and are likely to get worse in the future. Second, the only way to reduce these impacts is to reduce societal vulnerability to them. Third, reducing vulnerability can be achieved most effectively by encouraging democracy, raising standards of living, and improving environmental quality in the developing world. Fourth, such changes offer the best prospects not only for adapting to a capricious climate but also for reducing carbon-dioxide emissions.

The implicit moral imperative is not to prevent human disruption of the environment but to ameliorate the social and political conditions that lead people to behave in environmentally disruptive ways. This is a critical distinction—and one that environmentalists and scientists embroiled in the global-warming debate have so far failed to make.

To begin with, any global effort to reduce vulnerability to weather and climate must address the environmental conditions in developing nations. Poor land-use and natural-resource-management practices are, of course, a reflection of poverty, but they are also caused by government policies, particularly those that encourage unsustainable environmental activities. William Ascher, a political scientist at Duke University, has observed that such policies typically do not arise out of ignorance or lack of options but reflect conscious tradeoffs made by government officials faced with many competing priorities and political pressures. Nations, even poor ones, have choices. It was not inevitable, for example, that Indonesia would promote the disastrous exploitation of its forests by granting subsidized logging concessions to military and business leaders. This was the policy of an autocratic government seeking to manipulate powerful sectors of society. In the absence of open, democratically responsive institutions, Indonesian leaders were not accountable for the costs that the public might bear, such as increased vulnerability to floods, landslides, soil erosion,

drought, and fire. Promoting democratic institutions in developing nations could be the most important item on an agenda aimed at protecting the global environment and reducing vulnerability to climate. Environmental groups concerned about the consequences of climate change ought to consider reorienting their priorities accordingly.

Such long-term efforts must be accompanied by activities with a shorter-term payoff. An obvious first step would be to correct some of the imbalances created by the obsession with carbon dioxide. For example, the U.S. Agency for International Development has allocated $1 billion over five years to help developing nations quantify, monitor, and reduce greenhouse-gas emissions, but is spending less than a tenth of that amount on programs to prepare for and prevent disasters. These priorities should be rearranged. Similarly, the United Nations' International Strategy for Disaster Reduction is a relatively low-level effort that should be elevated to a status comparable to that of the Framework Convention on Climate Change.

Intellectual and financial resources are also poorly allocated in the realm of science, with research focused disproportionately on understanding and predicting basic climatic processes. Such research has yielded much interesting information about the global climate system. But little priority is given to generating and disseminating knowledge that people and communities can use to reduce their vulnerability to climate and extreme weather events. For example, researchers have made impressive strides in anticipating the impacts of some relatively short-term climatic phenomena, notably El Niño and La Niña. If these advances were accompanied by progress in monitoring weather, identifying vulnerable regions and populations, and communicating useful information, we would begin to reduce the toll exacted by weather and climate all over the world.

A powerful international mechanism for moving forward already exists in the Framework Convention on Climate Change. The language of the treaty offers sufficient flexibility for new priorities. The text states that signatory nations

have an obligation to "cooperate in preparing for adaptation to the impacts of climate change [and to] develop and elaborate appropriate and integrated plans for coastal zone management, water resources and agriculture, and for the protection and rehabilitation of areas... affected by drought and desertification, as well as floods."

The idea of improving our adaptation to weather and climate has been taboo in many circles, including the realms of international negotiation and political debate. "Do we have so much faith in our own adaptability that we will risk destroying the integrity of the entire global ecological system?" Vice President Gore asked in his book *Earth in the Balance* (1992). "Believing that we can adapt to just about anything is ultimately a kind of laziness, an arrogant faith in our ability to react in time to save our skin." For environmentalists, adaptation represents a capitulation to the momentum of human interference in nature. For their opponents, putting adaptation on the table would mean acknowledging the reality of global warming. And for scientists, focusing on adaptation would call into question the billions of tax dollars devoted to research and technology centered on climate processes, models, and predictions.

Yet there is a huge potential constituency for efforts focused on adaptation: everyone who is in any way subject to the effects of weather. Reframing the climate problem could mobilize this constituency and revitalize the Framework Convention. The revitalization could concentrate on coordinating disaster relief, debt relief, and development assistance, and on generating and providing information on climate that participating countries could use in order to reduce their vulnerability.

An opportunity to advance the cause of adaptation is on the horizon. The U.S. Global Change Research Program is now finishing its report on the National Assessment of the Potential Consequences of Climate Variability and Change. The draft includes examples from around the United States of why a greater focus on adaptation to climate makes sense. But it remains to be seen if the report will redefine the terms of the climate debate, or if it will simply become fodder in the battle over carbon-dioxide emissions.

Finally, efforts to reduce carbon-dioxide emissions need not be abandoned. The Framework Convention and its offshoots also offer a promising mechanism for promoting the diffusion of energy-efficient technologies that would reduce emissions. Both the convention and the Kyoto Protocol call on industrialized nations to share new energy technologies with the developing world. But because these provisions are coupled to carbon-dioxide-reduction mandates, they are trapped in the political gridlock. They should be liberated, promoted independently on the basis of their intrinsic environmental and economic benefits, and advanced through innovative funding mechanisms. For example, as the United Nations Development Programme has suggested, research into renewable-energy technologies for poor countries could be supported in part by a modest levy on patents registered under the World Intellectual Property Organization. Such ideas should be far less divisive than energy policies advanced on the back of the global-warming agenda.

As an organizing principle for political action, vulnerability to weather and climate offers everything that global warming does not: a clear, uncontroversial story rooted in concrete human experience, observable in the present, and definable in terms of unambiguous and widely shared human values, such as the fundamental rights to a secure shelter, a safe community, and a sustainable environment. In this light, efforts to blame global warming for extreme weather events seem maddeningly perverse—as if to say that those who died in Hurricane Mitch were symbols of the profligacy of industrialized society, rather than victims of poverty and the vulnerability it creates.

Such perversity shows just how morally and politically dangerous it can be to elevate science above human values. In the global-warming debate the logic behind public discourse and political action has been precisely backwards. Environmental prospects for the coming century depend far less on our strategies for reducing carbon-dioxide emissions than on our determination and ability to reduce human vulnerability to weather and climate.

Daniel Sarewitz is a research scholar at Columbia University's Center for Science, Policy and Outcomes. Roger Pielke Jr. is a scientist with the Environmental and Societal Impacts Group at the National Center for Atmospheric Research. They are the editors, with Radford Byerly Jr., of *Prediction: Science, Decision Making, and the Future of Nature* (2000).

From The *Atlantic Monthly*, July 2000, pp. 54-64. © 2000 by Daniel Sarewitz and Roger Pielke, Jr. Reprinted by permission.

A Politics for Generation X

Today's young adults may be the most politically disengaged in American history. The author explains why, and puts forth a new political agenda that just might galvanize his generation

by Ted Halstead

EVERETT Carll Ladd, a political scientist, once remarked, "Social analysis and commentary has many shortcomings, but few of its chapters are as persistently wrong-headed as those on the generations and generational change. This literature abounds with hyperbole and unsubstantiated leaps from available data." Many of the media's grand pronouncements about America's post–Baby Boom generation—alternatively called Generation X, Baby Busters, and twentysomethings—would seem to illustrate this point.

The 1990s opened with a frenzy of negative stereotyping of the roughly 50 million Americans born from 1965 to 1978: they were slackers, cynics, whiners, drifters, malcontents. A *Washington Post* headline captured the patronizing attitude that Baby Boomers apparently hold toward their successors: "THE BORING TWENTIES: GROW UP, CRYBABIES." Then books and articles began to recast young Americans as ambitious, savvy, independent, pragmatic, and self-sufficient. For instance, *Time* magazine described a 1997 article titled "Great Xpectations" this way: "Slackers? Hardly. The so-called Generation X turns out to be full of go-getters who are just doing it—but their way."

Stereotyping aside, some disquieting facts jump out regarding the political practices and political orientation of young Americans. A wide sampling of surveys indicates that Xers are less politically or civically engaged, exhibit less social trust or confidence in government, have a weaker allegiance to their country or to either political party, and are more materialistic than their predecessors. Why are so many young people opting out of conventional politics, and what does this mean for the future of American democracy? Might it be that today's political establishment is simply not addressing what matters to the nation's young? And if so, what is their political agenda?

THE DISENGAGED GENERATION

ALTHOUGH political and civic engagement began to decrease among those at the tail end of the Baby Boom, Xers appear to have enshrined political apathy as a way of life. In measurements of conventional political participation the youngest voting-age Americans stand out owing to their unprecedented levels of absenteeism. This political disengagement cannot be explained away as merely the habits of youth, because today's young are markedly less engaged than were their counterparts in earlier generations.

Voting rates are arrestingly low among post-Boomers. In the 1994 midterm elections, for instance, fewer than one in five eligible Xers showed up at the polls. As recently as 1972 half those aged eighteen to twenty-four voted; in 1996, a presidential-election year, only 32 percent did. Such anemic participation can be seen in all forms of traditional political activity: Xers are considerably less likely than previous generations of young Americans to call or write elected officials, attend candidates' rallies, or work on political campaigns. What is more, a number of studies reveal that their general knowledge about public affairs is uniquely low.

The most recent birth cohort to reach voting age is also rejecting conventional partisan demarcations: the distinction between Democrats and Republicans, which has defined American politics for more than a century, doesn't resonate much with the young, who tend to see more similarities than differences between the two parties. Even those young adults who are actively engaged in national politics see partisan boundaries blurring into irrelevance. Gary Ruskin, an Xer who directs the Congressional Accountability Project, a public-policy group in Washington, D.C., puts it this way: "Republicans and Democrats have become one and the same—they are both corrupt at the core and behave like children who are more interested in fighting with each other than in getting anything accomplished."

Surveys suggest that no more than a third of young adults identify with either political party, and only a quarter vote a straight party ticket. Xers are the group least likely to favor maintaining the current two-party system, and the most likely to favor candidates who are running as independents. Indeed, 44 percent of those aged eighteen to twenty-nine identify themselves as independents. Not surprisingly, young adults gave the strongest support to Ross Perot in 1992 and to Jesse Ventura in 1998.

More fundamental, Xers have internalized core beliefs and characteristics that bode ill for the future of American democracy. This generation is more likely to describe itself as having a negative attitude toward America, and as placing little importance on citizenship and national identity, than its predecessors. And Xers exhibit a more materialistic and individualistic streak than did their parents at a similar age. Moreover, there is a general decline in social trust among the young, whether that is trust in their fellow citizens, in established institutions, or in elected officials. These tendencies are, of course, related: heightened individualism and materialism, as Alexis de Tocqueville pointed out, tend to isolate people from one another, weakening the communal bonds that give meaning and force to notions of national identity and the common good.

EXPLANATION X

MANY explanations have been advanced for the political apathy of Generation X, but none seems to tell the entire story. One theory holds that television, which the average child now watches for forty hours a week, is to blame for the cynicism and lack of civic education among the young. Another is that growing up during the Reagan and Bush presidencies, when government-bashing was the norm, led many Xers to internalize a negative attitude toward politics and the public sector. A third theory blames the breakdown of the traditional family, in which much of a child's civic sensitivity and partisan orientation is said to develop. And, of course, the incessant scandals in contemporary politics deserve some blame for driving young people into political hiding. Each of these theories undoubtedly holds some truth, but a simpler and more straightforward explanation is possible—namely, that young Americans are reacting in a per-

fectly rational manner to their circumstances, at least as they perceive them.

As they enter adulthood, this explanation goes, Xers are facing a particularly acute economic insecurity, which leads them to turn inward and pursue material well-being above all else. They see the outlines of very real problems ahead—fiscal, social, and environmental. But in the nation's political system they perceive no leadership on the issues that concern them; rather, they see self-serving politicians who continually indenture themselves to the highest bidders. So Xers have decided, for now, to tune out. After all, they ask, what's the point?

To be sure, today's young have a great deal to be thankful for. Xers have been blessed to come of age in a time of peace and relative material prosperity—itself a significant historical aberration. And the positive legacy they are inheriting goes much deeper: Generation X enjoys the fruits of the civil-rights, women's-rights, and environmental-conservation battles waged by its parents. Finally, who could deny that today's young are benefiting from significant leaps in technology, science, and medicine? But for all these new opportunities, the world being passed on to young Americans is also weighed down by truly bedeviling problems. Prevailing ideologies have proved incapable of accommodating this seeming contradiction.

Ever since the pioneering work on generational theory by the German sociologist Karl Mannheim, in the 1920s, political generations have been thought to arise from the critical events that affect young people when they are most malleable. "Early impressions," Mannheim wrote, "tend to coalesce into a *natural view* of the world." At the very heart of the Xer world view is a deep-seated economic insecurity. In contrast to Baby Boomers, most of whom came of age during the period of unparalleled upward mobility that followed the Second World War, Xers grew up in a time of falling wages, shrinking benefits, and growing economic inequality.

Since 1973, while the earnings of older Americans have mostly stagnated, real median weekly earnings for men aged twenty to thirty-four have fallen by almost a third. In fact, Xers may well be the first generation whose lifetime earnings will be less than their parents'. Al-

ready they have the weakest middle class of any generation born in this century.

Falling wages and rising inequality have affected all young Americans, regardless of educational achievement. During the said-to-be economically strong years 1989–1995 earnings for recent college graduates fell by nearly 10 percent—representing the first time that a generation of graduates has earned less than the previous one. And circumstances are far worse for the roughly 67 percent of Xers aged twenty-five to thirty-four who don't have a college degree. In 1997 recent male high school graduates earned 28 percent less (in dollars adjusted for inflation) than did the comparable group in 1973, and recent female high school graduates earned 18 percent less. When politicians and the media continually extol the economy's performance, many Xers just scratch their heads in disbelief.

The economic hardship facing today's young cannot be overstated: America's rate of children in poverty—the highest in the developed world—rose by 37 percent from 1970 to 1995. During the same period the old notions of lifetime employment and guaranteed benefits gave way to the new realities of sudden downsizing and contingent, or temporary, employment. Forty-four million Americans lack basic health insurance today, and Xers—many of whom are part of the contingent work force—are the least insured of all. To compound these problems, many Xers received a poor education in failing public schools, which left them especially ill-prepared to compete in an ever more demanding marketplace.

A LEGACY OF DEBT

BESIDES struggling against downward economic mobility, Generation X is inheriting a daunting array of fiscal, social, and environmental debts. Although most media reports focus on the national debt and the likely future insolvency of Social Security, the real problem is actually much broader. When they envision their future, Xers don't just see a government drifting toward the political equivalent of Chapter 11; they also see a crippled social structure, a dwindling middle class, and a despoiled natural habitat.

Despite bipartisan fanfare about balancing the federal budget, the fiscal outlook remains quite bleak for young adults—and for reasons seldom discussed. Long before Social Security and Medicare go insolvent under the burden of Boomer retirement, entitlement payments will have crowded out the public investments that are essential to ensuring a promising future. Government spending on infrastructure, education, and research has already lessened over the past twenty-five years, from 24 percent to 14 percent of the federal budget, and the downward squeeze will only worsen. In other words, Xers will be forced to pay ever higher taxes for ever fewer government services.

Financially most frightening, however, are the nation's skyrocketing levels of personal debt and international debt. With all the focus on balancing the federal budget, not enough attention has been paid to the fact that American families, and Xers in particular, are increasingly unable to balance their own books. Xers carry more personal debt than did any other generation at their age in our nation's history; in fact, a full 60 percent of Xers carry credit-card balances from month to month. In addition, those who attend college face the dual burden of soaring tuition bills and shrinking federal education grants. From 1977 to 1997 the median student-loan debt has climbed from $2,000 to $15,000. The combination of lower wages and over-leveraged lifestyles is doubly worrisome to a generation that wonders if it will ever collect Social Security.

Then there is America's ballooning international debt. For the past two decades the nation as a whole has consumed more than it has produced, and has borrowed from abroad to cover the difference—nearly $2 trillion by the end of this decade, or more than a fifth of the total annual output of the U.S. economy. In the short life-span to date of most Xers, America has gone from being the world's largest creditor to being its largest debtor. At some point in the future, especially as interest on our international debt accumulates, investors in other countries will become reluctant to keep bankrolling us. When they do, we will have no choice but to tighten our belts by cutting both investment and consumption. In other words, just as Xers start entering their prime earning years, with their own array of debts and demo-

graphic adversities awaiting them, they may well find themselves having to pay off the international debt that Boomers accumulated in the 1980s and 1990s.

Despite the penumbra of long-term debt, the U.S. economy remains the envy of the world; U.S. social conditions, however, are certainly not. America has some of the worst rates of child poverty, infant mortality, teen suicide, crime, family breakup, homelessness, and functional illiteracy in the developed world. In addition, many of our inner cities have turned into islands of despair, a frightening number of our public schools are dangerous, and almost two million of our residents are behind bars.

Many Xers sense that the basic fabric of American society is somehow fraying. Traditional civic participation, community cohesion, and civility are in decline, and not just among the young. The long-held belief in the value of hard work is under assault, as many Americans work longer hours for less pay, watch the gap between rich and poor grow ever wider, and see their benefits cut by corporations with little allegiance to people or place. The result is a fundamental loss of trust: between citizens and elected officials, between employees and employers, and, ultimately, between individuals and their neighbors. Yet trust and civility are the pillars on which any well-functioning democracy and free-market economy depend.

Finally, Xers face large environmental debts that stem from the use and abuse of our natural resources. Well over half of the world's major fisheries are severely depleted or overfished; loss of species and habitat continues at an unprecedented rate, with some 50,000 plant and animal species disappearing each year; freshwater tables across the globe, including parts of America, are falling precipitously; each year America alone loses more than a million acres of productive farmland to sprawl; and emissions of carbon dioxide and other greenhouse gases continue to rise, threatening to raise global temperatures by two to six degrees within the next century.

Global warming is a revealing case study from the perspective of Generation X. There is nearly unanimous scientific agreement on the problem, and a consensus among economists that the nation could reduce its greenhouse-gas emissions without harming its economy. In

addition, there is ample evidence—ranging from temperature increases to abnormally frequent weather disturbances to icebergs breaking off from the poles—to warrant deep concern. Yet our political establishment has resigned itself to virtual inaction. Why act now, politicians appear to reason, when we can just pass the problem on to our kids?

How, Xers have every right to ask, can one generation justify permanently drawing down the financial, social, and natural capital of another?

But whining will do no good. The only way for Xers to reverse their sad situation—and to realize the promise of the economic opportunities and technological innovations of the next century—is by entering the political arena that they have every reason to loathe. After all, collective problems require collective solutions. Xers cannot reasonably expect the political establishment to address, let alone fix, the sobering problems they are to inherit unless they start participating in the nation's political process, and learn to flex their generational muscle. Whether or not they do so will depend on two more immediate questions: Does this generation share a set of political beliefs? And if so, how might these translate into a political agenda?

"BALANCED-BUDGET POPULISM"

THREE quarters of Generation X agree with the statement "Our generation has an important voice, but no one seems to hear it." Whatever this voice may be, it does not fit comfortably within existing partisan camps. "The old left-right paradigm is not working anymore," according to the novelist Douglas Coupland, who coined the term "Generation X." Neil Howe and William Strauss, who have written extensively on generational issues, have argued in these pages that from the Generation X perspective "America's greatest need these days is to clear out the underbrush of name-calling and ideology so that simple things can work again." If Xers have any ideology, it is surely pragmatism.

In an attempt to be more specific Coupland has claimed, "Coming down the pipe are an extraordinarily large number of fiscal conservatives who are socially left." The underlying assumption here is that the Xer political world view stems simplistically from a combination of the 1960s social revolution and the 1980s economic revolution. This kind of thinking has led some to describe young adults as a generation of libertarians, who basically want government out of their bedrooms and out of their pocketbooks. As it turns out, however, the political views of most Xers are more complex and more interesting than that.

Xers appear to be calling for a synthesis that unites components thought to be mutually exclusive. Like conservatives, they favor fiscal restraint. Like liberals, they want to help the little guy.

To say that Xers are fiscal conservatives is to miss half the economic story; the other and equally powerful force at play can best be described as economic populism. In fact, the Xer consensus represents a novel hybrid of two distinct currents of economic thought that have rarely combined in the history of American politics. It might well be called "balanced-budget populism."

On the one hand, many Xers are worried about the debts being loaded onto their future, and therefore support fiscal prudence, balanced budgets, and a pay-as-you-go philosophy. On the other hand, Xers are more concerned than other generations about rising income inequality, and are the most likely to support government intervention to reverse it. The majority believe that the state should do more to help Americans get ahead.

What makes the Generation X economic agenda so surprising is that its two main components have thus far proved to be mutually exclusive in contemporary politics. Fiscal conservatism, widely viewed as the economic philosophy of the Republican right, has generally been accompanied by calls for lower taxes, smaller government, and reduced assistance to the neediest. Meanwhile, concern about the distribution of wealth and helping low-income workers, customarily a pillar of the Democratic left, has been associated with notions of tax-and-spend liberalism and big government. Xers appear to be calling for a new economic synthesis. Like conservatives, they favor fiscal restraint—but unlike the conservative leadership in Congress, only 15 percent believe that America should use any budget surplus to cut taxes. Like Democrats, they want to help the little guy—but unlike traditional Democrats, they are unwilling to do it by running deficits.

The Generation X social synthesis is no more conventional. Although the young are presumed to be more tolerant and socially permissive than their elders, today's young are returning to religion, have family-oriented aspirations, and are proving to be unsupportive of some traditional liberal programs, among them affirmative action. There are numerous indications that Xers—many of whom grew up without a formal religion—are actively searching for a moral compass to guide their lives, and a recent poll suggests that the highest priority for the majority of young adults is building a strong and close-knit family.

Wade Clark Roof, a professor of religion and society at the University of California at Santa Barbara, who studies the religious life of Generation X, says, "It is too early to predict whether today's young adults will form lasting commitments to particular religious denominations or institutions, but it is quite clear that there is a renewed level of interest in religion and spirituality among the post–Baby Boom generation. Many, in fact, have embarked upon a spiritual quest." As if they were spiritual consumers, young adults are shopping around among a wide range of religious traditions. In the process they are finding new ways to incorporate religion into their daily lives: for instance, church socials are rapidly becoming the new singles scene for Xers who want to combine their devotional and romantic ambitions. A clear majority of older Americans believe that a more active involvement of religious groups in politics is a bad idea, but Xers are divided on the issue.

This revival of spiritual and family-oriented aspirations represents a partial repudiation of the moral relativism that took hold in the 1960s and has since become a mainstay of American pop culture. In essence, many Xers are struggling to find a new values consensus that lies somewhere between the secular permissiveness of the left and the cultural intolerance of the right.

When it comes to race relations, Xers are particularly difficult to categorize. They are the cohort most likely to say that the civil-rights movement has not gone far enough. Yet, like Americans of all ages, they register a high level of opposition to job- and education-related affirmative-action programs. The American National Election Survey has reported that 68 percent of Xers oppose affirmative action at colleges. This seeming paradox can be explained in part by the fact that most Xers—though genuinely concerned about improving race relations—are among the first to have felt the actual (or perceived) bite of the affirmative-action programs that their parents and grandparents put into place.

Improving public education is one of the highest policy priorities for Xers. In fact, when asked what should be done with any future budget surplus, nearly half favor increased education spending. They seem to understand that knowledge will be the key to success in the information- and service-based economy of the twenty-first century. Their strong emphasis on education betokens a larger belief in the importance of investing in the future. Rather than maintaining the social-welfare state, the Xer philosophy would favor the creation of a social-investment state.

Although Xers have forsaken conventional political participation en masse, it would be a mistake to assume, as many do, that they are wholly apolitical. There is considerable evidence to suggest that volunteerism and unconventional forms of political participation have increased among young adults. Local voluntary activities, demonstrations, and boycotts all seem to be on the rise within their ranks. Heather McLeod, a Generation X co-founder of *Who Cares* magazine, has provided the following explanation: "We can *see* the impact when we volunteer. We know the difference is real." The implication, of course, is that the conventional political system has become so ineffectual and unresponsive that young people can make a positive difference only by circumventing it.

Xers may be poorly informed when it comes to public affairs, but they know enough to believe that our political system is badly in need of reform. At a very basic level they recognize that the political system is rigged against their interests. For one thing, Xers continually see a large gap between the issues they care most about and the ones that politicians choose to address. For another, they understand that Democrats and Republicans, despite an appearance of perpetual partisan infighting, collude to favor upper-income constituencies and to prevent a range of issues (including campaign-finance reform) from being acted on. Seeing themselves as the "fix-it" generation, Xers long for leaders who will talk straight and advocate the shared sacrifices necessary to correct the long-term problems that preoccupy them most. But today's elected officials are far too deeply trapped in a politics of short-term convenience to deliver anything of the sort. Not surprisingly, then, Xers are eager to do away with the two-party system. They register particularly strong support for third parties, for campaign-finance reform, and for various forms of direct democracy.

The final core belief that helps to define the political views of today's young adults is their commitment to environmental conservation. Thanks to the advent of environmental education and the spread of environmental activism, Xers grew up experiencing recycling as second nature; many actually went home and lobbied their parents to get with the program. In fact, the environment is one of the rare public-policy arenas in which Xers are fairly aware. Many have incorporated their environmental values into their lifestyles and career choices. For instance, a 1997 *Harvard Business Review* article titled "Tomorrow's Leaders: The World According to Generation X" revealed that most current MBA students believed that corporations have a clear-cut responsibility to be environment-friendly in their practices. This generation does not believe that a tradeoff is necessary between a strong economy and a healthy environment.

Fiscal prudence, economic populism, social investment, campaign reform, shared sacrifice, and environmental conservation—this constellation of beliefs transcends the existing left-right spectrum. It should be immediately apparent

that this generation's voice is not represented by any of the established leaders or factions in the political mainstream. And Xers seem to recognize as much—61 percent agree with the statement "Politicians and political leaders have failed my generation." So how would American politics change if the voice of Generation X were suddenly heard?

A NEW POLITICAL AGENDA

DESPITE its feeble rates of political participation, Generation X has already—if unwittingly—exerted an influence on the substance of our politics. This may seem counterintuitive, but who would deny that young Americans were a major force in pushing the balanced-budget cause to the fore? In part this is owing to the large number of Xer votes cast in 1992 for Ross Perot, the candidate who staked much of his campaign on balancing the federal books. Though Perot lost, his pet issue gained momentum as candidates from both parties scrambled to win over Reform Party voters, and the young ones in particular. Recognizing that Generation X makes up a large and particularly unpredictable voting bloc, candidates from across the spectrum have gone out of their way to woo the youth vote, usually by paying lip service to some of young people's more obvious concerns, including, most recently, Social Security reform. Over time, however, Xer support for issues such as balancing the budget and saving Social Security will turn out to be only part of a much broader agenda, one that could come to challenge the status quo on everything from taxes to social policy to political reform.

For years the nation's tax debate has revolved around the question of how much to tax, with the left arguing for more and the right for less. In keeping with the concept of balanced-budget populism, the Xer economic agenda would start with the assumption that the government's share of national income should remain roughly constant. It would focus instead on a far more profound set of questions: What should be taxed? Who should be taxed? What should we invest in? and Who should get the benefits? Over the past several decades the tax burden has crept further and further down the income and age ladder, with the benefits going increasingly to the

elderly and the well-to-do—the government now spends nine times as much on each elderly person as it does on each child. If Xers had their way, the collection of taxes would become more progressive and the distribution of benefits more widespread.

One would never know it from partisan skirmishes over income-tax cuts, but the payroll tax actually constitutes the largest tax burden borne by 70 percent of working families and by a full 90 percent of working Americans under age thirty. It is also the most regressive of all taxes, because it kicks in from the first dollar earned, falls exclusively on wages, and is capped at $72,600. An appealing solution to this problem would be to replace payroll taxes with pollution taxes, thereby boosting wages, promoting jobs, and cleaning up the environment, all without raising the deficit. Taxing waste instead of work is precisely the kind of innovative and pragmatic proposal that could help to galvanize the members of Generation X, who have been put to sleep by the current tax debate.

Sooner or later Xers will figure out that America could raise trillions of dollars in new public revenues by charging fair market value for the use of common assets—the oil and coal in the ground, the trees in our national forests, the airwaves and the electromagnetic spectrum—and the rights to pollute our air. We currently subsidize the use of these resources in a number of ways, creating a huge windfall for a small number of industries and a significant loss for all other Americans. The idea of reversing this trend by charging fair market value for the use of common assets and returning the proceeds directly to each American citizen plays to a number of Xer political views—it is populist, equitable, libertarian, and pro-environment all at once.

The populist economic leanings of young adults will also lead them to rethink various other elements of the social contract between citizens, government, and business. For one thing, ending corporate welfare would appeal to a generation weaned on the principle of self-sufficiency. The hidden welfare state, composed of corporate subsidies and tax loopholes that overwhelmingly benefit the well-to-do, has grown several times as large as the hotly debated social-welfare state that benefits the disadvantaged through means-tested programs. Yet today's politicians are too much indebted to the beneficiaries of this governmental largesse to do anything about it. Here, then, may be the key to keeping the budget balanced while funding the social investments that are so important to Xers: all of the money raised or saved by charging for the use of common assets, ending corporate welfare, and closing unproductive tax loopholes could be used to make a topnotch education affordable and accessible to all and, just as important, to make every American child a "trust-fund" baby from birth.

Making economic incentives more progressive and redirecting budgetary priorities is only one part of an Xer economic agenda. Today's young adults, more than any other group at a comparable age, are concerned about their economic outlook and their ability to balance the conflicting demands of work and family. If such problems worsen as a result of economic globalization, then the populism of Generation X, which up to this point has been relatively mild, may suddenly become more pronounced. For instance, the 2030 Center, an advocacy group concerned about the economic well-being of Generation X, is launching a campaign to promote a contingent workers' bill of rights, which calls on employers to provide health care and other benefits to more of their workers.

Even as they were being told that education is the key to a promising future, many Xers were learning the hard way how bad our urban schools have become, and how inequitable is the access to a high-quality education. Neither party is providing a palatable solution: Republicans are all but writing off public schools by emphasizing vouchers that favor private schools, and Democrats are perpetuating many of the worst public-school problems by refusing to challenge the teachers' unions. There are no simple solutions to the predicament, but an obvious starting point would be to sever the traditional link between public-school funding and local property taxes, which only exacerbates existing socioeconomic inequalities. (Several states have already begun moving in this direction.) Another significant improvement would be to increase the skill level of our public-school teachers by imposing stricter standards and offering more-competitive salaries.

Xers would support enacting new policies to advance racial integration and civil rights in America—policies that avoid the divisiveness and unintended consequences of race-based affirmative action. Although such policies made sense when they were introduced, many Xers believe, race is no longer the determining factor in who gets ahead. In the twenty-first century poor black Americans will have more in common with poor white Americans than they will with upper-middle-class blacks. If the goal is to help those most in need, it would make a lot more sense to pursue class-based affirmative-action programs. Doing so would enable all those at the bottom—regardless of race—to get the help they need, in a way that promoted national unity and racial integration. Another promising alternative to race-based affirmative action is the Texas Ten Percent Plan, whereby all students graduating in the top tenth of their high school classes—whether in inner-city schools or in elite private ones—are automatically accepted into the state's public universities.

Fundamental campaign and political reform is the sine qua non of a Generation X political agenda. Like most Americans, Xers would like to see bold steps taken to get money out of politics. But persuading America's young that their individual votes matter is likely to require reforms far more radical than any currently under consideration.

Until recently most political-reform movements in the United States were based on the assumption that the problem was not the two-party system itself but rather its corruption by special interests and incumbency (hence the proposed cures of campaign-finance reform and term limits). But neither the reduction of private campaign contributions nor the implementation of term limits for elected officials will alter what seems to alienate Xers most of all: the political duopoly of Democrats and Republicans. The rules of today's two-party system actively discourage a third or a fourth party. Consequently, there is growing interest among the young in replacing our archaic electoral process (itself a remnant from eighteenth-century England) with a modern multiparty system. With three or four parties contesting many races, politics might become exciting enough to draw in disenchanted Xers who believe, correctly, that in most elections today their votes do not count.

As the vanguard of the digital age, Xers will also be inclined to support experiments with electronic democracy. For instance, one Xer has launched an effort to make information about the sources of campaign contributions immediately available to the public and the media over the Internet. But the full potential of digital democracy runs much deeper. Already groups are experimenting with electronic town-hall meetings and various forms of deliberative democracy, in which individuals are provided with a full range of information on a particular issue and can register their opinions with the push of a button. It is not hard to imagine a day when citizens will be able to register and vote online, and to monitor the performance of their elected officials with electronic scorecards.

The introduction of electronic communication within corporate America has helped to flatten organizational hierarchies, boost information flows, increase decision-making speed, and, most of all, empower workers. It is at least conceivable that the introduction of electronic forms of democracy could serve to re-engage a generation that has been alienated by today's money-, spin-, and celebrity-dominated politics. And if Xers do eventually enter the fray, their agenda will transform America's political landscape.

THE FUTURE OF AMERICAN POLITICS

REPUBLICANS and Democrats will be tempted to dismiss the Xer agenda, because it threatens their electoral coalitions and the politics of short-term convenience. But both parties will do so at their peril, because many of the issues that Xers care most about are already rising to the political surface.

A glimpse of the future may come, strangely enough, in the election of Jesse Ventura as governor of Minnesota. Much of Ventura's support came from young adults, who took advantage of Minnesota's same-day registration law and stormed the polls, helping to create a record turnout. This suggests that if a political candidate can somehow capture the passion of young adults, they will do their part. Ventura offered young Minnesotans something refreshing: a clear alternative to Democrats and Republicans, and a willingness to take on the status quo. But Jesse Ventura is no figurehead for Xers; he is just an early beneficiary of their pent-up political frustration.

As the Xer political agenda starts to take hold, it will further strain existing loyalties. On the Republican side, the odd-bedfellow coalition of social conservatives and economic libertarians that has defined the party for the past two decades is coming apart as a result of the Clinton impeachment saga, whose most lasting legacy may be that it dealt a coup de grace to the political aspirations of the religious right. The Democratic coalition is just as fragile, particularly since it has been losing its base of working-class white men, and the potential retreat of the religious right may deprive Democrats of an obvious opponent against which to rally. As these de-alignments unfold, major shifts in the makeup and core agendas of both parties become almost inevitable.

The stability of today's political consensus is also contingent on the promise of an economy that continues to expand. Take that away, and the props of the status quo—a balanced budget and the novelty of a budgetary surplus, a booming stock market and stable price structures, low unemployment and rising wages, falling welfare rolls and crime rates, and the illusion of a painless fix to Social Security—all topple at once. No business cycle lasts forever, and the global economic crisis of 1998 should come as a warning of what may lie ahead. The prospect of a significant recession leaves the future of American politics wide open.

Turning points in our nation's political history, occasioned by the collapse of an existing civic and political consensus, have usually been accompanied by rampant individualism, weakened institutions, and heightened levels of political alienation. On these scores Xers are playing out their historic role remarkably well. But such periods of civic unrest have also stimulated new political agendas, which eventually force one or both parties to remake themselves around new priorities and coalitions. Could the Generation X political agenda serve as the basis of America's next political consensus?

Balanced-budget populism, social investment, and other elements of the Xer agenda could resonate with Americans of all ages—and help to create the nation's next majoritarian coalition.

Balanced-budget populism, social investment, no-nonsense pragmatism, and shared sacrifice could resonate quite strongly with Americans of all ages—particularly the increasing number who are fed up with conventional politics. What is more, the Xer synthesis of a middle-class economic agenda with a moderate social one could remake the powerful alliance between progressives and populists that dominated national politics (and brought widespread upward mobility) from the 1930s to 1960s, when it was ripped apart by the cultural upheaval of the Baby Boom. In practical

terms this new politics—based on fiscal prudence, economic populism, family-friendly morality, social investment, campaign reform, environmental conservation, and technological innovation—could eventually take hold in either of the major parties, both of which are now searching for a coherent agenda and a lasting voter base. For Democrats it could mark a return to the party's New Deal roots, and for Republicans it could give substance to heretofore vague calls for a "compassionate conservatism."

Since this new politics could speak to many of those who are alienated by the current political order, Xers and older Americans alike, it could give birth to our nation's next majoritarian coalition. Such a coalition could do a great deal to reinvigorate our nation's democracy, benefit the majority of its citizens, and restore legitimacy to our political system.

When history books are written at the end of the twenty-first century, it is unlikely that the post–Baby Boom generation will still be referred to as a nondescript "X." One way or another, this generation will be judged and labeled by its legacy. Today's young adults will be remembered either as a late-blooming generation that ultimately helped to revive American democracy by coalescing around a bold new political program and bringing the rest of the nation along with them, or as another silent generation that stood by as our democracy and society suffered a slow decline.

The great question of twenty-first-century politics is whether a critical mass of Xers will eventually recognize the broader potential of their agenda, and outgrow their aversion to politics.

Ted Halstead is president and CEO of the New America Foundation, in Washington, D.C.

From *The Atlantic Monthly*, August 1999, pp. 33–42. © 1999 by Ted Halstead. Reprinted by permission of the author.

American Culture Goes Global, or Does It?

By RICHARD PELLS

Since september 11, newspaper and magazine columnists and television pundits have told us that it is not only the economic power of the United States or the Bush administration's "unilateralist" foreign policy that breeds global anti-Americanism. Dislike for the United States stems also, they say, from its "cultural imperialism." We have been hearing a good deal about how American mass culture inspires resentment and sometimes violent reactions, not just in the Middle East but all over the world.

Yet the discomfort with American cultural dominance is not new. In 1901, the British writer William Stead published a book called, ominously, *The Americanization of the World*. The title captured a set of apprehensions—about the disappearance of national languages and traditions, and the obliteration of the unique identities of countries under the weight of American habits and states of mind—that persists today.

More recently, globalization has become the main enemy for academics, journalists, and political activists who loathe what they see as a trend toward cultural uniformity. Still, they usually regard global culture and American culture as synonymous. And they continue to insist that Hollywood, McDonald's, and Disneyland are eradicating regional and local eccentricities—disseminating images and subliminal messages so beguiling as to drown out competing voices in other lands.

Despite those allegations, the cultural relationship between the United States and the rest of the world over the past 100 years has never been one-sided. On the contrary, the United States was, and continues to be, as much a consumer of foreign intellectual and artistic influences as it has been a shaper of the world's entertainment and tastes.

That is not an argument with which many foreigners (or even many Americans) would readily agree. The clichés about America's cultural "hegemony" make it difficult for most people to recognize that modern global culture is hardly a monolithic entity foisted on the world by the American media.

Neither is it easy for critics of Microsoft or AOL Time Warner to acknowledge that the conception of a harmonious and distinctively American culture—encircling the globe, implanting its values in foreign minds—is a myth.

In fact, as a nation of immigrants from the 19th to the 21st centuries, and as a haven in the 1930s and '40s for refugee scholars and artists, the United States has been a recipient as much as an exporter of global culture. Indeed, the influence of immigrants and African-Americans on the United States explains why its culture has been so popular for so long in so many places. American culture has spread throughout the world because it has incorporated foreign styles and ideas. What Americans have done more brilliantly than their competitors overseas is repackage the cultural products we receive from abroad and then retransmit them to the rest of the planet. In effect, Americans have specialized in selling the dreams, fears, and folklore of other people back to them. That is why a global mass culture has come to be identified, however simplistically, with the United States.

Americans, after all, did not invent fast food, amusement parks, or the movies. Before the Big Mac, there were fish and chips. Before Disneyland, there was Copenhagen's Tivoli Gardens (which Walt Disney used as a prototype for his first theme park, in Anaheim, a model later re-exported to Tokyo and Paris).

Nor can the origins of today's international entertainment be traced only to P.T. Barnum or Buffalo Bill. The roots of the new global culture lie as well in the European modernist assault, in the early 20th century, on 19th-century literature, music, painting, and architecture—particularly in the modernist refusal to honor the traditional boundaries between high and low culture. Modernism in the arts was improvisational, eclectic, and irreverent. Those traits have also been characteristic of, but not peculiar to, mass culture.

The hallmark of 19th-century culture, in Europe and also in Asia, was its insistence on defending the purity of literature, classical music, and representational painting against the intrusions of folklore and popular amusements. No one confused Tolstoy with dime novels, opera with Wild West shows, the Louvre with Coney Island. High culture was supposed to be educational, contemplative, and uplifting—a way of preserving the best in human civilization.

Such beliefs didn't mean that a Dickens never indulged in melodrama, or that a Brahms disdained the use of popular songs. Nor did Chinese or Japanese authors and painters refuse to draw on oral or folkloric traditions. But the 19th-century barriers between high and low culture were resolutely, if imperfectly, maintained.

The artists of the early 20th century shattered what seemed to them the artificial demarcations between different cultural forms. They also challenged the notion that culture was a means of intellectual or moral improvement. They did so by emphasizing style and craftsmanship at the expense of philosophy, religion, or ideology. They deliberately called attention to language in their novels, to optics in their paintings, to the materials in and function of their architecture, to the structure of music instead of its melodies.

And they wanted to shock their audiences. Which they succeeded in doing. Modern painting and literature—with its emphasis on visually distorted nudes, overt sexuality, and meditations on violence—was attacked for being degrading and obscene, and for appealing to the baser instincts of humanity. In much the same way, critics would later denounce the vulgarity of popular culture.

Although modernism assaulted the conventions of 19th-century high culture in Europe and Asia, it inadvertently accelerated the growth of mass culture in the United States. Indeed, Americans were already receptive to the blurring of cultural boundaries. In the 19th century, symphony orchestras in the United States often included band music in their programs, and opera singers were asked to perform both Mozart and Stephen Foster.

So, for Americans in the 20th century, Surrealism, with its dreamlike associations, easily lent itself to the wordplay and psychological symbolism of advertising, cartoons, and theme parks. Dadaism ridiculed the snobbery of elite cultural institutions and reinforced, instead, an existing appetite (especially among the immigrant audiences in the United States) for low-class, anti-bourgeois nickelodeons and vaudeville shows. Stravinsky's experiments with atonal (and thus unconventional and unmelodic) music validated the rhythmic innovations of American jazz. Writers like Hemingway, detesting the rhetorical embellishments of 19th-century prose, invented a terse, hard-boiled language, devoted to reproducing as authentically as possible the elemental qualities of personal experience. That laconic style became a model for modern journalism, detective fiction, and movie dialogue.

All of those trends provided the foundations for a genuinely new culture. But the new culture turned out to be neither modernist nor European. Instead, the United States transformed what was still a parochial culture, appealing largely to the young and the rebellious in Western society, into a global phenomenon.

The propensity of Americans to borrow modernist ideas, and to transform them into a global culture, is clearly visible in the commercial uses of modern architecture. The European Bauhaus movement—intended in the 1920s as a socialist experiment in working-class housing—eventually provided the theories and techniques for the construction of skyscrapers and vacation homes in the United States. But the same architectural ideas were then sent back to Europe after World War II as a model for the reconstruction of bombed-out cities like Rotterdam, Cologne, and Frankfurt. Thus, the United States converted what had once been a distinctive, if localized, rebellion by Dutch and German architects into a generic "international style."

But it is in popular culture that the reciprocal relationship between America and the rest of the world can best be seen. There are many reasons for the ascendancy of American mass culture. Certainly, the ability of American-based media conglomerates to control the production and distribution of their products has been a major stimulus to the worldwide spread of American entertainment. But the power of American capitalism is not the only, or even the most important, explanation for the global popularity of America's movies and television shows.

The effectiveness of English as a language of mass communications has been essential to the acceptance of American culture. Unlike, for example, German, Russian, or Chinese, the simple structure and grammar of English, along with its tendency to use shorter, less-abstract words and more-concise sentences, are all advantageous for the composers of song lyrics, ad slogans, cartoon captions, newspaper headlines, and movie and TV dialogue. English is thus a language exceptionally well-suited to the demands and spread of American mass culture.

American musicians and entertainers have followed modernist artists like Picasso and Braque in drawing on elements from high and low culture.

Another factor is the size of the American audience. A huge domestic market has made it possible for many American filmmakers and TV executives to retrieve most of their production costs and make a profit within the borders of the United States. That economic cushion has enabled them to spend more money on stars, sets, special effects, location shooting, and merchandising—the very ingredients that attract international audiences as well.

Yet even with such advantages, America's mass culture may not be all that American. The American audience is not only large; because of the influx of immigrants and refugees, it is also international in its complexion. The heterogeneity of America's population—its regional, ethnic, religious, and racial diversity—has forced the media, since the early years of the 20th century, to experiment with messages, images, and story lines that have a broad multicultural appeal. The Hollywood studios, mass-circulation magazines, and television networks have had to learn how to speak to a variety of groups and classes at home. That has given them the techniques to appeal to an equally diverse audience abroad. The American domestic market has, in essence, been a laboratory, a place to develop cultural products that can then be adapted to the world market.

An important way that the American media have succeeded in transcending internal social divisions, national borders, and language barriers is by mixing up cultural styles. American musicians and entertainers have followed the example of modernist artists like Picasso and Braque in drawing on elements from high and low culture, combining the sacred and the profane. Advertisers have adapted the techniques of Surrealism and Abstract Expressionism to make their products more intriguing. Composers like Aaron Copland, George Gershwin, and Leonard Bernstein incorporated folk melodies, religious hymns, blues, gospel songs, and jazz into their symphonies, concertos, operas, and ballets. Indeed, an art form as quintessentially American as jazz evolved during the 20th century into an amalgam of African, Caribbean, Latin American, and modernist European music. That blending of forms in America's mass culture has enhanced its appeal to multiethnic domestic and international audiences by capturing their varied experiences and tastes.

NOWHERE ARE FOREIGN INFLUENCES more evident than in the American movie industry. For better or worse, Hollywood became, in the 20th century, the cultural capital of the modern world. But it was never an exclusively American capital. Like past cultural centers—Florence, Paris, Vienna—Hollywood has functioned as an international community, built by immigrant entrepreneurs and drawing on the talents of actors, directors, writers, cinematographers, editors, and costume and set designers from all over the world. The first American movie star, after all, was Charlie Chaplin, whose comic skills were honed in British music halls.

Moreover, during much of the 20th century, American moviemakers thought of themselves as acolytes, entranced by the superior works of foreign directors. In the 1920s, few American directors could gain admittance to a European pantheon that included Sergei Eisenstein, F.W. Murnau, G.W. Pabst, Fritz Lang, and Carl Dreyer. The postwar years, from the 1940s to the mid-'60s, were once again a golden age of filmmaking in Britain, Sweden, France, Italy, Japan, and India. An extraordinary generation of foreign directors—Ingmar Bergman, Federico Fellini, Michelangelo Antonioni, François Truffaut, Jean-Luc Godard, Akira Kurosawa, Satyajit Ray—were the world's most celebrated auteurs.

Nevertheless, it is one of the paradoxes of the European and Asian cinemas that their greatest success was in spawning American imitations. After the release, in 1967, of *Bonnie and Clyde* (originally to have been directed by Truffaut or Godard), the newest geniuses—Francis Ford Coppola, Martin Scorsese, Robert Altman, Steven Spielberg, Woody Allen—were American. They may have owed their improvisational methods and autobiographical preoccupations to Italian neo-Realism and the French New Wave. But who, in any country, needed to see another *La Dolce Vita* when you could enjoy *Nashville*? Why try to decipher *Jules and Jim* or *L'Avventura* when you could see *Annie Hall* or *The Godfather*? Wasn't it conceivable that *The Seven Samurai* might not be as powerful or as disturbing a movie as *The Wild Bunch*?

It turned out that foreign filmmakers had been too influential for their own good. They helped revolutionize the American cinema, so that, after the 1960s and '70s, it became hard for any other continent's film industry to match the worldwide popularity of American movies.

Once again, however, we need to remember that Hollywood movies have never been just American. To take another example, American directors, in all eras, have emulated foreign artists and filmmakers by paying close attention to the style and formal qualities of a movie, and to the need to tell a story visually. Early-20th-century European painters wanted viewers to recognize that they were looking at lines and color on a canvas rather than at a reproduction of the natural world. Similarly, many American films—from the multiple narrators in *Citizen Kane*, to the split-screen portrait of how two lovers imagine their relationship in *Annie Hall*, to the flashbacks and flash-forwards in *Pulp Fiction*, to the roses blooming from the navel of Kevin Spacey's fantasy dream girl in *American Beauty*—deliberately remind the audience that it is watching a movie instead of a play or a photographed version of reality. American filmmakers (not only in the movies but also on MTV) have been willing to use the most sophisticated techniques of editing and camera work, much of it inspired by European directors, to create a modernist collage of images that captures the speed and seductiveness of life in the contemporary world.

Hollywood's addiction to modernist visual pyrotechnics is especially evident in the largely nonverbal style of many of its contemporary performers. The tendency to mumble was not always in vogue. In the 1930s and '40s, the sound and meaning of words were important not only in movies but also on records and the radio. Even though some homegrown stars, like John Wayne and Gary Cooper, were famously terse, audiences could at least hear and understand what they were saying. But the centrality of language in the films of the 1930s led, more often, to a dependence in Hollywood on British actors (like Cary Grant), or on Americans who sounded vaguely British (like Katharine Hepburn and Bette Davis). It is illustrative of how important foreign (especially British) talent was to Hollywood in an earlier era that the two most famous Southern belles in American fiction and drama—Scarlett O'Hara and Blanche DuBois—were played in the movies by Vivien Leigh.

The verbal eloquence of pre-World War II acting, in both movies and the theater, disappeared after 1945. After Marlon Brando's revolutionary performance in *A Streetcar Named Desire*, in the 1947 stage version and the 1951 screen version, the model of American acting became inarticulateness—a brooding and halting introspection that one doesn't find in the glib and clever heroes or heroines of the screwball comedies and gangster films of the '30s. Brando was trained in the Method, an acting technique originally developed in Stanislavsky's Moscow Art Theater in prerevolutionary Russia, then imported to New York by members of the Group Theater during the 1930s. Where British actors, trained in Shakespeare, were taught to subordinate their personalities to the role as written, the Method encouraged actors to improvise, to summon up childhood memories, and to explore their inner feelings, often at the expense of what the playwright or screenwriter intended. Norman Mailer once said that Brando, in his pauses and his gazes into the middle distance, always seemed to be searching for a better line than the one the writer had composed. In effect, what Brando did (along with his successors and imitators, from James Dean to Warren Beatty to Robert De Niro) was to lead a revolt against the British school of acting, with its reverence for the script and the written (and spoken) word.

Thus, after World War II, the emotional power of American acting lay more in what was not said, in what could not even be communicated in words. The Method actor's reliance on physical mannerisms and even silence in interpreting a role has been especially appropriate for a cinema that puts a premium on the inexpressible. Indeed, the influence of the Method, not only in the United States but also abroad (where it was reflected in the acting styles of Jean-Paul Belmondo and Marcello Mastroianni), is a classic example of how a foreign idea, originally meant for the stage, was adapted in postwar America to the movies, and then conveyed to the rest of the world as a paradigm for both cinematic and social behavior. More important, the Method's disregard for language permitted global audiences—even those not well-versed in English—to understand and appreciate what they were watching in American films.

Finally, American culture has imitated not only the modernists' visual flamboyance, but also their emphasis on personal expression and their tendency to be apolitical and anti-ideological. The refusal to browbeat an audience with a social message has accounted, more than any other factor, for the worldwide popularity of American entertainment. American movies, in particular, have customarily focused on human relationships and private feelings, not on the problems of a particular time and place. They tell tales about romance, intrigue, success, failure, moral conflicts, and survival. The most memorable movies of the 1930s (with the exception of *The Grapes of Wrath*) were comedies and musicals about mismatched people falling in love, not socially conscious films dealing with issues of poverty and unemployment. Similarly, the finest movies about World War II (like *Casablanca*) or the Vietnam War (like *The Deer Hunter*) linger in the mind long after those conflicts have ended because they explore their characters' intimate emotions rather than dwelling on headline events.

Such intensely personal dilemmas are what people everywhere wrestle with. So Europeans, Asians, and Latin Americans flocked to *Titanic* (as they once did to *Gone With the Wind*) not because it celebrated American values, but because people all over the world could see some part of their own lives reflected in the story of love and loss.

America's mass culture has often been crude and intrusive, as its critics—from American academics like Benjamin Barber to German directors like Wim Wenders—have always complained. In their eyes, American culture is "colonizing" everyone else's subconscious, reducing us all to passive residents of "McWorld."

But American culture has never felt all that foreign to foreigners. And, at its best, it has transformed what it received from others into a culture that everyone, everywhere, can embrace, a culture that is both emotionally and, on occasion, artistically compelling for millions of people throughout the world.

So, despite the current hostility to America's policies and values—in Europe and Latin America as well as in the Middle East and Asia—it is important to recognize how familiar much of American culture seems to people abroad. If anything, our movies, television shows, and theme parks have been less "imperialistic" than cosmopolitan. In the end, American mass culture has not transformed the world into a replica of the United States. Instead, America's dependence on foreign cultures has made the United States a replica of the world.

Richard Pells is a professor of history at the University of Texas at Austin. His books include Not Like Us: How Europeans Have Loved, Hated, and Transformed American Culture Since World War II *(Basic Books, 1997).*

Originally published in *The Chronicle of Higher Education*, April 12, 2002, pp. B7, B9. © 2002 by Richard Pells. Reprinted by permission of the author.

The Bubble of American Supremacy

A prominent financier argues that the heedless assertion
of American power in the world resembles a financial
bubble—and the moment of truth may be here

By George Soros

It is generally agreed that September 11, 2001, changed
the course of history. But we must ask ourselves why that
should be so. How could a single event, even one involving
3,000 civilian casualties, have such a far-reaching effect?
The answer lies not so much in the event itself as in the way
the United States, under the leadership of President George
W. Bush, responded to it.

Admittedly, the terrorist attack was historic in its own
right. Hijacking fully fueled airliners and using them as suicide bombs was an audacious idea, and its execution could
not have been more spectacular. The destruction of the Twin
Towers of the World Trade Center made a symbolic statement that reverberated around the world, and the fact that
people could watch the event on their television sets endowed it with an emotional impact that no terrorist act had
ever achieved before. The aim of terrorism is to terrorize, and
the attack of September 11 fully accomplished this objective.

Even so, September 11 could not have changed the
course of history to the extent that it has if President Bush
had not responded to it the way he did. He declared war on
terrorism, and under that guise implemented a radical for-
eign-policy agenda whose underlying principles predated
the tragedy. Those principles can be summed up as follows:
International relations are relations of power, not law;
power prevails and law legitimizes what prevails. The
United States is unquestionably the dominant power in the
post-Cold War world; it is therefore in a position to impose
its views, interests, and values. The world would benefit
from adopting those values, because the American model
has demonstrated its superiority. The Clinton and first Bush
Administrations failed to use the full potential of American

power. This must be corrected; the United States must find
a way to assert its supremacy in the world.

This foreign policy is part of a comprehensive ideology
customarily referred to as neoconservatism, though I prefer
to describe it as a crude form of social Darwinism. I call it
crude because it ignores the role of cooperation in the survival of the fittest, and puts all the emphasis on competition. In economic matters the competition is between firms;
in international relations it is between states. In economic
matters social Darwinism takes the form of market fundamentalism; in international relations it is now leading to the
pursuit of American supremacy.

Not all the members of the Bush Administration subscribe to this ideology, but neoconservatives form an influential group within it. They publicly called for the invasion
of Iraq as early as 1998. Their ideas originated in the Cold
War and were further elaborated in the post-Cold War era.
Before September 11 the ideologues were hindered in im-
plementing their strategy by two considerations: George W.
Bush did not have a clear mandate (he became President by
virtue of a single vote in the Supreme Court), and America
did not have a clearly defined enemy that would have justified a dramatic increase in military spending.

September 11 removed both obstacles. President Bush
declared war on terrorism, and the nation lined up behind
its President. Then the Bush Administration proceeded to
exploit the terrorist attack for its own purposes. It fostered
the fear that has gripped the country in order to keep the nation united behind the President, and it used the war on terrorism to execute an agenda of American supremacy. That
is how September 11 changed the course of history.

Exploiting an event to further an agenda is not in itself reprehensible. It is the task of the President to provide leadership, and it is only natural for politicians to exploit or manipulate events so as to promote their policies. The cause for concern lies in the policies that Bush is promoting, and in the way he is going about imposing them on the United States and the world. He is leading us in a very dangerous direction.

The supremacist ideology of the Bush Administration stands in opposition to the principles of an open society, which recognize that people have different views and that nobody is in possession of the ultimate truth. The supremacist ideology postulates that just because we are stronger than others, we know better and have right on our side. The very first sentence of the September 2002 National Security Strategy (the President's annual laying out to Congress of the country's security objectives) reads, "The great struggles of the twentieth century between liberty and totalitarianism ended with a decisive victory for the forces of freedom— and a single sustainable model for national success: freedom, democracy, and free enterprise."

> ## September 11 introduced a discontinuity into American Foreign policy. The abnormal, the radical, and the extreme have been redefined as normal. The advocates of continuity have been pursuing a rearguard action ever since.

The assumptions behind this statement are false on two counts. First, there is no single sustainable model for national success. Second, the American model, which has indeed been successful, is not available to others, because our success depends greatly on our dominant position at the center of the global capitalist system, and we are not willing to yield it.

The Bush doctrine, first enunciated in a presidential speech at West Point in June of 2002, and incorporated into the National Security Strategy three months later, is built on two pillars: the United States will do everything in its power to maintain its unquestioned military supremacy; and the United States arrogates the right to pre-emptive action. In effect, the doctrine establishes two classes of sovereignty: the sovereignty of the United States, which takes precedence over international treaties and obligations; and the sovereignty of all other states, which is subject to the will of the United States. This is reminiscent of George Orwell's *Animal Farm*: all animals are equal, but some animals are more equal than others.

To be sure, the Bush doctrine is not stated so starkly; it is shrouded in doublespeak. The doublespeak is needed because of the contradiction between the Bush Administration's concept of freedom and democracy and the actual principles and requirements of freedom and democracy. Talk of spreading democracy looms large in the National Security Strategy. But when President Bush says, as he does frequently, that freedom will prevail, he means that America will prevail. In a free and open society, people are supposed to decide for themselves what they mean by freedom and democracy, and not simply follow America's lead. The contradiction is especially apparent in the case of Iraq, and the occupation of Iraq has brought the issue home. We came as liberators, bringing freedom and democracy, but that is not how we are perceived by a large part of the population.

It is ironic that the government of the most successful open society in the world should have fallen into the hands of people who ignore the first principles of open society. At home Attorney General John Ashcroft has used the war on terrorism to curtail civil liberties. Abroad the United States is trying to impose its views and interests through the use of military force. The invasion of Iraq was the first practical application of the Bush doctrine, and it has turned out to be counterproductive. A chasm has opened between America and the rest of the world.

The size of the chasm is impressive. On September 12, 2001, a special meeting of the North Atlantic Council invoked Article 5 of the NATO Treaty for the first time in the alliance's history, calling on all member states to treat the terrorist attack on the United States as an attack upon their own soil. The United Nations promptly endorsed punitive U.S. action against al-Qaeda in Afghanistan. A little more than a year later the United States could not secure a UN resolution to endorse the invasion of Iraq. Gerhard Schröder won re-election in Germany by refusing to cooperate with the United States. In South Korea an underdog candidate was elected to the presidency because he was considered the least friendly to the United States; many South Koreans regard the United States as a greater danger to their security than North Korea. A large majority throughout the world opposed the war on Iraq.

September 11 introduced a discontinuity into American foreign policy. Violations of American standards of behavior that would have been considered objectionable in ordinary times became accepted as appropriate to the circumstances. The abnormal, the radical, and the extreme have been redefined as normal. The advocates of continuity have been pursuing a rearguard action ever since.

To explain the significance of the transition, I should like to draw on my experience in the financial markets. Stock markets often give rise to a boom-bust process, or bubble. Bubbles do not grow out of thin air. They have a basis in reality—but reality as distorted by a misconception. Under normal conditions misconceptions are self-correcting, and the markets tend toward some kind of equilibrium. Occasionally, a misconception is reinforced by a trend prevailing in reality, and that is when a boom-bust process gets under way. Eventually the gap between reality and its false interpretation becomes unsustainable, and the bubble bursts.

Exactly when the boom-bust process enters far-from-equilibrium territory can be established only in retrospect. During the self-reinforcing phase participants are under the spell of the prevailing bias. Events seem to confirm their beliefs, strengthening their misconceptions. This widens the gap and sets the stage for a moment of truth and an eventual reversal. When that reversal comes, it is liable to have devastating consequences. This course of events seems to have an inexorable quality, but a boom-bust process can be aborted at any stage, and the adverse effects can be reduced or avoided altogether. Few bubbles reach the extremes of the information-technology boom that ended in 2000. The sooner the process is aborted, the better.

The quest for American supremacy qualifies as a bubble. The dominant position the United States occupies in the world is the element of reality that is being distorted. The proposition that the United States will be better off if it uses its position to impose its values and interests everywhere is the misconception. It is exactly by not abusing its power that America attained its current position.

Where are we in this boom-bust process? The deteriorating situation in Iraq is either the moment of truth or a test that, if it is successfully overcome, will only reinforce the trend.

Whatever the justification for removing Saddam Hussein, there can be no doubt that we invaded Iraq on false pretenses. Wittingly or unwittingly, President Bush deceived the American public and Congress and rode roughshod over the opinions of our allies. The gap between the Administration's expectations and the actual state of affairs could not be wider. It is difficult to think of a recent military operation that has gone so wrong. Our soldiers have been forced to do police duty in combat gear, and they continue to be killed. We have put at risk not only our soldiers' lives but the combat effectiveness of our armed forces. Their morale is impaired, and we are no longer in a position to properly project our power. Yet there are more places than ever before where we might have legitimate need to project that power. North Korea is openly building nuclear weapons, and Iran is clandestinely doing so. The Taliban is regrouping in Afghanistan. The costs of occupation and the prospect of permanent war are weighing heavily on our economy, and we are failing to address many festering problems—domestic and global. If we ever needed proof that the dream of American supremacy is misconceived, the occupation of Iraq has provided it. If we fail to heed the evidence, we will have to pay a heavier price in the future.

Meanwhile, largely as a result of our preoccupation with supremacy, something has gone fundamentally wrong with the war on terrorism. Indeed, war is a false metaphor in this context. Terrorists do pose a threat to our national and personal security, and we must protect ourselves.

Many of the measures we have taken are necessary and proper. It can even be argued that not enough has been done to prevent future attacks. But the war being waged has little to do with ending terrorism or enhancing homeland security; on the contrary, it endangers our security by engendering a vicious circle of escalating violence.

The terrorist attack on the United States could have been treated as a crime against humanity rather than an act of war. Treating it as a crime would have been more appropriate. Crimes require police work, not military action. Protection against terrorism requires precautionary measures, awareness, and intelligence gathering—all of which ultimately depend on the support of the populations among which the terrorists operate. Imagine for a moment that September 11 had been treated as a crime. We would not have invaded Iraq, and we would not have our military struggling to perform police work and getting shot at.

Declaring war on terrorism better suited the purposes of the Bush Administration, because it invoked military might; but this is the wrong way to deal with the problem. Military action requires an identifiable target, preferably a state. As a result the war on terrorism has been directed primarily against states harboring terrorists. Yet terrorists are by definition non-state actors, even if they are often sponsored by states.

The war on terrorism as pursued by the Bush Administration cannot be won. On the contrary, it may bring about a permanent state of war. Terrorists will never disappear. They will continue to provide a pretext for the pursuit of American supremacy. That pursuit, in turn, will continue to generate resistance. Further, by turning the hunt for terrorists into a war, we are bound to create innocent victims. The more innocent victims there are, the greater the resentment and the better the chances that some victims will turn into perpetrators.

> **If we ever needed proof that the dream of American supremacy is misconceived, the occupation of Iraq has provided it. If we fail to heed the evidence, we will have to pay a heavier price in the future.**

The terrorist threat must be seen in proper perspective. Terrorism is not new. It was an important factor in nineteenth-century Russia, and it had a great influence on the character of the czarist regime, enhancing the importance of secret police and justifying authoritarianism. More recently several European countries—Italy, Germany, Great Britain—had to contend with terrorist gangs, and it took those countries a decade or more to root them out. But those countries did not live under the spell of terrorism during all that time. Granted, using hijacked planes for suicide attacks is something new, and so is the prospect of terrorists with weapons of mass destruction. To come to terms with these threats will take some adjustment; but the threats cannot be allowed to dominate our existence. Exaggerating them will only make them worse. The most powerful country on earth cannot afford to be consumed by fear. To make the war on terrorism the centerpiece of our national strategy is an abdication of our responsibility as the leading nation in the world. Moreover, by allowing terrorism to become our principal preoccupation, we are playing into the terrorists' hands. *They* are setting our priorities.

A recent Council on Foreign Relations publication sketches out three alternative national-security strategies. The first calls for the pursuit of American supremacy through the Bush doctrine of pre-emptive military action. It is advocated by neoconservatives. The second seeks the continuation of our earlier policy of deterrence and containment. It is advocated by Colin Powell and other moderates, who may be associated with either political party. The third would have the United States lead a cooperative effort to improve the world by engaging in preventive actions of a constructive character. It is not advocated by any group of significance, although President Bush pays lip service to it. That is the policy I stand for.

The evidence shows the first option to be extremely dangerous, and I believe that the second is no longer practical. The Bush Administration has done too much damage to our standing in the world to permit a return to the status quo. Moreover, the policies pursued before September 11 were clearly inadequate for dealing with the problems of globalization. Those problems require collective action. The United States is uniquely positioned to lead the effort. We cannot just do anything we want, as the Iraqi situation dem-

onstrates, but nothing much can be done in the way of international cooperation without the leadership—or at least the participation—of the United States.

Globalization has rendered the world increasingly interdependent, but international politics is still based on the sovereignty of states. What goes on within individual states can be of vital interest to the rest of the world, but the principle of sovereignty militates against interfering in their internal affairs. How to deal with failed states and oppressive, corrupt, and inept regimes? How to get rid of the likes of Saddam? There are too many such regimes to wage war against every one. This is the great unresolved problem confronting us today.

I propose replacing the Bush doctrine of pre-emptive military action with preventive action of a constructive and affirmative nature. Increased foreign aid or better and fairer trade rules, for example, would not violate the sovereignty of the recipients. Military action should remain a last resort. The United States is currently preoccupied with issues of security, and rightly so. But the framework within which to think about security is *collective* security. Neither nuclear proliferation nor international terrorism can be successfully addressed without international cooperation. The world is looking to us for leadership. We have provided it in the past; the main reason why anti-American feelings are so strong in the world today is that we are not providing it in the present.

GEORGE SOROS is the chairman of Soros Fund Management and the founder of a network of philanthropic organizations active in more than fifty countries. This essay is drawn from his book of the same name, to be published in January by Public Affairs.

From *The Atlantic Monthly*, December 2003, pages 63-66. Article derived from *The Bubble of American Supremacy*, Copyright © 2004 by George Soros. Reprinted with permission of George Soros and PublicAffairs.

The Case Against Perfection

What's wrong with designer children, bionic athletes, and genetic engineering?

By Michael J. Sandel

Breakthroughs in genetics present us with a promise and a predicament. The promise is that we may soon be able to treat and prevent a host of debilitating diseases. The predicament is that our newfound genetic knowledge may also enable us to manipulate our own nature—to enhance our muscles, memories, and moods; to choose the sex, height, and other genetic traits of our children; to make ourselves "better than well." When science moves faster than moral understanding, as it does today, men and women struggle to articulate their unease. In liberal societies they reach first for the language of autonomy, fairness, and individual rights. But this part of our moral vocabulary is ill equipped to address the hardest questions posed by genetic engineering. The genomic revolution has induced a kind of moral vertigo.

Consider cloning. The birth of Dolly the cloned sheep, in 1997, brought a torrent of concern about the prospect of cloned human beings. There are good medical reasons to worry. Most scientists agree that

cloning is unsafe, likely to produce offspring with serious abnormalities. (Dolly recently died a premature death.) But suppose technology improved to the point where clones were at no greater risk than naturally conceived offspring. Would human cloning still be objectionable? Should our hesitation be moral as well as medical? What, exactly, is wrong with creating a child who is a genetic twin of one parent, or of an older sibling who has tragically died—or, for that matter, of an admired scientist, sports star, or celebrity?

Some say cloning is wrong because it violates the right to autonomy: by choosing a child's genetic makeup in advance, parents deny the child's right to an open future. A similar objection can be raised against any form of bioengineering that allows parents to select or reject genetic characteristics. According to this argument, genetic enhancements for musical talent, say, or athletic prowess, would point children toward particular choices, and so designer children would never be fully free.

At first glance the autonomy argument seems to capture what is troubling about human cloning and other forms of genetic engineering. It is not persuasive, for two reasons. First, it wrongly implies that absent a designing parent, children are free to choose their characteristics for themselves. But none of us chooses his genetic inheritance. The alternative to a cloned or genetically enhanced child is not one whose future is unbound by particular talents but one at the mercy of the genetic lottery.

Second, even if a concern for autonomy explains some of our worries about made-to-order children, it cannot explain our moral hesitation about people who seek genetic remedies or enhancements for themselves. Gene therapy on somatic (that is, nonreproductive) cells, such as muscle cells and brain cells, repairs or replaces defective genes. The moral quandary arises when people use such therapy not to cure a disease but to reach beyond health, to enhance their physical or cognitive capacities, to lift themselves above the norm.

Like cosmetic surgery, genetic enhancement employs medical means for nonmedical ends—ends unrelated to curing or preventing disease or repairing injury. But unlike cosmetic surgery, genetic enhancement is more than skin-deep. If we are ambivalent about surgery or Botox injections for sagging chins and furrowed brows, we are all the more troubled by genetic engineering for stronger bodies, sharper memories, greater intelligence, and happier moods. The question is whether we are right to be troubled, and if so, on what grounds.

In order to grapple with the ethics of enhancement, we need to confront questions largely lost from view— questions about the moral status of nature, and about the proper stance of human beings toward the given world. Since these questions verge on theology, modern philosophers and political theorists tend to shrink from them. But our new powers of biotechnology make them unavoidable. To see why this is so, consider four examples already on the horizon: muscle enhancement, memory enhancement, growth-hormone treatment, and reproductive technologies that enable parents to choose the sex and some genetic traits of their children. In each case what began as an attempt to treat a disease or prevent a genetic disorder now beckons as an instrument of improvement and consumer choice.

Muscles. Everyone would welcome a gene therapy to alleviate muscular dystrophy and to reverse the debilitating muscle loss that comes with old age. But what if the same therapy were used to improve athletic performance? Researchers have developed a synthetic gene that, when injected into the muscle cells of mice, prevents and even reverses natural muscle deterioration. The gene not only repairs wasted or injured muscles but also strengthens healthy ones. This success bodes well for human applications. H. Lee Sweeney, of the University of Pennsylvania, who leads the research, hopes his discovery will cure the immobility that afflicts the elderly. But Sweeney's bulked-up mice have already attracted the attention of athletes seeking a competitive edge. Although the therapy is not yet approved for human use, the prospect of genetically enhanced weight lifters, home-run sluggers, linebackers, and sprinters is easy to imagine. The widespread use of steroids and other performance-improving drugs in professional sports suggests that many athletes will be eager to avail themselves of genetic enhancement.

Suppose for the sake of argument that muscle-enhancing gene therapy, unlike steroids, turned out to be safe— or at least no riskier than a rigorous weight-training regimen. Would there be a reason to ban its use in sports? There is something unsettling about the image of genetically altered athletes lifting SUVs or hitting 650-foot home runs or running a three-minute mile. But what, exactly, is troubling about it? Is it simply that we find such superhuman spectacles too bizarre to contemplate? Or does our unease point to something of ethical significance?

It might be argued that a genetically enhanced athlete, like a drug-enhanced athlete, would have an unfair advantage over his unenhanced competitors. But the fairness argument against enhancement has a fatal flaw: it has always been the case that some athletes are better endowed genetically than others, and yet we do not consider this to undermine the fairness of competitive sports. From the standpoint of fairness, enhanced genetic differences would be no worse than natural ones, assuming they were safe and made available to all. If genetic enhancement in sports is morally objectionable, it must be for reasons other than fairness.

Memory. Genetic enhancement is possible for brains as well as brawn. In the mid-1990s scientists managed to manipulate a memory-linked gene in fruit flies, creating flies with photographic memories. More recently researchers have produced smart mice by inserting extra copies of a memory-related gene into mouse embryos. The altered mice learn more quickly and remember things longer than normal mice. The extra copies were programmed to remain active even in old age, and the improvement was passed on to offspring.

Human memory is more complicated, but biotech companies, including Memory Pharmaceuticals, are in hot pursuit of memory-enhancing drugs, or "cognition enhancers," for human beings. The obvious market for such drugs consists of those who suffer from Alzheimer's and other serious memory disorders. The companies also have their sights on a bigger market: the 81 million Americans over fifty, who are beginning to encounter the memory loss that comes naturally with age. A drug that reversed age-related memory loss would be a bonanza for the pharmaceutical industry: a Viagra for the brain. Such use would straddle the line between remedy and enhancement. Unlike a treatment for Alzheimer's, it would cure no disease; but insofar as it restored capacities a person once possessed, it would have a remedial aspect. It could also have purely nonmedical uses: for example, by a lawyer cramming to memorize facts for an upcoming trial, or by a business executive eager to learn Mandarin on the eve of his departure for Shanghai.

Some who worry about the ethics of cognitive enhancement point to the danger of creating two classes of human beings: those with access to enhancement technologies, and those who must make do with their natural capacities. And if the enhancements could be passed down the generations, the two classes might eventually become subspecies—the enhanced and the merely natural. But worry about access ignores the moral status of enhancement itself. Is the scenario troubling because the unenhanced poor would be denied the benefits of bioengineering, or because the enhanced affluent would somehow be dehumanized? As with muscles, so with memory: the fundamental question is not how to ensure equal access to enhancement but whether we should aspire to it in the first place.

Height. Pediatricians already struggle with the ethics of enhancement when confronted by parents who want to make their children taller. Since the 1980s human growth hormone has been approved for children with a hormone deficiency that makes them much shorter than average. But the treatment also increases the height of healthy children. Some parents of healthy children who are unhappy with their stature (typically boys) ask why it should make a difference whether a child is short because of a hormone deficiency or because his parents happen to be short. Whatever the cause, the social consequences are the same.

In the face of this argument some doctors began prescribing hormone treatments for children whose short stature was unrelated to any medical problem. By 1996 such "off-label" use accounted for 40 percent of human-growth-hormone prescriptions. Although it is legal to prescribe drugs for purposes not approved by the Food and Drug Administration, pharmaceutical companies cannot promote such use. Seeking to expand its market, Eli Lilly & Co. recently persuaded the FDA to approve its human growth hormone for healthy children whose projected adult height is in the bottom one percentile—under five feet three inches for boys and four feet eleven inches for girls. This concession raises a large question about the ethics of enhancement: If hormone treatments need not be limited to those with hormone deficiencies, why should they be available only to very short children? Why shouldn't all shorter-than-average children be able to seek treatment? And what about a child of average height who wants to be taller so that he can make the basketball team?

Some oppose height enhancement on the grounds that it is collectively self-defeating; as some become taller, others become shorter relative to the norm. Except in Lake Wobegon, not every child can be above average. As the unenhanced began to feel shorter, they, too, might seek treatment, leading to a hormonal arms race that left everyone worse off, especially those who couldn't afford to buy their way up from shortness.

But the arms-race objection is not decisive on its own. Like the fairness objection to bioengineered muscles and memory, it leaves unexamined the attitudes and dispositions that prompt the drive for enhancement. If we were bothered only by the injustice of adding shortness to the problems of the poor, we could remedy that unfairness by publicly subsidizing height enhancements. As for the relative height deprivation suffered by innocent bystanders, we could compensate them by taxing those who buy their way to greater height. The real question is whether we want to live in a society where parents feel compelled to spend a fortune to make perfectly healthy kids a few inches taller.

Sex selection. Perhaps the most inevitable nonmedical use of bioengineering is sex selection. For centuries parents have been trying to choose the sex of their children. Today biotech succeeds where folk remedies failed.

One technique for sex selection arose with prenatal tests using amniocentesis and ultrasound. These medical technologies were developed to detect genetic abnormalities such as spina bifida and Down syndrome. But they can also reveal the sex of the fetus—allowing for the abortion of a fetus of an undesired sex. Even among those who favor abortion rights, few advocate abortion simply because the parents do not want a girl. Nevertheless, in traditional societies with a powerful cultural preference for boys, this practice has become widespread.

Sex selection need not involve abortion, however. For couples undergoing *in vitro* fertilization (IVF), it is possible to choose the sex of the child before the fertilized egg is implanted in the womb. One method makes use of pre-implantation genetic diagnosis (PGD), a procedure developed to screen for genetic diseases. Several eggs are fertilized in a petri dish and grown to the eight-cell stage (about three days). At that point the embryos are tested to determine their sex. Those of the desired sex are implanted; the others are typically discarded. Although few couples are likely to undergo the difficulty and expense of IVF simply to choose the sex of their child, embryo screening is a highly reliable means of sex selection. And as our genetic knowledge increases, it may be possible to use PGD to cull embryos carrying undesired genes, such as those associated with obesity, height, and skin color. The science-fiction movie *Gattaca* depicts a future in which parents routinely screen embryos for sex, height, immunity to disease, and even IQ. There is something troubling about the *Gattaca* scenario, but it is not easy to identify what exactly is wrong with screening embryos to choose the sex of our children.

One line of objection draws on arguments familiar from the abortion debate. Those who believe that an embryo is a person reject embryo screening for the same reasons they reject abortion. If an eight-cell embryo growing in a petri dish is morally equivalent to a fully developed human being, then discarding it is no better than aborting a fetus, and both practices are equivalent to infanticide. Whatever its merits, however, this "pro-life" objection is not an argument against sex selection as such.

The latest technology poses the question of sex selection unclouded by the matter of an embryo's moral status. The Genetics & IVF Institute, a for-profit infertility clinic in Fairfax, Virginia, now offers a sperm-sorting technique that makes it possible to choose the sex of one's child before it is conceived. X-bearing sperm, which produce girls, carry more DNA than Y-bearing sperm, which produce boys; a device called a flow cytometer can separate them. The process, called MicroSort, has a high rate of success.

If sex selection by sperm sorting is objectionable, it must be for reasons that go beyond the debate about the moral status of the embryo. One such reason is that sex selection is an instrument of sex discrimination—typically against girls, as illustrated by the chilling sex ratios in India and China. Some speculate that societies with substantially more men than women will be less stable, more violent, and more prone to crime or war. These are legitimate worries—but the sperm-sorting company has a clever way of addressing them. It offers MicroSort only to couples who want to choose the sex of a child for purposes of "family balancing." Those with more sons than daughters may choose a girl, and vice versa. But customers may not use the technology to stock up on children of the same sex, or even to choose the sex of their firstborn child. (So far the majority of MicroSort clients have chosen girls.) Under restrictions of this kind, do any ethical issues remain that should give us pause?

The case of MicroSort helps us isolate the moral objections that would persist if muscle-enhancement, memory-enhancement, and height-enhancement technologies were safe and available to all.

It is commonly said that genetic enhancements undermine our humanity by threatening our capacity to act freely, to succeed by our own efforts, and to consider ourselves responsible—worthy of praise or blame—for the things we do and for the way we are. It is one thing to hit seventy home runs as the result of disciplined training and effort, and something else, something less, to hit them with the help of steroids or genetically enhanced muscles. Of course, the roles of effort and en-

hancement will be a matter of degree. But as the role of enhancement increases, our admiration for the achievement fades—or, rather, our admiration for the achievement shifts from the player to his pharmacist. This suggests that our moral response to enhancement is a response to the diminished agency of the person whose achievement is enhanced.

Though there is much to be said for this argument, I do not think the main problem with enhancement and genetic engineering is that they undermine effort and erode human agency. The deeper danger is that they represent a kind of hyperagency—a Promethean aspiration to remake nature, including human nature, to serve our purposes and satisfy our desires. The problem is not the drift to mechanism but the drive to mastery. And what the drive to mastery misses and may even destroy is an appreciation of the gifted character of human powers and achievements.

To acknowledge the giftedness of life is to recognize that our talents and powers are not wholly our own doing, despite the effort we expend to develop and to exercise them. It is also to recognize that not everything in the world is open to whatever use we may desire or devise. Appreciating the gifted quality of life constrains the Promethean project and conduces to a certain humility. It is in part a religious sensibility. But its resonance reaches beyond religion.

It is difficult to account for what we admire about human activity and achievement without drawing upon some version of this idea. Consider two types of athletic achievement. We appreciate players like Pete Rose, who are not blessed with great natural gifts but who manage, through striving, grit, and determination, to excel in their sport. But we also admire players like Joe DiMaggio, who display natural gifts with grace and effortlessness. Now, suppose we learned that both players took performance-enhancing drugs. Whose turn to drugs would we find more deeply disillusioning? Which

aspect of the athletic ideal—effort or gift—would be more deeply offended?

Some might say effort: the problem with drugs is that they provide a shortcut, a way to win without striving. But striving is not the point of sports; excellence is. And excellence consists at least partly in the display of natural talents and gifts that are no doing of the athlete who possesses them. This is an uncomfortable fact for democratic societies. We want to believe that success, in sports and in life, is something we earn, not something we inherit. Natural gifts, and the admiration they inspire, embarrass the meritocratic faith; they cast doubt on the conviction that praise and rewards flow from effort alone. In the face of this embarrassment we inflate the moral significance of striving, and depreciate giftedness. This distortion can be seen, for example, in network-television coverage of the Olympics, which focuses less on the feats the athletes perform than on heartrending stories of the hardships they have overcome and the struggles they have waged to triumph over an injury or a difficult upbringing or political turmoil in their native land.

But effort isn't everything. No one believes that a mediocre basketball player who works and trains even harder than Michael Jordan deserves greater acclaim or a bigger contract. The real problem with genetically altered athletes is that they corrupt athletic competition as a human activity that honors the cultivation and display of natural talents. From this standpoint, enhancement can be seen as the ultimate expression of the ethic of effort and willfulness—a kind of high-tech striving. The ethic of willfulness and the biotechnological powers it now enlists are arrayed against the claims of giftedness.

The ethic of giftedness, under siege in sports, persists in the practice of parenting. But here, too, bioengineering and genetic enhancement threaten to dislodge it. To appreciate children as gifts is to accept them as they come, not as objects of our design or products of our will or instruments of our ambition. Parental love is not contingent on the talents and attributes a child happens to have. We choose our friends and spouses at least partly on the basis of qualities we find attractive. But we do not choose our children. Their qualities are unpredictable, and even the most conscientious parents cannot be held wholly responsible for the kind of children they have. That is why parenthood, more than other human relationships, teaches what the theologian William F. May calls an "openness to the unbidden."

May's resonant phrase helps us see that the deepest moral objection to enhancement lies less in the perfection it seeks than in the human disposition it expresses and promotes. The problem is not that parents usurp the autonomy of a child they design. The problem lies in the hubris of the designing parents, in their drive to master the mystery of birth. Even if this disposition did not make parents tyrants to their children, it would disfigure the relation between parent and child, and deprive the parent of the humility and enlarged human sympathies that an openness to the unbidden can cultivate.

To appreciate children as gifts or blessings is not, of course, to be passive in the face of illness or disease. Medical intervention to cure or prevent illness or restore the injured to health does not desecrate nature but honors it. Healing sickness or injury does not override a child's natural capacities but permits them to flourish.

Nor does the sense of life as a gift mean that parents must shrink from shaping and directing the development of their child. Just as athletes and artists have an obligation to cultivate their talents, so parents have an obligation to cultivate their children, to help them discover and develop their talents and gifts. As May points out, parents give their children two kinds of love: accepting love and transforming love. Accepting love affirms the being of the child, whereas transforming love seeks the well-being of the child. Each aspect corrects the excesses of the other, he writes: "Attachment becomes too quietistic if it slackens into mere acceptance of the child as he is." Parents have a duty to promote their children's excellence.

These days, however, overly ambitious parents are prone to get carried away with transforming love—promoting and demanding all manner of accomplishments from their children, seeking perfection. "Parents find it difficult to maintain an equilibrium between the two sides of love," May observes. "Accepting love, without transforming love, slides into indulgence and finally neglect. Transforming love, without accepting love, badgers and finally rejects." May finds in these competing impulses a parallel with modern science: it, too, engages us in beholding the given world, studying and savoring it, and also in molding the world, transforming and perfecting it.

The mandate to mold our children, to cultivate and improve them, complicates the case against enhancement. We usually admire parents who seek the best for their children, who spare no effort to help them achieve happiness and success. Some parents confer advantages on their children by enrolling them in expensive schools, hiring private tutors, sending them to tennis camp, providing them with piano lessons, ballet lessons, swimming lessons, SAT-prep courses, and so on. If it is permissible and even admirable for parents to help their children in these ways, why isn't it equally admirable for parents to use whatever genetic technologies may emerge (provided they are safe) to enhance their children's intelligence, musical ability, or athletic prowess?

The defenders of enhancement are right to this extent: improving children through genetic engineering is similar in spirit to the heavily managed, high-pressure child-rearing that is now common. But this similarity does not vindicate genetic enhancement. On the contrary, it highlights a problem with the trend toward hyperparenting. One conspicuous example of this trend is sports-crazed parents bent on making champions of their children. Another is the frenzied drive of overbearing parents to mold and manage their children's academic careers.

As the pressure for performance increases, so does the need to help distractible children concentrate on the task at hand. This may be why diagnoses of attention deficit and hyperactivity disorder have increased so sharply. Lawrence Diller, a pediatrician and the author of *Running on Ritalin*, estimates that five to six percent of American children under eighteen (a total of four to five million kids) are currently prescribed Ritalin, Adderall, and other stimulants, the treatment of choice for ADHD. (Stimulants counteract hyperactivity by making it easier to focus and sustain attention.) The number of Ritalin prescriptions for children and adolescents has tripled over the past decade, but not all users suffer from attention disorders or hyperactivity. High school and college students have learned that prescription stimulants improve concentration for those with normal attention spans, and some buy or borrow their classmates' drugs to enhance their performance on the SAT or other exams. Since stimulants work for both medical and nonmedical purposes, they raise the same moral questions posed by other technologies of enhancement.

However those questions are resolved, the debate reveals the cultural distance we have traveled since the debate over marijuana, LSD, and other drugs a generation ago. Unlike the drugs of the 1960s and 1970s, Ritalin and Adderall are not for checking out but for buckling down, not for beholding the world and taking it in but for molding the world and fitting in. We used to speak of nonmedical drug use as "recreational." That term no longer applies. The steroids and stimulants that figure in the enhancement debate are not a source of recreation but a bid for compliance—a way of answering a competitive society's demand to improve our performance and perfect our nature. This demand for performance and perfection animates the impulse to rail against the given. It is the deepest source of the moral trouble with enhancement.

Some see a clear line between genetic enhancement and other ways that people seek improvement in their children and themselves. Genetic manipulation seems somehow worse—more intrusive, more sinister—than other ways of enhancing performance and seeking success. But morally speaking, the difference is less significant than it seems. Bioengineering gives us reason to question the low-tech, high-pressure child-rearing practices we commonly accept. The hyperparenting familiar in our time represents an anxious excess of mastery and dominion that misses the sense of life as a gift. This draws it disturbingly close to eugenics.

The shadow of eugenics hangs over today's debates about genetic engineering and enhancement. Critics of genetic engineering argue that human cloning, enhancement, and the quest for designer children are nothing more than "privatized" or "free-market" eugenics. Defenders of enhancement reply that genetic choices freely made are not really eugenic—at least not in the pejorative sense. To remove the coercion, they argue, is to remove the very thing that makes eugenic policies repugnant.

Sorting out the lesson of eugenics is another way of wrestling with the ethics of enhancement. The Nazis gave eugenics a bad name. But what, precisely, was wrong with it? Was the old eugenics objectionable only insofar as it was coercive? Or is there something inherently wrong with the resolve to deliberately design our progeny's traits?

James Watson, the biologist who, with Francis Crick, discovered the structure of DNA, sees nothing wrong with genetic engineering and enhancement, provided they are freely chosen rather than state-imposed. And yet Watson's language contains more than a whiff of the old eugenic sensibility. "If you really are stupid, I would call that a disease," he recently told *The Times* of London. "The lower 10 percent who really have difficulty, even in elementary school, what's the cause of it? A lot of people would like to say, 'Well, poverty, things like that.' It probably isn't. So I'd like to get rid of that, to help the lower 10 percent." A few years ago Watson stirred controversy by saying that if a gene for homosexuality were discovered, a woman should be free to abort a fetus that carried it. When his remark provoked an uproar, he replied that he was not singling out gays but asserting a principle: women should be free to abort fetuses for any reason of genetic preference—for example, if the child would be dyslexic, or lacking musical talent, or too short to play basketball.

Watson's scenarios are clearly objectionable to those for whom all abortion is an unspeakable crime. But for those who do not subscribe to the pro-life position, these scenarios raise a hard question: If it is morally troubling to contemplate abortion to avoid a gay child or a dyslexic one, doesn't this suggest that something is wrong with acting on any eugenic preference, even when no state coercion is involved?

Consider the market in eggs and sperm. The advent of artificial insemination allows prospective parents to shop for gametes with the genetic traits they desire in their offspring. It is a less predictable way to design children than cloning or preimplantation genetic screening, but it offers a good example of a procreative practice in which the old eugenics meets the new consumerism. A few years ago some Ivy League newspapers ran an ad seeking an egg from a woman who was at least five feet ten inches tall and athletic, had no major family medical problems, and had a combined SAT score of 1400 or above. The ad offered $50,000 for an egg from a donor with these traits. More recently a Web site was launched claiming to auction eggs from fashion models whose photos appeared on the site, at starting bids of $15,000 to $150,000.

On what grounds, if any, is the egg market morally objectionable? Since no one is forced to buy or sell, it cannot be wrong for reasons of coercion. Some might worry that hefty prices would exploit poor women by presenting them with an offer they couldn't refuse. But the designer eggs that fetch the highest prices are likely to be sought from the privileged, not the poor. If the market for premium eggs gives us moral qualms, this, too, shows that concerns about eugenics are not put to rest by freedom of choice.

A tale of two sperm banks helps explain why. The Repository for Germinal Choice, one of America's first sperm banks, was not a commercial enterprise. It was opened in 1980 by Robert Graham, a philanthropist dedicated to improving the world's "germ plasm" and counteracting the rise of "retrograde humans." His plan was to collect the sperm of Nobel Prize-winning scientists and make it available to women of high intelligence, in hopes of breeding supersmart babies. But Graham had trouble persuading Nobel laureates to donate their sperm for his bizarre scheme, and so settled for sperm from young scientists of high promise. His sperm bank closed in 1999.

In contrast, California Cryobank, one of the world's leading sperm banks, is a for-profit company with no overt eugenic mission. Cappy Rothman, M.D., a co-founder of the firm, has nothing but disdain for Graham's eugenics, although the standards Cryobank imposes on the sperm it recruits are exacting. Cryobank has offices in Cambridge, Massachusetts, between Harvard and MIT, and in Palo Alto, California, near Stanford. It advertises for donors in campus newspapers (compensation up to

$900 a month), and accepts less than five percent of the men who apply. Cryobank's marketing materials play up the prestigious source of its sperm. Its catalogue provides detailed information about the physical characteristics of each donor, along with his ethnic origin and college major. For an extra fee prospective customers can buy the results of a test that assesses the donor's temperament and character type. Rothman reports that Cryobank's ideal sperm donor is six feet tall, with brown eyes, blond hair, and dimples, and has a college degree—not because the company wants to propagate those traits, but because those are the traits his customers want: "If our customers wanted high school dropouts, we would give them high school dropouts."

Not everyone objects to marketing sperm. But anyone who is troubled by the eugenic aspect of the Nobel Prize sperm bank should be equally troubled by Cryobank, consumer-driven though it be. What, after all, is the moral difference between designing children according to an explicit eugenic purpose and designing children according to the dictates of the market? Whether the aim is to improve humanity's "germ plasm" or to cater to consumer preferences, both practices are eugenic insofar as both make children into products of deliberate design.

A number of political philosophers call for a new "liberal eugenics." They argue that a moral distinction can be drawn between the old eugenic policies and genetic enhancements that do not restrict the autonomy of the child. "While old-fashioned authoritarian eugenicists sought to produce citizens out of a single centrally designed mould," writes Nicholas Agar, "the distinguishing mark of the new liberal eugenics is state neutrality." Government may not tell parents what sort of children to design, and parents may engineer in their children only those traits that improve their capacities without biasing their choice of life plans. A recent text on genetics and justice, written by the

bioethicists Allen Buchanan, Dan W. Brock, Norman Daniels, and Daniel Wikler, offers a similar view. The "bad reputation of eugenics," they write, is due to practices that "might be avoidable in a future eugenic program." The problem with the old eugenics was that its burdens fell disproportionately on the weak and the poor, who were unjustly sterilized and segregated. But provided that the benefits and burdens of genetic improvement are fairly distributed, these bioethicists argue, eugenic measures are unobjectionable and may even be morally required.

The libertarian philosopher Robert Nozick proposed a "genetic supermarket" that would enable parents to order children by design without imposing a single design on the society as a whole: "This supermarket system has the great virtue that it involves no centralized decision fixing the future human type(s)."

Even the leading philosopher of American liberalism, John Rawls, in his classic *A Theory of Justice* (1971), offered a brief endorsement of noncoercive eugenics. Even in a society that agrees to share the benefits and burdens of the genetic lottery, it is "in the interest of each to have greater natural assets," Rawls wrote. "This enables him to pursue a preferred plan of life." The parties to the social contract "want to insure for their descendants the best genetic endowment (assuming their own to be fixed)." Eugenic policies are therefore not only permissible but required as a matter of justice. "Thus over time a society is to take steps at least to preserve the general level of natural abilities and to prevent the diffusion of serious defects."

But removing the coercion does not vindicate eugenics. The problem with eugenics and genetic engineering is that they represent the one-sided triumph of willfulness over giftedness, of dominion over reverence, of molding over beholding. Why, we may wonder, should we worry about this triumph? Why not

shake off our unease about genetic enhancement as so much superstition? What would be lost if biotechnology dissolved our sense of giftedness?

From a religious standpoint the answer is clear: To believe that our talents and powers are wholly our own doing is to misunderstand our place in creation, to confuse our role with God's. Religion is not the only source of reasons to care about giftedness, however. The moral stakes can also be described in secular terms. If bioengineering made the myth of the "self-made man" come true, it would be difficult to view our talents as gifts for which we are indebted, rather than as achievements for which we are responsible. This would transform three key features of our moral landscape: humility, responsibility, and solidarity.

In a social world that prizes mastery and control, parenthood is a school for humility. That we care deeply about our children and yet cannot choose the kind we want teaches parents to be open to the unbidden. Such openness is a disposition worth affirming, not only within families but in the wider world as well. It invites us to abide the unexpected, to live with dissonance, to rein in the impulse to control. A *Gattaca*-like world in which parents became accustomed to specifying the sex and genetic traits of their children would be a world inhospitable to the unbidden, a gated community writ large. The awareness that our talents and abilities are not wholly our own doing restrains our tendency toward hubris.

Though some maintain that genetic enhancement erodes human agency by overriding effort, the real problem is the explosion, not the erosion, of responsibility. As humility gives way, responsibility expands to daunting proportions. We attribute less to chance and more to choice. Parents become responsible for choosing, or failing to choose, the right traits for their children. Athletes become responsible for acquiring, or failing to acquire, the talents that will help their teams win.

One of the blessings of seeing ourselves as creatures of nature, God, or fortune is that we are not wholly responsible for the way we are. The more we become masters of our genetic endowments, the greater the burden we bear for the talents we have and the way we perform. Today when a basketball player misses a rebound, his coach can blame him for being out of position. Tomorrow the coach may blame him for being too short. Even now the use of performance-enhancing drugs in professional sports is subtly transforming the expectations players have for one another; on some teams players who take the field free from amphetamines or other stimulants are criticized for "playing naked."

The more alive we are to the chanced nature of our lot, the more reason we have to share our fate with others. Consider insurance. Since people do not know whether or when various ills will befall them, they pool their risk by buying health insurance and life insurance. As life plays itself out, the healthy wind up subsidizing the unhealthy, and those who live to a ripe old age wind up subsidizing the families of those who die before their time. Even without a sense of mutual obligation, people pool their risks and resources and share one another's fate.

But insurance markets mimic solidarity only insofar as people do not know or control their own risk factors. Suppose genetic testing advanced to the point where it could reliably predict each person's medical future and life expectancy. Those confident of good health and long life would opt out of the pool, causing other people's premiums to skyrocket. The solidarity of insurance would disappear as those with good genes fled the actuarial company of those with bad ones.

The fear that insurance companies would use genetic data to assess risks and set premiums recently led the Senate to vote to prohibit genetic discrimination in health insurance.

But the bigger danger, admittedly more speculative, is that genetic enhancement, if routinely practiced, would make it harder to foster the moral sentiments that social solidarity requires.

Why, after all, do the successful owe anything to the least-advantaged members of society? The best answer to this question leans heavily on the notion of giftedness. The natural talents that enable the successful to flourish are not their own doing but, rather, their good fortune—a result of the genetic lottery. If our genetic endowments are gifts, rather than achievements for which we can claim credit, it is a mistake and a conceit to assume that we are entitled to the full measure of the bounty they reap in a market economy. We therefore have an obligation to share this bounty with those who, through no fault of their own, lack comparable gifts.

A lively sense of the contingency of our gifts—a consciousness that none of us is wholly responsible for his or her success—saves a meritocratic society from sliding into the smug assumption that the rich are rich because they are more deserving than the poor. Without this, the successful would become even more likely than they are now to view themselves as self-made and self-sufficient, and hence wholly responsible for their success. Those at the bottom of society would be viewed not as disadvantaged, and thus worthy of a measure of compensation, but as simply unfit, and thus worthy of eugenic repair. The meritocracy, less chastened by chance, would become harder, less forgiving. As perfect genetic knowledge would end the simulacrum of solidarity in insurance markets, so perfect genetic control would erode the actual solidarity that arises when men and women reflect on the contingency of their talents and fortunes.

Thirty-five years ago Robert L. Sinsheimer, a molecular biologist at the California Institute of Technology, glimpsed the shape of things to

come. In an article titled "The Prospect of Designed Genetic Change" he argued that freedom of choice would vindicate the new genetics, and set it apart from the discredited eugenics of old.

> To implement the older eugenics … would have required a massive social programme carried out over many generations. Such a programme could not have been initiated without the consent and co-operation of a major fraction of the population, and would have been continuously subject to social control. In contrast, the new eugenics could, at least in principle, be implemented on a quite individual basis, in one generation, and subject to no existing restrictions.

According to Sinsheimer, the new eugenics would be voluntary rather than coerced, and also more humane. Rather than segregating and eliminating the unfit, it would improve them. "The old eugenics would have required a continual selection for breeding of the fit, and a culling of the unfit," he wrote. "The new eugenics would permit in principle the conversion of all the unfit to the highest genetic level."

Sinsheimer's paean to genetic engineering caught the heady, Promethean self-image of the age. He wrote hopefully of rescuing "the losers in that chromosomal lottery that so firmly channels our human destinies," including not only those born with genetic defects but also "the 50,000,000 'normal' Americans with an IQ of less than 90." But he also saw that something bigger than improving on nature's "mindless, age-old throw of dice" was at stake. Implicit in technologies of genetic intervention was a more exalted place for human beings in the cosmos. "As we enlarge man's freedom, we diminish his constraints and that which he must accept as given," he wrote. Copernicus and Darwin had "demoted man from his bright glory at the focal point of the universe," but the new biology would restore his central role. In the mirror of our genetic knowledge we would see ourselves as more than a link in the chain of evolution: "We can be the agent of transition to a whole new pitch of evolution. This is a cosmic event."

There is something appealing, even intoxicating, about a vision of human freedom unfettered by the given. It may even be the case that the allure of that vision played a part in summoning the genomic age into being. It is often assumed that the powers of enhancement we now possess arose as an inadvertent by-product of biomedical progress—the genetic revolution came, so to speak, to cure disease, and stayed to tempt us with the prospect of enhancing our performance, designing our children, and perfecting our nature. That may have the story backwards.

It is more plausible to view genetic engineering as the ultimate expression of our resolve to see ourselves astride the world, the masters of our nature. But that promise of mastery is flawed. It threatens to banish our appreciation of life as a gift, and to leave us with nothing to affirm or behold outside our own will.

From *The Atlantic Monthly*, Vol. 293, No. 3, April 2004, pages 50-62. Copyright © 2004 by Michael J. Sandel. Reprinted with permission of the author.

Index

Index

Test Your Knowledge Form

We encourage you to photocopy and use this page as a tool to assess how the articles in *Annual Editions* expand on the information in your textbook. By reflecting on the articles you will gain enhanced text information. You can also access this useful form on a product's book support Web site at *http://www.dushkin.com/online/*.

NAME: _____ DATE: _____

TITLE AND NUMBER OF ARTICLE: _____

BRIEFLY STATE THE MAIN IDEA OF THIS ARTICLE:

_____

LIST THREE IMPORTANT FACTS THAT THE AUTHOR USES TO SUPPORT THE MAIN IDEA:

_____

WHAT INFORMATION OR IDEAS DISCUSSED IN THIS ARTICLE ARE ALSO DISCUSSED IN YOUR TEXTBOOK OR OTHER READINGS THAT YOU HAVE DONE? LIST THE TEXTBOOK CHAPTERS AND PAGE NUMBERS:

_____

LIST ANY EXAMPLES OF BIAS OR FAULTY REASONING THAT YOU FOUND IN THE ARTICLE:

_____

LIST ANY NEW TERMS/CONCEPTS THAT WERE DISCUSSED IN THE ARTICLE, AND WRITE A SHORT DEFINITION:

We Want Your Advice

ANNUAL EDITIONS revisions depend on two major opinion sources: one is our Advisory Board, listed in the front of this volume, which works with us in scanning the thousands of articles published in the public press each year; the other is you—the person actually using the book. Please help us and the users of the next edition by completing the prepaid article rating form on this page and returning it to us. Thank you for your help!

ANNUAL EDITIONS: American History, Volume 2

ARTICLE RATING FORM

Here is an opportunity for you to have direct input into the next revision of this volume.
We would like you to rate each of the articles listed below, using the following scale:

1. **Excellent: should definitely be retained**
2. **Above average: should probably be retained**
3. **Below average: should probably be deleted**
4. **Poor: should definitely be deleted**

Your ratings will play a vital part in the next revision.
Please mail this prepaid form to us as soon as possible.
Thanks for your help!

RATING	ARTICLE
	1. The New View of Reconstruction
	2. 1871 War on Terror
	3. Lockwood in '84
	4. Buffalo Soldiers
	5. Undermining the Molly Maguires
	6. African Americans and the Industrial Revolution
	7. The Death of Wilhautyah
	8. Where the Other Half Lived
	9. Our First Olympics
	10. Lady Muckraker
	11. Teddy in the Middle
	12. The Steamer Age
	13. The Ambiguous Legacies of Women's Progressivism
	14. The Fate of Leo Frank
	15. The Home Front
	16. Evolution on Trial
	17. Race Cleansing in America
	18. Marcus Garvey and the Rise of Black Nationalism
	19. 'Brother, Can You Spare a Dime?'
	20. A Monumental Man
	21. Birth of an Entitlement: Learning from the Origins of Social Security
	22. Japanese Americans and the U.S. Army: A Historical Reconsideration
	23. American Women in a World at War
	24. African Americans and World War II
	25. Dividing the Spoils
	26. The Biggest Decision: Why We Had to Drop the Atomic Bomb
	27. Baseball's *Noble* Experiment
	28. Truman's Other War: The Battle for the American Homefront, 1950-1953
	29. Women, Domesticity, and Postwar Conservatism
	30. The Split-Level Years
	31. The FBI Marches on the Dreamers
	32. The Spirit of '68
	33. Face-Off
	34. Dixie's Victory

RATING	ARTICLE
	35. The American Century
	36. What September 11th Really Wrought
	37. Breaking the Global-Warming Gridlock
	38. A Politics for Generation X
	39. American Culture Goes Global, or Does It?
	40. The Bubble of American Supremacy
	41. The Case Against Perfection

(Continued on next page)

NO POSTAGE
NECESSARY
IF MAILED
IN THE
UNITED STATES

BUSINESS REPLY MAIL
FIRST CLASS MAIL PERMIT NO. 551 DUBUQUE IA

POSTAGE WILL BE PAID BY ADDRESEE

McGraw-Hill/Dushkin
2460 KERPER BLVD
DUBUQUE, IA 52001-9902

ABOUT YOU

Name   Date

Are you a teacher? ❏   A student? ❏
Your school's name

Department

Address	City	State	Zip

School telephone #

YOUR COMMENTS ARE IMPORTANT TO US!

Please fill in the following information:
For which course did you use this book?

Did you use a text with this ANNUAL EDITION? ❏ yes ❏ no
What was the title of the text?

What are your general reactions to the *Annual Editions* concept?

Have you read any pertinent articles recently that you think should be included in the next edition? Explain.

Are there any articles that you feel should be replaced in the next edition? Why?

Are there any World Wide Web sites that you feel should be included in the next edition? Please annotate.

May we contact you for editorial input? ❏ yes ❏ no
May we quote your comments? ❏ yes ❏ no